PENGUIN BOOKS

GOD'S FURY, ENGLAND'S FIRE

Michael Braddick is Professor of History at the University of Sheffield. He has held fellowships from the British Academy and the Nuffield Foundation, a Major Research Fellowship from the Leverhulme Trust, and visiting scholarships at the Huntington Library, California, the Max Planck Institute for European Legal History in Frankfurt, and the Institute for Advanced Study in Princeton. He is the author of *The Nerves of State: Taxation and the Financing of the English State, 1558–1700* and *State Formation in Early Modern England, c. 1500–1700*.

D0863817

MICHAEL BRADDICK

God's Fury, England's Fire

A New History of the English Civil Wars

PENGUIN BOOKS

PENGUIN BOOKS

Published by the Penguin Group
Penguin Books Ltd, 80 Strand, London WC2R ORL, England
Penguin Group (USA) Inc., 375 Hudson Street, New York, New York 10014, USA
Penguin Group (Canada), 90 Eglinton Avenue East, Suite 700, Toronto, Ontario, Canada M4P 2Y3
(a division of Pearson Penguin Canada Inc.)
Penguin Ireland, 25 St Stephen's Green, Dublin 2, Ireland
(a division of Penguin Books Ltd)
Penguin Group (Australia), 250 Camberwell Road, Camberwell, Victoria 3124, Australia
(a division of Pearson Australia Group Pty Ltd)
Penguin Books India Pvt Ltd, 11 Community Centre, Panchsheel Park, New Delhi – 110 017, India
Penguin Group (NZ), 67 Apollo Drive, Rosedale, North Shore 0632, New Zealand
(a division of Pearson New Zealand Ltd)
Penguin Books (South Africa) (Pty) Ltd, 24 Sturdee Avenue,
Rosebank, Johannesburg 2196, South Africa

Penguin Books Ltd, Registered Offices: 80 Strand, London WC2R ORL, England

www.penguin.com

First published by Allen Lane 2008
Published in Penguin Books 2009
1

Typeset by Rowland Phototypesetting Ltd, Bury St Edmunds, Suffolk
Printed in England by Clays Ltd, St Ives plc

978-0-141-00897-4

www.greenpenguin.co.uk

Mixed Sources
Product group from well-managed
forests and other controlled sources
www.fsc.org   Cert no. SA-COC-1592
© 1996 Forest Stewardship Council
FSC

For Karen, Cora and Melissa

Contents

War, 1642–1646

Revolution, 1646–1649

CONTENTS

List of Illustrations

Maps

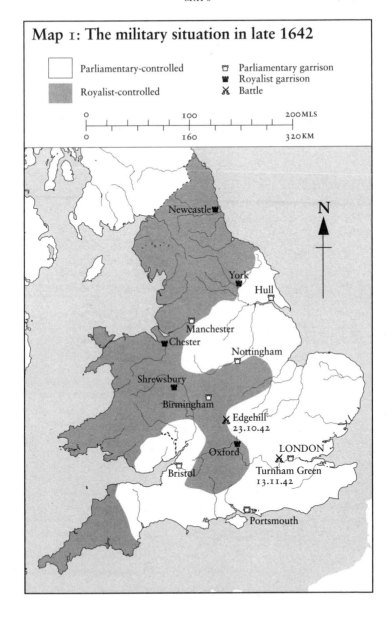

Map 1: The military situation in late 1642

Parliamentary-controlled

Royalist-controlled

☗ Parliamentary garrison
♜ Royalist garrison
✕ Battle

0   100   200 MLS
0   160   320 KM

N

Newcastle

York
Hull

Manchester
Chester
Nottingham

Shrewsbury
Birmingham

Edgehill
23.10.42

Oxford
LONDON
Bristol
Turnham Green
13.11.42

Portsmouth

Map 2: The military situation in late 1643

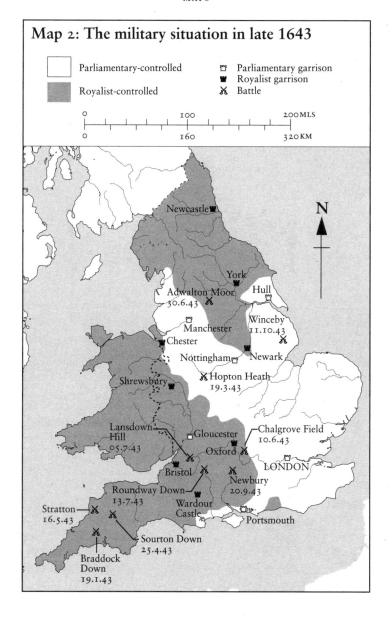

☐ Parliamentary-controlled   ♜ Parliamentary garrison
▨ Royalist-controlled   ♜ Royalist garrison
                           ✕ Battle

0   100   200 MLS
0   160   320 KM

N

Newcastle

York
Adwalton Moor
30.6.43
Hull

Manchester
Winceby
11.10.43

Chester
Nottingham
Newark

Shrewsbury
Hopton Heath
19.3.43

Lansdown
Hill
05.7.43
Gloucester
Chalgrove Field
10.6.43

Oxford
LONDON

Bristol
Newbury
20.9.43

Roundway Down
13.7.43
Wardour
Castle

Stratton
16.5.43
Portsmouth

Sourton Down
25.4.43

Braddock
Down
19.1.43

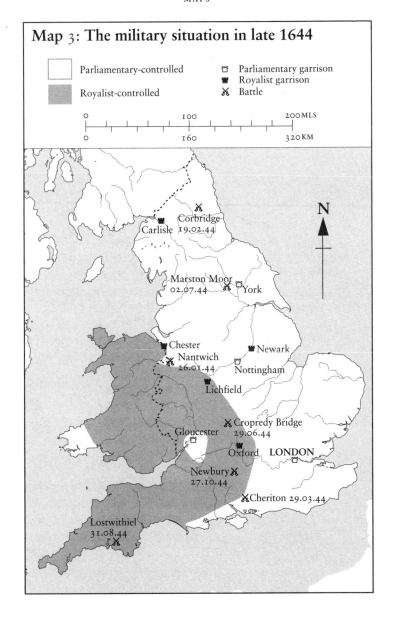

Map 3: The military situation in late 1644

Parliamentary-controlled

Royalist-controlled

Parliamentary garrison
Royalist garrison
Battle

| 0 | 100 | 200 MLS |
| 0 | 160 | 320 KM |

N

Corbridge
Carlisle 19.02.44

Marston Moor
02.07.44 York

Chester
Nantwich Newark
26.01.44
Nottingham

Lichfield

Cropredy Bridge
Gloucester 29.06.44

Oxford LONDON

Newbury
27.10.44

Cheriton 29.03.44

Lostwithiel
31.08.44

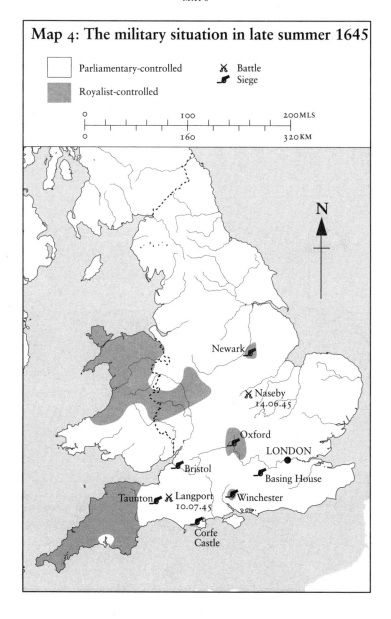

Map 4: The military situation in late summer 1645

Parliamentary-controlled

Royalist-controlled

Battle

Siege

| 0 | | | 100 | | | 200 MLS |
| 0 | | | 160 | | | 320 KM |

N

Newark

Naseby
14.06.45

Oxford

LONDON

Bristol

Basing House

Taunton Langport
10.07.45

Winchester

Corfe
Castle

Map 5: Principal battles in Ireland and Scotland

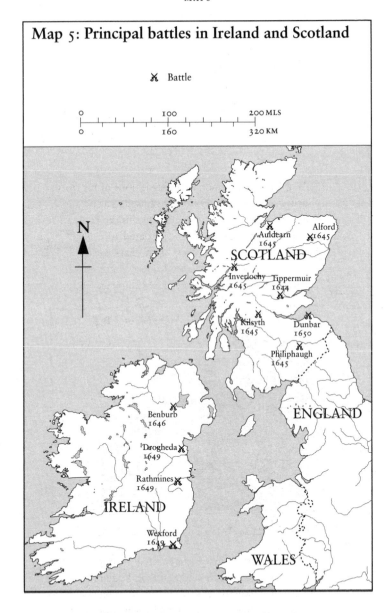

✗ Battle

0   100   200 MLS
0   160   320 KM

N

SCOTLAND

Auldearn
1645

Alford
1645

Inverlochy
1645

Tippermuir
1644

Kilsyth
1645

Dunbar
1650

Philiphaugh
1645

ENGLAND

Benburb
1646

Drogheda
1649

Rathmines
1649

IRELAND

Wexford
1649

WALES

Preface

In late April 1646 Charles I, a monarch very jealous of his dignity and personal authority, slipped out of Oxford disguised as a servant. A week later, after some apparently hesitant wanderings in the company of his chaplain and one personal friend, he surrendered to a Scottish army camped at Southwell, Nottinghamshire. Eight years earlier he had set out to crush religious protests in Scotland, never quite able to see the protesters as anything but rebels. But their campaign had set off a

Charles I leaving Oxford in disguise, April 1646

political and religious crisis that reverberated through all three of Charles's kingdoms – Scotland, Ireland and then England. Charles had been unable to establish military control in any of them and, following defeat in England, surrender to his original tormentors had come to seem his best option.

This personal humiliation signalled the end of one of the most destructive conflicts in English history, in which a larger percentage of the population may have died than in the First World War, and huge amounts of property had been destroyed. Armies had tramped the land, bringing in their wake terrible plagues. The coming harvest was bad, the crops ruined by wet weather, and over the next four years famine threatened. To many contemporaries these were unmistakable judgements of God on a sinful land: war, disease and famine, three of the Horsemen of the Apocalypse. After four years of war in England, however, there was still no agreement about which sins, specifically, were being punished.

Three days after the surrender of the King a London bookseller called George Thomason bought a tract, *Gods Fury, Englands Fire*, which promised the answer. Thomason, an avid (perhaps obsessive) collector of pamphlets, had acquired around thirty tracts published during or dealing with the events of that week. They were dominated by two issues: the surrender of the King and the chaos of religious opinion that many now saw in England. With the King defeated, God's judgement on the battle of arms now clear, it did not take much imagination to identify religion as the issue which should now be addressed. John Benbrigge, the author of *Gods Fury*, took as his text Isaiah xlii, 24–5:

Who gave Jacob for a spoil and Israel to the robbers? Did not the Lord? He against whom we have sinned? For they would not walk in his ways, neither were they obedient to his Law. Therefore he hath poured on him the fury of his anger, and the strength of battle, and it hath set him on fire round about; yet he knew not; and it burned him, and he laid it not to heart.

The general relevance was clear, but what was it that English sinners should lay to heart? Benbrigge promised to identify 'those spiritual incendiaries which have set church and state on fire' and exhorted 'all persons to join together in seeking to quench it'. He also promised to explain how to 'prevent the fire from being unquenchable in our ruin'. Like many others he set out his partisan view in a laboured and formalistic argument, based on scriptural authorities. His difficulty though was that reasoning of this kind, and scriptural authority, could not convince doubters. In the lush world of civil war print there were too many competing voices of reason, and divergent readings of scripture, to clinch an argument this way. Other partisans could make a competing case in the same style, from similar authorities, while some renounced scholarship and scripture altogether for these purposes. Benbrigge had nothing to say on this deeper problem, and is now forgotten.[1]

Thomason eventually bought around 20,000 tracts between 1640 and 1660, a collection which reveals another dimension of the crisis: the very wide publicity given to these fundamental political disagreements. From the very beginning of the Scottish crisis partisans had distributed tracts, mobilized petitions, organized demonstrations and, eventually, raised armies. Benbrigge was by no means the most obscure figure to be given a public voice as a result – leathersellers preached, women spoke of their visions to senior army commanders, men of pre-eminent obscurity purged churches of scandalous ministers and offensive images. Here was a challenge to the cultural authority not just of scripture and reason, but also of kings, bishops and gentlemen, of courts and institutions of government, of learning and universities. Contemporaries had no shortage of languages in which to describe the resulting chaos or to express anxiety: Thomason's collection is full of discussions of portents and wonders, and of the principles which, if agreed, might bring an end to fighting. But there were no such terms. As long as people like Benbrigge offered different versions of the nature of the problem, to a wide public and without finding new grounds on which to convince people, there remained a chaos of highly principled and competing certainties.

In one sense this was a crisis in Reformation politics – over the nature of the true religion, how to decide what that was, and of the proper relationship between religious and secular authority. In Scotland a religious party, the Covenanters, took control of the discontents, mobilizing pretty much the whole kingdom around a manifesto for a new settlement. They created a radical movement but one that had clear goals and, therefore, clear limits. The combination of a unified Scottish church and a revolutionary constitution gave control to identifiable political leaders: it was a revolution defined in theory and practice by Reformation politics. In Ireland, Catholic elites excluded from power on the basis of their religion took advantage of the crisis, seeking to recover their position by appealing to their king, in opposition to his English parliament and the Protestant political establishment. In the process they unleashed a popular revolt against Protestant settlement. Armies from Scotland and England were sent to defend the Protestant interest and Ireland eventually suffered the greatest devastation: a bloody, sectional conflict whose memory and relevance live on.

England's experience of this crisis was more hesitant, anxious and divided than Scotland's; but also more radical in its outcomes. And unlike Ireland the conflict was for most people an argument within a single church and state, about its true identity, past and future; it never quite became a war between rival confessions. Almost everyone was against popery (although they could not necessarily agree what it was) and the bitterest public recriminations about religious belief were often within the parliamentary coalition. England, the metropolitan kingdom, was the cockpit of the British crisis, its armies and battles the largest, its presses by far the most active, its public discussion completely open-ended and almost without social restriction.

This conflict over religion had profound political implications: Sir John Eliot, for example, thought 'religion it is that keeps the subject in obedience . . . [it is] the common obligation among men; the tie of all friendship and society; the bond of all office and relation; writing every duty into the conscience, the strictest of all laws'.[2] Confronted by the demands of the Covenanters, Charles had said that to concede would reduce him to the condition of the 'Duke of Venice': refusing to concede, it subsequently turned out, had reduced him much further. Criticisms of his rule implicitly raised fundamental questions not only about him, but about kingship, the normal form of government in seventeenth-century Europe (aside from city republics such as Venice that made do with a Doge). Over the coming decade the effort to make Charles see a different sense failed, and it became increasingly difficult to avoid asking what to do with a king who was unfit to rule, or to deal with. Fundamentally, that was a question about monarchy: a king governed by his subjects, or chosen by them, was a peculiar kind of king, perhaps no king at all; but a king who stubbornly led his people into religious error and civil war could hardly be said to be doing God's work, which was surely the purpose of kings.

Three years after his surrender to the Scots, Charles chose martyrdom to an ideal of the Anglican church and sacred monarchy rather than a deal with his English subjects. A powerful minority among his subjects, supported by the army, chose to execute him and establish a kingless government, rather than try any longer to get a deal from him. Fired both by a Reformation certainty (that God had called them to take charge of the commonwealth) and by an idea more associated with the Enlightenment (that the purpose of government was the good of the people, and should be answerable to their representative), these militants put their king on trial, then abolished the monarchy and the House of Lords. Like many modern revolutionaries they made this a year zero: according to their supporters this was the first year of England's freedom.

Out of a chaos of opinion and anxiety, and of the catastrophe and trauma of civil war, had come ideas about freedom and citizenship, religious toleration and the exclusion of secular power from matters of conscience. These arguments had deeper roots in the English past but were newly public, and newly in power. These English discussions about the origins and limits of political power were of profound significance for Enlightenment Europe – indeed, to the more celebrated revolutions in eighteenth-century America and France. But they were not, as far as we know, representative of average opinions: others sought resolutions to the crisis in astrology, the prosecution of witches, or the restoration of older forms of religious and political authority. Neither did this minority remain united, or command political power for very long – in 1660 a monarch was restored who indulged freely in the practice of touching for the King's Evil, curing a tubercular disease by virtue of his divinely sanctioned power. In that sense the revolution was of limited significance, and civil peace might have been established on other terms sooner than 1660.

It is conventional to tell that constitutional story – of a republican failure ending in restoration – but to do so is to limit the significance of the 1640s to that single constitutional question. There is much more to say, and to remember, about England's decade of civil war and revolution. Political and religious questions of fundamental importance were thrashed out before broad political audiences as activists and opportunists sought to mobilize support for their proposals. The resulting mass of contemporary argument is alluring to the historian since it lays bare the presumptions of a society very alien to our own. At the same time, by exposing those presumptions to sustained critical examination, this public discussion changed them. This was a decade of intense debate and spectacular intellectual creativity – not just in politics and religion, but in understandings of the natural world and in how political opinion was mobilized. The implications of this English experience reverberated around the world of the Enlightenment and English politics were permanently changed by the experience of popular mobilization: much more was at stake than the fate of Charles I and hence the restoration of his son did not settle the arguments, or erase the memory of what had been said.

England's civil wars were components of a larger crisis, of all three Stuart kingdoms. Nonetheless, although English experience cannot be understood outside that British context, this is a book about the distinctive English experience of that shared crisis. England was the last of Charles's kingdoms to rebel, and the one with the most spontaneous royalist party, but also the one with the most radical and creative politics. Part of the resolution of that apparent paradox is to study the conditions which made this extraordinary creativity possible. Crucial among them was the appeal to ordinary people, often those without a vote, to support particular platforms, and the creative dialogue between activists, opportunists and their wider publics. In this fluid and confused political world public support was courted, opinions were mobilized and, in the name of the people, a revolution was carried out. My aim here is to understand that political process in England, to capture the anxiety and trauma of civil war, the plurality of responses and the creative confusion to which it gave rise. To say that God's fury had caused England's fire was in these circumstances to start an argument rather than end one. Therein lay the crisis of Reformation politics.

The Crisis of the Three
Kingdoms, 1637–1642

I

From the Bowels of the Whore of Babel

*The Scottish Prayer Book Rebellion and the Politics
of Reformation*

It was more like a procession than an invasion. When a large Scottish
army passed through Flodden in 1640, their progress was 'very solemn
and sad much after the heavy form showed in funerals'. Trumpeters
decked with mourning ribbons led the way, followed by one hundred
ministers and, in their midst, the Bible 'covered with a mourning cover'.
Behind the ministers came old men with petitions in their hands along
with the military commanders, also wearing black ribbons or 'some sign
of mourning'. Finally came the soldiers, trailing pikes tied with black
ribbons, accompanied by drummers 'beating a sad march such as they
say is used in the funerals of officers of war'.[1]

This was a forceful demonstration about the death of the Bible, a
complaint about the fate of the true, scriptural religion in Scotland. The
origin of their protest was revulsion at a new Prayer Book, introduced
in 1637 and described by the Earl of Montrose as 'brood of the bowels
of the whore of Babel'. '[T]he life of the gospel', he said, had been 'stolen
away by enforcing on the kirk a dead service book'.[2] Here was its funeral.
In fact the army was not, strictly speaking, the army of the Scots but of
the Covenanters, men who had entered a mutual bond before God to
defend the true religion. Even at this stage there were Scots who were
not Covenanters, and that distinction was to become extremely significant in the coming years – Montrose, for one, was later to abandon this
version of the cause and become the champion of armed royalism in
Scotland.

This was not the first time that a Scottish army had taken this road,
inland from the fortified town of Berwick and crossing the river Tweed,
which marks the border between England and Scotland at its eastern
end, just south of Coldstream. The last time, in 1513, it had ended in
disaster: perhaps 5,000 Scots died, among them the Scottish king, eleven

earls, fifteen lords, three bishops and much of the rest of Scotland's governing class.[3] Fear of the arrival of armed Scots in the north had caused centuries of concern in England. Indeed tenants in the Borders had enjoyed unusual freedoms in return for an obligation to offer armed resistance to Scottish incursions, and the prevalence of cross-border cattle raiding had given rise to something like clan society. When James VI of Scotland ascended to the English throne in 1603, the Borders had, in his vision, become middle shires, and the problems had receded somewhat. Nonetheless, armed Scots were not regarded with equanimity in northern England.[4]

This time, however, they were barely opposed and the march past Flodden was the prelude to a successful occupation of northern England, achieved more or less without a fight. Alexander Leslie's Covenanting army were faced by 10,000 English troops with more in reserve further south. But this English force was easily discouraged. At Newburn on 28 August, just over a week after they had crossed the border, a short action saw the English routed and on 30 August the Scottish army marched unopposed into Newcastle, one of the nation's most significant cities.

This, then, was a very peculiar occupation: many Englishmen seem to have felt that the Scots had right on their side, or at least that the English army did not. When they reached Heddon-on-the-Wall, one of the invaders later recalled, 'old mistress Finnick came out and met us, and burst out and said, "And is it not so, that Jesus Christ will not come to England for reforming abuses, but with an army of 22,000 men at his back?"'[5] Certainly English forces, locally and nationally, were half-hearted in their responses. The Scottish party had actively courted, and clearly expected to receive, the sympathy of local people, and they were not disappointed.

England and Scotland were separate kingdoms under the same king – their churches, law, administration and representative institutions remained distinct. Like his father, who had first possessed the two crowns together, Charles governed Scotland from London, but he now hastened north. He intended to 'contain the Northern Counties at his devotion', fearing, it was said, that local people might 'waver' in their support for him. Opinion there had apparently been 'empoisoned by the pestilent declaration cast among them' by the Covenanters.[6] In their propaganda campaign of the summer of 1640, in print and in circulating

the English and Scotts Armies at first ready to fight, lovingly embrace each other, & part kinde freinds

Many English soldiers were said to be more sympathetic towards the Scots than to the King's cause in 1640

manuscripts, the Covenanters had made it clear that they had no quarrel with England but were forced to take these actions in order to defend their religion and liberties. Some of their papers and publications went further, suggesting that they intended to help England to complete its own Reformation, and that they were an instrument of God's providence in that respect.[7] Charles's government was palpably anxious about this propaganda effort.[8] Without the 'awe of his Majesty's presence' it was feared that local people might 'easily be tempted to fall to the Scottish party, or at leastwise, to let them pass through them without resistance or opposition'. It even seemed necessary to issue a proclamation that the Covenanters were 'Rebels and Traitors'. Only a nervous government would have felt it necessary to say so, or to add: 'so shall all they be deemed and reported that assist or supply them with money or victual, or shall not with all their might oppose and fight against them'.[9]

These fears about local loyalties were not groundless. The Covenanters had been amazed that Newcastle was surrendered without a fight[10] and within a week or so of arriving had made the town defensible, something the townspeople had neglected to do over the previous summer.[11] Prior to the crossing of the Tweed there had clearly been contacts with highly placed English politicians and the decision to invade had involved a careful calculation about the effect of crossing onto English soil on English sympathies.[12]

Although this episode is often described as a Scottish invasion it is better understood as a forceful demonstration of grievances by the Covenanters appealing to potential sympathizers in England. The royal proclamation had tried to obscure that distinction, but this was a religious protest intended to make common cause with fellow travellers in one of Charles's other kingdoms. It enjoyed some success in that respect and there are persistent suspicions about active collusion. Certainly a willingness to accept that the Covenanters were rebels (rather than, say, loyal petitioners with right on their side) became something of a political litmus test in England.[13] Reformation politics did not necessarily respect national borders or dynastic loyalties.

The Covenanting movement arose from attempts to harmonize religious practice in England and Scotland, which eventually raised fundamental issues in Reformation politics. In 1629, at the suggestion of William Laud, then Bishop of London, Charles had considered the introduction of the English Prayer Book into Scotland. The concerns of his Scottish bishops, however, had been sufficiently clear, and sufficiently substantial, to persuade him to back off.[14] Scottish practice was more rigorously Calvinist in its doctrine, liturgy and church government, and this purity of practice was defined in part in contrast to the 'halfly reformed' English church. Moreover, the influence of bishops and recent trends in Protestant practice in England seemed to threaten the Calvinist inheritance. These threats could be understood as differing facets of 'popery', a polemical escalation which made it hard to limit discussion to the specific measures being proposed. Ceremonial tinkering became emblematic of threats to the identity and future of Scottish Protestantism, which in turn raised questions about who should be custodian of that future, and the relations between church and state.

At the heart of the Reformation message was a rejection of the power of individual believers, or of the church acting on their behalf, to affect God's judgement about who should be saved and who should be damned. Martin Luther had been convinced, like Augustine, of the powerlessness and unworthiness of fallen humanity, and struck by the force of God's mercy. Good works could not merit this mercy, or affect a sovereign God: instead individual sinners were entirely dependent on

God's mercy and justified (saved) by faith alone. Jean Calvin, a generation later, developed more clearly the predestinarian implications – since some men were saved and some were damned, and since this had nothing to do with their own efforts, it must mean that God had created some men predestined for salvation (the elect). This seemed to imply that He must also have predestined other men for damnation (double predestination), a line of argument which led into dangerous territory. Some theologians, Calvin's close associate Beza among them, went further and argued that the entire course of human history was foreordained prior to Adam and Eve's fall in the Garden of Eden. These views (particularly the latter, 'supralapsarian' arguments) seemed to their opponents to suggest that God was the author of the sin, both in Eden and in those who were subsequently predestined for damnation. They also raised a question about Christ's sacrifice on the cross – had that been made to atone for the sins of all, or only of the elect? Because of these dangers many of those with strong predestinarian views were unsure about whether or not the doctrine should be openly preached. Clever theologians, like expensive lawyers, are adept at failing to push arguments too far and there were many respectable positions short of the one adopted by Beza. But predestination was for many Protestants a fundamental – retreat from this doctrine implied a role for free will expressed in works rather than a justification by faith. It thus reopened the door to the corruptions of late-medieval Christianity.[15]

In defending these views Luther and subsequent reformers took their stand on scripture, the Word, rather than the accumulated tradition and wisdom of the church. This too became central to Reformation argument. It led to an emphasis on the relationship between the individual believer and God, mediated by scripture rather than a priesthood interceding on behalf of the flock, and elevated preaching of the Word at the expense of many forms of shared ritual. Scriptural warrant was found for only two sacraments – baptism and communion. Much of the rest of the ceremonial life of the church gave way to exposition of scripture. Placing the Word at the centre of the religious experience led to a suspicion of potentially distracting ritual or imagery and practices which had previously been regarded as central to worship. What had previously been seen as important for fostering a sense of fellowship or edifying the believer was now often seen as superstitious or idolatrous.[16]

Emphasis on the Word therefore had implications for forms of public worship, and controversy over matters of faith frequently centred around these visible expressions of religious belief: these questions were of much more widespread and immediate significance to ordinary Christians. They also drove the roots of these theological controversies very deeply into European society. What happened at each moment of each occasion of religious worship in every corner of Europe could provide the focus for a debate which was literally more important than life or death. More than Luther, Calvin and his followers tended towards an austere view of the role of ritual and image in communicating religious truth, placing great emphasis on scripture, expounded by ministers who were expected to be effective preachers.

There were differences of degree and opinion on these matters, which divided not only Protestant from Catholic, but Protestant reformers from one another. Predestination was urged with caution, and although religious practices were tested more stringently against scripture this did not lead to the abandonment of all traditional practices. Importantly, it was possible to defend 'harmless' practices which were not specified in scripture, but which were not counter to it. In particular a residual role was reserved for edification – sensitizing the believer to the saving message – which allowed for the preservation of parts of the medieval tradition.

Similarly, respectable reformed opinion was not anti-clerical. Most reformers believed that scripture was not self-explanatory, and needed to be expounded by those with a gift for such exposition. There were good reasons to be careful about pushing the argument against an intercessory priesthood too far – it might entail standing idly by while misinformed brethren with a poor understanding of God's Word pursued their own damnation. Equally, there were concrete fears about the consequences for this world of allowing misinformed brethren to follow what they mistakenly understood to be their conscience. The Münster Anabaptists who had held property in common or the German peasants who had engaged in social protest during the 1520s were remembered as the exemplars of the dangers of ungoverned spiritual life. The pursuit of reformation often entailed a reduction in the space allowed to clerical authority, therefore, but almost always stopped short of allowing individual believers complete freedom to define their own relationship with God.[17] Priest became minister and teacher; the individual believer was by no means left isolated.

At the centre of the Reformation message was the view that individuals were saved (justified) by faith, not works; a greater emphasis on scripture as a guide to the Christian life; and a pared-down sacramental and ceremonial worship focused more clearly on the Word. These issues, although fundamental, were not without ambiguities – over the doctrine of predestination and its implications, over which elements of the received tradition were acceptable, and over which particular practices edified, or were superstitious, idolatrous and distracting. The Reformation was not a completed event but a process and the Protestant faiths were recovered rather than founded: Reformation politics were not driven by a desire to establish a new church but the urgent need to purify the old one. This might mean stripping out of the liturgy, ritual and physical fabric of the church those corruptions which were counter to the true scriptural religion, or removing the vestiges of the papal corruption of the constitution of the church which had allowed errors to flourish. But in Scotland, as everywhere else, the nature of the task and its limits were contested.

Although there was no unambiguous agreement about what a restored church would look like, it did seem clear to many Protestants that the principal enemy of that restoration was the Bishop of Rome. The favoured term of abuse for unwelcome practices was therefore 'popery': a term which gave a comforting polemical clarity when debating complex issues. Polemic about the nature of the true church, or of its opponents, was often couched in terms of anti-popery, and the language of anti-popery was used to mark the boundaries of acceptable belief and practice. What popery might mean in any particular context was highly contestable, of course – it was the opposite of truly Christian belief and practice, but if people differed on what true belief and practice were, they automatically identified popery differently too. The Pope, in this view, was the agent of the Antichrist, or even actually the Antichrist – the promoter of practices and beliefs inimical to the salvation of good Christians. The control exercised by the Bishop of Rome over the church was the equivalent of the Babylonish captivity of the Israelites. Complex debates about scriptural justification for particular elements of belief and practice, about the authenticity of the tradition that they represented, or about the effects of political compromise on the promotion of reform, might easily dissolve into shouting matches about popery and the Antichrist.[18]

This radical simplification could raise the issues to apocalyptic levels since it was often said that these battles corresponded to the battles in the biblical last days: the triumph of reformation over popery would, it was hoped, lead to the reign of Christ and the saints. Obviously, the radicalism, and simplicity, of this rhetoric made the negotiation of a harmonious consensus difficult. The clarity of the polemic was a contrast to the complexity of the identity problem to which it related; the certainties it offered were perhaps comforts in the face of the anxieties generated by that complexity. Popery was an important discourse within Protestantism precisely because the boundary between the purified church and the corrupt Roman Catholic church was both crucial and indistinct.

These arguments about reformation raised questions about how churches should be governed and about the relationship with secular authorities which would protect these churches. On both of these crucial questions, however, the reformers' message was pragmatic, and therefore a little ambiguous. Calvin's first, and most influential, publication was the *Institutes*, which was the first statement of Protestant belief to discuss civil government at length. This interest in the relationship between religious and secular authority was a product of the experience of the second generation of religious reformers, who were frequently men forced into exile by the hostility of their own rulers to reform. In exile in Geneva, Calvin oversaw the establishment of a Presbyterian ecclesiastical organization, which was often catering to the needs of an exile community. This stood alongside a secular authority, membership of which was not open to refugees. The refugee experience therefore fostered, in practice and theory, parallel systems of religious and secular government: two kingdoms, in fact. Secular and religious affairs were separated, and placed in the hands of different kinds of authority. Pushed to an extreme position, this might suggest that secular rulers had no role in religious affairs.[19] Most monarchs were very suspicious of 'two kingdoms' theory, for obvious reasons.

Although Calvin had developed an influential argument about the appropriate constitution of the church, and its relationship with civil authority, that was not the essence of the Reformation message, even for Calvin. Calvin had distinguished four functions for the clergy – doctors, ministers, elders and deacons – but these four functions were not associated with any particular form. Doctors ensured the purity of doctrine, ministers preached, elders oversaw discipline and deacons gave an example of Christian charity. All four functions could be identified in scripture, but there was no clear prescription as to how to allocate these disparate functions in actual offices.[20] There was no necessary assumption that in following Calvin's teaching in other political contexts it was necessary to establish Presbyterianism on the Genevan model. The Presbyterian organization of Calvin's church offered a model for others, but by comparison with the fundamentals – preaching, sacraments, reformation – how the church was governed was of secondary significance, a practical question. Reformation came to different places by various means, resulting in a variety of settlements of this practical question.

Rather than a prescriptive view of how churches should be organized, Calvinists looked for signs that particular churches had the marks of a 'true church'. Even those who held very strict predestinarian views agreed that it was not possible to be certain about who was a member of the elect and who was damned. This gave rise to a distinction between the visible church of all practising Christians and the invisible church of the elect. Protestants tended to assess visible churches according to the agreed marks of a true church – the signs that members of the invisible church might be present. Naturally enough, there was room for disagreement about what the marks of a true church were, but they always included the preaching of the Word and administration of the sacraments (rightly understood).

Beza and others added discipline to the list – a collective effort to combat sin and teach the true religion. For the very reason that it was not possible to know who was saved and who was damned, it was incumbent on everyone to secure the purification of the visible church, and also of the society around them. Avoiding sin, and abhorring the sins of others, did not secure a place in heaven, but they might be evidence of membership of the invisible church. In alliance with the secular power, the ecclesiastical authorities should put down sin wherever possible: an alliance of magistrate and minister aimed at the eradication of sin transformed a church reformation into a societal one. The discipline of the flock – both in worship and in their everyday lives – was therefore of central concern to the reformers.

It was these fundamentals – Word, sacrament and (for some) discipline – which marked out a true church. If these things were present there was ample room for accommodation to apparently uncongenial forms of ceremony, and no significant school of thought identified a particular form of church government as one of the marks of a true church. It also became common among Calvinists to distinguish between churches which were under the Cross – that is, those which did not enjoy the protection of a godly civil authority – and those which did.[21]

When Charles proposed changes in Scottish practice emphasizing formality and ceremony in worship he was not necessarily betraying the Reformation message, even if he was denounced by his opponents as popish; and using his authority as monarch to achieve this was not necessarily a betrayal either. Many Protestants might have viewed these ceremonies as harmless and remained confident that the kirk remained a true church under a godly civil authority. But that is clearly not how it seemed in Scotland. That fact owes as much to the history of the Scottish Reformation as to the nature of the changes actually being proposed.

Reformation had come to Scotland by means of a coup against royal authority in 1560. The 'Lords of the Congregation', a group of Protestant nobles, led an armed rising against the unpopular French regent, Mary of Guise. Following their success French interest was excluded from Scotland by the Treaty of Edinburgh and a parliament was called which, among other things, legislated for a reformation. John Knox, recently returned from religious exile in Calvin's Geneva, gave spiritual leadership to the movement and in doing so imported the Calvinist vision of reformation. But the coming of reformation nonetheless involved compromises. The parliament of 1560 had legislated in the light of a confession of faith and a Book of Discipline. According to later legend this was the result of the irresistible pressure for Protestant reformation, but in fact it owed much to opportunism and political chance – the Scottish Reformation was not completed in a single step or according to a blueprint.[22]

Important practical compromises were made in the interests of domestic peace. The bishops, who after all were not the means by which reformation had arrived, were not allowed to say Mass but they were not compelled to subscribe to the confession of faith either, and neither was anyone else. Some of the bishops joined in the promotion of reform and their efforts were supplemented rather than supplanted by superintendents, appointed to direct the pastoral effort in areas without a sympathetic bishop. These new offices were not really rivals to the episcopal office, therefore, but a means of strengthening its pastoral role where that was perceived to be weak.[23] Since the monarch was a devoted Catholic she could not oversee the Reformation in Scotland and as a result a General Assembly was formed modelled on the composition of the Scottish parliament.[24] The role of the parish was perpetuated in the kirk sessions, later claimed on dubious authority to have grown out of voluntary Protestant congregations – privy kirks – operating prior to 1560. This version of the history of the Reformation emphasized again the roots of the Reformation among the flock, rather than its debt to the head. If their significance to the origins of the Reformation has been exaggerated or distorted, however, they were certainly of crucial significance to the subsequent development of Scottish Protestantism. Through the sessions the parish remained the fundamental unit of church organization, providing preaching, sacraments and discipline of the flock. It was these institutions which, over time, became the motor of Scottish reformation.[25] Finally, weekly exercises took root, meetings where preaching could reach an audience beyond the parish, or reach parishioners not well served with a preaching ministry at home.[26] In all, this was a hybrid and pragmatic solution, which supplemented the ancient institutions of the church by giving some of its functions to new bodies, and it developed over time in an organic way.

A second ambiguity, or compromise, was that the legislation setting up these new arrangements was not ratified. When Queen Mary returned from France in August 1561 she issued a proclamation enjoining obedience to 'public and universally standing practices' then current. While this did allow for the prosecution of 'mass mongers' it did not validate or endow the new church. Only after 1567, when Mary was deposed in favour of her infant son, James VI, was legislation counter to the Reformation rescinded. The provisional nature of the arrangements of the 1560s is also reflected in the fact that in 1573, when the position of Protestantism was clearly established, it was suggested that the General Assembly had served its purpose and the stewardship of the church might now return to the crown.[27] It was certainly not the case that the General Assembly was by law the supreme authority in ecclesiastical matters. The founding vision of reformation in Scotland had not given the kirk a clear constitution or an unambiguous relationship to civil authority.

Over the following years there was growing pressure to adopt a Presbyterian model of church government in order to promote reformation, but this met with monarchical resistance. The institutions of the reformed church had been set alongside those of the old church, supplementing rather than supplanting them in order to promote the pastoral work of the reformers. The priority was the promotion of a pastoral ministry – supporting the preaching of the Word, true sacramental worship and discipline. As time passed, however, the institutional compromises of the 1560s came increasingly to be seen as presenting obstacles to that. Old church institutions were deprived of their pastoral role but not of their endowments, whereas the new institutions were given pastoral functions but inadequate endowments.[28] Evangelists pushing for the establishment of a more active ministry might easily identify kirk sessions, weekly exercises, superintendents and the General Assembly as their allies; bishops and the monarch, however, were less unambiguously on the side of the saints.

As a result there was a tendency for convinced Calvinists to push for greater institutional security for an independent kirk. This was also associated with a desire to secure the four functions of the clergy in a form more akin to Genevan Presbyterianism, to develop the new institutions established alongside the skeleton of the old church in a Presbyterian direction and to separate their authority from that of the crown. The guiding spirit for this is usually assumed to have been Andrew Melville, former exile in Geneva and close ally of Beza, although there is little direct evidence to show that he did direct these developments. But from the 1570s onwards it was thought that the promotion of reform meant endowing the pastoral ministry at the expense of the remnants of the pre-Reformation church, and making it more answerable to the needs of the flock. This created a pressure to transform the kirk sessions, weekly exercises, superintendents and General Assembly into a fully developed Presbyterian church.[29]

Melville was certainly influential in the General Assembly which adopted the second Book of Discipline in 1578. This stated that the authority of the kirk flowed directly from God and had no temporal lord, and condemned the office of bishop. Bishops were excluded from the General Assembly and from 1581 membership depended on nomination from the kirk sessions. The political influence of Presbyterians was enhanced during a Catholic scare around 1580, when the dominance of the Earl of Lennox in secular affairs seemed to threaten rapprochement with the Roman church. In 1581 a Negative Confession was drawn up, denouncing popery in general and in a number of particular forms, and Lennox agreed to subscribe, again seeming to confirm that the kirk, not the civil power, was the guardian of the reformed faith.[30] It was to become a key text in the Covenanting crisis, a benchmark of shared belief, promoted in the face of an ungodly civil power.

Although the General Assembly could adopt the second Book of Discipline as a programme, it would require crown and Parliament to give it legal force and the assembly certainly could not prevent the continued appointment of bishops by the crown. In 1582 Lennox was overthrown as a result of the Ruthven Raid, in which several prominent Presbyterian nobles, led by William Ruthven, Earl of Gowrie, abducted James VI while he was staying at Ruthven's castle. The King was kept in captivity for a year and during that time government was in Ruthven's hands. A series of pro-Presbyterian proclamations followed, but when James was eventually free of the power of the Raiders he quickly revealed a determination to curb Presbyterianism. Legislation the following year (later known as the Black Acts) reasserted episcopal and royal authority. An Act of 1592 recognized the jurisdiction of Presbyterian courts and removed the bishops' jurisdiction, but did not acknowledge that Presbyterian discipline drew its authority directly from God. Neither did it abolish episcopacy, and although the General Assembly was given a statutory authority to assemble every year, the crown could still name the time and place of the meeting.[31]

James's hostility to Melville's views is often attributed to his political rather than strictly theological preferences. Indeed, there were few if any monarchs who would have welcomed Presbyterianism, because it was associated with 'two kingdoms' theory. The initial triumph of Protestantism, and the subsequent elaboration of Calvinist reform in Scotland, had come in opposition to a weakened monarch (and, indeed, with the military help of the English). Doctrines stressing a very clear separation of church and state were therefore a particularly worrying threat to monarchical authority in Scotland, where the nobility had plenty of recent 'form' in this respect. At a conference in 1596 Melville notoriously told James that he was 'God's silly vassal': His representative in civil affairs but just another member of the kirk. By the late sixteenth century there were two respectable views of the Scottish kirk – one based on 'two kingdoms' theory, and associated in particular with Melvillians; and another based on 'one kingdom' theory, which emphasized monarchical authority over all the bodies and institutions of the kingdom, including the church.[32]

James may therefore have had particular reasons for hostility to Presbyterianism, but he was not flying in the face of the reformed tradition in Scotland in seeking to preserve a role for bishops and the crown, and his views were not completely outside the mainstream of Scottish Protestant opinion. In fact, Melville's outburst in 1596 more or less coincided with a reaction against the very clericalist view of Presbyterianism. Ironically, by emphasizing the separation of kirk and state matters, and arguing that authority in the kirk was a manifestation of divine will, Melville could appear to be raising up the clerical caste once more. *Jure divino* presbytery – Presbyterian organization justified as by the law of God – might seem little more than the old popery writ large, and was certainly not the only authentic view of authority in the reformed church. James had some support in resisting it. In 1600 'parliamentary bishops' were appointed – they sat in parliament as representatives of the church but did not have any ecclesiastical jurisdiction. Within the kirk, commissioners had been appointed to oversee its discipline, and over the years these positions sometimes went to parliamentary bishops: clearly this pointed towards a revival of modified episcopacy.[33]

Following his accession to the English throne James also tried to make Scottish and English practice more alike, both in matters of church government and in forms of worship. He successfully manipulated a series of General Assemblies to establish the reality of his power to summon them and to secure meetings more amenable to his views. By 1610 he had intruded bishops first as permanent moderators of kirk sessions and then of synods, and the admission of ministers was made their responsibility rather than that of presbyteries. Estates and consistorial powers were restored. In the same year, normal episcopal succession was restored by the consecration of Scottish bishops, normal except that it was done in Westminster by English hands.[34]

All this was more offensive to the chattering classes than to the parishioner in the pew, for whom the daily functioning of the kirk was largely unchanged. In any case these constitutional questions were of secondary significance. Changes to forms of worship, however, were far more likely to evoke a reaction in the localities. It was in forms of worship that the signs of a true church were manifest – preaching and sacraments – and it was in worship that ordinary Christians encountered the visible church. In Scotland discipline was often seen as a mark of a true church, and the kirk sessions, which assumed responsibility for discipline, had planted deep roots in the religious and political life of local communities.[35] The kirk had deep local roots and it was of course a formal presumption of Reformation thought that the laity should be well-informed. The radical potential of Reformation ideas was not socially restricted and the details of local religious practice were habitually invested with considerable, even apocalyptic, significance. Changing local religious practice ran the risk of arousing principled resistance from the whole Christian congregation. It is not perhaps surprising, therefore, that James met more significant resistance to proposed changes in worship after 1612 than he had to his reforms of church government.

Worship in the kirk had initially used the English Prayer Book of 1549, but this had given way in the early years of the Reformation to a more austere Book of Common Order, although there is some evidence that it was sometimes used alongside the English Book. Dissatisfied with the Book of Common Order, James promoted a new Prayer Book. He was not alone in thinking that the Book needed attention, and it may have been falling out of use through neglect in the early seventeenth century. James's new Book went through three drafts after having been commissioned at a General Assembly in 1616, the final one closely resembling the English Prayer Book. However, although it was ready for printing in 1619, it was never issued, a reflection of hostility to these changes in the form of worship. In the meantime the Five Articles of Perth (enjoining the observance of the main holy days in the Christian calendar, kneeling at communion, private communion, private baptism and confirmation by bishops) had caused serious difficulty at a General Assembly in 1617. Although they were bullied through an assembly at Perth in 1618 and a parliament in 1621, they were not subsequently enforced, and in securing consent James had promised not to promote any more changes. In the meantime the Prayer Book was dropped.[36]

By the 1620s Scottish Presbyterianism stood in a rather uneasy tension with the episcopal authority favoured by the crown. Episcopal authority was not particularly welcome, and for sound historical reasons many thought that Scottish Christians could not depend on the crown to promote godliness. But changes in church government were of far less immediate and widespread concern than changes to forms of worship –

James had secured some success in turning back the tide of Presbyterianization in the kirk, but had been forced to leave off attempts to change the liturgy. Many Scottish Protestants had by the 1620s developed a pretty austere view of appropriate forms of worship. Unlike many other Protestant churches, for example, it had abandoned the celebration of Christmas. This strand of opinion was again at odds with the preferences of the monarch. A greater emphasis on ceremonial was likely to be seen as a retreat from reformation, particularly if it was associated with the authority of bishops, and there were also plenty of vested interests hostile to the increasing political and administrative power of the bishops. Crucially for the mobilization of the Covenanting movement, the Presbyterian system had deep roots in Scottish society: kirk sessions exercised an often quite effective control over the lives of the local population and integrated local worship into a national church. It was probably parochial self-determination, as much as the precise content of worship, that mattered.[37]

The Scottish Reformation had left unresolved tensions about both the internal organization of the kirk and its relationship with the secular power of the monarchy. There was a strong but not unchallengeable case that the purity of Scottish religion depended on the independence of the kirk from monarchical and episcopal control. At the same time, in the localities, a Calvinist discipline had developed with a far closer embrace of social life than had been achieved in England.

These big issues in Reformation politics acquired a particular edge in the years following the outbreak of war in Bohemia in 1618. What became the Thirty Years War engulfed much of the Holy Roman Empire, which dominated central Europe, and involved armies from the whole continent. Lands gained for Protestantism in the sixteenth century fell to Catholic forces, and for some publicists this came to represent a battle for the future of the true religion.[38] Of course, it was in reality both more and less than this, but the implications of that battle were relevant in every place of worship in Christendom. As Protestant armies fought for the future of the true religion, so creeping popery at home seemed more shocking. Many Scots left to fight these wars in the 1620s and 1630s,[39] and the battle on the home front was not neglected.

At the same time Calvinist orthodoxy was challenged by forms of Protestantism which questioned predestinarian theology, and placed a greater emphasis on ritual and edification. These tendencies were denounced as 'Arminian', creating an association with a bitterly divisive controversy in the Dutch republic in the early seventeenth century provoked by the anti-predestinarian preaching of Arminius. His followers, who became known as the Remonstrants, rejected double predestination and supralapsarian beliefs on the grounds that they made God the author of sin. But this reopened the possibility that responsibility for damnation lay with the sinner – as if free will, or the actions of humans, might affect the will of God – a question at the heart of the Reformation. It was also overlain with political significance, since the Arminians were associated with those supporting peace with Catholic Spain after nearly fifty years of war, and the abandonment of the southern Netherlands to Catholicism. In 1618 a synod was called at Dort, at which representatives of reformed churches from all over Europe were present. Stern predestinarian views were confirmed as the principal tenets of mature Calvinism, Arminianism was roundly condemned, and the Remonstrants were politically defeated in an associated coup.[40]

From the later 1620s onwards Charles was associated with changes in the English church which were denounced as Arminian, and this weakened respect for the English church in Scotland, which had in any case been very measured. England's Reformation had also been marked by pragmatism and compromise. There, as in Scotland, predestinarian thought had been very influential, but Presbyterianism, 'two kingdoms' theory and austere views of worship were much less so. The 'official Reformation' of the 1530s had been primarily jurisdictional, excluding the authority of the Pope from the affairs of the English church, rather than doctrinal: 'Catholicism without the Pope', as its detractors have claimed ever since. Thereafter the Royal Supremacy in the Church was a vehicle for quite different purposes, not just under Henry VIII, whose official policy shifted somewhat, but much more so under his evangelical Protestant son Edward VI and Catholic daughter Mary. It was only with the accession of Elizabeth in 1558 that the Reformation was securely established, particularly if that is taken to imply the widespread acceptance of Protestantism among the English population. Even in the 1590s, as Elizabeth's death approached, with no heir named, there were fears (or hopes) that the Protestantization of England might falter.[41] Sir Cheney Culpeper was not alone in dating the start of the Reformation to Elizabeth's reign, or in seeing it as unfinished business in the 1640s:

writing in 1646 he thought that the imperial Antichrist (the Pope) 'was (through God's providence) pulled down 80 years since', but the 'spoil [was] divided between the King [*sic*] and bishops'. Now, in the excitement of the 1640s, he could see hopes for the completion of the process, the full liberation of Christians from such spiritual bondage.[42]

As Protestantism took firm root under Elizabeth a broad Calvinist consensus around the doctrine of predestination developed which survived into the reign of James I. University doctorates and official policy consistently defended the doctrine, which acted as an 'ameliorating bond' among men divided on other issues. In particular, the English Reformation was unusual in leaving the institutions of the medieval church more or less completely intact. Bishops, cathedrals and church courts were preserved as the vehicle for the reformation of the faith, and the only (albeit very notable) casualty of reform was the regular clergy – the monasteries and nunneries had gone, alongside chantries, mainly as an act of asset stripping in order to finance war. Associated with the persistence of the institutions of the medieval church was the survival of traditional forms of worship: for example, the wearing of surplices by the clergy, kneeling at communion and other relatively formal tastes in worship. This ceremonialism was particularly prevalent in cathedrals (and Westminster Abbey) where professional musicians were also employed to help in the edification of the believers.[43]

Defence of tradition had been an important part of English Protestantism throughout the Elizabethan and Jacobean period, on the grounds that things which were not commanded by scripture might be demanded by the secular authority, so long as they were not actively against scripture. Many Calvinists could live with this without discomfort. Again this relates to the distinction between the visible and invisible church. Since it was not possible to know who was saved or damned it was quite reasonable to focus attention on the visible church of all believers. Such 'credal' Calvinists were also relatively reluctant to have predestination emphasized in preaching, fearing that it might encourage despair and sin in those who feared that they were not of the elect. The view that in matters 'indifferent' the preferences of the secular authority should be obeyed was most influentially argued by Richard Hooker in his *Laws of Ecclesiastical Polity* (published in instalments from 1593 onwards). To Hooker the ceremonies of the medieval church were a treasured inheritance, guaranteeing the unbroken succession of Christian community. Where they did not conflict with scripture they had an important positive role in the faith. He was even willing to defend the Church of Rome as a part of the visible church on these grounds. This last step of the argument points to the explosive tensions that might be released if the Calvinist consensus broke: many Protestants would balk at such a claim, given the common identification of the Pope with the Antichrist.[44]

For some Calvinists, however, it was not enough to admit the doctrine of predestination but to concentrate on the visible church; they felt driven to seek signs of their own election. This view – 'experimental' ('experiential' might be a better term) Calvinism – was associated with intense personal piety, often very introspective, and a desire to associate with others of a similar mind. This hotter sort of Protestant sought the signs in others of what they felt in themselves, forming networks of fellow travellers with an often critical view of the ceremonies and practices of the church. To such people ceremonialism and the continued existence of bishops and cathedrals might have been intolerable had the Church of England not borne the signs of a true church – the presence of the Word and the sacraments rightly administered. Labelled Puritans by their opponents, they could be driven to separate from the church over particular issues, or more commonly to live in a position of semi-separation, conforming to the Church of England but seeking supplementary spiritual comforts.[45]

Overall, then, the impact of Calvin on English Protestantism was more clearly felt in terms of theology than in matters of ecclesiastical organization. Predestinarian thought was very influential, but 'two kingdoms' theory was much less so. An Elizabethan movement to establish a national Presbyterian system was defeated and by the early seventeenth century those seeking further reformation focused more on invigorating the life of the parish.[46] By 1640 Elizabeth was remembered in England as a champion of English Protestantism, successor to Bloody Mary and victor over the Spanish Armada – here was a model monarch for the English to remember. In the survival of medieval institutions and on ceremonial issues too, such as the wearing of vestments, the English embrace of Calvinism was less complete than the Scottish. But, and importantly for the politics of the Prayer Book rebellion, there were many English Calvinists who agreed with the Covenanters about Charles's religious reforms, although they found themselves able to conform, in some degree, most of the time.

From the late 1620s Charles was closely associated with an influential reaction against even this dilute form of Calvinism, building on a shift of emphasis which had begun in the later years of James I. Prominent positions in the church were taken by men willing to challenge the hold of Calvinism on doctrine and practice. Charles came to embrace this programme and to promote this tendency more systematically. Underlying many of his religious preferences was a concern for order and decency, something that led him to back the authority of bishops and forms of ritual and church decoration that emphasized the holiness of worship. Under the authority of William Laud, initially as Bishop of London and later as Archbishop of Canterbury, and with the evident sympathy of Charles I, the English church became a safe haven for those opposed to predestinarian views and for those with relatively ceremonial tastes in worship. This was an important connection, too: a suspicion of, or hostility to, predestination gave renewed importance to the visible church as a means to salvation. Finally then, associated with this pursuit of beauty, order and decency in the visible church was a greater emphasis on the dignity and authority of the clergy. This 'Laudian' or 'Arminian' movement was not as unpopular in England as it would have been in Scotland. The danger, though, was that far from edifying believers this emphasis on holiness was a distraction, something that filled the senses, drawing attention away from the Word, and might even become an object of worship in itself.[47]

If the crown and bishops were not seen as the natural ally of reformation in Scotland, therefore, Charles I, his English church and Archbishop Laud were regarded with particular suspicion. As war between Protestant and Catholic powers broke out in Bohemia there was violent opposition to anti-predestinarian preaching in the Dutch republic. In England the promotion of ceremonialism was the really divisive issue, although it was also true that preaching predestination became more difficult under the government of Charles and William Laud. For informed and concerned Calvinists the danger was the same – that in the very period in which Protestantism was under sustained military assault, it was being weakened from within by the erosion of some of its fundamental theological commitments. Still worse, the Stuarts failed to intervene on the side of the true religion, despite the fact that James's son-in-law was at the heart of the political crisis that had precipitated the war.

Popery was not necessarily about Catholics since weak Protestants (variously identified) could be popish too. Nonetheless the dangers of popery were (naturally enough) particularly associated with the Pope, and his agents. Especially reviled were the Jesuits, an order founded directly by the papacy in response to the challenge of the Protestant Reformation, and seminary priests trained in order to regain ordinary Christians for Catholicism in Protestant areas. It was unfortunate for Charles that the popishness of his Protestantism could so easily be associated with actual Catholicism at his court. Charles was married to a Catholic – Henrietta Maria – and under her influence his court was open to Catholic influences. From a certain point of view, therefore, the popishness of Laudianism was associated with an actual Catholic influence, which could only have adverse effects on the true religion under the Stuart crown. On past experience, this could become the basis of a conspiracy theory – that actual Catholics could, through the manipulation of weak and corrupt Protestants, subvert the true religion in England.[48]

To many Scottish Protestants the English court and church seemed to be betraying the Reformation message and the Protestant cause. This confirmed a lesson of history held with increasing conviction in Scotland – the kirk was not securely under a godly civil authority so long as kings, bishops and the English could determine matters of doctrine and liturgy. As the Prayer Book crisis unfolded, it was these very large issues in Reformation politics, about the constitution of the church and its relationship to secular authority, which came to predominate.

Given the stakes we might wonder why Charles introduced these ceremonial changes in Scotland. The answer, in part, is that since the stakes were so high he could not afford not to. Charles's relatively ceremonial sensibilities were out of tune with mainstream Scottish opinion and it may have been what he saw on his coronation visit to Scotland in 1633 that convinced him of the need to introduce changes to the Scottish Prayer Book. The practice of extempore prayer was particularly offensive to him: he preferred by far the solemnities and order of a set service. In any case, it was in 1634 that his Scottish bishops were invited to consider what changes were necessary to the English book in order to make it acceptable in Scotland. New ecclesiastical canons in January 1636 touched on these Scottish sensitivities about the creeping influence of bishops and of the Church of England. They confirmed the Five Articles of Perth but did not mention the General Assembly, presbyteries or kirk sessions by name. More troubling, or more obviously troubling, they placed restrictions on preaching which were enforced by episcopal licence.[49]

A willingness to press these sensitive reforms was not simply the product of personal conviction, however. Charles was monarch and head of the church: an important part of his sacred trust as he understood it was care for the salvation of his subjects. There were more practical concerns too. Charles had to govern three kingdoms (since 1541 monarchs of England had also been monarchs in Ireland) and live with three national churches. It was widely acknowledged in Reformation Europe that a people divided from their monarch on matters of religion could not be depended upon as loyal subjects. Monarchs in multiple monarchies faced the additional problem that if religion in their various realms was not uniform then it was an invitation to dissenters in one kingdom to make trouble on the basis of more favourable conditions offered by the same monarch to his or her subjects elsewhere. Like his father, Charles seems to have wanted to make the three churches more like one another, and to achieve that by applying pressure towards a form of worship with which he was more comfortable, but his preferences led him to make changes in all three kingdoms. Charles and Laud were probably pursuing greater conformity rather than uniformity, but it is also clear from their measures in relation to the Channel Islands and Massachusetts and stranger churches (congregations allowed in England to cater to the needs of foreign Protestants) that a common vision was at work: harmonization in fact meant altering the practice of all the churches under his crowns.[50]

Charles did less than he might have done to allay the fears provoked by these policies. His political style made him particularly unlikely to cope well with dissent, especially when expressed immoderately, and this contributed to his difficulties. He was far less pragmatic than his father in political negotiation and his preference for religious order seems to have been related to a well-developed sense of the dignity of monarchy. The portraits painted by Van Dyke during the mid-1630s

Portraits of Charles I from the 1630s

were and are the most recognizable images of Charles. The widely disseminated state portrait of 1636, while constrained by convention, conveys the same political image as the more freely composed portraits of the same period.[51] It was surely an image he was eager to project. A short man, Charles was habitually portrayed from below in order to enhance his stature, but this also increases the impression of hauteur. He engages the viewer directly but coldly, suggesting perhaps a monarch willing to listen but also one who felt no obligation to agree or to act or persuade. In real life he certainly favoured a political style in which his concern for his subjects was exercised at some distance, and with regal dignity. In the face of turbulent politics in England in the late 1620s Charles had turned away from his people, refusing to resort to print to woo public opinion as his opponents were doing. During the 1630s his court, although open to a range of opinion and a variety of talents, was austere in its regality and concern for order. This was a monarch who strove for the good of his people, not their approval; and those who seemed too eager to court public opinion were disparaged as popular spirits, or seekers after a vain popularity.[52]

Since 1603, when James VI had succeeded to the English throne and moved to London, the Scots had grappled with life under an absentee monarch. This became a more serious problem under Charles, who was brought up in England and had not visited Scotland before 1633. He had a poor feel for Scottish affairs, and his personal style accentuated the problem. Notoriously, Charles launched a 'Revocation' scheme which aroused deep suspicion. Passed only months after his accession it reclaimed titles to lands sold or granted (alienated) from the crown since 1540. This was a variation on an established practice allowing kings when they came of age to recover lands alienated during their minority. In this case, however, the variations on this more or less clearly established practice all favoured the crown. Charles had not ruled as a minor, for example. There were problems of presentation too: Charles almost certainly intended to impose fines on these alienated lands, rather than to dispossess people, but he did not feel it necessary to offer this reassurance publicly. It was associated with an attempt to recover church lands alienated at the Reformation in order to re-endow the church, but here the vested interests of those who held those lands cut across their commitment to the well-being of the church. The Revocation raised almost no money, as the local commissioners fought trench warfare over the legal technicalities, and without particularly wanting to win. But the political cost in suspicion of the absentee king was significant. It may be that a fair-minded observer would see the problems as lying with Scottish perceptions as much as Charles's intentions; but it was certainly the case that Charles was regarded with suspicion after this initiative.[53]

Charles was not just absent and distant in the more political sense – he was anglicized. This, of course, was a related problem and became all too evident on his coronation visit to Scotland – made eight years after his coronation in England. His journey through England lasted as long as his stay in Edinburgh, and his conduct in Scotland was altogether more stately and remote than was comfortable for his Scottish subjects. English manners were sufficiently widespread amongst the Scottish nobility to attract criticism but not so widespread as to secure approval.[54] So too the religious ceremonies. Revealingly, however, Charles seems to have taken the absence of open hostility to this ceremonial as evidence that Scotland would stomach pressure to conform more closely to the English liturgy.[55]

His impatience with dissenting views was also manifest during his coronation visit, when he had received petitions calling for further reformation of one kind or another. A supplication was drawn up for presentation to Parliament concerning a mixture of religious and secular grievances, but was not presented to Charles since he had made it clear that he would disapprove. The following year, James Elphinstone, Lord Balmerino, was found to have a copy in his possession and was arrested for 'lease-making', that is, slandering the King or his council. This was perhaps an over-reaction, but even more startling was the sentence of death handed down on Balmerino. Worse still, it was only passed on the casting vote of the foreman of the jury, John Stewart, the Earl of Traquair, a close adviser of the King. Balmerino was pardoned in November 1636 but what was intended to terrify opposition into silence probably had a counter-productive effect: encouraging the thought that if possession of a copy of a supplication was treasonous then only more forceful expressions of dissent would suffice.[56]

Against the backdrop of these larger concerns, and of the reaction to the new canons of 1636, it is easier to understand the hostility aroused by the new Prayer Book ordered in October that year. This was to be the guide to worship in every parish of the kirk, the standard against which local practice should be held. Tinkering here was of concern to every informed Christian in Scotland, and there were plenty of them. It was indeed based on the English Prayer Book but had been much altered over two years of consultation between Charles, Laud and the Scottish bishops. That, of course, did little to smooth its path in some quarters.[57] News that a new book was in preparation alerted the kirk to the imminence of reform without explaining its substance and gave plenty of time to imagine the worst. Many Scots seem to have been convinced of the evils of the book without actually having read it.[58] In the months before the introduction of the book an effective campaign of meetings and then demonstrations was organized, which probably drew on contacts between malcontents stretching back for several years. Given the treatment of Balmerino, however, it is not surprising that traces of this organization are hard to find. Nonetheless, in late 1636 discussion was sufficiently public that evidence has survived. When parts of the book were read at a synod in Edinburgh it was said to contain popish errors and by early 1637 concerned parties were calling meetings specifically to discuss the new book. Writing much later, Henry Guthry claimed that a meeting took place in Cowgate, Edinburgh, in April 1637 between two radical ministers, Alexander Henderson and David Dickson, and various Edinburgh 'matrons'. They had already consulted with Balmerino and the King's advocate, Sir Thomas Hope, and prior to the meeting in Cowgate secured their approval for opposing the Prayer Book. Public demonstrations (to be led by women) were apparently planned against the first public use of the book and certainly by the early summer of 1637 synods and meetings of ministers were openly discussing it. In June the Scottish Privy Council was forced to threaten punishment for those who had failed to buy the book. The introduction of the book in Edinburgh was advertised a week in advance.[59] As it turned out, this seems to have allowed time to co-ordinate protests by the disaffected.

On 23 July at St Giles in Edinburgh a distinguished group of worshippers, including privy councillors, a number of bishops and other dignitaries, joined a large congregation for a service to be held according to the new Prayer Book. As soon as the dean began to read, however, insults were thrown both at him and at the bishop. Some worshippers stood up and threw their stools before leaving the kirk. Women, perhaps including the Edinburgh matrons who had met with Henderson and Dickson, were prominent among the protesters. Although the service

The Arch-Prelate of St Andrewes in Scotland reading the new Service-booke in his pontificalibus assaulted by men & women, with Crickets stooles Stickes and Stones.

The Prayer Book disturbances in Edinburgh

continued, there were disturbances outside and the bishop, on leaving the kirk, was stoned and pursued by the crowd. An afternoon service was held according to the new liturgy, apparently without incident, but the Bishop of Edinburgh was again pursued to Holyroodhouse in the Earl of Roxburgh's coach, stoned all the way, and was said to have soiled himself as he reached safety. The dean, meanwhile, had taken refuge in the steeple. The Tolbooth kirk, which met in the partitioned west end of St Giles, also saw disturbances, and James Fairlie abandoned reading from the book. He too was pursued home by a cursing mob. Meanwhile, Henry Rollock, one of the more enthusiastic supporters of the new book, clearly sensed something was up. At Trinity kirk he was probably in the presence of particularly highly motivated protesters, and he decided not to begin reading until news of the reception in other kirks was in. Having heard about the disturbances elsewhere he made no attempt to use the book.[60]

Ultimately, these disagreements touched on an unresolved tension over who was in charge of the Scottish kirk. The new Prayer Book was being promoted not only by Scottish bishops, but from England and by a monarch and his archbishop widely regarded in Scotland as unsound on religion. Many Scots apparently needed little convincing that a new Prayer Book promoted by these bodies, and these people, could only represent a retreat from reformation. For those afraid of Charles I's policies, both in England and in Scotland, they evoked anxieties about the purity of the faith, about the boundaries of Protestantism and the encroachments of popery. In Scotland this boundary issue focused in particular on the role of bishops and the influence of English practices, and the introduction of the Prayer Book touched on deep fears about the future of reformation. These perceptions, and the heated rhetoric to which they gave rise, provided much of the energy for the subsequent Covenanting movement. But it was also driven by the ways in which Charles himself was perceived. Geographically and by personal style a distant monarch, Charles did little to soothe the feelings of his concerned subjects. When his policies were misunderstood, or evoked unreasonable fears, his instincts were authoritarian. He certainly seems to have felt no need to reassure – to do so would surely flirt with 'popularity'; and few people have ever thought that Charles was a popular king.

The underlying religious tensions were common to much of Reformation Europe and they created potentially intersecting problems for Charles I. This protest would clearly be of comfort to English and Irish opponents of Laudianism. Other European states had been undone by religious rebellion, and other European monarchs had faced severe problems in governing multiple kingdoms. There were many who might have liked to throw a stool at their clerics, few who did not appreciate the significance of the gesture. John Castle wrote to the Earl of Bridgewater as this crisis unfolded: 'the theatre for these kingdoms has now for a good while been chiefly placed at Edinburgh and what should be acted there hath been the expectation of all the Princes in Christendom, who are to frame the scene of their own interests accordingly'. It did not look good: 'They will now behold . . . that in the last Act, all things are like to go off in perplexity and trouble'.[61] There was certainly much more at stake for Charles than what his Scottish subjects did in church.

In the aftermath of the riots the Scottish Privy Council was divided and irresolute. There was little support for the King's policy, except from the bishops, and even they were unconvinced by his political strategy. The King's chief adviser in Scotland was the Earl of Traquair, who has suffered badly at the hands of his historians. Having risen to influence as Lord Treasurer as a result of his acumen, he was found wanting in political skill once he came to dominate the Privy Council. He was widely regarded as vain, bullying and so committed to his own advancement as to be untrustworthy both as an ally and as a source of information. In the ensuing crisis it is quite possible to demonstrate his duplicity. Although he had subscribed to the Five Articles of Perth he was no supporter of the King's policy over the Prayer Book, and had squabbled with the bishops on the council for several years. It seems that he deliberately fed fears about the King's intentions while exaggerating his own influence with the King, presumably in order to cement his position. Perhaps the most remarkable feature of his reputation was that he was suspected both of popery and also of having instigated the riots in Edinburgh – a singular achievement but not one that bears testimony to his political skills.[62]

Some people blamed Traquair for the way in which the introduction of the book had been handled. However, at a meeting of the council attended by him and his supporters there was more discussion of the failings of the bishops, a line of analysis which had a much wider resonance, of course. The King's advisers were clearly feeling pressure from below and a subsequent petitioning campaign maintained the pressure on men who were palpably unwilling to face down the opposition. At the same time, however, the same men were unwilling to state their opinion clearly to Charles, since it was an opinion they were sure he did not want to hear. Their immediate response was to suspend further attempts to introduce the Prayer Book pending Charles's response to their letter outlining the hostility of its reception. When it came, on 4 August, it was uncompromising, insisting on full implementation and the punishment of offenders. The Privy Council agreed half-hearted measures of suppression but also requested a personal audience with Charles in order to explain the full dimensions of the problem. They renewed their insistence that ministers would face punishment if they did not buy the book, but when this produced further petitions they made it clear that they were only enforcing purchase, not use. This was hardly the crackdown that Charles wanted.[63]

This pattern persisted over the next three months, as widely spaced and long-awaited meetings of the Privy Council were arranged in anticipation of the King's replies to their letters. In advance of these meetings, which took place on 20 September, 17 October and 15 November, opponents of the Prayer Book were able to organize petitions and demonstrations at their leisure, so that at each meeting the councillors were clear that they were caught between two more or less immovable forces. As it went on, this petitioning campaign was able to muster impressive displays of solidarity. At the time of the meeting in October a 'multitude' gathered at the Tolbooth in Edinburgh, in 'high mood', threatening to lynch the council if they denied the crowd's demand for the appointment of commissioners. On 15 November the meeting of the Privy Council was moved out of Edinburgh to try to relieve some of this pressure, although this effectively conceded the capital city to opponents of the Prayer Book.[64]

Clearly the management of this difficulty was less than ideal. The Scottish council was divided and there was competition among his councillors for the King's ear, which centred on getting permission to attend him in person. Traquair was advising compromise both on the liturgy and on the role of the bishops in the process since, by September, many of the petitions were quite openly anti-episcopal in tone. Charles was reluctant to allow his councillors to come south since that would concede to his opponents that he was shaken by the protests, and when Traquair was eventually given permission to go to London it was publicly stated that it was because there was Exchequer business to discuss. Because of this reluctance Charles was in the hands of men locally, and unable to respond quickly to events on the ground. Possible solutions might have been to follow their advice, grant them more power, or put in place men to whom he would grant sufficient authority and whose judgement he would trust. In fact he did none of the above, preferring to put pressure on those on the spot to counter the pressure they were feeling from below.[65]

Whereas the response of the government was hesitant and slow-footed, the campaign of the opponents of the Prayer Book, now known as the Supplicants, was impressively effective. Little is known about the local history of this campaign and little can be said about how this impressive mobilization was achieved, but it clearly owes much to the Presbyterian organization of the kirk. Behind that lay the growing importance of the Scottish middling sort. The increasing economic power of a middling group of landholders found expression in the kirk sessions.[66] Such men had been hostile to the Revocation scheme and a number of economic issues – taxation, monopolies and the proposal for a British fishery that would give English fishermen equal access to Scottish waters.[67] Crucial too seems to have been the absence of a loyal reaction among the Scottish nobility. It was not until the autumn of 1638 that rivalries among the nobility began to create the possibilities for mobilizing a loyalist response. Here again, the nature of Charles's government prior to 1637 seems to have been an important reason for the absence of a loyal reaction, particularly concerns about the exclusion of the nobility from political influence and the suspicions surrounding the Revocation.[68] Another important factor in the developing solidarity and tactics of this campaign was the importance of 'bands' in Scottish politics and Covenant thinking in Scottish Protestantism, both of which offered means for the mobilization of nationwide religious campaigns.[69]

As the campaign to get Charles to listen escalated, the Suppliants had sought to explain themselves more publicly. In December a 'historical narration' was prepared, and when Charles was finally persuaded of the value of talking to Traquair personally, the Suppliants succeeded in getting Traquair to take it with him. In publicizing their cause they were appealing to opinion in England too, and it is clear that they were being kept well-informed about developments in the south by some well-placed sympathizers in the English government. For those whose notion of reformation conflicted with that of Laud and Charles there was a common cause here, in opposition to a common threat to the progress of reform. The Suppliants were quick to realize that they could make this common cause and there were many others in England who can be presumed to have been hesitant about supporting a war against such an influential vision of reformation.[70]

When the Scottish Privy Council met at Stirling on 20 February 1638 it provoked a further escalation: the transformation of the Suppliants into the Covenanters. Traquair returned from London armed with an uncompromising proclamation from Charles which declared, among other things, that future meetings of the Suppliants would be deemed treasonous. The Suppliants had known something of its contents from their English friends before Traquair published it, and that perhaps allowed them to consider their response. Far from backing down, they raised the stakes, forming a band for mutual support. The petitioning campaign of the Suppliants had been organized informally through the bodies representing the four estates of Scotland, and through the presbyteries. Now a new organization was formed, called the Tables.

The four estates were represented as in the Scottish parliament – nobles, barons, burgesses and clergy – but in this case the clerical estate was comprised of ministers and excluded (of course) the bishops. Each of the estates had a Table, and a fifth Table, composed of the nobility and representatives of the other three estates, assumed overall control of the campaign. Much of the energy for this mobilization came from Alexander Henderson, a radical minister and, as we have seen, one of the leading figures in the co-ordination of the protests in Edinburgh in the previous July. Equally prominent was Archibald Johnston of Wariston, a lawyer of intense personal piety and considerable energy.[71]

A week after the fifth Table acknowledged itself to be head of this movement, the National Covenant was promulgated. It opened by re-affirming the Negative Confession of 1581, the national manifesto prompted by fears of the popish influence of the Earl of Lennox over the crown. It was expressed in terms of opposition to false doctrine and in particular to a number of specific Roman Catholic teachings which were explicitly condemned. Since its initial promulgation, the confession had been reaffirmed in 1590, this time in association with a general band to maintain the true religion thus defined. This Scottish confession had been 'established and publicly confirmed by sundry Acts of Parliament; and now of a long time hath been openly professed by the King's Majesty, and whole body of the realm': there is a fairly plain view of its relationship to royal authority here, albeit one only implicitly stated. A (selective) account of subsequent resolutions by Parliament follows which again serves to establish the historical legitimacy, and legality, of the demands being made. This is followed by a two-fold band between God, king and people, once again on the basis of historical and legal precedent: the first bound subscribers to defend the true religion; the second committed them to 'maintaining the King's Majesty, his person and estate'. Of course, from at least one perspective, the need to defend the true religion was currently in conflict with the maintenance of the King's majesty, but the text does not acknowledge the tension explicitly. Instead it insists, on the basis of past experience, that 'the true worship of God and the King's authority being so straitly joined, as that they had the same friends and common enemies, and did stand and fall together'.[72]

Finally, there is a long oath, arguing that the measures complained of by the Supplicants contravene the Word of God, and 'are contrary to the articles of the aforesaid confessions, to the intention and meaning of the blessed reformers of religion in this land, to the above-written Acts of Parliament, and do sensibly tend to the re-establishing of the popish religion and tyranny, and to the subversion and ruin of the true reformed religion, and of our liberties, laws and estates'.[73] All subscribers became collectively responsible to the utmost of their power, and with their lives, to 'stand to the defence of our dread Sovereign the King's Majesty, his person and authority, in the defence and preservation of the aforesaid true religion, liberties and laws of the kingdom'. This explanation was intended to free them from 'the foul aspersion of rebellion' since their actions were 'well warranted' and arose from an 'unfeigned desire' to defend the true religion, the majesty of the King, the peace of the kingdom 'for the common happiness of ourselves and our posterity'.[74] This was not, in short, treason.

While it is clear that obedience was due to a covenanted king, however, the real question was left hanging in the air: the Covenant is silent on the obligations due to the king who is not defending the true religion. Given the campaigning of the previous year, this might seem like a statement of conditional loyalty. The King had been bound to this confession by his coronation oath, and if he was not with the Covenanters, they might seem to be suggesting, then he was in contravention of that oath. The double Covenant placed a not very coded limit on obedience.

In the wider context of the European Reformation this can be read as an example of fairly orthodox resistance theory. Protestants had grappled with the problem of the legitimacy of resistance to earthly powers from very early on because it had quickly become clear that the progress of the Reformation might often be blocked by ungodly kings. Resistance was difficult to justify, though, since St Paul had told Christians to 'obey the powers that be'. One solution to this problem was to concede the right to resist to lesser magistrates: they too were powers enjoying divine sanction, and so they could lawfully use their office to resist another magistrate who was neglecting his. Another solution was federal theology – that a covenanted people constituted a divinely sanctioned power, which might resist an ungodly ruler.[75]

In this context the Covenant represents a manifesto for revolution, not in the sense that it called for kingless government, or for the right of any individual to resist an anointed monarch, but because it asserted a corporate intent on the authority of the body of the kirk. Mobilized through a novel institution, the Tables, it made authoritative claims on behalf of the covenanted people about the interpretation of the 1581 confession and subsequent legislation: it appeared, in fact, to make the Tables the custodian of the collective interest.[76] In principle, this made the authority of the King conditional, even if the text did not spell out what to do when obligations to godly reformation and kingly authority were in tension. The implication was clear to Charles though, who wrote to Hamilton: 'so long as this Covenant is in force . . . I have no more Power in Scotland than as a Duke of Venice; which I will rather die than suffer'.[77] But these menaces are present only in the silences – it is also possible to read this as an ambiguous or evasive document, and that was probably a source of its effectiveness. It was possible to commit to this programme without saying out loud that it was a licence to resist an anointed monarch.[78]

What gave the Covenant its power was widespread acceptance. This owed much to the organizational powers of the presbyteries and Tables, and probably much also to positive commitment to this vision of Scotland's past. There was also a degree of coercion, however, in that admission to communion was made conditional on subscription.[79] Although the Covenant was a religious document, the movement clearly drew on other currents in Scottish society, and almost certainly other sources of discontent. Significant among these other issues was the difficulty many people found in trusting Charles. At the very least, it cannot be explained simply as a response to what the new Prayer Book actually contained or how it had been introduced.

Much as he might have disliked it, Charles faced a nationally effective mobilization based around something like Calvinist ideas of lawful resistance to an ungodly monarch. It was far more than a rebuttal to a potential treason charge and the Scottish Privy Council was clearly surprised by this escalation, something made obvious at meetings on 1 and 3 March. Attempts to enforce use of the book were suspended and the Privy Council agreed that it could do nothing since the firm royal proclamation of 19 February was being widely ignored.[80]

This finally persuaded the King to take more direct control. Arrangements were made for a visit by James Hamilton, Marquess of Hamilton, the most prominent Scot at Charles's court. He was a veteran of the Thirty Years War, having led a British force under Gustavus Adolphus in 1631–2. His politics were firmly anti-Spanish and he had good Protestant credentials. But he was not 'rigid'; that is, he did not pursue policies which were not viable when to pursue them threatened the health of the kingdom. This made him appear to some as pliable and untrustworthy, and he 'changed sides' several times in the coming years. In the late 1630s, however, he had influence with the King and yet was free of association with the popish religious policies; in fact he held deeply anti-episcopal views. He also had some credit in Scotland: he had lived abroad for much of his life without ever relinquishing his contacts and political influence there.[81] As the King's commissioner, armed with the trust of his king, he had broader powers to deal with the problems in Scotland although he was still limited in his freedom of action.[82]

Even now, though, with the stakes very obviously high, it took Hamilton three months to arrive. A Privy Council meeting was arranged for 6 June 1638, by which time the Covenant had gathered signatures widely and in every part of the country except Aberdeen. Hamilton was carrying two proclamations demanding obedience, although one was slightly more conciliatory in that it did not demand surrender of all signed copies of the National Covenant. Moreover, the fact that the King had also begun military preparations suggests that Hamilton was not being sent primarily to listen. The Covenanters clearly had word of this and were also planning firm responses. When Hamilton became aware of these tensions, by the time he had got to Berwick, he wrote to the King advising him to accelerate military preparations.[83]

When Hamilton stepped off the boat at Leith he must have lost any lingering illusions about the possibility of overawing the Covenanters. Thirty nobles were waiting for him at the end of the sands between Leith and Musselburgh and the gentry were standing in ranks all along the sands for a distance of a mile and a half. At the end of Leith links stood 600 ministers and between Leith and Edinburgh another 20,000 people were said to be waiting.[84] If accurate, these estimates reflect an astonishing level of mobilization: there were 105 Scottish nobles in 1641, and between 900 and 1,000 parishes: one third of the nobility were present and up to two thirds of Scottish parishes were physically represented. The total population of Edinburgh and its suburbs was probably between 25,000 and 30,000 at this time.[85] It was a demonstration of the whole community – nobility, pastors and people. The political costs of confronting this phalanx of opinion would not be restricted to Scotland, either. On 20 June Hamilton wrote to Charles that he could not see how the King could impose his will in Scotland 'without the hazarding of your three Crowns'.[86]

The political situation was now pretty intractable since bullying would not work and Charles would not make concessions, fearing the larger implications of accepting this lay influence over the direction of his church. Even given the intractability of the problem, however, it is difficult to fathom Charles's tactics: he had made almost no effort to court moderate opinion in Scotland and nor was he careful to win the support of his English subjects. Although he was preparing to use English military and financial resources to resolve this problem he did not formally raise the issue with his English Privy Council until 1 July. This was the correct position in constitutional terms, since the two kingdoms shared a king but not their other governing institutions: Scottish affairs were for the Scottish Privy Council, and there was no formal body with responsibility for British affairs. But the consensus of most modern commentators is that this was stiff-necked as much as it was principled.[87] In any case, it clearly left Hamilton with little more room for manoeuvre than had been enjoyed by the reviled Traquair. There is certainly little doubt that Hamilton, on behalf of the King, was seeking to buy time rather than to resolve the conflict.

On 9 September 1638 Charles withdrew the Prayer Book and affirmed the Negative Confession of 1581. These measures would have had more effect had they not come after failed attempts to face down opposition: a temporary suspension in August 1637 would almost certainly have been a more effective response, politically. It seems clear, though, that Charles had already decided on English military intervention. On 21 September, when further conciliatory measures were unveiled at a meeting of the Scottish Privy Council, Charles mentioned in a letter to Hamilton that cannon were being sent north to Hull.[88] Nonetheless the concessions were significant: a General Assembly was summoned to meet in Glasgow and, in a shrewd manoeuvre, the 'King's Covenant' was launched as an alternative to the National Covenant. This was based on proclamations affirming the 1581 confession and an anti-Catholic band of 1589. Its potential for cutting the ground from under the feet of the Covenanters was immediately appreciated by some of them, and wrangling followed as to whether it was inherently anti-episcopal (as some Covenanters liked to claim) and whether subsequent measures had been compatible with the 1581 confession. Although it did not succeed, it went further towards disrupting the Covenanters' solidarity than any other measure promoted by Charles.[89]

When the General Assembly met, the Covenanters were once again successful in mobilizing crowds: there was such a huge press of people around Glasgow Cathedral on the morning of the first meeting that members of the assembly had trouble taking up their places. A week of procedural wrangling was resolved in their favour too and Hamilton, recognizing defeat, walked out of the assembly. Unfortunately his dramatic exit was marred by the fact that the door had been locked behind him and he had to break his way out. The assembly continued to sit and to pass radical measures, all of which were dismissed by the King, who denied the legal powers of the assembly once his commissioner had dissolved it.[90]

Charles now planned military action for February or March 1639 using, in part, English money and men, but he did not plan to call an English parliament. The campaign against the Covenanters in 1639 therefore went ahead using prerogative powers. But Charles also intended to draw upon the military resources of his other (largely Catholic) kingdom, Ireland. The prospect of a papistical army being used to put down calls for further reformation was clearly an alarming one. In both respects – the reliance on the prerogative rather than Parliament and the use of armed papists – this policy touched on sensitivities in England about the nature of the regime. Certainly, when mobilization came it did not prompt a straightforwardly loyal response. By the time that Leslie crossed the Tweed, the English army had already been faced down once, and a parliament had failed to support the King's cause.

2

Self-Government at the King's Command

Politics and Society in Caroline England

On the face of it Charles's English subjects were more reconciled to his rule when the Prayer Book rebellion broke out than they had been a decade earlier. In the late 1620s a number of interrelated grievances had reached a public climax, in parliaments, alehouses and presses. The main target of this discontent was the King's favourite, George Villiers, Duke of Buckingham.

On 23 August 1628 the duke was in Portsmouth preparing an expedition to aid the French Protestants in La Rochelle, then besieged by Catholic forces. Between nine and ten o'clock in the morning, having taken breakfast with 'men of quality and action', he left the chamber where he had eaten, intending to take his carriage to see the King. In a small passageway outside the chamber, however, he was stabbed by John Felton. The blow was so quick that those around the duke did not see it. Villiers himself said only one word, 'villain', before plucking the knife from his wound. In fact, those around him thought that it was a fit of 'apoplexy', until, that is, they saw the blood gushing from the duke's mouth. Felton was probably motivated by bitter experience of service under the duke, whose influence over the King and conduct of the military campaigns were widely resented. The parliament of 1626 had prepared charges against Buckingham, intending to impeach him as responsible for a number of perceived acts of misgovernment. However, in killing Buckingham, Felton effectively sacrificed his own life 'for the honour of God, his King and country'.[1]

Felton had obviously expected to die in the act of committing the murder, and for that reason had sewn a note explaining his actions into his hat. The note has not survived, but the various accounts of what it said agree on the main points. The fullest reads:

That man is cowardly base and deserves not the name of a gentleman or soldier that is not willing to sacrifice his life for the honour of his God, his king and his country. Let no man commend me for doing it, but rather discommend themselves as the cause of it, for if God had not taken away our hearts for our sins he would not have gone so long unpunished.[2]

Felton's claim, then, was that this assassination – of the King's favourite in the midst of military preparations – was a godly and patriotic act, and one intended for the service of the King.

Felton could have escaped following the murder, since in the surprise no-one tried to stop him. Indeed no-one seems to have known who had struck the blow, and while people rushed to help the duke and to secure the gates and the ramparts of the town, Felton was able to walk to the nearby kitchen unmolested. As a group of soldiers went through the house calling out for the 'villain' and 'butcher', Felton, drawing his sword, stepped out 'amongst them, saying boldly, "I am the man, here I am"'. It was only hasty action by some of those present that prevented him being killed there and then.[3]

Following his capture Felton explained that he was owed £80 for previous military service and had been passed over for command of his company, but he also claimed to be acting for the Protestant religion. Significantly, too, he said that while 'reading the Remonstrance of the House of Parliament it came into his mind, that in committing the act of killing the Duke he should do his country good service'.[4] In all then, Felton's was a premeditated, political act, in the commission of which he claimed some legitimacy, even perhaps a degree of parliamentary sanction. According to one eyewitness he said, 'God have mercy on thy soul' as he struck the fatal blow.[5] It turned out that there were many others who thought that Felton had done a public service, but in committing the murder Felton had also accepted his own death, apparently preparing for it and eschewing the chance to escape. Several months later, having been found guilty of the murder, he was hanged at Tyburn and his body was taken to Portsmouth, where it was hung up in chains 'in manner as is usual upon notorious murders'.[6]

While in prison awaiting trial Felton became something of a celebrity and was frequently visited by people anxious to 'see the man who had committed so bold a murder' and others wishing 'to understand what were the motives and inducements thereunto'. His captors in fact were a little concerned that he was becoming 'puffed up with the vain applause of the multitude'. Felton admitted that he had committed the murder and that he was wrong to have done it, but he told his visitors that 'he had long looked upon the Duke as an evil Instrument in the Commonwealth and that he was convinced there for by the Remonstrance of Parliament'. Such considerations, 'together with the instigation of the Evil One', had led him to his action. Under examination before the council he expanded on some of these comments, saying that he had killed the duke, 'partly for private displeasure, and partly by reason of a Remonstrance in Parliament, having also read some books which he said defended that it was lawful to kill an enemy to the republic'.[7]

The Privy Council was anxious to discover who had incited him to commit the murder, suspecting the 'Puritans', but Felton insisted that he had acted alone and had not told anyone of his intentions. In the face of this insistence William Laud, then Bishop of London and emerging as an influential anti-Puritan, threatened him with the rack. But Felton was clearly made of stern stuff, and even though he was a 'person of little stature' he had 'a stout and revengeful spirit'.[8] In these tense moments he demonstrated considerable *sang froid*, replying that if he were put to the rack:

he could not tell whom he might nominate in the extremity of torture, and if what he should say then must go for truth, he could not tell whether his Lordship (meaning the Bishop of London) or which of their Lordships he might name, for torture might draw unexpected things from him.

After this there were no more questions for the prisoner.[9]

Legal proprieties were observed throughout. Charles wanted to put Felton on the rack but respected the judges' unanimous opinion that it would not be lawful.[10] At his trial, on 27 November, Felton offered 'that hand to be cut off that did the fact', but even though the offer was made by him the court found that it could not inflict this further punishment. Once again this decision was made despite the evident wishes of the King, who had 'sent to the judges to intimate his desire that his hand be cut off before execution'.[11]

On the scaffold Felton would have been expected to make a good end. Felons often made, or were said to have done, 'last dying speeches' which affirmed the validity of social and political order and the rightness of their own execution. The drama on the scaffold was a crucial demonstration of the power of the state, and its claims to legitimacy.[12] Felton seems to have done his part. A pamphlet recounted his 'prayer and confession' on the scaffold, 'word for word'. According to this account he asked several times for the forgiveness of God, acknowledging the punishments that he deserved and admitting that he had been driven by the Devil. He also sought the pardon of the Duchess of Buckingham and her household, including 'the veriest scullion of her kitchen'. Better still, from an official point of view, he told his auditors: 'That which drew me to this horrid sinful fact, was some foul reports, which though they had been true it was damnable in me, in committing so foul a sin'. He wished the King long life and hoped that 'the parliament may agree, and be united in one'. He went further, expressing gratitude for official mercy: 'I did not think but that I should come to a crueller death, as I have deserved'. On this account, then, Felton was a model of contrition on the scaffold: 'I beseech you, none of you think that the fact was done well, it was abhorrent, I have so much dishonoured God in it, Lord forgive me this bloody sin, and all my other sins'.[13] This printed version accords with other, briefer, descriptions which noted the depth of his repentance and the dignity of his death.[14] The power of the regime, it seems, was unequivocally affirmed and the drama of the scaffold vindicated.

It was a feature of these dramas, however, that they were not closely controlled: the leading players were the condemned felon and the crowd, and there were occasions when they departed from the script. The execution scene was a moment of negotiation, where claims to legitimacy were not simply asserted, but also tested.[15] Although in this case the condemned man seems to have played his part, there are hints that the audience might have been less willing. Felton was quite aware of the possibility that his audience might think his action justified, or even laudable, and he twice asked that the executioner should not be held to account for his death.[16]

There is other evidence of public sympathy for Felton and approval of the murder. Drinkers in Dover were in trouble for drinking a health to Felton only a week after the assassination, and as he passed through Kingston on his way to London from Portsmouth an old lady shouted out, 'God bless thee, little David'. As he arrived at the Tower by water crowds gathered to see him. When he asked that they pray for him they, 'with a general voice cried "Lord comfort thee", "The Lord be merciful unto thee", or such like words'.[17] His trial was brought forward and expedited[18] and the execution may not have been a very public spectacle: one correspondent reporting the scene was not sure on which day it had been enacted, having heard different days from different sources.[19] Charles's advisers could not have been sure it would be a good death.

After the execution Felton continued to elicit sympathy and even approbation. At Trinity College, Oxford, in 1628, Alexander Gil, later to be schoolmaster to John Milton, got into trouble for proposing a toast to Felton's health 'saying that he was a sorry fellow and had deprived him of the honour of doing that brave action'. Many of his hearers, apparently, approved the sentiment. This, and other outrages such as suggesting that Charles would make a better shopkeeper than king, earned him a summons to appear before Laud. Under examination he claimed that such toasts were common in London and elsewhere.[20] Numerous poems survive which applaud or excuse Felton along with many others abusing Buckingham, whose funeral was marked by public contempt for the dead duke.[21] In 1629, during a quarrel in Middlesex, a man threatened to 'Felton' his adversary, and as late as 1645 a London woman was reported to have asked, 'Is there a Felton yet living?' 'Her target seems to have been the "stuttering fool", Charles I'.[22]

Felton had touched a deep vein of hostility to Buckingham and the policies associated with his influence over the King. Against the assassin was ranged a Privy Council convinced that this reflected a deeper subversive movement, associated with Puritanism, which was self-evidently both populist and lawless. Felton himself respected the course of the law, and Christian strictures against murder, and regretted that they had not restrained him earlier. Many of those who might have wished Buckingham dead were presumably less willing to see that happy day arrive by these means. That both Felton and Charles I were denied permission to get the fatal hand severed revealed in extreme circumstances a fundamental respect for the rule of law which was second nature to Stuart Englishmen, and which was deeply offended by lawless violence. But these were obviously very troubled times: on one hand there was a strong sense that there was a populist Puritan conspiracy whose agents claimed some excuse in the attitude of Parliament; on the other there was a regime that, even on the eve of an expedition to help besieged Protestants, tested the conscience of the godly and patriotic soldier, anxious to do good service to the King and to the 'commonwealth' or 'republic'. This debate was not restricted to the councils of the powerful: it was carried out before a public audience, on the scaffold, in print and through the networks of gossip and rumour that bound English political society together.

This assassination occurred close to the climax of a crisis of parliaments. During the 1620s James and Charles had faced pressure to join the defence of Protestantism in the Thirty Years War, particularly in pursuit of an actively anti-Spanish foreign policy. They had not been able to get the money from parliaments to pay for it, though. The crown blamed this on the reluctance of parliaments to pay on a realistic scale; in fact, it seems, the reluctance arose at least as much from a sense that the crown was fighting the wrong wars, in the wrong way. At the same time Charles in particular was castigated for extending patronage and favour to Arminians. The difficulties of raising money and men for war had also intersected with divisions over foreign policy. Political difficulties over money and troops led to policies which raised constitutional concerns, while the direction of foreign policy alarmed the hotter sort of Protestant, a reaction compounded by the promotion of anti-Calvinists. It was not only the paranoid who could see here an intertwining threat to religion and liberty.[23]

War with Spain came in 1625, but its fruit was a disastrous expedition to Cadiz, where, among other problems, some soldiers found that their muskets did not have fire holes and that many of the bullets were the wrong size. Parliament met the following February but failed to produce more money for war, preferring instead to impeach the Duke of Buckingham. Exasperated, Charles sought to raise money without Parliament by means of a forced loan. Direct pressure was applied to individuals, and those who refused to pay risked having troops billeted on them, or imprisonment. Five prominent resisters were imprisoned at the King's pleasure. When they sued for the protection of *habeas corpus* (the fundamental right of the accused to have cause for their arrest shown), the King successfully sought to persuade Attorney Heath that he had the right to imprison in these circumstances without showing cause. It is likely that these men, the 'Five Knights', had intended to secure a day in court in order to test the legality of the loan; instead their cause had become a test case of the King's right to arbitrary imprisonment. It was later said that Charles had caused the records of this opinion to be falsified, in order to make it a matter of record that he had the right to imprison without showing cause: the judges claimed that they had merely adjourned the matter for a later hearing. This use of the prerogative powers of the crown, and possibly felonious falsification of judicial records, raised questions not just about foreign policy and military affairs, but about the balance of the constitution. It caused a sensation in the parliament of 1628.[24] If Felton threatened a lawless politics so too, in a way, did arbitrary royal power.

In the meantime England had gone to war with France as well and in 1627 an expedition was launched to La Rochelle and the Île de Ré. Once again it was a military disaster, which came nowhere near achieving its objective despite the cost in lives and money.[25] Although the military dividend was negligible the expeditions to Cadiz and La Rochelle had imposed considerable burdens on the country – impressment of troops, rates to pay for the food and clothes, billeting and martial law.[26] The disaster at La Rochelle was freely criticized when a new parliament met in its aftermath and this gave encouragement to Felton in his murderous response. The attacks on Buckingham in the 1628 parliament further soured relations between crown and Parliament, and fears about the crown's attitude towards the law culminated in the passage of the Petition of Right. Once thought to be a manifesto for parliamentary resistance to the crown, it is now often seen as a measure specific to its time – offering statutory protections against forced loans and the unpopular measures taken to achieve the failed military expeditions. Charles at first gave it an unwelcoming response but was persuaded to accept it. With the King's approval secured, it was enrolled on the parliament roll, with a number, which seemed to suggest that it had the power of a statute. When it was printed, however, there was no statute number, and it was published with both the King's answers, not just the more welcoming one. Charles's line, throughout, was that it simply declared the situation as it existed: Parliament had won nothing from him.[27] It was in the course of these debates about the Petition of Right that the House of Commons had drawn up a remonstrance against Buckingham; in the aftermath, a new force was gathered at Portsmouth for a renewed assault on La Rochelle. While it was in harbour, waiting for parliamentary moneys to arrive, Felton had struck his fatal blow against the regime. A few weeks earlier Dr Lambe, Buckingham's doctor, had been attacked and killed by a crowd in a London street, amidst accusations of witchcraft.[28]

In one sense these were symptoms of practical problems, matters of policy; but they revealed and helped to harden quite different views of the political world. English constitutional thought was a common-sense system, not a theoretical one. It had many elements, some of which were apparently contradictory, but which could co-exist so long as it was understood that particular arguments worked in particular circumstances and not others. While the common law and parliamentary statute were acknowledged to be supreme, the royal prerogative existed to deal with areas or circumstances beyond their reach. So, for example, the prerogative was used to regulate international affairs and to deal with conditions of emergency. A number of monarchs had raised revenue using the prerogative by imposing duties on overseas trade (impositions), or by creating monopolies over particular trades and raising fines for breaches of the monopolies. To the extent that these were measures for the regulation of trade these were clearly matters for the prerogative. To the extent that they were revenue devices they threatened the role of Parliament in authorizing taxation, and the common law in protecting the property of the subject. There was then a crucial ambiguity as to whether the impositions should be seen as illegal taxes, or revenues arising from the legitimate use of the prerogative to regulate international trade – an area beyond the common law. The trick was to avoid making people have to choose, but in the later 1620s and then again during the 1630s the questions were put quite clearly by a number of financial and military policies.[29] When consensus failed, fundamental issues were raised: about the relationship between the subject and the crown, the nature of political liberty, and the means by which it was to be preserved.[30]

An important element of fears about fundamental threats to liberty was of course anti-popery: those seeking to subvert religion would first need to subvert the law. Buckingham had also been a prominent patron of Arminians or anti-Calvinists in the English church. This rising tendency was characterized by a suspicion of predestinarian preaching, even an active hostility to the doctrine, and a correspondingly stronger emphasis on the practices and rites of the visible church. It had roots in the tradition represented by Hooker, and enjoyed increasingly powerful backing during the 1620s, but it elicited stringent criticism from opponents and disrupted the uneasy Calvinist consensus that had prevailed in the English church under Elizabeth and James. These anti-Calvinist churchmen tended to be less worried by the threat of the Antichrist than their opponents and more concerned about stability and order in the visible church. The best hopes for salvation lay in the educated ministry, acting under episcopal authority. Doctrinal Arminians shared a taste for more ceremony and order in the visible church with a wider group – the link between the theology and the liturgical preferences was not exact, but it all looked like popery to hotter Protestants. A number of these ceremonialists were also identified with a defence of the aggressive use of the prerogative and the apparently casual attitude of Charles and his advisers towards the authority of parliaments and the common law. For example, Roger Maynwaring, a royal chaplain, and Robert Sibthorpe, rector of Brackley, caused a storm during the Forced Loan controversy by preaching that the monarch did not need the consent of his subjects in order to raise financial supply.[31] This kind of argument seemed to threaten property rights – what could an Englishman call his own if the monarch could make financial levies without securing consent? In the 1629 parliament heated rhetoric about the popery of Arminians was closely tied to threats to liberty, the threat of the introduction of a 'Spanish monarchy'.[32]

Richard Montague, Bishop of Chichester, had gone further than most anti-Calvinists in his *New Gagg for an Old Goose* (1625), arguing that double predestination was a false doctrine and attacking the view that the Pope was the Antichrist. In 1626 Buckingham had hosted a meeting convened to discuss this, the most inflammatory anti-Calvinist publication of the period, and the meeting had failed to condemn it.[33] Those who defended or failed to condemn Montague's views, or those like them, enjoyed increasingly powerful patronage under Buckingham, William Laud and Charles, fostering considerable anxiety among the godly. The increasing prominence of this strand of opinion reinvigorated the longstanding debate about the identity of English Protestantism, a debate which was almost as old as English Protestantism itself.

This debate had often been very public and fractious. On the Puritan side the language of anti-popery was very prominent and often associated with accusations about plots to undermine law and religion. Hostility to popery was set against the background of a view of English history in which God had intervened repeatedly to deliver His chosen people from these dangers. John Foxe's 'Book of Martyrs' made this case in numerous editions, and it drew further strength from the defeat of the Spanish Armada and the thwarting of the Gunpowder Plot.[34] Inevitably, this view of English history intersected with a view of England's place in the world, with its foreign policy. In 1623 Charles had travelled in secret to Madrid, accompanied only by Buckingham, in the hope of securing the hand in marriage of the Spanish infanta. His mission failed – the Spanish had been stringing the English along for diplomatic reasons, hoping to prevent their entry into the European war on the wrong side, and were embarrassed by the arrival in town of the English sucker. Charles's return to London was triumphant, rather than sheepish, however, as bonfires were lit and the bells rung out to celebrate another delivery from the clutches of the Antichrist, harbinger of a 'blessed revolution' in foreign policy.[35]

Zealous opponents of popery, those offended by ceremonialism and medieval survivals, were on the other hand branded in conversation, pamphlets and on the stage as Puritans – their hypocrisy and sanctimoniousness were pilloried in stereotypes such as 'Zeal of the Land Busy'. The term 'Puritan' really described a relationship to current orthodoxy rather than a fixed body of ideas. It was a label (often used with hostile intent) for those pushing for further reform, or offended by some aspect of the current settlement: those labelled Puritans in the later sixteenth century were people agitated by different aspects of church practice than those labelled Puritans in the 1630s.[36] As Francis Rous put it, the word 'Puritan' was an 'essential engine' of the attempt to push English religion towards conformity with Rome, a word consisting of only a few letters, but one of which the Devil could make manifold use: 'this word in the mouth of a drunkard doth mean a sober man, in the mouth of an Arminian, an Orthodox man, in the mouth of a papist, a Protestant. And so it is spoke to shame a man out of all religion, if a man be ashamed to be saved'.[37] One man's Puritanism was another man's quite reasonable concern about the encroachments of popery – the terms were two sides of a polemical battle about the boundaries of purified Christian practice.

At stake too was the location of the Royal Supremacy. 'Puritan' opponents of crown policy looked to the King-in-Parliament as the seat of the Royal Supremacy – it was a parliament which had given Henry VIII power over the English church – and sought an active foreign policy in defence of the Reformation in Europe at large. Hooker offered an authority for this view too.[38] The battle might erupt over any number of issues, and when it did the means of publicity, and handy stereotypes, lay close to hand.

Print was not the cause of this, nor its only medium, but the growth of printing in England in the later sixteenth century had been associated with the development of a pamphlet culture encouraging open debate of political issues in print. Much printed matter was in expensive formats, large bibles or learned tracts written in Latin and not intended to inspire reflection on current affairs by the vulgar. But there were also genres of cheap print which targeted wider audiences. In particular ballads were produced in huge numbers, illustrated and set to well-known tunes with the intention of amusing but also educating audiences in alehouses and elsewhere. Although literacy in England may have been as low as 30 per cent among the male population, and less than that among the female population, this form of print was not primarily textual. Ballads were sung, and pasted on the walls of village alehouses, their woodcut images offering a spur to the memory of what the text contained. In the second half of the sixteenth century there may have been 4 million of these ballads in circulation – nearly one each for the whole population.[39]

Many of these ballads were entertainments, dealing with chivalric stories or romances between young swains and country maids. They also had a didactic function, of course, giving their audiences examples with which to think about, for instance, moral qualities and the dangers of adolescence. Others were intended to educate the populace about the demands of a Protestant life, and, by the 1640s in any case, about tyranny and virtuous government.[40] Alongside these religiously improving ballads and stories of civic virtue huge numbers of printed catechisms circulated, teaching people to read at the same time that they offered religious instruction. In the early seventeenth century there were about half a million official catechisms in circulation, as well as three quarters of a million alternatives.[41] An unknown number of broadsides – large single sheets illustrated with a woodcut – were also in circulation, again often with the purpose of offering religious instruction that reached beyond the formally literate population. By the late sixteenth century more elaborate works were making their way in a more sophisticated print market – the chapbook. Costing a penny or two, and consisting of up to twenty-four small unbound pages, many of these books also took up the themes of love and chivalry, but they might also seek to edify and inform about more narrowly religious or political issues.[42]

In the later sixteenth century and the first half of the seventeenth century there was also a steady growth in the publication of 'news pamphlets', alongside ballads and broadsides. They were not serial publications, but were one-off, topical and (at least ostensibly) factual.[43] Many of these pamphlets sought to give advice or example about the active Christian life by lending a providential meaning to disasters, murders, monstrous births and unusual natural phenomena. The hand of God could be discerned in the life and repentance of a Puritan, for example, evidence of the need to avoid excesses of zeal, introspection and spiritual pride. Once again, this was a form of print that intersected with a common cultural form – many parishioners were exposed to these providential lessons every Sunday. Print circulated and fixed accounts of events which were at the same time politicized. Its messages were intended to reach well beyond the formally literate.[44]

These news pamphlets fed, and fed upon, what was pretty clearly a growing appetite for news, fuelled by rumour and circulating manuscripts as well as print. This caused unease among the country's governors, but the circulation of news was restrained rather than controlled. Semi-regular news pamphlets, the 'corantos' (the name is related to *courant*), appeared in the 1620s. Forerunners of the later newsbooks, they published news of European affairs, respecting the ban on domestic news but still causing enough concern for them to be closed down during the 1630s. An unfulfilled appetite existed, and reliable news (and reliable guidance as to its meaning) was at a premium, even for those who could pay around £20 a year for the services of a manuscript newsletter writer. For governments the destabilizing effects of the news culture lay partly in the danger of misinformation – ill-founded rumours had played a part in riot and rebellion – and their solution was to try to stop the circulation of news rather than to improve its quality. When governments sought to regulate information, therefore, they were not simply seeking to safeguard hierarchy. It was a losing battle however: it is clear that comment on public affairs was opinionated, common and widely circulated. Libels and seditious verses, penned in response to particular incidents or personalities, circulated in manuscript copies, and news spread orally with the passage of trade around the country. Alehouses and taverns were often alive with the buzz of news.[45]

In all this represented an increasingly sophisticated print market, reaching a wide section of the population directly, and much of it

The Royal Exchange in 1644: a centre of trade, gossip and news

intended to be passed on to the non-literate by being read out or sung. Official publications circulated too, pasted up or fixed to posts in prominent places – the marketplace or the porch of the church. They could be deciphered by the literate for their neighbours, reaching into every corner of the kingdom. Oral and literate forms of communication overlapped and informed one another – print seeping into networks of gossip and rumour, rumours and stories finding their way into print from these conversations.[46] Central to this world of opinion was religious and political awareness, often attached to critical views of particular events or personalities.

The royal court was the nerve centre of the political system, the seat of royal patronage and the place at which the fortunes of particular views of church, state and foreign policy were most easily to be followed. Here was another source of the hostility to Buckingham – he had managed to become a favourite both of the old king and of the new, so that those who had hoped he would fall with the death of the father were disappointed. In fact, there was a persistent rumour that the change of master had been facilitated by the poisoning of James I, arranged by Buckingham and even, perhaps, connived at by Charles. At court in the later 1620s 'new counsels' were increasingly influential, advising against participation in the European war, advocating support of Laud and the anti-Calvinists, very hostile to 'popularity' and in favour of avoiding parliaments. These voices did not have a monopoly at court, but they were increasingly powerful.[47]

Parliaments, presses and crowds offered opportunities to try to pressure the royal court, the affairs of which were a frequent topic of public comment. Periodically since the reign of Elizabeth prominent politicians, including courtiers, had appealed to wider publics, often presenting current political issues in terms of highly polarized language, or the stereotypes of Puritan hypocrite or popish agent of the Antichrist. These stereotypes were associated too with conspiracy theories – in a political system so dependent on personal authority, personal intrigue was an obvious means of securing political ends. Another theme in such conspiracies was the corruption of political virtue by private interest, a politics of commonwealth which drew on classical histories for its view of republican virtue.[48]

Meetings of Parliament might stoke all this up, particularly in London. Felton, after all, had been encouraged to murder Buckingham not just by the promptings of his conscience, but by a declaration of Parliament and by what he had read. He clearly moved in a world of easy private connections. Two of his lodging house acquaintances were later examined about the assassination. Elizabeth Josselyn, the wife of a stationer, testified that she and her mother lived in part of the same house as Felton in Fleet Lane, and that she had lent him several books. The only one he did not return was a 'History of the Queen of Scots'. Like many others she found him a melancholy man 'much given to reading of books, and of very few words. She never saw him merry'.[49] But he had spent two hours discussing a copy of Parliament's remonstrance with Richard Harward at the Windmill in Shoe Lane. Felton knew a scrivener – a professional writer of manuscript copies – by the name of Willoughby who had written petitions for him in the past. It was from Willoughby that Harward had got his copy of the remonstrance. After the murder of Buckingham, Willoughby was found to have copies of a verse in his desk – 'Let Charles and George [Buckingham] do what they can / Yet George shall die like Doctor Lambe'.[50] Books and declarations could be dangerous things, and they circulated easily in the taverns and lodging houses of early Stuart London. Felton's own fate, of course, also became a public issue – in his scaffold scene, and in the circulation of opinions and verses about him. In the late 1620s Charles not only turned his back on parliaments and Puritans but on the public too, refusing to resort to print to explain himself.[51]

In these public controversies – over religion, foreign policy and pre-rogative powers – religious, legal and political concerns intersected. This was true at several levels: the fact that prominent Arminians seemed to support a generous view of the prerogative or that Puritans sought also to clip the King's wings; an argument about how far to emphasize the King-in-Parliament as the seat of the Royal Supremacy; that foreign policy was irreligious and could not be funded because of the corruptions of the court; that harmless ceremonies should be respected as the preference of the monarch and the legal heritage of the church.

It was a matter of faith that the common law enshrined human reason, arrived at by accretion of the ages. So too the view that the Reformation had been achieved by statute, and that the law was literally omnicompetent – able to provide solutions to all social and political questions and the ultimate safeguard of civil and religious rights. Over the sixteenth and seventeenth centuries this view had been entrenched as governments used the law to widen the scope of their powers. Paradoxically, therefore, as the governments became more ambitious they became more trammelled by the common law – the uses of the prerogative in the 1550s resembled those of the 1620s, but caused much less alarm.[52] Part of this mix was a language of commonwealth which drew, ultimately, on the classical heritage that was a standard part of the education not just of Stuart gentlemen but of anyone who had been at a grammar school. This education, broadly termed humanist, informed a sense of public activism among these men as holders of public office and, more generally, as leading figures in local society.[53] More theoretical questions were open too: Roman histories of 'free states' were widely available in early Stuart England, to the extent that they had become, in effect, works of English political theory, at least in some circles.[54]

It is at least possible, for example, that one of the books that Felton had read 'which defended that it was lawful to kill an enemy to the republic' was Thomas May's translation of Lucan's *Pharsalia*, published the previous year. *Pharsalia* was a poem about the civil wars from which Julius Caesar emerged as dictator. It championed the virtues of the republic against Caesar, and dealt with his murder by Brutus. May's edition was dedicated to figures associated with support of the international Protestant cause and opposition to an extensive view of royal prerogative powers. The poem itself is ambiguous: it is clear about the horrors of civil war but claims that imperial peace is worse; it recognizes virtue in Caesar while despising his victory; it champions the republican armies, but blames their defeat on a lack of will. At one point May commends the war, for having produced Nero – critics differ as to whether this is an ironic point or not. But in the context of early Stuart England republican virtue lay in the selfless service of the public, not in government without a king. Readers of *Pharsalia* could be found on both sides at the outbreak of civil war in 1642, and it was more than possible to read it without approving of Felton's actions. Nonetheless, May's translation was sufficiently sensitive, politically, that the dedicatory pages were removed from many of the early editions.[55]

Felton's fate was marked and celebrated in an outpouring of 'underground verse', like that found copied out in the desk of his friend the scrivener. This was an important feature of the political culture of the 1620s: poems circulated in manuscript, employing rough verse and expressing anti-courtly sentiments, in marked and deliberate contrast to the refined culture of the court. In Felton's case there was an ambivalence, akin to his own, between a Christian revulsion at murder and sense of civic virtue in his dramatic act on behalf of the commonwealth. The classical heritage offered a fund of republican thinking, and practical examples, on which those anxious to defend the commonwealth could draw. One of the verse epitaphs to Felton contains very clear echoes of *Pharsalia* – if Felton had not read May then some of his supporters certainly had. The republican virtues of active citizenship which animated much of the government of the kingdom offered too the resources with which to criticize royal government, and to imagine alternative political worlds.[56]

Charles's policies, then, caused outrage but also outrages. In 1629, Parliament met again, following Buckingham's death. Hostility to Arminianism and the collection of tonnage and poundage (customs duties with disputed legal status) led to speeches which came close to personal attacks on Charles, and which seemed to make radical claims for the constitutional position of Parliament. Charles moved to adjourn the sitting, but the Speaker of the House of Commons was not allowed simply to call an adjournment by members anxious that they were about to be deprived of a platform. The Speaker was physically held in his chair while resolutions hostile to Arminianism and tonnage and poundage were read. In the meantime the door was barred to Black Rod, who had arrived to end the session.[57] For Charles, this sudden dissolution of Parliament was a repudiation of Puritan populism in more than one sense, a solution to the problem posed by the plotting of 'envenomed spirits which troubled ... the blessed harmony between us and our subjects'.[58]

Compared to the fraught politics of the late 1620s it could be claimed with some reason that the 1630s were halcyon days in England. Two crucial elements of the situation had changed – the country was not at war, and parliaments were not meeting. The dissolution of Parliament in 1629 signalled the opening of the 'Personal Rule', what turned out to be eleven years of government without recourse to Parliament. Without parliaments England was still an informed and participatory political society, in which classical and Christian notions of an active life enjoyed much currency. War, money and religion remained potentially controversial and so the absence of parliaments, and the heated publicity of the late 1620s, was a palliative, not necessarily a cure. It was, though, undoubtedly a palliative and by 1637 Charles probably had good reason to be pleased with the Personal Rule. England remained much more governable than it had been at the time of Buckingham's assassination.

Doing without Parliament was not in itself a violation of constitutional principle. The institution had no continuous existence, but was an assembly called at the royal will for a particular purpose – Parliament was in that sense an event rather than an institution. Parliaments could provide money (only parliaments could grant taxation) and legislation. They might also offer counsel on the basis of wide knowledge of the affairs of the kingdom, and give voice to the grievances of the subjects, asking for redress from the monarch. But the crown had many sources of revenue that were not, formally speaking, taxes; and if there was no need for new laws then there was no need for parliamentary legislation. Parliament was not an executive body, and had no permanent place in government – if the King did not want taxes, legislation or the advice of Parliament there was no obligation on him to call one. In practice, it is difficult to see how such circumstances could persist for long, however: Parliament had no right to existence, but it was not easily disposable either. Nonetheless, James I had called only one parliament between 1610 and 1621, and in the reign of Elizabeth parliaments met on average once every three and a half years, for sessions lasting only ten or eleven weeks. Even during the 1620s, parliaments were in session only 20 per cent of the time.[59]

During the 1630s, in the absence of parliaments and war, it was clear that in many respects English government was in rude health. Notably, local government was clearly capable of energetic and effective action. The strengths of this system, frequently described as 'self-government at the King's command', had been clearly revealed in its response to rapid social and economic change. Population growth over the previous 130 years had placed great strain on the economy. The supply of necessities did not expand rapidly enough to meet demand, and there was rapid inflation in the price of basic foodstuffs. At the same time, economic growth did not create employment quickly enough to absorb the increased population. As a result there seems to have been an over-supply of labour and the value of wages fell. Over the long run this was bad news for those who bought more food than they sold, and those who earned wages rather than employing labour. England's economy was regionally diverse and all sorts of social practices served to mitigate these crude economic facts, but it is clear that there was a large increase in the number of people suffering some degree of want as basic food prices rose and wages failed to keep up. In bad harvest years food prices went up even further, since food was an absolute necessity, no matter how scarce it became. At the same time there was less work in agriculture, and less demand for non-agricultural goods, so that employment in the whole economy was affected. With work and wages less easy to find and food prices steepling upwards serious privation threatened for many people. In Cumberland, in 1623, some people starved.[60]

Others thrived. Those who sold food and employed labour prospered, particularly if they owned their own land, or held long leases at fixed rents. In arable areas there was a tendency for village society to polarize, as wealthier farmers bought out their less successful neighbours, creating a newly assertive middling sort, below the level of the gentry but very clearly distinguished from their poorer neighbours. Those who had been bought out turned to wage labour or took to the roads for places where a living could be made without land – town, forest and fen were common destinations. In arable villages in particular the prospering middling sort confronted a society of labouring poor, chronically vulnerable to want and, in periods of harvest failure, threatened with catastrophe. They were also acutely conscious of the tramping vagrant poor, moving across the country in search of work or a livelihood without land.[61]

In the face of these problems there was a remarkable harmony between crown policies and local officeholders: an ideological consensus among social elites supported active government and underpinned the social and political position of those benefiting from economic change. The deserving poor (the old, the young, the sick and, increasingly, the honest but unemployed) were offered help; the undeserving were set to work or punished. Vagrants were whipped and sent home. Many of these measures, and the refinements that accompanied them, originated in local solutions. Boroughs, in particular, faced the social problems associated with migration, a population with a high proportion of wage earners and a dependence on the market to supply food. Statute and Privy Council urgings lent authority to local initiative as much as they gave leadership. Where particular measures were ignored this was not because they were disapproved of in principle, or were thought to be of dubious legality, but because they were thought to be inappropriate to specific local conditions. There might be a preference in some places for Christian charity rather than bureaucratic dole as the solution for the deserving poor, but these were differences of accent rather than language.[62]

Over three generations prior to 1640 this system had developed flexibly and without significant tension between national and local governors. This harmony of vision reflected a harmony of interest. Local government was staffed by volunteers, who held office in order to cement their local social standing and, no doubt, out of a sense of duty. Measures intended to protect social order and the commonwealth also served the interests of these local elites. Village constables, who served for one year at a time without payment, were drawn from the middling sort, the group prospering from long-term economic change, and they were implementing measures to control the adverse consequences of the change, not to reverse it. In offering relief to their poorer neighbours, or imposing discipline on them, they reinforced their own social position. There was in general no tension for them in co-operating with national legislation or the promptings of the Privy Council. Above them stood high constables – responsible for numbers of parishes within a county and drawn from a slightly more elevated social rank – and magistrates (Justices of the Peace) – county gentlemen serving voluntarily in the Commission of the Peace appointed by the crown. These men higher up the ladder of local government and of correspondingly higher social status had no more reason to resist these measures than the village constables. In general the hierarchy of local officeholders corresponded pretty closely to the hierarchy of social status, and measures designed to preserve social order drew on this congruence of political and social aspirations. The result was successful, if we measure success in terms of a harmony of purpose between national and local governors.[63]

This was no less true during the 1630s than over the previous three generations. Prompted by harvest failures between 1629 and 1631, and by outbreaks of the plague, the Privy Council drew up Books of Orders which regularized practices that had evolved over a number of years. Dearth orders requiring magistrates to seize and sell stocks of grain at a fixed price were implemented in the bad harvest year of 1631 but not in the later 1630s, and this might reflect some disaffection with the implications for the property rights of the middling and richer sort. But there were marked continuities in these social policies into the 1640s: the Earl of Manchester was author both of the Caroline and of the parliamentary plague orders, and the hard years of the later 1640s seem to have witnessed a fairly uncontroversial use of the powers regularized in the 1630s in the absence of Privy Council oversight.[64]

The system of local government which generated and enforced these measures also bound Stuart England together as an intimate political community, densely populated with officeholders. Communications were slow by modern standards although not quite as slow as is sometimes imagined. Between 1570 and 1620 royal posts took, on average, 65 hours to reach Newcastle, 80 to reach Berwick and 95 to reach Penryn. A region bounded by Newark, Chester and Exeter was within 40 hours of London, although letters slowed down considerably once they were off the main highways.[65] For private letters speeds were more variable. One letter reached Ludlow in 36 hours from Charing Cross but this was unusual. Although the Harleys of Brampton Bryan in Herefordshire might know in advance of business coming before Parliament, news from London was often two weeks old by the time it got to them.[66] In that sense many areas of England were somewhat remote from the seat of government.

But the chains of government were comparatively short: the localities were not in that sense at all remote from the centre of political authority. Every parish had at least one resident who was representing royal government, as a petty constable. A crude indication of what this implies is that a total population of 5.1 million was divided into about 9,000 parishes, an average of 570 people in each. Of that number 285 were men, of them 140 or so over the age of twenty-five.[67] Since parish constables held office for one year at a time, there might be a dozen or more men who held, had held, or would hold office: nearly one in ten of adult males, or one in forty of the total population. Moreover, there were not many degrees of separation between a parish official and the King. A demand for reports on the implementation of the Books of Orders passed through a small number of hands before arriving in a village: from Privy Council to magistrates' bench to the high and then petty constables. Ordinary English people had little formal influence over the executive: parliaments met infrequently, the franchise was restricted, there was no ballot box, and parliamentary elections were frequently acclamations of candidates put forward by the county elite. But much more than in a modern bureaucratic state there was an intimate and continuous connection with the *exercise* of political power and, also, a degree of control over the detailed implementation of general instructions.[68]

The practice of active self-government connected with and confirmed the commonwealth and Calvinist ideals that were common amongst the gentry, and which were broadcast to inferior officers and wider publics in church and in court. This was particularly true among the university-educated gentry, of course, but a practical ideal of active citizenship was common too in the towns. The same period that saw the rise of the middling sort also saw a rapid increase in the number of towns enjoying independent legal powers – the boroughs. In 1640 England and Wales boasted 194 boroughs, of which only forty-eight had achieved that status a century earlier. Collectively they represented a kind of urban network, or system, in which active self-government was connected with ideals of civic identity, and civic virtue. With or without the gloss of a classical education many of the country's governors were acting under the influence of republican values, ideals that saw in the virtuous man an active servant to the commonwealth.[69] This system of participatory administration was a means of exclusion too, of course, for those outside the ranks of the village elite, those who were governed, not governors. But the language of commonwealth, in fact, was another means by which the governed could hold their betters to account – it was a term frequently invoked against grasping landlords or neglectful magistrates.[70] Of course, even if neither side was genuinely interested in civic virtue, by choosing it as their battleground they nonetheless gave the ideas wider currency.[71]

Participatory administration brought politics into the villages and towns of early modern England in a more direct sense too. Those in the officeholding population, which included men of relatively humble status, as well as those with whom they dealt, made decisions about how to interpret general policies in the light of local circumstances. This served as a political education for a still wider group. Grain riots, for example, reveal both an awareness of official policies and ideals on the part of the poor, and a capacity to deploy those ideals to their own advantage. Local officeholders proclaimed themselves to be fathers of their country, taking on a duty of care for their inferiors as a consequence of their social position. When grain prices were high this paternal responsibility required them to intervene in the market to restrain profiteering and to ensure that the local population was fed. On numerous occasions the local poor acted on their own initiative, stopping and distributing loads of grain destined for the market, imposing a fair price or calling for magistrates to take up their duties. The same seems to be true of the parish poor, who were able to deploy a language of entitlement in order to secure supplements to their income. The politics of subsistence, and of the parish, brought even the poor into contact with official prescription and practice.[72] During the later 1640s, when there was no Privy Council to prompt local governors to implement dearth orders, they may in fact have been responding to pressure from below, as petitioners called them to account. In doing so they used the values and terms routinely employed to justify the authority of magistrates.[73] This is not evidence of informed opinions about the membership of the Privy Council, or the trend of episcopal appointments, but it does bear testimony to the administrative and political integration of seventeenth-century England.

It was not just in routine administration that politics resonated in local life. Quarter sessions were convened and presided over four times each year by the Justices of the Peace. The sessions were both a criminal court and an administrative authority, and operated with the help of juries composed of substantial freeholders – village worthies. Twice each year judges from the central courts in London went on circuit, hearing more serious criminal cases and bringing with them messages about current priorities at the heart of government. Here, too, local office-holders and jurymen (drawn from the ranks of the local gentry and middling sort) were brought into direct contact with essential functions of government. Many of them would have had experience of the law in more local settings too: in manor or borough courts, defending their property rights or participating in the regulation of local society.[74]

English criminal law was not inquisitorial – crimes were presented to the courts, rather than sought out and investigated by officers of the court. Here, too, local discretion was a regular and informed feature of the system and in many cases it seems that there was a preference for more informal sanctions. Those cases that did come to court usually required the agreement of juries that there was a case to answer, and the judgement of juries about the guilt or innocence of the accused. This participatory legal system overlapped with the institutions of local government, and was dependent for its life on the voluntary action of substantial local inhabitants.[75] Institutional connections between the political centre and the English localities therefore offered a practical political education, both about what was going on and how things worked, and the social depth of that political education was marked. In some institutions, such as the assizes, quarter sessions or Parliament, national and local interests mixed. At the assizes local legal and administrative issues took their place alongside the transmission of ideas and policies from the King and Privy Council.[76]

Godly Protestants, the Puritan populists of hostile stereotype, were as likely as anyone to see the virtue in measures of social regulation, perhaps more so. Most of those who saw popery in the religious policies of the late 1620s were not natural rebels; nor were they necessarily radical on social questions.[77] In fact, many of the leading figures behind secular policies of social discipline were 'Puritans' in relation to the established church. In the Essex village of Terling, for example, illegitimacy rates were successfully reduced in the early seventeenth century, suggesting that an alliance of magistrate and minister could affect the most intimate areas of human life. In Dorchester, after a catastrophic fire in 1613, a similar alliance of magistrate and minister sought to appease God's righteous anger through an assault on sin, and an invigoration of charity, again with notable results.[78] Similar alliances have been observed in the Stour Valley, on the Essex and Suffolk borders, in Gloucester, Salisbury and Ipswich. In such places, before popery was intruded into the church, there was no necessary tension between local views of the correct form of reformation and royal government. There might be a difference between an indulgent paternalism, willing to wink at the harmless festivities of the poor, and a more austere Puritan social discipline; but it was certainly not the case that all disciplinarians were Puritans or that there was anything socially levelling or necessarily anti-monarchical about Puritanism.[79] For those who were not particularly offended by Laudian practices the tensions were even less marked. But the smooth running of local government rested on informed consent among county and village elites: the King's command was hugely influential, but so too was the practical reality of self-government. In that sense there was a republic of officeholders, acting independently and with discretion to preserve local religious and social order. No doubt many of them had not read Lucan, but many of them knew about the importance of active service of the commonwealth. That could clearly work for the crown.

In the absence of parliaments and active warfare some of the heat had gone out of English politics. Charles, an art collector of refined and fashionable tastes, was entertained at court with elaborate masques, designed by Ben Jonson and at the cutting edge of literary and dramatic fashion. Criticism was voiced, but so too was compliment, and a prominent theme was the reconciliation of conflict through the love and wisdom of the monarch.[80] However, some of the problems with parliaments were problems not only for parliaments but also for local governors, and they had not gone permanently away. Military mobilization, for example, was close to the heart of the political difficulties with parliaments and tensions were to re-emerge in the mid- and later 1630s even in the absence of parliaments.

Across the whole of Europe the increasing use of gunpowder weapons by infantry made it more expensive to equip soldiers, and increasingly important that foot soldiers were properly trained and drilled. This too was expensive and a number of governments in sixteenth- and seventeenth-century Europe got into financial trouble as a result of over-spending on military mobilization. England had been relatively protected from these developments by the sea, a far more effective defence. Over the long term, however, there were attempts to improve the military potential of the nation through reform of the militia. In the end, then, this made it a problem for local officeholders.

There was a longstanding obligation on adult males to present themselves at the general muster each year, and to offer military service when called upon. From the mid sixteenth century onwards this peasant army was gradually transformed and from within the general body of able-bodied men a more select group – the Trained Band – was given something more like proper equipment and training. This was supported by local rates so that for many people an obligation to serve in the militia was transformed into a cash payment to support the Trained Bands.[81]

Naturally enough, this created frictions. From the 1590s onwards the militia was increasingly run by Lords Lieutenant – usually relatively prominent noblemen – responding directly to the promptings of the Privy Council. They passed on their instructions via deputies to village constables. General demands from the Privy Council were translated, in a short series of steps, into the imposition on particular villages and towns of the duty to provide a particular number of men, armed and equipped according to a specified standard. It was not necessarily a smooth process, however. Rates were unpopular, and it proved impossible to establish a basis on which they could be raised without also producing wailing and gnashing of teeth about inequalities. There was also a legal difficulty in that the statute which empowered the Lords Lieutenant was repealed in 1605, leaving them with duties but perhaps no legal authority. The mustering and drilling of the Trained Bands was a palaver, causing considerable inconvenience both to the mustered and to those mustering them. Many of the local officeholders responsible for achieving all this – even Lords Lieutenant, but certainly village constables – clearly thought it a chore that was not worth losing much sleep over. These were men, after all, who held office in order to cement their social standing and the good opinion of their neighbours. Mustering and raising rates, in other words, offered little by way of direct benefit to local people, and the level of co-operation achieved was often unimpressive.[82]

As a result militia reform was at best patchily and intermittently impressive. Attempts at reform under Charles I were no more popular than previous efforts. After 1625, in the light of the war in Europe, Charles had pursued an 'exact' or 'perfect' militia. Pressure was applied to hold regular musters, at which meaningful training took place and appropriate weapons were produced. In order to overcome a common evasion, weapons were to be marked, so that the same weapon could not be produced in different places on different days. Overall, said Charles, he was no longer prepared to accept the appearance; he wanted a real performance. After the fractious parliaments of the 1620s Charles had sought peace in order to avoid having to call them, and treaties were signed with France and Spain. In the early 1630s, it seems that there was little pressure to improve the militia, but with a worsening diplomatic situation in 1635, the Privy Council turned once again to militia reform. One feature of this campaign was to ensure that local militias appointed, and paid, muster masters – men of professional experience who could oversee the arms and training of the militia, and ensure that higher standards of preparedness were maintained. This was not the first time that this had been urged and, not for the first time, it produced political problems in the counties.[83]

Administration by local officeholders did not just bring the burden of military mobilization into the villages and towns, but also the negotiation of that burden – the politics of administration. Questions about the wisdom and legality of crown policies could get a wide airing. For example, in Shropshire at the Easter meeting of the quarter sessions, the Grand Jury presented the muster master's fee as a grievance, saying that the office was unnecessary.[84] In making presentments Grand Juries responded to the information and representations of a wider circle of men of similar status – village constables and their superiors, the high constables. A presentment by the Grand Jury, therefore, was understood to be the voice and opinion of the county, expressed by its respectable inhabitants to leading figures from gentry circles, sitting as JPs. It was also a very public statement since meetings of the sessions were major events in the county year. In addition to the JPs, jurymen and constables, they were attended by the sheriff and numerous petitioners. The promulgation of Privy Council orders, the hearing and redress of grievances, and the prosecution of crime were the focal point of a larger event, and the practice of meeting in a number of towns in rotation may have reflected a desire to spread the commercial benefits.[85]

There had been grumbling and foot-dragging in Shropshire over the muster master and his fee for many years. In fact, Edward Burton, the muster master during the 1630s, had himself opposed the establishment of the office during the 1620s.[86] The Grand Jury's position was shrewdly chosen: they did not complain that it was illegal, although it was possible to make that case, but rather that it was unnecessary. Even if this was at root tight-fistedness, it was politically informed. Local reputations were at stake, though, in such a public forum and the Lord Lieutenant, the Earl of Bridgewater, felt his honour had been slighted. At the sessions his interest had been defended by Timothy Tourneur, JP and close associate of the earl, who had told the Grand Jury that they were 'too busy' in making this presentment. This was a common insult for minor officials, suggesting that they should be less meddlesome. Such rebukes exercised a considerable influence over how officeholders behaved towards their neighbours.[87]

But the Grand Jury had an eminent defender: John Corbett, another JP. He leaped to their defence, saying that they were simply doing their job, and calling for a reading of the Petition of Right. When the statute book was produced, despite Tourneur's objection, Corbett pointed to the relevant section. Tourneur said that he need not 'digitate', to which Corbett replied, 'Nor you be so touchy'. This evidently counted as a serious defeat in a battle of wits and news of this public embarrassment spread rapidly. It seems to have encouraged resistance in the rest of Shropshire later in the year, and Bridgewater heard of the exchange by 'flying report' before his subordinates had had a chance to write to him: 'I heard a great noise of the business about the town before I was able to give any answer to such questions (upon such an occasion) might have been demanded of me'. The Privy Council could not afford to ignore this public expression of dissent, and Corbett ended up in prison in London during a plague outbreak. He also had to enter a bond of £2,000 to answer for his conduct before Star Chamber, a central law court with a particular responsibility for overseeing the conduct of officeholders.[88]

This was more than a kerfuffle, since Corbett at least was willing to risk death in prison rather than apologize. Shropshire was not alone in hearing these arguments. Essex also produced a petition at quarter sessions and in many counties there is evidence of reluctant or partial payment of the fee.[89] In Leicestershire opposition to the militia pro-gramme was led by Sir William Faunt and Sir Arthur Haselrig, both JPs, who were hostile to the Lord Lieutenant, the Earl of Huntingdon. Faunt refused his contribution to the muster master's fee, publicly declared that Huntingdon was oppressing the county and questioned whether the money was actually being spent on the militia. He may have had some grounds in the latter case – Huntingdon was more eminent than rich and it seems he was not above using public or family money to help him over short-term problems. Here too a division in the county's governing elite ended up in Star Chamber. The authority of the Lieutenant was upheld by a swingeing fine, which at this distance in time seems to be barely warranted by the evidence produced.[90]

In the absence of Parliament, problems relating to military and financial questions continued to resonate deeply in English society. Local officeholders had an eye on what would make them popular or unpopular, and what would be difficult to achieve, or lead to accusations of 'busy-ness'. This made local government responsive to influential local opinion since it depended on a degree of consensus-building and informal negotiation. It also delivered significant practical power to local officeholders, who were expected to be representatives as well as leaders of their local community and who, for practical reasons, had to respond to wider local opinion. Policies which were potentially unpopular, or not in the immediate interests of local elites, might not be vigorously enforced: on receipt of administrative instructions local officeholders took decisions about what to push and what to leave alone; and institutions such as the Grand Jury and quarter sessions offered a platform for the expression of these local preferences. Sanctions existed to discipline officeholders, and were effective on individuals who might be quite anxious to retain their position, but the crown could not dismiss all its volunteers. A powerful man like the Earl of Bridgewater could bully and cajole, but there were evidently limits there too. Policies that were widely unpopular, such as expensive militia reform, created a level of foot-dragging and evasion that was difficult to deal with.

Problems with reform of the militia reveal these features of political life, and they were not the only controversial aspects of Caroline government in England. During the 1630s Charles's government responded imaginatively to its financial problems. Frustrated at the experience of the 1620s, when parliaments had been productive of political argument rather than cash, Charles raised money by other means during the 1630s. Prerogative rights were exploited for their revenue potential – for example, in a concerted campaign to raise fines for encroachments on the ancient bounds of the royal forests, or in the granting of monopolies in return for payments or loans. In 1629 the Council began to impose fines on men worth more than £40 per annum (not a large sum) who had failed to acknowledge their ancient duty of presenting themselves for knighting at the coronation – a wheeze known as distraint of knighthood. Of course, showing imagination about fiscal solutions is not an easy route to popularity and there were significant signs of dissatisfaction. In some localities the resurrection of forest jurisdictions caused considerable local conflict and in Leicestershire the fines for distraint of knighthood raised very large sums from a large number of people. By 1635 £174,000 had been raised from 10,000 landowners. Similarly, fines imposed for enclosures of common land that led to depopulation, while laudable for their concern for the victims of economic change, were widely seen as a revenue device. Once again, in Leicestershire, they raised considerable sums of money and again the hostility seems to have attached above all to the Earl of Huntingdon.[91] These were useful sums, but not a long-term solution: as the Venetian ambassador noted, fines were 'false mines for obtaining money, because they are good for once only, and states are not maintained by such devices'.[92] And this money came at a high price.

The most unpopular of these non-parliamentary revenues was ship money.[93] This transformed a duty on port towns to supply ships for royal service into a payment to build them, and the payment was soon imposed on the whole country, not just in the ports. Like the militia reforms, then, this was an attempt to commute an established duty of service into a cash payment. Although it did not cause a tax rebellion it did cause widespread disquiet and there was a very public dispute about whether or not ship money was legal. In 1637 Charles wrote to the judges asking whether the monarch had the power to command the provision of ships in times of danger, to enforce payment and act as the sole judge of the danger. Five days later all twelve judges replied affirmatively. Their ruling was entered in the courts and publicized at assizes. The danger, of course, is that this procedure gives publicity to the doubts rather than the certainties, and we know that it led to informed debate among the Kentish gentry.[94] Elsewhere, refusals continued.[95]

In Buckinghamshire the doubts were pressed further by John Hampden, who went to court. This was almost certainly promoted as a test case, with the co-operation of William Fiennes, Viscount Saye and Sele. A man of firm and godly religious conviction, Say and Sele became prominent in the parliamentary cause in the 1640s. During the 1630s he was an important member of the Providence Island Company, founded to fund settlement in the New World. This colonization scheme attracted the support of others who became prominent parliamentarians, including John Pym and the Lord Brooke. Say and Sele was a supporter of the international Calvinist cause and no friend to the policies of the Personal Rule. He had intended to bring his own case against ship money, but instead seems to have co-operated with his nephew, Sir Peter Temple, who issued a writ against John Hampden. The King, probably fortified by the judges' ruling, allowed the case to be heard in the Court of Exchequer, even though to lose would be to lose the whole revenue.[96]

The Earl of Clarendon later recalled that Hampden 'grew the argument of all tongues, every man enquiring who and what he was that durst at his own charge support the liberty and property of the kingdom, and rescue his kingdom from being made prey to the court'. The hearings were well attended, even by some relatively humble observers, and provincial newsletters reported the arguments widely. As should be expected, with expensive lawyers involved, the issues were not straightforward. Charles's case rested on the fact that ship money was not a tax – something regulated by common law and statute – but an aspect of his prerogative power. Ship money could be justified as an emergency measure and therefore as one relating to areas not covered by the common law. Oliver St John, representing Hampden, did not challenge the King's prerogative powers in general terms, arguing instead on a more narrow point: the writ had been issued six months prior to the collection. If there had been an emergency the writ should have mentioned it, and six months clearly permitted the summoning of a parliament to deal with the emergency. Holborne, Hampden's other lawyer, argued more broadly about the prerogative, and the subsequent hearings ranged over both broad principles and narrow technicalities. Each judge found slightly differently on each issue, so that the count in favour of the King, normally rendered as 7–5, was actually reckoned differently by different observers. Crucial judgements by Bramston and Davenport made it appear closer, but their view was based on a technicality. The writ had demanded a service, which Hampden could not in practice provide (the provision of a portion of a ship). He was being prosecuted for a debt, however. The crown could not have this both ways: if he owed a debt, then this was an unparliamentary tax, and therefore illegal;

if it was a service to be performed in emergency conditions he could not be sued for a debt. On the broad principles the King's victory was clearer.[97]

This public debate about the legality of the levy had resonances at the lowest levels of the administration because constables were being required by sheriffs to assess their neighbours. Debate about whether they had such a power, or about whether it was enforceable, was clearly relevant to local politics and administration. Reluctance to pay was almost universally expressed in technical or bureaucratic complaints – disputes about the details of ratings or the conduct of distraint and so on. For those unwilling to presume much about the political conscious-ness of ordinary people, this form of expression is often accepted at face value: that there was no larger political or legal principle involved. However, given the level of administrative participation and the elabor-ated consciousness of legal matters which is evident across the country, it seems difficult to believe that in every case reluctance was only the product of administrative detail. Local officeholders seem to have been increasingly reluctant to take up office, something attributed to the unpopularity of ship money which was surely not simply a matter of rating difficulties. As a result of this reluctance, and unlike the parliamen-tary taxes of the early seventeenth century, ship money also began to suffer from problems of collection. Clarendon went so far as to claim that the judgement had 'proved of more advantage and credit to the gentleman condemned, Mr Hampden, than to the King's service'. Hind-sight no doubt exaggerated his view, but it is true that after the crown's legal victory in 1637 the difficulties of collection in many counties continued to mount.[98]

English people were encouraged by practice and precept to be active for the public good. Self-government was crucial to the order of local communities and also to the public image of those individuals respon-sible for it – officeholders cultivated the image of virtue necessary to carry out their duties to the public good. In general this self-government was supportive of, and dependent on, the King's command, but the two might not always sit well together. Responses to the King's command were not simply passive and unthinkingly obedient, even when they were in fact obedient. Where there was reluctance, or resistance, it might not be the result of principled objection, but whether for reasons of narrow advantage – personal or local – or because of a wider vision of the public good, the King's command was appraised and interpreted as well as acted upon. Government depended on the voluntary efforts of substantial local inhabitants, and during the 1630s the imposition of ship money and militia reform made their lives difficult. Those difficulties were not eased by the legal question marks which hung over the extent of their powers. Other grievances affected those in more elevated circles – for example, monopolies and distraint of knighthood – while the forest policy had a deep impact in some regions.

Behind all these policies lay legal questions which were potentially of very general significance and some people certainly invested them with that general significance. The absence of parliaments removed one important means of voicing grievances and the use of the Court of Star Chamber (the authority of which rested on the royal prerogative) to enforce them seemed to be increasingly politicized.[99] This was not the stuff of revolution, or even of civil war, but it gave grounds to be reluctant to supply money, men and arms to fight the Covenanters; and to want the King to call a parliament instead.

In 1629 a sub-committee of the House of Commons had complained that persons maintaining 'papistical, Arminian, and superstitious opinions and practices . . . are countenanced, favoured and preferred'. An associated protestation of the Commons was one of the measures passed while the Speaker was held down. It announced that anyone promoting Arminianism or popery should be 'reputed a capital enemy to this Kingdom and Commonwealth'.[100] The continued and apparently triumphant rise of Laudianism during the Personal Rule was not likely to have spread the blessings of ecclesiastical peace, therefore.[101]

Closer restrictions on preaching, which affected the freedom to preach predestinarian views, were clearly inflammatory but had less immediate impact on the experience of worshippers than the campaign to promote decency and order in public service and the beauty of holiness: moving the 'communion table' 'altar-wise', and placing it at the east end of the church, there to be railed off in a raised chancel; bowing to the altar; reintroducing decorative features such as paintings and statues; and reincorporating a number of ceremonies and rituals into worship. Thus, for example, worshippers were expected to register reverence and obeisance to God as a uniform body, so that 'the whole congregation shall appear in the presence of God as one man, decently kneeling, rising, standing, bowing, praising, praying together . . . like men of one mind and religion in the house of God'. This was contrasted with a stolid immobility, likened to posts and stones; for its opponents it smelt of popish ritual, a form of mechanical worship which did not encourage a questing, demanding personal piety. A corollary of this was a campaign to enhance the dignity and authority of the clergy. Vestments worn by the clergy were regarded by opponents as 'rags of popery' but had previously been defended as adiaphora – 'things indifferent' which were not necessary but which were demanded by the civil authority. They were now defended as signs of the special and elevated status of the clergy, an argument that smacked of popery to many hot Protestants. Ceremonial changes, and changes to the decoration and architecture of the church, were intended to set a clearer boundary between the sacred and the profane, and to concentrate the mind of the worshipper on the presence of the former.[102]

Once he became Archbishop of Canterbury in 1633 Laud used his powers of visitation – to send questions to the lower clergy and church-wardens demanding reports about conformity and standards of practice – to promote the new ceremonialism. These initiatives were not universally disliked, nor were they only grudgingly enforced in every parish. Anti-Puritanism was an established strand of opinion, just as anti-popery, and these reforms might give comfort to ordinary worshippers. They drew on ceremonial traditions which can be identified much earlier in English Protestantism than the rise of anti-predestinarian divines, and owed something at least to Charles (who was not an Arminian): it was not simply an expression of the theological preferences of William Laud. Nonetheless, it was the use of the metropolitan visitation in the mid-1630s – enquiry into parochial practice in response to the archbishop, not the diocesan bishop – that caused friction in many places.[103]

Clearly, to many Protestants this campaign smacked of idolatry and superstition, rather than edification.[104] And although this was the more immediate experience of Laudianism, shifts in theological taste were manifest in what preaching was available – both who was licensed and who was not. Thus, to opponents of these policies, the church was simultaneously promoting idolatry and suppressing the preaching of the Word: substituting popery for the edifying exposition of scripture. As in Scotland, the boundary between what edified and what was idolatrous could be marked out polemically in terms of popery. On the wrong side of the line stood the whorish allurements of Babylon, ensnaring the unwary believer into an anti-Christian captivity. Any parish church might become an arena for the battle against popery; far more than was the case with the secular complaints, these policies lent themselves to simple sloganeering.

Laudianism was made to look worse by the presence of actual Catholics at the royal court. Charles's wife, Henrietta Maria, was allowed to practise her religion freely by the marriage treaty: her faith was a matter of state. It was also very devout, and public. Inigo Jones designed a beautiful chapel for her at Somerset House, decorated in a style very offensive to many Calvinist sensibilities. The dedication service attracted hundreds of observers and at its consecration in 1635 papal mass was sung amidst festivities lasting three days. A dozen Capuchins – the vanguard of Catholic reform in France – were sent to minister to her. She also protected other Catholics at the court and from 1636 George Con, a papal representative, was permanently resident at Henrietta Maria's court. Ironically, Laud was resentful of the influence of both Henrietta Maria and Con, but the association of Laudianism with Arminianism, and of both with a court friendly to Catholicism, produced a heady mix of provocations to the godly. At the same time, a shift in foreign policy towards neutrality in the Thirty Years War, which was effectively a shift to a pro-Spanish policy, fuelled the suspicion that the King was being influenced by a Catholic conspiracy: the Spanish monarchy was routinely assumed to be a secular arm of papal ambitions. 'Court Catholicism became associated with papal meddling, Spanish intrigue, and repressive domestic policies, and the king with all of these'. Rumours of the King's imminent conversion were taken seriously in Rome.[105]

Even with a full-blown episcopacy it was very difficult simply to impose the Laudian programme, however. Lay influence was entrenched in the institutions of the church. For example, the crown and its bishops did not have secure control over parochial appointments. The right to present men to parochial appointments, 'livings', was often attached to a piece of land, and that land was often in the hands of laymen. Although whoever was presented had to be licensed by a bishop, the bishop and the crown did not control the patronage of the church. Nor could the ecclesiastical authorities easily prevent the development of parallel forms of religious practice. Attendance at parish church was enforced, but it was not straightforward to prevent other, supplementary, gatherings. Moreover, a shortage of preaching in the early years of the Reformation had encouraged private benefactors, especially corporations, to establish lectureships – paid preaching posts not attached to a parish. In the mid-1620s the Feoffes for Impropriations had been established to purchase alienated church revenues and use them to fund preaching: a laudable project, but one which threatened Laudian discipline over the teaching of the church. It was closed down, but the provision of preaching outside the parish church was difficult to abolish; not least, of course, because it was often blameless and helpful to the cause of reformation as the ecclesiastical hierarchy understood it.[106]

Ecclesiastical authorities were dependent on local people to volunteer information about local practice and for the imposition of sanctions. The church courts, responsible for enforcing observance of the rites of the established church, also depended on participation. Business could be brought before them by individuals – instance business, akin to civil actions in the secular courts – or by churchwardens – office business, akin to the criminal law. Churchwardens, like constables, took account of local opinion in the discharge of their office. In either case, it was difficult for ecclesiastical authorities simply to implement or enforce policies. The inquisitorial power that they did possess lay in the visitation – the power to demand answers to specific questions. But there was no easy way to check the accuracy of the replies and so once again the ecclesiastical authorities were to a significant degree in the hands of their inferiors. Finally, some ecclesiastical policies demanded action from secular officeholders: for example, in fining recusants (those not attending church). Local officeholders often appear to have responded to local preferences in interpreting their obligations, favouring the maintenance of good local relations over the national imperative of religious unity.[107] In other words lay influence in the church intersected with local self-government in ways that limited the practical power of the head of the church.

All this did not mean that local practice was automatically at odds with official policy, but it did mean that the propagation of the faith, and even the nature of the faith that was propagated, was coloured by local lay preferences. Administrative patterns allowed for distinctive local responses to official policy on how to submit with one's fingers crossed, as it were. Thus, even if at a certain time on a certain day everyone in England could be made to bow to the altar, this uniformity of practice might still have concealed a great variety of belief: what bowing meant, if anything, could not be, as it were, divined. Lay influence within the church made the promotion of reformation dependent on a degree of voluntarism, and that voluntarism produced plurality.

As with secular matters, consent in the localities was usually informed. Protestant worship, like local administration, served as an education. Parishioners were expected in church each Sunday, on pain of a fine imposed by the government, not the ecclesiastical authorities. Those who came heard a powerful message about Christian submission, but also about Reformation history. Worshippers attending their local parish church were frequently encouraged to place their local experiences in the context of a larger, international and apocalyptic history of the Christian community. In March 1629 the minister at St Helen's, Ashby-de-la-Zouch, delivered a powerful sermon on the need for Protestant solidarity across the whole of Europe: 'Say not thou art a member of the Church of England, thou art a member of the Church of France, or of Germany, or of Bohemia: for all the Churches of the world that profess the same faith and religion, are but one body'. He went on to lament the lack of 'fellow-feeling with their miseries'. Although these sufferings were commonly heard and talked about, and news circulated in the corantos, as much as any other news, it was treated 'as if a matter that concerns not us at all'. This indifference risked provoking God 'by our profane stupidity'.[108]

Of course, the need for the harangue suggests that many of his audience did not acknowledge these truths, but as war raged in Germany, a war perceived by many as crucial to the future of the church, it seemed to some observers that they were witnessing the battles of the last days. Many Scots had gone to serve in these wars, and some Englishmen too: according to one estimate 3,000 volunteers each year from 1562 to 1642, not counting those in the service of the English crown. Collections for distressed Protestants, and to support wounded veterans of the wars, were relatively common in English parish churches.[109]

Local worship was also about the celebration and formation of local community, of course. It was a ritual moment of common prayer in which hierarchy was reconciled with community. The moral and spiritual boundaries of community were physically represented in the decoration of the church and the disposition of its internal spaces. Pews were increasingly likely to be personally allocated, the best seats going to the local quality, their social inferiors ranged behind them. This was in fact one common problem in railing off the altar, that it might disturb the seating arrangements which were so carefully calibrated to reflect the local social order. Through the ritual year communal life was marked out and reproduced – even the physical boundaries of the community were marked by Rogation-tide processions, when the minister 'beat the bounds' with his parishioners. The life cycle was marked out by communal events – baptism, marriage and death. In a ritual much despised by the godly but promoted by the Laudians, women were formally received back into the congregation after childbirth, a ceremony known as churching. Sinners did public penance and were readmitted to the bosom of the Christian community. Ritual forms might carry a considerable freight of local social and political significance; and that significance was in turn located within an apocalyptic scheme that embraced the whole Christian community.[110] Sin and popery in (as it might be) Ashby-de-la-Zouch had a potentially cosmic significance, and Protestant preachers were anxious to make that clear. Episcopal authority in England therefore provided the framework for a participatory, and active, Christian practice; and that practice was, by principle, socially and politically engaged.

Although lay influence diluted the power of the head of the church, it was not nullified. As we have seen, during the 1630s, as episcopal powers were brought to bear, there was a distinct change in tone in many localities and changes to the internal arrangements of many churches. Some people, among them both the humble and very influential, clearly felt concerned about the future of reformation. During the 1630s, some of the godly in England fled to the New World (along with those motivated by more secular concerns), hoping to establish a new Zion, and many others seem to have gone to Europe.[111] But separation from a church in which the Word and the sacraments could be found was no easy step. Even after the church did begin to appear popish, there were powerful reasons for thinking that the cloud might pass, and that in the meantime enough of the Word, the true sacraments and of religious discipline was present to allow a good Christian to endure with a good conscience. The ideals of the common prayer gave a powerful incentive to stay, and to hope for better days.[112]

Central to this agonizing problem was the common Reformation view that reform should produce a purified church, not a sect or heresy.

Arguments between those who stayed and those who left were to become quite heated once the tide of Laudianism had been turned back in England. For those who felt these difficulties, however, the way forward was not clear and for those who stayed it was not clear how far resistance should go. The Covenanters' publicists recognized the dangers of setting religious obligations against political duties and had thought carefully about the limits of legitimate resistance: for many reformers a world reformed in line with scripture was a hierarchical one, in which everyone knew their place and their calling. Active encouragement of civil and political unrest was clearly ungodly and religious diversity in England did not automatically create rebels.[113]

Those who stayed, and protested loudly, might fall foul of Laudian authoritarianism. Most famously Henry Burton, John Bastwick and William Prynne stood trial before Star Chamber in 1637 as a result of publishing offensive tracts. Their sentence was the pillory and to have their ears cropped. Prynne's ears had already been cropped, but the remaining stumps came off nonetheless, and his cheeks were branded 'SL' for 'seditious libeller'. Burton's left ear was cut so close to the head, and so clumsily, that he lost a lot of blood. Throughout it all they bore their sufferings with Christian patience, turning their punishment into an example of the futility of physical punishment in the face of godliness. All three had been in trouble before without exciting nationwide sympathy, and their publications were acknowledged even by many of the godly to have gone far beyond the bounds of acceptable public criticism. They were given ample opportunity to speak at their trials, and to seek some relatively mild punishment, but there is a suspicion that they sought martyrdom. Certainly, in the pillory, they were transformed into suffering saints. Both during and after their brutal public mutilations they were given a warm welcome. Prynne was feasted in St Alban's and Chester, for example, and the Privy Council came to think that it had lost a propaganda battle. The spectacle prompted Sir Thomas Wentworth to remark to Laud that 'A Prince that loses the force and example of his punishments loses withal the greatest part of his dominion'.[114] Of course, hardly any anti-Laudians ran the risk of similar treatment, but through their transformation into Puritan martyrs these three came to represent the more general suffering of the godly under Laud's episcopal authoritarianism. Their views were not universally liked, their preferred mode of expression even less so, but these were men of status – a doctor, a

William Laud and Sir Thomas Wentworth (soon to become the Earl of Strafford): the two royal advisers held most responsible for the misgovernment of Charles's kingdoms

lawyer and a divine. That status should have protected them from this fury; their sufferings became a symbol of something much bigger.

Grumbling, foot-dragging and some sharp intakes of breath at the mutilation of the Puritan martyrs were a fair exchange for the problems of a decade earlier, perhaps. There was an informed, principled and critical public in England, but it was not ungovernable. It is true that there were many grievances in the 1630s, but they did not all irritate the same people to the same extent, and there were few Englishmen who would have argued that royal government was not in itself a good thing. Things had been much easier in the absence of war, and of parliaments. Clearly, however, some secular policies were producing tensions between the crown and some of its natural governors in the localities. Charles won his legal battles but there is little doubt that in some minds the imaginative use of the prerogative to raise money, associated as it was with a reluctance to call parliaments, represented a shift in the balance of the constitution. There is also little doubt that this question of legality hampered administration either because of principled objection or because it offered plausible cover for tight-fistedness. It was probably both, but in either case legal debate gave public airing to constitutional questions, and these were of relevance to lives of the middling sort, and open to discussion at relatively humble levels of English society.

Opposition to Laudianism made a connection between religious and civil liberties – it was partly driven by a fear of clerical authority. The Reformation in England rested on statute and threats to it arising from episcopal authority were easily connected in the minds of the godly with the threats posed by an extensive view of the royal prerogative. It was as much clerical ambition as popery that made Laudianism seem threatening, or at least the religious 'innovation' was identified by opponents with an expanding royal prerogative.[115]

It was not only Puritans who were anxious about Laudianism, therefore. Central aspects of Calvinism in England appealed beyond the ranks of those known as Puritans and it is not possible to draw a distinction between hotter Protestants and others simply on the grounds of their attitude towards Calvinism: the doctrine of predestination had held together people who were divided on questions of ceremony and church government. By the same token, it was not only Puritans who might sympathize with the plight of the Covenanters – Calvinists who were similarly offended by Laudian policy – and such sympathy as there was did not necessarily depend on an admiration of Scottish practice either. Most English people would probably not have willingly signed up to join the church of Alexander Henderson, but many of them might see in that church a potential ally against Laudianism.

For men schooled in English history and Renaissance values, as local magistrates were, there were abstract principles at stake here. Classical values of republican virtue, manifest in active citizenship, were widely known among the English gentry; so too was a deep attachment to the 'ancient constitution', unique liberties which formed the inheritance of Englishmen, and which they owed a profound duty to protect. Of course, their opposition might arise from narrow local interest or even self-interest and personal ambition, but the ethos and practice of Stuart government dignified their opinions as crucial to the health of government. Renaissance republicans were not necessarily more altruistic than twenty-first-century democrats, but the principles they asserted still mattered to the conduct of government. Inf rmed local officeholders, when making judgements about particular policies, were equipped with the knowledge and understanding to arrive at an independent view about the direction of religious and political affairs. Their education might tell them that this independent view, their 'discretion', was a personal virtue essential to their public role.

English government depended on active involvement, sometimes informed explicitly by classical histories, which prompted action for the public good, but which might be critical of the crown. Felton had demonstrated the existence of these ideals of active Christian citizenship, capable of opposing the King's favourite and military commander in the interests of the commonwealth. His actions also demonstrated the tensions caused by Caroline policies in the fraught conditions of Reformation Europe. These elements of Caroline political culture, and Caroline politics, were exaggerated by the personalities – Felton's own, the melancholy loner, and Buckingham's – and by war, financial problems and meetings of fractious parliaments. The 1630s were calmer – with no Buckingham, parliaments or war and a lower intensity of public debate – but the calm was not a dumb obedience. The issues that concerned Felton – religion, the King's advisers, money and war – were concerns shared by many others, well beyond the ranks of those willing to applaud the assassination. During the 1630s English government continued to depend on active local officeholders; political issues and argument continued to circulate, and fuel discussion; and some tensions remained.

We cannot say that these questions were the talk of every alehouse, and it seems unlikely, but it is practically possible that they might have been. Political awareness was available to the villagers of Stuart England, and their participation was essential to the functioning of government. Practice and precept made them self-activating for the public good, defined in terms common with the magisterial class. Local misgivings about particular policies could be expressed through foot-dragging and legal challenge and, to some extent, through the normal channels of government leading up to the court. During the 1630s, however, they could not be expressed in Parliament and so local grievances accumulated. The problems of the 1620s had not gone away, although the absence of war, and of a talking shop, clearly helped to reduce the temperature. But the apocalypse continued to threaten and militia reform proceeded: fighting a war against fellow Protestants in the light of all this was unlikely to meet uncritical obedience.

3

Drawing Swords in the King's Service

The English and the Bishops' Wars

As far we can possibly tell, Alexander Powell, of Holt, Cheshire, was not a natural rebel or traitor. His background and personal history, though, to the extent that we can reconstruct them, did make him likely to oppose the war against the Covenanters. In 1638 he had been accused of attending church to hear preaching by a minister who had been suspended for his advanced Protestant views. These meetings, labelled conventicles by the ecclesiastical authorities, had been winked at by the churchwardens, reflecting perhaps the extent to which 'Puritan' sympathies were entrenched among village worthies in that part of the country. Puritan preaching had certainly enjoyed some success in fostering hotter forms of Protestantism in the county. It was quite possible for 'Puritans' such as Powell to be active in their local communities, pursuing charitable work or fostering an alliance between magistrate and minister aimed at the eradication of sin. But in 1638 Powell turned a beggar away from his house, saying, 'No sirrah, you shall have no alms here for shortly you will be pressed to war, and then you will fight against us'. Soldiers were about to be pressed in the north-west to fight against the Covenanters, and when the press was used it was exactly such men who were vulnerable: it was not unlikely that this man may have been on the verge of being pressed for service against the Covenanters. Powell seems then to have been asserting the importance of a religious affiliation with the Covenanters over obligations to his ungodly but vulnerable neighbours.[1] The pressure of events was making plain potential contradictions in the world view of Charles's subjects.

We do not know how many people there were like Powell, but we do know that military mobilization by prerogative power in order to enforce Laudian ceremonialism would have plenty of opponents. A

Buckinghamshire gentleman came to the attention of the authorities for saying that 'he cared not [for Laud], for he has been the occasion of this strife between the Scots and us, and I care not if he heard me'. Libels in Ware (Herts.) proposed delivering Laud to the Scots rather than being eaten up with superstition and idolatry, and claimed that the conflict with the Covenanters arose from their resistance to idolatry and the Mass. Others were willing to blame the King, who, according to a man in Pembrokeshire, wanted 'a good headpiece', unlike his wise and learned father. A vicar in Northamptonshire who preached obedience was interrupted by a parishioner who said the King should yield to the Covenanters, and another argued that God's will might be that England's pride should have a fall. In Newcastle a man was reported to have argued that the Covenanters 'did nothing but in defence of their own right and maintenance of the Gospel, and did but defend themselves against those that would have brought in popery and idolatry among them'. He declared himself unwilling to fight, 'for unless his conscience moved him to it, he would not fight for any prince in Christendom'. Perhaps even more significantly, he was provoked by someone saying 'beshrew the Scots that stand out against the King, for they are likely to put us to a great deal of charge, and it is likely we shall all go and fight against them': hardly the most positive statement of support for the King's position.[2] Lurking behind all this must have been some sense that this was the wrong war – Charles had been at pains to stay out of the European wars but was now raising troops against his own, Protestant, subjects. Since many others were keen to have a parliament to discuss secular and religious grievances, it was not only opponents of Laudianism and militia reform that were qualified in their support for the King.

The demands of the wars had an impact on an informed and engaged political society in which a degree of consensus and co-operation was essential to successful government. There was no such consensus behind the policy of armed intervention against Scottish Calvinists: opinion was instead divided. Laudianism and militia reform clearly had supporters in England or they would have made no headway. Neither were opponents of these policies necessarily advocates of the Covenanters' religious views, or political tactics; nor were they necessarily equally offended by all these policies. Still less were they in favour of the dissolution of royal government. Reluctance to support the war effort might proceed from a positive sympathy for the Covenanters' cause, an unwillingness to support the use of the prerogative or armed Catholics against the cause, or a sense that this crisis might be useful as leverage in securing redress of English grievances. There was a difference, in other words, between being pro-Covenanter and being not anti-Covenanter, and different arguments might support either of these positions. For Charles the issue was plain – this was a rebellion. For others the issue was more complicated and this undoubtedly added to the normal problems of mobilizing for war in early Stuart England. English opinion was far more ambivalent and divided than opinion in Scotland, but a King seeking to raise an army by prerogative power would clearly have hoped for less ambivalence and more commitment.

These complex responses help to explain why building the necessary consensus around military mobilization proved so very difficult. Among those in trouble in Exeter were the mayor and two aldermen.[3] At the King's rendezvous in York in late April 1639 two peers refused the military oath. They were Viscount Say and Sele, member of the Providence Island Company and supporter of Hampden's case, and Lord Brooke, another member of the company and a man of godly piety.[4] Others clearly thought it inadvisable to proceed without the support of a parliament: extraordinarily this was the first time since 1323 that England had gone to war without the summoning of a parliament.[5] Winning this one would be uphill work.

Divisions in England came into the open, and came to matter, because Charles had to rely exclusively on English forces to crush the rebellion of his Scottish subjects. This had not been his original intention. In Scotland his hopes rested on George Gordon, Marquess of Huntly, who had offered protection to the Aberdeen Doctors, an eminent minority who had supported the royal position against the Covenanters. During Hamilton's mission Charles had encouraged Huntly's efforts to resist the promotion of the Covenant in the north-east and he now hoped that Hamilton could join Huntly, who was raising forces in Aberdeenshire.[6] In Ireland Charles hoped for help from Randall MacDonnell, the Catholic Earl of Antrim. Antrim also had claims to land in Scotland and he hoped to pursue those claims through opposition to the Covenanters. As early as January 1638 he had offered to raise troops for the King in Ulster and he now hoped to make good on that offer.[7] With forces moving south from Aberdeenshire and across the North Channel into the western highlands, Charles hoped to bring an English force to the Borders, forcing the Covenanters to fight on three fronts.

This strategy, however, quickly collapsed. In Ireland, Charles was in the hands of Sir Thomas Wentworth, the Lord Deputy. Schooled in the harsh world of Yorkshire politics, Wentworth had made his way by appealing to the royal court for patronage and protection and, when it suited, to the country as a champion of local interests. He was prominent in the parliaments of the 1620s as a critic of the court, but rose to be president of the Council of the North, vanquishing local rivals in the process. He was then made Lord Deputy in Ireland, the kind of promotion which can also be seen as an exile. In Ireland he acquired a reputation for authoritarian government, partly because he was indeed authoritarian and partly because he attacked all vested interests equally boldly. His service there was valued by the King, however, who gave him the title of Lord Lieutenant in January 1640 and elevated him to the peerage shortly after as the first Earl of Strafford. In England, in more normal circumstances, he would have been less authoritarian than in Ireland, but in the Scottish crisis he counselled Charles to take a strong line.[8] Nonetheless, he opposed Antrim's mobilization, and doubted the usefulness of his troops. In north-east Scotland, Huntly was outfaced by a better-mobilized Covenanter force, which took a number of castles, leading Huntly to disband his forces rather than risk defeat, and Hamilton was diverted from his rendezvous with Huntly to the Firth of Forth. There he found landing unsafe, not least because his own mother appeared in public with a pistol and threatened to shoot him if he came ashore. Charles had also sought help from the Dutch and the Spanish. The Dutch were completely uninterested and the Spanish claimed that they could not commit troops because suitable bread ovens would not be available in England. That the Privy Council explored the range of available bread ovens perhaps reflects a certain desperation, or an inability to take a hint.[9]

Despite his initial intentions, therefore, Charles had to rely entirely on his English forces. The achievement was not negligible: two large armies were mobilized to fight the Covenanters in just over a year, 15,000 in May 1639 and nearly 25,000 in August 1640.[10] But the Earl of Northumberland, commander of the English forces, had counselled against going to war in July 1638, on the grounds that 'The People through all England are generally so discontented, by reason of the multitude of projects daily imposed upon them, as I think there is reason to fear that a great part of them will be readier to join with the Scots, than to draw their swords in the King's service'.[11] Things were little better once war broke out. On their way to fight in the second of the Bishops' Wars, in 1640, some English troops did in fact behave as if they were on the other side, carrying out iconoclastic acts to purify parish churches and refusing to obey papistical officers. English opinion was divided, and complex, not uniformly hostile to the war, and we should not ignore the achievement; but division was not what Charles had expected, and it was not welcome. It precipitated the end of his Personal Rule in England and prompted a crisis which ultimately led to the dissolution of his authority in England, Scotland and Ireland.

On 9 February 1639 the Privy Council had conceded that members of the Trained Bands (that part of the able-bodied population summoned to muster which had been equipped and trained to modern standards) need not serve. They could instead send substitutes, an important concession to anticipated resistance.[12] Many others were pressed from the general population – the common practice in the case of foreign service since the Trained Bands were too precious to be sent abroad. Impressment, by contrast, was often the occasion for ridding villages of undesirables. Officeholders in place for perhaps one year would have to live with their neighbours for much longer than that. It is easy to see why, when asked to pick some men to serve abroad, they might not choose the most popular and hard-working lads in the village or their neighbours' most promising sons. The home counties were responsible for equipping conscripts from local rates, and paying their expenses to the point of embarkation.[13] The mobilization against the Covenanters might have been regarded as a defensive action, allowing the use of the Trained Bands rather than conscripts, and in allowing the use of substitutes the Privy Council had significantly weakened the potential of the war effort.

Pressing men for military service was never easy, but in early 1639 it intersected with domestic discontents. George Plowright, constable of Burton Latimer, Northamptonshire, was the kind of village worthy who provided the backbone of English local government. His family had been freeholders in the village for over a century and he had served not only as constable but also as an overseer of the poor, sidesman and churchwarden.[14] However, conflicts over royal policies during the 1630s intersected with local rivalries to make his life very difficult. When he went to Northampton in 1638/9 to pay ship money receipts to the sheriff his horse was requisitioned for the royal posts, even though he was himself on royal service. He blamed Thomas Bacon, with whom he had clashed previously over religion and the forced loan, and with whom he had been in dispute over ship money since 1635. In retaliation Plowright brought a case against Bacon in Star Chamber. In March 1639 Plowright was pressed for service against the Covenanters: something highly unusual given his status and office. He again blamed Bacon, who had been accused of using impressment maliciously in the past and who had been served with a writ to appear in Star Chamber five days before Plowright was pressed. Conveniently, it would mean that Plowright would be in York when the case came before the court.

Forced to intervene, the Privy Council was in an uncomfortable position. It could hardly leave Sir Rowland St John, the Deputy Lieutenant ultimately responsible for the impressment, twisting in the wind. On the other hand, from the point of view of the Privy Council, Plowright was clearly on the side of the angels in Northamptonshire. He had the support of Robert Sibthorpe, a scourge of the local Puritans and an almost embarrassingly keen supporter of Charles and Laud in ecclesiastical matters, who during the Forced Loan controversy had preached that consent was not necessary for the King to raise money from his subjects. Sibthorpe interceded with St John on Plowright's behalf, enabling Plowright to send a deputy to join the army, and his intervention clearly reflected political solidarity. Sibthorpe had brought a case against Bacon over ship money, and noted Plowright's service in collecting the duty despite the hostility of local 'Puritans', expressing regret that his reward might now be to risk perishing at the hand of the Scottish Puritans. Before the Privy Council, though, St John maintained that Bacon had had no role in the pressing of Plowright, and that Plowright had been guilty of malpractices. The Privy Council had little choice but to uphold the authority of the Deputy Lieutenant, and Plowright was imprisoned and landed with the costs of both parties.[15]

Here and elsewhere, the local met the national. Rivalries and hostilities among the local gentry and middling sort might become invested with a larger political and religious significance. This does not reflect a fatal weakness of the whole mobilization since large numbers of men were raised, but it does demonstrate the potential of the Covenanters' cause to polarize English opinion. Latent conflicts were coming into the open, or were allowed freer expression.

By design, and because of the substitution clause, the infantry contained large numbers of pressed men. Even husbandmen (small farmers) and agricultural labourers seem to have been spared, so that labourers in non-agricultural trades predominated – men without the status or patrons to protect them from service.[16] They were often untrained and poorly armed or even unarmed. Although Charles raised significant sums in loans and contributions from prominent individuals, there was not enough money to make up the lack, since coat and conduct money barely covered the costs of getting soldiers to camp. It was also of dubious legality, raised by the lieutenancy, whose powers in that respect had been left poorly defined by the repeal of legislation in 1605. It had previously been used to get soldiers destined for foreign service to port, and was reimbursed (in theory at least) from parliamentary grants. Neither of these things was relevant to the current case, since this was not a force being raised for foreign service, and no parliament was planned. People were quite capable of making a connection between this and ship money. Many of the nobility were reluctant to serve in arms and the officer corps was inexperienced. England's arms industry had not had regular business under Elizabeth or the early Stuarts, and it had atrophied during the Caroline peace. As a result ordnance was difficult to find.[17] These latter problems reflect the relative lack of active warfare over the previous generation rather than a political weakness: no arms industry could thrive in the absence of a lively market.[18]

Contemporaries, not least the Covenanter leadership, were not convinced that the English forces were inferior to the Covenanters', but there is little doubt that the Covenanters enjoyed more support in Scotland than Charles did in England. They were able to draw on the military experience of large numbers of men who had served in the continental wars, and that experience also informed the methods of mobilization, which was further inspired by the preaching of a committed clergy. There were fewer pressed men, and behind the whole effort lay greater enthusiasm for the cause.[19]

Despite the apparent problems of the English mobilization and the relative success of the Covenanters, the English defeat was by no means assured.[20] It is clear though that the English camp at Birks, just south of the border, was an unhappy place – poorly provisioned, of uncertain morale and the rump of a once much more impressive strategy. Reservations were expressed there about whether to proceed, given the weakness of the army. In the event, the English threw in the towel without much of a fight. The Earl of Holland, second in command in the English army, advanced to Kelso, where he was probably fooled by Alexander Leslie into thinking that the Scottish forces were more numerous than they actually were. Holland withdrew, and when the Covenanters advanced to Duns Law on 5 June, the king agreed to negotiate.[21]

In seeking negotiation Charles was following the advice of the nobility in his camp and the decision probably rested as much on political as military calculation. The weakness of Scottish opposition to the Covenanters, the divided and often lukewarm English response and the threat of calling an English parliament persuaded him to do a deal.[22] A Pacification was agreed at Berwick but it seems to have fudged the key issues. In return for the summoning of a General Assembly and parliament the Covenanters agreed to disband, free royalist prisoners and hand back royal castles. However, on the powers of the General Assembly (and hence, by implication, the future of episcopacy) the two sides seem to have had a quite different impression of what had been said. The King issued a declaration denying the legality of the measures taken by the General Assembly in Glasgow the previous year, but promised to deliver on the promises made by Hamilton. For the future, he said, ecclesiastical matters would be in the hands of a lawfully constituted General Assembly and all secular matters in the hands of the Scottish parliament. The Covenanters interpreted this as a victory for the independence of the kirk, and it could be presumed that the end of the bishops was not far off. Charles later disavowed this interpretation without offering another, but notes made by one of the English delegates suggest that the difference may have lain in what was meant by the phrase 'lawfully constituted': for Charles this clearly implied the persistence of episcopal representation in the assembly. That such a crucial detail could be fudged probably reflects how much both sides wanted to end the armed conflict.[23]

In the aftermath of the Pacification it was clear that Charles was not altogether trusted and that his royal word was regarded by some as worth less than the parchment on which it was not written. An indication of the underlying attitude, to which he might well require obedience when he had the opportunity to command it, was the public burning of a Covenanter paper giving their interpretation of these events, which had circulated widely in England. For the Covenanters this reinforced the sense that the real security for their reformation lay in a sympathetic settlement in England.[24]

Management of the King's interest at the resulting General Assembly was handed back to Traquair, Hamilton clearly calculating that there was little pleasure or advantage to be had from this role.[25] Traquair presided over an assembly that confirmed most of the decisions reached by the 'illegal' assembly in Glasgow the previous year and went further on episcopacy. He also agreed that a parliament would be called in the expectation that these measures would be ratified. He failed to manage the legislative programme of that parliament, with the result that by November it was clear that Parliament had claimed more than the King would actually grant. The King intervened, dissolving Parliament on 14 November 1639, but the acquiescence of the parliamentarians was publicly stated alongside the view that it was an illegal dissolution.[26]

From here it was a relatively short and predictable step to renewed hostilities. In early February, Edinburgh Castle was garrisoned with English troops and, although Edinburgh's governors did not interfere, this did spur the Covenanters to renewed military preparations. One ill-advised initiative in this respect was a letter to Louis XIII asking him to intercede with Charles on behalf of his Scottish subjects.[27]

Charles had resolved to call an English parliament for this second war and clearly expected to find support. His sole purpose was to raise money to fight the Covenanters and he certainly had no intention of justifying the war, or of having to redress other grievances before receiving supply. He was also clear that if Parliament failed, he would be willing to proceed by other means, and in order to have some room for manoeuvre he had taken out loans. Many of his subjects, it would soon become clear, saw things differently. To Charles, King of three kingdoms, the Covenanters were rebels, and there could be no question of the need to crush rebellion, but to his English subjects this was a proposed invasion, or at least a war with another kingdom. In that respect there was some concern that an army was being raised prior to Parliament.[28]

Certainly, after an eleven-year intermission, the summoning of a new parliament was the occasion of much excitement. The Earl of

The House of Commons in the Short Parliament

Bridgewater had some difficulty in securing a place at a window from which his wife could watch the opening procession. When a place was found on King's Street she was advised to take up her place by six o'clock at the latest, since the streets would be full by five and after six it would be impossible to get into the house from the street.[29] Sixty-two elections were contested (by comparison with twenty to forty during the 1620s), and since most of these were in two-member constituencies, this meant that around one quarter of the members of the new Commons had arrived as a result of contests. In some cases this reflected a campaign by the godly, to get their own men in.[30]

Charles and his subjects clearly had different expectations of this parliament, and Charles's willingness to go to war without a parliament if necessary was almost self-fulfilling since to bring his subjects along would need patience. The royal view was clear, however. Lord Keeper Finch opened the parliament by asking for immediate supply to support the war while holding out the promise of another session later in the year in order to pursue the redress of grievances. Charles then handed him the letter written by the Covenanters to the French king and Finch read it out, claiming that it was treasonous.[31] The letter was subscribed 'au roy', a form of address which was only used by Frenchmen when addressing their own king. Charles claimed that this was treasonous – that the Covenanters were recognizing Louis to be their sovereign.[32] The defence offered by Loudon, one of the signatories, that he did not have enough French to understand the niceties of the letter, may not have been completely dishonest,[33] but what is most striking about this is the lack of excitement caused by the revelation of apparently treasonous activity.

On the following day, in the House of Commons, Secretary Windebank opened business with a restatement of the need for immediate supply, and offered to read the letter again, in both French and English, for those who had not been able to hear clearly at the crowded opening the previous day. This he did, but the first speakers offered little comfort to the crown. Harbottle Grimston stood up, acknowledging the importance of the King's business in fairly brisk terms before concentrating the burden of his remarks on other issues altogether: 'I am very much mistaken if there be not a case here at home of as great a danger'. This was a case that the King, confronted by armed rebels, would find hard to accept, but it was made at length by Grimston and others. Grimston was also innocent of understatement, to say the least:

the Commonwealth has been miserably torn and massacred and all property and liberty shaken, the Church distracted, the gospel and professors of it persecuted and the whole nation is overrun with multitudes and swarms of projecting cankerworms and caterpillars, the worst of all the Egyptian plagues.[34]

Sir Benjamin Rudyerd and Sir Francis Seymour spoke next, building on Grimston's concerns about the lapse of liberties granted by Magna Carta and the Petition of Right, but concentrating in particular on the circumstances of the dissolution of the previous parliament in 1629.[35]

This desire to secure redress of grievances before granting supply was widely but not universally shared, and it might arise from a variety of political concerns – it was by no means the same thing as supporting the Covenant, although it seems reasonably clear that the Covenanters had friends in the English parliament.[36] Many seem to have been hoping that the parliament would succeed – producing both supply and redress – but there were those who were not at all anxious that it should.[37] As the debates on grievances unfolded over the next few weeks, some speakers hinted at opposition to the war, but that was not on the surface of the debates.

These are important distinctions, but behind these various positions there was also a clear political message: Parliament, and not just the Commons, showed very little interest in shelving grievances in the interests of supplying the impending war. John Pym, a veteran of the parliaments of the 1620s, emerged as an influential speaker early on. He was an unusual parliamentarian in that he lacked a large landed estate. A convinced godly Protestant, he enjoyed the patronage of the Earl of Bedford and had held office in the Exchequer. This latter experience seems to have made him more responsible and realistic about the financial needs of government than many of those whose opinions he courted. On 17 April he spoke for two hours on a threefold threat: to the liberties of Parliament, to religion and to the law ('affairs of state or matters of property'). In most of these respects he was speaking to the mood of the House, but he went further in arguing that these were symptoms of a single malaise: 'the intermission of parliaments have been a true cause of all these evils in the Commonwealth, which by law should be once every year'. The liberty of Parliament, he was arguing, was the safeguard of religion and law.[38] When he sat down a string of county petitions were presented in what seems like a co-ordinated move, perhaps reminiscent of Covenanter tactics.[39]

Over the following weeks unsuccessful shuffling could not overcome this essential impasse – that Parliament wanted redress before supply, a procedure which Charles said 'put the cart before the horse'. Some members of both Houses supported the King's position, but Ralph Hopton seems to have spoken for the majority in the Commons when he drew the analogy with a servant who held his master up to remove a thorn from his foot. Such a delay was not the same as disobedience; Parliament, as a dutiful servant, had an obligation to remove the thorns from the King's foot.[40] Deals were proposed to give up unpopular revenue sources in return for parliamentary supply, and the crown tried to enlist the help of the Lords in persuading the Commons to grant supply and put the grievances on hold. This suggestion, however, made the Commons bristle, acutely conscious of any threat to the constitutional principle that supply could only be initiated in the Commons. Rather than acknowledge the immediate and unquestioned necessity of supplying the King's needs, MPs continued to call for redress of their grievances. And these grievances ranged widely – the long intermission of parliaments and the administrative measures Charles had taken in that time had created a backlog of moaning, and it seems that many MPs were keen to give it full rein. If the problems of mobilizing for war earlier in the year had disappointed the monarch, the attitude of his parliament was still more frustrating and after only three weeks he dissolved it.

Five or six days prior to the dissolution rumours had gone round London that in the event of a dissolution, Lambeth Palace (the seat of the Archbishop of Canterbury) would be burned down, with William Laud inside it. This proved to be not far from the truth. On 8 May 1640, after the dissolution, the words 'bishop's devils' were scrawled on the walls of the Royal Exchange. Placards soon followed there and elsewhere, urging an assembly at St George's Fields of 'all gentlemen 'prentices that desire to kill the bishops, who would fane kill us, our wives and children'. Apprentices were also invited to join in the hunting of 'William the fox'. The assembly was planned for the following Monday morning, 11 May. Although threats and rumours circulated about a number of royal ministers identified as public enemies it was clear that the real target of this hostility was Laud (who was also rumoured to have become a Roman Catholic) and bishops more generally. The Southwark militia were mustered at St George's Fields all day but people simply waited. About midnight, after the departure of the militia, a crowd gathered. One report had it that 1,200 'prentices and others' (probably an over-estimate) had knocked at the gate and 'said that they must needs speak with his Grace, of whom they would ask (as they termed it) but one civil question; and it was who was the cause of breaking up the parliament?' Laud had been forewarned and was not in Lambeth Palace when the crowd got there. They stayed for two and a half hours, until they were convinced that he was not inside, but left saying 'they would be shortly there again, and would not leave until they had spoken with him either by hook or by crook, sooner or later'.[41] In fact, he did not return to his palace until 27 May.[42] Their anger was instead expressed in damage to the garden and orchard. On the following Thursday crowds gathered again, and broke into the White Lion prison to release men awaiting trial for their part in these events.[43]

Despite hostile contemporary comment, these were not the actions of a mindless mob. It was an organized, targeted protest which had a clear (if not necessarily sophisticated) political agenda.[44] In the following days, anxious authorities responded edgily to reports of a gathering of

The attack on Lambeth Palace, May 1640

thousands of armed men on Blackheath. In fact it was local people being summoned to work on the roads by the beat of a drum. But this was symptomatic of an atmosphere in which rumours circulated freely, threatening more drastic action. Armed watches were set in the city and the suburbs, and guards placed outside St James's Palace and Whitehall. The militia was augmented by men drawn from the surrounding counties and a Provost Marshal with a company of horse and foot was appointed to keep order on the South Bank. St James's was home to actual Catholics, possibly agents of international Catholicism. It was the residence of the French Queen Mother, Marie de Medici, who had arrived in mid-October 1638. Another Catholic chapel had been opened there, served by a Jesuit confessor, and she was a strong presence at the court. The rioters reportedly said that the guard there was for the 'defence of the French'. The Queen Mother ignored advice to move out, fearing that if she left she would never come back.[45]

It may have been the threat to his family, or memories of anti-Buckingham disturbances in the late 1620s, that prompted Charles to particularly stern measures. A royal proclamation declared these events to be rebellious and called for the apprehension of three ringleaders. Two of the rioters were brought to trial in Southwark on 21 May at a special session of Oyer and Terminer (a court empanelled by a specific writ to investigate particular crimes). A man called Archer, who had beaten a drum to summon the crowd, was put on the rack to discover whether he had been put up to it. This was the last use of judicial torture in English history, and the warrant for it is in Charles's hand throughout. The eventual victim was Thomas Bensted, probably a mariner but described in some sources as a tailor from Lambeth or a cobbler. Bensted had been the only casualty of the initial riot, when he sustained relatively minor injuries. Having been injured, however, he said, 'come follow me, seeing I am hurt I will be your captain'. It was enough to get him a death sentence. He was kept in Newgate prison prior to his execution in the early hours of the morning in Southwark. He met his end on gallows constructed overnight under guard of the militia. His head was displayed on London Bridge and the rest of his body, cut into quarters, at four of the city gates.[46]

Parliaments coincided with meetings of the clergy of the diocese of Canterbury in Convocation to discuss ecclesiastical matters and to provide clerical taxation. Convocation's important decisions were ratified in Parliament: those who believed that the Royal Supremacy in the church resided in Parliament (by no means all of them Calvinists) were very hostile to the view that a Convocation could issue canons on its own authority. Customarily, Convocation dissolved with Parliament, but on this occasion it continued to sit and, moreover, produced controversial new canons. This was highly unusual, and was clearly Charles's personal decision – the Council minute expressing support was intended as a statement about whose idea this was. Charles claimed that the new canons would reassure opinion about the future of the faith, a prominent concern in the just-dissolved parliament, but it is more likely that he hoped by these means to flush out those of his subjects who were supporting the Covenanters. The canons therefore represented a characteristically forthright statement of royal intent – they defended the Laudian policies from the charge of innovation. The chief controversy arose from the disastrous 'etc oath', however. Clergy were required to swear never to alter the government of the church by 'archbishops, bishops, deacons, and archdeacons etc'. This kind of open-ended commitment was unacceptable to many people in a culture in which swearing was taken extremely seriously. The clause was probably the result of sloppy rather than deceitful drafting, but it provoked fears that something terrible might be intended.[47]

Charles had lost patience with his parliament and dissolved it: his needs unsupplied, the grievances of the country unaddressed. The response revealed a powerful strain of anti-popery, associated with hostility to Laud and an attachment to parliaments. A failed parliament did not provide the best basis for renewed war in defence of Laudian ceremonial: indeed, it was worse than no parliament at all.[48]

Unsurprisingly Charles's military preparations for the 1640 campaign were once again problematic. The intention, as in 1639, had not been to depend on English resources alone. Once again, however, the strategy disintegrated and Charles depended entirely on a response in England that was measured, to put the best gloss on it. When Wentworth had returned from Ireland the previous September he had urged Charles to form a committee for Scottish affairs. It was at a meeting of that body in the aftermath of the dissolution that he suggested to Charles: 'you have an army in Ireland that you may employ here to reduce this kingdom'. From the context there is no doubt that he meant that the 8,000 men in Ireland could be used in Scotland, but the accusation that he meant to use an Irish army to enforce the royal will in England was later to be a crucial charge against him.[49] In the event the Irish army did not materialize, and neither did the foreign mercenaries or money which Wentworth, now the Earl of Strafford, had advised Charles to seek.[50]

Political will was failing, both in the Privy Council and out in the provinces, and in this tense political situation rumour and news assumed a crucial importance. The Lord General and commander of Charles's army, the Earl of Northumberland, was dismayed by the attempt to pursue the war without parliamentary supply, not least because of the public knowledge of this financial weakness: 'What will the world judge of us abroad, to see us enter into such an action as this, not knowing how to maintain it for one month'. The Earl of Northumberland confessed that 'It grieves my soul to be involved in these counsels',[51] but if the newsletter writer John Castle is to be believed he was soon to be in an even more uncomfortable position. In May, Castle wrote to Bridgewater that at a Privy Council meeting the King had complained of 'the liberty the people took to discourse of his action intended for the North, as if he had not means to make a war, but was calling back his troops'. He bade his councillors to 'publish the contrary'.[52]

This was one battle that the King was certain to lose: there was a lively and unstoppable appetite for news and rumour. The speeches by Pym and Rous on 17 April had been delivered from scripts, which may have reflected an intention to circulate them outside the walls of the chamber. It was a practice that was frowned upon, but became increasingly common. Certainly these two speeches circulated widely and Pym's speech of 17 April was circulated in manuscript by Edward Rossingham, the newsletter writer, as an account of the grievances of Parliament.[53]

In fact, the buzz of rumour and news made life difficult for a newsletter writer. Castle was always eager to name and weigh his sources when reporting to Bridgewater: 'This relation, because it comes from Mr Kellaway, one that waits very near him [Charles], I have thought fit to advertise your lordship of it, as a matter that is likely to be true'; 'I was told by an inward confident of his [Secretary Coke]'; 'This morning, meeting with a friend of mine who dined yesterday with my Lord Keeper, I was confidently assured by him, that he had heard the news there'. Similarly, he distinguished between the varieties of news, rumour and gossip that he heard: 'On Tuesday last there went a rumour very current both here and at court'; 'here hath been a rumour somewhat constantly maintained for these 5 or 6 days'; 'there come every day such contradictory reports from out of the north, that I know not how to advertise any thing that may deserve to be believed'. This left even a prominent nobleman oversupplied with information, in want of certainty while away from the centre of events: 'I confess the various reports of the news of this time be such that no great credit be to be given to the rumours spread abroad, yet I shall be willing (at this distance) to hear of the several occurrences as they be divulged, or talked of; some use I may make thereof though I do not purpose to make them all to be part of my creed'.[54]

As the summer progressed there were further disorders in London, which seem to have been fuelled by religious fears arising from Charles's use of Convocation.[55] The capital was intimately connected to the provinces by networks of trade, kinship and power; news and rumour travelled alongside these things. In Shelley, Essex, a villager regaled his neighbour with an account of the attack on Lambeth Palace and claimed that the soldiers of the militia, far from suppressing the rioters, would instead 'fall upon' those that were on the side of the bishops. He also predicted imminent risings against Laud's favourites and supporters of the Bishops on the grounds that 'there was not laws now'.[56]

Further out, on the evening of 25 July at about 5 p.m., William Hawley overtook Thomas Webb, a clothier from Devizes, on the road just outside Wantage. Friendly greetings and discussion of wool prices were interlaced with more painful topics. Webb had asked if there had been soldiers on the move in the area, this being the period of the build-up to the second Bishops' War, and this may have prompted Hawley into some unguarded political comment. Hauled before a local magistrate the next day, he had to answer to charges that he had said the apprentices had risen against Laud and that it would be a pitiful time, that Laud was the cause of the raising of the armies and that the King was 'ruled' by him. He had also attributed the riots to rumours that Laud had turned papist and indeed that it was well known that he was in fact a papist. Much of this was denied, of course, but so seriously was this taken that a report of the examination ended up on the desk of the Secretary of State, Francis Windebank.[57]

Mobilization in England in 1640 was even more reluctant than in the previous year. In many parts of the country the collection of ship money, which had slowed down in advance of the parliament, now seems to have collapsed entirely. This was selective inaction – it seems clear that other aspects of local government continued to operate.[58] Financial difficulties led to disastrous expedients – the seizure of Spanish bullion in the Tower, the threat to issue brass money and the seizure of pepper belonging to London merchants for sale at about 30 per cent below its market value. These manoeuvres cost the crown friends abroad and in the City, although the brass money plan was so obviously bad for the economy that it may have been a threat to the City, intended to encourage the provision of a loan which would prevent the need for this drastic measure.[59]

Given the crown's dependence on officeholders, the lack of consensus made mobilization very difficult, and morale was low. John Castle's letters from court are filled with bad news – the reluctance of the City to lend money, and the attempts to bully it, the supply of 'stinking' victuals, the impossibility of setting an expedition out to sea, all combine with a sense of foreboding. The difficulties of raising troops were at least as bad as in the previous year because the Trained Bands were if anything more reluctant to serve and the substitution clause was more widely invoked.[60] Shortly after the end of the parliament it was rumoured that 'the people' in Norfolk 'like the sea will surely rise upon the first wind that blows upon them'. The same 'ill news' came from the west, where the clothiers had been laying off workers because they could not sell the cloth. 'The ball of wildfire that is kindled here above will fly and burn (it is feared) a great way off, where there will not be so good means to quench it as here under the King's window where his person strikes more terror than the Trained Band with their arms'. Sir Jacob Astley was assembling a force of some 6,000 at Blackheath from among the Trained Bands of Kent, Surrey, Essex and Middlesex. Ostensibly for service against the Covenanters, it was said that this force was secretly intended to be available 'as the occasion may arise to suppress any insurrection'.[61]

This climate proved unfavourable to raising troops. In late June there were reports of men refusing to serve in Norfolk and the Lord Chamberlain went to Wiltshire in person to quell disturbances there. Troops imprisoned for refusing to pay coat and conduct money had been freed from gaol by some of their colleagues and it was said that the men raised there would not march unless the King came in person. Similar stirs were reported in Huntingdon, Warwickshire and Cambridge.[62] Men raised in Essex were reported to have slain some of their officers and beaten a deputy lieutenant, those in Norfolk to be refusing to embark and those in Cambridge to have beaten their officers at Newmarket.[63] The Earl of Northumberland was sure that the army would be under-strength given what he knew of the restiveness in London, Kent, Surrey, Essex, Hertfordshire, Buckinghamshire and Bedfordshire while in Lincolnshire the deputy lieutenants threatened to resign their positions in the face of the rebelliousness of the pressed men.[64]

Some of this was motivated by resentments over pay and conditions,[65] but it seems that much of this restiveness was related to religious feelings. Francis Windebank, son of the Secretary of State and a man of fairly Romish sensibilities, was responsible for raising men in Devon. On first meeting his men he was told that 'if they found we were papists they would soon despatch us'. In order to counteract this threat, on the first day's march 'I desired them all to kneel down and sing psalms, and made one of my officers to read prayers, which pleased them not a little'. He had also plied them with drink and tobacco, with the result that 'they all now swear they will never leave me so long as they live, and, indeed, I have not had one man run from me yet in this nine days' march'. Other captains of similar bands were in fear of their men, who were very threatening. Behind all this lay 'the Puritan rascals of this country [who have] strongly possessed the soldiers that all the commanders of our regiment were papists'. Credulous popular anti-popery may well have lain behind many of the discipline problems, fuelled by rumours about the papistical purposes and leadership of the army. This anti-popery was centrally concerned with ritual forms: 'I was forced for two or three days to sing psalms all the day I marched, for all their religion lies in a psalm'. Soldiers in Warminster (Wilts.) insisted that their commanders take communion with them before setting out.[66] In Daventry (Northants.) troopers said that they would not fight against the gospel and would not be commanded by papists.[67]

We know for certain that two officers were murdered on the grounds that they were papists: William Mohun suffered a terrible beating and eventual death in Farringdon at the hands of soldiers raised in Dorset; and Compton Evers was killed three weeks later by men raised in Devon. An illustration of the spread of rumour, but also of its potential unreliability, is Castle's report on the death of Mohun, to whom he gave the rank of captain rather than lieutenant. He said that Mohun had been hanged; in fact he was forced out of the window of his lodgings, from where he fell to the ground. He was severely beaten, dragged by his hair through the town and left in a ditch for dead. Regaining consciousness he made it to a nearby house, where medical care was interrupted by the arrival of soldiers. Cornered, he pulled a knife, which was dashed from his hands with a cudgel. His brains were then knocked out, the job completed this time, and the corpse was placed in the pillory.[68]

Some of the soldiers heading north engaged in informed acts of iconoclasm. On 15 August soldiers calling themselves 'London Prentices' arrived in Marsworth, Buckinghamshire, on their way to Aylesbury and indulged in some unofficial reformation. They demanded the key to the church from the parish clerk and 'broke down the rails at the upper end of the Chancel where formerly the Communion Table stood, and beat down all the painted glass in the windows'. They then went to the minister's house, in search of the service book and surplice, telling him 'that if he did not deliver them to them, they would pull down his house over his head'. Told that the minister did not have them they went back to the church, and 'finding them there, first tore the two Service books all to pieces, scattering some of the leaves about the streets, and carrying the rest away upon the points of their swords'. Afterwards 'one of them

The Souldiers in their passage to York turn unto reformers pull down Popish pictures, break down rayles, turn altars into Tables.

English soldiers purging churches on their way north in 1640

took the Surplice and put it on him, as the Minister useth to do, and so marched away to Aylesbury triumphing in contempt and derision'.[69]

Their targets were clearly not indiscriminate, and they were not unique to these men: reports of similar attacks on altar rails, communion tables, stained glass and vestments recur in other parts of the country. These items were often ritually degraded, not simply destroyed. Some of these acts aped official ritual practice – like poor Mohun, objects taken from churches were displayed in pillories, for example. Others were tried in 'court' or burned. Church services were disrupted too, but at critical moments – such as immediately after the sermon. This may suggest a tenderness about disrupting the preaching of the Word among those intent on attacking idolatry. These acts were informed by a popular anti-popery, in which the dangers of corruption were attached to specific aspects of the physical environment, and particular moments in religious ritual: they were not apolitical or irreligious, since they shared the vocabulary of state and church. The dates of these acts seem also to have had some ritual significance – incidents were reported on 5 November, Plough Monday and Candalmas, all of them important dates in the ritual calendar. The humour of the participants (their 'triumphing in contempt and derision') again suggests a political intent rather than an inchoate violence. Rough music parodied the sacred music of Laudian ritual and the mock courts and trials of offenders were clearly occasions of raucous humour. Iconoclasts relished their temporary power.[70] Elsewhere soldiers did 'justice' on secular issues – in helping to break down enclosures, breaking open prisons to release debtors and deserters or smashing windows and tools in a House of Correction in Wakefield (an institution in which the able-bodied but unemployed poor were incarcerated and set to work).[71] These were overturning times, when poor men could do justice on their oppressors – enclosers, creditors and Poor Law officers – and purify churches.

To say that soldiers were doing this is in some degree misleading for, of course, prior to their muster these were not soldiers at all, but simply men of low status. Evidence is difficult to come by, but there is enough to suggest that these attacks by soldiers sometimes enjoyed the support of the local godly, and might be related to previous disputes and local preferences. In Radwinter, Essex, for example, Richard Drake had been in conflict with a section of his congregation since his arrival in 1638. He favoured relatively high ceremonial, and that had led to a running battle with the local godly. He had raised the chancel, railed the altar and refused to church women (that is, ritually receive them back into the congregation after childbirth) unless they came up to the rails. Similarly, he would not administer communion at Easter and Christmas to those who did not come up to the rails. One hundred of his parishioners had been excluded from communion at Easter 1640, and this had led to a direct confrontation with the godly. The godly had their moment later in the summer, however, when fifty men who had assembled at Saffron Walden passed through the village on their way to war. On a fast day in early July they pulled down the altar rails and some images erected by Drake. The images were tied to a tree and scourged, before being taken back to Saffron Walden, where they were used as fuel to roast the soldiers' meat. En route they were taunted: 'if ye be Gods deliver yourselves'.[72] Clearly, in this case as presumably in many others, it makes little sense to separate the violence of the soldiers from a broader culture of anti-popery, and from a local history of conflict over ceremonial forms.

Certainly Essex was alive with this popular anti-popery. On 26 May, Colchester had erupted in panic when two young girls reported having seen two men, both strangers, acting suspiciously the previous night. According to one of the girls, who had been playing in the street, one of the men had been pushing rags through the window of a house into which he was peering. The mayor, informed of this, put the town in a state of defence, on suspicion that the men were trying to fire it. Seventeenth-century towns were built largely of flammable materials and full of open fires: fire was a constant threat and, in an age before insurance, a total disaster. Reports of attempts to fire a town touched on real sensitivities. The following morning, the danger became widely associated with another great fear of Stuart England – plotting Catholics. It was rumoured that a large number of papists had gathered at Berechurch (the house of a prominent recusant, Lady Audley), planning to bring the Queen Mother, William Laud and the Bishop of Ely there. The details were disputed – which bishop and whether it was to Berechurch or Monkwick. The following afternoon a drum was beaten through the town summoning apprentices to go to Berechurch and Monkwick 'to see what company was there'.[73] In a locality where men would try to beat a drum to the house of local recusants on information as flimsy as this, it is easy to understand why following the drum to the Scottish borders was regarded with a critical eye.

To the extent that Charles's problems arose from an attempt to connect and harmonize practices in his three churches we can presume that this opposition to Laudianism, popery and the influence of French papists was also, potentially, connected. This all impinged on the royal family: in late September the Queen Mother's carriage was pelted with carrots by women while passing through Kingston, Surrey. Abuse was also thrown, and one 'rude fellow' struck one of her guards.[74] Among the soldiers heading north, it seems, were armed men likely to sympathize with their enemy rather than their king. Not only were these soldiers not hurrying to fight the Covenanters, they were taking the opportunity to make their own protests against royal ecclesiastical policy.

The point is not that Charles was facing two armies, of course, since a large English force was successfully mustered near the border. At the Green Dragon, in Bishopsgate Street in London, two clothiers from Dedham, in the same godly corner of Essex, fell into conversation with two officers about to go to fight the Covenanters. When they revealed their hostility to the enterprise the officers called them Puritans, to which they responded, in the style of Francis Rous, by asking what a Puritan was. This so enraged one of the officers that he threw his meal at the clothier and hit him on the head with the flat of his sword. Other soldiers had to be restrained from attacking Lord Loudon on no other grounds than that he was Scottish. This is evidence of division in an integrated and informed political society, rather than fickleness among 'soldiers'.[75] Charles's English army was not opposed to him, but the evidence suggests that the English mobilization was hesitant and compromised, and that this reflected a wider polarization of English opinion.

As military preparations in England faltered, the Covenanters, untroubled by such divisions, seemed to be in the superior position. At the English court the preference seemed to be to postpone war for a year, or to limit it to a defensive war. But the Covenanters forced the issue, perhaps in the knowledge that this was their moment.[76] The Scottish parliament reassembled, ignoring Charles's desire for a further prorogation, and carried through further dramatic constitutional changes. In England two years later, when Parliament seemed to be moving in a similar direction, it generated a strong royalist party; but not in Scotland in 1640, although there was some division. The Earl of Argyll had emerged as a dominant figure, and there was some suspicion about his motives and plans, but the Covenanters faced little organized opposition. A General Assembly called in Aberdeen, territory friendly to the King's cause, was actually free of external pressure to moderate its policies – even there the Covenanters' military and political position was unchallenged.[77]

Nonetheless, the Covenanters invaded England with some reluctance. They had been unsure of their reception and had maintained correspondence with the English peers. The question of whether to invade was also divisive in Scotland, and seems to have precipitated the first sign of serious division in Covenanter ranks. The Earl of Montrose had organized the Cumbernauld band, which claimed that the purposes of the Covenant were being subverted by a minority, and promised to pursue the original aims by another means. This was perhaps the first sign of his move towards support of the King, and was certainly evidence of a growing suspicion of Argyll. In the end, the Covenanters probably invaded because of the difficulty of maintaining an army off the land north of the border.[78]

As in the first war, we cannot be certain how disabling English foot-dragging was, because at Newburn, the only significant engagement of the war, the crucial problem for the English was not the quality of their men or arms, but that they chose the wrong ground. The Covenanting army may not have been easy to sustain for a long period, so the outcome of a single battle exaggerates the relative importance of the problems on the English side.[79] Against this, however, it is a poor army, or one with very limited political capital behind it, that collapses in the face of relatively small casualties. Exact figures are lacking, but it is unlikely that either side lost more than several hundred men: significant for a day, but hardly the destruction of an army said to have numbered 25,000 overall. In the end, the dismal military performance reflected a lack of political will, a product of divisions felt at all levels of English society from the peerage to the beggar turned away by Alexander Powell.

On the same day that the two armies clashed at Newburn, twelve peers petitioned the King to call a parliament and from that point there is clear evidence of co-ordination between the Covenanters and those anxious to secure the meeting of another English parliament – Nathaniel Fiennes, son of Saye and Sele, was certainly in correspondence designed to secure a treaty and a parliament. Charles bowed to this pressure, summoning a Great Council at York on 24 September. He opened proceedings by announcing his intention to call another parliament, although he took some persuasion that defeat at Newburn necessitated recognition of the Covenanters' political victory.[80]

These twelve peers were the most confident of a wider circle of aristocrats opposed to the policies of the Personal Rule: the Earls of Essex, Hertford, Bedford, Warwick, Exeter and Rutland and Lords Saye and Sele, Brooke, Mandeville, Howard of Escrick, Mulgrave and Bolingbroke. The Earl of Manchester, a future parliamentarian general, also urged the calling of a parliament. The Earl of Northumberland, another prominent parliamentarian during the civil war, had been in charge of the war effort against the Covenanters. The political role of the aristocracy is a neglected theme in civil war studies, but it has been plausibly suggested that a group of radical peers had ridden this crisis intent on engineering exactly this outcome – an opportunity actually to reduce the King to the position of a Doge of Venice.[81] It is certainly clear that Charles's policies divided the ruling class, and debates resonated outside it. There were imitators of the twelve peers' petition in York and Hereford, although those petitions were not delivered for fear that they would prove fractious, and in London, where the inhibitions were fewer.[82]

Once a parliament had been called the City of London advanced £200,000. Delegates from the Great Council, those most sympathetic to settlement with the Covenanters, were sent to negotiate the Treaty of Ripon. Under its terms the Covenanters were to stay in the six northern counties of England and to be paid £850 per day. A full settlement was to await, and be ratified in, an English parliament. In effect, what had been agreed was a ceasefire, pending a treaty in London, and the terms of the ceasefire clearly suited the Covenanters and their English friends – the costs of the army were placed on the English taxpayer, which gave a guarantee that the next parliament could not be a short one. Ripon not only ended the attempt to crush the Covenant, therefore, but also cemented the connection between the fate of reformation in Scotland and the redress of grievances in England. For those in England who were primarily interested in religious grievances, Ripon also established the connection between the position of the English parliament and the future of reformed religion. Influential men, like Pym, took full advantage of this association between the defence of Parliament's constitutional position and the promotion of reformation.[83]

During this crisis the Earl of Lindsey had been presented with a severed toe by a woman from Boston, Lincolnshire. The toe had previously belonged to her husband but he had cut it off so that he would not have to fight. It is difficult to be sure that this was an ideological statement.[84] There was nothing particularly new about English military failure or lack of political support: even during the Armada year there were signs of reluctance to support the war effort.[85] But the Bishops' Wars proved particularly damaging to Charles's English regime. Prerogative rule, particularly the use of prerogative powers to secure military resources, had caused significant resentments during the 1630s. Using those same powers to cow the godly Scots was little more popular, and by the late summer of 1640 it had failed.

It was John Knox, father of the Scottish Reformation, who had asked Heinrich Bullinger in 1554 'Whether obedience is to be rendered to a magistrate who enforces idolatry and condemns true religion'. Bullinger had flannelled in response and not surprisingly, for this was the most loaded political question in Reformation Europe.[86] It was close to being posed by some of Charles's Scottish subjects in 1640. Generally recognized obligations to obey both God and the King were coming into conflict in the Prayer Book crisis, as obedience to the King's commands seemed to offend against godliness.

Alexander Henderson, leading light in the Covenanting movement, dealt with these questions in his tract 'Instructions for Defensive Arms', which is a little puzzling to modern readers in its silences and hesitations. The key question was not whether to honour the King, or to render unto Caesar what was Caesar's, but 'whether honour should be given to evil and wicked superiors in an evil thing?' In the normal course of events evil and wicked superiors should be honoured, since they might have been sent as a punishment, but not, Henderson argued, when they commanded evil things. In that case, he said, they could be resisted, even by private citizens, although it would be better if this was done by inferior magistrates. A chief magistrate commanding evil things had stepped out of the line of divine hierarchy so that his inferior was acting in direct response to God.[87]

All this is blunt, and bracing. But Henderson was less clear on the more fundamental question: who was to judge when the chief magistrate was out of line? This was really the nub, and a king who accepted the argument about an errant chief magistrate was unlikely to accept that a self-appointed group like the Covenanters should be judges of when it had happened. At least the Covenanters had produced authoritative texts against which the judgement could be made – the Negative Confession of 1581 and subsequent declarations. England, as events over the next two years showed, lacked such texts. Although it seems to avoid the most pressing question – who should be the judge – this tract was persuasive enough to be reprinted in 1642 for the guidance of English readers facing a similar dilemma. The dangers inherent in opening up these lines of argument, and the reasons for imposing limits on the right to resist, were exemplified, however, by the words of Roger Moore, in Middleton (Westmorland) in 1640: he was accused of saying that if the king commanded him to turn papist, or do anything against his conscience, then he would rise up against him and kill him.[88] An unlimited licence to follow conscience rather than to obey the powers that be might quickly lead to chaos if individuals could claim the right to kill a king.

In the Short Parliament, of course, these questions had not been asked, and the debates were in the main revisiting the grievances of the 1620s.[89] But as we have seen, on the streets of London and among the troops going north there were signs that a new and more radical kind of politics was emerging: not just anti-Laudian but in favour of pushing the Reformation further, perhaps openly anti-episcopal. At some point in the summer of 1640 an underground press kicked into life in London, publishing Covenanter texts almost simultaneously with the presses in Edinburgh.[90] This could even have been construed as treasonous after the royal proclamation of August 1640 that all those who 'shall not with all their might oppose and fight against' the Covenanters would be deemed rebels and traitors. But there was worse. The same press published two tracts arguing that the Church of England was anti-Christian – so corrupt that true believers should withdraw. Instead Christians should separate themselves completely from the established church, forming independent congregations, gathered voluntarily. These arguments had a hinterland in discussions within radical Protestant circles during the 1630s, but now they were breaking cover and they were to be of profound significance to the politics of the 1640s. Even more disturbingly, Samuel How's pamphlet, *The Sufficiencie of the Spirits Teaching*, argued that human learning about the scriptures might not be merely wrong but positively dangerous. This cut the ground from under the entire ministry, not just bishops, justifying lay preaching and even suggesting that the minds of the poor and unlearned, whose thinking was unadulterated by human learning, were more receptive to the teaching of the Spirit. These too were radical claims, again with an established heritage in Reformation thought, that were to be of profound significance to the politics of the following decade.

Perhaps the most inflammatory of the pamphlets produced from this press was *Englands Complaint to Jesus Christ Against the Bishops canons*. This argued that there was a popish plot which had infected government right up to the King himself, who was personally implicated because he had fallen for the Devil's snares. To allow such a faction to flourish threatened the people's laws and liberties, and the good of their souls. This, it was claimed, breached a covenant between the King and the people in existence since the Norman conquest. An argument in this form hinted, to put it no more strongly, at a positive right to resist. These were by no means standard, or normal, responses to the Covenanter crisis, and in arguing for congregational separatism, they were in fact going far further than the Covenanters. It may have been that this press started up having been brought back from Amsterdam, a centre of clandestine and radical publication in Reformation Europe.[91]

London crowds mobilized in response to libels, pasquils and papers may also have been consuming the output of underground presses.[92]

Nehemiah Wallington, a London wood turner and avid reader of the press, was often among the crowds in London in these years. He was an unusually pious man, who paid painstaking attention to his own spiritual well-being and the health of the community in which he lived. He has left hundreds of pages of notes on his own affairs, and on public issues, all seeking to come closer to an understanding of God's purposes in the world. Among his notes on the canons of 1640 is a paper outlining orthodox resistance theory and relating it directly to the situation of the Covenanters.

It was in the form of an answer to the concern that for subjects to bear arms against their king 'upon any pretence whatsoever' was to resist 'the powers ordained of God'. It was acknowledged that private individuals could not resist. However, if the King maintained a faction which oppressed the whole kingdom and the 'people in their law and liberties and most of all in the true religion', ruling not by law, but seeking to 'make all his subjects slaves by bringing their souls, bodies, estates under a miserable bondage'; and if the breach could not be healed, and there was no alternative, then it was acceptable for the whole people 'to stand up as one man to defend themselves and their country'. He noted that 'this point trencheth upon the Scots at this time', who were standing to the defence of their laws, liberties and religion:

> when a whole Nation thus universal and unanimously stands up in such a quarrel it cannot but be ascribed to the overruling and righteous hand that thereby thou might both defend the people's rights and preserve the State of the Kingdom to the King himself and his posterity, which otherwise by oppression and Tyranny would be brought to confusion . . .

The royal office was a sacred one, but numerous biblical sources justified the view that kings were bound by the law, covenants and conditions agreed between them and their people. Those that 'persuade Kings, that they are no way bound, but have liberty to rule as they list, by an independent prerogative these are they that are traitors both to God and to the King, and to the Realm and to the peace and prosperity thereof'.[93]

Whether informed directly from the presses or not, the politics of crowds in London and of some of the troops conscripted for service against the Covenanters indicate that English politics were entering some of the more dangerous waters in post-Reformation Europe. Tensions between religious and political duties such as those being experienced in Scotland and England were not unusual in Reformation Europe, and had tremendous radical potential. The classical heritage was rich in resources for those who would oppose tyranny, champion virtue or promote freedom. These may have been some of the books that encouraged Felton to think that 'it was lawful to kill an enemy to the republic', or that those who were not free to exercise their own judgement free of interference were in bondage or slavery: an argument that became prominent in 1642. England was not full of revolutionaries in 1640, but its cultural heritage – biblical and classical – furnished materials with which to think radically about political crises when they erupted. And it was true of the popular culture too. Scottish troops on the march through Flodden in 1640 were encouraged by an ancient prophecy of Merlin, circulating in both Latin and 'Scottish verse', which could be read as predicting success in their venture. Such prophecies were widely thought to be potential solvents of political order, lending a kind of supernatural authority to resistance, upheaval and changes of regime.[94]

It is tempting to dwell on this radicalism because of its implications for the future, and there was very obviously much more at stake in this public contestation than a failure to deal adequately with a 'Scottish invasion'. But English opinion was on the whole expressed in conventional terms, and seems to have been more divided and irresolute than it was revolutionary. John Castle, for example, drew a ready but not particularly helpful analogy between natural events and the political crisis. Strafford's crossing from Ireland in 1640 had been rough, and there were fears that the ship might be lost. The ride, and the fear it induced, brought on his gout and he finished his journey to London on a litter. His condition had ruled out the possibility of serving as Lord High Steward of Parliament. A month later, following the failure of the Short Parliament, Castle reached for the obvious analogy: 'God I trust will guide the rudder of this ship, and give you a healthful body to support the concussions and tossings of these stormy times'. Reporting assaults on their officers by troops in Essex, later in the summer, he concluded equally piously, 'God amend all, and defend this great ship from breaking upon these rocks'. In June he wrote:

there is at this time reigning here at Westminster a disease . . . wherein they that labour of it, complain of a stifling at heart and distemper in the head; and there is cause to fear that almost generally through the kingdom, the common people are sick of those parts; they labour of a suffocation of their hearts in the duty and obedience they owe to his Majesty's service and commands, and they are stricken in the head that they rave and utter they know not what against his Majesty's government and proceedings in the present action in hand.[95]

Looking for signs or portents in the natural world was commonplace. For example, English troops in the Borders had been intimidated by an eclipse on 22 May 1639, two days after a skirmish at Wark that marked the first action of the first Bishops' War. Troops summoned suddenly to Newcastle were overtaken by the eclipse, and feared for the worst. John Aston started his journey late in the afternoon, just at the time of eclipse. '[I]t was not superstition stayed me, though rumours being then uncertain, and our departure sudden, there wanted not those who construed this eclipse as an ominous presage of the bad success of the king's affairs'.[96] This habit of thought helped to make sense of an insecure natural and political world, but it was not a very effective guide to action.

The Covenanting movement drew on deep wells of support in Scotland and appealed to English opinion through declarations that circulated in manuscript and were printed by presses in Edinburgh and London. Mobilization in England was supported from the pulpits and demanded action from village officers. Political engagement, in other words, was invited at relatively low levels of society in both countries. In Scotland control was exerted by an oligarchic group, whose authority resided in the Presbyterian church and in the Tables. 'Oligarchic centralism' allowed for a degree of co-ordination and ideological control that under-pinned a dramatic political success and also set limits to the radicalism of the movement: the whole campaign, in fact, was framed by a document which reflected, and respected, informed Protestant opinion about the limits of legitimate resistance.[97] In England, over the next two years, similar tensions were not controlled, and armed conflict was not re-strained: as proponents of reformation pushed for more fundamental changes, and accompanying shifts in constitutional arrangements, others pulled back, wary of what this radicalism meant for political order. Greater hesitancy and a lack of clarity about the aims of the opposition to the crown paradoxically led to a much more bloody conflict and, eventually, much greater radicalism on both the royalist and parliamentary sides.

Armed petitioning was a well-established form of politics. Leslie's army, processing in the form of a funeral march for the Bible, had been led by ministers and the greybeards of Scottish society: the soldiers came last. But the soldiers were there, and if the King would not listen to the leaders of the community, then they would have to defend their corner by force of arms. The difficulty was that force, or the threat of it, might be a cure that was worse than the disease – indeed, one that was fatal to the patient. 'God grant this viperous brood so freely received into the body of the Kingdom, do not eat through the belly of their fosterers; for I assure you where they shall govern we shall find them proud lords', wrote one correspondent from Newcastle a little more than a week after its occupation by Leslie's army. A week of Scottish occupation had been an education for the author: 'For my part, I assure you had I known what I now find, I should have preferred by much to have suffered as a martyr for my religion, than to run the hazard of being a traitor to mine own country'. Manuscript copies seem to have circulated widely.[98] The costs of the Treaty of Ripon, and the realities of occupation, created a political opportunity for those anxious for change in England. But the Covenanters' occupation also, potentially, changed the balance of priorities for many English people between the maintenance of normal civil government and the defence of the true religion or redress of secular grievances. England's tragedy in the coming years was to be that so many continued to feel that they had to make this choice. When they did, the ideals and experience of active citizenship, and of informed Protestant faith, were available to guide them.

4

We Dream Now of a Golden Age

The Long Parliament and the Public Sphere

Failure in the Bishops' Wars forced Charles to call a parliament which he could not dissolve until the Covenanters were paid and a treaty ratified. From an English point of view this meant that there was now ample opportunity to air eleven years' worth of grievances. When Parliament met in November 1640, therefore, there was plenty to talk about, but that talking was structured by a number of concerns which were already becoming clear. Aside from, or behind, the immediate problems of undoing the religious innovations and abuses of the prerogative during the 1630s there lay an influential body of opinion in favour of further reformation. There were potential tensions in this coalition, however. Over the previous summer pressure for reformation had seemed to threaten political and social decency: a willingness to collude with the Covenanters was by no means the same thing as a desire to import their reformation, or an even more radical one; still less did it imply approval of unofficial iconoclasm. The previous summer had seen politics in the hands, to some extent, of Scottish soldiers inspired by Merlin and led by ministers and English soldiers eager to make a statement of their own about the future of the church. The potential for political debate to spill out of the usual channels was becoming plain: this was true out in the counties but it is revealed most clearly in London, which now replaced Edinburgh as the theatre of events.

Looking at Wenceslaus Hollar's 1647 engraving, drawn from an imaginary spot high above Bankside, we see the two sides of the heart of the English kingdom. On the right, below the only bridge, ships are massed on the river, carrying goods into and out of the greatest port in the country. London's trade was increasingly reaching not only into the Baltic and Mediterranean, but also across the Atlantic and even into

London in 1647

the Indian Ocean. London was also an important manufacturing centre, with more diverse trades and industries than any other city in England. With a population of 400,000 it dwarfed its nearest provincial rivals, which mustered only 20,000 inhabitants, and it was second only to Paris in the whole of Europe. It dominated the economy more completely than the capital cities of other major kingdoms and its position was more akin to that of a city republic like Amsterdam or Venice, but with a larger hinterland. On the left, centred on the great medieval buildings of Westminster, is the seat of government, a magnet for petitioners, lobbyists and those with political ambition, as well as increasingly large numbers of litigants. This was the most litigious age in English history, with great tides of suits washing over the courts each year. The market for manufactures, the level of litigation and the expansion of overseas trade reflected increasing domestic wealth. The beneficiaries of increasing population growth were spending on exotic luxury items, manufactures and the pursuit of grudges. London benefited from all three.[1]

This drove a massive expansion of population despite the fact that London was a death trap: year after year the death rate far exceeded the birth rate. A flood of immigration replaced not just the annual loss of population but fed spectacular growth. By 1650 London contained about 8 per cent of the total population of England and Wales. A substantial part of that migration was motivated by a desire for betterment, of course, but an even larger part was probably motivated by hardship. In arable communities farms were getting bigger as those able to profit from rising prices and falling wages bought out their smaller neighbours. These large farms generated profits which helped to create the market for London's trades and services and therefore fed the city's growth. These changes also led to improvements in agricultural effici-

ency, helping to create the food surpluses necessary to support London and other large towns. But they also tended to employ less labour than a larger number of small farms and therefore created conditions which forced young people off the land. One of the places where it was possible to secure a living without land was obviously a town; and the pull of London·for that kind of migration was mighty indeed.[2]

London was a densely governed as well as a densely populated city. Within the ancient bounds of the City power lay with the Corporation: the Lord Mayor, Court of Aldermen and Common Council. Below them lay the wards, which took on a wide range of administrative tasks. According to one estimate, one in ten adult males in London held office. Alongside these civic offices stood the Companies, which took on a variety of social and welfare roles, integrating a broad swathe of London's population into a complex associational life. Finally, the City contained a large number of parishes and numerous lectureships. There was not a free market in religious belief, but, on the other hand, an interested worshipper would not have to try very hard to find alternative visions of proper Christian worship. One element of this relatively diverse religious life was a 'puritan underground'.[3]

Beyond the lines of the medieval City walls and the boundaries of Westminster, densely settled inner-city parishes gave way to more sprawling suburbs. Unlike the modern city, however, the suburbs were not havens of semi-rural retreat, but sprawling settlements of new arrivals, often of low status. Here the structures of authority were less well-established. South of the river too, in Southwark and Bankside, the growth of population placed strain on political and religious institutions which had evolved in very different conditions. These places were associated, often without good reason, with a lack of order.[4]

This sprawling metropolis was the centre of a demonstrative, theatrical street politics. London crowds had been prominent in politics throughout the sixteenth century and during the 1620s. Particular dates such as Shrove Tuesday, and particular forms of demonstration such as attacks on brothels, formed a recognizable repertoire of protest, which could be used to express political views. Bonfires and street celebrations marked an official Protestant calendar, celebrating the accession of Elizabeth or deliverance from the Armada, but these same celebrations of Protestant triumph might be the means to express more limited victories. Charles I's ignominious return from Madrid in 1624, for example, a defeat for diplomacy aimed at securing him a Spanish bride, was enthusiastically celebrated in London's streets as another delivery from popish threat.[5]

Talk on the streets, and in the shops and markets, was crucial in unleashing this political energy. Richard Beaumont, an apprentice apothecary, while visiting one of his master's patients in May 1640, had heard from members of the militia about the assaults on White Lion prison and other prisons in Southwark to release those arrested for attacking Lambeth Palace. In conversation with his master's sister-in-law, who lived by the Old Exchange, he heard forecasts of further intended outrages which were confirmed and augmented in conversation with other apprentices. They in turn circulated the street talk. Back in his master's shop he passed on the highlights of these conversations to a waterbearer, telling him that apprentices planned attacks on popish royal chapels and the Earl of Arundel's house, and passing on the rumours about Laud's conversion.[6] London's streets, it seems, were alive with engaged political comment, and ambitious plans for action. An attack on a bawdy house off Golden Lane also seems to have had some connections with these protests against Laud and Laudianism: two of the main actors, when asked about the recent proclamation against disorders in the City, were said to have replied: 'tumultuous persons God bless them God prosper them, let them go on'.[7] As the disorders in May had demonstrated, action or talk on London's streets could accelerate, or rarefy, political issues, raising the stakes in public controversies. Behind these events lay a political energy that could only be restrained by the authorities with some difficulty.

The potential for more direct political interventions by this mobilized citizenry was clearly demonstrated in September, after the defeat at

Newburn, when a petition with 10,000 signatures was presented to the King. Like that of the twelve peers, who had petitioned the King on the same day as the battle of Newburn, the petition called for a parliament. Unlike the peers, however, the petitioners were citizens 'of every condition' and they added a list of specific grievances in need of remedy, including ship money, impositions, monopolies, innovations in religion and complaints about the sudden dissolution of parliaments. It also contained explicit statements of hostility to the campaigns against the Covenanters. Signatures had been systematically gathered in the City's wards and at one such venue 300 people queued to read and subscribe the petition, twenty or thirty at a time. Although four aldermen signed the petition, it was not organized or condoned by the Corporation. Indeed, while it was being mobilized, from August onwards, the Privy Council repeatedly urged the Corporation to stop it, but they could not. The Lord Mayor was reported to have refused to present it and on 22 September the Court of Aldermen officially disowned it. It was presented instead by four citizens, including two prominent radical merchants, Maurice Thomson and Richard Shute. Like Captain John Venn, another of those who presented the petition, these men were to be prominent in radical politics in London in the following years.[8]

It had been clear in May that the atmosphere in the teeming streets of the City and its sprawling suburbs could be febrile – rumour and argument swirled around the streets and the pressure of the vulgar was felt by those in authority. Mobilization in the City ran beyond the control of the Corporation. The Covenanters, as we have seen, appealed downwards as well as upwards. News of Charles's domestic political woes was clearly in circulation in provincial England. Political debate was spilling out onto London's streets and into the provinces. This was not politics as it should be; negotiation in such an atmosphere was going to be difficult.

When Parliament met, much was at stake for Scotland, England and (in the eyes of many) for Europe at large. The anticipation that had attended the Short Parliament (when the Earl of Bridgewater had paid through the nose for his wife's place at a window) was reinforced. Sir Henry Slingsby, in Yorkshire, expected 'a happy parliament where the subject may have a total redress of all his grievances'; John Bampfield, in Somerset, wrote: 'For ever be this parliament renowned for so great achievements, for we dream now of nothing more than of a golden age'. In part this was a religious hope for redemption, very marked among the godly – Stanley Gower wrote to Sir Robert Harley: 'We cease not to pray for you and that great assembly . . . if the Lord turn away our captivity we shall be like them that dream'.[9] Exiles returned and foreigners arrived hoping that this was a moment for the perfection of reformation – the eyes of Christendom were now on the negotiations in London.[10] Perhaps the most significant fact about the new parliament was that it could not be dissolved – whereas in May no-one could have known that they were witnessing the summoning of the 'Short' parliament, it was more obvious in November that they were witnessing the meeting of a long one. The price of the money to pay for the Treaty of Ripon was to be the redress of grievances. And, after eleven years, a relatively unpopular ecclesiastical policy, an invasion from Scotland and the collapse of financial reforms based on the prerogative, there were a lot of potential grievances to hear.

Elections in the autumn of 1640 were, like those earlier in the year, unusually contentious and eighty-six elections were contested. Since many of these were two-member constituencies, it seems that one quarter of the Commons had gained their seats through a public contest. Inflation had reduced the real value of the property qualification in the counties – fixed at possession of a 40 shilling freehold, which was now a relatively small sum. As a result the electorate was expanding. In the boroughs it was increasingly common to challenge the right of the Corporation to select members on behalf of the inhabitants. Such disputes were referred to the Commons Committee for Privileges, which frequently ruled in favour of wider franchises. As a result of these developments perhaps one in three adult males had the right to vote in 1640, and in many cases they had a choice of candidates too. Although in many elections only two candidates were presented for the two seats, reflecting an aversion to public contests and a preference for 'selection' over 'election', even where no effective choice was offered to electors there were still opportunities for the middling sort to apply independent pressure. In eighteen counties, and a number of significant boroughs, petitions were drawn up in the name of the candidates, and presented to them for delivery to Parliament. In some cases they had been read out and acclaimed at meetings of the county court when the elections had been organized.[11]

It is certainly clear that many members arrived with a powerful sense of the strength of provincial feeling, and of their obligation to represent it. When official business opened in the Commons speaker after speaker presented petitions covering what was quickly to become pretty familiar ground. Among the petitions piled up on the desk of John Rushworth, the clerk of the House of Commons, was the text of a speech by Sir John Colepeper, member for Kent. 'I stand not up with the petition in my hand, as others have done', he declared, 'I have it in my mouth, and in charge from them that sent me hither to present the grievances of the county of Kent'. Like many others he expressed concern about the fate of religion, complaining both of the great increase of papists due to the neglect of the laws against them and of the 'intruding and countenancing of divers new ceremonies in matters of religion'. This dislike of Laudian-ism was particularly evoked by the placing of the communion table altar-wise and 'bowing or cringing to or towards the same'. His com-plaints against the Convocation, although they included the 'etc oath', were primarily constitutional: the canons had been passed by a Convo-cation which had turned itself into a synod, without warrant, following the dissolution of Parliament. It had, in effect, taken unto itself the power to make laws and impose benevolences. Along with many others Colepeper was also concerned about financial measures of the 1630s, especially coat and conduct money, the rising cost of gunpowder, and the taking of arms from Kent to Scotland the previous summer, which had not been returned. He was particularly bothered by ship money, however, claiming that the legal position on which it was based threat-ened property rights: 'If the laws give the king power in any danger to the kingdom whereof he is judge, to impose what and when he please, we owe all that is left to the goodness of the king'. Finally, he complained of the monopolists, 'a nest of wasps or swarm of vermin which have overcrept the land' who invaded the households of the English like 'the frogs of Egypt'. These are the 'leeches that have sucked the common-wealth so hard it is almost become hectical'.[12]

Colepeper fought for the King in the civil war, like nine of the fifteen other speakers recorded by Rushworth in the collection of these speeches published later.[13] Although Colepeper's language was ripe, and the griev-ances very serious, there was no constitutional radicalism here, or any clear desire to pursue further reformation. Most of the speeches from these early days make similar recitations of threats to the true religion, bemoan the long intermission of parliaments and the uses made of the prerogative during the 1630s. Many of them attributed these problems to poor advice, and called for a change in royal counsels. But that was it. The programme represented by these speeches, which claimed to reflect provincial opinion in general, was in that sense limited: parliamentary control of taxation, the end of the Laudian experiment, and a balance between prerogative power and other sources of law which gave greater security to the subject.[14]

A number of overlapping concerns were at the heart of these provincial and parliamentary complaints: resentment of some of the religious and secular policies of the 1630s; of those who promoted them, and towards the influence of Catholicism at court; and of the powers that had allowed these counsellors to implement their policies. On secular matters these were calls for redress, rather than a positive programme for a new settlement – the removal of specific counsellors and the abolition of particular powers. The same was true in religious matters – there was a widespread grievance, but no agreed programme for a new settlement.

One of the first measures taken by Parliament was to release Burton and Bastwick, two of the Puritan martyrs pilloried and whipped in 1637, in response to petitions from their wives presented to the Commons by Pym. The case for the third, William Prynne, was made by one of his servants and presented by Rous.[15] On 28 November, Prynne and Burton, released from prison and heading for London, were met at Brentford, where an escort was established. They proceeded to London accompanied by more than one hundred coaches and by thousands of men and women. Those escorting them carried rosemary for remembrance and laurel in token of joy and triumph. What could this triumph possibly be but the defeat of Laudianism? Crowds gathered in the city, 'the common people strewing flowers and herbs in the ways as they passed, making great noise and expressions of joy for their deliverance and return'. According to one observer they were received almost with 'adoration, as if they had been let down from heaven'.[16] Bastwick was similarly greeted at Blackheath a few days later. Although Charles, incensed by the reception afforded to Burton and Prynne, had issued instructions that no more than 800 horse should accompany Bastwick into town, he was not obeyed. Twenty-seven coaches and 1,000 horse formed a convoy into London, where Bastwick was greeted with jubilant crowds and the sounding of trumpets.[17]

Demonstrations added to political pressure, but also fed fears about the breakdown of normal politics. Edward Hyde, MP and later the Earl of Clarendon, became a prominent loyalist. In November 1640, however, he shared many of these grievances about Laudianism and other policies of the 1630s but he could not distinguish between this obviously peaceful demonstration celebrating the return of Burton and Prynne and an 'insurrection (for it was no better) and frenzy of the people'. Nothing provided clearer illustration than these scenes of 'the unruly and mutinous spirit of the city of London, which was the sink of all the ill humour of the kingdom'.[18] These tensions were plain over the next two years – sympathy with the pressure for further reformation was in tension with its implications for authority, and the threat that it might proceed in an unlicensed way, on the streets.

Moreover, these demonstrations combined opposition to Laud, anti-popery and hostility to bishops. These were different issues, of course, and not everyone who was happy to see the Puritan martyrs returned had the same view of what their return signified, and some were not happy at all that they had been returned. For example, Nehemiah Wallington, the pious London wood turner, rejoiced at the liberation of 'those worthy and dear servants of God'. Robert Woodford, steward of the Earl of Northampton and another godly man, was also there, and his zeal also rings down the years: 'oh, blessed be the Lord for this day! This day those holy living martyrs Mr Burton and Mr Prynne came to town . . . My heart rejoiceth in the Lord for this day; it's even like the return of the captivity from Babylon'. But Peter Heylyn thought their release reflected the machinations of the Puritan faction in London and Southwark. Behind this suggestion lay the view that being anti-Laudian was something rather less radical than was intended by the men mobilizing these crowds: one observer noted that cries against the bishops had mingled with the acclamations of the crowds. Others saw these demonstrations primarily as an affront to the courts that had condemned these men, rather than as a religious deliverance. It was in the words of Thomas May the 'greatest affront that was ever given to the Courts of Justice in England', and contributed to the eventual abolition of the courts of Star Chamber and High Commission.[19] All the signs are that in November 1640 England was in the grip of a powerful anti-Laudian reaction, but this was a rather disparate coalition. A profound hostility to aspects of Laudian ceremonial was shared for example by Colepeper, the future royalist, and Pym, the future champion of Parliament's cause.

Despite these divisions all this was, for Charles, unpromising. He had called a parliament to meet the costs of an army of occupation, but faced calls for the redress of the grievances of his English subjects while also seeking to negotiate terms for the withdrawal of the Covenanters' army. He could not dissolve Parliament, because of the costs of the Treaty of Ripon, and in order to get the money he was clearly going to have to listen to a lot of rather inchoate bellyaching, including pressure for a significant change in his ecclesiastical policies. Concessions were inevitable, but painful for a monarch for whom his public front was a crucial political matter. Charles set about minimizing the impact on his regality, and on the frame of well-ordered monarchy and religion. Here he had two pre-eminent advantages: the very general commitment to the principles of monarchy (even among those with concerns about this particular king) and the lack of unity among his critics about what positive measures should be taken beyond the redress of particular grievances.

A remarkable feature of the first six months of the Long Parliament was that it produced very little by way of legislation. In part this was due to the double fact that grievances were at once so loudly expressed and so very miscellaneous. Much business was passed on to committees: five Grand Committees were established to consider matters relating to general areas of concern and select committees proliferated to discuss particular issues. The first of a number of attempts to reduce the number of these committees took place in January 1641, resulting in a list of sixteen committees alongside the five Grand Committees. But the tendency was to sclerosis. The Houses usually sat for three hours each day, from 9 a.m. to noon, occasionally starting earlier, and afternoon sessions were relatively rare. In November and December 1640 only a little more than one in twenty sittings were in the afternoon. Even in November of the following year, a month of intense crisis, only one quarter of sittings were in the afternoon. In the absence of effective management, business tended to drift. Parliaments were not designed as executive bodies, but as occasions where the ills of the kingdom were resolved through a union of monarch and people. As a result, grievances and disputes were brought before the Houses in an apparently random manner and important discussion was hived off to the committees. The intention was that committees would produce legislation that would be passed effectively, but in these months the impression is more of drift than of efficiency.[20]

On top of this flood of petitions came numerous private legal suits to the House of Lords. During the 1620s the House of Lords revived its judicial function, responding to massive demand from the increasingly litigious population. The lower courts were overcrowded, plagued with complex and overlapping jurisdictions, procedural irregularities and peculiarities, and appeal from some of the busiest courts was not possible. Measures of reform in Parliament had been considered, but not produced, and so the Lords became an attractive alternative forum. This development was at first slow – there was a rising trend through the 1620s, but only about 200 petitions in all during that decade. The first three months of the 1640 session brought 200 more. In addition to the kinds of suit brought in the 1620s, the Lords was now inundated with petitions from people who claimed to have fallen foul of what they said was the abuse of the legal system by crown officials during the 1630s. The Lords was flooded with petitions relating to the imposition of Laudian policies and the enforcement of unpopular fiscal expedients, and, from the summer of 1641, another round of litigation was opened up when Parliament abolished some of the courts that had enforced these measures. Officials of those courts were forced to seek protection from prosecution for their actions while the courts had been in existence, and those who would have used those courts in the past were forced to go to the Lords instead. By the middle of 1641 the Lords had received some 500 petitions and by the end of the year the figure had reached 650.[21]

Another reason for slow progress was the close relationship between the fate of reform and redress in England and the negotiations for a Scottish treaty. The Covenanters had agreed eight negotiating points, each of which was to be settled in turn. Nothing was to be formally agreed until all eight had been dealt with, and then the whole package was to be ratified by the English parliament once everything had been agreed. In the later stages of the negotiation this raised the stakes, since earlier agreements could come unstuck in the light of later discussions, and each party was responding throughout to external circumstances in the hope of securing more of their aims. The eighth negotiating point included the demand that the religious practices of the two kingdoms would be harmonized around a single confession of faith, something which was in practical terms essential to the security of the Scottish settlement. The first seven points were agreed by February, leading to fears among English parliamentarians that they might be abandoned by their Covenanting friends. Fortunately, and perhaps not entirely to the regret of the Covenanters and their English friends, discussion of the vague eighth point dragged on until June. Business in the Long Parliament was tied to these negotiations formally but also because it was Parliament which paid the costs of the Scottish army and which would have to finance their eventual disbandment. There was also more or less obvious co-operation over particular demands, for example the removal of Laud and Strafford.[22]

Anglo-Scottish affairs were intertwined in less formal ways too. One of the first acts of the parliament was to institute fast days on which sermons would be heard by the members. The first two preachers were Stephen Marshall and Cornelius Burges, both famous Puritans. They both preached on the theme of the Reformation in danger and Burges went further, dwelling on the story of Israel's delivery from Babylon by an army from the north.[23] On their arrival in London the Covenanters' commissioners were greeted by cheering crowds ('this libertine populace', according to the Venetian ambassador) and it is clear that there were close connections between the commissioners and their friends in Parliament. However, at the heart of this friendship lay the emotive, but potentially problematic, issue of the ecclesiastical settlement.[24] As we have seen this was not the only grievance brought to Parliament by the county petitions, and to the extent that it was a prominent concern in England, there was room for doubt that the Covenanters represented a more viable position in England than the Laudians.

Parliament met, then, with a variety of secular grievances to settle and a strong reaction against Laudianism in progress. But it was not clear what measures, precisely, would satisfy the country in secular and religious matters; and in the religious sphere the attempt to turn an anti-Laudian moment into a positive programme of further reformation, or to 'Scottify' the church, was not going to have an easy passage. These English issues were further complicated by the formal and informal connections with the Scottish settlement and the danger that reformation, even if it was desirable in itself, was proceeding without proper licence. Parliament was a deliberative body, with procedures designed to facilitate the airing of grievances and the generation of consensus. It was not an executive body, and there was no very developed machinery of management – certainly there were no party organization, no whips, no front bench, no Prime Minister.

The most coherent proposals for settlement were promoted by the 'Junto', a group associated with John Pym in the Commons and the Earl of Bedford in the Lords. They had no formal position: their authority rested not on office, but on the extent to which they were able to guide business in the direction of their preferred settlement by domination of committees, effective speech-making and the creative use of the power of the purse to secure redress of grievances.[25] Members of the Commons were also apparently willing to co-ordinate their efforts with pressure from outside Parliament – the presentation of petitions and the assembling of crowds. If this was happening, however, it did not always favour the Junto's programme – here and elsewhere they could hope to guide or harness the larger forces at work but they could not control them. There is no reason, beyond hindsight, to think that Charles ought to have seen a deal with the Junto as the centre of his political concerns. They were not an elected party and had no formal role: their authority was informal, and negotiated, and their command of business in the two Houses was imperfect.[26]

Pym had been a relatively prominent figure in the parliaments of the 1620s, and was in the Short Parliament one of the two most experienced members. He had achieved prominence in that parliament also by his electrifying speech on 17 April, which had fused religious and secular grievances around the need to protect the liberties of Parliament: Parliament was the guarantor of both.[27] He established himself in the new parliament with a similarly powerful speech made on 7 November. The burden of his two-hour speech was similar, but introduced a new element. Once again he suggested that law and religion were so necessarily joined that 'with the one, the other falls', but he now identified a single and compelling threat: a plot by the papists to alter both. This case had been made by Rous in the Short Parliament but was now taken up with vigour by Pym. The agents of this plot were evil counsellors, corrupt clergy that 'finds a better doctrine in papists to serve their turns better than that of our church', and those who were not particularly concerned about popery and, through their inaction, allowed it to flourish. Part of his appeal was his ability to meld the miscellaneous grievances being expressed into a single problem, with a clear diagnosis and a suggested remedy: he consistently argued, and at times convinced many other members, that the problems of popery and arbitrary government were bound together by a single popish plot.[28]

For much of the first session of the Long Parliament, however, Pym was a significant but not quite dominant figure, and was not the manager of business that his later reputation as 'King Pym' suggests. His views were compelling, but not universally held. Colepeper's speech, for example, bears many similarities with Pym's: they could more or less agree on all the symptoms that were in need of attention, but their diagnosis of the cause was different. Pym saw a fundamental corruption, caused by a malign and identifiable agent, whereas Colepeper saw examples of misgovernment. As the symptoms were alleviated over the coming months it became clearer that men like Colepeper were working to a different, and less demanding, agenda from men like Pym. In the early months of the parliament, in fact, much of Pym's energy was engaged in liaising between the two Houses, seeking to establish a coalition in difficult circumstances.[29]

Hindsight leads historians to emphasize the role of the Commons, but in Tudor and Stuart parliaments the Lords often took the lead. They did not initiate supply bills (taxation), but networks of patronage and connection often meant that business in Parliament was dominated by peers. Clarendon thought that it was Pym's patron in the Lords, the 4th Earl of Bedford, who really could have brokered this settlement. A Calvinist who favoured bishops and disliked sects, someone who distrusted this king but did not like the stronger arguments for restraint on the monarchy, Bedford represented a kind of par position that might have been the basis for settlement. He was undoubtedly a respected figure in both Houses: when he died, in early May 1641, the Commons adjourned all committees in order to allow members to attend his funeral – no-one else was honoured in this way by the early Stuart parliaments. But his views were not shared by the majority in the Lords, many of whom were more wary than Bedford about the direction of secular and religious redress.[30]

The Privy Council showed some interest in achieving a settlement through a change of counsel, by bringing in prominent men from among the twelve peers who had petitioned for a parliament the previous August. Bedford was a key figure here, and there is evidence that the plan for settlement favoured by him and Pym made some headway between January and March 1641. Their settlement required the removal of Strafford, Laud and others associated with the policies of the 1630s. They also sought a number of 'bridge appointments' intended to surround the monarch with more reliable advisers. Naturally enough, Bedford and Pym were in the frame here, as Treasurer and Chancellor of the Exchequer respectively. They wanted permanent, parliamentary additions to the revenue in order to compensate the crown for the loss of ship money and other prerogative revenues. That had constitutional implications, of course, in shifting the balance of royal revenue towards sources granted by Parliament. Beyond that they do not seem to have wanted to go: their own authority as counsellors, of course, depended on the preservation of a reasonable freedom of action for the monarch. A third important element of the projected settlement was the regulation of episcopacy, along lines proposed by James Ussher, the Calvinist archbishop of the Church of Ireland, a scheme in which bishops were to act in consultation with the clergy and to be bound by law; the analogy was with the regulation of the divinely ordained powers of the monarchy by the laws of the community.[31]

It seems that Charles was reluctant to abandon his counsellors, willing to accept augmentation of his revenue, but not at all willing to allow reformation to reach to the abolition of bishops. On the other hand, the inducement of a sufficient financial settlement, based on parliamentary grants, was attractive to the King but less so to many Members of Parliament, who favoured the abolition of ship money more than they did the creation of new sources of revenue. Meanwhile, the Scots were seeking the abolition of episcopacy in England in order to secure their own church settlement; any settlement in England short of that was unacceptable to them. This was a tricky negotiation, which foundered for a mixture of reasons, including the failure of the money to arrive in return for attacks on prerogative revenues. But what really did for it was the failure to reach an agreement over church government. Bedford and Pym were closely tied to the Covenanters, who made it clear that the abolition of episcopacy was an unshakeable demand.[32] The failure of this proposed settlement would not have mattered if there had been a ready alternative, but there was not.

Religious settlement was just as problematic outside Whitehall and Westminster. As parliamentary business and the treaty negotiation with the

Covenanters meandered along, religious debate in England began to range well beyond the attack on Laudianism, and as it did it became more divisive. This was a very public debate, which had immediate relevance to every churchgoer in the land. In the parish of All Hallows, Barking, for example, a week before the triumphal return of the Laudian martyrs local enthusiasts sawed wooden angels off the altar rails and took them to the House of Commons as evidence of popish innovation, without the approval of the vestry. There were clearly divisions in this parish, however: in August 1638 the vestry had agreed to the creation of an altar. There was such an outcry from other parishioners that the bishop's chancellor had to intervene in January 1640.[33] It is highly likely that these decisions were taken, and perceived, against the background of the Scottish crisis, of course; in any case they bear testimony both to the divisiveness and the immediate local significance of these arguments about the future of the true religion.

Parish radicalism underpinned the mobilization of London's Root and Branch petition, presented on 10 December. The petition denounced ecclesiastical hierarchy in comprehensive terms and became a focus for subsequent discussion of religious reform in Parliament. Its tone was inflammatory: 'the government of archbishops and lord bishops, deans and archdeacons, etc, with their courts and ministrations in them, have proved prejudicial and very dangerous both to the church and commonwealth'. Such government was 'found by woeful experience to be a main cause and occasion of many foul evils, pressures and grievances of a very high nature unto his Majesty's subjects in their own consciences, liberties and estates'. The particular offences of this church government were miscellaneous and grave: it had allowed the decay of preaching or was actively hostile to it; discountenanced the magistracy; failed to identify the Pope as Antichrist and therefore fostered a continued resemblance between practices in England and Rome, particularly in 'vestures, postures, ceremonies and administrations'; abused its legal power; failed to enforce observance of the Sabbath; and allowed pluralism – ministers holding more than one appointment in the church. In suppressing godly and painful preaching, the bishops had fostered:

The great increase of idle, lewd and dissolute, ignorant and erroneous men in the ministry, which swarm like the locusts of Egypt over the whole kingdom, and will they but wear a canonical cap, a surplice, a hood, bow at the name of Jesus and be zealous of superstitious ceremonies, they may live as they list, confront whom they please, preach and vent what errors they will, and neglect preaching at their pleasures without control.

The net result was that 'only papists, Jesuits, priests and such others as propagate Popery or Arminianism' had prospered, with three particular consequences: the encouragement of popery and papistical party; the forced migration of godly men, particularly to Holland, resulting in the decay of trade; and the likelihood that the 'wars and commotions' between the King and his subjects in Scotland would be perpetuated, making all his kingdoms 'prey to the common enemy'.[34] Hostility to Laud's policies had been radically elaborated here, and the final implication that the Scots were not the real enemy was pretty incendiary – something close to treason on one reading of the King's proclamation of the previous August.[35]

Printed copies of the petition had circulated for some time, and between 10,000 and 20,000 signatures were eventually gathered, all of them, or so it was claimed, from citizens. On the day of its presentation the petition was accompanied by a large crowd, of around 1,500 people, that gathered in Westminster Yard. Although most observers agreed

New Palace Yard and Westminster Hall in 1647

that this was a socially respectable and well-behaved assembly, it was nonetheless politically unsettling. The menace of such forceful demonstrations threatened political propriety.[36]

Metropolitan mobilization soon produced provincial imitations. During January, as the Commons prepared to discuss the petition, similar petitions were produced in thirteen counties. One more was delivered in

January, from Devon; another two, from Lancashire and Nottingham-shire, followed in April; Lincolnshire petitioned on 27 May and Oxford-shire on 27 July. Somerset brought up the tail in December.[37] The Kentish petition was presented by Sir Edward Dering, with some reluctance and in response to pressure from some of his constituents. He had disliked the tone of the London petition and in subsequent debates expressed a willingness to see reformed episcopacy survive.[38] In this case, as in many others, it is clear that the petition was not simply got up by MPs, although it is also clear that we should not see it as the consensual voice of the county either.[39] Instead petitions represent successful efforts at mobilizing wider opinion – making use of networks of officeholders, gentlemen and ministers, appealing to issues recognizable to larger con-stituencies. Whatever the opinions being represented, however, the increasing sophistication of the petitioning process was in itself a remark-able political development. These petitions seem to have been timed to maintain the momentum of a parliamentary debate: the Commons held significant debates on Root and Branch reform on 8/9 February and 27 May, and the process approached conclusion in late July.[40] Provincial petitions were almost direct contributions to specific parliamentary debates and this phenomenon of mobilizing opinion in order to influence the political process became a source of concern in itself.

The first of the Root and Branch debates, on 8 February, lasted eight hours and involved sixty speakers. The question was whether to commit the petition to the consideration of a committee. It was renewed the following day, when the exchanges were even more divisive.[41] There was an issue of substance here, about whether the faults of Laudian bishops justified such radical measures. But there was also a debate about the means being used, about the threat of street politics. As Lord George Digby put it: there was 'no man of judgement, that will think it fit for a parliament, under a monarchy, to give countenance to irregular, and tumultuous assemblies of people, be it for never so good an end'. On the other hand, Nathaniel Fiennes was willing to defend mass petitioning, arguing that the crowds proved that the thousands of signatures were genuine, and that the weight of numbers was a reason for Parliament to take the petition seriously. Others supported this view and emphasized the respectability of the crowd.[42] Not only did Fiennes make this case, but it was published to an audience outside the House: both he and Digby saw their speeches in print.[43] Parliament was clearly a permeable institution, and that was a political issue in itself. Some members were willing to exploit or respond to audiences beyond the chamber, others feared the implications of that for the authority and dignity of government, but it did not necessarily stop them going into print too.

On 9 February a compromise emerged: the petition was referred to a committee, but the issue of episcopacy was reserved for the House. Chastened by the divided response to radical reform, the 'rooters' in Parliament proceeded cautiously over the spring, aiming, as their Covenanting friend Baillie put it, 'to take down the roof first to come to the walls'. Committee meetings over the following month received presentations from citizens and ministers, and came to concentrate on the secular powers of bishops. A well-prepared measure to remove their legislative and judicial powers was approved by the Commons on 10 March and, on the following day, so was their exclusion from the Sessions of the Peace and Star Chamber. This paved the way for a bill to exclude bishops from secular employments and from the House of Lords, which passed the Commons and was sent to the Lords on 1 May. There it had a rough ride, and relations between the two Houses were made worse by proceedings which were also, by that time, under way against the Earl of Strafford. Bringing the tussle to a head, a Root and Branch bill was presented, rather half-heartedly, by Dering on 27 May (coinciding with the Lincolnshire petition). Dering made clear that he had not abandoned all hope of reviving 'the primitive, lawful and just episcopacy', and it may have been that the presentation of this bill was tactical – intended to pressure the Lords into accepting the exclusion of bishops from their House. They did not accept it, and that meant that a Root and Branch bill would not get through the Lords either. A contentious committee stage for the legislation between 27 May and 11 June was followed by nearly two months of wearisome debate. The last discussion took place on 3 August, and thereafter the bill was lost in the tide of events.[44] Neither the modified episcopacy promoted by Pym and Bedford nor more fundamental reform was a live political option.

By the spring of 1641 little of the Pym–Bedford plan had been achieved. There was no consensus about what the post-Laudian church should look like and there was no financial settlement either. In the first two and a half months of the parliament the Lords initiated ten bills, of which two had made it to the statute book by the end of January: a bill to allow the Marquess of Winchester to sell some of his lands and a bill relating to the Queen's jointure (the provision made for her in the event of her husband's death). The Commons were in one way even less effective, initiating twenty-six bills, of which only one became law. But that Act was of fundamental political and constitutional importance: the Triennial Act, passed on 16 February.

Henceforth, it said, Parliament should meet at least every three years, and each sitting should last at least fifty days. This right to sit was, or so the preamble claimed, already established in laws and statutes which, as experience had shown, should be 'duly kept and observed'. It was in part a measure necessary to secure public credit: in order to pay off the Scots the King needed to borrow and his personal credit was low. Over the previous two generations the crown had been increasingly reliant on intermediaries for its credit, since the word of a king was of no value to a businessman. Behind the intermediary stood the assets of the crown – its lands, its rights to raise revenue and its powers to grant monopolies and licences. Now, however, these things were increasingly under pressure, and parliamentary revenue was the best security for loans. Regular meetings of Parliament would offer a reasonable security for lenders. Although these suggestions may have persuaded the King, the Act meant much more than this: if ship money had arguably affected the constitutional balance then the Triennial Act certainly did.[45]

Progress on crown income had also been limited. Ship money collection had collapsed over the summer of 1640 but there had been no permanent parliamentary grant to replace it. In the meantime the costs of the two armies continued to mount. A grant of four subsidies, first proposed in November 1640, was not finally made until 16 February 1641. Two more were proposed on 20 February, but 129 members spoke against them, and it took until May to get them onto the statute book.[46] If this reflected a lack of financial realism in Parliament it was reflected in the provinces too. The subsidy imposed a fixed rate of taxation on the wealth of the population, assessed in either lands or goods. But the assessment of the wealth on which that rate was levied was in the hands of local men – the sort of people who served as constables or Justices. This was one of those tasks in which they did not impose the letter of the law. Beyond straightforward under-assessment, there were more elaborate evasions, such as the use of bearers, described by Henry Best in 1641. According to that scheme a small number of inhabitants were returned on the tax assessment, with others agreeing to bear the burden with them. This, and similar scams, had led to a catastrophic decline in the overall value of subsidies from the 1560s onwards, which was offset but not overcome by the habit of granting more and more of them at once.[47] Pym had been aware of the need to reform the subsidies early on, and had proposed an obvious solution – that Parliament should grant a lump sum, sufficient for the intended purpose, that could then be divided up as a specific sum due from every county and borough, and eventually every village and ward.[48] But this was an uphill battle, quickly abandoned in the autumn of 1640. In Norfolk and Cheshire yields of the subsidies of 1640/41 were no higher than they had been in the late 1620s, and in Norfolk that meant that an individual subsidy was worth about 30 per cent as much as it had been in 1589.[49]

Customs revenues were in general more important to overall crown finances since they provided a large part of the ordinary revenue, for the normal costs of government, whereas parliamentary subsidies were occasional additions intended to meet extraordinary costs.[50] The customs consisted of several elements: the ancient customs which belonged to the crown by prerogative right; tonnage and poundage, which rested on statute, but which had from the fifteenth century been routinely granted to a monarch for life in the first year of his reign; and impositions, more recent additions raised without parliamentary sanction. The rates at which these duties were raised was determined by the Books of Rates, which laid out the schedule of liable goods. This was negotiated between the crown and merchant bodies. Impositions were raised by prerogative power either openly, as a means to regulate trade, or through the manipulation of the Books of Rates. Like ship money, they looked like taxes imposed without consent; but as in the case of ship money there was a defensible legal case that they were a reasonable use of a long-established legal power. By 1640 the impositions and the 'pretermitted custom' (another duty raised by prerogative power) brought in £250,000 per annum.[51] Overall, therefore, the customs, and their yield, were largely outside parliamentary control.

Both tonnage and poundage and the impositions were grievances in 1640 and, true to form, Parliament was keener to abolish than to replace them. Particular duties among the impositions had been the subject of legal challenge, and although (or because) the crown won, they remained a grievance. In 1625 Charles had not been granted tonnage and poundage for life by his first parliament, as the grant was held up as part of a negotiation about the unpopular impositions. It seems clear that the intention had been to make the grant for the monarch's life once the negotiations were concluded, and a one-year grant was made to tide the King over. Events overtook these negotiations, with the result that the grant was not renewed. Charles continued to collect the duties. In 1626 it was declared illegal, but a bill was prepared to indemnify the King from prosecution. The issue was not resolved in the next parliament either, and so Charles collected the duties without parliamentary sanction throughout the 1630s.[52] Now, the grant of tonnage and poundage was deliberately used as a negotiating counter: successive short-term grants were made in order to lever concessions from the King, on the promise of a long-term settlement. Moreover, when a new tonnage and poundage bill was proposed, in March 1641, it contained a Book of Rates set by Parliament rather than the crown – both measures reflect a determination to secure greater parliamentary control over the grant, and yield, of the customs.[53] Neither bore immediate fruit, partly because of parliamentary resentment at the King's determination to resist pressure to institute thoroughgoing persecution of Catholics.[54] By the summer of 1641 there was no financial settlement either.

The one area of substantial progress in redress of provincial grievances was in the removal of Charles's counsellors, in particular Laud and Strafford. There were few defenders of either in Parliament, among the Covenanters or in Ireland, and the attacks on both resonated powerfully in the streets. Laud was impeached in mid-December, the beginning of a slow march to the scaffold which did not finally end until January 1645. In the meantime he was imprisoned in the Tower of London in March 1641, his arrival greeted by jeering crowds, and throughout his incarceration suffered neglect and indignity at the hands of the godly. Other committees were also pursuing particular people: Bridgewater and other parties to the dispute about the muster master in Shropshire were brought to book and so was the Earl of Huntingdon, brought low by his adversary Sir William Fawnt.[55]

The first real victim, however, was Strafford, who was impeached on 10 November, a week after the meeting of Parliament. He was accused of trying to subvert Parliament, or to find ways of avoiding having to summon it at all. It was said that he had intended to have some of the leading figures in the Commons arrested and tried on charges of treason on the grounds that they had co-operated with the Scots, or even actively encouraged the Covenanters' invasion. He may have done that, just as they may have. His strong line on the need to crush the Covenanters made him few friends in Scotland. In Ireland he had imposed an oath in Ulster, heartland of Scottish Presbyterian settlement in Ireland, disavowing support for the Covenant. This 'Black Oath' outraged influential Protestant opinion in Scotland and Ireland. It was also said, plausibly but almost certainly inaccurately, that immediately after the failure of the Short Parliament he had suggested using an Irish army to bring the English kingdom to heel.[56]

Whatever the truth, Strafford came to personify an apparently lawless defence of the King's interests in the face of all political difficulties; a willingness to subvert the constitution in defence of otherwise indefensible policies. But, although Strafford had few admirers, the manner of his trial and execution compounded fears that the political process was becoming dangerously corrupted. It was close to judicial murder, informed in no small part by the threat of public disorder if his neck was saved.

On 30 January 1641, when Strafford was called to Westminster to hear his charge, he travelled by water under armed guard. In the event he suffered nothing worse than shouts and curses from the crowd and the early stages of the trial were uneventful. However, as the likelihood that he might escape with his life increased, so did the temperature on London's streets. On 23 March Strafford's trial opened on the rather frail-looking charge of 'cumulative treason'. It was likely that Strafford would have beaten this particular rap, since those accusing him of this previously unknown crime were themselves motivated in part by fears about the erosion of legal protections for the subject. Tiring of this procedure, Arthur Haselrig introduced a bill of attainder of Strafford on 10 April. Here, by vote, was the possibility of simply declaring Strafford to be guilty, and the bill had passed its third reading in the Commons on 21 April. Avoiding the complexities of a trial, it had the advantage of achieving an obviously necessary political end by efficient means. 'Stone dead hath no fellow', as one wry observer put it. In April petitions circulated in the City calling for swift action, despite a personal request from the King to the mayor to put a stop to this activity. The petitions made a connection between the slow progress in Parliament and economic problems, and attributed the decay of trade to political uncertainty. This agitation was taken up by those anxious for the attainder to make progress. The suggestion that animals of prey (like Strafford) did not deserve the same protections as the creatures they hunted was politically convenient but worrying in principle. Even more worryingly, the names of those who had voted against the attainder (the 'Straffordians') were published, and those named feared for their lives in the face of angry crowds. In the Lords there was hostility to these pressures from the Commons and the trial continued.

Not trusting to the course of law, however, some of Strafford's friends, with Charles's knowledge, hatched a plot to spring him. On 3 May, fearing that Strafford was not going to survive the attainder, Charles sent loyal troops to take control of the Tower, but they were foiled by the lieutenant of the Tower and vigilant citizens. The public failure of the plot, 'the first army plot', did Strafford no favours.[57]

Nehemiah Wallington was among the huge crowd that gathered at Westminster the same day, prompted by a declaration that Charles would not allow the attainder to succeed. Several thousand gathered in the morning and by the afternoon the crowd had swelled to perhaps 10,000. The demand, paradoxically perhaps, was for justice and execution. When the Earl of Arundel arrived his way was deliberately blocked, and he was forced to say that he was working to achieve the execution of Strafford. These words, reassuring in one way, were met with the threat that 'they would have justice, or take it'. As for Arundel, they said, 'we will take his word for once'. At midday the Lords adjourned and many peers left by water. Some of those who took coaches were subject to personal abuse – the Earl of Bristol, for example. Pembroke, a supporter of the attainder, was able to pacify the crowd. John Lilburne, the celebrity radical, was also among the crowd. A London apprentice, originally from the north-east of England, he came from a minor gentry background and had a grammar school education. In the house of Thomas Hewson, a Puritan clothier, he had immersed himself in the Bible and emerged with an intense personal piety. During the 1630s he had been imprisoned for helping to distribute Burton's publications. Present at most of the crucial disturbances of the period 1640–42, Lilburne became a successful soldier and then a prominent controversialist in print and in the courts. He was questioned the day after these events for some treasonable words, and at this distance in time it sounds like it was a fair cop.[58]

Despite the efforts of the Lord Mayor crowds assembled again on 4 May in the feverish atmosphere created by the revelation of the army plot. Some of the crowd were indeed armed, as had been threatened the previous day and the social profile was, if contemporaries are to be believed, less respectable. In the Commons the main business was the drafting of what became known as the Protestation, intended as a litmus test of political reliability. Those swearing to it would bind themselves to protect the true religion, and its passage seems to have calmed fears about the direction of events. The crowd eventually dispersed in the late afternoon, when the text of the Protestation was read out by Cornelius Burges, a well-known radical divine, client of the Earl of Bedford and a key figure in the London Puritan brotherhood.[59]

More excitement followed the next day, when a rumour swept the City that the House of Commons was being besieged by papists. Wallington closed his shop and rushed to the defence of the Commons, along with many others. When an old woman interrupted the sermon at St Anne's, Blackfriars, with the news, people 'ran up and down as if they had been wild'. As armed men hurried through Moorfields on their way to Westminster, women wept in the streets.[60]

Hostile contemporary accounts habitually claimed that the crowds in London's streets in May and November 1640, and May 1641, were a low-born rabble. Those that can be identified, however, were often socially respectable, and more fair-minded commentators noted the social mix of these crowds. The leadership and organization seem to have been generated in London, within the City's middling sort or from activists. There were continuities in the participation of Lilburne, Wallington and others, and there is no reason to suppose they needed, or wanted, the support of MPs in order to mobilize. Indeed, there is every reason to think that they felt the pressure should be operating in the opposite direction. The placards, petitions and crowd mobilizations drew on the crowded commercial society of the City, not on the natural obedience of thousands of inhabitants to MPs representing other constituencies.[61]

When the Lords did pass the attainder, on 8 May, therefore, there were good grounds for thinking that this significant political gesture, arguably the most significant so far achieved by the parliament, owed something to the pressure of London's crowds. This was certainly true of the royal assent – the final necessary step to pass the bill into law.

Charles was by no means inclined to give his assent – his loyalty to Strafford, and determination to save him, had already been amply demonstrated. But his judgement was affected by the arrival in Whitehall of a crowd said to number four or five thousand, among them armed men. Charles was advised by the Privy Council and the Archbishop of York that the only way to quell these disorders was to sacrifice Strafford. He regretted submitting to this pressure for the rest of his life.

In the days before the execution tensions continued to run high. Rumours spread of a planned French invasion to save Strafford, an attack on a bawdy house served as a guise for economic and social protest, there were attacks on the Queen Mother and a guard was placed on St James's Palace. The execution itself drew a crowd of 100,000, also immortalized by Hollar, and following Strafford's death celebrations

The execution of the Earl of Strafford

continued long into the night. Bonfires were lit and those who failed to join the celebrations had their windows broken. Strafford had not made a helpful 'last dying speech', with the result that it was necessary to pretend that he had, and a pamphlet was published purporting to be a repentant speech he had made prior to reaching the scaffold. It was immediately denounced as a hoax.[62] In all sorts of ways the virtue of the outcome – Strafford's death – was undermined by the unseemliness of the means.

Strafford died unlamented except perhaps for the way that he had come to his end. Here were populism and something close to judicial murder in tandem. Strafford himself thought that the Lords had been affected by the crowds.[63] A second important reason for acquiescence in these dubious proceedings was the vividness of fears about a popish plot, but this too was felt differently by different people. On 19 May a board in the gallery of the House of Commons had cracked and Walter Earle's son had 'cried out Treason, Treason and many of the burgesses had run away with swords drawn'. Other members, however, merely laughed at the panic and remained in the House. Arthur Haselrig, a notoriously hot Protestant who had clutched hold of an image in his alarm, was jeered for flying to the horns of the altar. Anti-popery, in other words, was extremely powerful, but its more extreme manifestations were not universally persuasive. It is significant both that there were parliamentary proposals in the summer of 1641 to geld Jesuits and that they were not accepted.[64] Those anxious about legal propriety or political decency could take little comfort from Strafford's trial or the crowds that (successfully) bayed for his blood during the passage of the attainder.

In May, seven months after the assembly of the parliament, some progress was finally being made but the principal achievement, the execution of Strafford, left a legacy of division and bitterness which further undermined attempts at settlement. Certainly, these proceedings against Strafford were a final nail in the coffin of the Pym–Bedford plans: their association with these events is unclear, but they finally ended their hopes of retaining the King's favour. Equally, the army plot to seize Strafford increased fears that Charles might employ a military coup against the troublesome parliament. Committed to the abolition of episcopacy by their alliance with the Covenanters, and now tarred with the brush of populism, these were people with whom Charles would not deal. Bedford was in any case dying – he caught smallpox in the first week of May and died on 9 May.[65] Strafford's end was in some ways a consummation of the politics of 1640: opposition to royal policies was most powerful as a movement of redress rather than rebuilding, and drew considerable strength from opinion outside Whitehall and Westminster. But these events also accelerated some of the divisive political trends that had emerged since November 1640: rebuilding would be difficult in the atmosphere of distrust and mutual recrimination which now reigned.

In particular Parliament's search for security for the future led it onto new constitutional ground, fuelling fears of a Puritan populist conspiracy against the monarchy. On the day of the attainder of Strafford, Parliament had passed an Act against its own dissolution. If the Triennial Act had tiptoed awkwardly round the implications of such measures for the prerogative, there was no such hesitation after the army plot. At this point over half of the members of Charles's Privy Council in November 1640 were dead, under arrest or in exile, but further safeguards seemed to be necessary to some MPs.[66] The political context for this was clear: the revelation of the army plot and the fear that all the talking about grievances would come to nothing because of the King's advisers.

Immediately, however, the prospects looked good as a constructive legislative programme finally materialized. Revenue measures were not necessarily far-sighted, although they had far-reaching implications. On 12 May the Houses voted on a bill based on Pym's earlier proposal for grants of a fixed sum, in this case the £400,000 subsidy. The bill was not treated with urgency until December, but it is a sign of the growing seriousness of measures to settle the financial question.[67] In the meantime, a poll tax was granted in June 1641, with high hopes. It passed from first reading to royal assent in only eleven days and in some places appears to have captured a large slice of the population, but the yield was disappointing (£250,000 compared with the £1m some had hoped for). This reflected widespread evasion, and there was also a problem of slow payment.[68] Its failure made the adoption of the £400,000 subsidy more or less inevitable. A Tonnage and Poundage Act was finally passed on 22 June. This was in one sense a tactical measure, since it granted the duties for less than two months, starting retrospectively on 25 May, and there were frequent subsequent renewals as negotiations continued. But the effect of the Act was to transform the customs into parliamentary taxes. It abolished those impositions which had been taken without 'common consent in Parliament', setting almost all the various duties instead on a statutory basis, and it stated that the rates at which the duties were to be imposed would 'be hereafter in this present Parliament altered in such manner as shall be thought fit'. Parliament had taken control of the Books of Rates too.[69]

With new sources of revenue available the legal basis of the fiscal expedients of the 1630s was taken away: on 7 August ship money and forest fines were declared unlawful; knighthood fines were abolished on

10 August. Collectively, these measures had profound implications for the basis of crown finances. Prior to 1640 only about 25 per cent of crown revenue depended on parliamentary sanction, and that figure was probably falling. When Charles's son took possession of his throne in 1660 it was on the terms of these 1641 reforms. During his reign about 90 per cent of his revenue depended on parliamentary sanction.[70]

There was rapid progress towards the redress of grievances, too. The courts of Star Chamber and High Commission, the two courts most responsible for the enforcement of Laudianism, were abolished on 5 July. All these measures enjoyed considerable political support, but, collectively, they represented a redrawing of crucial aspects of the constitution, changes which were never reversed. This rapid progress owed something to the need to get things done before members returned home for the harvest. Attendances were dropping and there is evidence of anxiety that constituents would not be happy at the return on a year of talking.

Another development that focused minds was Charles's decision to go to Scotland. In itself this was a reasonable enough enterprise – it was after all one of his kingdoms and he was in the process of finalizing a treaty with a Scottish army. But in the atmosphere of distrust and anxiety that lingered after the attainder of Strafford, and the first army plot, this trip to Scotland was regarded with deep concern. There were signs in Scotland that the remarkable unity of the Covenanting movement was beginning to fracture. A number of leading noblemen had come to feel that the restraint of royal power was going too far, and that a new danger was emerging. Prominent among them was James Graham, later first Marquess of Montrose. It has been said persistently that Montrose was ambitious rather than anything else. His undoubted enthusiasm for the Covenanting cause – he played a prominent role in its mobilization – was attributed to disappointment at his reception at the English court in 1637. If that was part of his motive he must have been frustrated by the dominance of the Earl of Argyll – his superior in wealth and influence. But it was also conviction that made him pull back and by the time of the second Bishops' War he was no longer a prominent Covenanting leader. He had also been significant in the organization of the Cumbernauld band, partly in opposition to the growing dominance of Argyll.[71]

Montrose and others encouraged Charles to come to Scotland as early as March, and Charles had announced his intention to do so in April.

Quite what he intended is not clear, but he was suspected in Scotland of planning some kind of move against the Covenanters (those who had written to him are known to posterity as the 'Plotters'). In England it was feared that he intended to raise Scottish support for moves against Parliament, or that he intended to use the northern army to impose his authority. In the spring, at the time of the plot to spring Strafford from the Tower, there had also been discussions about the possibility of bringing the English northern army south in order to teach Parliament some discipline. These two army plots reflected the fact that the northern army had become resentful about the reluctance of Parliament to pay their wages and board, and come to regard Parliament with hostility. Lavish grants of money to enable the disbandment of the armies certainly owed something to the desire to see them gone before Charles went north.

A short-term problem – the difficulty of trusting this particular king to pass through two large armies without causing trouble – again led to proposals which had far-reaching implications and which raised the political stakes. This was compounded by a continuing fear of court Catholics – that the King was not reliable so long as he was surrounded by agents of the plot to subvert the law and religion. The Ten Propositions, agreed on 24 June 1641, arose from 'A large conference with the Lords, concerning several particulars about disbanding the army, the Capuchins &c.' They made demands which would have been quite startling a year earlier. As well as calling for disbandment of the English army and appealing to the Covenanters to withdraw part of theirs, the Houses asked Charles to delay his journey until more business in England was settled (including the tonnage and poundage bill). Beyond that the proposals clearly encroached on royal power: a wish not only to remove but also propose royal counsellors; a desire to restrict the religious freedoms enjoyed by his wife; the proposal to take over the education of the princes (to ensure that they grew up good Protestants); the view that anyone entering the kingdom as a representative of the Pope was committing treason; that the militia and defensive resources of the kingdom be placed in reliable hands; that the King should be more sparing in inviting Catholics to court; and that pensions should be withheld from recusants 'held dangerous to the state'. It was clear who would do the 'holding' in this case. The militia demand ('That there may be good lord-lieutenants, and deputy-lieutenants; and such as may be faithful and trusty, and careful of the peace of the kingdom') was later to harden into a demand for parliamentary control – a precipitant of the war, and a sticking point in all subsequent negotiations.[72] This was well short of that, but the direction of politics was plain. The difficulty that prominent politicians had in trusting Charles was radicalizing demands, and this despite the substantial legislative programme achieved in the early summer. This was a truly worrying sign, since it is difficult to see how Charles could have rebuilt this trust, or his opponents suspended their distrust.

A second significant obstacle to a lasting settlement was the very public and divisive religious debate. The failure of Root and Branch proposals had amplified that debate without offering a resolution. The Protestation, passed in the aftermath of the revelation of the first army plot, exacerbated religious conflicts, both in Parliament and in the provinces. The preamble made no bones about the popish plot to subvert law and religion and about the dangers presented by a plot to move the army against Parliament. It was, to say the least, tendentious and provocative, but this account of recent history justified an oath of association to defend 'as lawfully I may with my life, power and estate, the true reformed Protestant religion expressed in the doctrine of the Church of England, against all Popery and popish innovation'. Those who subscribed were collectively bound to maintain the King's royal person and estate, the power and privilege of parliaments, and the rights and liberties of the subject.[73] In structure it was much like the Scottish National Covenant, therefore, and Baillie made the comparison directly. But it was shorter – there was no historical account of what the doctrine of the Church of England was. More importantly still, it was deliberately silent on the discipline of the church. In the frenzied debate of the Protestation a number of members who saw some 'hint intended' against bishops and the liturgy argued that 'the word discipline might be adjoined to the word doctrine'.[74] They failed, and the Protestation became, for those in the know, a defence of the doctrine but not necessarily the discipline of the church.

Rather than becoming a unifying force, therefore, the Protestation divided: it went to the heart of the problem of the post-Laudian church. Beyond the defence of the church from popish innovation, was it necessary to push for further reformation of its discipline? Some of the promoters of the Protestation were quite aware that it would have this function, serving as a shibboleth 'to discover a true Israelite', a means of identifying who was really committed to the pursuit of reformation.[75] Imposing it in Westminster was a means of intimidation, although the fact that the bishops were able to take it devalued it in the eyes of Robert Baillie, the acute Covenanting observer of English affairs. Reported, debated, amended in one day, this demonstrated the power of Parliament to act when it felt the urgency. It also took the debate out into the country. On 5 May the Commons ordered that it be printed and on the following day a bill was read requiring all adult males to take the Protestation by Christmas. The Lords refused to pass it, but subscription to the printed Protestation became a national campaign, nonetheless.[76] Alongside the official copies went unauthorized manuscript and print copies, not all of them accurate.[77]

The divisions caused by the Protestation were evident in print – Henry Burton saw it as a licence for radical reformation, others as a threat to the authority and responsibilities of the godly magistrate; the easy phrases, about the powers and privilege of Parliament and the rights of the subject, were all contestable. So too was the doctrine of the church. The text did nothing to answer doubts on these points and there was a healthy public debate.[78] Copies of the Protestation eventually became talismans, worn in hats, thrown in the King's coach and, later, affixed to muskets and ensigns, and the text was later treated as the parliamentarian's 'title to be in arms'.[79] But it was controversial, and that controversy was deliberately exported from Westminster to the rest of the country. Across the country, at assizes and quarter sessions, the Protestation was subscribed by officeholders and the better sort. London led the way in its systematic arrangements for subscription. In Essex the following spring swearing of the Protestation was not always limited only to the men of the parish – women and youths took it too. It was done in church, following a sermon and, in some places, was accompanied by communion.[80]

For radicals, the Protestation gave further legitimacy to iconoclasm. There is evidence in Essex that religious protests moved beyond anti-Laudian gestures such as attacks on altar rails, on to attacks on the liturgy of the Prayer Book and the use of clerical vestments.[81] In Cheshire, during the spring, painted windows and images had become targets for iconoclasts.[82] At Radwinter, where there had been attacks on altar rails the previous summer, one of the churchwardens began to refuse to co-operate with the minister over matters of ceremony – locking away the vestments, refusing bread and wine at communion, and moving the communion table from its elevated position.[83] Iconoclasm in London seems to have picked up pace and there were the first signs of the cleansing of chapels in the universities of Oxford and Cambridge.[84]

It was not just the Protestation which prompted or gave legitimacy to these radical acts. The parochial energies which had prompted the Root and Branch campaign had not been dissipated, and gained some legitimacy from parliamentary debate. Following the presentation of the original petition a committee had been established to consider the decay of preaching, scandalous ministers and the increase of popery soon after the presentation of the London petition. On 31 December, Simonds D'Ewes proposed a bill to abolish idolatry, heresy, superstition and profaneness, a measure attached to the subsidy bill. A committee report led to further consideration of idolatry, and on 23 January 1641 this resulted in an order from the Commons for 'commissions, to be sent into all countries, for the defacing, demolishing, and quite taking away of all images, altars, or tables turned altarwise, crucifixes, superstitious pictures, monuments, and relics of idolatry, out of all churches or chapels'.[85]

The fact that the Commons was pushing for reform in these directions lent legitimacy to local initiatives. In the light of this parliamentary pressure, for example, Cheapside Cross, in London, came to stand for, even personify, the dangers of popery and superstition. It had been erected in the late thirteenth century, one of a series of Eleanor Crosses built around the country to commemorate Edward I's wife. An elaborately carved and very public monument, decorated with images of angels, the cross was a very familiar landmark. It had been the target of hostility in Elizabeth's time, and at the beginning of the seventeenth century, and now, once again, came under scrutiny. Henry Burton, preaching in Parliament in June 1641, had called on Parliament to cast down idols, beginning with the Cheapside Cross, and a flutter of pamphlets followed. On the whole, however, these pamphlets were satirical, sending up the radicals who made such a fuss about so little, likening the cross, for example, to Dagon, the filthy God of the Philistines.[86] The cross survived again, in 1641, but remained a focus for religious controversy.[87]

The attack on Laudianism was readily expressed as an assault on popery (spiritual bondage), but that language might lead in the direction of more radical reform, undertaken without magisterial direction. As

Cheapside Cross, a focal point of civic life

this line of polemic about popery and reformation developed so did a counterpoint: attacks on episcopacy opened the way for religious licence and sectarianism (spiritual anarchy). There was a long tradition of anti-Puritan polemic, stretching back to the 1560s, in which hot Protestants were denounced as hypocrites and sectarians, and this provided a means to understand the threat now being posed by the challenge to ecclesiastical hierarchy. Such fears seem to have exercised a powerful effect in the Lords. Most notably, having been informed about the activities of sectarians in Southwark on 15 January, the Lords ordered

That the divine service be performed as it is appointed by the Acts of Parliament of this realm; and that all such as shall disturb that wholesome order shall be severely punished, according to law; and that the parsons, vicars, and curates, in several parishes, shall forbear to introduce any rites or ceremonies that may give offence, otherwise than those which are established by the laws of the land.[88]

The order was to be read publicly in all the parish churches of London, Westminster, Southwark and their surrounding liberties and suburbs. This fear about spiritual anarchy gained strength from stories of iconoclasm in the provinces. As radicals in Parliament pressed for the abolition of episcopacy, iconoclasts in the country attacked the outworks of popery in their own church. For hesitant reformers such as Dering, these stories of provincial iconoclasm only added to their hesitancy about the abolition of episcopacy. In June, at the time of the Protestation controversy, and the exchanges over Cheapside Cross, Dering seems to have had a change of heart. He abandoned attacks on episcopacy and the cause of Root and Branch reform, informed once again by concerns in his home county about religious order. Others, like Sir John Colepeper and Sir Thomas Aston, also seem to have been driven towards royalism by attacks on episcopacy and the Prayer Book.[89]

From late 1640 through 1641 there were intermittent attempts at local reformation, as activists took up the call to arms. These local initiatives stood in uneasy relation to the parliamentary debates on religion, which gave out an intermittent and often contradictory message. As the events of the previous summer had shown, local activists did not need explicit parliamentary prompting: attacks on altar rails, surplices and images were reported in the summer of 1640, all associated with hostility towards Laudianism, but without explicit parliamentary sanction. When Parliament did begin to discuss Root and Branch reform there was a well-grounded fear that this would invite, or license, unofficial and disorderly reformation. It does seem that indecisive debate in Parliament legitimated local action without setting limits to it.

Church government had become crucial because, following the impeachment of Laud, episcopal authority was collapsing: the archbishop was in the Tower, after all. But the politics of reformation were also coming to centre on the material dimensions of worship – the fabric of the church, the arrangement of its internal space, dress and gesture during worship. It was in these details that the boundaries between the practices of a true church and the corruptions of Rome could be marked out. It is impossible to quantify these local controversies, or to attempt an account of their geography, but attacks on church furnishings and decoration, and demonstrations against particular forms of worship, across the summers of 1640 and 1641 were clearly informed and calculated acts. These were interventions in the liturgical and ritual calendar, gesturing towards a purified form of religion; they were not ill-informed, violent or particularly spontaneous. Behind each lay local histories too, as at Radwinter. It is a mistake to see the iconoclasm of the 1640s as a new Puritan zealotry. Those who undertook these actions were aware of their place in a longer Reformation history, and so can we be.[90]

Radical debates in Parliament, and their local resonances, were taking politics beyond the redress of grievances towards the creation of a renewed moral order. Exuberant hopes lay behind these measures, but they also excited dark fears. Although it is plain to us that this was not indiscriminate or anti-religious violence, for many contemporaries it was difficult not to see this popular agency as anything other than sedition. It may not actually have been the case that this presaged anarchy, but it was an important political fact that many respectable people thought it did. This unofficial iconoclasm in the counties created fear that religious authority was no longer in safe hands. Matters of high politics, the most important matters of state, were now being canvassed quite deliberately on the streets of London and in the counties. The political issues being thrashed out in Parliament were available to a broad section of the population, particularly in London but also in the provinces. Politics had gone public.

By the time the King eventually left for Scotland on 13 August he had consented to a major constitutional reform: the very halting progress made before the death of Strafford had given way to rapid and important legislative action. But the experience of debate up until May is important in understanding why this substantial legislative programme did not produce a permanent settlement. By the early summer of 1641 the removal of evil counsellors had been successful, but the death of Strafford seemed to illustrate the threat of mob rule. Religious debate was both inconclusive and very public: there was a gathering reaction against radical reformation which was soon to take defence of the English Prayer Book as its talisman. The Pym–Bedford plan, which in retrospect appears to have been the most constructive one available in Parliament, was now dead. Charles was not inclined to settle with Strafford's killers, or those who consorted with a popular reformation that was tending towards anti-clericalism. On the other hand, revelation of the army plot had reinforced a sense that the King could not be trusted and his trip to Scotland had produced radical demands intended to offer security for the gains already made. Just as attacks on Laudianism had given rise to attacks on episcopacy, attacks on particular policies and counsellors had begun to give way to proposals for more profound and durable constitutional change. When Parliament went into recess on 9 September, therefore, much had been done to redress the grievances of November 1640, but there were new difficulties that it seemed hard to settle. Most obviously, the shape of a religious settlement in England was unclear and the King was not trusted.

During the harvest recess, in September 1641, George Thomason acquired two pamphlets which clearly reflected the fear that reformation was tending towards licence and spiritual anarchy: *A Discovery of 29 Sects here in London* and *A Nest of Serpents Discovered*.[91] The latter described the practices of the Adamites, a sect said to have been active in fifteenth-century Bohemia and now alive in London. Most of *A Nest of Serpents* was taken up with a recitation of previous denunciations of religious enthusiasts who went naked in imitation of Adam's innocence before the Fall. The cover featured eight naked figures, three of them clearly women and four very conspicuously men. One of the women is flagellating a man whose penis is erect, alongside the banner 'Down lust': the exhortation, we are invited to believe, was not being honoured. *A Discovery* also placed the Adamites alongside other historic errors, sects and schisms. Religious order and decency depended on tradition, and the authorities cited in *A Nest of Serpents* made an implicit case for the importance of tradition alongside scripture. These pamphlets belong to a growing genre of shocking revelations about sectarian threat – the polemical accompaniment to the concerns enshrined in the Lords order of 16 January 1641. Adamites had been mentioned in the controversy over the Protestation and pamphlets over the summer and autumn of 1641 built on the conceit.[92] As the anti-Laudian cause splintered, and many committed themselves to the Protestation, which had been explicitly designed not to make commitments about the discipline of the Church of England, anti-sectarian polemic made the case about where this was leading.

In fact, in this case, this polemic about spiritual excess probably tells us more about a particular form of anxiety than it does about actual conditions. *A Nest of Serpents* offers almost nothing of substance about the actual practices of modern-day Adamites: 'Their meeting is sometime at Lambeth, at other times about Saint Katherine's, sometimes in the fields or in woods, at sometimes in cellars'. It does offer, perhaps ironically given the subject matter, to reveal more. The authorities are after their leaders, and there is little doubt that they will be caught 'in the midst of their lewd and abominable exercise, which is so scandalous, blasphemous, heathenish and abominable. At their discovery more shall

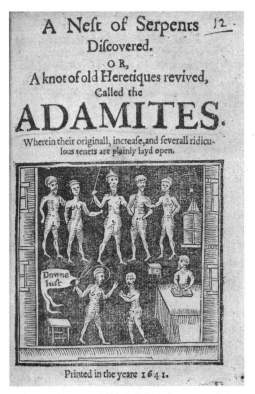

The dangers of sectarian excess

be written'.[93] The style of attack was to become familiar through the rest of the decade. The falsity of the Adamites' teaching was addressed not through doctrinal debate but on the basis of its obviously sinful fruit: 'By their fruits shall ye know them'. There was also a strong desire to enumerate and taxonomize, as in *A Discovery of 29 Sects*: the intention was presumably to alarm and perhaps titillate, and the numbers (which tended to grow bigger) had that effect. But they were also precise – lending credibility perhaps, but also limiting the threat at the same time that it was being publicized. By historicizing, taxonomizing and enumerating sects these pamphlets captured, and to some extent contained, the dangers of spiritual excess.

There is no independent evidence of the existence of the Adamites, and Ephraim Pagitt wrote about them in his 1645 compendium of religious errors as a historical, rather than a contemporary, phenomenon. Thomas Edwards, in his even more compendious catalogue of schisms and errors, did not mention them at all.[94] Prior to 1640 there had undoubtedly been sectarian congregations, separating from the national church, in London and elsewhere. There was also a long tradition of semi-separatism, of groups remaining within the church but also pursuing their faith in voluntary settings. It seems unlikely that the pressure for further reformation, and in particular the attacks on episcopal power, did not lead to an actual increase in these forms of religious practice: although bishops were not abolished, the fact that the suggestion was in the air eroded their cultural legitimacy and, therefore, their practical powers. Church courts had lost their teeth. Nonetheless, although these fears were plausible, it seems that they were exaggerated. By the autumn of 1641 there were probably fewer sectarians in London than there were Catholics – seven congregations have been identified, with perhaps 1,000 adherents – and the evidence we have suggests that lay preaching was being restrained too.[95]

That the fears being expressed in print were probably exaggerated does not diminish their political significance, and actions in Parliament fed them. Root and Branch reform was a victim of the impending recess, as debate had led to an elaboration of proposals, making agreement more difficult and discussions more complex. On the day before the recess, 8 September 1641, the Commons passed an order for the suppression of innovations, which pushed the cleansing of the church further than before and did so by authority of the Commons alone. The pressure for further reformation was becoming increasingly easy to associate with threats to order and decency. It was, for its proponents, an epochal moment in a larger history; for its opponents a resonance of other periods of over-zealous interpretation of the gospel message. The Lords responded to the Commons order by publishing their order of 16 January calling for worship according to the law established.[96] But such calls were not unifying – the refusal in the Protestation to demand support for the 'discipline' as well as the doctrine of the church could assume considerable importance in that respect. If the Protestation appealed to those hot for the fight with popery, the defence of the Prayer Book and discipline of the church was attractive to those resisting both popery and Puritan populism.

Over the coming months opinion was successfully mobilized in support for the Prayer Book as a defence against the sectarian threat. In September 1641 the Essex Grand Jury, which contained a number of hotter Protestants, with connections in both Houses, had made a declaration which failed to defend the Prayer Book. This seems to have prompted an attempt in the county to set in train a petition in favour of the book, citing instances of religious disorder as evidence of the need to uphold the decencies it enshrined. This was part of a wider phenomenon: between September 1641 and May 1642 twenty-two English counties sent up petitions in defence of the Prayer Book, twelve of them in November and December 1641.[97] They had in common a desire to reaffirm fundamentals – episcopacy and the Prayer Book. Stories of the mocking or desecration of the Prayer Book justified an appeal to the established liturgy, authenticated by long custom.[98] Often promoted by the clergy, some of these petitions gained very large numbers of signatures – 14,350 in Somerset, 6,000 each in Cheshire, Devon and Nottinghamshire, 30,000 in the six counties of north Wales.[99]

There were now two clear slogans in religious debate: the Protestation was a totemic expression of defence of the doctrine (but not the discipline) of the Church of England, and a bulwark against popery. The Prayer Book, by contrast, expressed both the doctrine and the discipline of the Church of England, and was therefore a bulwark against both sectarianism and popery, so long as it could be agreed that it was not itself popish. These Prayer Book petitions were driven not just by fear of course, but by an attachment to the forms of religion currently established. Nonetheless, the necessity of petitioning in order to sustain the status quo reflected anxiety that that settlement was not safe. In at least sixteen counties there were clashes between those promoting rival petitions, and those clashes were related to opposition to the Protestation.[100] Anti-Laudians, of whom there seems to have been no shortage, might sign up for either.

Successive drafts of one of these petitions survive from Essex and they reveal the tensions that might lie behind these campaigns. The drafts survive among the papers of Henry Nevill, a prominent supporter of the Personal Rule in Essex and an opponent of the Puritan networks protected by the Earl of Warwick. It told of the need to protect the Prayer Book in the light of local disorders. The detail and the way in which the stories were redrafted suggest that, although the petition was addressed to the King, the audience for the petition was as much opinion in the county. It highlighted not only how the Protestation had been used as a pretext for religious disorder, but also how attempts to restore order had been obstructed by the Grand Jury. Close analysis of who was on the Grand Jury suggests that it had indeed been captured by the local godly. Actual desecrations of the Prayer Book and disruptions of the observance of the liturgy bear testimony to local support for the view (stated in the first Root and Branch petition) that the Prayer Book was 'a plain device to usher in the mass'.[101] In Essex, as elsewhere, there was a developing battle between rival fears of popery and religious anarchy – emblematically expressed in attachment to the Protestation or the Prayer Book.[102]

The anti-sectarian pamphlets of September point to a further change in the means by which political debate was being conducted. A consequence of the abolition of High Commission and Star Chamber in July was not only to further reduce the effective influence of church discipline, but also to end controls on printing. George Thomason, the London bookseller, had been collecting pamphlets since early 1640. Prior to the meeting of the Long Parliament he had collected seventeen, over nine months. Between November 1640 and May 1641, the month of the attainder of Strafford, he had amassed a further 116. From May onwards he was collecting around sixty per month, and in September amassed eighty. There was more to come, but the rising political temperature, the collapse of effective censorship and the increasing willingness to resort to print were transforming the market for print.[103] Parliamentary declarations and speeches were printed, partly it seems to satisfy the country that MPs were active on their behalf. The open expression of religious and political differences now spilt onto the streets, not only in the form of crowd actions and the circulation of partisan statements. In Cornwall the promotion of the Prayer Book petition was linked explicitly to ill-affected pamphlets, 'which fly abroad in such swarms as are able to cloud the pure air of truth and present a dark ignorance to those who have not the two wings of justice and knowledge to fly above them'.[104]

This growth of publicity was troubling for a monarch who felt, probably correctly, that the security of the monarchy lay ultimately in the deference of his subjects. Charles's refined sense of his regality emphasized respect for the King, and entailed an extensive, perhaps jealous, view of the *arcana imperii*. He was not alone in feeling uneasy about the growing publicity afforded to fundamental political and religious controversy. By late 1641 religious and political anxieties were finding regular expression in print: this was no longer a matter simply of parliamentary politics and the politics of the day were reported in an increasingly luxuriant print culture.

In debate and in practice it was proving difficult to foster a positive alliance around the promotion of the true religion or to maintain a negative alliance on the basis of a ragbag of grievances such as those expressed in the opening months of the parliament. As reformers took advantage of their position of strength not only to dismantle Laudian innovation but also to mark out the new boundaries of the true church, fundamental questions were publicly raised but not resolved. Polemically this gave great prominence to anti-popery; practically it centred on matters of church decoration and ritual practice. Here, though, was a potential problem of order – the thought that groups of individual Christians could take it upon themselves to mark out these new boundaries could bring little comfort to many people. The resonances of this pressure for reform on the streets of London and in the provinces were not always welcome. As in the 1630s, shifts in national policy preferences could be taken up by willing local parties, but in the early 1640s those responding sometimes came from outside the ranks of the 'natural governors'. It was not just the content but also the conditions of religious and political debate which had been transformed in the first year of the Long Parliament: the mobilization of opinion for partisan purposes in crowds, petitions and now print.

In both secular and religious matters the debate during 1640–41 was moving from particularities to general principles: from the policies of the 1630s to the constitution; from attacks on Laudianism to the problem of reformation. In November 1640 the Covenanters had been useful to a broad coalition of English people – not simply admirers of Scottish Presbyterianism but also those who wanted reformation of a different kind, as well as those with the more modest hope of rolling back Laudianism or those who wanted to force Charles to summon, and listen to, a parliament. Everyone in November 1640 was a monarchist, but almost everyone was also opposed to at least one of the following: Laudianism; financial devices based on the prerogative; court Catholicism; some of the leading royal counsellors. In its first year the Long

Parliament produced no clear programme of redress and no definitive text on which such a thing could be built. Instead debate escalated without resolution, and the political process became increasingly public, as demands relating to political principle were made by crowds and petitioners and were debated in print.

As Parliament went into recess for the harvest after a year of parliamentary activity, the King was in Scotland finalizing a settlement there, and substantial measures of reform had been achieved in England with (grudging) royal assent. Although some did not trust this particular king, no-one seems to have advocated a political settlement that was not monarchical. In the autumn of 1641 everyone was still a monarchist and more or less everyone believed in the necessity of a national church. Laudianism and the unpopular financial policies of the 1630s were dead, and the counsellors of the 1630s were out of power. But new dangers seemed to have arisen in their place. Differences were emerging between those afraid of the King's role in relation to the true religion and those afraid of the corrosive effects on church and monarchy of a populist Puritan campaign for further reformation. The latter was a principled position and one which underpinned the commitment of some of Charles's supporters when war broke out. It was not simply, or necessarily, a reactionary position since it sought a balance, not a retreat to the 1630s; and it was not simply aristocratic – it too found support on the streets and in the provinces, just as influential peers were pushing policies of radical reform. Petitions and pamphlets sought to mobilize opinion among wider publics. Their appeal was overlapping, not mutually exclusive, and therein lay the problem. What the English lacked in 1640, by comparison with the much more successful campaign of the Covenanters in Scotland, was a rallying point for a settlement – a text like the National Covenant, around which a coalition could mobilize and on the basis of which specific measures could have been agreed. What they had instead, by the summer of 1641, was the Protestation, seen by some as a shibboleth, intended to sort the sheep from the goats. Against that stood the Prayer Book, seen by some as a threat to the true religion. Many were able to support both. As they were urged as alternatives, however, the possibility of a deep divide had emerged, and one that might run through not just the heart of government but also through the towns and villages of England.

5

Barbarous Catholics and Puritan Populists

The Irish Rising and the Politics of Fear

Parliament reassembled on 20 October 1641 and soon after it was presented with a utopian tract called *A description of the famous king-dome of Macaria*. It was consciously modelled on Thomas More's *Utopia* and Francis Bacon's *New Atlantis* and took the form of a dialogue in which a traveller, someone with practical knowledge, described Macaria to a scholar in straightforward terms, in the course of a walk from the Exchange – centre of news and trade – out into Moorfields. The traveller's spare description of the institutions and political practices of Macaria made it clear how political arrangements could be made to deliver fundamental social reform. Some of the institutional practices in Macaria were of direct topical interest in England – for example, that the ruler's council met annually, and heard complaints only about ministers, judges and officers, whom 'they trounce soundly, if there be cause'. Others were less immediately topical, but were intended to help 'this honourable court [to] lay the cornerstone of the world's happiness'. Five under-councils sat briefly each year, dealing with economic matters (agriculture, fishing, land and maritime trade, and new colonies, or plantations). Any divine who published a new doctrine was considered a disturber of the peace, and suffered death for it, but in order to prevent the persistence of error, a Great Council met each year to debate new opinions. Those that won out in argument were adopted; those that did not were declared false. A college of experience took responsibility for new medicines, and those who produced them were rewarded out of the public purse. These features of life in Macaria, and the enlightened laws passed by the councils, promised not just political peace, but 'plenty, prosperity, health, peace, and happiness, and ... not half so much trouble as they have in these European countries'.[1]

This was an indirect, and belated, product of the high hopes of the previous autumn. Soon after the Long Parliament had instituted fast days, John Gauden and George Morley were invited to preach. They had both spoken on the theme of the need to pursue peaceful reformation and Gauden had made very positive mention of two leading figures in European Protestantism: John Dury and Jan Komensky (better known to posterity as Comenius). These two were already in correspondence with Samuel Hartlib, a Protestant refugee from the Thirty Years War. Hartlib was, like Comenius and Dury, well-connected with John Pym. He also had the support of Elizabeth of Bohemia and many other prominent politicians. These connections linked parliamentary pressure for the redress of English grievances with the larger European struggle for religious reform and Hartlib was asked to invite Dury and Comenius to London. As with so many other schemes in the first year of the Long Parliament's life, nothing much had happened to deliver on these high ideals. In the summer of 1641, however, as the political logjam appeared to move and hopes rose, Dury and Comenius finally arrived. Dury had arrived by the end of June, and Comenius came on 21 September, in time for the re-assembly of Parliament.[2]

Dury was the son of a Scottish minister who was banished to the Netherlands when Dury was ten years old. Dury himself became minister to the Scottish and English Presbyterian community in Leiden and had, therefore, good credentials as a Calvinist involved in the international cause. He had made his name as a campaigner for religious unity, an irenic approach to religious difference intended to produce solidarity in the face of irreligion. Comenius was a victim of the Thirty Years War, a Bohemian exiled repeatedly by the military advance of Catholicism in central Europe. His distinctive contribution to Protestant thinking had been an emphasis on education: appropriate socialization would create good Christians and, therefore, a good society. For him, the pursuit of God entailed, and was promoted by, the pursuit of understanding. In the Garden of Eden, Adam had been blessed with a perfect knowledge of nature, knowledge which was lost at the Fall. To recover that knowledge of nature was therefore to undo some of the effects of the Fall and to come closer to God. Here he was influenced by Francis Bacon's vision of a unified human knowledge based on experience, tried and proved using the powers of reason.[3]

It was these ideals which lay behind the utopian tract now before Parliament, proposing a college of experience, rational debate of doctrine and the use of government to make fuller use of economic resources. *Macaria* was almost certainly written by Gabriel Plattes, one of the 'impecunious but ambitious innovators whose cause was taken up by Hartlib'.[4] In 1639 Plattes had published treatises on mining and agriculture and he had a significant posthumous impact, but his immediate fate was perhaps symbolic of the disappointment of utopian hopes more generally: in December 1644 he was said to have been 'suffered to fall down dead in the street for want of food, whose studies tended to no less than providing and preserving food for all nations'.[5] Others took up these schemes for improving social conditions and knowledge of the natural world, and with some effect, but these hopes do not appear to have caught a very general mood during the years that followed.

Certainly, in October 1641, many people would have been content with a more limited settlement than the extravagant promise of *Macaria*. The most significant secular grievances from the 1630s had been redressed the previous summer. Charles's settlement with the Scots entailed the abandonment of his attempts at reform of the kirk in return for a withdrawal of their army. This not only drew some of the sting about Charles's intentions for the English church, but in leading to the end of the occupation offered financial relief and the possibility of dissolving the English parliament. The Prayer Book was becoming a rallying point for those as worried (or even more worried) by sectarianism as they were by popery. Meanwhile, in Edinburgh the King had begun to present himself as a focus for loyalty, emphasizing his regality. He had even offered to touch approved legislation with his sceptre, imbuing it with his sacred royal authority. This was a gesture unlikely to endear him to his Scottish subjects, implying as it might that the legislation was not valid until it had been so touched. It was, therefore, one with powerful resonance, and his Scottish subjects managed to put him off.[6]

In these circumstances the hopes of Pym and his allies may have had less potential appeal than their fears: anti-popery offered a better basis for a wider coalition than utopian hopes of the kind expressed in *Macaria*. Arguments about a popish plot found a ready audience, and were plausible in view of recent events. Charles had been seeking outside support throughout the last two years. He had seemed willing to do deals with Catholics, and against Covenanters and parliamentarians, and was now in Scotland perhaps conspiring against the people with whom he had just done a deal. This might seem to be the conduct of a king in the grip of a papistical conspiracy, or at least of a duplicitous or shifty individual, and many historians have taken essentially this latter view of him. But his behaviour seems more reasonable if we look at these things from a 'three kingdoms', or Stuart, perspective. It was not inherently unreasonable of Charles to seek support for his policies in all three of his kingdoms, and to try to use support in one kingdom to help him to govern the others. And he was, of course, acting out of principle, in defending the church and the crown from attack: he owed it to his successors to do exactly that. Nonetheless, it was not surprising that some at least of his English subjects regarded him as unreliable. The plot to get Strafford out of gaol had demonstrated that he was willing to resolve his political difficulties by unparliamentary means; reasonable enough from his point of view but not a welcome thought to parliamentarians. In June we know, although contemporaries did not, that he had considered a plan to use the northern army to overawe Parliament: the so-called second army plot. In July he had entertained discussion of the use of an Irish army to do the same thing. Thus, his negotiation in Scotland had certainly proceeded alongside discussions about how to do away with the English parliament; and those discussions had included consideration of some unconstitutional measures.[7]

This had certainly been reflected in his actions in Scotland. In October he had tried to carry out a coup against his chief Scottish opponents, the 'Incident'. How far the King was involved in the attempt to seize Argyll, Hamilton and Lanark is not clear; nor what was to be done with them once they were taken, although assassination was a possible intention. Hamilton's misfortune here was considerable: a member of the English parliament working for settlement, he had established links with many of Charles's leading critics; in Scotland he had good relations with Argyll. Rather than putting him in a strong position, as a close adviser of the King, this laid him open to a hostile whispering campaign at court. The man who as Charles's representative had had to kick his way out of the Glasgow assembly, and whose own mother had threatened to shoot him if he landed in Scotland, may now have been the target of a royalist assassination plot in which the King himself had a hand. Amidst rumours of royalist plotting, Charles attended Parliament to explain himself, but unfortunately agreed to be accompanied by several hundred armed men. Hamilton and the others fled, although

Charles strenuously denied that they had anything to fear, and claimed in fact that the plot was invented solely to discredit him. Amazingly, Hamilton seems to have believed him: he returned with the King to England in November.[8] For others the Incident made Charles difficult to trust and it continued to be possible to claim that this pattern of behaviour reflected the machinations of international popery. Despite the revelation of the Incident, however, opinion in England was probably drifting in his favour in the autumn of 1641.

It was in that sense convenient, perhaps, that on the same day that *Macaria* was presented to parliament, 25 October, fresh evidence of papistical perfidy also became available to the English parliament. John Pym received a letter on the floor of the House which purported to contain the dressing from a plague sore. Plague had been prevalent the previous summer but in England, unlike some other areas of Europe,

The dressing from a plague sore delivered to John Pym on the floor
of the House of Commons

the accusation of deliberate plague spreading was not usual. In fact, there do not appear to have been any other accusations like this in England during the period of the plague's greatest incidence. Nonetheless it was a disease with political resonances, associated with disorder and divine wrath. Here, though, the problem in the body politic was not internal distemper, but foreign infection. 'How bold was this attempt of inhumanity . . . But see the subtlety of the damnable project compiled without all Christianity'. Could papists possibly stoop lower? They would have to, of course, because God's providential defence of Protestantism forced them to it: 'God beholdeth all your mischief and saves the righteous from the cruelty'.[9]

Pym's apparent brush with death was politically useful, perhaps suspiciously so.[10] The fear of popery was a potent tool in fostering support for reform, and offered a powerful means of distracting attention from the perceived corrosion of religious and political decencies over the previous two years. English history, as generations of people had now been taught, gave manifest evidence of the desire of Catholics to defeat English Protestantism and to reintroduce popery: the effort to purify the church by eradicating popery existed alongside a vividly expressed fear of plotting by actual Catholics. In November, Pym was to take respectable anti-popery and use it to support a more or less direct attack on the King. With many secular grievances settled, peace in Scotland and fears about religious anarchy calling forth a Prayer Book petitioning campaign to rival that for Root and Branch reform, anti-popery may have represented a last refuge for some scoundrels.

Religious and political debate in the first year of the Long Parliament had been both open-ended and very public; unlike the Covenanting movement it had been constrained neither by organizational structures nor by a clearly stated programme. The content of the debate can be characterized both in terms of extravagant hopes, particularly for religious reformation, and of deep anxieties about the dangers of popery, sectarianism and what was being said, by whom and to what audiences. Charles's public performances communicated a regality that was surely appealing to people becoming anxious about social, religious and political order. In the opening weeks of the second session fear was a more potent political emotion than hope, and fears of popery and Puritan populism were quite evenly balanced. That probably put the King in a strengthening position, particularly since so many of the grievances voiced twelve months earlier had now received a statutory redress.

If there was a drift of opinion towards the King, however, it was abruptly reversed in early November, when Pym was delivered more promising material than a surgical dressing. On 1 November, seventeen senior privy councillors came to the Commons to inform them 'of certain intelligences, that were lately come, of a great treason, and general rebellion, of the Irish Papists in Ireland; and a design of cutting off all the Protestants in Ireland; and seizing all the King's forts there'.[11] This was sterner stuff than the attempt on Pym's life, and offered a clearer reminder of the need to show solidarity in seeking to preserve the true religion.

Since 1541 Ireland had been regarded by the English as a sister kingdom. Gaelic elites had been invited to surrender their lands to the crown, accepting them back on feudal terms: the initial intention was to transform the Gaelic chiefs into aristocrats like their counterparts in England. Had this succeeded there is no particular reason to believe that the Tudor and Stuart monarchs would have favoured expropriation. That it did not succeed was due in part to the vested interests of Gaelic lords. The crown wanted succession to follow the principles of primogeniture, which lent stability and order to hierarchy, but in Ireland this would have meant cutting off the prospects of younger sons and others who could, under Irish law, hope to succeed through competition. The failure to transform the Gaelic elite into a court aristocracy was exacerbated by the failure of the Reformation, which also created a rift between the crown and its natural allies in Ireland – the group increasingly known as the Old English. Descendants of Anglo-Norman settlers, these groups were, in theory at least, culturally and politically closer to London than their Gaelic counterparts. In practice this was not true, and when both Gaelic and Old English groups failed to accept Protestantism a layer of religious conflict came to overlay these other political problems. A series of rebellions under the Tudors had led to an increasingly hostile policy of expropriation, culminating in the 1590s. In that decade rebellion in the Gaelic heartland of Ulster was eventually defeated and the landowning elite was replaced, largely by Scots. What was once close to the core of Gaelic society was now dominated by Protestant settlers. During the 1590s too, Spenser, one of the flowers of the English Renaissance, had written his *View of the Present State of Ireland*, a text used to appal modern sensibilities. It argued that the 'wild Irish' lived in barbarous conditions, bringing waste to a potentially fruitful island as a result of the corruption of their religion and manners (that is, the codes of social and political life by which they lived). Plantation of laws, civility and religion was the only way to redeem the waste. The creation of this Protestant, 'New English' presence in Ireland was a considerable threat to existing Gaelic or Old English elites. By the early seventeenth century

Ireland seems to have been regarded by mainstream English opinion as both a problem of order and, under the influence of writers like Spenser, a heartland of barbarity and irreligion.[12]

It is to their credit that the early Stuart kings did not necessarily share these views, or give in to them, and in the late 1620s the crown, anxious to secure financial support from Ireland, adopted a conciliatory attitude towards Gaelic and Old English opinion. Both groups were concerned about the policy of plantation, seeking secure title for their lands, and some freedom to follow their religion under the crown. The Old English, previously regarded as the natural agents of the crown, sought to defend their political and social status from the newcomers. A miscellany of concessions, known collectively as the Graces, was negotiated in the later 1620s in return for the promise of money intended to make the Irish government self-sufficient, and able to withstand a Spanish attack without drawing on English money. Prominent among them was a recognition of title to lands which had been held for more than sixty years: a safeguard against expropriation and plantation. This echoed concessions granted elsewhere under the Stuart crown, and offered considerable reassurance to Irish landholders. The Graces also offered to relieve Catholics from some of the civil disabilities under which they lived – being barred from office and practising the law, for example.[13]

There were influential sources of opposition to the Graces, however. Both the Church of Ireland and the Dublin administration opposed them, or at least the most significant of them. Under James Ussher the Church of Ireland had taken a distinctly Calvinist direction, in advance of the Church of England. In fact worship was governed by Irish articles drawn up by Ussher, rather than by the Thirty-Nine Articles of the Church of England, and although they did not directly conflict, they differed in emphasis in the direction of a more thoroughgoing Calvinism. The Church of Ireland, a hot Calvinist church amongst a majority Catholic population, was hostile to Catholicism in principle and a natural ally of those hostile to the interests of Catholics. New English settlers were often convinced Calvinists and many of them, particularly of course the Scottish settlers in Ulster, were not particularly sympathetic to the Laudian church. They had a material interest in the protection of the interests of existing planters, and of their church, and religious, political and strategic interests in the further promotion of plantation. The Dublin administration, not unnaturally, tended to regard the Church of Ireland and the New English as its most important allies. As a result concessions by the crown to Gaelic or Old English interests were not likely to be welcome to the church, New English settlers or the Dublin administration.[14]

On the promise of grants of taxation the crown had negotiated the Graces in spite of these complexities, but they were never finally conferred. In 1628 peace with Spain and France reduced the need for money, and the Graces were a casualty of the changed political environment. Hopes rose again in 1634 when Thomas Wentworth, now Lord Deputy in Ireland, called a parliament. He hoped to put Irish government on a secure financial footing – to make it pay for itself – and this led him to seek means of conciliating Gaelic and Old English interests. In return for financial support granted in the first session of the parliament Wentworth had held out the promise of a revival of the Graces, and an end to the imposition of recusancy fines on those who failed to attend the national church. Justified as a spur to conversion and therefore a godly measure, they had also proved an attractive financial expedient in the past. As it turned out, however, the parliament granted the money without, in the second session, giving the promised concessions. Indeed, it was clear that Wentworth favoured further plantation, for financial reasons and the other standard arguments: the promotion of civility and Protestantism, and therefore of loyalty and security.[15]

But this did not create the basis of a close alliance between Wentworth and the Protestant interests in Ireland. Wentworth also favoured bringing the Church of Ireland in line with the Church of England, which meant pushing it in a Laudian direction, and he was suspicious of the vested interests in the Dublin administration. In both cases a central priority was to uphold the direct authority of the crown, and these policies bear some resemblance to the priorities pursued in both England and Scotland during the same period. As in England the religious issue was particularly divisive. In 1634 Wentworth compelled adoption of the Thirty-Nine Articles in Ireland, and this was a prelude to sustained pressure to move Irish doctrine and practice in a Laudian direction. These measures acquired a directly political and strategic importance in the light of the Prayer Book rebellion. For many Protestants in Ireland, particularly in Ulster, the religion of the Covenanters was much more congenial than that of the Church of England. It was as a means of discouraging that alliance that Wentworth imposed the Black Oath –

requiring them to abjure the Scottish National Covenant and to swear allegiance to King Charles.[16]

Crown policy was creating a common cause for advanced Calvinists in all the three kingdoms. Catholic leaders in Ireland, both Gaelic and Old English, on the other hand saw an obvious threat in the rise of the Covenanters and, in the Long Parliament, of English 'Puritans'. Both Covenanters and English Puritans were hostile to Irish Catholicism and therefore relatively favourably inclined to plantation and the interests of the New English. But Gaelic and Old English leaders were also hostile to Wentworth because of his evident desire to promote Protestant interests in general, and their failure to secure the Graces. Thus, although there were obvious conflicts between the interests of Ireland's various political groups, hostility to Wentworth was a common cause, and many parties in Ireland went along with the attack on Wentworth in the English parliament. This also reflected a more general pattern in Irish history – a willingness to go over the head of the Lord Deputy or Lord Lieutenant, and to appeal directly to the King. In 1640 the Irish parliament sent a remonstrance denouncing Wentworth's government, and covering the whole gamut of Irish political interests, to the English parliament. This was, constitutionally speaking, something of an innovation. The English parliament had no direct role in the government of Ireland, but bringing Irish grievances to the English parliament gave that body a pretext for discussion of Irish affairs.[17] Since the English parliament was a safe haven for anti-popish feeling of all sorts, this was not in the long-term interests of Irish Catholics – clearly the King was likely to be a better friend for them.

Hoping to make capital out of this obvious point, Charles had offered concessions to Old English leaders during Strafford's trial. In return for financial support he promised to cancel future plantations, recognize the security of title of lands held for sixty years or more and to confirm other concessions initially offered in the Graces. Further concessions were offered in July, again in return for promises of financial support. These offers were tactical, of course, and the tactics soon changed. The Edinburgh parliament took up the case of an Ulster settler who suffered as a result of the Black Oath, forwarding his case to the English House of Lords. As the temperature rose in London, the offer to confirm the Graces was withdrawn and the Irish parliament was formally subordinated to the English one.[18]

These political disappointments led some prominent Irish leaders to rebel. In its inception the rising was an elite movement intended as a coup against the Dublin administration, which did not have the interests of many Irish people at heart, and against strongholds in Ulster which might become a threat to Catholic interests. The aims of the risings were to secure parliamentary independence under the crown, security of title to lands and freedom of worship without financial or political penalty. This was a form of politics familiar from Tudor England: a loyal rebellion, designed to present grievances from a position of strength. It was not conceived as a separatist, nationalist or even anti-Protestant movement, but an attempt by elite figures to secure extra leverage in making their case to their king. Magnates in Tudor England had made a similar case, that their Catholicism could be reconciled with political loyalty to the crown. Force was a means to secure a change of policy, typified in the proposal that the Earl of Ormond, who was both Protestant and of Old English extraction, should replace the despised Lords Justice in Dublin.[19] Significantly, however, most of the leaders of aristocratic rebellions in Tudor England had ended up dead.

The initial plan had been that on 23 October risings in Ulster would coincide with an attempt to seize Dublin Castle but the Dublin conspiracy was betrayed the night before and the chief conspirators arrested. Ormond had already withdrawn to the family seat at Kilkenny, and it remains unclear whether or not he knew about the impending attack on Dublin Castle. The Ulster risings did bear fruit, however. Building on a coalition against plantation and in favour of the Graces, it brought together the aspirations of the Gaelic and Old English leadership. Increasing indebtedness had led to hostility against the settlers in Ulster and that also fed into the support enjoyed by the leader of the rising there, Phelim O'Neill. The Ulster rebels declared themselves to be in arms in defence of their liberties, not against the King – a claim typical of risings in fifteenth- and sixteenth-century England. It seems clear that at this stage the Irish Catholic nobility felt that they could call off the rising if their political demands were met – they seem to have made that offer explicitly.[20] Outside Ulster, however, in the other three provinces, and in Ulster once the rising was underway, significant social tensions were released.[21]

For Protestant settlers the rising evidently came as a surprise: they said so, and it is clear from statements taken about the rising that

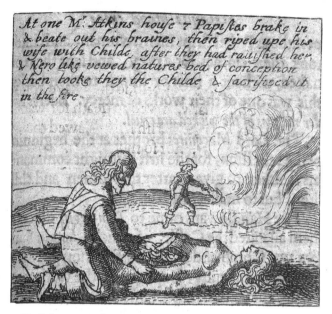

At one M.ʳ Atkins house 7 Papistes brake in & beate out his braines, then riped upe his wife with Childe, after they had ravished her, & Nero like vewed natures bed of conception then tooke they the Childe & sacrificed it in the fire.

English reports of atrocities in Ireland were wildly exaggerated

many of them had not fortified their houses or taken serious measures to protect themselves. However, although it was not in origin a religious protest, it came to be one, and was certainly seen that way in England. Forceful expropriation led to physical violence and there was at least an element of religious hostility in those attacks.[22] It is difficult to believe that the rising had no basis in real tensions between 'natives' and 'newcomers'.

Whatever the actual course of events on the ground, atrocity stories quickly began to circulate in England, both orally and in print, along with fevered rumours that the Irish were coming. *VVorse and worse nevves from Ireland* reprinted a letter read to the House of Commons on 14 December, reporting how in Munster the 'rebels':

exercising all manner of cruelties, and striving who can be most barbarously exquisite in tormenting the poor Protestants, wheresoever they come, cutting off the privy members, ears, fingers, and hands, plucking out their eyes, boiling the heads of little children before their mothers' faces, and then ripping up their mothers' bowels, stripping women naked, and standing by them being naked, whilst they are in travail [labour], killing the children as soon as they are born, ripping up their mothers' bellies as soon as they are delivered . . .[23]

And so on. The pamphlet goes on to name names, dates and places, but the modern consensus is that these pamphlets reveal more about the imaginations of the authors and readers than about events in Ireland. Although there were more measured voices, these stories offered for a receptive audience in England a manifest proof of the existence of the popish plot and the horrors to which it could give rise.

Worse still, on 4 November, Sir Phelim O'Neill published what purported to be a commission to him from the King. His purpose was to claim support for his Irish aims, by claiming to act to preserve the King from the hostility of Puritans and Parliament.[24] The impact on Charles's prospects in England could hardly have been worse. The rebellion fused with the already extant fear that Charles was either untrustworthy or in the hands of a papist plot which aimed to extinguish English liberties and to corrupt the English church. These and similar responses in Scotland persuaded the Old English that the prospects for Catholics in Ireland were dismal and in December 1641 they declared their support for the Ulster rising. O'Neill's tactics therefore triggered an unhealthy set of reactions with apocalyptic views in England and Scotland of the Irish and of Catholics. The result was to transform what was perceived to be a Catholic rising against Protestants into an actual rising of Catholics against Protestants.

Little more than two months after news of the Irish rising reached London any pretence of normal parliamentary government had collapsed. At the point when news of the rising reached London, parliamentary commissioners were in Edinburgh with the King. They were sent Additional Instructions about the necessary armed response to the Irish rebellion which could hardly have been more inflammatory. The seventh instruction attributed the great 'miseries, burdens and distempers' in the King's dominions over recent years to the 'cunning, false and malicious practices' of men close to the King's counsels. This party had been 'favourers of Popery, superstition and innovation, subverters of religion, honour and justice' and 'factors for promoting the designs' of hostile foreign powers. Not only this, but they had also sought to disrupt the relationship between the King and his parliament. Money granted by

Parliament had been spent unprofitably, or on schemes which were positively detrimental to the state, and while Parliament had laboured to purge 'corruptions' and restore 'decays' in church and state this same party had laboured to suppress the liberty of Parliament. In response to the power of this group, and the threat that it posed to Parliament and religion, Parliament had to attach strings to any money granted to deal with the Irish rising. The eighth instruction, accordingly, called for the King to change his counsels, listening to such men 'as shall be approved by his Parliament . . . that so his people may with courage and confidence undergo the charge and hazard of this war'. This was a crucial escalation from the Ten Propositions of June, which had asked the King to remove counsellors unsound on 'religion, liberty, [and] good government', and to replace them with men 'his people and parliament may have just cause to confide in'. The new demand, for active approval by Parliament of the advisers, was accompanied by a threat that made an important distinction, by citing the 'trust which we owe to the state and to those whom we represent'. That could, potentially, justify their finding another way of 'securing ourselves from such mischievous counsels and designs' and giving control of money for Ireland to 'such persons of honour and fidelity as we have cause to confide in'.[25]

On the same day, 8 November, Pym tabled what has become known as the Grand Remonstrance. A committee on the state of the kingdom had been at work on 'a remonstrance of all the present evils and griev-ances of the kingdom, to present to the King' as early as January. While Pym sought to maintain a sense of impending crisis in Westminster, it was clear by early August that it was not shared in the provinces, and the original committee of twenty-four was replaced by a committee of eight, which evidently made rapid progress. In the autumn one more meeting sufficed to add thirty-four clauses relating to the second army plot and the Irish rising. In the subsequent debates eight more clauses were added, and six were enlarged, but the Grand Remonstrance as we have it was largely the view of the world that Pym's circle had held in August.[26] The Irish rising confirmed them in their views, reinforcing the message of the plague sore about the real problem that confronted the English state.

The Grand Remonstrance elaborated on the themes of a popish plot to subvert religion and liberty, detailing specific instances from the date of Charles's accession onwards, and citing resistance to the wholesome reforms promoted during the previous year. This was done at very great length – a total of 204 individual points were made for the King's consideration. The preamble went further than the Additional Instructions by naming the actors in this plot. They were not only the 'Jesuited Papists' but also the bishops and 'corrupt part of the clergy, who cherish formality and superstition' as the best means of sustaining their own 'ecclesiastical tyranny and usurpation'. These two were joined by counsellors and courtiers who for private reasons had found it helpful to pursue the interests of hostile foreign powers. The aim of this plot was to cause differences between the King and his people over the prerogative, to suppress the purity and power of religion, to unify those most friendly to these aims and to sow division in the ranks of those most likely to oppose it, and to disaffect the King from his parliament. It was a complex phenomenon, of course, but there was a clear essence: 'As in all compounded bodies the operations are qualified according to the predominant element, so in this mixed party, the Jesuited counsels, being most active and prevailing, may easily be discovered to have had the greatest sway'.[27]

This was a remarkably provocative document intended to firm up support for further reform, and support for the King in resisting the threat of religious and political disorder. It followed on from anti-Catholic measures taken on 1 November but escalated the claims of anti-popery.[28] In effect, the Grand Remonstrance presented the King to himself as the stooge of a conspiracy dominated by Jesuitical aims, supported by corrupt churchmen and counsellors pursuing private interests. Of course, such a government could not be trusted with the prosecution of the war in Ireland and this latter point was spelt out for good measure in the accompanying petition. The malignant party, in addition to all the aims already enumerated, had sought 'the insurrection of the Papists in your kingdom of Ireland, and bloody massacre of your people'.[29] To support the war without first changing the counsels of the King would be to give money and arms to those responsible for the rebellion in the first place. Thus, although it had moderated certain key demands – in particular dropping Root and Branch reform – it did not find the middle ground.[30]

Even for those who believed all this, in every detail, it was difficult to believe that you could talk to a king this way, or at least do so with any hope of success. Looking back on it later, Clarendon remarked more on the divisiveness of this means of proceeding than on the rights and wrongs of the particular grievances:

It contained a very bitter representation of all the illegal things which had been done from the first hour of the King's coming to the crown to that minute, with all those sharp reflections which could be made upon the King himself, the Queen, and Council; and published all the unreasonable jealousies of the present government, of the introducing Popery, and all other particulars which might disturb the minds of the people, which were enough discomposed.[31]

To many contemporaries this was simply wrong in principle, but even if it was not, it was impolitic to proceed in this way since it gave the King no real option but to reject the analysis.

After a twelve-hour debate on 22 November the remonstrance was passed by the Commons by the narrowest of margins: 159–148. It was even more impolitic, and an even greater breach of decorum, to make this case and the associated demands publicly, but this too was done after an even more controversial debate. By a vote of 124–101 it was agreed that the remonstrance could be 'published' but not 'printed': that it could be circulated in manuscript copies, in other words. In the course of the debate Geoffrey Palmer had threatened to enter a protestation against the decision to publish, an intervention which nearly caused a fight and was later considered to have been intended to. The inhibition about printing lasted until 15 December, when the Commons voted by 135–83 to allow the printing of the remonstrance. These divisions reflected the growing difficulty of sustaining consensus in Parliament and the growth of open division. In going ahead without the Lords, the Commons were also, perhaps, making a point. There were significant misgivings though. As Dering put it: 'I did not dream that we should remonstrate downward, tell tales to the people, and talk of the king as a third person'. Increasingly obvious partisanship in Parliament represented a significant political change.[32]

Clearly, what gave strength to those pushing these measures forward was a belief in the imminent danger of the popish plot. Over the winter of 1641–2 politics in England was conducted against the backdrop of terrible stories from Ireland, and the fear of popery in the provinces was all too evident. Security measures taken in Parliament helped fuel rumours in Norwich, Guildford and London that papists were going to fire the town. A troop of forty armed Catholics was reported in London, and a few days later it was said another troop had arrived from Lancashire. A recusant in Buckinghamshire caused panic when he was stopped with letters that he had carried through Lancashire, Staffordshire and Warwickshire, and which he destroyed when captured. Searches of recusants' stores of arms took place in many parts of the country and mysterious movements or assemblies caused panics in Bedfordshire and Berkshire. Portsmouth was gripped with a fear that the governor was going to take the fortress, in preparation for a French or Irish invasion, and in Staffordshire, it was reported, people were so frightened by rumours of popish plots to attack them while they were defenceless in church that 'they durst not go to Church unarmed'. Rumours spread through the West Midlands in late November, from Lichfield to Ashby-de-la-Zouch, and from Kidderminster to Bridgenorth. Ludlow, Bewdley and Brampton Bryan spent the night of 19–20 November 'in very great fear'. A similar panic spread in West Riding towns early in 1642. Civic authorities in Newcastle, Hull and Berwick all appealed to Parliament for protection in late 1641, Berwick on two occasions. Panics also seized Liverpool, Conway and Beaumaris, and Lancashire towns ordered the arrest of strangers, Catholics or men riding at night. In January 1642 a skirmish took place resulting in the death of Catholics and Protestants. This was the third of five such peaks of anti-Catholic panics between 1640 and 1642, all of them related to particular political crises. It was over by the early summer, but revived again in August.[33]

This panic about popery fed, and probably fed upon, the output of the presses.[34] During the third week of November letters reporting events in Ireland had flooded into London and this gave rise to a publishing innovation: the newsbook. On 29 November, the *Heads of Severall Proceedings* appeared, published by John Thomas. The appetite for news was well-established, and had been satisfied in previous years by manuscript newsletters or 'separates'. There had been hostility to publishing Parliament's proceedings in print, and Dering had got into quite serious trouble for doing it. In fact during the Short Parliament note-taking had been banned, and, in the Long Parliament, John Rushworth was regarded with some suspicion because of his proficiency in shorthand, leading to a formal investigation.[35]

At the same time that inhibitions in Parliament were lifting, the apparatus of control was dissolving. News-related pamphleteering was peaking: Thomason had collected around sixty titles per month since the trial of Strafford, and that total now reached ninety. The publication of the Grand Remonstrance both recognized and encouraged the growth of this political world of print, by addressing 'the people' as competent judges of history and politics. At the same time, country petitions were being printed – their appeal thereby directed not just to the named recipient but to a wider political world of potential fellow travellers. The brakes were now completely off and January 1642 was the biggest month in Thomason's whole collection – 200 titles, dropping back to ninety by May. This was the spring of the 'paper war', in which fundamental political questions were canvassed before a print audience.[36]

This is the context of John Thomas's decision to publish his newsletter of parliamentary business. He had connections with Pym, who had proved himself an eager publicist over previous months, and was a prime mover behind the publication of the Grand Remonstrance. Earlier in the week Thomas had published a pamphlet reporting the Incident. What was particularly important about the *Heads of Severall Proceedings*, however, was that it was a serial. He published another the following week, and soon had numerous competitors. The boom lasted until March 1643, when Parliament successfully enforced licensing.[37] By that time a series of long-term newsbook titles accounted for half of Thomason's collection – clearly the newsbook eroded the market for the one-off political pamphlet.[38]

An immediate implication of this was an increase in the supply of news. During the 1630s the services of professional letter writers seem to have cost around £20 p.a. The Earl of Bridgewater seems to have paid something like this to John Castle in return for perhaps three letters every two weeks.[39] A little over a year later 1d bought 5,000 words of news each week; for his £20 Bridgewater could have had 4,800 titles (more than ninety each week). More important than the potential banquet that this provided for Bridgewater was that readers who could not possibly have enjoyed the services of a newsletter writer could, for less than one ninetieth of the price, have a weekly newsletter which was fuller, and not necessarily less well-informed, than that of a professional letter writer of the 1630s. Increasing the supply of information is not, of course, a guaranteed way to foster clear understanding, and many readers may have felt that they enjoyed fewer certainties as a result of this news revolution. John Castle had been scrupulous about identifying and weighing sources, advertising particular reports as 'likely to be true', distinguishing between rumour, report and news in complex ways. Nonetheless, Bridgewater was unsure what to believe: 'the various reports of the news of this time be such that no great credit be to be given to the rumours spread abroad'.[40] Newsbook writers were evidently aware of this difficulty and quickly came to proclaim their bona fides on their title pages: *The kingdomes weekly intelligencer: sent abroad to prevent mis-information; Mercurius Civicus; Londons Intelligencer as truth impartially related from thence to the Kingdome to prevent mis-information; The moderate: impartially communicating Martial affaires to the Kingdom;* or the *Mercurius anti-mercurius,* which claimed to be 'Communicating all humours, conditions, forgeries and lies of mydas eared newsmongers'.

There are some suggestive connections here. The pamphlet about the plague sore had been printed for 'W.B.', possibly the bookseller William Bowden, who was active in these months. Bowden is known to have published a number of tracts recounting stories of Catholic plotting and in December he published a number of pamphlets retailing the atrocities of the Irish rebels. John Thomas's pamphlet about the Incident used the same woodcut as W.B.'s pamphlet about the plague sore. Like Bowden, Thomas was also active in publishing pamphlets about the atrocities carried out by Irish Catholics. It may be that this reflects a network of printers and booksellers working hard to promote awareness of the popish plot and the image of Pym as the main bulwark against its

John Pym portrayed in the forefront of the battle against popish conspiracies

success.[41] It is clear that the plague sore and the Irish rising were useful to Pym and he may actually have used them.

Fear about the popish plot fed on uncertainty about events, an uncertainty that in turn fed rumour and anxiety. These issues were reaching out beyond Parliament; perceptions of local events were coloured by these larger anxieties while at the same time reports of these events fuelled the crisis of confidence that lay at the heart of the failure of the political process. Pamphlets sold by their covers – the titles are actually abstracts which sell the book from the shelves of the stalls. What publishers and authors put on the covers probably reflected their sense of the market and it may therefore be significant that in 1641 'plot' and 'conspiracy' were unusually prominent terms.[42] Excluding official publications and newsbooks, the impression is quite dramatic: in November 1641 Thomason collected eighty-eight pamphlets, of which nine had 'plot' in the title, two more promised discussion of 'conspiracies', and others discussed 'bloody plots' and 'bloody attempts'.[43] An increased supply of information did not in this case solve the central political difficulty of uncertainty and the problem of establishing trust, but it greatly amplified rumours. In March it was reported that 154,000 settlers had been killed (the real number may have been nearer 4,000)[44] and some estimates went as high as 200,000.[45] And, to reiterate, this Catholic rising was said to have enjoyed the support of the English king.

Fear of the popish plot was driving political action beyond the bounds of decency and was reciprocally related to the growing publicity given to political discussions. This produced a polarization of political opinion, however, not simply a drift of opinion to Parliament. By the time that the Grand Remonstrance had been passed Charles was back in London. His progress southwards from Scotland was marked by conspicuous displays of loyalty, and his entry into London on 26 November was the occasion for another lavish display. This was a deliberate political manoeuvre of course: Charles had not previously indulged in a formal entry into his capital city, a lack that has struck subsequent commentators as significant by comparison with the greeting accorded to the Puritan martyrs the previous year.[46] The King was, of course, the essential element of any settlement, and this interest in public political theatre surely rested on that knowledge.

On entering London, Charles was 'brought in with a *Hosanna* at one end of Town, [but] he found a *Crucifige* at the other', wrote James Howell a short time later. In the light of the controversy over the Grand

Remonstrance and the warmth of his own reception in the City, Charles cannot be blamed for thinking that his opponents in England might now have gone too far and that this division of opinion could play in his favour. In any case, Charles could hardly be expected to concede to the demands of the Grand Remonstrance, given the public analysis on which those demands were apparently based. Thus, while he was feted in the City, the 'Remonstrance framed' in Westminster could expect 'but cold entertainment with His Majesty'.[47]

Charles, by emphasizing the threat of Puritan populism, played to a resurgent royalism based on a concern to preserve political and religious decencies. Acknowledging the petition and the 'declaration of a very unusual kind attached thereunto', his answer first objected to the publication of the petition and remonstrance. He would have hoped for a chance to answer but this decision robbed him of the time to consider his response. He had also hoped that their own 'reason' and regard to the King would have dissuaded them from proceeding in this way, or at least that his express view that they should not would have restrained them. He was, he said, 'very sensible of the disrespect' that it implied. Beyond these concerns about the integrity of the political process, he naturally rejected the history presented in the petition and remonstrance, and promised to consider the proposals in a 'parliamentary way', although his answer sounded dubious about all the principal proposals – removing the bishops' votes in the House of Lords, alienating control of his choice of counsellors and giving undertakings about Irish lands before the war was even fought. It was significant, perhaps, that the answer said that Charles was in search of support for the 'royal estate', in contrast to their concern for the state and those they represented. But the key issue was that Charles could plausibly suggest that he was the safeguard of parliamentary courses, rather than these populist hotheads and, perhaps, that their views of the interests of the state were corrosive of the royal estate.[48]

If Charles was harsh on popularity he was also stringent on Puritans, without using either term. On 10 December he issued his own declaration on religion, which largely echoed the Lords declaration of 16 January, calling for worship according to the laws of the realm, and for severe action against those who undermined that worship: 'the present division, separation and disorder about the worship and service of God, as it is established by the laws and statutes of this kingdom . . .

tends to great distraction and confusion, and may endanger the sub-version of the very essence and substance of true religion'.[49] An attack on a conventicle in the City on 19 December shows that crowds could be mobilized against sectaries as well as against bishops.[50] In a sense this was a battle for the middle ground. The Grand Remonstrance had accused papists of driving a wedge through Protestantism and here was the counter-charge – that Puritans were splintering and weakening the practice of the true religion. In the coming years it was partly on these grounds that radical Protestant sects were to be accused of popery.[51]

The passage of the Grand Remonstrance was a pivotal moment in English politics in several ways. It crystallized a conflict between the popish plot and the fear of Puritan populism; those promoting concern at the machinations of Jesuits, their allies and dupes were appealing out-wards, confirming fears about populism and making it increasingly dif-ficult to secure concessions which left the dignity of the crown intact. There was a widening gap between the rhetoric of the two sides: Thomas May (writing in 1647) thought that it was at this point that 'ordinary discourse' became polarized.[52] The constitutional implications of the remedies proposed by the Grand Remonstrance further confirmed that political demands had escalated uncomfortably. For those actively engaged in national politics, it would be difficult to get out of this not simply because the claims being made were so likely to be rejected, but because the way that political negotiation was being conducted was dangerous in itself. Many who felt Parliament had right on its side on religion, foreign policy and the prerogative might well come to feel that the greater threat to political well-being was posed by democracy or anarchy.

Above all, this was a triumph for coalition-building on the basis of fear rather than hope. There had been a drift of opinion towards the King over the summer, and at the heart of this revival of Pym's fortunes were fear and distrust; and in particular the impossibility of trusting the King and his advisers. Simonds D'Ewes noted in his diary during this tense autumn that 'The logicians say that the final cause is the first in intention though it be the last in execution: and so here let us but look to the ultimate end of all those conspiracies and we shall find them to be to subvert the truth'.[53] Extravagant anti-popery was combined with conscious popular appeal, and this found echoes on the streets and in the counties. Much of the appeal of the Grand Remonstrance lay in the purchase of anti-popery, which was greatly increased in the wake of the Incident and the Irish rising, and the burgeoning print market escalated the uncertainty in more than one way. It also began to justify increasingly direct attacks on the Queen's freedom of worship.

Pushing through the Grand Remonstrance, however, and moving against the Queen in this way, came close to over-bearing the weight that could be sustained by anti-popery and the King was not in an isolated political position in taking a strong line against it. If conspiracy theorists could see in the demands of the Irish leaders the machinations of the popish plot, others could see in the Additional Instructions and the Grand Remonstrance the clear imprint of Puritan populism. The polarized opinion manifest at the heart of government was manifest too in the counties, where the Prayer Book petitioning campaigns were taking off. With the benefit of hindsight it is possible to see that this was good news for the King: there had been no such polarization when Parliament had assembled in November 1640.

Politics in London were also becoming more polarized. The triumphant entry of the King had rejuvenated street politics, and in late November and December it was calls for further reform that dominated. In Common Council elections in late November the balance of power shifted towards those promoting reformation, and this was associated with constitutional change in the City and in many vestries.[54] A second Root and Branch petition was presented on 11 December to mark the anniversary of the first one. In the final days of December crowds thronged around Westminster demanding a response, and seeking the exclusion of the bishops and popish lords from the House of Lords while the future of episcopacy was being discussed. They were also confronted by Colonel Lunsford, a clash which revealed the currency of two stereotypes of enormous significance for the future. Lunsford's men were referred to as 'Cavaliers' while the apprentices were derided as 'Roundheads': party affiliations were becoming visible among the populace at large. Demands for Lunsford's removal from command of the Tower of London became another rallying point, and one of constitutional significance.[55] Violence was barely constrained and increasingly partisan, and there can be little doubt that these disturbances affected parliamentary business.

Charles now embarked on a high-risk strategy, against this background of increasingly unruly politics in London, and fear that his wife (who was increasingly openly attacked as the heart of Catholic influence at court) was becoming the target of the kind of campaign that had killed Strafford. On 4 January 1642 he entered Parliament with a body of armed men in search of five members of the Commons and one of the Lords whom he had identified as the principal architects of his troubles.[56] He had intended to try them for treason on seven counts: attempting the subversion of the laws of the kingdom and depriving the King of his regal power; attempting to alienate the people from their King; attempting to draw the army from its obedience to the King; inviting and encouraging a foreign power (Scotland) to invade; attempting to subvert the right 'and the very being of Parliaments'; in order to do this, attempting 'by force and terror to compel the Parliament to join with them in their traitorous designs, and to that end have actually raised and countenanced tumults against the King and Parliament'; and conspiring to levy, and actually levying, war against the King.[57] This was not perhaps as unprovoked as is sometimes implied: it followed immediately after an accusation of treason against twelve bishops. Nehemiah Wallington certainly seemed to appreciate the significance of the juxtaposition, giving the running heads to these pages of his notebook 'xii bishops charged with treason justly' and 'Six worthy members of the house charged with treason unjustly'.[58]

The attempt on the Five Members was a bold move, which would certainly have broken the deadlock, but it is difficult to see it as anything other than politically foolish, although the charges were no more extravagant than those laid at Charles's door by the Grand Remonstrance. There is evidence of co-ordination between Pym's circle and the Scots prior to the invasion of 1640, and of Pym's connection with the incitement and countenancing of tumults.[59] Of course, the worst outcome was to suffer the outrage without bagging the targets. Famously, when Charles arrived the birds had flown, forewarned that something was up. This ensured that the coup was a failure, and left the Commons free to express its unrestrained outrage at this invasion of its privileges. The declaration 'touching a late breach of their privileges' made no bones that the King had come to Parliament with 'many soldiers, Papists and others, to the number of about five hundred'.[60]

On the following day Charles went into the City to demand that the members be handed over but this visit revealed the extent to which he had lost control of his capital. Common Council men elected in

November had taken their seats early, and the City was already in the hands of men with whom Charles was unlikely to want to deal. The meeting became disorderly, as cries of 'Parliament, privileges of Parliament!' mingled with cries of 'God bless the King!' Charles withdrew, but as he did so the outer hall rang with the cries of assembled citizens, 'Privileges of Parliament!' Such was the hostility on the streets of London that, on 10 January, Charles left his capital.[61] As has often been noted, Charles was not to return until he himself was tried for treason in 1649.

Parliament had adjourned its sitting on the grounds that it was not safe at Westminster. On 11 January its sitting was resumed. Having left town the previous day Charles was spared the sight of a triumphant return of the Parliament men, the accused members among them. It was

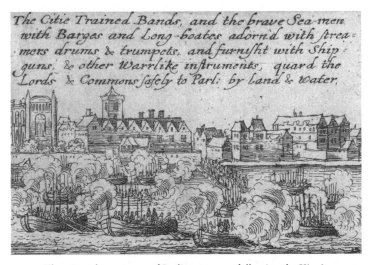

The triumphant return of Parliament men following the King's departure from London

an orchestrated demonstration of support for Parliament, marked by banners and streamers, celebratory volleys and a flotilla on the Thames. Shouts against bishops and popish lords were heard and, along with copies of Parliament's condemnation of the breach of its privileges, copies of the Protestation were prominent – fixed to the tops of pikes and sticks or on muskets, worn in hats, pinned to coats or attached to banners. A copy of the Protestation had also been thrown into the

King's coach on his retreat from the Guildhall. The message was clear: Parliament was the guardian of the Protestant faith: its privileges and the true religion stood together.[62]

If the English response to the Covenanters' invasion in 1640 had disappointed the King, the response to the Irish rising must have come as a blow to the solar plexus. The question of whether the King could be trusted with an army to put down the rising was immediately at the forefront of English politics. Even if this doubt was groundless, of course, it did not make it any more likely that the King would seek to conciliate it. Both sides played on commonly held fears, rhetorical exchanges heated up and an increasingly polarized political argument spilled out onto the streets, into the presses and out into the counties. The high hopes expressed in *A description of the famous kingdome of Macaria* had not held the centre of political debate; fear was triumphing over hope. Indeed, 1641 had become the year of plots – fears of popish plots in rural England fed on the revelation of actual plots in London. Two army plots, the attempt on the Five Members and the Incident, the revelation of Strafford's plans for the Irish army – all this created a political atmosphere in which trust was at a premium. But it was not all on one side – on 5 January 1642 an associate of one of the constables of the Tower had claimed that Pym and the others accused of treason 'did carry two faces under one hood' and that Puritans, not papists, were at the root of the current trouble.[63] The vastly increased output of pamphlets and then newspapers did little to lower the temperature either. If titles are a guide to what publishers thought would sell, it is clear that they saw a large market in this uncertainty.

These panicky politics had led to political escalation. Parliament was no longer acting as a consensual body, but was increasingly partisan. Members were actively courting public opinion and were certainly not trying particularly hard to put an end to street politics. Executive powers were being claimed too: in the fevered last weeks of December, Parliament had called out military forces on its own authority, and the Common Council of the City of London had formed a Committee of Safety with similarly questionable powers. Most importantly of all, the King had removed himself from London. In that sense, and many others, parliamentary politics in England had collapsed; the nation's ills were no longer being addressed by the King-in-Parliament.

6

Paper Combats

The Battle for the Provinces

Parliament had failed as a forum in which to express and reconcile
political differences and could not hope to enjoy that function again
until the King returned, along with those members who now defected.[1]
A recurring theme of subsequent negotiations was to find terms on
which the King could return to London, a necessary preliminary to the
resumption of this role. In the spring of 1642, however, parliamentary
politics as they were normally understood had broken down, but there
was no alternative way forward. As a consequence emerging royalist
and parliamentarian parties battled for control of the language of constitutional moderation and of provincial institutions, appealing to wider
publics and mobilizing support for their favoured projects and
platforms.

In the immediate aftermath of the attempt on the Five Members the
political temperature was very high. The arsenal assembled for the
Scottish wars was in Hull and the King made a preliminary attempt to
take control of it by issuing the Earl of Newcastle with a commission as
governor of the town. Parliament hastily empowered Sir John Hotham
to secure the arsenal in the name of King and Parliament, and a hasty
journey up the Great North Road thwarted the royal plan. On
12 January, Colonel Lunsford assembled some of his Cavaliers at Kingston, where the Surrey arsenal was kept. There they met Lord George
Digby, sent over from Hampton Court, and it was assumed that the
plan was to arm enough men to secure Portsmouth for the King. When
the King moved from the palace at Hampton Court to the castle at
Windsor, on 13 January, it was easy to believe the worst, and there were
rumours of wagons of arms heading for Windsor in the days afterwards.[2]
On 15 January men of strong convictions in the Commons, including

Oliver Cromwell, called for the creation of a committee to put the kingdom into a posture of defence and on 18 January that committee proposed that the militia should be mobilized by the authority of a parliamentary ordinance – that is, without the King's assent. This was an issue of unmistakable constitutional significance, and one which forced many allegiances later in the summer. The previous day, prompted by Pym, a Committee of the Whole House requested the dismissal of the King's entire Privy Council, to be replaced by men appointed with the advice of the Houses. The Attorney General was impeached for agreeing to issue the charges against the Five Members and on 20 January the Commons ordered that a printed letter be sent to the sheriffs in all counties requiring all adult males to swear the Protestation.[3]

Taken together these were remarkably provocative measures. Parliament would have taken control of the militia and of whom the King should take as advisers, and was at the same time appealing directly to the people as the defenders of the Church of England. The use of ordinances (legislation passed on the authority of Parliament but without royal consent) seemed also to threaten fundamental constitutional principles. It was certainly a ticklish issue. No-one argued that Parliament could legislate alone: statutes required the royal assent. Parliament, however, could be said to be serving as a Great Council to the monarch, akin to the Privy Council. Just as the King could make proclamations in the absence of a parliament, so long as they did not make new law, so the Privy Council could issue executive orders in the King's absence. Now, it was claimed, Parliament acting as the King's Great Council could make such orders. While the King had been in Scotland the previous August, Parliament had passed five ordinances with this logic, and the constitutional principle does not appear to have caused outrage even though the fifth order, for disarming recusants, arguably went beyond existing law.[4] On the other hand, this constitutional device coincided with more aggressive claims for Commons influence over policy, and this political issue did cause dissent – resentment against the growing pretensions of 'King Pym', the programme suggested by the Ten Propositions and the Commons order of 8 September for the purification of the churches.[5] The proposals put forward in the fevered aftermath of the attempt on the Five Members accelerated this process. In the Lords there was considerable disquiet about these developments, and active opposition to the national imposition of the Protestation.[6]

These measures were taken against a background of continuing crowd activity in London and a renewed round of county petitioning strengthened Pym's hand: on 25 January he personally delivered four massive county petitions to the Lords, throwing the weight of the Commons behind their demands (among which were the removal of bishops and popish lords from the upper House). Some London petitions were now making a connection between the failure to reach a political settlement and the decay of trade, and between January and March eleven counties and six towns petitioned Parliament on this issue. Clothworkers in Essex, Suffolk and the West Riding were among those who made this connection, and with some justification. Fearing forced loans and debasement of the coinage in the summer of 1641 many merchants had avoided tying up their capital in stocks of cloth. This, in turn, meant that work in clothing districts dried up and these conditions apparently persisted through the winter. In Essex, at least, this sectional economic interest fused with anti-Catholicism and popular parliamentarianism. In London, the slump led to the intervention of 'poor labouring men, known by the name of porters, the lowest members of the City of London'.[7]

On 31 January, for the first time in this crisis, a petition was presented by women, specifically 'many poor and distressed women in and about London'. To some extent these petitioners stayed within the bounds of the public role afforded to women by claiming that because of the slump they could not feed their families. Women had an established role in this sense, and were frequently prominent in food riots for this reason: as the family members most involved in the food market it was they who were most aware of corruption and exploitation within it. Petitioning on behalf of their families, and in these terms, avoided any challenge to the patriarchal assumptions governing political participation. But this posture could not conceal the fact that these women were making direct political interventions in a less than deferential way. Like the clothworkers and porters they attributed the slump to the political crisis, arguing that a popish plot existed to plunge England into a war, once Ireland had been overrun. This line of argument led to the extraordinary spectacle of poor women attending the Houses demanding that the kingdom be put in a posture of defence, that popish lords and bishops should be excluded from the House of Lords and that those who were hindering reformation should be identified and punished. The following day, 400 women attended the Houses for an answer and became involved in a scuffle with the Earl of Lennox. 'Away with these women, we were best to have a parliament of women,' he apparently said, only to have his staff broken as they tried to block his path. Philip Skippon, who was guarding the House, was told that for every woman there today there would be 500 the following day, since they might as well die there as at home, and they had also apparently threatened to bring their children to starve at the door of the Lords rather than watch them die at home. Lennox and Lord Keeper Littleton were both mobbed by a crowd of women and porters when they left that evening.[8]

In response to the provocations of Parliament's measures, and against the background of these developments in crowd politics, Charles adopted a surprisingly conciliatory tone. He had gone to Windsor on 13 January partly in fear for his safety, since it was rumoured that 1,000 citizens were on their way to Hampton Court with a petition. At Windsor he kept a rather thin and depressing court, which can have done little for his morale.[9] On 20 January he wrote to the Houses in fairly emollient terms, acknowledging 'the manifold distractions which are now in this Kingdom which cannot but bring great inconveniency and mischiefs to this whole government'. Accordingly he asked the Houses to consider what was necessary 'for the upholding and maintaining of His Majesty's just and regal authority, and for the settling of his revenue, as for the present and future establishment of their privileges, the free and quiet enjoying of their estates and fortunes, the liberty of their persons, and security of the true religion now professed in the Church of England, and the settling of the ceremonies in such a manner as may take away all just offence'. He hoped that, digested into a single document, this would provide the basis for progress, and disavowed 'intending or designing any of those things, which the too great fears and jealousies of some persons seem to apprehend'.[10]

This restrained public response was probably a reflection of his desire to get his wife safely across the Channel. Whatever its motives, it did not satisfy the more radical spirits in Parliament. On 20 January the Commons had received a petition from Colchester which was hostile to the Prayer Book and a move to refuse to give thanks for the petition was overruled. The following day, in a debate about a forthcoming declaration of their position, the Commons voted in favour of a clause arguing that the ills of the kingdom were due to the want of reformation of church government and the shortcomings of the liturgy. When the Protestation had been passed the previous spring it had silently excluded a commitment to defend the discipline of the Church of England. Now the Commons were actively refusing to defend the Book of Common Prayer. Meanwhile, John Hampden called for parliamentary control of military strongpoints, including the Tower.[11]

Such developments had often been obstructed by the House of Lords over the previous fifteen months. But there was a committed core of activists who fought for, indeed sought to lead, the cause during the 1640s in co-operation with fellow travellers in the Commons. Their effectiveness in the Lords was increased by the defection of those who had restrained them.[12] In early February Charles gave fourteen peers leave to absent themselves from the House, some of whom joined him. Others took the opportunity to leave the House: on 9 February sixty-seven Lords were absent and attendances in both Houses fell further during the early spring.[13]

This exodus allowed the passage of the Bishops Exclusion Bill and the Impressment Bill in early February. Most provocatively of all, the reduced House immediately welcomed the proposed Militia Ordinance when it was presented on 15 February. The ordinance suggested that the King was being misled by the counsels of papists and other ill-affected persons and that as a result, in this time of imminent danger, Parliament should take over the King's military authority, appointing dependable men as lieutenants and deputy lieutenants. As a practical political measure this is easy enough to understand, given what many people thought they knew about Charles. As a constitutional issue this was outrageous: what kind of king was it who did not control the military resources of the realm?

Throughout this period Charles held fire, agreeing to the Bishops Exclusion Bill and the Impressment Bill, dropping the charges against the Five Members and agreeing to place the command of the Tower of London in the hands of Sir John Conyers. Even in this mood, however, the Militia Ordinance was impossible for him to accept, but he signalled this only with a fairly moderate prevarication. By the time Henrietta Maria was safely embarked, on 23 February, Charles had made spectacular concessions, and London's streets were quiet once again. Pym pressed on, however, securing the passage of the Militia Ordinance on 5 March.[14]

*

These measures were hardly likely to be seen as solutions to ills of the kingdom – parliamentary government as it was normally understood had collapsed. An important reason for this political failure was the way in which political argument had spilled out beyond the walls – in the mobilization of opinion in petitions, demonstrations and printed polemics. Following the breakdown of parliamentary government this process was virtually unrestrained. From March onwards battle was joined for the hearts, minds and military resources of provincial England.

After Henrietta Maria's departure Charles had returned to Greenwich where, despite the wishes of Parliament, he met up with his eldest son. While he was there he finally responded to the Militia Ordinance, in strongly negative terms. This rejection led to a further escalation of the constitutional terms of the conflict. An important argument in justification of the ordinance was that there was a state of emergency manifest in the various military threats to Parliament. Tackling this emergency required Parliament to have control of defensive military forces and, in the absence of the King, that could only be achieved by an ordinance. This was, in other words, presented as an executive measure rather than a new law. When the King rejected the measure, according to this line of argument, it confirmed the emergency and the absence of the King. As Simonds D'Ewes, a member with a keen eye for legal matters, wrote: 'if the king should be desperate and lay violent hands upon himself [we] must not only advise but wrest the weapon, so too if he should seize the helm of a ship in a storm and threaten to drown them all, only one course of action was possible'.[15]

With affairs in this posture, the King began a leisurely progress to York, taking eighteen days for a journey that was possible much more quickly. En route he was warmly received in Cambridge and enjoyed a day of hunting at Little Gidding, but his reception at York was disappointing. In the meantime he had exchanged declarations with his parliamentary critics. In these exchanges his absence, the nature of the emergency and the extraordinary political and constitutional postures adopted by Parliament were all debated at length and in historical detail. Both parties sought to attribute blame for the breakdown of the political process to the other party in an exchange that has been likened to a marital dispute – a series of mutual recriminations rather than an attempt to resolve the dispute, almost incomprehensible in its detail to non-participants.[16] But it was also intended for public consumption: to extend

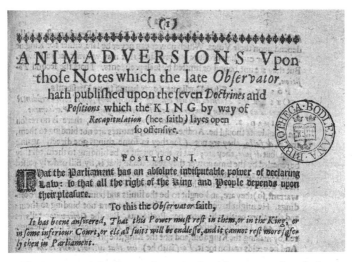

The 'paper war': fundamental constitutional issues argued out before
a print audience

the analogy, it was communication in the form 'tell your father that he's the one who is jeopardizing the constitution'.

These mutual recriminations were aimed at a print audience, and were intended to recruit allies as much as to resolve differences. Proclamations, petitions, ballads, pamphlets and scandalous verse brought the issues of this paper war to the provincial middling sort. Letters accompanied pamphlets sent down to the country, fuelling tavern conversation that was engaged, irreverent and often satirical. The response could be informed and critical, as in Colchester, where Stephen Lewes was disgruntled at the suppression of royal propaganda: 'why should not we know the King's mind as well as the parliament's mind?'[17]

Behind these public and widely discussed exchanges, a parliamentary constitutional theory was taking shape: claims for the rights of subjects to exercise key restraints over the powers of their monarch. The argument for the executive powers of Parliament as the Great Council of the kingdom solidified – the King's absence was said to be part of the crisis which necessitated the emergency measure (an argument which duly infuriated the royalists). By the early summer Parliament had staked out political territory which could only be justified by these arguments with a dose of goodwill and a following wind. A key issue in these exchanges was the King's 'Negative Voice'. To become law, a bill had to pass both Houses and then receive the royal assent. This effectively gave the monarch a veto – a Negative Voice which allowed him to stop legislation which had been passed by both Houses (hence, for example, the slight delay in securing Strafford's death). According to the Great Council argument now being made, the use of the Negative Voice could necessitate an ordinance. Where the King was not willing to assent to necessary measures the Houses had to act in his absence.[18] This, of course, implied something very profound about the relative powers of King and Parliament, and their relationship to the good of the kingdom. Charles was upholding his right to withhold consent, arguing that without that power he was no longer a king in a meaningful sense. In that, surely, he must have had a lot of support, and there were few who would have drawn the conclusion that England would therefore be better off without a king. Advocates of Parliament's position, on the other hand, seemed to be suggesting that the King was answerable to his advisers' sense of what was good for the kingdom – if something was unacceptable to them then the King could not insist upon it.[19]

Throughout the life of this parliament there had been a tendency for political difficulties with Charles to lead to constitutional resolutions affecting all kings. Control of the militia was accelerating this process, and leading to startling claims. Even though the sternest opponents of these measures were now likely to be absent from the Houses, it took considerable political skill on Pym's part to maintain the momentum, and to carry increasingly radical policies despite the qualms of many more moderate spirits.[20] In his public declarations Charles was guided by moderate, constitutional royalists, like Edward Hyde, later the Earl of Clarendon, who aimed to undercut the political and constitutional radicalism of Parliament's position. An opponent of abuses of the prerogative, he supported episcopacy and the Church of England, but without an insistence on enforcing ceremonial issues that were 'indifferent'. His trajectory from the 'opposition' of 1640 to royalism in 1642 is fairly clear, and similar to that of others. By the summer of 1641 Hyde had been working informally to achieve a full settlement in co-operation with Sir John Colepeper and Lucius Cary, Viscount Falkland, the latter two parliamentary critics of the Personal Rule who, as defenders of the rule of law and religious decency, drew back as the measures of reform pressed further. Together they co-ordinated court attempts to influence the Commons in late 1641 and were widely suspected of being the authors of Charles's propaganda. On concrete policy, however, Charles seems to have been heavily reliant on the forthright advice of Henrietta Maria, who had consistently counselled him to settle matters by force, foreign force if necessary. Disappointed by the rather lukewarm reception in York, Charles decided on two inflammatory courses of action – to go to Ireland personally to settle the political conflict there, and to wrest control of the arsenal in Hull from Sir John Hotham. Both suggestions were provocative in a situation where the King was thought to be in the hands of an armed papistical conspiracy, and was known previously to have considered bringing Irish forces into England in order to exert a bit of discipline on his behalf.[21]

The journey to Ireland did not materialize, but the attempt on Hull did, and it resulted in one of the most famous confrontations of the decade. The King's second son, the Duke of York, and Charles's brother-in-law, the Elector Palatine, had visited Hull on 22 April and been well entertained, but when the King made the journey there in person the following day the reception was much cooler. Four miles from town he sent ahead a letter saying that he had come to inspect the arsenal and that if his request was refused he would make his way into town 'according to the laws of the land'. Forewarned Hotham decided to stick by his orders from Parliament. Aware that around forty-five strangers had arrived the previous day in the train of the princes, and that the King was accompanied by 300 horsemen, he shut the gates of the town and sent a message ahead to the King telling him 'with all humble submissions' that he would not break his trust to Parliament. In the rain, outside the walls, Charles's supporters called on the garrison to kill Hotham and throw his body over the wall, but they did not; and Hotham refused Charles's request to enter with just twenty of his men. Charles called on the heralds to proclaim Hotham a traitor, and rode away. He had given such ample notice of his arrival that it is hard to believe that he simply wanted to take control of the arsenal – arriving unannounced he would almost certainly have been able to do it. It seems likely that this was intended to be the symbolic moment that it subsequently became – demonstrating that Hotham was in rebellion against his king.[22]

Hotham's position had not been an enviable one. His defence against the charge of rebellion rested on a well-established (though now rather incredible) line of argument. In January, when Parliament had sent him to take control of Hull, the order had been not to deliver it without 'the King's authority signified unto him by the Lords and Commons now assembled in Parliament'. The King, and some Members of Parliament, could not believe that this stretched to refusing entry to the King himself, and he rather cleverly put Hotham in the position of arguing that it did. The justification was that the authority of the King was separate from his physical body, that his authority could be present where his private person was not. For example, when a judge gave a judgement in court, it was considered to be the King's judgement, underpinned by royal authority, even if the King did not agree with it. The argument went, therefore, that Parliament could express itself with the King's authority in ways with which the King as an individual disagreed. All very clever, but rather cleverly nailed by Charles in a subsequent proclamation: 'these persons have gone about subtly to distinguish betwixt our person and our authority, as if, because our authority may be where our person is not, that therefore our person may be where our authority is not'. For him the case was clear – these people were in open rebellion against him.[23]

Although he scored a fundamental political point, Charles had lost the arsenal. He had also by this time lost Portsmouth, the other great provincial arsenal, and the navy. After his initial departure from London in January it seems fairly clear that Charles was manoeuvring to take control of Portsmouth but it was for the time being under the command of George Goring on behalf of Parliament.[24] Parliamentary attempts to influence the choice of naval commanders had been going on since 1640. In March 1642 the Lord High Admiral, Lord Northumberland, declared himself too unwell to go to sea and was persuaded by the House of Lords to nominate the Earl of Warwick in his stead. Warwick's naval credentials were good, but his political and religious views persuaded the King to resist this nomination. He sought instead to secure the appointment of Sir John Pennington, a man who had commanded the fleet since 1639. Parliament launched an investigation of his conduct as a means of subverting this appointment, and persuaded Northumberland to confirm Warwick's appointment on 4 April. The King, faced with a fait accompli, even failed to accept by way of consolation the appointment of Sir George Carteret, a man trusted by him, as vice-admiral. The military effects of this were soon to be felt, for Warwick, acting under Parliament's orders, had sent warships to lie in the Humber before the King's confrontation with Hotham. Their presence there had strengthened Hotham's position, of course, and in May the fleet brought the arms to London. Having ignored direct orders from the King the commanders of the fleet were thanked for their fidelity by the House of Lords. The military benefits of parliamentary command of the navy were significant in the coming years.[25]

In the aftermath of these events the constitutional struggle and attendant pamphlet war reached new heights. In this round of argument the intention seems even more clearly to have been to appeal for support rather than to achieve reconciliation.[26] On 5 May, Parliament ordered that the Militia Ordinance be put into execution, provoking an immediate printed answer from the King and, on 27 May, a formal proclamation against the ordinance and those who obeyed it. On 6 May a parliamentary declaration had put the Great Council argument particularly pungently:

The High Court of Parliament is not only a court of judicature, enabled by the laws to adjudge and determine the rights and liberties of the kingdom, against such patents and grants of His Majesty as are prejudicial thereunto . . . but is likewise a council, to provide for the necessities, prevent the imminent dangers, and preserve the public peace and safety of the kingdom, and to declare the King's pleasure in those things as are requisite thereunto; and what they do herein hath the stamp of the royal authority, although His Majesty, seduced by evil counsel, do in his own person oppose or interrupt the same; for the King's supreme and royal pleasure is exercised and declared by this High Court of law and council, after a more eminent and obligatory manner than it can be by personal act or resolution of his own.[27]

Invited by people within the royal camp to state its terms for settlement, Parliament produced the Nineteen Propositions on 1 June. Here the claims of Parliament to an executive role were unmistakable and prompted a further round of escalation in the constitutional argument. Accepted as a whole they would have made Parliament the sovereign power. Parliament would have had the power to approve who the King chose as councillors, officials and judges. Following the implementation of the Militia Ordinance, the disbandment of the King's personal forces, and the placing of fortresses in the hands of men approved by Parliament, parliamentary control of military resources would have been complete. Parliament demanded that the church be reformed and governed according to Parliament's wishes and that no peers created subsequently would have been allowed to sit without the consent of both Houses. It also sought to dictate the King's foreign policy. These were demands which would have permanently shifted the constitutional position of Parliament. There were also other demands relating to the education of the King's children and the arrangement of their marriages, the enforcement of the recusancy laws, and the punishment of delinquents.[28] Distrust of this particular king had led Parliament into proposing a constitutional revolution; this radicalism and the public insult to the King could hardly be plainer.

The King's *Answer to the XIX Propositions* stated the royalist position in terms of established and respectable political theory. It was drafted by Falkland and Colepeper, who took their stand on the law. Parliament's propositions, they said, were an attempt to remove a 'troublesome rub' from their path – that is, the law of the land, which was the birthright of every Englishman. To accept the propositions would have overthrown not just personal monarchy but also a mixed monarchy, in which the authority of the crown and Parliament were combined. Authority lay with the King-in-Parliament – the King was a part of Parliament, and could not simply be dictated to by the other constituent parts. They also gave a commitment to remove illegal innovations that had crept into the church – a commitment to the preservation of the Reformation within the law which implied again the importance of the law in the regulation of political and religious life. The argument about the estates of the realm had a very respectable lineage, but there was room for disagreement here. Hyde held to the view that the three estates of the realm were the Commons, the Lords spiritual (the bishops) and the Lords temporal (the peers). He felt that Colepeper and Falkland had conceded too much in taking the (equally venerable) line that the King was one of the three estates – making him an equal partner, rather than the King over the three estates. In effect, however, they had mounted a defence of a limited monarch, something that had been taken for granted in 1640.[29] Indeed, Colepeper had been a vociferous petitioner in the opening days of the Long Parliament, in defence of the lawful government of the country, and now found himself the spokesman for moderate royalism on the eve of a civil war.

In response to the *Answer*, Henry Parker, something of a veteran pamphleteer and controversialist, published his *Observations on some of His Majesties Late Answers and Expresses*. This broke new ground in a number of ways. Unperturbed by the royalists' claim to be the defenders of the constitution, he pushed ahead, spelling out very clearly the implications of the recent declarations and demands. In an emergency which threatened the state the King was obliged to follow Parliament's advice. Parliament was the state itself, with a sovereign power of its own, capable of addressing dangers by legislative, executive or judicial means. Its advice was crucial to supplying the defects of monarchy and if the King did not follow it then the ultimate moving force of all human laws – individual self-preservation and the good of the people (*salus populi*) – justified the Lords and Commons in acting without him.[30] Even more daringly, he argued that the King's Negative Voice rendered all Englishmen slaves. It was based on an argument about freedom which can be traced before 1642 in parliamentary speeches and elsewhere, not least in the controversy over the Petition of Right. To be free, it was said, it was necessary not only to be able to exercise all your rights and freedoms in practice; you also needed to be free, in principle, from any *possible* constraint. This was because fear of censure or hope of reward would act as a bridle or a spur, distorting your actions as a free man and rendering you, in effect, the creature of another. This was used as an argument in favour of the Bishops Exclusion Bill in January – they should not sit in the House of Lords since their position depended on the King, and they were not, therefore, free to exercise their rights and liberties as free men. Parker now yoked it to the controversy about the Negative Voice, the existence of which rendered all Englishmen 'slaves', since it was a continual potential limit on the exercise of their rights and liberties.[31]

But was Parker speaking for anyone but himself? It is significant here that Parker was probably also involved in drafting two declarations of May which had flirted with these ideas and his argument about slavery. Parker was secretary to the Committee of Safety established in the summer of 1642, and clearly had a role in drafting many of its papers and letters. From July onwards the committee also had a primary role in drafting declarations and, although Pym was the most prominent member of the committee, it is unlikely that an experienced polemicist like Parker was there only to take dictation.[32] Parker's argument about slavery was taken up in other pamphlets later in the summer – among them a pamphlet called *Reasons why this Kingdom ought to adhere to the Parliament*. This has plausibly been shown to have been published by presses run by George Bishop and Robert White, who evidently had a line in radical parliamentary publications. Even more intriguingly, they seem to have had connections with Pym and with William Walwyn, the later Leveller. Pym may have been complicit in floating these arguments but, at the point where a very significant line was crossed, the views were expressed as private opinion, not as the official parliamentary line. Instead they appeared as the private opinion of polemicists like Parker or anonymously, as in the case of *Reasons* (which bore the name of neither author nor publisher).[33]

If it is true that Pym was to some degree complicit in this ideological radicalization, seeking either to fly kites or to soften up the public with a clever manipulation of the press, it bears testimony to an increasingly complicated relationship between politicians and the press.[34] For example, the publication of parliamentary speeches seems to have been both commonplace and a breach of a longstanding inhibition on publicizing the deliberations of Parliament.[35] Nonetheless, from very early in the Long Parliament speeches had been printed, and there were also, from very early on, publications purporting to be speeches which were clearly fictitious – because the supposed speaker had not spoken in the relevant debate or was no longer even a member of the House. Even this did not automatically cause offence, however. Many of John Pym's printed speeches seem to have been fabrications, for example: an observation that both cuts him down to size a little, while at the same time inflating his importance as a figurehead for influential views.[36] But on occasion what was said, or who said it, or the timing, clearly did cause offence and on those occasions sanctions were imposed which might have seemed to some to have been inconsistent.

Sir Edward Dering offers an instructive case. It was he who famously objected to the printing of the Grand Remonstrance: 'I did not dream that we should remonstrate downward, tell tales to the people, and talk of the king as a third person'. The experience of these debates was an important moment in his 'defection' from the parliamentary cause. He had himself been chair of a committee dealing with ministers' grievances and charged with the licensing of books – he made an early speech complaining about the licensing of crypto-popish books. He had also seen many of his speeches in print, or circulating in manuscript copies, however. On 16 January 1642, at the height of the security scare following the attempt on the Five Members, a collection of his speeches appeared. Styled as moderate, they were highly inflammatory, and very critical of the more radical positions being taken by Parliament. But his parliamentary colleagues were most offended by the irreverent tone, and the public display of this dirty linen (sentiments not unlike his own reaction to the publication of the Grand Remonstrance). This offended against the view that free speech depended on civility, freedom from public opprobrium and, therefore, secrecy. On 2 February the collection was condemned by the Commons and ordered to be burned by the public hangman. Dering himself was expelled from the House and sent to the Tower, where he remained until discharged on his own petition on 11 February.[37] The spectacle of politicians appearing on all sides of these questions about the propriety of publication invited satire. John Taylor, one of the most prolific satirists of the period, for example, published a pamphlet (under the anagrammatic pseudonym Thorny Ailo) which promised on its title page that it was based on shorthand notes taken at a sermon.[38]

Such a public breakdown of government by the King-in-Parliament was bound to resonate more widely and the snowstorm of official and semi-official declarations was part of a larger paper war. Thomason acquired more pamphlets per month in this period than during any other: an average of 165 titles each month, with peaks of 200 in January and 231 in August.[39] Much of the output consisted of the official statements of the two sides, published speeches or news items, but there was clearly a much wider mobilization of opinion. This was manifest too in petitions and battles for control of local institutions, and in this mobilization there was a concerted attempt to harness existing metaphors and images to fit the current situation. The issues which seemed irreconcilable in national institutions were represented differently in local situations, but this was clearly a crisis which affected all levels of English government.

In the paper war between Parliament and the King secular issues were at the cutting edge of the conflict. But the motor behind the radical constitutional position, and the grounds on which Parliament's cause often seemed to rest, was the defence of the true religion.[40] This was certainly prominent on both sides of the conflict in the larger pamphlet campaign. Anti-popery, of course, played well for those who had remained in Parliament. In the light of what were seen as recurrent attempts to use force to overawe the guardians of the true religion – the two army plots, the Incident and the attempt on the Five Members – popery could now be seen as an active military threat. This was not new, but was newly urgent, and gained a further impetus from the Irish rebellion. Anti-popery as a polemical argument for further reformation was fused with this more restricted and dangerous form of anti-popery attached to a specific Catholic threat. It served to mobilize opinion in support of radical constitutional as well as religious positions.

Ireland was a dominant presence in print: in October 15 per cent of the tracts collected by Thomason were concerned with Ireland, rising to 22 and 28 per cent in the following two months. Between January and June 1642 nearly 23 per cent of the collection concerns Ireland, with peaks of one third or more of the total in February and April. In this massive print output stories of Catholic atrocities were clearly exaggerated, and the authors and publishers of those accounts were men with an agenda close to that championed by Pym. An important strand of writing related these atrocities directly to a strong tradition in English Protestantism celebrating the sufferings of true believers, and some passages apparently describing contemporary atrocities seem to have been lifted almost directly from Foxe's 'Book of Martyrs'.[41]

They had detractors in the presses, willing to denounce the 'many fabulous pamphlets that are set out concerning the rebels in Ireland of their outrages and bloody proceedings', and which identified this episode with a history of the evils of rebellion rather than of Protestant sufferings. But these brave voices were shouting into a strong wind. By late 1641 fears of an Irish invasion were alive in England and Wales, along with the (groundless) fear that recusants would join forces with them.[42] In January, John Thomas, likely associate of Pym and inventor of the newsbook, published 'a true relation' of a bloody popish plot in Derbyshire, an attempt to blow up the parish church of Bingley, which must have been intended for this audience.[43] The title page is larded with promises of details: names, dates and places, as well as a full inventory of a store of arms seized from a Catholic recusant. This plain factual reporting countered the charge of exaggeration, but the pamphlet had a clear and partisan political implication. Thomas Needham, a prominent local recusant of substantial means, employed John Simonds to place thirty-four barrels of gunpowder, faggots, old iron and stones in the vault of the church, with the intention of blowing it up during divine

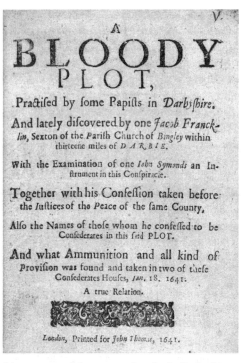

A

BLOODY
PLOT,

Practifed by fome Papifts in *Darbyfhire*,

And lately difcovered by one *Jacob Franck-lin*, Sexton of the Parifh Church of *Bingley* within thirteene miles of *DARBIE*.

With the Examination of one *John Symonds* an Inftrument in this Confpiracie.

Together with his Confeffion taken before the Iuftices of the Peace of the fame County,

Alfo the Names of thofe whom he confeffed to be Confederates in this faid PLOT.

And what Ammunition and all kind of Provifion was found and taken in two of thefe Confederates Houfes, *Jan.* 18. 1641.

A true Relation.

London, Printed for *John Thomas,* 1641.

The pamphlet account of the gunpowder plot in Derbyshire, which was probably fictitious, despite the assurances on the title page

service, 'when the church was filled with a full number of parishioners'. God's providence averted the catastrophe, however, when Jacob Francklin, the sexton, arrived at the church to toll the 'passing bell' for a parishioner who was gravely ill. Hearing noises in the vault he investigated and disaster was averted. Following investigations by the local magistrates a search of Needham's house revealed a stock of arms, enough to set out at least one hundred men for war.[44] The pamphlet is written with a little style – the narrative is dramatically recounted – but there are some printing errors, so it may have been a rushed production. Given what else we know about Thomas's publishing, it seems likely that revelation of this store of arms was intended to support the case for the radical security measures promoted in the Commons during January: it was on 18 January that a parliamentary committee had proposed the

Militia Ordinance and, a couple of days later, that John Hampden had called for parliamentary control of strongpoints, including the Tower.[45]

This was also a story to be understood in the light of previous Catholic plots, of course: the resonances with the Gunpowder Plot are strong in general and in the details (Fawkes and his associates had used thirty-six barrels of powder, along with faggots and other materials), and placed this story in a longer history of providential deliveries from Catholic plots. It was this general lesson which was, ostensibly, the main concern of the pamphlet: 'This kingdom hath had too frequent experience of their mischievous intentions and plots, which had the all-seeing eye of Heaven not prevented, we would long ago been brought to utter ruin and destruction'. Like the plague sore of the previous autumn, the inhumanity of the plot revealed the corruption of the beliefs from which it sprang. Providential delivery bore testimony to God's favour, and to the persistent blindness of Catholics to His purposes. Their resilience in the face of constant frustration was thus evidence of a more fundamental error: 'Mischief, the child of heresy, cannot want instruments to prosecute and bring it to perfection, and the devil, who is the author of all unlawful attempts is always ready at hand to further and set forward any dissensions, and damnable enterprises'.[46]

Anti-popery was not necessarily about Catholics – it was a language with which to denounce the danger of all threats to the Reformation. In the past, it had been possible to distinguish between the threat of popery and the more acceptable presence of Catholic recusants and it is well attested that practical local toleration of Catholics existed alongside a keen awareness of the threat of popery in the abstract.[47] In these fraught political circumstances, however, these distinctions were in danger of breaking down. Pym and others had conflated popery with Catholic conspiracy for months, but the Irish rebellion and the year of plots gave this line of argument its maximum appeal. Many parts of the country experienced Catholic scares during these months, fuelled by knowledge that violence in Ireland was extending widely in January and February.[48] There is some evidence that it began to erode the practical toleration of recusants in provincial England, and in August anti-Catholic scares were to give way in Essex to attacks on the houses of Catholics.[49] This atmosphere was also bad for the prospects of those Catholic priests unfortunate enough to be arrested. Seven priests were arrested and executed in the aftermath of the Irish rising. Two of them, a Benedictine called Alban Roe and an ageing secular priest, Father Thomas Greene, met their ends at Tyburn in late January, and on 22 March further executions followed. This was despite, or perhaps because of, the King's record in securing reprieves for Catholic priests. Such deaths were gleefully reported in pamphlets, of course. Arthur Browne, a seminary priest, was condemned at Dorchester assizes on 16 August, and his public recantation was reported for the edification of a wider audience in London nine days later. Hugh Green, condemned at the same assizes, met a grotesque end, which reportedly culminated in a game of football using his severed head.[50]

This heady mix of anti-papistical writing seems to have underpinned mobilizations across most of the country in support for the emerging parliamentary position. In the aftermath of the attempt on the Five Members, a number of county petitions were submitted, co-ordinating provincial concerns about the future of Protestantism with the defence of parliamentary liberties. In fact, between December 1641 and May 1642, thirty-seven of England's forty counties petitioned Parliament, along with a number of Welsh counties and boroughs. Some counties petitioned more than once, and Westmorland added its petition to the pile in August. The contents of these petitions suggest that those promoting Pym's position were more successful at mobilizing provincial opinion than those with alternative visions. Most concentrated on anti-popery, evil counsellors, preaching and scandalous ministers, the decay of trade and the militia. Rather than talk of confrontation they tended to set out terms for an accommodation; but of course to urge accommodation was to urge that someone shift their position, and that often entailed taking a position on the national debate.[51] Many of these petitions, of course, were printed, suggesting that these 'county' postures were intended as contributions to the wider debate.[52]

National subscription to the Protestation was not uncontroversial, but it was very successful – so successful in fact that the extant returns are one of the most complete English population listings for the seventeenth century. The Protestation had already become a token of allegiance and now 11,000 copies were printed to be circulated with a letter expressly tying the defence of English Protestantism to the defence of parliamentary liberties. Subscription was required as a sign of 'good concurrence with the Parliament' and was more urgent than ever because of the discovery of 'many dangerous designs plotted against Parliament'.

Parliament required the names of refusers as well as of subscribers, and many local returns obliged, with explanations for refusals or absences. Although the clearly partisan nature of this national subscription prompted new debate about the propriety of subscription, and many took the subscription with some mental reservation or explicit limitation, there is ample local evidence of widespread subscription and of the great pains that were taken to achieve that. On the other hand, the evidence of the reservations with which people might subscribe suggests that some could still separate subscription from a partisan parliamentarianism.[53]

Anti-popery was a powerful means to mobilize opinion in favour of Parliament's actions, and it was promoted in the press, petitions and the Protestation campaign. It also involved the institutions of local government in partisan politics. Given the wide purchase of the call to defend English Protestantism it is not surprising that proto-royalists did not tackle anti-popery. Instead, they played on fears about religious and political order. For example, those who expressed more restrained views of the Irish rebellion did not distance themselves from anti-popery, but did place greater emphasis on the evils of disorder and rebellion.[54] This concern for order resonated more widely. As we have seen, religious debate could now be expressed in terms of a choice between totems: the Protestation and the Prayer Book. The Commons vote of 21 January, which attributed the ills of the kingdom to the want of good reformation in church government and liturgy, had lent official weight to attacks on the Prayer Book, and reinforced attempts to rally to its support.[55]

Standard metaphors and literary forms were put to service in this mobilization too – God's judgements were detected in the misfortunes of sectarians as well as popish plotters. One such was Richard Stichberry, churchwarden in Towcester in Northamptonshire, whose punishments were reported in a pamphlet of June 1642. He had broken a stained-glass window, 'fairly painted', leaving 'God's house so miserable mangled and torn, which ought to be used with an holy respect'. The patron of the church refused to make good the damage, insisting instead that those who had done it make the repair. God could not see such sins unpunished and within two days of the iconoclasm Stichberry's wife 'was exceedingly tormented on a sudden in her limbs, raging and crying most fearfully with the extreme anguish and pain she did endure, that she could not rest till such time as the violence thereof brought her to her last end'.

Stichberry himself suffered an agonizing death shortly afterwards, 'raving' in such a way that five or six men could not control him, 'howling and making a noise until he died'. Stichberry's sister, Anne, had made scorn of the Prayer Book for the previous 'two years': in other words, more or less since the failure of the Short Parliament. She too was punished when she tore her Prayer Book out of a volume in which it was bound up with her Bible. God dealt harshly with this 'poor silly creature'. Her hands began to rot 'in a most strange manner . . . the flesh flying from the bones: and so continues to this present, rotting in a most fearful and loathsome manner'. Something of a local attraction, large crowds of onlookers came to see her, and 'being so extreme loathsome' she had been moved a mile out of town by her neighbours. The lesson was clear, that it was rash to attempt anything against sacred places, or to 'vilify those things which have any part of holy Writ in them'. It was clearly unwise to attempt to alter anything in church, or about the Prayer Book established by 'Authority' until Parliament should determine otherwise. To that end the pamphlet reproduced the Lords order of 16 January 1641 calling for worship to be performed according to the statutes currently in force.[56]

This pamphlet invested a local event with cosmic significance and used it to underline the importance of order in worship, and of legitimate authority in achieving religious change. It also offered God's special providence as a source of authority in uncertain times.[57] Another, published by Richard Harper later in the summer, told of the punishment of those who resisted harmless ceremonies on the basis of ignorant zeal.[58] Mary Wilmore, wife of John Wilmore, a rough mason in Mears Ashby (Northants.), had become concerned about the religious rituals that attended a birth while expecting a baby. In particular, she was concerned about the use of the sign of the cross during baptism, a ritual moment subject to some criticism in these months. In Essex, attacks on the practice, like attacks on the Prayer Book and the use of surplices, had been justified with reference to the Protestation and the obligation it imposed on people to resist popery.[59] Mary persuaded her husband to visit one Master Barnard, a 'reverend Divine' in the village of Hardwick, not far away. Barnard's answer was a learned and moderate one: the use of the sign of the cross 'was in no ways necessary to salvation, but an ancient, laudable and decent ceremony of the Church of England'. On hearing this verdict Mary apparently declared that 'I had rather my child should be born without a head than to have a head to be signed with the sign of the Cross'. Tragically, this wish was granted, and she gave birth to a child with no head and a sign of the cross on its chest.[60]

According to the author, John Locke, cleric, the responsibility for this tragedy lay either in Mary's 'weakness' or in her 'too much confiding in the conventicling Sectaries', whose claims that the practice was a 'pernicious, popish and idolatrous ceremony' were refuted with scriptural citations. The judgement was set in the context of the fate of Julian the apostate, who pissed on the altar in Antioch to demonstrate his belief that 'Divine providence took no care of outward ceremonies'. His punishment was 'a disease that rotted his bowels [so that] his excrements leaving their wonted course, ran through his throat and blasphemous mouth in as stinking a manner as the poisoned trash and beggarly rudiments are fomented nowadays from the impudent mouths of unlearned and ignorant Teachers'. The fruits of their 'pernicious and illiterate doctrine' were exemplified in the terrible fate of Mary's child, which reflected 'God's wrath and judgments to over curious and nice zealots of our times'. Locke's own learning was evident not just in his command of scripture, and his knowing awareness of the danger of pursuing 'unprofitable questions' in public disputations, but in the Latin phrases which pepper the text.[61]

Religious contention in Northamptonshire was not restricted to pamphlet wars. On 28 June a party of volunteers raised for Parliament entered the village of Isham and destroyed its cross. This led to a charge of riot, prosecuted by Thomas Jenison, a neighbouring Justice. But the two men most likely to judge the case at a special sessions called to consider the matter were also likely to sympathize with the iconoclasm, and the commander of the troop was himself a JP. On 6 July, Jenison went to Wellingborough and found Puritan JPs at lunch in the Hind, after the regular lecture, discussing the incident. Their conclusion was that it was not a riot and that he was interfering unnecessarily. A heated argument ensued but the matter was eventually brought before a special sessions on 11 July. There the men were found guilty, but not without problems. The foreman of the jury had apparently disheartened the jury, and as they withdrew to consider their verdict one of the presiding magistrates, Mr Sawyer, lectured them about the superstitious nature of crosses, citing the Commons order of 8 September 1641 as justification for the action of the volunteers. This led to an argument between Jenison and Sawyer in which Jenison accused him of seeking to pervert the jury. The Commons order had mentioned crucifixes not crosses, but Isham Cross was not the last victim of this zeal.[62]

Defence of the liturgy in pamphlets like those describing the torments of Stichberry and the Wilmores supported a programme of order based around the dignity of the clergy, learned divinity, and a nuanced approach to the authority of scripture and tradition in liturgical matters. The zeal of the humble, Puritan scriptural preciseness and public contestation were in this view not means to promote reformation, but a threat to the faith. Again, this seems to represent a modulation and radicalization of longer-standing polemics. Since the reign of Elizabeth at least there had been an anti-Puritan polemic, which had often focused on the hypocrisy and self-love of Puritans. Starting with the line of anti-sectarian writing in the autumn of 1641, however, anti-Puritanism seemed to concentrate almost exclusively on the question of order, the dangers of schism and the folly of unlearned preachers.[63]

This anti-Puritanism was not necessarily the same as support for Laudianism, but it was certainly beginning to play better for the royalists than for Parliament. It was reflected, for example, in Ludlow, on 1 May, where a maypole was adorned with the head of a Roundhead and pelted with stones. Puritan excess in suppressing communal festivities was harnessed to attacks on Parliament's partisans. Wallington noted, alongside 'God's judgements on them that set up the cursed maypole', judgements on 'mockers especially that new reproachful name ... Round heads'.[64] At Croft images were shot at 'in derision of roundheads' and a 'Roundhead sermon' in Hereford Cathedral was silenced. It was a term now juxtaposed to loyalty and constitutional royalism and it began to erode deference to the godly elite. Lady Brilliana Harvey wrote to her husband in June 1642 that:

They are grown exceeding rude in these parts. Every Thursday some of Ludlow, as they go through the town, wish all the puritans of Brampton [the home of the Harleys] hanged, and as I was walking one day in the garden ... they looked upon me and wished all the puritans and Roundheads at Brampton hanged.[65]

Another sign of irreverence is in the spread of the nickname King Pym. It apparently arose from the publication of an order of the House of Commons in a form resembling that of a royal publication, appearing over the name of John Pym.[66] It became a means of ridiculing the presumption of the parliamentary leadership. On 15 March 1642 the Commons sent for Mr Shawbery, who was reported by two witnesses as having said in the Spread Eagle in Gracechurch Street 'That he would cut [Pym's] throat, and his sinews in pieces', and referring to him as 'King Pym, and Rascal'. Another witness reported him as saying that 'he could find in his heart to cut King Pym in pieces'.[67]

It was in these months that Prayer Book petitioning was widespread. These campaigns were clearly partisan, related to local mobilizations against parliamentary radicalism.[68] The best known was that in Kent. At the assizes on 25 March, Sir Edward Dering, the disgraced MP, successfully engineered a confrontation with a rival Puritan and parliamentary faction, associated with Sir Anthony Weldon and Sir Michael Livesey. As chairman of the Grand Jury, Dering managed to steer through the assizes, after three drafts, a petition in defence of the existing liturgy and church government, and against sectarianism. The Grand Jury had been empanelled by Justice Malet rather than the sheriff, and was clearly managed, but even so nine members of the jury disowned it. One of the grounds for speaking against it was that it contradicted petitions previously sent up – clearly a tactical argument but one that arose from the increasingly partisan use of institutions previously understood to serve as the 'voice of the county'. These struggles were revisited at quarter sessions in Maidstone in April, and at the summer assizes in July. The Commons sent a committee to sit on the bench at the summer assizes, but this was resented by those on the bench legally, and there was even some jostling as they tried to take their seats and their colleagues failed to make room for them. At another point rival groups 'hummed' each other as they tried to speak. Henry Oxinden complained that 'I have heard foul language and desperate quarrellings even between old and entire friends'. This partisan struggle was very public too: it was said that 2,000 people witnessed the reading of the petition on 25 March.[69]

In these partisan battles standard metaphors – such as providence or natural wonders – were deployed with precise partisan purposes, and some of the staple elements of local life – the history of Protestant sufferings or the Prayer Book – became invested with partisan meaning. Newsbooks inhabited this same world of polemic and were often produced by men with a record of contentious pamphleteering and a line in other kinds of writing: Richard Harper was soon to launch an apparently very successful line in prophecy pamphlets, having published 'pleasant histories' during the 1630s. John Thomas and Bernard Alsop, both associated with newsbooks and publication of parliamentary news, had also been up before Parliament for publishing scandalous pamphlets.[70] Unsurprisingly, therefore, news stories were often explicitly intended as moral or religious exempla. Nathaniel Butter, better known to posterity as a newspaper pioneer, published a number of wonder pamphlets, including the story of a giant toad fish caught at Woolwich and displayed at Glove Alley in London in 1642. Its appearance was attested by many witnesses, among them gentlemen, and that it meant something was attested by classical sources including Pliny and Josephus as well as more contemporary examples: large fish coming ashore had meant, throughout history, trouble for reigning monarchs. 'These unnatural accidents though dumb, do notwithstanding speak the supernatural intentions and purposes of the Divine powers, chiefly when they meet just at that time when distractions, jars, and distempers are afoot in a Common-weale or Kingdom'. 'It is further observed by those that profess skill in prognostication, that of how much the monster is of feature or fashion, hateful and odious, so much it portends danger the more dreadful and universal'. Appended to the story is news of a more conventional kind – a skirmish outside Hull.[71] News was partisan and reports of human and natural events were of equal value in coming to terms with the times.

But this literature too was open to satire. In January 1642 a marine monster was reported to have appeared to six sailors near the mouth of the Thames. The monster 'was very terrible; having broad fiery eyes, hair black and curled, his breast armed with shining scales, so that by the reflection of the sun they became so blind and dazzled, that he might have taken or slain every man of them, he having a musket in one hand, and a large paper in the other hand, which seemed to them a petition'. Able to travel at miraculous speeds he left the sailors to observe the French fleet on its way to Catalonia, returning within minutes with news of it. In discussion with the amazed sailors the monster emphasized to them the dangers faced by the kingdom, a clear warning about the consequences of divisions. Appended was a report of a minor victory in Ireland, a providence of God and an encouragement to the Protestants. The six sailors were named, and the story was said to have been taken down by a gentleman – a contemporary code for the reliability of the testimony. The names of the witnesses, however, suggest a satirical intent.[72] Perhaps the point was to make fun of the influence of rumour on menacing petitioners. In January fear of the crowd was certainly vying with fear of armed Catholic conspiracy. In any case, this subverted more than just the use of monsters to tell political tales, since a plain, factual style was in itself a persuasive technique. The bloody plot in Derbyshire was reported with the full apparatus of sober reporting, for a clearly identifiable political purpose but in the hope that it would be inoculated against the charges of fantasy and exaggeration being levelled against some of the pamphlets about the Irish rebellion. There does not seem to have been a parish called Bingley, though, and there is no independent evidence of the existence of this plot. This was not uncommon: in such publications 'moral verisimilitude' was as important as 'circumstantial accuracy'.[73] But at this juncture such ambiguities made it even more difficult to know not only what to believe, but also whom to believe.

A substantial number of pamphlets sought to expound the fundamental issues using the common metaphors of political life, but in these increasingly polarized political conditions their meaning was elusive. For example, an important metaphor for contemporaries in understanding political relationships, and dysfunctions within them, was that of the body politic. Over the summer of 1640 the court had been afflicted by disease, as had the Earl of Strafford. In August, after this summer of disease, uncertainty and discontent, John Castle prayed for his patron's 'safety and health in these valetudinous times, when all is sick and ill at ease'.[74] Where did the sickness lie? In Parliament, following the revelation of the Irish rising and the suspicion that it was prompted from above, Pym had said 'diseases which proceed from the inward parts, as the liver, the heart or the brains, the more noble parts, it is a hard thing to apply cure to such diseases'.[75] In December, William Montagu wrote to his father that 'sects in the body and factions in the head are dangerous diseases and do desperately threaten the dissolution of a well governed estate'.[76] A shared language did not enable the resolution of the conflict, but it might be a means to express it. Thomas Knyvett wrote to his wife on 31 May 1642 about the paper war, expressing his frustration that both sides claimed to be seeking the maintenance of the laws: 'the question is not so much how to be governed by them, as who shall be master and judge of them'. 'A lamentable condition', he continued:

to consume the wealth and treasure of such a kingdom, perhaps the blood too, upon a few nice wilful quibbles. Out of these prints you may feel how the pulse of the King and kingdom beats, both highly distempered, and if God doth not please to raise up skilful physicians that may apply lenatives and cooling Julips, phlebotomy [blood letting] will be a desperate cure to abate this heat.[77]

Provincial opinion was not leading events, but it is certainly clear that the issues being thrashed out in Parliament and at court resonated powerfully in the localities. Local conflicts were interpreted in the light of much larger, even apocalyptic issues, and as such were represented in print for the edification of a non-local audience. Standard metaphors and forms of explanation were appropriated to the highly unusual conditions of incipient civil war. Providence, wonders and signs were good to think with. These pamphlets were being published into a market, and intersected with attempts to mobilize provincial opinion via press and pulpit or to take control of local institutions like the militia or law courts. Anti-Puritan and anti-Catholic pamphlets clearly resonated in local panics and controversies. By refining political differences into polemical positions, and soliciting support for these positions among wider publics, print had helped to corrode normal political processes. Events were over-interpreted in a febrile atmosphere, in which passions were inflamed, animosities were stoked up in print, and plots were detected everywhere.

7

Raising Forces

The Slide into War

Speaking in July 1642, in the course of a Commons debate about whether Parliament should raise an army in its own defence, Bulstrode Whitelocke reflected on how Parliament had

insensibly slipped into this beginning of a civil war by one unexpected accident after another, as waves of the sea which have brought us thus far; and we scarce know how, but from paper combats by declarations, remonstrances, protestations, votes, messages, answers and replies we are now come to the question of raising forces.[1]

As fear drove partisanship beyond the bounds of accepted convention, institutions of local government became sites of partisan conflict: institutions intended to give voice to the local community, and to represent and reproduce its social order, became the focus for explicit political conflict. Like Parliament these institutions were no longer acting as the embodiment of an organic political community and for some people resistance to this process became the primary concern, overriding the issues which had spilled out of Parliament. Such men forged neutrality agreements, seeking to protect county government from the spirits and afflictions which had eroded parliamentary government. But they did not succeed: there were always activists who could see religious and political debates clearly, and were willing to subvert political decencies in order to defend their corner. As this battle for military control of the provinces got under way, local people were able, or were forced, to take sides. Not only were national political issues of the most fundamental concern now being discussed before the public, but ordinary people were making active choices based on their understanding of the issues.

*

Central to this was a slow-motion battle for military resources, justified as a necessary security measure. In January measures to take control of stores of arms and strongpoints and to disarm papists had been easily carried. This had been followed by the Militia Ordinance, eventually passed on 5 March. In early June, as musters began to take place under its authority and following the exchanges over the Nineteen Propositions, the King issued Commissions of Array so that in the late summer local communities were choosing not just whether to obey an ordinance for the militia, but whether to obey it in preference to a commission from the King. The Commissions of Array were also more warlike than simply implementing the muster, allowing individuals to raise troops under their command.

A further key escalation came on 12 July. Parliament voted to raise an army, and appointed the Earl of Essex its general – this was also going beyond taking control of the musters. A failure as a courtier, Essex had significant military experience (like his father the Elizabethan traitor); in fact there was no aristocrat of his rank who could match it. He was an assiduous parliamentarian, often associated with anti-court positions, and a man with an acute sense of personal honour, who felt his political disappointments keenly. When Charles raised forces Essex's military experience had initially suggested that he would be second-in-command, but he lost out to Henrietta Maria's favourite, the Earl of Holland. By 1640 he was almost certainly in sympathetic contact with the Covenanters, and with John Pym was fully involved in the petition of the twelve peers calling for a parliament and presented to Charles on the day the armies clashed at Newburn. He was, in short, one of a number of leading aristocratic figures with a record of resistance to Charles's misgovernment, and the one with the most impressive military experience.[2]

It was at the point of Essex's commission to lead the army that, Whitelocke felt, through paper combats Englishmen had brought themselves to a real clash of arms. By then there had been a tussle over the command of the navy, in March, with the outcome confirmed in a further argument in late June. In early August the Commons accepted a declaration of the case for arms which claimed that the King had started a war and declared that those who assisted him were guilty of treason. On 22 August the King raised his standard at Nottingham, summoning his loyal subjects to join him in fighting Essex's rebellion, and declaring Essex a traitor.[3]

Mobilization was leading to polarization: the dispute about military resources meant that confused political discussion had to be resolved in concrete, and simple, choices. In particular the controversy over the Militia Ordinance produced clear statements of constitutional theory, some of them quite novel and of lasting significance, probably for the very reason that it was the moment at which a painful choice became necessary. In the process, the local role of the militia and other governing institutions was transformed.

Parliament's attempt to take control of the militia was significant to every town and village in England, and was a struggle for a much larger prize. There had been some jostling over the King's attempt to raise a lifeguard in late May, and there was some flapping in Parliament about an assembly of Yorkshire gentry called by the King on Heyworth Moor on 3 June. Whatever the King intended there, he found the gentry sympathetic but not particularly warlike. Parliament responded with measures to prevent the movement of arms, to enforce the Militia Ordinance in Leicestershire, Lincolnshire and Cheshire, and to raise money by loans – the Propositions. To the King, not unreasonably, these things looked like aggressive moves and he responded, on 12 June, by beginning to issue Commissions of Array. The commissions, issued in Latin under the Great Seal, were directed to each county and major borough, naming those whom the King expected to raise troops on his behalf. The instrument rested on an unrepealed statute of Henry IV and had been obsolete since 1557. It was, therefore, something of a legal anachronism, and there was some suspicion that the use of Latin served to bedazzle the unlettered. Commissions were accompanied by a letter detailing how to proceed which was tailored to local circumstances, and a signed warrant for a muster, with the time and place left blank.[4]

The existence of these rival authorities posed a potentially agonizing choice for those who received demands for compliance with both commands and raised questions about the legality of the use of local arms for these purposes. Thomas Knyvett described vividly how on receipt of his commission under the Militia Ordinance he had avoided argument and said that he needed time to think about it. Only a few hours later he received the declaration 'point blank against it by the King'. His obedience to Parliament was limited from thenceforward by his concern to ensure that it 'trenches not upon my obedience against the King'. In similar circumstances Henry Oxinden complained that he was caught between Scylla and Charybdis.[5]

At the same time Charles began a fairly concerted attempt to tune quarter sessions and assizes. These bodies, and the Grand Juries within them, had played a key role in many petitioning campaigns, and the Kentish petition of the summer of 1642 had been mobilized in part by virtue of sound management of the assizes.[6] Starting two days before the first Commissions of Array, surely not coincidentally, a series of changes were made in the Commissions of the Peace around the country. Between 10 June and 7 August 177 men were purged from fourteen county benches, and 154 added. These changes were quite clearly politically motivated – all of the Deputy Lieutenants named in the Militia Ordinance for Northamptonshire were dismissed from their office as JP, for example, and the bench in Monmouthshire was packed with dependants of the Earl of Worcester, who was very reliable from Charles's point of view. Parliament took this seriously enough to appoint a commission to investigate on 23 August, but the King had achieved another coup which rather limited its effectiveness. In mid-May the Lord Keeper had sent the Great Seal to York and followed himself a few days later, giving the King control of the issue of Commissions of the Peace. The practical effect of these moves is hard to gauge: it caused complaint from a Grand Jury of Hampshire, and from other local officers, and there are few correlations between purged counties and those which successfully implemented Commissions of Array.[7] Perhaps the interference was counter-productive: it was certainly a manifestation of the same process that was causing disquiet across the country.

On 4 August the King sent an open letter to the assize judges, setting out four key elements of his position and calling on Grand Juries to petition in response, so long as it was 'in a humble and fitting way'. Charles proclaimed a commitment to the defence of Protestantism from the threats of both popery and sectarianism; a determination to govern by law and not arbitrarily; to uphold the privileges of Parliament and the honour of the crown.[8] The Grand Jury in Worcester seems to have obliged, more or less parroting the letter. They declared a commitment:

to defend and maintain the true protestant religion, by law established, against popish recusants, Anabaptists, and all other separatists. And that the laws of the land shall be the rule of his Majesty's government, whereby the Subject's liberty and property is defended: And that his Majesty will preserve the freedom, and just privilege of parliament.[9]

The gap between this language and that of the proto-Parliamentarians was not very great. For example, earlier in the summer the knights, gentry and freeholders of Lincolnshire had declared themselves willing:

> to spend our lives and estates, in defence of his Majesty's person, the true Protestant religion, the peace of the realm, the maintenance of the rights and privileges of Parliament, the law of the land, and the lawful liberty of the subject according to our late Protestation against all such as shall attempt to separate his Majesty from his great and faithful counsel of parliament.

Many would presumably have signed up for both, or all, positions, but were increasingly unable to. However, one key issue in distinguishing the positions was trust of the King: in Worcester they declared that 'we do not any way distrust His Majesty's constancy in these resolutions'. While it was difficult to say that you did not trust the King, it was possible to say, as they had in Lincoln, that they were concerned about 'the malicious practice of a malignant party, labouring to breed jealousies between the King and his People'. Once again, significantly, these local resolutions were published and became part of the national public debate.[10]

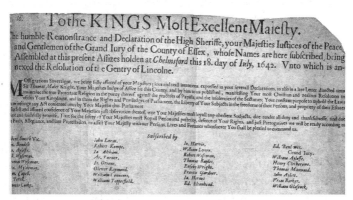

Declarations and resolutions of local bodies broadcast to a national audience

Grand Juries, Commissions of the Peace and the assizes, like the militias, were being drawn into partisan political conflicts. Declarations in court about political propriety might do much to advance or hinder the battle for local forces. Parliament responded to the King's assize letter by asking the judges to read the Commons order declaring the Commission of Array to be illegal. Most contemporary observers felt that Parliament had come off worse in this particular exchange, and in Worcester and Cornwall the subsequent successful implementation of the commission was attributed in part to the attitude of the assizes.[11]

The launch of the Commission of Array was a prelude to open tussles over control of local militias. Muster under the authority of the Militia Ordinance had started in May, and gathered pace in June. By the middle of July fourteen English counties had put the ordinance into effect, although in Cheshire and Lancashire it had proved so divisive that the process was never completed. Although much depended on firm action by Lords Lieutenant and MPs, in the counties where it was most effective this seems to have reflected genuine support. Volunteers proved easy to find in many places and at musters in some places further petitioning campaigns were launched.[12] In these cases a defensive muster, against a danger perceived to be very real, provides something of a contrast with the atmosphere at musters for the Bishops' Wars.

By mid-July, however, implementation of the Militia Ordinance represented not just obedience to a parliamentary order of dubious legality, but a failure to turn out for the King's Commission of Array. From August another nine counties saw musters under the authority of the ordinance, the last two in September and October.[13] Ten English counties saw attempts to implement the Commission of Array, too, but in Cheshire and Lancashire this was very divisive, and in a further twelve counties the attempt collapsed because strongpoints had already been taken, or because of local antipathy. In Leicestershire and Warwickshire, both counties that had seen the Militia Ordinance implemented early, there was a fierce contest later in the summer.[14]

Alongside these rival mustering campaigns ran an intensified struggle over the control of other military resources. The King attempted decisive action on the navy in June. The Earl of Northumberland, who had named Warwick his deputy in defiance of the King's preference for Sir John Pennington, was now dismissed. At the same time the King informed Warwick that his authority as deputy to Northumberland was therefore void, Pennington was appointed in his stead and letters were sent to all captains apprising them of this fact. In the ensuing show of strength in the fleet Pennington and the King lost: Warwick's warrant was the one with practical effect.[15]

On land such manoeuvres might make local musters redundant. In Kent, for example, promising signs of the formation of a royalist party were cut off by brisk action by Edwin Sandys. Dover Castle was seized on 21 August and this was followed by raids on stores of arms and potential royalist strongholds. Arms and munitions stored in the Deanery in Canterbury were captured and soldiers were said to have been involved in the breaking of images, or perhaps desecration. The effect was decisive: despite local divisions, Kent was secured for Parliament and remained so throughout the first civil war.[16]

Slowly, but perceptibly, a civil war was breaking out and a crucial third element of this descent was the raising of field armies. In addition to the Commissions of Array, which gave power to muster the Trained Bands and to secure local strongpoints, Charles issued commissions to individuals to raise troops on his behalf. This was the seed of a field army with which to fight a war, rather than a defensive force designed to thwart the machinations of an opponent. Technically distinct, these diverse elements often intersected with the execution of the Commission of Array. The experiences of the Earl of Hertford illustrate this process. He was appointed by Charles to execute the Commission of Array in the western counties (Hampshire, Wiltshire, Dorset, Somerset, Devon and Cornwall) and to secure Portsmouth for the King. He started his work in Wells, in the centre of Somerset. This was considered friendly territory for the King and a number of men (including Lunsford) were already at work on the King's behalf. But on 1 August rival musters almost came to blows at Shepton Mallet, where 1,200 parliamentarians faced Ralph Hopton's men, who had been sent by Hertford to prevent the muster. Three days later, at Marshall's Elm in Somerset, eighty royalists under the command of Lunsford outfaced 600 parliamentarians, using only forty rounds of musket fire. They had lined up in a way that gave an exaggerated impression of their numbers. Despite this setback, however, the parliamentarian mobilization was to prove more successful. On 5 August 12,000 people assembled to resist Hertford, fearing that he was going to break the peace of the shire, and motivated by resentment of key gentry figures, vivid anti-Catholicism and Puritan enthusiasm. According to royalist estimates 10,000–12,000 men were mobilized in east Somerset by the late summer and Hertford decided to withdraw to Sherborne Castle. There, on 2 September, his forces were confronted by those of the Earl of Bedford – 7,000 men drawn from Devon and Dorset as well as from Somerset. Once again the royalists showed themselves more cunning, and the 600 defenders secured the withdrawal of 7,000 parliamentarians, to Yeovil, on 6 September.[17]

But this was too late to help Portsmouth. The second most important provincial magazine, after Hull, Portsmouth was also in parliamentarian hands, but the commander, George Goring, was considering a change of sides by the summer of 1642. Hertford had intended to strengthen Goring's hand, but the imminent arrival of parliamentary reinforcements from London under William Waller had forced Goring to declare his intentions early. By the time Bedford's men had withdrawn from Sherborne, Portsmouth was securely in Waller's hands.[18]

Following the fall of Portsmouth, Hertford withdrew northwards, towards Bristol, before deciding to cross to Wales, via Minehead, in order to gather troops to join the main royalist field army. Ralph Hopton was sent westwards to raise forces in Cornwall, a mission which Bedford did little to prevent. Despite the later reputation for royalism, the balance of forces in Cornwall was quite even in the summer of 1642. Only 180 men had attended musters at Bodmin, calling on the authority of the Commission of Array, but now the value of a friendly reception at the assizes became clear. Hopton submitted to a trial at Truro assizes for bringing armed men into the county, in what turned out to be a successful political manoeuvre. Not only did the Grand Jury acquit him, but it thanked him for coming to their aid and by early October he had secured the loyalty of the Cornish Trained Bands. He also raised a force of volunteers willing to leave the county, and managed to lay siege (albeit unsuccessfully) to Portsmouth.[19]

These tussles for control of local military resources – magazines, the loyalty of the Trained Bands and strongpoints like Sherborne Castle – were common across England in the summer of 1642. Inevitably, given that in some localities activists were mobilizing for both sides, tensions increased. In Manchester, on 15 July, an affray had broken out when Lord Strange, the Earl of Derby, was being feasted by the chief townsmen. Tensions were clearly running high, since on his way into town Strange had apparently instructed those with him 'not to shoot any pistol or offer any violence, nor to light off their horses while they stayed in the town'. While he was dining one of his servants came in to say that a drum was being beaten and soldiers were being assembled: apparently three deputy lieutenants had called out the militia in protest.[20]

In a subsequent statement sympathetic to Strange, leading figures in Manchester were at pains to say that they were amazed at this, and that they had tried to get Strange and his men safely away. The sheriff called on Mr Holcroft, one of those who had summoned the militia, to keep the peace and lay down his arms as Strange, against the advice of some of those around him, stood alongside. Holcroft and his company withdrew 'with many curses and great shouting'. In confused scenes Strange's company found their path blocked by a company under the command of Captain Birch, and Sir Thomas Stanley, another of the local men, fired a pistol from a window. It was later said that as Birch's company closed on them, Birch was heard to give a command to fire. Birch himself was disarmed and ran for cover under a cart, where he might have been killed but for the intervention of Strange. Thinking that the trouble had been averted Strange and his men then made their way towards Sir Alexander Ratcliffe's, where they had planned further entertainment, but turning around they saw that fighting had started and that four men had been knocked from their horses. In all the confusion a militia man had been killed.

It was symptomatic of these tense and anxious months that there was an immediate local concern to disavow responsibility for breaking the peace.[21] Sixty or eighty women from Manchester approached Strange the next morning 'weeping and wailing and beseeching his lordship not to think any thing of them in the town for that which was done over-night'. Leading townsmen also came to excuse themselves, and were reassured that Strange believed them to have been innocent of any role in the trouble, promising he would be 'as ready to relieve them and their town as any town in the country'. Twenty-two witnesses, including two constables, attested that Birch, Holcroft and Stanley had been the disturbers of the peace.[22] Nonetheless, it was this resistance in Manchester that prevented the whole of Lancashire falling to the royalists.

As war broke out, piecemeal, the gap between the rhetoric of the two sides remained narrow. At Shrewsbury, early in the autumn, the King pledged 'to the utmost of my power, [to] defend and maintain the true reformed protestant religion established in the Church of England . . . govern by the known law of the land, and that the liberty and property of the subject may be by them preserved . . . and I do solemnly and faithfully promise, in the sight of God, to maintain the just privileges and freedom of parliament'. The Earl of Essex's commission from Parliament, issued earlier the same month, was 'for the just and necessary defence of the protestant religion, of your majesty's person, crown, and dignity, of the laws and liberties of the kingdom, and the privileges of parliament'.[23]

Although the rhetorical differences were slight, the consequences of disagreement were increasingly lethal. At dawn, in the rain, on 9 August, Captain John Smith led a troop of royalist cavalry into Kilsby, Northamptonshire. There they found a crowd armed with muskets and pitchforks. They stopped Thomas Wrinkles and asked him who he was for, and when he replied 'for the king and parliament' it was enough to identify him as an enemy. He was shot dead. Thomas Marriot protested and was hit on the head several times with swords and shot as he ran away. John White was speared with his pitchfork as the soldiers searched the village for arms, but as a crowd gathered they found it increasingly hard to move. Armed men appeared at upstairs windows and Smith ordered everyone not to shoot, but they did. Smith's troops returned fire, killing three or four, and all the crowd ran, except an old man who ran at Smith with his pitchfork. He hit him without much effect, ignoring warnings to desist, before 'a pistol quieted him'.[24]

Prior to 1640 the militia had served better as a vehicle for honourable display by the county elite than as a fighting force. In this it had much in common with other local institutions which reflected and expressed the local social order. Social and political power were closely entwined, and these institutions represented the face of that order to local society. In Tudor and Stuart England there was a horror of exposing divisions among the governing elite, but that inhibition seemed now to be giving way under the pressure of events.[25] It had happened to Parliament and now it happened to the institutions of local government and in some places this dawning realization led to attempts to pull back from the brink. Although the language used was similar, the meanings attributed to it were quite different, and increasingly irreconcilable.

Fear of division was probably more significant than the reality for, despite the purges and the increasingly partisan role of quarter sessions and assizes in the conflict, the general impression seems to be that county government continued to operate reasonably normally into the autumn.[26] But there were reports of enclosure and other disturbances in which social insubordination seemed to be a clear threat. The rival mobilizations clearly affected village relations, and were often interpreted in the light of a popular anti-Puritanism or anti-Catholicism.[27] Gentry figures remarked on the strain placed on the normal courtesies of county society by political differences. Fear of disorder and division, and of military conflict, was potent and drove some gentry to try to demilitarize their counties. In Derbyshire neither the Militia Ordinance nor the Commission of Array was implemented, as the gentry united in order to keep war out, and a similar process led to a long delay in implementing the Militia Ordinance in Suffolk and Norfolk. In Staffordshire the sheriff, Justices and Grand Jury agreed a declaration at the Sessions of the Peace on 15 November – three weeks after the first battle of the war. They made arrangements for a force 'for the defence of the county' motivated by 'the many outrages, riots, routs, and unlawful assemblies that have been made and committed in divers parts of this county by certain persons in arrays and warlike manner' to 'the great fear of all the inhabitants in general'.[28]

This is usually referred to as neutralism but 'neutralization' is often a better term – it did not necessarily reflect the absence of local ideological conflict or dispute, but an attempt to contain its consequences. In Staffordshire, for example, Henry Bagot and Philip Jackson, both signatories of the pact in November 1642, were in arms against each other a year later.[29] Neither was this 'localism' necessarily a reflection of a parochial view of the issues – there might be deep ideological divisions among men with well-informed views of national politics, but war might still seem worse than peace. Contrarily, allowing one set of partisans uncontested control of the county might also be better than fighting, even if there was a strong current of opinion against them. In Buckinghamshire, Essex, Herefordshire, Lancashire, Shropshire and Worcestershire the unchallenged triumph of either the Militia Ordinance or the Commission of Array seems to have been a means of preserving unity.[30] Local 'neutralism' of these various kinds was not evidence of disengagement from the issues, or of the irrelevance of these questions to local life, but of the difficulty of reducing these questions to a choice between two sides, or fear of the consequences of settling them by force of arms.[31]

In Norfolk and Lincolnshire, as in Staffordshire, there were attempts to raise a third force, something that looks more like an authentic neutralism or local-mindedness, albeit in reaction to the activities of local partisans.[32] In Lincolnshire, for example, there had been considerable unity of purpose behind the implementation of the Militia Ordinance in June and in July the influence of Lord Willoughby of Parham was reflected in a powerful declaration of the parliamentary position. But when the King appeared in person in the county there was also a powerful display of loyalty to him: there seems to have been a genuinely divided response in the county. It was this partisanship, and the threat of radicalizing resistance to fen drainage, which seems to have informed the development of armed neutralism:

> The rein of government has been so slackened as now is cut in pieces amongst us, many men of desperate fortunes . . . live together without the acknowledgement of any law . . . They resist it in a warlike manner, accumulating all manner of insolencies, by adding to their rebellion violences upon men's houses, goods and lands, burning, stealing and devastating of them, so as men of fortune had need to serve them against such spirits.[33]

Much of this is county-minded, preoccupied with local law and order, and when a force was raised in Worcester it was justified in terms which more or less suited either side. But although the range of action was geographically limited, the ideological horizons were not. Attempts to use the institutions of the county, particularly the military institutions, for partisan purposes naturally produced attempts to stop them being used in this way – to take the Worcestershire horse beyond the county was to participate in a war. The desire to pacify was expressed through county institutions, but may have related to a much wider political consciousness. Nationally and locally the justification for mobilization was defensive, and that naturally meant that county arms were used to defend the county.[34]

In Yorkshire a neutrality pact was the product of deep divisions rather than of local unity. Early in October prominent Yorkshire gentlemen concluded a treaty of neutrality. Ferdinando, Lord Fairfax, who had raised forces on behalf of Parliament, and the Earl of Cumberland, the King's commander in Yorkshire, were both signatories. Ferdinando's father had fought in the continental wars and was a committed supporter of the military defence of international Protestantism. He had been disappointed in Ferdinando's martial qualities after he sent him to the Netherlands in the 1630s, but Ferdinando was to prove a successful parliamentary general. His son, Sir Thomas, had been schooled in the

virtues of armed Protestantism by his grandfather more than by Ferdinando, and was to rise to the very top of the parliamentarian armies in
1645. The desire to exclude the war from Yorkshire was thought by
some to be improper. Fairfax had insisted that it be approved by Parliament and Sir John Hotham, an old rival of Fairfax, denounced it in print
as an affront to the judgement of Parliament. His son went further,
taking armed men to the walls of royalist-held York, and capturing the
Archbishop's seat at Cawood Castle on 4 October. The following spring
both Hothams deserted the parliamentary cause, and their attitude to
this neutrality deal may have reflected hostility to Fairfax as much as it
did commitment to parliamentary authority. It also reflected how
exposed the Hothams would have been by a neutrality pact – they had
ventured far more than the Fairfax family at this point, not least in
refusing the King entry to Hull.[35]

Whatever the local politics of neutrality in Yorkshire, it did not work.
Parliament condemned the treaty, and a military contest for control
of the county ensued. The Earl of Newcastle, a regional magnate of
considerable influence, was able to bring men south, while the Fairfaxes
were able to draw on considerable support in the clothing towns of the
West Riding. Hull, perhaps the best-fortified town in England, was
securely in parliamentary hands. The East Riding was in the control of
the Hothams, on behalf of Parliament, but their relationship with the
Fairfaxes was not easy.[36] It seems equally true that neutrality reflected
deep divisions in Lancashire and Cornwall.[37]

The varieties of neutralism – genuine refusal to join either side, or
more prudential calculations about how to limit the impending war –
were also visible in the towns. Towns were very obvious military targets,
and faced the possibilities of long-term garrisoning and sieges. Although
some towns were well-fortified most were not, and there was a clear
incentive to submit to the nearest strong military force. Bristol, for
example, seems to have been largely non-aligned prior to 1642, pursuing
primarily economic grievances and allowing, rather than seeking, parliamentary occupation. Worcester's royalism was similarly passive, York
was not clearly committed and even Oxford, soon to become the royalist
capital, owed that position to the University more than to the citizens.[38]
Nonetheless, it does seem that on balance Parliament enjoyed more
support from the towns: in October 1642 all the major towns were
in parliamentary hands with the exception of Chester, Shrewsbury and

Newcastle. In Coventry an attempted royalist occupation led by the King himself was defeated by citizens in August, an event crucial to the course of the war in Warwickshire. This citizen activism tipped the balance between rival groups in the governing elite, a balance which had until then pointed towards neutralism.[39]

One particular special case was the English colonies abroad. Their legal existence depended on the prerogative and, unlike most other areas of English jurisdiction, there was a close relationship between their legal powers and their actual existence: robbed of the protection of a charter they might disintegrate, or disappear altogether. All strands of opinion were represented, but perhaps a poll of settlers in the New World might have revealed a stronger backing for further reformation than was evident in the Old World. Nonetheless, as corporate entities the colonies were not free to take sides. Thus, although New Englanders fought as individuals, either in the armies or in the pamphlet exchanges, their colonial governments tried to remain uncommitted as corporate entities. Virginia, under the governorship of Sir William Berkeley, kept the royalism of its nascent elite undeclared until after the regicide in 1649. Even after that, a formula was found for an accommodation with the King's killers.[40]

By the autumn, in England, the military geography was fairly clear. Waller had taken Portsmouth on 7 September and the south of England had been secured for Parliament, with the exception of Sherborne Castle, which was in the hands of Hertford. East Anglia, subsequently notoriously parliamentarian, in fact had a more complex history in 1642. A group of gentry tried to get the support of the Grand Jury at the Suffolk assizes for a neutralist petition and both the Commission of Array and Militia Ordinance were left unenforced for much of the summer. There it may have been fear of social disorder which created this attitude among the gentry, and once parliamentarians had taken the initiative support for them posed less of a threat to local social order than contesting control. Essex, Cambridgeshire, Hertfordshire and Norfolk also saw attempts to prevent political dislocation.[41] The royalists had control of Cornwall, Wales and the north. Lancashire was disputed territory, thanks to the resistance to the royalists of districts around Manchester. Yorkshire was in parliamentary hands but the Earl of Newcastle had secure control further north. Parliament had Portsmouth, Hull, London, Bristol and many more minor, and less defensible, towns (see Map 1).

Military and political control of a territory might conceal divisions in local opinion, and such control was rarely treated as unquestioned by either side. The Marches of Wales became renowned as heartlands of royalism, but there is little sign of royalism prior to the mobilizations of 1642, except perhaps in Herefordshire – it seems to have been a product of mobilization rather than a cause of it.[42] In Cornwall and Kent, as we have seen, it was decisive action by Hopton and Sandys not uniform local support that underpinned military command. Even in London there were divisions of opinion. Given these histories, it is no surprise that maintaining control over territory was an important part of the military history of the war, as much so as the grand marches which form the meat of most military accounts of the war.

Finally, in the late summer, the field armies gathered. When Charles raised the royal standard on Castle Hill in Nottingham on 22 August, summoning his loyal subjects to his side, few people came. The small crowd flung their caps loyally in the air and cheered 'God save King Charles and hang up the Roundheads', but the standard blew down in the night and, according to Hyde, 'a general sadness covered the whole town'. It was the culmination of a disappointing peregrination of the Midlands. At Lincoln, Charles had been met by 30,000 people anxious to get a glimpse of their king and to listen to the loyal addresses, but there were few troops from Lincolnshire to see the standard on 22 August. The gentry of Yorkshire and the burgesses of Coventry seem to have been equally lacking in fighting spirit. At Nottingham Charles may have had 2,000 horse, but he had very few foot and by early September he may have had only a quarter as many troops as Parliament had managed to move to Northampton.[43]

Disappointed, the King set off for Shrewsbury, disarming the Trained Bands as he went. He had already taken the weapons of the Lincolnshire Trained Bands on 16 August. Here too war was raising the stakes in mendacity, since he had promised that he was fighting to defend property. Equally, or even more alarmingly, local communities were being stripped of their defensive arms after fifteen months of very public anxiety about popish plots. West of the Pennines, however, his fortunes improved and an army gathered. The Earl of Derby successfully recruited in south Lancashire, perhaps coercively. Troops began to arrive from north Wales and the Marches in the last week of September and into mid-October. On 23 September he was given a heartwarming welcome at Chester and, if Strange's recruiting methods were coercive, it seems that Sir Edward Stradling and Thomas Salusbury were able to draw on deep wells of support in Wales. The troops were also paid, of course, and this may have helped – at Myddle Hill, in Shropshire, Sir Paul Harris was offering a very generous 4s 4d per week, and he found twenty volunteers at that price. In Monmouthshire it was the prestige and power of the Earl of Worcester that delivered troops to the King. Despite these more hopeful signs Charles still felt he needed to relax the policy on Catholics. He had officially declared that 'No papist of what degree or quality so ever shall be admitted to serve in our army', but in a letter of 19 September to the Earl of Newcastle he took a more pragmatic line:

this rebellion is grown to such a height that I must not look of what opinion men are who at this time are willing and able to serve me. Therefore I do not only permit but command you to make use of all my loving subjects' services, without examining their consciences – more than their loyalty to us – as you shall find most to conduce to the upholding of my just legal power.[44]

Newcastle's army was renowned as papistical through the rest of the war.

Parliament's success was much more immediate. In May the earls of Essex, Holland and Northumberland had attended a muster of 8–10,000 men in London. Subsequent attempts to enforce the Militia Ordinance were largely successful, particularly in the south-east. A committee for printing had been re-established in June 1642 which seems to have been energetic in publicizing the cause – there were 9,000 copies of a declaration of 4 July against the Commission of Array for example. The House of Commons itself failed the test of raising money on the Propositions, but it was successful in Hertfordshire and elsewhere, funding a productive drive to recruit volunteers in London and the south-east. On 8 August six bands of foot (4,800 men) set out for Warwick, accompanied by eleven bands of horse. When the Earl of Essex left London to join the army on 9 September he was watched by the full City militia, in arms.[45] When he got to Northampton he was at the head of 20,000 men. This might have threatened a quick resolution given the unimpressive response to royalist recruiting at that stage. Sir Jacob Astley, the King's infantry commander, was said to have been worried that the King was so poorly supported that he might be 'taken out of his bed if the rebels should make a brisk attempt to that purpose'.[46]

It is difficult not to think that Charles had the worst of all this. Petitions for accommodation between King and Parliament, and of loyalty to bishops, had come in from all around the country, but the King struggled to find men willing to fight for him in the Midlands. West of the Pennines he had more success, although it is difficult to see this as building on a long-term commitment to the cause, at least in most of the Marches. Elsewhere royalists manoeuvred, with mixed success, for local control. The success of individuals established the roots of regional royalist armies in the north and west but the King's own field army was slow to build in the Midland counties. It created a federation of regiments under particular commanders as much as an integrated army.[47] A map of military outcomes – strongpoints and towns held, musters achieved, armies assembled – is probably not a map of enthusiastic royalism. For both sides mobilization through print, preaching and the use of local institutions as a platform for partisan politics had been crucial. There were more musters by the authority of the ordinance than the Commission of Array, and petitions in support of Parliament were offset more by petitions for accommodation than by positive support for the King against Parliament. There were plenty of signs of reluctance to go to war, but far fewer that many people thought Parliament should concede.[48]

Two military parties were forming but it is by no means clear that opinion at large was dividing neatly into two camps. There was no National Covenant, but instead a series of contentious slogans – the Prayer Book or Protestation – and attempts to read in natural and supernatural events signs of God's purposes. Amidst all the shouting it is possible to discern the formulation of coherent, and radical, constitutional theories, but they were not always officially owned, and neither did they command universal assent. Neither was there an equivalent of the Covenanters' Tables: a revolutionary body responsible for the campaign. Instead there were contests for existing institutions of national or local government – Parliament, quarter sessions and assizes. There is very little evidence of pure neutralism, in the sense of a disengagement from the political issues, but there is plenty of evidence of hesitation in committing to one 'side' or to resolving the conflict by force. For individuals this posed crises of conscience, in choosing between propositions which had not previously been understood as alternatives, or using established arguments in ways that must have flirted with insincerity. The apparent need to secure political and religious ends had produced a constitutional crisis, and as that crisis played out largely consensual values were presented as alternatives. Potential conflicts in a common-sense system were being forced into the open: quite different meanings were applied to an apparently shared language of politics, with increasingly lethal consequences. But it was both common and understandable to try to contain these conflicts within existing languages of honour, loyalty and legality and so forth.

How people chose was a product of circumstance as well as conviction. Explanations for patterns in these choices vary according to who was making the choice, under what circumstances, and what the question was. Signing a Root and Branch petition in December 1641 might reveal a religious sensibility most likely to lead to an affinity with Parliament, but a lot could have changed by August 1642. It was certainly a different kind of choice from acquiescing in the use of a Grand Jury to support a partisan use of the militia, or to signing up for military service against the King's army. Different kinds of choice were being made at different moments, and there was always an element of calculation about local conditions, too. It was also the case, of course, that there were more than two sides to the arguments, and many more than two possible positions. In other words, numerous choices confronted people without a clear sense of two sides. Choosing sides in such circumstances was painful and, probably, conditional.

The difficulty and complexity of these choices are made clear for almost any individual whose thoughts about the issues have come down to us. Sir Edmund Verney famously overcame his personal political preferences and joined the King's army, admitting as much to Hyde: 'My conscience is only concerned in honour and gratitude to follow my master. I have eaten his bread and served him near thirty years, and will not do so base a thing as to forsake him; and I choose rather to lose my life (which I am sure I shall do) to preserve and defend those things, which are against my conscience to preserve and defend'. He was indeed to die in the first major battle of the war, bearing the King's standard with great courage. Of his four sons three joined him in the royalist cause. His second son, another Edmund, had fought for the Protestant cause in the Low Countries, and heard the news of the army raised to fight the Scots with 'sorrow'. But he did not hesitate to join the King's army and castigated his parliamentarian brother Ralph for his desertion of the King. It was, he said, 'unhandsomely done'. 'I am tooth and nail for the king's cause, and shall endure to the death, whatsoever his fortune be'. '[C]onsider that majesty is sacred; God says "touch not mine anointed" . . . you say you intend not to hurt the king, but can any of you warrant any one shot to say it shall not endanger his very person?' Ralph stayed firm to the parliamentarian cause until late in 1643, but then retired to France to consult his conscience, suffering expulsion from the Commons and sequestration. Despite these sufferings, however, he did not renounce his parliamentarianism.[49]

Many of those who faced these choices thought long and hard about them. The godly, following the advice of casuists, prayed, read the Bible (perhaps even opening it at random to see if God guided them to a relevant chapter), discussed and reflected. Lord Paget, a moderate reformer, became a royalist general following such a period of reflection:

It may seem strange that I, who with all zeal and earnestness have prosecuted (ever since the beginning of parliament) the reformation of all disorders in Church and Commonwealth should now (in a time of great distraction) desert the cause. Most true it is that my ends were the common good, and whilst it was prosecuted I was ready to lay down both my life and fortune, but when I found a preparation of arms against the King, under shadow of loyalty, I rather resolved to obey a good conscience than particular ends.[50]

The dictates of a good conscience drove a wedge between old friends and fellow travellers Sir Ralph Hopton and Sir William Waller. Hopton became a successful royalist general, Waller enjoyed a period of press coverage as 'William the Conqueror' in Parliament's service. On the eve of their encounter on the battlefield at Roundway Down, Waller wrote his much-quoted letter to Hopton:

That great God who is the searcher of my heart knows with what a sad sense I go on upon this service, and with what a perfect hatred I detest this war without an enemy; but I look upon it as sent from God . . . God . . . in His good time send us the blessing of peace and in the meantime assist us to receive it! We are both upon the stage, and must act such parts as are assigned us in this tragedy. Let us do it in a way of honour and without personal animosities.[51]

Lady Sydenham wrote in similarly civil terms to Lady Verney that her son Sir Ralph had 'chosen the strongest part, but I cannot think the best'. 'It staggers me', she wrote, that he could believe that he was fighting for the liberty of the subject when his partisans 'take all from them that are not of their mind, and . . . pull down their houses and . . . imprison them, and leave them to the mercy of the unruly multitude'. Nor could she find it is 'in God's law to take up arms against their lawful King to depose him; for sure they have not made his person known to all those that they have employed in this war to spare him and not to kill him'. But still, she trusted his good faith: I 'am confident he does believe it is the best, and for that he chose it'.[52]

In these difficult circumstances, with allegiances to the King, friends and family cutting across political priorities, civil war allegiances are difficult to predict on the basis of previous behaviour. Attitudes in the 1630s, or even in 1641, are no clear guide to civil war allegiance, although general patterns do emerge. At the core of royalism were ideas of loyalty, but also concern for the constitution and the integrity of the national church. A group of influential figures arrived in the emerging royal camp by this route. Opponents of Laudianism, they became more concerned about the threat of religious disorder posed by the campaigns for Root and Branch, and by the ways in which Pym and his allies had overridden the law. These men – the Duke of Richmond and Lennox, the Earl of Hertford, the Earl of Dorset and his younger brother Sir Francis Seymour, the Earl of Southampton, Lord Willoughby of Eresby, Sir Edward Hyde, Viscount Falkland, Sir John Colepeper and Sir John Strangways – followed a trajectory similar to that of Sir Edward Dering. Colepeper, for example, had been quick on his feet in November 1640 with a vivid denunciation of the Personal Rule, but had co-operated with Dering to organize the controversial Kentish petition of 1642.[53]

Others, as we have seen, were sceptical that raising an army against Charles could be seen as a loyal act, or that it could be guaranteed that in fighting his army one was not endangering the King himself. There was also a royalist war party, keen to see opposition crushed, regality restored and the rebels brought to heel: Charles's nephew Prince Rupert, his wife Henrietta Maria, as well as Lord George Digby and John Ashburnham.[54] Prince Rupert was the son of the exiled Elector of the Palatinate. In 1637 he had done service in Germany and was captured in 1639, at the age of twenty, and held prisoner in Linz, Austria. There he studied military arts, and he joined the King's ranks with practical and theoretical experience of war, as well as some iron in his soul. In

England he established a well-deserved reputation as a hot-head and he took a firm line with rebels. Digby had credentials as a reformer in the early months of the Long Parliament, but was driven into active royalism by the attacks on episcopacy and by the attainder of Strafford. He was, throughout the war, conspicuously loyal, although embroiled in a developing rivalry with Rupert.[55] Catholics, like the rest of the population, were more likely to be uninvolved than to be military partisans, but they were disproportionately royalist. These were quite different registers of royalism.[56]

On the other hand, men like Pym could see such a clear threat to religion and liberty that qualms about the means seemed secondary to the ends. The motives for individuals in taking sides were manifold, of course, and the implications of their doing so equally varied. What is clear is that the two sides consisted of complex coalitions of allies, with varying concerns and differing degrees of conviction and commitment. Polemic and local circumstance might serve to reduce complexities to polarities – Militia Ordinance or Array, Prayer Book or Protestation, King or King and Parliament – but in reality there must often have seemed to be right on all sides.

It is relatively easy to lay out the issues, but very difficult for all these reasons to find out who identified with which arguments and even more difficult to say why. This has been at the heart of academic debate about the civil war for several generations as models have been found to relate ideological preferences to economic and social interest, religious background or age. The data is often good enough to disprove these models, but has never proved sufficient to clinch an argument in favour of any of them. Not the least of the problems, of course, is that the vast bulk of the population, even those of high status, left little direct evidence about their allegiance, still less the reasons for that allegiance. But it is also clear that what was at stake in supporting one side or another changed over time, and between places. It was one thing to have a preference for a party position, another to sign up to fight, or to refuse to.

In most places, however, the establishment of local military control was not the outcome of democratic consultation, but of opportunism. Maps of military control are not maps of popular allegiance. For example, Oliver Cromwell's decisive action in seizing the store of arms at Cambridge for the parliamentary side is more significant for who Cromwell became than for its immediate military significance. Nonetheless, because of who he subsequently became, we can tell quite a lot about the motivation of this particular opportunist. Son of a minor gentry family, Oliver Cromwell had hit hard times during the 1630s, perhaps slipping below the level of the gentry and into the ranks of the husbandmen. Educated by the famous Puritan author Thomas Beard, Cromwell clearly grew up with a godly piety, and had considered emigration to the New World. But it was probably at some point in the late 1630s that he had what turned out to be his formative experience, something akin to the modern experience of being born again. From then on his life seems to have been driven by an intense providentialism. At difficult moments he often seemed paralysed as he searched for signs of God's intentions for him, but once he felt sure what they were he was capable of decisive action. He had played a minor role in the Commons following his election to the Long Parliament, but did make some important interventions, perhaps at the prompting of John Pym, to whom he was related by marriage. But it was surely his convinced providentialism that allowed this minor gentleman to seize plate belonging to Cambridge colleges and intended for the King – something close to theft and treason.[57] Cromwell's politics were not despised in his local area but in the City of Cambridge, and particularly in the University, there were plenty of people who might have wanted to support the crown.[58] In Kent, Cornwall, East Anglia and even the Marches of Wales, apparent military control concealed local divisions. The military geography of the country, therefore, cannot be taken to reflect the complexion of local political and religious opinions.

Attempts by individuals to mobilize for one side or the other were not always successful, however. On the day that the King raised his standard at Nottingham, Charles Lucas set out to raise forces in support of him. In stepping out of his house he was stepping almost straight into the pages of history. He was observed by a watch set by the Corporation of Colchester, who raised the alarm in town. Crowds attacked his home the next day, discovering a store of weapons and effectively thwarting his plans. Over the subsequent weeks roving crowds attacked the homes of other prominent local recusants and royalists. This popular parliamentarianism had roots in the local economy and social structure, but was also the product of local history. The local politics of the Lucas family, and their relations with the borough of Colchester, and the perceived role of local recusants and royalists in mobilizing the county,

A later compendium of Bruno Ryves's *Mercurius Rusticus*
which reported the actions of the 'Colchester plunderers'
and other parliamentarian barbarities

created quite clearly identified targets for crowds fired up by a commitment to Parliament as the defender of liberty and Protestantism. These ideas were mobilized among a population bound together by the cloth trade, and suffering a recession widely blamed on the failure of settlement, and on the papists in particular. They drew on parliamentary measures such as the Protestation, calls for the disarming of papists and recusants, and on the 8 September order, and were not quite disowned by Parliament either. Although local courts continued to operate, and records survive, there is little evidence of a concerted local effort to quash this insurrection.[59]

Such popular agency was not unique. Royalist mobilization in Somerset was halted by apparently spontaneous resistance from below, leading to a massive mobilization of the local Trained Bands. When the Earl of

Bath tried to publish the Commission of Array in South Molton, Devon, in the spring of 1642, he was met by a hostile crowd, estimated to contain 1,000 people or more. An eyewitness claimed 'the common sort of the town . . . fell in a great rage . . . and swore that if . . . [the royalists] did attempt any thing there, or read their Commission . . . they would beat them all down and kill them, aye, if they were all hanged for it; and thereupon betook themselves to arms, both men, women, and children'.[60] The earl was more interested in his position in London than in the county, and that may have affected his local influence when he succeeded to the lieutenancy, but this was, nonetheless, a powerful demonstration of popular agency. When the gentry of North Devon came out in support of the Commission of Array it was observed that 'those men will never get renown and credit again of their Country'.[61] Cheshire royalists were clear that they did not enjoy unanimous popular support and when William Davenport asked his tenants for support in the King's service they wrote that although they would not 'harbour a disloyal thought' against the King, 'yet we dare not lift up our hands against that honourable assembly of parliament, whom we are confidently assured do labour both for the happiness of his Majesty and all the kingdom'. Davenport noted in his diary that the next day, a sabbath no less, 'not staying or belike caring much for me or my answer', they had enlisted for parliamentary service.[62] In Warwickshire, the godly activist Lord Brooke appealed below the ranks of the gentry, who were disproportionately royalist. In alliance with the middling sort, some of whom can be positively shown to have been ideologically motivated, he took military control in a county where the gentry were twice as likely to be royalist as parliamentarian. In Gloucester, too, activists below the level of the gentry took the initiative as their social superiors hesitated.[63]

Where relatively free political choices were being made, as in the Stour Valley, they reflected local politics, local histories of economic and social change, and of religious affiliation. Putting together all the evidence for Devon, for example, creates a complex picture but one in which those below the gentry frequently had an important voice. This seems also to have been true elsewhere in the country: contemporary perceptions that particular areas were more prone to support one side or another can be mapped against their religious complexion and that, in turn, seems to have owed something to social structure and patterns of economic activity.[64] To put it the other way, though, military command did not depend on ideological unanimity,[65] and one universal finding of studies of allegiance is the existence of division in every locality that has been studied.[66]

Local political ecologies clearly did not make choices inevitable, therefore, although they did create conditions that might make them, on the whole, tend in one direction rather than another. It might be better to think in terms of the responses to particular mobilizations rather than a fixed allegiance to one of two sides. Looking back across the two years of campaigns – the elections, petitioning, promotion of the Protestation, implementation of the Militia Ordinance or the Commissions of Array, and then the raising of money and men for the field armies – it is clear that different questions were being posed at different times. At particular moments MPs, printers, local officeholders and ministers sought to galvanize support for a specific project or policy. They were presented as parts of larger visions, but it was quite possible these various projects might meet different responses in the same places, or for apparently rival mobilizations to succeed in the same localities. There were patterns in the way these things were mobilized – in the networks which promoted them and the ideological temper of the locality in question – but they also have a history, an element of contingency, calculation and mutability. For example, when the King crossed the Pennines seeking support in the summer of 1642, some Derbyshire miners signed up in return for remission of the tithe of tin. Many models of popular allegiance would suggest that these miners should be parliamentarian. They worked as independent men, had a long tradition of defending their rights at law and in demonstrations, and this sturdy individualism is usually seen as a basis for support for Parliament, as opposed to a more deferential support for Charles. But this calculating response to a specific question was just as much a product of the history and political culture of the Derbyshire tin miners as enlistment in the parliamentarian army would have been.[67]

In the early 1640s a large number of agrarian and industrial grievances found expression in collective action and it is always possible, of course, that they were motivated mainly, or solely, by agrarian and industrial discontents. It is tempting to see in these and other agrarian or industrial protests elements of class hostility. Clearly, however, these economic grievances could be coloured by other concerns: in the Stour Valley the politics of cloth and class intersected with godliness in the popular parliamentarianism that was so decisive. At various points throughout the 1640s it is possible to see that 'bread and butter' issues caused discontent, and that these discontents were not being addressed by the war: there was a potential for radical social change which was sidelined by the politicians, in other words.[68]

Enclosure rioters in Lincolnshire, for example, had good reason to be hostile to the crown, which had sponsored large-scale drainage and enclosure projects during the 1630s, but little subsequent reason to be grateful to Parliament, which came to support further drainage schemes. Fenlanders had enjoyed extensive common rights to benefit from the riches of the fens, but these resources disappeared with drainage and those who lost rights did not always feel adequately compensated. Drainage schemes had been an issue in elections both to the Short and Long Parliaments and hopes for redress of grievances seem to have prompted direct action. In April 1640 commoners forcibly entered drained lands, and this was a prelude to two years of disturbances. Hopes were raised when the Commons established a Committee for the Fens, but frustration with its slow progress led to direct action in the winter of 1641–2. Another wave of disturbances started in late 1641, running through the summer of 1642, by which time the local agencies of law and order seemed powerless to stop it. This seems to have galvanized gentry solidarity in these areas – a desire to limit the political damage of the incipient conflict in the interests of social order. Subsequently the commoners and their opponents took advantage of political circumstances to push their case, adjusting their language to meet the expectations of their rulers, or to call them to account. Drainers complaining about disorder identified it as a seditious conspiracy against the King in the 1620s, in the 1640s as a benighted rabble careless of the benefits to the commonwealth of agricultural improvement, then as Levellers seeking a violent change of government in the 1650s. The fenmen, for their part, shifted the emphasis of their addresses away from humble supplication for the protection of their governors towards their fundamental rights, particularly in property.[69]

Between 1640 and 1642 the House of Lords heard many such complaints, as its legal jurisdiction opened up new possibilities of redress. The resulting flood of petitions is a goldmine for social historians and the peak of disputes over economic and social grievances has been interpreted as evidence of an actual peak in a rising trend in economic conflict.[70] Perhaps, though, these things reflect the legal awareness of people whose interests were closely entwined with the law. When enclosure rioters in Waltham Forest in May 1642 claimed that there was 'no law settled' and that killing deer was therefore outside sanction, they may have been making a claim more limited than that anarchy was engulfing the country. Rights of access to the forest, or rights to build fences there, were regulated by courts whose jurisdiction had now been thrown into doubt. During the 1630s Waltham had seen the revival of a regime hostile to the common rights of local people, taking an aggressive view of the limits of the forest. In 1642, with the legal basis of those policies removed, local people went into the forest to kill deer. Threatened by the keeper of the forest, they joked that 'if they complained of offenders, to complain of a good store of them, that if they went to prison they might be merry together'.[71] 'Riot', here, was a kind of festive expression of a new, but quite specific liberty, and an adjunct to litigation. It seems clear that in breaking open deer parks, and killing deer, there was something more than the politics of hunger at work: opportunities were being taken up. At Corse Lawn, Gloucestershire, in October 1642, 600 deer were not eaten, but rather slaughtered in 'a riotous, devilish way'. Deer hunting was central to ideals of gentility, and venison was widely used as a gift, circulating not in markets but as tokens of mutual respect and honour. The massacre of the deer at Corse Lawn was a direct, festive transgression of the ideals of gentility, a slap in the face for the aristocratic landlord, the Earl of Middlesex. His unpopular administration of the forest during the 1630s had made use of Star Chamber and was regarded locally as unjust, ignoble and unneighbourly. The massacre of his deer, a kind of desecration, was a political act, a response to the change of the times.[72] A leading figure in the renewed attacks on enclosures on Berkhamsted Common in Hertfordshire in 1641 and 1642 was William Edlyn. He was also the first man in the neighbouring settlements of Berkhamsted, Great Gaddesden and Northchurch to make a voluntary contribution to support the Scottish army when it joined the parliamentary alliance in January 1644. Attacks on Wortley Park, in Yorkshire, seem also to have a partisan context.[73]

Such engagements with the national crisis, like the examples of gentry feuding, can appear instrumental or tactical, but they might not be so different, in their way, from Pym and Bedford's deployment of the popish plot as a means of securing the bridge appointments to major offices of state in early 1641. They were certainly part of a longer tradition of riot, petition and demonstration, in which suppliants represented their grievances in terms of the larger ideals of government, or larger concerns of the nation's rulers. Grain rioters, and those seeking poor relief or redress of some other material grievances, had demonstrated this capacity to take advantage of the rhetoric of their governors over previous generations, trying to persuade or embarrass them into acting on their behalf. This might be said too of the London petitions of the previous winter, or of City interests in the rest of the decade.[74] It is unlikely that the allegiance of many people was simply determined by the preferences of their social superiors: that the gentry were more powerful than their neighbours did not mean that they were all-powerful. Fear of this popular agency – termed riot and disorder by hostile contemporaries – fed into the decisions about allegiance. Pamphleteers were quick to publicize these events, placing them in the context of a longer history of peasant insurrection stretching back to the Peasants' Revolt of 1381. There is plenty of evidence from around the country that this fear played well for the royalists.[75]

Drawing a line between instrumental and sincere appeal to these issues is difficult of course, and misses a more fundamental point – that the political argument was available throughout the provinces and down the social scale, and that creative use could be made of this opportunity. Local and popular allegiance may have had an impact on the military geography of the war then, at least in limiting what activists might achieve. Much of the war was fought in these local arenas: a series of essentially local struggles for control of garrisons and territory. This was an ongoing process as war, and politics, moved on. Mobilizations entailed continuous coalition-building.

As political negotiation foundered and the resort to arms appeared more likely, people of all ranks were confronted with the practical consequences of failed negotiation. Rents were appearing in the fabric of political authority and conflicts which in normal times could only have been expressed in the expectation of exemplary punishment were publicly voiced. But with a division in national government increasingly obvious it was possible for these languages and disputes to be appropriated to local conditions and in those local conflicts a voice was given to those normally excluded from the counsels of government. This was not simply a matter of the people being given a voice by the revolution, however, for the people were also in some circumstances making it: the Stour Valley riots helped to shape national political action. Print created reciprocal relationships between national and local issues, connecting parochial battles with conflicts of national significance and advertising local examples of general threats.

Some kind of strategic position emerged from these local battles but the complexities of allegiance are liable to be flattened out in maps of that position. It would certainly be a mistake to conclude from the military geography either that people did not have opinions, or that areas under the military command of one side or the other were homogenously and unequivocally in favour of that cause. All the evidence suggests that the nation was divided from top to bottom, and that every village had its royalists and parliamentarians. Nonetheless, we can discern geographies of allegiance, starting with broad national distinctions and leading to more subtle anatomies of particular areas. Clearly local political cultures were significant in moulding these choices, but so too were local political contingencies.

The war was starting with a series of whimpers rather than a bang, but it was starting nonetheless. In the arguments urged in favour of these mobilizations two fears stand out: for the future of reformation and the security of the gains already made; and for the security of the social, religious and political order in the face of ignorant zeal. Religious conflicts were increasingly expressed as a choice between Protestation and Prayer Book; between defence of the doctrine of the church, or both the doctrine and the discipline. Fear of popery was juxtaposed to fear of religious and social anarchy. The really pernicious thing about these concerns was, of course, that it was possible to be equally worried by them all: the real political failure of the Long Parliament lay in the fact that they came to be seen as alternatives. Similarly, the 'just' prerogatives of the King were juxtaposed with the 'just' rights and privileges of Parliament: who was there who didn't believe in both? But as activists sought to take control of military resources, it became harder to sustain a complex attitude – the Hull magazine was either with Parliament or with the King, and it was difficult to find a third way, particularly after the King disavowed the authority of the King-in-Parliament as superior to his own personal word.

As war erupted a third anxiety came to lie alongside these fears for religion and the balance of rights, powers and privileges: that this was not worth a war. Awareness of the costs of war, already evident in the Covenanters' occupation of the north-east or the apparent spiral of social disorder that was being unleashed, informed attempts to pull back from the brink, or to stay out of the fighting. In the first eight months of 1642 all but two English counties generated petitions which used the language of accommodation, but even this was a language used for partisan purposes.[76] Caught between these competing concerns 'choosing sides' was not an easy or once-and-for-all thing. An important strand of opinion was bewilderment at a world out of joint, at a body politic so diseased as to be monstrous. Above all, though, among those activists driving events, fear was triumphing over hope. For most active participants this was to be a defensive war, defined by what it was intended to prevent rather than what it was hoped it would achieve.

War, 1642–1646

8

Armed Negotiation

The Battle of Edgehill and Its Aftermath

In September 1642, as the King moved westwards from Nottingham in search of support, he was shadowed by the Earl of Essex. Both sides had an eye on Worcester. Sir John Byron was heading there with a large amount of plate from Oxford, intended to finance the King's war effort – a parallel to the operation foiled by Cromwell in Cambridge in August – and Prince Rupert was sent to secure the city for the King. On arrival Rupert concluded that it could not be defended and by the time that Essex had sent Colonel John Brown ahead to scout the approaches to the city, the royalists were already withdrawing. Rupert posted 1,000 dragoons at Powick Bridge to cover their rear, however, and it was this force that Brown stumbled into on 23 September. Surprised by the encounter, Brown nonetheless ignored the advice of more cautious men, and rushed into an engagement. So hasty was he, in fact, that it was said that resting royalists did not have time to put on their armour. But the surprise did not help Brown – his men were caught in a defile, and met with a counter-charge, and a rout ensued. The psychological impact of this defeat was considerable, enhancing Rupert's reputation and inducing caution in Essex. However, since the royalists had withdrawn, Essex was able to enter Worcester on 24 September and so both sides were able to claim victory. Once in Worcester, or at least so it was later claimed, the parliamentary troops defiled the cathedral.[1]

Although there had been clashes and skirmishes over the previous summer, this was the first encounter between elements of the field armies – by most reckonings the first battle of the war. Much worse was to come, of course. On 12 October the King felt able to leave Shrewsbury and seek an engagement with the parliamentary army. Avoiding what had become parliamentary strongholds such as Warwick and Coventry the King moved towards London as fast as possible. On 22 October his troops were quartered in Edgecott, north of Banbury, when he was informed that Essex had moved close to intercepting him, lying only seven miles away at Kineton. The King saw the opportunity to strike a significant blow, and so it was that battle was sought at Edgehill.[2]

Prior to 1639 England had enjoyed a long peace. Expeditions to Cadiz, the Île de Ré and Germany in the 1620s had been both unimpressive and the sum total of England's official involvement in European war. Writing in the 1630s with their eyes on continental Europe, and in the 1640s with their eyes on England in the throes of civil war, many people thought of this period before the Bishops' Wars as England's halcyon days. While from these two viewpoints that is a reasonable opinion, it should not be taken as evidence that England was a completely demilitarized society prior to the Bishops' Wars, or that there was no military experience in the English armies of 1642.[3]

Military knowledge arrived in England by a variety of routes. Significant numbers of Englishmen had experience of service as volunteers in the European wars, among them a number of significant commanders on both sides: Essex, Hopton, Waller, Sir Thomas Fairfax, Astley, James King (Newcastle's chief of staff), Ruthven, Lindsey and Prince Rupert to name only a few who figure in this chapter.[4] We know more about the Scottish volunteers in those wars, but it seems that, in addition to those in royal armies and navies, an average of 3,000 Englishmen were in Dutch or French Protestant service each year between 1562 and 1642.[5] Some of that direct personal experience of warfare had been passed on during the 1630s to the Trained Bands. The appointment of muster masters with military experience, and of the Low Countries captains, was a minor, but nonetheless significant, attempt to update the expertise of the English military. Those who had served also passed on their experience, both about techniques and about their experience of warfare, through personal testimony. The fledgling news industry, permitted to publish foreign news during the 1620s and '30s, reported military affairs on the continent. This, and the oral networks with which it intersected, spread awareness of war and its costs to many English people. Maimed soldiers, and swaggering veterans, were familiar stereotypes during the 1630s. The escalating conflict and changing military tactics spawned an impressive technical literature and this too was current in England. This was of significance not just to armchair generals, but to aspiring combatants too: Edward Harley, evidently anticipating the onset of war in March 1642, paid a bookseller's bill in which at least one third of his thirty purchases were directly concerned with military matters. This no doubt informed his transformation from scholar at Lincoln's Inn to colonel in the parliamentary armies. Obviously, such technical advice was available to many others.[6]

Although the crown had complained about the Trained Bands for much of the three generations prior to 1640, they did nonetheless provide a basis for military mobilization. Some, particularly those in London, were significant forces, well-armed and regularly drilled. Despite local apathy, or hostility, energetic lieutenants had in some places managed to foster a degree of military training. In Great Yarmouth in 1638, and in London the following year, there had been military exercises which gave a taste of what was to come. Of course, the Trained Bands were less than perfectly armed and drilled, had no experience of actual combat and had been the object of governmental concern for years, even generations. Nonetheless, in 1642 they provided a useful stock of arms, and some useful military skills. The King, on his progress from York to Shrewsbury, had tried to muster the bands, or take their arms, and the London Trained Bands provided the core of Essex's army.[7]

Warfare did not come to Englishmen from a clear blue sky, therefore. There was a limited but still significant pool of direct experience, evident in the command of both sides, and a wider pool of second-hand, drilled or theoretical knowledge. This extended to the rank and file, in the form of experience in the Trained Bands. It was some time before these rudiments were transformed into armies to impress the major European powers, but the thousands of men gathered between Kineton and Edgehill in October 1642 were not completely unprepared for what was about to happen. However, although there was enough expertise available to hold a proper battle, the experience that followed was undoubtedly shocking for many participants and observers.

Edgehill presents a steep scarp face to the plain below, reaching 1:4 in places, and it was below this commanding promontory that Charles's army took up position to confront the parliamentary army.[8] Essex was apparently surprised by the news that battle was about to be joined – he was on his way to church at 8 a.m. on the morning of 23 October when intelligence was brought to him of Charles's movements. The standard battle formation in the seventeenth century was for infantry to line up in the centre, flanked on either side by cavalry regiments, and this the royalists did at the foot of the hill. But this precipitated the first of many quarrels in the royalist command. The King's general, Lindsey, favoured ranging his infantry according to Dutch practice, a preference which reflected his own experience of service under Maurice of Nassau. Prince Rupert, although only a cavalry commander, had been granted a commission which meant that he took orders directly from the King, not the general. He favoured the more complex Swedish infantry formation, which had been very successful under the command of Gustavus Adolphus. Others present had experience of these questions – Ruthven, who had served with Gustavus, and Astley, who had served with Maurice. If this exchange reveals a relatively informed expertise among the command it also reveals the problems of command structure which bedevilled both war efforts, but particularly that of the royalists. Lindsey, having lost the argument, told the King that he would prefer to serve as a colonel facing Essex, since the King did not trust him as his general. This he did, and he received a fatal wound in the ensuing battle.

Essex would have preferred to wait for reinforcements, which were known to be on their way, but could not avoid battle with the royal forces in such close proximity. The parliamentary force was, accordingly, drawn up with infantry in the centre, cavalry and dragoons on either side and, crucially as it turned out, two regiments of cavalry in the rear. They were perhaps caught on the hop, trying to move to reinforce the cavalry facing Rupert but failing to make the manoeuvre before battle was joined. In any case, the battle opened with exchanges of artillery fire which lasted an hour, but did little damage. It was Rupert, commanding the cavalry on the royalists' right wing, who initiated the real fighting, when he led a devastating charge against the parliamentarian cavalry. At almost the same time Wilmot, on the other royalist flank, led a similarly successful charge, and a second wave of royalist cavalry charges joined the pursuit of the fleeing parliamentarians.

This pursuit was unfortunate, and a sign of inexperience. A royalist victory would have been much more likely had the cavalry regrouped and supported an assault on the parliamentarian infantry. As it was, with the royalist cavalry in exultant pursuit of the parliamentarians through Kineton, Astley was left to lead the royalist infantry forward without cavalry support. The second line of cavalry had disobeyed an

At Ege-hill 16 peeces of Cañon shot againft 80 of E: of Essex
Liffegard & not one man hurte, & thofe 80 broke in upon
1600 of the Kings, 4. of yᵉ Parliā: Reg: ran a way, & 16 troops
of Horfe, fo wee warre 6000 & ther 18000, yet wee tooke yᵉ
Standerd & Clefte Sᵗ Ed: Varney Standerbearer in the head
& Slew the Lord Lindfey Generall of the Fielde.

The battle of Edgehill

order from Rupert not to quit the field, perhaps confused by the shape
of the battle, and something similar seems to have happened on the
other wing, where it was not immediately clear that the parliamentary
cavalry had indeed been scattered.

With the cavalry gone, the infantry battle came to a grim 'push of
pike'. As the infantry closed they faced each other at close range, firing
volleys, until hand-to-hand combat was joined. Safety depended on
mastering fear and maintaining the ranks, which could also withstand
a cavalry charge, since horses would turn away from a solid rank of
men. Among these raw recruits, however, that discipline was not easy
to maintain and Nathaniel Fiennes remembered many years later the
sight of four regiments fleeing their colours without a fight in the face
of an intimidating cavalry charge.[9] As the two bodies of infantry closed
with one another the parliamentarian cavalry regiments that had been
held in reserve were able to advance through the gaps in the parliamentary infantry formations and inflict heavy losses on the royalist infantry.
These were terrifying moments for foot soldiers, what all the drill was
designed to avoid, when they enjoyed little protection:

when the horsemen fall in amongst the infantry and cruelly hack them; the poor
soldiers the while sheltering their heads with their arms, sometime with the one,

then the other, until they be both most cruelly mangled: and yet the head fares little better the while for their defence, many of them not escaping with less than two or three wounds through the skull into the membranes, and often into the brain.

But flight was hardly an attractive option either if the enemy pursued, 'his hinder parts meet with great wounds as over the thighs, back, shoulders and neck'.[10] If Rupert had not belatedly succeeded in rallying some of his cavalry and returning to the field, the parliamentarian cavalry might themselves have secured an outright victory for their army.

When night fell, however, the two sides had fought themselves to a standstill. They slept in the field and overnight there was a sharp frost. Sir Adrian Scrope was among those seriously wounded. Left for dead and stripped, he spent the night among the fallen. It was common throughout the war for the fallen to be stripped, so that in the morning the field was covered with naked corpses. Waking in the morning he pulled a corpse on top of himself for warmth, and survived. William Harvey, the great anatomist and physiologist, to whom we owe this story, noted that the cold had probably saved Scrope's life by slowing his bleeding.[11] Harvey himself had left London with Charles and at Edgehill was given care of the Prince and the Duke of York (it was the later recollections of the latter that furnish us with important details about the battle). Taking cover behind a bush, he took out a book and read 'but he had not read very long before a bullet of a great gun grazed on the ground near him, which made him remove his station'.[12]

Harvey was probably not the only one to receive a rapid education at Edgehill. The King, shocked by the sight of sixty corpses piled up where the royal standard had flown, huddled over a small fire through the night, unable to sleep because of the moans and cries of the wounded. At Edgehill as elsewhere, the proportion of wounded to dead was higher among officers, probably because they received medical help more promptly. When the two sides faced each other the following morning it was clear that many men had been less fortunate than Sir Adrian Scrope: according to one account 'the field was covered with the dead, yet no-one could tell to what party they belonged'. Cold and hungry, many witnesses seem to have experienced a kind of lethargy, a numbness that made further action difficult. Sir William Le Neve, sent by the King to demand surrender, was rebuffed, but he reported 'trouble and

disorder' on the faces of Essex and other senior officers.[13] Soldiers had
not eaten for a day, and the horses were also probably unwatered.[14]
There was little willingness or capacity on either side to renew the
engagement.[15] Among the dead was Sir Edmund Verney, committed to
the cause against his political judgement, but in gratitude for the patronage he had enjoyed from the King. He died carrying the standard in the
royal lifeguard, apparently having killed two men with his own hands,
including the man who killed his own loyal servant. He had broken
the point of the standard at push of pike. One story had it that the
parliamentarian soldiers had to cut his hand off in order to take the
standard, and that he was also wearing a small ring with a miniature
portrait of the King.[16]

About 1,500 men had died, evenly divided between the two sides, and
the battle is usually reckoned a draw. But the royalists emerged with a
clear advantage since the road to London was now open. Essex had
withdrawn northwards to Warwick, allowing the King to move south,
securing first Banbury and then Oxford. A rapid advance might have
taken him straight to London, with enormous political dividends, but
he hesitated, resisting the suggestion that a flying column of 3,000
men be despatched to arrive in London in advance of the regrouped
parliamentary forces. This fateful decision may have been taken on the
morning after, to allow time to bury the dead, treat the wounded and
to take stock, but it seems more likely that the discussion took place
some days later. Either way, and although there was perhaps a clear
chance to capture London, it is probably an exaggeration to say that it
was Charles's chance to win the war, at least if that is taken to mean his
chance to impose his own terms for a settlement. Certainly, a decisive
victory at Edgehill, if it had been achieved, would not in itself have
ended the war: it is very unlikely that resistance elsewhere would have
ceased, or that the Scots would have stood by while the royalists imposed
terms on Parliament.[17]

In London, news of the battle, and the face-to-face meeting with the
horrors of war, affected the political will to fight, partly because reporting was so confused. Three days prior to the battle Stephen Charlton
recorded in a private letter reports of a great battle in which, some said,
Charles had been captured, and Rupert and Essex (according to varying
reports) had been killed. In fact, of course, there had been no battle at
all, but Charlton spent an entire morning at Westminster trying to find

out more. It was symptomatic of an atmosphere of fevered speculation, of a massive appetite for news which was fed by rumour and flying report. On the day of Edgehill the people of Alveston heard the cannon and, a short while later, saw terrified parliamentarian deserters streaming through the village. Royalist deserters arrived in Oxford the next day, with exaggerated stories of defeat told to excuse their own flight. Two days after the battle villagers of Alveston were able to visit the field to see for themselves and the same day parliamentarian scouts arrived in Oxford, broadcasting news of a crushing parliamentary victory. The reporting in London was understandably confused. Two days after the battle a hurriedly produced pamphlet reproduced a letter from 'a gentleman of quality'. It claimed a total parliamentarian victory and the capture of Rupert. Two more pamphlets that were no more accurate appeared over the next two days and it was only six days after the battle that firmer news was available in print: a group of parliamentary officers, including Denzil Holles, published their account of the battle. On 2 November a royalist rival was available, smuggled from Oxford.[18] In the meantime, it seems safe to assume, rumour was rife.

Chastened, the Commons agreed with the Lords on 2 November to reopen peace negotiations and Sir John Evelyn and other parliamentary commissioners caught up with the King at Reading. Evelyn was refused access, however, on the grounds that he stood charged of treason, and the royalist advance continued. Rupert stormed Brentford, ten miles west of London, on 12 November, allowing his troops to sack it. Sir Thomas May was later to say that this was the date on which the word 'plunder' entered the English language. In fact the word was known during the 1630s from reports of the wars in Germany: it was the experience rather than the word that England was now learning. Brentford made clear what to expect from triumphant troops under Rupert's command. Although Essex had by this time returned to London, the political and military momentum was with the King. On the day before Brentford was sacked the King had agreed in principle to peace negotiations, and suggested Windsor as a venue, but the military option still clearly appealed as his army advanced on London.[19]

On 13 November the royalist army faced London's citizenry at Turnham Green. Six thousand men of the Trained Bands had mustered at Chelsea Fields the previous day. At Turnham Green the ranks of London's defenders had swollen to 24,000, comprising members of the

Trained Bands of Hertfordshire, Essex and Surrey, as well as willing apprentices and Essex's army. Supported by enthusiastic camp followers and with much superior numbers, this people's army successfully out-faced the royalist forces. Essex's guns fired a few shots but there was no substantial engagement before the royalists withdrew. This non-battle was in some ways as important as the actual battle at Edgehill. The King returned to winter quarters in Oxford on 23 November.[20]

Military campaigning was an adjunct to, rather than an alternative to, negotiation. In some places the formation of parties did not really take place until 1643 as an early settlement was sought.[21] Peace proposals were more or less continuously in the air, and fighting was undertaken with an eye on the eventual peace. On both sides a significant body of opinion was reluctant to pursue an outright victory for this reason – it would make an honourable peace more difficult to achieve. In fact negotiation had continued almost until the last minute. On 25 August, only three days after raising his standard, Charles sent peace com-missioners to Parliament, but they received a very frosty reception. It is hard not to believe that Charles's approach, and its firm rebuff, reflected a mutual awareness of the disappointing state of the King's military preparations at that point. Parliament demanded the withdrawal of treason charges and that Charles should take down his standard. These terms were, of course, unacceptable, and the incivility with which the King's commissioners had been received reflected a fair degree of confi-dence at Westminster.[22] On 5 September, Falkland was sent to West-minster again to canvass peace and holding out the hope of a 'thorough reformation in religion', but the approach was once again rebuffed. This seems to have reflected the distrust of Charles among those who remained at Westminster. In its public response Parliament called for the withdrawal of the King's protection from all those who might subsequently be prosecuted as delinquents, and that his protection be extended to all those who had stood firm to Parliament's cause. This amounted, more or less, to a public statement that Parliament represented the nation and that Charles's party was composed of delinquents and traitors.[23]

How these approaches had been received, and the improvement of the royalists' military position, seems to have strengthened the hand of hardliners of the royalist camp. Henrietta Maria was particularly influential as an advocate of this hard line, and thought that the message of 25 August had threatened to ruin Charles altogether.[24] Parliament's rebuff may also have been a factor in the King's increasingly successful recruiting drive.[25] In any case, by late September, Parliament had become the suitor receiving rebuffs. On 26 September, shortly after the first and disappointing encounter at Powick Bridge, Essex wrote to the Earl of Dorset asking what kind of approach might be acceptable. The response, although receptive in principle to an approach, presented the same stumbling block – the King would not receive anyone who stood charged with treason. By 20 October, Parliament had become convinced of the futility of this initiative and it was declared dead, only three days before Edgehill.[26] Pym took this moment, of the dropping of a peace initiative, to launch a proposal for an oath of association, apparently seeking to cement the coalition now that further fighting was inevitable.[27]

These to-ings and fro-ings have a pattern which persisted for much of the war. The Earl of Essex had delayed his departure from London in early September as he sought the title Lord High Constable of England. This was not (or not only) a personal vanity – what he wanted was the power to negotiate with the King independently of parliamentary control.[28] The desire to unite military command with negotiating power offers further demonstration that for many participants the main purpose of the fighting was to negotiate from a position of strength. Throughout the conflict, negotiations took place in the light of calculations about military strength – the actual position and course of the war, and the prospect of outside help. In the autumn of 1642 both these calculations played well to royalist hardliners, as Henrietta Maria's efforts on the continent seemed to offer a further strengthening of their military position. Her reception in Holland had been disappointing, but in late November she was offered money, and there were soon hopes of help from Denmark and even France. She was also trying to recall English soldiers from service in the continental armies, although it is not clear how many returning soldiers fought for Parliament rather than the King. It is certainly true that Parliament was already currying favour with the Covenanters, offering the abolition of episcopacy in response to the General Assembly's declared view that unity of religion in the two kingdoms was the best way forward. These undertakings about the future of the English church in the event of a parliamentarian victory further strengthened the resolve of royalists in refusing to deal.[29]

Over the winter of 1642–3 there was little in the military fortunes of the war, or the diplomatic position, to shift the weight of royalist opinion. Powick Bridge and Edgehill did wonders for royalist morale and, although Turnham Green had raised parliamentary spirits, the fortunes of the field armies had not bolstered their negotiating position. Neither, on the whole, had the numerous regional campaigns. In the autumn of 1642 the royalist forces from Cornwall crossed the Tamar and put pressure on Plymouth. Privateers raised in Cornwall successfully evaded Warwick's ships and the situation was sufficiently serious by December that the Committee of Safety turned its attention away from the defence of London to the situation in the south-west. Although the royalists did not succeed in taking Plymouth they did summon (that is, demand the surrender of) Exeter on 30 December and stormed Topsham, cutting the city off from the sea, before they were forced to pull back, having over-extended themselves.[30]

In the north, Newcastle advanced successfully in December, taking York on 1 December, engaging Fairfax at Tadcaster on 6 December and forcing his retreat to Selby the following day. By establishing his position at Pontefract, Newcastle cut communications between what had emerged as important parliamentary bases in the West Riding cloth towns and the strategically crucial port of Hull. The capture of Newark secured communications with Oxford. However, royalist victories for Saville at Leeds and Wakefield were not followed up: Bradford and Halifax resisted successfully and both Leeds and Wakefield were retaken. Nonetheless, the parliamentary hold on Yorkshire was weakened through the autumn and winter, and neighbouring parliamentary commanders – Gell in Derbyshire and Irby in Lincolnshire – were unwilling to help. The capture of Nantwich by Sir William Brereton served to make the military position in the north appear more balanced, but it was really the royalists who had more to be pleased about. Although Newcastle could not easily move south, given the sustained strength of Parliament's forces in the West Riding and at Hull, his was the better position.[31]

In Oxford the King's position was consolidated by the establishment of garrisons at Banbury and Brill. The parliamentary forces had abandoned Worcester on 5 November, and on 5 December Marlborough was stormed (and ruthlessly plundered). As the Earl of Stamford marched to the south-west to support resistance to Hopton, Gloucestershire was left weakened and the Earl of Hertford advanced through the gap with his Welsh regiments to Oxford, taking Cirencester at the second attempt on 2 February. By early December, Charles was also in a strong position internationally: the Danish court had given encouraging signs of support and the death of Richelieu and the succession of Mazarin as chief minister in France seemed to offer the prospect of French support too.[32]

Through the autumn and winter, therefore, the King's military position had become clear: his base in Oxford was consolidated and Cornwall and Wales were in the hands of his supporters. The Earl of Newcastle had established a strong position in the north. His three forces were, however, separated by significant parliamentary forces: Hopton's advance was blocked in Devon and by Bristol and Gloucester; Newcastle was hampered by Brereton, the West Riding and Hull. Parliament's power base was also clear: London and its resources were the foundation on which Parliament's position was established, Sir William Waller had established a powerful position in the southern counties and Parliament had secure control over the south-east.[33] Overall, the King's position was not bad, which meant that his opponents' position was not good (see Map 2).

The rebuff received by Sir John Evelyn at Reading in early November was of a piece with the military action at Brentford and the attitude displayed afterwards: it reflected the growing confidence on the royalist side. On 6 December, John Lilburne, a prisoner from the fighting at Brentford, was charged with treason. Sentenced to death he was only saved by a declaration of the Houses that, if he were hanged, the same punishment would be meted out to all prisoners that fell into parliamentary hands.[34] Little had happened since August to dispirit the royalists, or to convince them that they might have to pay a price for high-handedness after the war, although fear of reprisal clearly continued to serve as a restraint.

Parliament, on the other hand, faced more difficulties in stiffening the sinews of its coalition. By November there were two positions emerging in parliamentary ranks as to what would be a sufficient settlement. A number of members, prominent among them Denzil Holles, were horrified by the potential costs of war, as revealed at Edgehill and, in Holles's case at least, Brentford. Holles had an honourable record as a parliamentary defender of law and religion, and his views were close to Pym's. He was a much less effective speaker, often referred to as intemperate, but he had also been in at least as much trouble. In 1629 he had helped to hold the Speaker down in his chair to prevent him dissolving Parliament until some final business was rushed through, and had read a paper which denounced Arminianism and unparliamentary customs duties as treasonous. He was arrested, released and finally tried in 1630, living under a whopping bail for the rest of the decade. Given his record it is little surprise that he was prominent in supporting Pym's programme, including a proper revenue settlement, although he actively worked to save Strafford's life, presumably because he was his brother-in-law. On two other issues, he tended to caution – in early April 1641 he had spoken about the threat of mechanic preachers and in late 1642 he had direct experience of the trauma of war. Given a military command in the West Country he was present at the parliamentary defeat at Sherborne Castle, where more than half his men were lost. He returned to London, where he recruited his regiment back to strength in time to join Essex at Edgehill, where he was praised for his role. But at Brentford his regiment was surprised. Holles was not there, but one third of his men were killed, and the others captured. According to D'Ewes, writing in late November, he 'was much cooled in his fierceness by the great slaughter made in his regiment at Brentford'.[35] In order to achieve a settlement Holles was willing to see concessions to Charles on the control of civil government, so long as religion was made safe. Throughout the spring of 1643, and the rest of the 1640s, he was a supporter of settlement whenever a formal peace seemed to be possible.

A harder line was taken by others, prominent among them Pym, who thought no settlement was safe without constraints on the King's freedom to choose officers of state. In his view the King was in the hands of military hardliners, and no peace could succeed while their counsels prevailed.[36] Henrietta Maria's apparent success in raising money for Charles provided the context for the first Assessment Ordinance on 29 November, which imposed a tax by the authority of an ordinance. It was the first of many and, in fact, the form of the tax became the basis for direct taxation for the following 140 years.[37] It was also far heavier than ship money and arguably even less legally justifiable, resting as it did on an ordinance. Three days earlier, the Commons had heard a suggestion that a strict league should be entered into with the Dutch republic, an initiative which presumably grew out of the same apprehension.[38] On 15 December the counties of Leicester, Derbyshire, Nottinghamshire, Rutland, Northampton, Buckingham and Bedford were combined in a single Midland Association – an attempt to bolster the war effort by giving it a basis larger than a single county. On 20 December the Eastern Association was formed and, on 31 December, Warwickshire and Staffordshire were associated under the command of Lord Brooke.[39] These measures, necessary to secure a stronger bargaining position, were in themselves problematic, both locally and nationally. Pushing ahead with the war effort created new pressures for peace, and reinforced many of the existing ones.

London was also divided between those keen to prosecute the war and those keen to secure an early peace. Although a deputation from the City had approached Parliament on 13 November petitioning against any accommodation[40] and made a loan, there was by now a powerful peace movement in London which produced petitions for accommodation through December and January. Throughout the war, in fact, there was a popular royalism in London, drawing on resistance to godly reformation, the financial demands of the parliamentary war effort and loyalty to the monarch. The extent of this can be gauged from the known support offered to the royalists from London and the prosecutions for words spoken against the parliamentary cause. On 8 December a crowd gathered at Haberdashers' Hall, site of the meeting of the Committee of Both Houses for the Advance of Money: originally responsible for raising supplies for the army it had oversight of the imposition of penal taxation on neutrals or passive royalists who had failed to lend money or supplies voluntarily. It was one of the nerve centres of the war effort, in other words, and active parliamentarians present that day were jostled. Four days later a meeting of the City's Common Council was disrupted by a large crowd. They were identified as royalists by their opponents, but what they demanded was peace: when someone shouted 'Peace and truth' someone else immediately replied 'Hang truth! We want peace at any price'. There was violence outside, prompted by the arrival of soldiers going about other business, and petitioners were openly threatening to pursue more violent courses if their demands were not met. Pressure was maintained through the rest of the month, and peace petitions were presented on 17, 19 and 22 December. They drew on the ranks of prosperous and middling tradesmen, and men of relatively conservative religious views can be identified as prominent among them. They seem to have identified the Lords rather than the Commons as their most sympathetic audience.[41] The threat of disorder may have lain behind the closing of the theatres in September and the ban on bear-baiting on 12 December.[42] In early January a further escalation took place, when a large number of apprentices gathered in Covent Garden to call for peace, threatening to plunder houses there. Their petition claimed 20,000 signatures (probably an exaggeration), but it was agreed that it could be presented only by a delegation of twenty.[43]

Maintaining the war effort in Parliament and London was a political problem, just as it was for the King in Oxford and the royalist heartlands. The seriousness of the problem entered the calculations of each side about the military strength of their enemy's position. Two days before the apprentices' peace petition was presented Edgehill was in the news again. On 1 January, between 3 and 4 p.m., ghostly apparitions appeared there that seemed to point to God's desire for peace. '[F]earful and strange apparitions of spirits as sounds of drums, trumpets, with the discharging of cannons, muskets, carbines, petronels' caused 'terror and amazement of all the fearful hearers and beholders'. Four days later people in Kineton heard 'the doleful and hideous groans of dying men ... crying revenge and some again to ease them of their pain by friendly killing them'. Trembling in their beds, they heard what appeared to be the beginning of an assault, which sent many to hide in corners or under their bedclothes. Those brave enough to look out of their windows saw horsemen riding against one another before vanishing. The following night a strong watch was set and many people witnessed a full-scale battle, which began at midnight and ended 'in the twinkling of an eye' at daybreak.

These events were reported to the King by Samuel Marshall, the minister of Kineton, and Charles sent six men from Oxford to investigate. Having stayed several days they saw and heard these phenomena for themselves and were able to identify a number of the apparitions, including Sir Edmund Verney. Robert Ellit, who claimed to be an eyewitness to these events, had a pamphlet published, as did Thomas Jackson, whose pamphlet rehearsed essentially the same story, with more detail, and was certified not only by Marshall but also by William Wood, JP.[44] Sky battles such as this were an unusual but not unknown phenomenon, and were widely regarded as having a contemporary political meaning.

They could be seen as a kind of 'special providence', a direct message from God, and certainly belong with a wider interest in such wonders: these years seem to have been good ones for such wonder pamphlets.[45]

That such phenomena meant something was obvious, but it was less clear what they meant, and authors were characteristically wary about interpreting them very directly. *The New Yeares wonder* was cautious but did note a fairly limited meaning: some learned observers suggested that a search be made for unburied carcasses, which, being duly done, revealed that there were indeed some.[46] *A great vvonder* was bolder. Historical precedent suggested that such diabolic visitations 'appear either in premonstrance of God's Judgements, or as fatal ambassadors to declare the message of mortality and destruction to offending nations'. Following such signs God afflicted Germany and other places 'with the horror of a civil and foreign wars'.[47] The fact that this apparition appeared at Christmas-time suggested that 'the saviour of the world who died to save mankind, had been angry that so much Christian blood was there spilt'. But here, of course, interpretations might differ as to the fault, or even the response that was required. Ellit concluded that it was the significance of the New Year that really counted: 'the hopeful and believing Christian to put on new obedience unto heaven, and begin with the New Year, a newness of life and conversation'.[48] Both authors concluded that these terrifying apparitions should induce men to seek peace, but Jackson seemed to place the onus for this on the royalists. It was at Edgehill, he rather controversially claimed, that Essex had 'obtained a glorious victory over the cavaliers':[49] surely such an interpretation suggested a view about whom God might be speaking to. But his conclusion was more neutral: 'What this does portend, God only knows, and time perhaps will discover; but doubtlessly it is a sign of his wrath against this land, for these civil wars, which He in his good time finish, and send a sudden peace between his Majesty and Parliament'.[50] But what, specifically, was the cause of His anger, and against whom was it directed?

These pamphlets saw in the horrors of Edgehill an argument for a speedy peace, and that probably resonated with many people both at the centres of power in Westminster and Oxford, and in the country at large. January saw many petitions for peace or accommodation, and a 'pleasant dialogue . . . suitable to the times' called *Peace, and No Peace*.[51] Open warfare had changed the terms of political debate, and choices made in the tense summer of 1642 might well now seem misjudged; and continued warfare did not seem to be favouring the parliamentary cause either.

On the other hand, pressure for peace raised the spectre of a capitulation, moreover a capitulation to someone who was not trustworthy. Two pamphlets from this period, *Plaine English* and *An Answer to Mis'Led Dr Ferne*, gave intellectual support to a stronger parliamentarian line. This is, of course, only a minor part of the press output in these months, but the arguments are significant, and part of a wider pamphlet exchange. *Plaine English* was sufficiently provocative to produce explicit responses and Richard Baxter, the Shropshire Puritan, religious writer and active parliamentarian, was to claim it marked the death of constitutionalism.[52] The fear that Parliament would conclude a weak peace prompted a profoundly radical response.

During the previous autumn a number of pamphlets had considered the right of a parliament to depose a king. *An Answer* took a strong line on this question, arguing that the authority of all kings was essentially elective, deriving from a view that the authority of the most numerous opinion should prevail. A similar argument was preached before the Lord Mayor in March 1643, the same month that Prynne, one of the three Puritan martyrs of the Personal Rule, published a pamphlet rehearsing numerous historical precedents for deposition. Henry Marten, who had apparently favoured deposition as early as 1641, was imprisoned in August 1643 for supporting such views, but his was clearly not a completely isolated case. Prynne had by that time published the fourth part of *The Soveraigne power of Parliaments and Kingdomes*, which translated the key arguments of the notorious *Vindiciae, contra tyrannos* in favour of tyrannicide.[53]

Implied in this power of deposition was a renunciation of the idea of constitutional balance which had characterized the *Answer to the XIX Propositions*. In December 1642 the *Discourse between a Resolved and Doubtful Englishman* had said this explicitly – necessity allowed Parliament to set aside constitutional and legal precedent and the King had no power to reject legislation. This truth about where power lay had been revealed only slowly and that had made it more palatable: 'that necessity might make the people know that that power was just and reasonable, as fearing the people's weakness could not digest these strong and sinewy truths, whereunto their stomachs had not of long time been accustomed'. Such truth was all that made us 'firm, and resolute, and true Englishmen', however. *The Privileges of the Commons* had argued, in December 1642, that the Commons was superior to the Lords and in the following March *The Priviledges of Parliament* argued that the Houses could impose legislation on a dissenting monarch.[54]

Such claims were difficult to justify on the basis of precedent and rested instead on a radical view of the basis of political authority. They were suggesting in effect that the ancient constitution – the complex of rights and liberties enshrined in the common law and customs of the kingdom – should give way before parliamentary sovereignty. As the author of *Touching the Fundamental Laws* put it in February, the ultimate authority was not Parliament but that 'universal and popular authority, that is in the body of the people, and which (for the public good, and preservation) is above every man and all laws'. It was here that *Plaine English* made its distinctive claim – that the people could renounce the authority of parliaments too, if that body threatened to betray their interests. In the immediate circumstances of January 1643, this threat lay with the dominance of proponents of an easy peace in Parliament, and the absence on business of the more resolute members. The danger was that Parliament 'out of an intolerable weariness of this present condition, and fear of the event [outcome], agree to the making up of an unsafe unsatisfying accommodation'. War weariness, and fear of the outcome, threatened a betrayal of the cause and of the sacrifices already made which was here being countered by the assertion of political fundamentals.

Jeremiah Burroughs had made a similar argument in December 1642 in response to a direct challenge by Henry Ferne, the royalist propagandist. Ferne had asked: 'But if Parliaments should degenerate and grow tyrannical, what means of safety could there be for such a State'. What he seems to have hoped would make the claim for parliamentary sovereignty look ridiculous actually prompted a more revolutionary argument.[55]

Burroughs's argument rested in part on English freedoms, which distinguished free men from slaves:

There is no country in the world where country men, such as we call the yeomanry, yea and their farmers and workmen under them, do live in that fashion and freedom as they do in *England*; in all other places they are slaves in comparison, their lives are so miserable as they are not worth the enjoying, they have no influence at all into the government they are under, nothing to do in the making of laws, or any way consenting to them, but must receive them from others, according to their pleasure; but in *England* every freeholder has an influence into the making and consenting every law he is under, and enjoys his own with as true a title as the nobleman enjoys whatsoever is his.[56]

Here, perhaps, is an echo of the neo-Roman ideas of freedom expressed the previous summer, now cast as a potential source of resistance to Parliament.[57] But there was also an Old Testament view of justice – that the shedding of innocent blood required expiation in order to avoid God's fury. Bowles put this argument too, in *Plaine English*:

how can the land by this accommodation be cleansed from blood, that crying sin, which has been contracted by this quarrel ... God will not prosper an accommodation without the execution of justice upon these bloodthirsty men ... If the people, especially the parliament does not their utmost to wash their hands, and cleanse the land from this innocent and precious blood that has been shed; I fear that blood ... will be avenged upon them, which they will believe, when they see their accommodation turned into an assassination.[58]

This hard line depended for its appeal on a conviction that Parliament was in defensive arms and that Charles could not be trusted – the latter point though was difficult to express or justify in respectable circles. This, and his improving military position, gave the King little incentive to deal with the hardliners, and the open expression of this more radical position was probably more useful in stiffening royalist than parliamentarian resolve. These pamphlets reflected a developing radicalism on the parliamentarian side which was an embarrassment to mainstream parliamentarians and a gift to royalist propagandists.

Arguments about the basis of political authority were of great significance for the future but were not very prominent in the peace proposals which were eventually sent to the King at Oxford in early February. Parliament's discussion of the propositions for peace through the winter of 1642–3 took place against a complicated but generally deteriorating military position, and complex responses to this new political world. Drafting lasted for several weeks, from late December onwards, in the light of pressure from London crowds. Propositions drawn up in the Lords on 20 December were considered by the Commons two days later. These initiatives were given final form in the propositions presented to the King at Oxford on 1 February. They called for the disbandment of the royal army, the settlement of the church and militia on the advice of Parliament, parliamentary power to make a number of judicial appointments, and pardon and restitution for parliamentarians facing charges or who had been deprived of office. The King's rejection of these proposals was almost instantaneous. His public tone was sorrowful, but in a private letter he wrote candidly that he thought 'no less power than he who made the world can draw peace out of these articles'. A victory for Prince Rupert at Cirencester on 2 February further convinced Secretary Nicholas that the parliamentary commissioners would have to settle for less.[59]

Doomed from the start, negotiations nonetheless continued through February and March. Charles responded with six demands of his own, including restoration of his revenues, towns, forts and ships, and a cessation as a prelude to negotiation. Formally speaking, therefore, the discussion never got to point one of Parliament's demands – that the royal army disband as a prelude to treaty. The prospects for peace were not promising and (perhaps because) the weight of military advantage was clearly with the King. By late March, Parliament was willing to negotiate its first two demands without a cessation but nothing much in the military situation encouraged flexibility on the King's part, and the tensions within the parliamentary coalition can only have encouraged him too. By mid-April the negotiations seemed to Parliament to be pointless and the commissioners were withdrawn. Both Whitelocke and Clarendon felt that hardline royalist counsels had prevented progress, although Clarendon felt that this reflected the King's natural preferences too, whereas Whitelocke felt that the King might have been inclined to conclude a peace.[60] In any case, the war had been continuing around the country, and was sure now to last for at least one more campaigning season.

The City authorities, informed by discontent within the City, had sent a peace petition to the King on 2 January 1643. Charles's reply to the City, received on 13 January, had given little ground. He was clearly no longer averse to publicity, however, seeking to have his answer read at the City Companies. This was presumably a more or less direct appeal to wavering opinion in London. When Charles's response to the City's peace petition was read out at the Guildhall, it was clear to Pym (who was present) and others that the King's commitment to peace was questionable.[61] It was this view that eventually won out in the spring of 1643. An easy peace might simply allow Charles the freedom to renege on all the commitments extracted from him. It was this issue, in March, which seems to have cut the ground from under the feet of the proponents of peace in Parliament.

The failure of the Oxford propositions could only mean that the war would escalate in the coming year. The march of Prince Rupert on Bristol in early March sent a clear message, as did the publication of an intercepted letter from Charles I to Henrietta Maria in which he acknowledged the lack of serious intent behind his participation in negotiations. By the spring, those in both Oxford and London who had been hoping and working for peace were despondent.[62] The coming year saw successful efforts at administrative and political escalation on the parliamentary side.

In the meantime the influence of 'peace party' arguments in the Commons had persisted throughout the Oxford treaty negotiations. By the spring of 1643 this produced little by way of realistic hopes for settlement and drove some writers to think out loud about what to do if Parliament let them down in their fight against tyranny. Secular radicalism, in other words, was in the air, informed by classical and humanist political thought. Motivated by mistrust of the King and fear for the future of the true religion their intention was to break an impasse in constitutional thinking.[63] Politics were being transformed by war: the reasons for fighting in the autumn of 1642 might no longer seem sufficient in the spring of 1643; the cause being defended might also seem to have been changed. Escalation of the military conflict seems to have posed new difficulties in deciding political allegiances. War was fought in the light of, and as a means to affect, these political choices.

9

Military Escalation, Loyalty and Honour
The English War Efforts in 1643

On a 'calm, clear and fair' day a little over two weeks after the failure of the Oxford treaty a gang of workmen set about the demolition of Cheapside Cross in the commercial heart of London. Over the next three days, as they went about their work, they were watched by a large crowd, whose response was divided: 'the majority blessing the deed but others, although of the same religion, detesting and deploring it'. A troop of horse and a troop of foot were on hand in case of trouble.[1]

This was the final act of a long drama. The cross, standing twelve

The destruction of Cheapside Cross, May 1643

yards high, was richly decorated with images of the saints and the Virgin Mary, and was surmounted with a crucifix. It was a focal point for commercial life and both civic and royal pageantry. Under the Tudors and Stuarts it had been refurbished a number of times, but periodically since the Reformation it had also been attacked, verbally and sometimes physically. Attempts to deface it in 1581 and 1595 had forced the authorities to the expense of repairs, and in 1601, when refurbishment was being considered, George Abbot had been asked for his religious opinion of the cross. The Vice-Chancellor of Oxford and future archbishop had supported the case for repairing it, but had suggested changes to the imagery. In particular he had suggested that the crucifix should be replaced with a pyramid in the hope that people would stop calling it 'the Cross in the Cheap'. While acknowledging the case for iconoclasm, he had been committed to lawful reform – only the magistrate was empowered 'to redress such enormities'. His advice on reformed refurbishment was ignored, however, and following its restoration in 1601 it was attacked once again. Attacked in print in 1641, and physically in January 1642, the cross nonetheless survived until 1643, despite active hostility and the qualms of the more moderate. The Venetian ambassador described it at that point as 'a most beautiful pyramidal cross surrounded with figures of saints of exquisite workmanship'.[2] But then he was a papist.

From 1581 onwards it had been regularly claimed that the cross was a comfort to papists and even that they surreptitiously nodded when they approached it. Hotter Protestants had for years attacked the cross as an idol, while others, convinced of its harmlessness, beauty and civic value, had satirized them for their painful consciences. The cross, among many other things, was a symbol of the divisions within English Protestantism. In the tense atmosphere of January 1642, when London's streets were alive with fear of armed popery, the cross was physically attacked and as a result a protective guard had been posted around it. There remained, nonetheless, a strong current of opinion that the cross was 'an offence and grief of heart to the strong Christian, a stumbling block to the weak, and a very downfall to the stubborn and wilful'.[3]

In throwing their weight behind this view, Parliament and the City authorities were making a clear statement. The troops previously there to protect the cross were, in April, changing sides to protect those charged with its destruction. Armed with an order from the Common

Council and prompted by a parliamentary initiative to purge London of such idols, the workmen set about their task on 2 May: maypole season, a part of the old ritual calendar particularly offensive to godly sensibilities. Superstition was being abolished by authority, but in line with the hopes of many ordinary Londoners. Such purgation did not represent a consensus within English Protestantism, but was one of the actions through which its identity was contested: as our eyewitness noted, the destruction of the cross in 1643 elicited a divided response from a crowd 'of the same religion'.

Cheapside Cross was in one sense a victim of a desire to cement the parliamentary cause. As the Oxford negotiations meandered towards oblivion the fighting had favoured the royalists, and this gave strength to those promoting administrative and ideological radicalization. Hopton had continued to prosper in the West Country in the first months of 1643, turning back a parliamentary advance under Stamford and drawing Ruthin into battle at Braddock Down. There, on 19 January, the royalists won a decisive victory, forcing Ruthin to flee Saltash on 22 January, where the royalists captured arms and ammunition. Attempts at further advances into Devon in February were repelled, however, and after a skirmish at Chagford and a more substantial battle at Modbury, a local cessation was agreed.[4]

Royalist advances in the north were impressive and Henrietta Maria was able to land at Bridlington on 22 February, bringing with her money and supplies assembled in the Netherlands. Unable to prevent her landing, the only parliamentary resistance was an ineffective barrage from ships off the coast while her ships were unloading. According to Clarendon, the hundred-cannon bombardment was primarily a threat to her lodging, 'whereupon she was forced out of her bed, some of the shot making way through her own chamber; and to shelter herself under a bank in the open fields'.[5] Newark resisted a concerted parliamentary assault at the same time, and Scarborough was handed over to the royalists by Sir Hugh Cholmley, who had experienced a change of heart. It was in resistance to further southward advances that Oliver Cromwell began to establish a reputation as a cavalry commander, and a major relief for Parliament was the victory at Grantham on 13 May. Two days later, however, Henrietta Maria's convoy of arms arrived in Oxford and the Queen herself, the 'she-generalissima', was able to move fairly freely from York to Newark and then to Oxford, eventually joining forces with the King on 13 July.[6]

The only encouragement for Parliament in the north came from Lancashire. The Earl of Derby had taken Lancaster for the royalists, but then burnt it, thereby grasping a political defeat from the jaws of military victory. Local opinion, which was by no means uniformly parliamentarian, turned against him and, following a defeat at Whalley Abbey on 20 April, he fled into exile on the Isle of Man. He returned in early 1644, when the arrival of Prince Rupert's troops in Lancashire made it safe for him, but in the meantime the Stanley (and Stuart) interest in Lancashire was defended by his wife. The Countess of Derby held out at Lathom House in one of the more celebrated acts of heroism from this period of the war. This was of larger military significance too, since it tied down parliamentarian forces that might otherwise have been engaged elsewhere.[7]

The Earl of Essex was based at the eastern end of the Thames Valley, and Waller to the south and west of the main royalist forces, centred in Oxford. Waller became something of a darling of the parliamentary side in these early months of the war. Between January and March he won a string of victories at Winchester, Farnham Castle, Arundel Castle and Chichester. Although these were relatively minor victories, they earned him the title 'William the Conqueror' from the London press, not least perhaps because the picture elsewhere was so discouraging for Parliament. In central England the balance of advantage swung quite rapidly. Royalist control of Banbury and Brill gave solidity to the position in Oxford, while Waller's victories had given Parliament secure control of the areas south of the Thames as far west as Devon. In the late spring he won victories against Herbert's forces in Gloucestershire and Monmouthshire, but his advances were halted by Prince Maurice at Ripple Field, north of Tewkesbury (13 April). In the north Midlands, Brereton held much of Cheshire, but not Chester, for Parliament, and Sir John Gell held much of Derbyshire. But in Lichfield local royalists seized control of the cathedral close and in the course of the ensuing siege Lord Brooke was killed by a single shot from the roof of the cathedral. At Hopton Heath (19 March) royalist forces under Compton and Hastings won an important battle over Gell and Brereton, although the loss of the Earl of Northampton was a blow to the royalists. That, and the successful defence of Lichfield by parliamentary forces, prevented a significant follow-up to the victory. Rupert took and sacked Birmingham on 3 April, but, on 21 April, Lichfield Cathedral was captured by Parliament, albeit briefly.[8]

It has been widely accepted that the King had a consistent concern to capture London, and that during 1643 this involved a three-pronged advance from the west, centre and north. In fact, it is not clear that there was a general strategy, or at least one that could be executed. Command structures were rather confused, and communications imperfect, so much of the war had the quality of separate, reactive and tactical skirmishing. At the same time, Parliament's strategy was probably clearer than was once argued – seeking to push back the regional armies sufficiently to allow Essex to move on Oxford from the lower end of the Thames Valley. In either case, it seems that Parliament had little to be cheerful about in strategic terms by late spring 1643 (see map 1).[9] Before the cessation in the west the advantage had clearly been with Hopton, and in the north the war had gone badly for parliamentary forces everywhere except in Lancashire. In the Midlands the picture was more confused, but it is hard to make a case that the parliamentary cause was thriving. The death of Lord Brooke and the victory at Hopton Heath certainly seemed to give the advantage to the royalists.

Told as a series of regional stories, some order can be imposed on the campaign history, but as a week-by-week account, as it might have been heard in Oxford or London, the war made much less sense. In these circumstances rumour and news about particular triumphs or failures had a great impact on morale. Waller's campaign was a huge boost to parliamentarian spirits, for example, although its effect on the outcome of the war is difficult to chart; so too individual setbacks such as the surrender of Scarborough or the death of Lord Brooke. For this reason it was important to try to impose a meaning on events. The death of Brooke, for example, was reported by royalists as a divine judgement on a rebel: an amazing shot that clearly reflected the divine hand. It was reported in the parliamentary paper *Mercurius Britannicus*, on the other hand, as evidence that the cathedral was a 'Monster' with '*bloody Anthems*' and 'murdering *Organ-Pipes*'.[10] It was not only the meaning of the news that was disputed, however, but also its accuracy – the royalist press reported with some glee that 'Sir Jacob Astley, lately slain at Gloucester, desires to know was he slain with a musket or a cannon bullet'.[11] These minor paper skirmishes were probably as significant to morale at any particular point as the realities of the broader strategic position. Nonetheless it is hard to make a case that Parliament's military or political position had been improving between January and April.

In late March, as the Oxford treaty failed and Parliament's military campaigns failed to thrive, there are clear signs of a desire to stiffen the sinews of the parliamentary war effort. However, this administrative problem was inextricably entwined with a desire to define the cause, while at the same time seeming to some people to transform it. Behind the noise of the day-to-day news it was possible to perceive larger trends and deeper problems – the reluctance of armies to move, the difficulties of securing an effective strategic control of particular commanders, the problems of co-ordinating effort, and of supplying the armies. At various points, both sides had experienced these handicaps, but they seemed more urgent for the parliamentarians by the spring of 1643.

One important innovation was the formation of regional armies. In 1642 troops had been mobilized through county institutions, and by custom, tradition and sentiment they identified their role with the defence of that county. Throughout the war troops proved reluctant to cross county boundaries, although this was not a universal phenomenon. The London Trained Bands were willing to march out of London to support the larger cause, and parliamentary armies at Turnham Green and Sherborne included levies from outside the county. Nonetheless, it was recognized as a problem very early on, and Hopton, for example, had raised volunteers willing to travel once he had secured control of the Cornish Trained Bands. The royalists depended more on regiments raised by particular men acting under a direct commission, and these tended to be more mobile, but on the parliamentary side part of the answer was seen to lie in the association of contiguous counties into regional bodies.[12]

Early parliamentary measures of defence had suggested that counties might call on neighbours for assistance in the case of a royalist attack and in October 1642 that had become a formal prescription, extended to the eastern, midland and western counties in ordinances passed between mid- December and early January.[13] The measures taken in October had been associated with a move to create a political bond too, when Pym 'with very great vehemence' promoted a 'covenant or association that all might enter into' to help link 'ourselves together in a more firm bond and union'. Parliament agreed to publish its intention to draw up a Covenant with God to defend 'his truth . . . with the hazard of our lives against the King's army'. In East Anglia, however, there was more support for the military reform than for the proposed oath or covenant. Even so, attempts in the late autumn to co-ordinate efforts in the various associated counties had limited effect and it was not until 11 January that it was agreed to put the ordinance for the Eastern Association into effect. No action was taken until 9 February, when local committee men met in Bury St Edmunds. The vision at Westminster had been of an oath of association supporting an army supplied from the voluntary contributions of those associated. Locally it was decided to proceed by imposing a rate instead – evidence of the tricky local negotiation necessary to secure consent to military mobilization.[14]

Despite the difficulties, both sides saw the need for regional military organizations. The royalists attempted to create associations and Parliament launched a number through 1643, in a rather uncoordinated way. Confused and ad hoc measures layered associations on one another as each ordinance failed to repeal previous measures. As a result some counties were formally associated in different ways – Shropshire, the most extreme example, was in five different associations in six months. More coherence was emerging by 1644, but there were two features of these early measures: their lack of coherence and suspicion at the county level of the new regional committees. Even in East Anglia – according to popular legend a hotbed of Puritan enthusiasm for the parliamentary cause – these measures required careful handling and caused considerable friction.[15]

Military measures on the parliamentary side were imposed by the power of ordinances, and some of the people who had held their noses during the crisis following the attempt on the Five Members might now be more uneasy about the long-term implications of these innovations. During February and March a loan was raised and repaid to set the navy to sea, and an ordinance passed to find sailors to man the ships.[16] On 7 March the Lord Mayor and citizens of London were given the necessary powers to fortify London, allowing them to trench, stop and fortify the highways leading into the City, and to raise a local rate to pay for the work. In next to no time, in the light of the obvious military threat through the spring and summer of 1643, London was turned into a fortress. Towns elsewhere felt vulnerable – obvious targets of military action and not easily defensible – so co-operation with this project was not in itself a measure of allegiance to the parliamentary cause. If the royalists came, they would not necessarily be careful to damage only the property of committed parliamentarians. Surely one of the largest public construction projects in early modern England, the construction of London's defences was turned into a moment of civic celebration, at least if some observers were to be believed.[17] Not all the massive burdens being imposed by the war were met with such enthusiasm: not all had such an obvious and necessary function.

The most powerful demonstration of the potential of ordinances, however, was the creation of an elaborate and productive financial apparatus. In late February, Parliament had imposed a national tax, the Weekly Assessment, on the authority of an ordinance. It was a measure of fearful power, successfully circumventing the problem of local evasion which had drawn the teeth of the main parliamentary tax before 1640, the subsidy. Faced with a demand for a parliamentary subsidy local assessors had winked at or actively supported under-assessment at a staggering level, an administrative weakness which rendered the tax increasingly inadequate to the needs of the crown. In Norfolk, for example, the value of an individual subsidy had fallen by 70 per cent between 1590 and 1630, a crippling loss in a period of inflation, and this was not untypical. The assessment avoided this problem by imposing a fixed sum on the whole country, stipulating how much was to be raised in each county and borough. Local assessors then divided this burden – this system retained local discretion about relative liabilities, but not the power to determine the overall yield. The yields were phenomenal by pre-war standards. Hunstanton, Norfolk, had paid £5 18s for the subsidy of 1626. In 1640 the subsidies cost £10 12s and the poll tax £58 2s 6d. In the twelve months to December 1643 it paid £138 12s. In Hanworth, Norfolk, the assessment was imposed at an annual rate nine times higher than ship money. Examples of this kind could be multiplied endlessly. The burden never went away, either – this was the dominant form of direct taxation for the next 140 years. The financial success of the measure during the 1640s did not recommend it to many contemporaries, however, nor the fact that it was raised by ordinance.

Even more alarmingly, on 28 March, Pym proposed an excise – a tax on consumption which was regarded with deep hostility in Stuart England. There was no current means of taxing commercial wealth, since taxes fell either on the value of land or on personal goods. Taxing consumption provided a means of getting at commercial wealth, but this awful expedient was regarded with horror. In 1628, it has been said, 'excise' was almost a swear word. Faced with Pym's suggestion in 1643 one speaker expressed astonishment 'that he who pretended to stand so much for the liberty of the subject should propose such an unjust, scandalous, and destructive project'.[18]

Although the excise was too loathsome to be countenanced Parliament had, the previous day, found it possible to stomach the Sequestration Ordinance. To the modern eye this was hardly a less objectionable measure, and was certainly extraordinary by pre-war standards. It established local committees with remarkably wide powers to seize the estates of 'notorious delinquents [who] have been causers or instruments of the public calamities'. The profits of the estates would thereafter be 'applied towards the support of the great charges of the commonwealth and for the easing of the good subjects therein, who have hitherto borne the greatest share in these burdens'. The definition of 'notorious delinquent' was a generous one. A number of bishops were named but the act extended well beyond them to all persons 'Ecclesiastical or Temporal' who had raised arms, voluntarily contributed to the royalist war chest, supported the royal armies in any other way, co-operated with robbery and spoil of parliamentarian activists, taken any oath or association against Parliament, or imposed any tax or assessment on behalf of the royalist forces. Such powers were justified in the light of the 'unnatural war raised against the Parliament', but it is possible to imagine that such measures might begin to erode support.[19]

In early May the principle that the royalists should pay was taken further with the imposition of the Fifth and Twentieth Part. Those who had not contributed or lent to the parliamentary cause, or at least had not done so in proportion to their wealth, were to be subject to formal taxation of up to one fifth of the yearly value of their real estate and one twentieth of the value of their personal goods. This was placed in the hands of yet more committees.[20] Here were taxes far heavier than Charles had imposed, with little better legal justification; and financial penalties with a much wider impact than the notorious fines of the Personal Rule. There was a real risk that the cure might begin to seem worse than the disease.[21]

Parliament was in effect improvising a system of government, since it had never previously been an executive body, and many of the functions it was now forced to undertake were therefore pretty much unprecedented. Although this gave it greatly increased powers, it did not necessarily foster efficient use of them. In military matters Parliament ended up with two parallel systems: the defensive forces mustered under the deputy lieutenants and the field armies under the command of the Earl of Essex. As other volunteer forces were raised they were subject to Essex, but the militias continued under local command. When the associations were formed Parliament nominated a major-general for each, but the commissions were formally given by Essex, who also licensed the subordinate commissions issued by regional commanders.[22] Essex's commission had been issued by the parliamentary Committee of Safety, which had been created on 4 July 1642, replacing the Committee of Defence. The liaison between the civilian and military authorities was not always smooth, however. The Committee of Safety was not regularly informed by local military bodies, and suffered from the subsequent appointment of committees with overlapping responsibilities. It was composed of members of the two Houses, served as the supreme council of war, and as an executive body, but in both respects was more reliant on parliamentary votes than the Privy Council, or previous councils of war, had been. As a form of military command it was less than perfect. There was also a Committee for the Navy and for the Mint, the Ordnance, the Posts and the Tower of London. Particular measures taken to mobilize the parliamentary war effort called forth further committees – for the Advance of Money, for Compounding (penal taxation) and for Sequestration.[23] Each committee was called into existence by a particular piece of legislation – it was not a planned constitution, and arose from particular decisions rather than a coherent policy. Government by committee then supplemented the decision-making by committee which had characterized the political sclerosis in the first two years of the Long Parliament.

Central committees were mainly staffed by MPs, and struggles within Parliament over policy can be followed through the memberships of these committees. Other committees had a combined membership of MPs and others. For example, there was no central committee for assessment but there were commissions empanelled in the localities instead, and the same was true for the militia and sequestration. In these cases the system owed something to patterns of pre-war administration of the subsidy and militia, but in many counties local committees for the militia, assessment and sequestration coalesced into a single county committee, whose powers and composition came to be resented. On the other hand, these local committees might come into conflict with other arms of the parliamentary administration, and there were many local disputes over these issues. Each source of revenue had a committee responsible for raising but not spending the money, and in practice they worked through county committees nominated by Parliament, while the money was disbursed by a number of different treasuries. Not the least of the complications was that military effort was increasingly co-ordinated on a regional basis whereas the basis for finance remained the county. This was confused, giving many opportunities for jurisdictional rivalries, and more or less invited conflict between bodies with different territorial interests in view.[24] Much of this was in place by the summer of 1643, and certainly the general pattern of ad hoc accretion of committees on the parliamentary side was well-established. It looked quite different from the system of government in place a year earlier, and which the parliamentary armies were supposedly defending.

Administrative innovation went in tandem with attempts to define and publicize the cause. On 24 March, Edward Husbands had been given copyright for an *Exact collection* of official declarations and messages of Parliament and the King. A careful and painstaking production, it seems, for example, to have followed the typeface of each declaration as it was originally published, black letter (a kind of Gothic used in particularly important declarations) and Roman type used as appropriate. The text, which ran to 955 pages, was followed by a chronological table of contents. It was an invaluable source of reference, was bought by local authorities, and has been drawn on extensively by historians ever since. It must have been a significant investment of time and money for a commercial printer, and that was presumably the justification for giving copyright to an individual. There is no surviving commission for the work, but the suspicion must be that Husbands was asked to enter into this financially risky enterprise, which tied up capital in a large stock of paper and relatively expensive typesetting. Penny pamphlets offered much more rapid turnover with a much smaller initial investment. This was not necessarily good business. Certainly when he produced a continuation, in August 1644, it was definitely in response to a commission.[25]

Husbands offered no editorial comment, but the scope of the collection is revealing. It opens not with the first ordinances (of the summer of 1641), nor with the opening of the parliamentary session in October 1641, but with the King's first speech to Parliament following his return from Scotland, on 2 December 1641. It ends with the Assessment Ordinance and related measures in late February and early March 1643. The King's speech had expressed disappointment that the legislation of the previous summer had not achieved settlement and attributed that to fears and jealousies about his government. There then follows an escalating dispute about the King's interference with parliamentary privilege – he had given an opinion on a measure in Parliament before it was presented to him, something which breached the privilege of free speech. From December 1641 onwards, of course, it was easy to make a case that the privileges of Parliament were increasingly threatened by violent intervention, culminating in the attempt on the Five Members. This selection seems therefore to have silently narrated a history, in which the fears and jealousies identified by the King as the cause of the trouble were shown to be justified by the actions of those around the King. It culminates in the military measures necessary to open a new military campaign in the spring of 1643. The preamble of the Assessment Ordinance, which is reproduced in full, depends on such a history:

The Lords and Commons now assembled in Parliament, being fully satisfied and resolved in their consciences, that they have lawfully taken up arms: and may and ought to continue the same for the necessary defence of themselves and the Parliament from violence and destruction, and of this Kingdom from foreign invasion, and for the bringing of notorious offenders to condign punishment, which are the only causes for which they have raised and do continue an army and forces.[26]

They were forced to raise an assessment as the fairest way to support this necessary effort. It is difficult not to see this as a propaganda exercise, an attempt to define the cause which was about to make renewed financial and administrative demands. Of course, as propaganda, it was aimed at the very committed reader: perhaps those local officeholders on whom the administrative burden of the war was falling. One such committed reader was John Lilburne, who was later to use it to hold Parliament to account.[27]

Defence of Parliament had been closely linked to the defence of reformation, and here we come to the demise of Cheapside Cross. On 30 March, three days after the Sequestration Ordinance and two days after the proposed excise, a committee was despatched from the Houses to arrest the Capuchins, a calculated insult to Henrietta Maria, and her chapel at Somerset House was purged of images and idols. Among them was a painting by Rubens, valued at £500, which was thrown into the

Henrietta Maria charged with treason and royal houses purged of popery, May 1643

Thames.[28] Like Cheapside this had been the focus of hostility for a long time, in this case restrained by diplomatic pressure from the French ambassador and by deference to the King. Inhibitions were lifting, however. The previous week a group of London ministers had been asked to view the windows of the Guildhall chapel, and their hostile report went further, expressing concerns about Cheapside Cross and other images in the City. On 24 April a committee was appointed under Sir Robert Harley to 'receive information, from time to time, of any monuments of superstition or idolatry in the Abbey Church at *Westminster*, or the windows thereof, or in any other Church or Chapel, in or about *London*: and they have power to demolish the same, where any such superstitious or idolatrous monuments are informed to be'. All churchwardens and other officers were required to help in this work and the committee was to meet at 2 p.m. that day.[29]

Their work began immediately – windows were smashed and idols defaced in Westminster Abbey and St Margaret's, Westminster, on 25 April and a regular team subsequently carried out an orderly and systematic purgation of the royal chapels at Whitehall, Greenwich and Hampton Court, as well as at St Paul's. The Common Council of London took up the campaign and on 27 April ordered the destruction of Cheapside Cross, which was begun on 2 May, and, on 27 May, Temple church was purged. This was a prelude to a sustained round of iconoclasm in the capital, lasting into 1644.[30]

This amounted to official backing for zealous reformation which went far beyond the anti-Laudian iconoclasm of 1640–41. It embraced 'all superstitious and idolatrous images and pictures' which were 'inconsistent with, and scandalous to the true Protestant reformed religion'. Purgation of St Margaret's, Westminster, and of the Abbey, intended that 'no Roman relics may remain to attract the simple devotions of ignorant and illiterate Popish people'. Crosses, windows and images were all now legitimate objects of attack, and there is evidence of enthusiasm for this work. Sir Robert Harley had called for the demolition of Cheapside Cross in 1626 and had confiscated and destroyed a picture of God belonging to one of his tenants in 1639. Emboldened by the Commons order of September 1641 he had championed the attack on images in his native Herefordshire during the parliamentary recess of that month. At Wigmore a church cross was not simply removed, but 'caused to be beaten in pieces, even to dust with a sledge, and then laid . . . in the footpath to be trodden on in the churchyard'. At Leintwardine offensive windows were 'broke small with a hammer' and thrown into the River Teme, 'in imitation of King Asa 2 Chronicles 15:16: who threw the images into the brook Kidron'.[31] But this zeal was empowered, and therefore restrained, by law: radical reformation by committee.

Purgation took other forms. Since its first meeting Parliament had been flooded with complaints about scandalous clergy, charges which ranged across the board from insufficiency (a predilection for drink and adulterous or lecherous behaviour) to religious error and malignancy (hostility to Parliament). In December 1640 a committee for scandalous ministers had been established in order to try to deal with this business, but it struggled to do so. Perhaps 800 petitions were received in its first few months of business and its capacity to deal with this volume of complaint was hampered by constant interruptions. The committee was dissolved at least five times only to be revived again following revelation of some new outrage. It was not clear if the committee was intended to actually deal with all these grievances, or to propose legislation that would do so, but in either case it failed. Legislation was introduced in June 1641 but made slow progress before being forgotten in the crisis of that autumn and winter. There was no progress either on particular cases.[32]

After this slow start there is clear evidence of greater urgency in 1643. There was an immediate political interest in this oversight of the clergy, of course, since the pulpit was crucial to publicizing the rival causes, and this may have had something to do with it. In any case, key procedural changes speeded up the process. Initially the committee had proceeded case by case – having heard the details the committee recommended a decision to the Commons and it was then passed on to the Lords, who heard it all again. Rather than submit to this painful doubling of effort, the Commons after June 1643 proceeded by orders for sequestration rather than by ordinance of both Houses. Moreover, the criteria for starting the process were relaxed and the definition of malignancy was broadened. Initially only ministers who had joined the King needed to fear the committee, but now those who had spoken in his favour, or read his proclamations, could be charged as malignants. Ministers were accused of betraying their hostility to Parliament by reading its publications 'with a low voice' or confusedly, but those of the King 'very audibly', or 'with great carriage and seeming joy'. In December 1642 the work had been handed over to a new Committee for Plundered Ministers – something of an Orwellian name, since much of its work consisted of ejecting ministers from their benefices. The measure was proposed by the Lords as a means to provide for ministers ousted by Cavaliers by ejecting unfit ministers from other benefices. During 1643 scores of clergy were ejected, although the Commons remained unsatisfied with the rate of progress in July 1643. Even as the definition of malignancy was being enlarged, the committee also began to authorize proceedings against popish and scandalous ministers, even if they were not malignant.[33] Reformation was therefore in the hands of committees: on superstitious monuments and on scandalous or plundered ministers.

These measures gave parishioners the power to denounce their minister on political grounds and to secure his removal by Parliament, not a bishop. It had been immediately apparent that there was a local appetite for such powers. The committee had its origins in a sub-committee of the Committee of Religion, established on 12 December 1640, to investigate the scarcity of preaching ministers. On 19 December the Commons renewed the order to the committee to investigate the scarcity of preaching, but added to it the power 'to consider of some Way of removing of scandalous Ministers, and putting others in their Places'. To this end, MPs were to report within six weeks on 'the State and Condition of their Counties, concerning preaching Ministers, and whence it arises, that there is such a Want of preaching Ministers, through the whole Kingdom'. A pirate edition of this order was published, suggesting that the Commons would welcome certificates from the public too, of 'persecuting, innovating or scandalous ministers, that they may be put out'. The publisher was mildly rebuked, but the pamphlet enjoyed a wide circulation.[34]

By 1644 the lid was completely off, and ministers around the country were being forced to defend themselves against disapproving parishioners. Maptid Violet, for example, had to answer charges about his drinking habits, and the suggestion that he was an antinomian (someone who denied the reality of 'sin' for those who were pure in heart). He also expressed the dangers of this new aspect of parishioners' power, asking that those hearing his case 'would be pleased to take into their consideration in this time of distractions how easy a thing it is for men abounding in malice to find witnesses to accuse men of our profession to accomplish their own ends'.[35] Fostering the parliamentary cause and further reformation here went hand in hand, but with profound implications for local social relations: the boundary between radical reformation and social levelling seemed to many contemporaries difficult to discern.

This was not all. On the day that the Common Council ordered the destruction of Cheapside Cross, the House of Commons ordered that Charles I's *Book of Sports* should be burnt 'in several places in the City of London by the common Hangman'.[36] Such burning punctuated the life of the capital, from the reign of Henry VIII onwards, but the Stuarts seem to have elaborated on the ritual at the same time that they employed it more frequently. Prior to 1640 it had often been associated with the physical punishment of the author as well as the destruction of books, but there had always been books burned without their authors. James I ordered a dozen or so books to be burned, many of them obscure foreign publications: this was a statement of disgust rather than a coherent act of censorship.[37]

Under Charles I, Alexander Leighton and William Prynne suffered alongside their books. In fact Prynne suffered the revival of burnings by the public hangman, in 1634. His *Histrio-Mastix* had denounced stage plays, and included attacks on female actors, at just about the time that Henrietta Maria appeared in a court masque. The timing was ambiguous – the criticism might have predated knowledge of the Queen's participation – but the implication was a damaging one. However, *Histrio-Mastix* was dangerous as much for its tone – highly intemperate and disrespectful – as its content and this earned it special treatment. Lord Cottington, the Chancellor of the Exchequer, ordered it to be 'burnt in the most public manner that can be. The manner in other countries is . . . to be burnt by the hangman, though not used in England. Yet I wish it may, in respect of the strangeness and heinousness of the matter contained in it, to have a strange manner of burning, therefore I shall desire it may be so burnt by the hand of the hangman'. It was on this occasion that Prynne lost the first parts of his ears: set in a pillory at Westminster and Cheapside, one of his ears cropped in each place and copies of his book burned before him. It was said that he nearly suffocated from the smoke.[38]

Burnings characteristically took place in large public spaces – Westminster, St Paul's Churchyard (heart of the book trade), Smithfield, Cheapside. A pamphlet of 1642 describes one such ritual. Scottish texts were burned in 1640, presumably some of those that cultivated support for the Covenanters and thereby encouraged the King to issue a proclamation declaring it treason to assist them. If it was these texts, the point was reinforced with some dramatic theatre:

the common hangman, . . . came in great state, as if he had been to bishop or brand Bastwick or Burton again, to the palace yard (alias the prelates purgatory) with a halter in each hand and with two trumpeters before him, and two men with a few loose papers following him; where after reading of the proclamation, Gregory very ceremoniously put fire to the faggots, and so the poor innocent papers paid for it. When he had done he cried, 'God save the king', and flourished his ropes, [adding] 'if any man conceal any such papers, he shall be hanged in these halters'; with which words I was so afraid, that I ran home and burnt all my papers, and so saved him a labour.[39]

During the 1640s book-burning took off, alongside publishing: perhaps with greater freedoms came greater anxiety and increased severity at the margins. Certainly books were burned in far greater numbers in these years: thirteen in 1642 alone, another nine during 1646. Alongside three newsbooks, sixty pamphlets, books and broadsheets were condemned between 1640 and 1660. It was now separated from the physical punishment of the author, and was much more clearly a dramatic statement of anathema. Sir Edward Dering, John Milton, Richard Overton and John Lilburne (the latter the most burned author of the period) all saw their books burned without suffering any physical mutilation themselves. This could not serve to censor, either: Dering noted that 4,500 copies of his speeches had already been printed, and more were on the way. The fires did not consume them all and, in fact, a number of contemporaries noted that a book-burning was good for sales.[40] Burning the *Book of Sports* was political theatre as much as an act of censorship, and it made a very clear point.

Hostility to the *Book of Sports* was another touchstone of reformers, and another point at which concerns about religious decency intersected with questions of social order. 'This book', according to *Certaine informations*, was 'first made and allowed in the reign of King James, and since his decease, it hath been pressed by the Bishops with such rigour, that many ministers, which refused only to read it in their Churches, have been [?] and deprived of their benefices, contrary to all laws both civil and ecclesiastical'.[41]

In 1635 controversy had broken out over church ales (a kind of fund-raising knees-up) in Somerset. An assize judge, motivated as much by personal animosity as religious conviction, had banned the ales on the grounds that they promoted disorder, but Charles and Laud took a different view. Enquiries made locally found evidence that they were harmless affairs, and that they encouraged attendance at church, and this led to the issue of a new *Book of Sports*. It defined those recreations that were lawful on the Lord's Day but was seen as far too indulgent by advanced Protestants, among whom there were many with strict sabbatarian views. Although it appears that many ministers had been able to avoid condoning its provisions, the Caroline *Book of Sports*, first issued in 1634, was much disliked in certain circles. It allowed dancing, May games and archery, but not before the end of divine service, and disallowed more harmful pastimes such as bear- and bull-baiting.

However, what was in one sense a measure of discipline – making it clear what forms of recreation were allowable – was in another a measure of licence, and it allied Laudian ceremonial with a relatively relaxed view of popular festive culture.[42]

Condemnation of the *Book of Sports* had been added to a Commons order on religion on the eve of the recess in 1641 by Simonds D'Ewes. While a law student D'Ewes had been disgusted by the spectacle of the Lords of Misrule – a ritual of inversion in the Christmas season in which someone was elected to preside over 'revels' in a great man's house. A convinced Puritan hostile to such festive pastimes – not harmless sociability, but a celebration of sinfulness – D'Ewes was naturally opposed to the licence that the *Book of Sports* offered. The initiative to abolish it ran out of time before the harvest recess, however. In 1643 the *Book* was unrepealed, but also unenforced. Moves against it were recommenced in February, in the weeks of the crucial measures of financial and administrative reorganization. On 15 February an ordinance had been passed exhorting all good subjects in England and Wales to repent their sins, which were the cause of the war, so that 'we may obtain a firm and happy peace both with God and Man'. Among the sins enumerated were 'wicked prophanations of the Lord's Day, by sports and gamings, formerly encouraged by authority'.[43]

Burning the *Book of Sports* was further testimony to the fact that the material and administrative radicalism of the parliamentary cause was in the support of a social and cultural reformation. It may have had a more immediate meaning too: one of the places at which the *Book* was burnt was the now empty site of Cheapside Cross. The destruction of both the cross and the *Book* took place in maypole season, and maypoles had become something of a rallying point for anti-Puritanism.[44] What was aimed at here was an orderly but zealous reformation, the use of secular power to achieve godly aims. Iconoclasm by committee was allied to a godly reformation of manners, and the promotion of a more sober devotion. It was an assertion of the proper relationship between zeal, law and social order.

Although there seems to be a connection between these reforming impulses and military fortunes in the war, it is difficult to know exactly what the connection was. The day before the order was given for the cross to be demolished the Earl of Essex had captured Reading. To some observers there was a direct connection – reformers had been

The burning of the *Book of Sports* at the site of Cheapside Cross

emboldened by victory. Others thought that recent successes showed God's favour for earlier measures of purgation – for example, the purging of Henrietta Maria's chapel and the expulsion of the Capuchins – and hoped that renewed zeal would bring more victories. Robert Harley and Isaac Pennington seem to have thought the cross and similar symbols were an active impediment to victory, and their destruction a means of propitiating and assuaging God. For others orderly reformation like this might help to assure those concerned about social order that reformation could proceed by authority, without sedition.[45] These measures might also have been intended to strengthen commitment, win God's favour or, by the summer of 1643, to woo Scottish opinion by putting the parliamentary cause at the vanguard of advanced Protestantism.[46] Among advanced Protestants, ensuring the preaching of the Word by purging the ministry, improving Sabbath observance, restricting the more ungodly elements of festive culture and combating idolatry were all more or less uncontroversial issues.

In the space of a few weeks in late spring and early summer Parliament had accepted the Weekly Assessment and Sequestration ordinances, and given serious consideration to an excise. These were no longer measures to defend the country from the innovations of the Personal Rule, but measures necessary to support Parliament in defensive arms – a case made at some length by Husbands' collection of declarations. But it was also a war in defence of the Reformation, something now given clearer official licence and put in the hands of committees. This pre-empted but did not defeat the polemical counter-case, that this was an ignorant zeal, associated with religious and social disorder. This debate about discipline centred on church government, which remained a potentially divisive issue within the parliamentary coalition – defined in these terms more by anti-episcopal views than by a positive vision of the proper constitution of the church. Progress on images and the Word avoided saying anything much about what changes in church government were necessary for the promotion of reformation – for the early reformers the Word and the sacraments had been the priority. But this remained an uneasy truce. Mechanic preachers and sectarians were no more welcome to Presbyterians than bishops.

Further reformation was the justification for vigorous military action by Parliament in defensive arms. But this identified the parliamentary cause ever more clearly with religious and constitutional innovation. Neither were these things abstract questions – they resonated deeply in parish conflicts about religious practice and in the material demands the war was now making. An increasingly clear identity as 'well-affected' took shape amongst those raising money, purging churches and ejecting scandalous ministers, in contrast to those identified as 'malignants'.[47] The royalists picked at these problems very effectively. Early in January, *Mercurius Aulicus*, a royalist newsbook, had begun to appear in Oxford. Authorized by the King himself, it represented quite a change of posture since the 1630s. The first editor, Peter Heylin, was succeeded by Sir John Berkenhead, but the approach was fairly consistent. It was written in a relatively plain style, but with substantial editorial comment, much of it bitingly satirical, and it was clearly intended as a counter-blast to the parliamentary press in London. It affected a higher literary style than the 'Puritan' papers and was also better produced. It asserted, in other words, the literary and cultural superiority of the royalist cause.[48] In May, perhaps prompted by the new wave of iconoclasm, a second and equally scabrous newsbook appeared: *Mercurius Rusticus*, subtitled *The Countries Complaint of the barbarous Outrages committed by the sectaries of this late flourishing kingdom*.[49] Much of the coverage was retrospective, and the first issue opened with the Stour Valley riots of August 1642. Eventually, it gave a very full catalogue of the depredations of crowds and soldiers, and of iconoclasm. Separate editions were produced covering attacks on the cathedrals and universities. It has proved an attractive source for subsequent generations, and it is unlikely that much of it was completely invented, but there was a consistent polemical purpose.

Bruno Ryves, the editor of *Mercurius Rusticus*, reported on the actions of parliamentarian soldiers, crowds and religious radicals, juxtaposing their behaviour with their claim to be acting to preserve religion and liberty. The detail was often significant in these narratives: for example, soldiers were frequently said to have entered houses by the window, having failed to secure access by the door. In common law this made entry necessarily forced and therefore felonious. Servants frequently appear loyally defending their master's interests, their loyalty and deference a sharp contrast with the fury of their attackers. Women and children too were roughly handled, as they intervened to protect the head of the household. Among goods taken were clothes, including 'wearing apparel', that is everyday and necessary clothes, not valuable and luxurious clothes. Ryves's polemical purpose was plain – this felonious and furious behaviour was entirely at odds with the claimed defence of true religion and liberty. The spoil of houses included the destruction of recently fashionable adornments – windows, panelling, paintings, furnishings; in churches it included windows which commemorated noble benefactions. Such refinements were an expression of social status, which carried with it a right to rule, and to deference. Whatever the propaganda said, in other words, the destruction was wanton, and socially levelling. In the autumn, when the work of the Harley Committee was effectively extended to cover the whole country, Ryves began to publish accounts of parliamentary iconoclasm. These measures were presented as desecration, which did a similar job on parliamentarian claims to godliness. Attacks on funerary monuments in churches made this point particularly clearly.

In which the world may observe that these men are the sworn enemies, not only of pretended superstition but of the ensigns of nobility and gentry, that if their *Diana*, I mean their *parity*, may take effect, posterity may forget and not read the distinction of noble from ignoble in these venerable monuments of ancient nobility: there being in these windows something indeed to instruct a herald, nothing to offend the weakest Christian.[50]

Here Ryves was establishing the historical record in a controversial way, and that controversy went to the heart of social order. Cast in the form of reportage this was a powerful polemic, placing before the public the facts of the case and pointing towards the obvious conclusion. In a sense, therefore, by reporting the facts he was rising above the cacophony of public controversy in a way rather like Edward Husbands. It certainly undercut the claims for the necessity of defensive arms which ran throughout the *Exact collection*.

For those who gravitated to the royal standard in late 1642, on the other hand, little had happened to make that seem like the wrong decision. There was, of course, no fundamental difficulty for Charles in assuming an executive function. Military affairs were handled by Charles personally, with a council of war, consisting of both military men and civilians, taking the place of his Privy Council. The Earl of Lindsey was initially Lord General of the royalist forces, and following his death at Edgehill his position was taken by Patrick Ruthven, Lord Forth. Rupert commanded the horse, by virtue of a commission direct from the King, something which caused conflict with Lindsey before the battle of Edgehill. Similar tensions about Rupert's command erupted later in the war, and with Prince Maurice, who was also commissioned directly by the King although not formally superior to other commanders. Sir Jacob Astley was in overall command of the infantry. Relations within the council of war were not always easy, and it is generally said that there was a tension between the relatively hardline royalism of the military men and more moderate counsels in the council of war and the court. The council was not always obeyed, and was not always in regular contact with the men on the ground, but at least there was a clearer executive authority. There might also be a question about the quality of advice and experience of his advisers however. Many senior figures from the 1630s had fled, or were dead or in prison, or fighting against him: Hyde, Ashburnham, Digby and Prince Rupert had not been at all significant in royal counsels three years earlier. The range of opinion available to him was relatively broad, reaching to much ground shared with the parliamentary coalition, but the loss he suffered in the quality of his advice is more difficult to measure.[51]

Charles also had less need for innovation in his central administration since the bulk of his officeholders had joined him in Oxford. His appointments rested on clearly established legal powers, and in local government he preferred to work through the established institutions: as commissioners in the Marcher counties put it in 1645, it was hoped 'that during this war your Majesty will order that as near as the necessity of the times can admit, our ancient laws shall be observed in force and reputation'. In areas of royalist control there was an evident desire to work with the authority of Grand Juries, assizes and quarter sessions, whereas in many parliamentarian areas the new committees largely took over from these bodies.[52]

The royalists were also slower to use new forms of taxation, for example adopting an excise only in December 1643. In part this was because of their dependence on individuals to raise regiments and on contributions from particular individuals. Sixty-seven men paid £70,000 between them for baronetcies, and the Marquess of Worcester paid £318,000 in one go. Lord Herbert was said eventually to have spent £1,000,000 in the royal service and Henrietta Maria's gallant exploits during the year had yielded very significant benefits. Moreover, the King had taken most of the traditional offices and revenues with him – Chancery, Exchequer and the Court of Wards continued to act, and in the first year of the war nearly one third of the revenues came from traditional sources. The royalist equivalent of the assessment, the contribution, was not a fixed burden but a payment related to the number of troops in arms in each county, and consent was sought from the Grand Jury or an assembly of freeholders. Similarly, the sequestration policy on the royalist side was tempered by a desire to see victims indicted for treason at common law and, where that had not been done, to allow them to appeal against sequestration at the next assize. This system was sufficient until royalist control of its heartland slipped in 1645 – until then, the royalist financial administration sufficed, and gave less offence to pre-war scruples than the parliamentarian equivalents.[53]

On the whole, therefore, innovative committee government was more clearly a parliamentary phenomenon, and it was possible for royalists to make great play with the constitutional impropriety of the parliamentarian effort. And it was not just royalists or moderate parliamentarians, either: on 1 May, Parliament sent embassies to Scotland and Holland, but this prompted Henry Marten to ask, rather unhelpfully, whether Parliament could enter such negotiations without first claiming sovereign power.[54] Once again, the more vigorous proponents of the parliamentary position were not necessarily helpful in maintaining the integrity of the alliance.

For propaganda purposes, however, this respectable royalism had an obvious Achilles heel: the behaviour of some elements of the royalist army. Rupert's behaviour at Brentford, Marlborough and Birmingham gave him an unsavoury contemporary reputation which he has never entirely shaken off.[55] The Earl of Derby's decision to torch Lancaster lost him his war and led more or less directly to his exile on the Isle of Man.[56] Such actions were defensible, or at least arguable, under the laws of war. Belligerents recognized three kinds of constraint on their actions – the laws of nature and nations (which defined what might be expected of a reasonable, moral Christian); the laws of war (an informal international code of customary expectations); and the military law which formally codified the expectations of particular armies, drawn up specifically for them. While these overlapping codes restrained violence they also of course licensed it, and there was often room for interpretation about the extent of that licence. For example, an order backed by military law might seem to contravene the laws of nature and nations, and behaviour licensed by the laws of war might also seem to breach the expectations of those laws. Sacking captured towns was a case in point here: according to the laws of war it was illegitimate to sack a town that had surrendered, but not illegitimate if the town had not surrendered. This served to encourage surrender, once it was clear that the town would fall, and therefore limited bloodshed.[57] But it did not mean that it was *compulsory* to sack towns that had not surrendered. In their judgement of this issue the royalists, or at least Rupert and Derby, appeared more ruthless than their parliamentarian opponents.

In the long run, it is often said, this hampered the royalist war effort. As early as January 1643, at least if the London press is to be believed, the course of military events could be affected by local people in arms but not in the paid service of one side or the other. The desperate defence of Bradford against the royalists by local people in arms was celebrated in London newsbooks as a revival of club law – the use of the club to secure obedience, the triumph of force over argument – and the example was urged on the rest of the country. It was soon taken up in Rotherham.[58] In April, the Earl of Derby was reported to have gone from Manchester to Whalley with 500 horse, 500 foot and about 2,000 'clubmen'. There they seized the town, and got into the church and steeple, but were flushed out by 200 musketeers, thirty horse and 200 clubmen. Having regained the town they were challenged by the earl to come out and fight, which they did, 'and routed all his Army, and chased them about six miles'. Anticipating scepticism, the writer added: 'which is firmly verified by letters from those parts'.[59]

As spring turned to summer, there were no active peace negotiations in train and parliamentary efforts to strengthen the war effort were offering further ammunition for their opponents in the paper war. As Parliament's war effort escalated, the 'cause' was more clearly defined, but in ways that left a flank exposed to propagandists such as Ryves. The royalists did not have it all their own way, however. While they were more conservative in their demands from the civilian populations under their control, and in the ways in which they made those demands, they too were vulnerable – the relatively maximal view taken by a number of royalist commanders about honourable behaviour in war did the cause long-term damage. If the political battle was poised, however, for Parliament the military news got worse.

For much of the spring the Earl of Essex had been relatively immobile, covering the western approaches to London. On 13 April he left Windsor and laid siege to Reading, which had the effect of forcing Rupert to come south from Lichfield, but this attempted relief of Reading failed and it was surrendered on 26 April. This victory was important for parliamentary morale, but it was not followed up – Essex's army, hampered by disease and lack of pay, did not leave Reading until 10 June.[60] This lack of mobility on the part of the main army proved a problem for the overall fortunes of Parliament's forces, something which was held against Essex.

On the day before the surrender of Reading, William Waller's parliamentary forces had surprised Hereford, and James Chudleigh's had fought an inconclusive engagement against Ralph Hopton at Sourton Down. These were good days for Parliament but Sourton Down was followed by an important royalist victory at Stratton (16 May). Hopton then advanced into Somerset, despite the fact that it left parliamentary strongholds (Bideford, Barnstaple, Plymouth, Dartmouth and Exeter) to his rear, and the gamble paid off. Having joined up with Prince Maurice and the Earl of Hertford in early June his advance continued. Waller had in the meantime been forced to abandon Hereford and failed to take Worcester on 29 May, and Hopton was advancing rapidly through the south-west. When Essex was eventually able to leave Reading to advance on Oxford, he met a decisive defeat at Chalgrove Field

(18 June). Once again particular details were as important to morale as the overall position: John Hampden received two shots in the shoulder at Chalgrove Field and made his way painfully to Thame, where he died six days later in agony from his wounds. The plunder of Wycombe on 25 June led to panic in London and criticism of Essex's generalship. Pym's reaction was characteristic – recommending the tendering of a new oath, the Vow and Covenant, to Essex's troops. On 28 June, instead, Essex tendered his resignation, though it was not accepted.[61]

As Hopton swept all before him he was brought into direct confrontation with Waller's army. Battle was avoided at Chewton Mendip, 12 June, and the royalists instead swung round Waller's army through Frome and Bradford-upon-Avon. Manoeuvring continued, leading to a skirmish at Monkton Farleigh on 3 July and to the pitched battle at Lansdown on 5 July. Victory there was hard won for the royalists, who found themselves too short of supplies to lay effective siege to Bath. Instead they moved on towards Devizes and Waller was able to meet them again at Roundway Down on 13 July. Waller's army was destroyed in a battle more remarkable for bravery than tactical shrewdness, but the impact on the military and political landscape was no less significant for that. Waller was critical of Essex for failing to prevent the march of royalist forces from Oxford to support Hopton's campaign: it seemed strange 'that he, lying with his whole army within ten miles of Oxford, should suffer the chief strength of that place to march thirty [sic] miles to destroy him'. Following this catastrophic defeat Waller withdrew to Gloucester, then Evesham and finally London. The royalists now moved easily in the West Country, Bath was abandoned on 23 July and, on 26 July, Rupert stormed Bristol and the parliamentary commander, Nathaniel Fiennes, was court-martialled for surrendering too easily.[62]

In the meantime, Newcastle had won a significant victory at Adwalton Moor on 30 June, leading to an undignified retreat by the parliamentarians to Hull. They were only able to do that because the townspeople had prevented Sir John Hotham surrendering the town to the royalists. As the summer progressed, therefore, it was most certainly the royalists rather than the parliamentarians who had most to cheer. Although complete disaster had been averted following Adwalton Moor, when the surrender of Hull was prevented, the picture in the north was bleak indeed for the parliamentarians. The Fairfaxes had been driven out of the West Riding after that defeat, and were cut off from other parliamentary forces. As a result, all of the north was in Newcastle's control, with the exception of Hull.[63]

On the day of the great victory at Roundway Down, Henrietta Maria met Charles on the field at Edgehill, bringing with her 3,000 men, eight or nine artillery pieces and 100 wagons of supplies. By late July it was feared that Hull would not be able to stand and Cromwell and Meldrum were sent to support the parliamentary position at Gainsborough. Having taken Burghley House, Cromwell's troops were able to relieve Gainsborough on 28 July owing to disciplined and heroic cavalry action. This boosted morale, but hardly turned the tide of the war in the north. There were not enough infantry to hold Stamford and Cromwell drew back to Spalding and Peterborough. This scanty band was all that stood between Newcastle and an advance on London, and the Earl of Manchester was given a commission to command the forces of the associated counties to resist this advance. Early August saw further royalist triumph in the west, too: soon after the capture of Bristol came the capture of Dorchester, Weymouth and Portland. Erle abandoned the siege of Corfe Castle, and Dorset, with the exception of Poole and Lyme, was in the hands of the royalists. Waller was given an independent command, a reflection of the disaffection with Essex after his failure to advance from Reading: many seem to have shared Waller's view that his defeats reflected a lack of support from Essex.[64]

So compelling were the royalist advances of these months that this may have been another moment when they might have won the war. Victories at Hopton Heath, Roundway Down and Adwalton Moor, the surrender or capture of Bath, Bristol and a number of more minor towns, the death of Hampden and the political vulnerability of Essex all posed a serious problem of morale to the parliamentarians, besides the obvious military advantages that had been won. Parliamentary forces were everywhere under pressure and resources to renew them not yet available, and political will among the leadership in London was clearly measured.

As it turned out, however, the royalists did not press home this advantage. The Yorkshire levies refused to move south and Newcastle was forced to besiege Hull, while Hopton's Cornish levies similarly wanted to stay at home to protect their county from the garrison at Plymouth. Welsh troops refused to cross the Severn until Gloucester was taken. Since neither the northern nor the western armies were willing to advance further the real question was what to do with the armies in central England. With Waller beaten and back in London the way was clear for an advance on the capital, but Prince Rupert was instead sent to take Gloucester. The Parliamentary commander there, Massey, was thought to be wavering in his loyalty to Parliament, and certainly Gloucester was no more defensible than Bristol. Taking Gloucester would cement the royalist position, clearing communications between Oxford and south Wales and giving control of the Severn Valley. But posterity has blamed the royalists for failing to move decisively on London. As on the other side there was division over war aims too: between those who simply wanted to win the war and those who wanted to win the war in order to preserve the constitutional settlement of 1641, those who 'wished to carry on the war with a view to the eventual peace'. This division erupted between Prince Rupert and the Earl of Hertford and between Prince Maurice and the Earl of Caernarvon over their conduct following victories in Bristol and Dorset. There were military arguments in favour of the more cautious strategy and it is not clear that the royalist armies were really in a position to advance at this moment. But the relatively conservative decision to move on Gloucester rather than London probably reflected the influence of moderate counsels as much as military considerations. In any case it was this decision which probably saved Parliament's bacon: if the three royalist forces had pushed on in concert towards London victory might well have been possible.[65]

When Rupert arrived before Gloucester, Massey refused to surrender and this led to a second crucial decision – to lay siege to the city rather than storm it. This decision arose, it is said, from Charles's own distaste for the human costs of the storming of Bristol, and to that extent it can be admired, but from a military point of view it was a questionable judgement. Gloucester could probably have been stormed quite quickly, whereas a siege tied down a large number of troops and gave Parliament time to levy a relieving force. On 27 August, Essex led out an army of 15,000 men, including men of the London Trained Bands, which entered Gloucestershire at Stow-on-the-Wold on 4 September. There an attack by Rupert failed and Essex reached Gloucester on 5 September. It was not a moment too soon, since Massey had only three barrels of powder left when they arrived, but their arrival had an immediate effect. Charles, unwilling to be caught between Essex's army and the Gloucester forces, withdrew rather than risk losses and Essex was able to raise the siege on 8 September. There then began a race to prevent Essex reaching London. This relieved an appalling position, and boosted morale, but military advantage still lay with the royalists. Rupert still intended to engage Essex, but not in front of a hostile city, and further west royalist successes had continued as Barnstaple, Bideford and Exeter surrendered between 28 August and 4 September. West of Poole only Lyme, Plymouth, Dartmouth and Wardour Castle now held out for Parliament.[66]

Between late February and late April important measures had been taken to stiffen the parliamentary alliance, but the military tide had certainly not turned. Parliament also faced enemies within. In March, Charles encouraged the development of what became known as Waller's plot.

The revelation of the Waller plot

He issued a commission to seventeen prominent London citizens, empowering them to lead an armed rising on his behalf. It was not activated until May, but the effort reveals the insincerity of Charles's interest in the Oxford treaty. Edmund Waller, one of Parliament's commissioners at Oxford, was the chief conspirator, and the list of his contacts was impressive – the Earl of Northumberland, John Selden, Bulstrode Whitelocke and Simonds D'Ewes, for example, all of them prominent Puritan critics of Charles I's government. The plot was revealed theatrically, at the end of May, for propaganda effect: news was deliberately withheld until the fast day on 31 May, when MPs were summoned from morning worship to hear the revelations. By that point there was, of course, no danger since the chief conspirators were already under arrest, but the announcement and the precautionary mustering of the militia caused a considerable stir. Two of the chief conspirators were hanged in front of their own houses. Waller himself escaped, however, through a 'combination of bribery and informing on his contacts'. He was fined £10,000 and banished.[67]

The execution of the plotters

London's allegiance was not certain. Since January a radical caucus had been agitating for more rigorous prosecution of the war effort, their petitioning matched by practical measures to raise men and money through a committee at Salters' Hall, established in March. But the leading figures in these initiatives were new men, and their activities cut across the powers of existing bodies, such as the City's militia committee. In July a more radical step was proposed in a scheme for a general rising – intended primarily as a means to support more thorough prosecution of the war under Waller, and independent of Essex's command, the City would raise a volunteer army, funded directly from sources intended for that purpose. The initiative was associated too with attempts to dictate the membership of the parliamentary committee to oversee its use. These radical initiatives were a direct counterpoint to the activities of the Harley Committee and the progress of radical reformation in the City and the construction of extensive fortifications.[68]

But although the revelation of the Waller plot made it unwise to speak in favour of peace in London, it seems clear that the city was divided. In August the Lords prepared peace proposals which abandoned the position adopted in the Oxford negotiations, terms so soft that Essex refused to subscribe. News that they had been passed by the Lords, and that the Commons had agreed to consider them, led to consternation in the City. A co-ordinated attempt was made to exploit fears for the future of Protestantism in order to scupper what would have amounted to a capitulation. Some 5,000 men were reported to have demonstrated on 7 August in the Palace Yard against the proposed treason to the commonwealth. On 8 and 9 August, however, Parliament was surrounded by large crowds of women, wearing white ribbons, and calling for peace. The Commons was driven to publish a long explanation of their reasons for rejecting these proposals.[69]

The theatrical revelation of the Waller plot had been a prelude to further measures to stiffen the ideological and administrative sinews of the parliamentary war effort. On 9 June, Parliament imposed the Vow and Covenant. It was justified by the 'popish and traitorous plot, for the subversion of the true Protestant reformed religion, and the liberty of the subject', pursued by a popish army and manifest in the 'treacherous and horrid design lately discovered, by the great blessing and especial providence of God'. These popish forces had been 'raised by the King'. In view of the 'constant experience, that many ways of force and treachery are continually attempted, to bring to utter ruin and destruction the Parliament and Kingdom, and, that which is dearest, the true Protestant religion . . . all who are true-hearted and lovers of their country should bind themselves each to other in a Sacred Vow and Covenant'. Subscribers were to acknowledge these distractions to be a punishment for their sins, and to promise not to lay down arms while the papists were in arms; to disavow the late plot and report any future ones; and most importantly, 'according to my power and vocation, assist the forces raised and continued by both Houses of Parliament, against the forces raised by the King without their consent'. By declaring that 'I do believe, in my conscience, that the forces raised by the two Houses of Parliament are raised and continued for their just defence, and for the defence of the true Protestant religion, and liberties of the subject, against the forces raised by the King', the Vow had in effect dropped claims that the armies were fighting for the defence of the King's honour and person. This was made the substance of a separate short declaration of 'loyalty to the King's person, his crown and dignity'. To some extent, or on some readings, it was in direct conflict with the Protestation, and royalist commentators were quick to say so.[70] The purpose was clear enough, however: to shore up support for the continued war effort – this was the oath urged by Pym on Essex's troops following the defeat at Chalgrove and the sacking of Wycombe.

On 12 June the future of the Reformation, a core element of the cause defined by the Vow and Covenant, was put in the hands of an assembly of divines, the Westminster Assembly. This was a consistent part of the negotiation platform of course, but a highly contentious issue – arguably the one at the heart of the instability of the parliamentary coalition. There was a suggestion that this was a means of kicking the issue of church government into the long grass while drawing the Scots back into English politics. Certainly for Sir Cheney Culpeper, a Kentish gentlemen of radical views but no great political influence, this initiative was closely related to the desire for an alliance with the Covenanters and to separate the sheep from the goats. On 16 June he wrote to Samuel Hartlib, with whom he maintained a regular correspondence, commending the 'covenant lately made for the uniting of ourselves' but also hoping for another 'which I hope shortly to see for the stronger union of the 2 kingdoms in their common interest of religion and liberty'. Both would benefit from a confession of faith which in turn would be the basis of 'a better union and correspondency between all the reformed churches and states, against the civil and ecclesiastical Babylon which God will certainly bring to judgement'. Although the military support from the Covenanters was shortly to be adopted, and was associated with just such a covenant, Culpeper was disappointed in his hopes for a confession of faith. When it became clear that the Covenanters intended to impose a Presbyterian church settlement Culpeper became quite scathing about our 'geud brethren'. Initially, however, he was hopeful that 'the well affected in both nations being united by Covenant first with themselves and then with one another, our strength and our enemy's may be fully known'.[71] This mirrored an element of the Waller plot, which had been to take a census of royalist sympathizers in London, parish by parish.[72]

On 14 June there followed a renewal of press licensing, suggesting that this desire to get the message out was closely associated with a desire to suppress rival or misleading messages and to preserve decency. A Commons order of August 1642 had sought to impose a crackdown on publication by re-establishing the partnership between government and the Stationers' Company, and in March another order turned the parliamentary committee for examinations into a kind of Star Chamber for the press by giving it powers of search, seizure and imprisonment. These elements of the policy were now brought together. The officers of the Stationers' Company along with the Gentleman Usher of the House of Lords and the Sergeant of the House of Commons were given powers of search, seizure and arrest of authors and printers. It was partly in response to lobbying from the company, whose commercial interests had been damaged by the collapse of their monopoly. But there was also a clear political purpose, to suppress 'the great late abuses and frequent disorders in printing many false, forged, scandalous, seditious, libellous, and unlicensed papers, pamphlets, and books' which had been published 'to the great defamation of religion and government'.[73]

This redefinition and restatement of the parliamentary cause called forth from Charles a declaration that Parliament was not free and anyone abetting it in its usurpations was guilty of high treason. On the other hand, with some named exceptions, those who joined him in Oxford would be pardoned. This caused more than a little unease at Westminster.[74] Seven lords did indeed abandon Parliament and three of them went to Oxford, but Charles hesitated to welcome them, aware of the hostility to converts among those who had been there from the start. Henrietta Maria was prominent among those hostile to such fair-weather friends and in the end the opportunity was missed. Although only Clarendon seems to have recommended a warm welcome at the time, most royalists subsequently came to see the coldness of the reception as a mistake.[75] Although military success concealed the fact, there were divisions at Oxford. Moderate counsels, associated in particular with the 'constitutional royalists', were competing with a much harder line taken by military men and championed by Henrietta Maria. If failure to take advantage of the military position in the high summer of 1643 in order to impose terms had reflected the continuing influence of moderates, there were signs that the position was shifting. As Henrietta Maria's influence became increasingly important, the moderates were to find it harder to make their case.[76]

These noble defections from Westminster reflected the despondency of those hoping to negotiate a settlement. The revelation of Waller's plot had led more or less directly to measures to confirm the ideological basis of Parliament's cause, and their treatment in Oxford confirmed that opinion there was hardly more conciliatory. Charles was known to be negotiating for a cessation in Ireland in order to bring forces back to

England. The continuing failure of parliamentary forces to make ground in the war and the dismal prospects of negotiation provide the context in which the inhibition about the excise was finally broken.

On 22 July, Parliament adopted the excise and thereby completed the administrative and financial revolution which underpinned its war effort. A central committee was established, co-ordinating the efforts of professional tax gatherers. Previous taxes depended on local officeholders acting voluntarily, which obviously increased the possibilities for evasion but also softened the edges of any potential confrontation. Excise men were soon widely loathed, denounced as a biblical plague in terms strongly reminiscent of the denunciation of monopolists. The tax was also regressive, raised as a flat rate and imposed on (among other things) meat, salt and beer, all of them staple elements of the diet of the poor. Butchers and saltworkers were prominent in the subsequent resistance to the tax. Despite these problems the excise survived and was, like the assessment, retained by the restored monarchy to become a staple element of public finances throughout the eighteenth century. Parliament had, between October 1642 and July 1643, created the financial instruments which supported the eighteenth-century empire.[77] But it did not make them popular; nor did it make them very plausible as defenders of the ancient constitution.

Three days earlier Parliament had formally requested military aid from the Covenanters. The Westminster Assembly had begun work on a new church settlement, acting under the authority of Parliament and with the abolition of episcopacy certainly on the agenda. Parliament had become an executive body, raising taxes, seizing property, ejecting ministers, licensing the press, setting armies in the field and fleets out to sea, all on the authority of ordinances which had originally been justified as measures necessary owing to the absence of the King. A careful reading of Husbands' *Exact collection* revealed the case for defensive arms, in defence of religion, law and the liberty of Parliament. But iconoclasm, the burning of the *Book of Sports*, the (possibly malicious) ejection of parish clergy, not to mention the constitutional and administrative radicalism of the parliamentary war effort, all threatened to open a fatal gap between the rhetoric and the reality of the parliamentary cause. This was a carefully chosen and cautiously staged answer to the common concern that zealous reformation led to social disorder, but it was clearly much beyond the aims of redress in 1640. So too, the Vow and Covenant had severed the defence of the King's person, crown and dignity from the defence of the true religion and the liberties of Parliament. Even before a military alliance with the Covenanters was ratified, these developments had put a strain on the loyalty men felt to the choices they had made in 1642. Bruno Ryves clearly recognized the potential here.

The relief of Gloucester had required the loan of fifty subsidies from London, ten times as many as had been granted at any one time during the 1620s, which was forced out of the city on 18 August. At the same time the Commons felt the need to rebuke John Saltmarsh, the increasingly radical divine, for some apparently derogatory remarks about the royal family. When the issue was discussed Henry Marten defended Saltmarsh, saying 'it were better one family were destroyed than the whole kingdom should perish' – a not very coded statement of conditional loyalty to the King. Challenged, he said without hesitation that he did indeed mean the royal family. He was imprisoned in the Tower and excluded from the House for three years.[78] Parliamentarians trod an increasingly thin line: as the measures necessary to fight the war became more radical, the claim to be in defensive arms to protect monarchical government seemed increasingly difficult to justify. The King's posture of respect for local offices was undermined by the behaviour of some royalist troops, but it is easy to see why those who had chosen Parliament might have begun to feel that they had chosen wrongly, or were backing a losing side.

Sir Hugh Cholmley, for one, had acted reluctantly in taking up arms for Parliament. He later claimed that he had regarded the Militia Ordinance as an act of war against Charles and the Nineteen Propositions as unjust and unreasonable. However, ties of friendship (most of his friends were parliamentarians) and hostility to Strafford's friends and allies, who were throwing in their lot with the King, had persuaded him to accept a commission from the Earl of Essex. Acting decisively, he took control of Scarborough Castle and led 500 men in a successful action at Guisborough on 16 January 1643. Slingsby, his royalist opponent, died of his wounds three days later. Although this was a relatively minor skirmish, which figures barely at all in the military histories of the war, Cholmley was sickened by what he saw. He had refused to lead his forces into the West Riding in support of the Fairfaxes, convincing his commanders in London that this was prudent, rather than treacherous. When the Queen arrived in York from Bridlington, however, in March 1643, he changed allegiances. He claimed now to be certain that Pym, not Charles, was the warmonger; and he admitted to acting to defend his home, tenants and constituents from invasion and plunder by the royalists. He subsequently held Scarborough for the King, stubbornly in 1644 after the war in the north had turned against the royalists, and went into exile after he eventually surrendered it. He returned to England in the 1650s, but was widely distrusted, and even despised.[79] Cholmley was later able to present all this as consistent and personally honourable, placing it squarely in the context of oaths of allegiance and the Protestation, which he had sworn.[80] But for those who had commissioned him, or who had thought him an ally, it was clearly possible to take another view.

Clarendon believed that Cholmley had initially accepted the parliamentarian commission because of his friendship with Sir John Hotham, who had refused the King entry to Hull in April 1642. Hotham too had second thoughts. Late in 1642 he promised Lord Digby, a prisoner in his charge, that he would surrender the town to the King. When it came to it, he changed his mind and drove away the besiegers, but by April 1643 he and his son were at odds with other parliamentary commanders. Troops under the command of the younger Hotham were ill-disciplined and this had led him into conflict with the Fairfaxes, Cromwell and Hutchinson. The elder Hotham, in the course of this dispute, had referred to Cromwell and Hutchinson as 'Anabaptists', suggesting that he, at least, was unimpressed by the attempt to identify the parliamentary cause with more advanced reformation. By the early summer of 1643 their disaffection with the parliamentary cause had led both Hothams into correspondence with the Earl of Newcastle about changing sides. In mid-April the younger formally approached Newcastle promising to do the King good service. When their intentions became public on 18 June the younger Hotham was imprisoned in Nottingham Castle. In his defence he alleged that the strength of the parliamentary forces was restricted to defacing churches. He escaped from Nottingham and contacted Henrietta Maria, who seemed willing to welcome his defection, before going to Hull to see his father. By the time he got there, however, the Commons had ordered the traitors' appearance at Westminster, and he was arrested from his bed on the authority of the mayor.

The defences were put in the hands of the citizens, and his father Sir John, hearing what was up, fled in a hurry on horseback. He was knocked off his horse at Beverley, however, and returned to Hull, whence father and son were sent to London by sea. Their court-martial was long delayed, suggesting that there was some sympathy for their position in London, but they were eventually found guilty and executed in January 1644.[81]

Although Henrietta Maria had seemed willing to welcome this kind of friend, many other royalists took a sterner view. Sir Edward Nicholas, Secretary of State to Charles during the war, wrote of the father: 'The rebels have seized him, his son, their wives and children, and sent them all prisoners to the rebellious city, London, where the justice of God will, I believe, bring him to be punished by the same usurped power that at first did encourage him in his first act of rebellion; for falser men than he and his son live not upon the earth'. Others thought him proud and covetous. There was a more charitable view, although not an entirely positive one: that he was a man of judgement, albeit one whose passion and pride overbore that judgement on occasion. Views of the son were less equivocal: Clarendon thought him full of 'pride and stubbornness' and Cholmley, who was after all on thin ice here, described him as 'a very politic and cunning man, [who] looked chiefly at that which stood most with his own particular interest'.[82]

Fighting alongside Cholmley at Guisborough was Sir Matthew Boynton, a gentleman of sufficiently significant standing to have been knighted on 9 May 1618 and created a baronet the following week. Member of Parliament for Heydon in the 1620s, he had by 1637 become sufficiently concerned about the direction of affairs in England to have sold lands in the Tees Valley, intending to follow the Pilgrim Fathers to the New World. He pulled out at a late stage but joined the Independent church at Southwark. When war broke out he acted quickly, raising troops for Parliament, and it is easy to see the roots of this political and military history in his previous history. It was Boynton's second son who took Sir John Hotham (his own uncle) prisoner at Beverley on 29 June 1643; and it was Sir Matthew himself who on 22 July 1645 captured Scarborough from Sir Hugh Cholmley, after an arduous and destructive siege.[83] In 1648, however, the younger Boynton was to desert his parliamentary command in the hope of a royal military victory in the second civil war.[84]

The realities of war, and the lack of clarity in war aims, caused divisions on both sides, but on the parliamentary side the overall military situation encouraged defeatism among the less committed. The litany of military reverses, which continued more or less without interruption through the summer of 1643, was accompanied by a series of treasons and betrayals. Essentially personal decisions, by Hotham and his son and by Cholmley, had a decisive military impact, delivering secure control of the north to the royalist forces under Newcastle.[85] The fall of Bristol in July was of even greater significance to the war in the west and here, too, questions were asked about military honour and loyalty. In this case, with no very good reason, treason charges were successfully made against Nathaniel Fiennes, who was sentenced to death and only reprieved at the request of the Earl of Essex. According to contemporary understandings of the laws of war to continue in a forlorn defence was to cause unnecessary loss of life and in those circumstances surrender was the honourable military decision. Most modern commentators agree that Fiennes had judged this correctly, but to contemporaries who had witnessed side-changing and plots, and whose knowledge of conditions on the ground was hazy, it was a decision that could easily be suspected.[86] Fiennes was forced into a public vindication of his actions.

Honour was an elusive quality, difficult in these circumstances to define. It could be recognized in opponents, and difficult to discern in apparent friends; but sticking to an initial commitment was not necessarily what honour dictated either. It is not clear that the behaviour of Hotham and Cholmley was in any simple way less principled than that of Boynton: they might have argued, in fact, that their changing allegiances arose from a surfeit of principle. Cholmley was certainly insistent that his position was principled, and Boynton's son clearly felt by 1648 that the cause had shifted and that he no longer wanted to support it. Given the costs of the war, and the shifting basis of the two coalitions, it is certainly possible to see a refusal to carry on fighting as an honourable position. Sir John Hotham had after all accepted a commission to take control of Hull in the face of armed popish conspiracy against Parliament; not for the cause that was now taking shape. The case of Fiennes makes it appear rather more complex: there was an honour code governing surrender, but in the heat of battle a surrender offered too easily might look quite like a change of sides. These questions were posed continuously for those in arms. In May, James Chudleigh had deserted the parliamentary cause, following his capture at the battle of Stratton Hill, and wrote to his father encouraging him to do the same. It had been widely thought among royalists that Massey would surrender Gloucester in the summer of 1643, since he seemed unwilling to resist the King in person, but his resolve was apparently strengthened by feeling within the city. Sir Alexander Carew rethought his allegiance in August, following the fall of Bristol and the deterioration of the military position in the west, and contacted Sir John Berkeley with a view to changing sides. He delayed, however, 'so sottishly and dangerously wary of his own security . . . that he would not proceed till he was sufficiently assured that his pardon was passed the Great Seal of England'.[87]

Amidst these ambiguities it is plain that some men had a clear view about honourable conduct. Following defeat at Adwalton Moor, Sir Thomas Fairfax had stayed in Bradford until all was lost, fighting his way out and leaving behind his wife and many followers. En route to Hull he had abandoned his small daughter, who could not bear the hard ride to Hull, apparently thinking she would die. His daughter joined him a day after his arrival in Hull, revived after a night's sleep, and his wife was 'sent to him with all courtesy by the stately Newcastle, who was too gallant a cavalier to make war on ladies'. Similar courtesies were observed at the siege of Arundel Castle in January 1644. Once negotiations for a treaty had been opened, the parliamentary commander, Sir William Waller, invited Lady Bishop, the wife of the royalist commander, and her daughters to dine with him.[88] Such things clearly mattered. On 10 August 1643, when Charles summoned Gloucester to surrender, a soldier and citizen came out to deliver the reply. The city was at His Majesty's orders as soon as it was signified to them by the two Houses of Parliament, they said. Having delivered their message they wheeled around, turning their backs on the King; and putting on their hats in which the orange ribbons denoting their allegiance were prominently visible, they rode off. This was a gross breach of etiquette, which evoked laughter among the courtiers, but strengthened the King's determination to press on with the siege. In July, frustrated by his failure to bring the royalists to battle, Essex had proposed to the Speaker of the House of Lords that the terms rejected by the King in Oxford should be offered again. If he refused them, then the King should be asked to withdraw and the two armies be allowed to fight a single battle to settle the quarrel. The idea was studiously ignored.[89] Insistence on honourable, civil, courteous behaviour was an understandable response to the moral ambiguities confronted by those seeking to act in a principled and consistent way. Whether, in these conditions, honour had any clear meaning was less certain.

Settling into a longer campaign created new political issues, arising from the war itself. Those who were fighting to preserve legal propriety and those fighting to defend religious decency might change their mind about which side best represented their views. Clearly, there were different views among the parliamentarians about what the war was for and how the cause could be strengthened. From the spring of 1643 until the early autumn, military fortune favoured the King, and this tended to make these questions very pressing on the parliamentary side. Relative military failure, in itself, posed problems for the solidarity of the parliamentary coalition, but it did so in less direct ways too. At Edgehill and Turnham Green there had been an element of excitement, or even euphoria, about the response of the troops. During the following years the hard realities of soldiering became obvious. The horrors endured in Germany during the Thirty Years War were well-known, and fears that England might 'turn Germany' were common. They were quickly reinforced by Edgehill, Brentford, Marlborough, Birmingham and Lancaster. The almost forgotten skirmish at Guisborough was sufficiently appalling to shift Cholmley's allegiance, and the agonizing death suffered by Hampden had many fellows. Charles was in the end reluctant to storm Gloucester, having seen the aftermath of the storming of Bristol, where, as one participant put it, 'as gallant men as ever drew sword . . . lay upon the ground like rotten sheep'.[90] Given the political uncertainties about war aims the problems raised by these terrible experiences were more complicated than simple revulsion at the experience of warfare: what was this suffering supposed to achieve, and was it doing so?

Military campaigns imposed heavy burdens on individuals and communities and continued fighting posed a problem of political and religious mobilization. But as the campaigns became more destructive, without being more decisive, and novel institutional measures were taken to support them, the war became a political issue in itself, complicating the choices made in 1642. In justifying new measures and trying to stiffen the sinews, again particularly on the parliamentary side, more radical religious and political arguments were voiced. Parliament's war effort, increasingly closely associated with zealous reformation, was stepped up in two distinct phases: one towards the end of the Oxford negotiations and extending into late April, the other in June and July. This process too led to some revision of the choices of 1642. By late summer, Parliament's military fortunes were at a low ebb, radical administrative measures were being taken, supported by rhetoric which would not have commanded much support a year earlier. The core of the parliamentary cause was being more clearly defined and could not easily be presented as merely defensive. The problems this posed were obvious in the defections of 1643. Domestic radicalization had benefits in fighting the war, but also costs in threatening the solidity of the coalition of 1642. This was to become still more the case in the autumn, as Parliament concluded a military alliance with the Covenanters, and Charles negotiated a cessation in Ireland in order to allow him to bring troops across the Irish Sea. Meanwhile, Parliament had not really enjoyed the fruits of this escalation either, although the relief of Gloucester had lifted spirits.

Bruno Ryves's strategy in *Mercurius Rusticus*, of contrasting the actions of parliamentarians with their rhetoric, was a common one, and manifested the much larger problem posed by the contested meaning of key terms. Publicity magnified the obvious problem: conditions of necessity had made the meaning of apparently plain words (law, reformation, treason, honour) obscure. The truth in these conditions was very elusive – both in the sense of reliable accounts of what was happening and, more importantly, what it meant. Versions of the truth could not be taken on trust either, as polemics consistently undercut the authority of the other side. Meanwhile, for an uncommitted reader of the flood of pamphlets that swept from the presses, it was difficult to identify the grounds of honourable personal conduct.

10

The War of the Three Kingdoms

The Irish Cessation and the Solemn League and Covenant, 1643

By late 1643 both sides had secured outside help, further complicating the politics of mobilization and the difficulty of negotiating an eventual peace. The King sought a truce in Ireland to release troops for service in England; Parliament sought military help from the Covenanters. The English civil war had been a consequence of crises in the other kingdoms; England was now to become the cockpit of a war of all three kingdoms.

There were three armies in Ireland. The confederated Catholics, the original rebels, had risen against the government, having been frustrated in their hopes of securing concessions from Wentworth in return for financial support for the crown. They were now seeking freedom of worship and security of their estates and religion. Given the climate in England freedom of worship was unthinkable, but security of estates and religion were, potentially, negotiable. The Confederates had been sensitive to the realities of English politics – for example, they did not refer to their assembly in Kilkenny (which met two days after the battle of Edgehill) as a parliament because the oath of confederacy had bound them to acknowledge the King's rights, among which was the sole authority to summon parliaments. They also recognized the authority of English common law and statute, so long as they did not infringe the liberties of the Irish people or the free exercise of their religion. There were of course divisions over what these demands meant in practice, and it is significant that they were the confederated Catholics, rather than the united Catholics, or simply the Catholics. It was a loose coalition, formed in the months after the rising, in the light of military needs. Its politics are best understood in terms of a tension between a peace party, anxious for a rapid settlement with the King, and a clericalist wing, seeking to extract maximal religious concessions from the King now that a rising was underway. There was also a middle group, negotiating between these positions, led by Nicholas Plunkett, a distinguished Dublin lawyer. Plunkett had acted against Wentworth on a number of occasions during the 1630s. Initially opposed to the rising he had risen rapidly in the ranks of the Confederacy once he had committed himself to its cause. He was one of the most prominent Catholic politicians of the mid seventeenth century, but his politics were not dogmatically confessional – his was a campaign for the rights of Catholics under the crown. His sense of what kind of peace would suffice was at odds with that of other influential figures in the Confederacy. Nonetheless, and despite their internal differences, the Confederates were surely correct in thinking that the King was a more likely friend than the English parliament and in October 1642 they had petitioned the King in these terms, 'which granted, we will convert our forces upon any design your majesty may appoint'.[1]

English forces in Ireland were based in Dublin under the command of James Butler, Earl of Ormond. The son of a prominent family (he was the 12th earl), he is normally commended above all for his loyalty. The Butlers had remained Catholic at the Reformation and so, despite a long record of crown service, had become subjects of suspicion. James was taken into royal wardship in 1614, however, and educated under the austerely Calvinist eye of George Abbot. Although his education was otherwise rather neglected, this created a breach with the Catholic past of the family and opened the door to service of the crown, something essential to the interests of ambitious landowners and something that Ormond pursued enthusiastically ever after. Sympathetic to the royalist cause in England, and serving under a royal commission, he was securely royalist. But this was less true of other figures in the Dublin government. Fear of popery and (Catholic) rebellion, such a prominent part of the English parliamentarian case, played powerfully among Ireland's Protestant elite. In October 1642, the month of the assembly at Kilkenny and of the battle of Edgehill, Parliament sent commissioners to Dublin hoping to get this army to renounce its loyalty to the King.[2]

A third army had been sent by the Covenanters in April 1642 to make Ulster safe for Presbyterianism, under the command of Robert Monro, and partly funded by the English parliament. A veteran of French, Danish and Swedish service, Monro had shown no hesitation in throwing in his lot with the Covenanters, and when he took up the commission of Major-General of the Covenanting army in Ireland he was probably

in his mid-forties. The proposal for a Scottish army to preserve Protestantism in Ireland had initially come from both Parliament and the
King, but by the time that the army was sent the King was no longer
behind it. This army was obviously more likely to fight for Parliament
than for the King, should it become interested in joining the English
war. There were also a number of regiments raised in England, the
Adventurers, on the promise of reward from confiscated lands, whose
loyalties were clearly far more likely to be parliamentarian.[3]

Of these armies in Ireland the Confederates were most likely to be
royalist, but an alliance with Irish Catholics would cost Charles support
everywhere else. Monro, of course, was unlikely to be anything but
pro-parliamentarian, but the allegiance of the English forces under the
command of Ormond might be contested. Viewed strictly as a matter
of military policy the King's best option was to seek peace with the
Confederates, hoping thereby to release Ormond's forces for service in
England. Early in 1643 Charles ordered the expulsion of the parliamentary delegation from Dublin, and sent a commission to Ormond and
others to hear the grievances of the Catholics. This process went ahead
despite a military initiative from Dublin, and despite the demands of the
Confederates, which were too far-reaching to be granted. By April, a
ceasefire seemed plausible, but not a full settlement, and over the summer
of 1643 this is what was negotiated. On 15 September, after a year of
military failure, Ormond managed to secure a twelve-month cessation
of arms in Ireland, leaving only very limited royal outposts on the east
coast and around Cork in the south-west, and some fortresses in the
north and west. Ormond's misgivings were shared by other influential
figures such as Murrough O'Brien, Earl of Inchiquin (a Protestant of
distinguished parentage and commander of the government's forces in
Munster), and Barnabas O'Brien, Earl of Thomond (governor of County
Clare). But the larger logic of the arrangement was plain. Ormond's
hesitations fed doubts about this peace party strategy among the Confederates: that the bargaining position was being given up too easily or to
someone who could not be fully trusted.[4]

The Cessation was (to put it no more strongly) unlikely to be well-
received in England and Scotland, particularly since its purpose was to
allow troops to be brought back and used against the English parliament.
It brought an end to Sir Edward Dering's flirtation with royalism, for
example. Returning from Oxford he was examined at Westminster, and

said 'that since the cessation in Ireland, and seeing so many papists and Irish rebels in the king's army and the anti-parliament set up at Oxford, and the King's counsels wholly governed by the popish party, his conscience would not permit him to stay longer with them'. He was allowed to compound for his delinquency, his treatment to be a model 'for all others that would come in after him who was the first'.[5] Perhaps more damagingly, the Cessation made Charles's hopes of getting Scottish support seem even more remote. The truce left Monro with a choice: to enjoy the benefits of the Cessation or to face the Confederate army without support from Ormond. Ormond's diplomacy therefore also aimed at preventing Monro fighting for Parliament, if possible. By early November the arrival of Irish troops had been negotiated and on 15 September a cessation was agreed, to last twelve months.[6]

While backing the plan for the Cessation in Ireland, Charles had also sought support in Scotland, hoping to exploit cracks in the Covenanting coalition, but these were more or less contradictory policies. He did not seem concerned that his Irish policy would upset others among his allies, or that Sir Edward Hyde (supporter of the policy of winning the war by subverting London through such means as the Waller plot) was not aware of these plans for Ireland. Hyde had been knighted as recently as February, joining the Privy Council and being appointed Chancellor of the Exchequer shortly afterwards – he was apparently a rising man in Charles's counsels, but he was in the dark about the Irish policy. Hamilton, the leading Scot at the English court and long-suffering adviser to Charles, who currently enjoyed Charles's confidence, thought that by normal means of aristocratic intrigue he would be able to generate support for the King in Scotland. In particular, the leading role played by the Earl of Argyll in the Covenanting movement was generating hostility in Scotland, particularly among his rivals, and this might form the basis for a royalist party without the necessity of making war in Scotland. The price of such a deal was likely to be a secure Presbyterian settlement, but making such guarantees appear convincing would be even harder than before as a result of his Irish policy.[7] Charles clearly saw his government in a 'three kingdoms' perspective, and was alert to the implications of dissent in one kingdom for the good order of the other two. It is hard to credit, therefore, how relaxed he was about the obvious difficulties of promoting a royalist alliance in three kingdoms, or at least one that was not obnoxious to many of his subjects.

An alternative vision for Scotland was the more militant one proposed by the Earl of Montrose. He was keen to create a royalist force in Scotland, and met Henrietta Maria soon after her landing in Bridlington, hoping to get the King's support for a rising in Scotland. Later in the year he met Charles in person outside Gloucester during the siege, to discuss this plan, which was less palatable than more moderate advice but probably more realistic. As early as 1640, when the Covenanters had been divided about the wisdom of crossing into England, Montrose had been able to gain support for an anti-Argyll covenant and hostility to Argyll remained significant. Another potential ally was the Earl of Antrim, anxious to regain his lands in Ulster from occupation by Monro, and also hostile to Argyll's domination of the west coast of Scotland. In the late summer of 1641 the Earl of Antrim had received orders from Charles I to raise troops in Ireland for deployment in Scotland. Now Montrose backed a plan (the 'Antrim plot') to use 2,000 Irish Catholic troops under Antrim to invade Argyll's estates in western Scotland, while Antrim was also commissioned to send 10,000 men to England to fight for the royalists.[8]

Hamilton's hope was that a moderate royalist cause could be built in Scotland without resort to war, but the Irish policy certainly made this uphill work. Montrose's militancy, while not necessarily the best thing for Scotland, was the better pair for the policy of Cessation in Ireland. However, further to Hamilton's policy a convention of estates was summoned in April 1643, but when it eventually met in June 1643 it was solidly pro-parliamentarian. This was perhaps predictable given that the English parliament had been seen as the guarantee of the Covenanting revolution in 1641, and the prospects of a cessation can only really have reinforced this view. Revelation of the Antrim plot was certainly the nail in the coffin of the moderate alliance. Its effect in London was also dramatic: according to Simonds D'Ewes, 'The discovery of this plot did more work on most men than anything that had happened during these miserable calamities and civil wars of England, because it seemed now that there was a fixed resolution in the Popish party utterly to extirpate the true Protestant religion in England, Scotland, and Ireland'.[9]

Charles's strategy, of pursuing all options at once – peace in Ireland, armed intervention in Scotland using Catholic troops, the capture of London from within and negotiated support in Scotland – was understandable, but untenable.[10] The Scottish convention of estates was dominated by Argyll and his supporters. Argyll was a supporter of the parliamentary cause and on good terms with Pym, and after the Antrim plot the game was up for moderate royalism in Scotland. Antrim, whose capture had led to revelation of the plot, was imprisoned in Carrickfergus, from where a dramatic escape allowed him to join the Confederates in Waterford. Meanwhile commissioners were sent from England to Scotland to negotiate a civil league and a religious covenant, arriving in August: what had seemed to be the likely outcome was indeed the eventual result – that Parliament would secure the help of the Covenanters. This produced a substantial army the following spring.[11] Charles, by negotiating a truce in Ireland, would be able to deploy the Dublin government's troops in England.

The Covenanters wanted the same thing from Parliament that they wanted from the King – security for a Presbyterian settlement. Here was one group who could certainly tell everyone what the war was about. But although there was much common ground about the preaching of the Word and purification of the church and liturgy, it was not clear that Parliament had been fighting to establish Presbyterian church government in England. The Westminster Assembly had been convened in order to discuss the form of a church settlement in England and so, in a fundamental sense, the divines were debating war aims. These discussions were therefore crucial to the military alliance with the Covenanters, and might offer the means to make common ground ideologically. Certainly its composition pointed that way – no Episcopalians sat, for obvious reasons – and it is also clear that the temper of the assembly owed something to Scottish influence. The task in front of it was both very difficult and of fundamental importance, and the assembly showed every sign of wanting to move at a pace appropriate to that task. From its first meeting, on 1 July, it proceeded slowly over issues of procedure and the rules for debate. From mid-July onwards a painstaking discussion of the Articles began. But it was undertaking that task in conditions of civil war, and with the urgent need to foster unity not only within England but also between the parliamentarians and Covenanters.[12]

When parliamentary commissioners had arrived in Scotland on 7 August, their priority was to secure troops. The Covenanters, however, were more concerned with securing closer union of the churches, or were at least more concerned with extracting that as the price of military support. A precondition of the military alliance became, for the Covenanters, a joint band or covenant to pursue shared religious objectives. In other words, where the parliamentarians were seeking a civil alliance, the Covenanters wanted a covenant; and for reasons internal to England that meant that the English commissioners had to try to restrain the influence of strict adherence to Presbyterian discipline on the shape of the covenant.[13] The weakness of Parliament's military position in England did not allow for robust negotiation.

This was the context in which the Solemn League and Covenant was produced. It was the document that the Covenanters wanted, not a straightforward statement of the parliamentary cause as seen by its English adherents. It was intended that the covenant would be sworn by all the inhabitants of the three kingdoms and would commit them to the promotion of a common religious practice. Significantly that entailed the *preservation* of the kirk, but the *reform* of the English and Irish churches. This reform was to be undertaken according to the example of the best reformed churches, and since no reform was proposed of the kirk, it is pretty clear which churches the drafters had in mind. Henry Vane, the chief parliamentary negotiator, is credited with securing a little wriggle room for those uncomfortable with Scottish presbytery: a clause was changed in Westminster so that reform should be pursued 'according to the word of God' rather than by the 'same holy word' that governed the kirk. It was not simply a religious covenant, since subscribers were also bound to preserve both Houses of Parliament and the King's person and authority, and to seek the punishment of malignants as well as opponents of religion. In fact only two of the six clauses were purely religious.[14] Nonetheless, the religious bond was close to the heart of the military alliance, and like all religious commitments it posed potentially very serious problems of conscience.[15]

There can be little doubt that this religious programme was closer to the mainstream of Scottish opinion than of English, or even the centre ground of the parliamentary coalition. For the Covenanters the best security for the gains they had made in 1640 and 1641 lay in the export of their church settlement, and that was in hand here, but many of those who fought for Parliament in England had not taken up arms for that. Moreover, the covenant pledged to extirpate heresy and schism. Sectarians could hope for little sympathy here, and respectable Congregationalists might look askance too. The pay-off for the English parliament was priceless, however: alongside this mutual covenant to pursue reformation the Covenanters demanded £30,000 per month from the English parliament in return for sending 21,000 men to bolster Parliament's ailing cause.[16]

The Scottish Convention adjourned on 26 August, the day that the draft of the Solemn League reached Westminster, where it was forwarded to the Assembly of Divines. Amendments were added in early September but negotiations were taking place with Gloucester under siege and Parliament's military fortunes far from thriving: nice distinctions over the precise form of the most desirable form of Protestant worship were allowed to slip notice, in the interests of political and military expediency. Scots commissioners arrived on 7 September and the covenant was finally sworn to by the Commons and the Assembly of Divines on 25 September.[17]

By October the assembly had returned to the business of a confession of faith for the English church, but again these careful deliberations were overtaken by the more pressing concern with the unity of the parliamentarian–Covenanter alliance. On 12 October the assembly was busy on the sixteenth of the Thirty-Nine Articles, especially 'upon that clause of it which mentions *departing from Grace*'.[18] At that point the Houses ordered the assembly, with some urgency, to consider the discipline and liturgy of the church instead. Although opinion on the issue of church government was poised between Presbyterians, Independents and Erastians, its deliberations took place in the light of the clear military and political significance of an alliance with the Presbyterian Scots. In this new work on discipline and liturgy, the hand of the Scottish commissioners can clearly be seen. The five Scottish commissioners had originally been chosen by the Scottish General Assembly, 'to treat with the English parliament or Assembly for the union of England and Scotland in one form of kirk government, one confession of faith, one catechism and one directory for worship'.[19] The Houses empowered the Westminster Assembly to elect a committee to treat with the Covenanters, and this standing committee came to exercise a considerable influence over the deliberations of the assembly as a whole. Initially it was a means of agreeing the Solemn League and Covenant, but on 17 October, as a result of Scottish pressure, another standing committee was formed to discuss the union of the churches – what had initially been a means of securing a political and military alliance had mutated into the instrument for the achievement of a union of the churches.[20] Robert Baillie, the leading Scottish Presbyterian minister, who was one of the commissioners, claimed that the influence of this committee was pervasive, and the records of the assembly seem to bear out that view. From the autumn onwards debate in the Westminster Assembly took a distinctly Presbyterian direction, one which was to cause significant problems within the parliamentary alliance.

Parliament was now co-ordinating a military campaign built around the call for further reformation defined ever more closely not simply in anti-episcopal but also in actively Presbyterian terms. The anti-Laudian alliance which had sustained opposition to the crown at the opening of the Long Parliament was far easier to mobilize than one in favour of this particular brand of reformation, but for the time being it was not in anyone's interest to dwell on the potential difficulties.

There was much common ground, of course. The Solemn League and Covenant committed its signatories to the extirpation of 'Popery, prelacy (that is, Church government by Archbishops, Bishops, their Chancellors and Commissaries, Deans, Deans and Chapters, Archdeacons, and all other ecclesiastical officers depending on that hierarchy), superstition, heresy, schism, profaneness, and whatsoever shall be found to be contrary to sound doctrine and the power of godliness'.[21] Much of this was dear to the hearts of English parliamentarians: popery, superstition and profaneness certainly; prelacy almost certainly; and heresy, subject to negotiation over definitions. Schism, however, was a much more controversial term, bearing on the nature of church government to follow from the abolition of prelacy.

As we have seen, and perhaps not coincidentally, the campaign against popery, superstition and profaneness had been stepped up during 1643. Scottish commissioners in London during the spring and summer of 1643 were witness to a more advanced process of purification than anything that had previously been undertaken as the Harley Committee, supported by the authorities in London, had started its campaign against exactly these things. Reformation of the physical space of English churches and towns, and purification of the liturgy, could be identified as pushing forward the preaching of the Word, and the right administration of the sacraments. Completion of the military alliance with the Covenanters coincided with an escalation of this second phase of iconoclasm, a campaign which was apparently more top-down than the relatively spontaneous reactions against Laudianism in 1640–42. On 26 August, the day that the Solemn League and Covenant was received at Westminster and immediately referred to the Westminster Assembly, the Lords approved an ordinance 'for the utter demolishing, removing and taking away of all monuments of superstition or idolatry'. It had been in production since June, and the terms echoed the Commons order of 8 September 1641 and the remit of the Harley Committee. But it was also broader in scope, more detailed and conducted nationally on a legislative basis. It called for the removal of altar tables and tables of stone. Communion tables were to be moved away from the east end of the church and all rails removed; tapers, candlesticks and basins taken off the communion table and no such things to be used. Crucifixes and crosses, images and pictures of the Virgin Mary and the saints, and superstitious inscriptions were all to be removed. This was a far wider campaign than the attacks on Laudian innovations in 1640–42: Michael Herring, for example, the churchwarden of St Mary Woolchurch, London, had at that time been reprimanded for defacing superstitious inscriptions. In adding crosses, the saints and superstitious inscriptions the legislation went further than previous orders, and also embraced not just the interiors of places of worship but also churchyards and other places belonging to churches and chapels, and 'any other open space'. The orders were not simply for removal either, but that these things should be defaced.[22]

It was this ordinance that set in train one of the more remarkable careers of the 1640s. Through the following spring an otherwise obscure man, William Dowsing, set about his own work in God's cause with great energy. A working farmer of relatively modest means, Dowsing was clearly a godly man. He collected a serious library of religious books, the earliest acquisitions illegal imports from the Low Countries dealing with separatism. In his mid-forties by the time war broke out, he served as Provost Marshal to the Eastern Association armies from August 1643 – responsible for military discipline. In December of that year, however, he surrendered his commission in favour of appointment as commissioner for removing the monuments of idolatry and superstition from the churches of the Eastern Association. This he did, with tremendous commitment, and over the next four months he visited 200 churches. On 15 April he visited three churches near his home in Suffolk, removing fifty-six superstitious pictures. This was the end of his most vigorous phase: in the coming five months he visited barely thirty more.[23] Perhaps his farm absorbed his energies over the summer, and by the autumn the Earl of Manchester's command was no longer secure. Thereafter, this kind of purification became the responsibility of churchwardens. In a relatively brief period, however, the first third or half of 1644, a yeoman farmer had cleansed most of the churches in Cambridgeshire and, with at least eight deputies, most of those in Suffolk too. There are signs of his presence in Essex and Norfolk too.[24]

In all this Dowsing was careful to act within the law, interpreting the ordinances empowering him very carefully: what he took into account changed as the legislation changed, and he sometimes argued the case with local authorities. The actual work of destruction was often left in the hands of churchwardens, constables or respectable local gentlemen. Here, as in the destruction of Cheapside Cross or the activities of the Harley Committee, was iconoclasm shorn of any association with sedition or lawlessness. As with those measures too, here was an opportunity for godly solidarity. Dowsing, almost certainly an Independent by inclination, was acting under orders from Manchester, a godly man who inclined towards Presbyterianism. Manchester, although conservative on church government, was very active in promoting the ejection of scandalous ministers and his father had, in the 1630s, taken a sympathetic view of the famous iconoclast Henry Sherfield. He was one of the members of the Lords who had supported the Commons order of September 1641, suggesting a long-term commitment to this issue.[25] Dowsing's books contain annotations which reveal a loss of confidence from 1645 onwards, as divisions among the godly and anxiety about the abuses of religious liberty by sectarians sapped his confidence about the authority of the cause.[26] But in 1644 these concerns lay in the future – here was a high-water mark of godly activism, in which differences over church government were marginal, or not of the essence.

The uncontroversial core of the alliance with the Covenanters was the promotion of the preaching of the Word, and the attack on idolatry and superstition.[27] Although this had been an important element of the parliamentary coalition in 1642, further reformation was controversial in England. Escalation of the war effort in the first half of 1643 had been accompanied by the definition of the cause – defensive arms (Husbands) and further reformation (the Harley Committee and Cheapside Cross). The Solemn League and Covenant reinforced this latter element, of purgation, making Parliament ever more committed to reform of forms of worship and the ritual calendar. This was of real significance to every parish in the country – the demands of this alliance were considerable. The more so, too, since this effort at purgation was closely tied to the negotiation of a Presbyterian church settlement in England. As events would prove, this was highly controversial even among those committed to the other features of this further reformation.

Royalist politics were hardly straightforward, either. Charles's diplomacy threw into sharp relief the longstanding question about his trustworthiness. The Cessation was difficult to reconcile with an attempt to woo moderate opinion in Scotland or England, and his major initiative of the final months of 1643 seems similarly instrumental. On 22 December he summoned all those who had left the Westminster parliament to attend a parliament in Oxford, along with all those who might now be willing to come. It was to meet on 22 January. This was a shrewd move, of course, raising in acute form the question of what kind of parliament was now sitting at Westminster – armed with legislation preventing dissolution without its own consent, and following the departure of the King and many members of both Houses, and the assumption of unprecedented executive powers, it was reasonably easy to question the extent to which this could still be considered a parliament. When the Oxford parliament met, 44 peers and 137 commoners were said to have attended – the majority of able-bodied peers and a substantial proportion of the Commons – which represented a considerable propaganda coup. In fact, if those willing but unable to attend are added, Charles would have had the support of 175 members of the Commons. Between the autumn of 1642 and January 1649 average attendance at the Westminster House of Lords was less than twenty, and the active membership of the Commons was below 200.[28]

But this is difficult to interpret as a genuine commitment on Charles's part to the virtues of parliaments. He had been reluctant to call the parliament, fearing that it would just press him to make accommodation and peace. On the other hand, it promised to rally support against a proposed invasion by the Scots, and given the balance of the political arguments, he seems to have been persuaded by the constitutional argument. He was restrained from dissolving the Westminster parliament, as advised by hardliners, on the grounds that this would be in breach of legislation he himself agreed in the summer of 1641, and would therefore both cancel the advantage he was seeking to claim, and make him appear untrustworthy, a primary charge against him.[29]

The force of the charge derived from his simultaneous pursuit of different and sometimes contradictory policies. Prior to the negotiation of the Cessation he had sought further help from Denmark, which had supplied arms in November 1642, but the terms demanded in May 1643 included handing over the Orkneys and Shetland, terms which would cost him dear in Scotland. From November 1643 an envoy was in Paris seeking French help. The Cessation was the best deal he could get, not necessarily the one closest to his heart. Over the winter of 1643–4, he was persuaded by the hardliners of Henrietta Maria's circle to seek a final peace in Ireland, while at the same time he was open to 'plots' – a plan to secure the delivery of the garrison of Aylesbury by disgruntled separatists called the 'Ogle plot' and another attempt to divide the authorities of the City of London from Parliament, called the 'Brooke plot'.[30]

All this has often persuaded historians that Charles was indeed untrustworthy. For many historians it has seemed easy to add a list of pejoratives – inept, calculating, instrumental, inconsistent, and so on. He was not unprincipled, however. His primary purpose was to preserve the dignity of the crown and integrity of the church, duties for which he was answerable to God. Those with whom he was dealing were rebels and traitors; they were not his equals, and did not share his obligations. Later in the 1640s this principled position was transmuted into an image of the suffering monarch – bearing burdens on behalf of his ungrateful subjects, and willing to suffer at their hands rather than surrender his sacred obligations.[31] These principles were consistent and sincere, and made his behaviour internally consistent and honourable; but it made him appear slippery and untrustworthy. He was a difficult king to like. Of course, another pressure making for apparent inconsistency was division among his counsellors, and as their influence waxed and waned so did royalist policies – in this respect the royalist coalition was no more shifty than the parliamentarians. Parliament, for example, was quite capable of negotiating for peace on the basis of established rights and liberties while at the same time seeking to win the war using administrative instruments which undoubtedly violated those principles. In a peculiar way, then, Charles and his critics agree on one thing – that he should be judged by different standards.

The Cessation also introduced an ethnic dimension into the conflict in England. Irish involvement in the war was easily misrepresented, and prompted reactions which were, to the modern observer, grotesque. Newspaper reports over the coming years gave a cumulative estimate that more than 22,000 troops had arrived from Ireland, of whom the majority might have been native Irish rather than Protestant troops returned from service against the Catholics. Clearly an army of this size would have had a very substantial effect on the fighting, but this almost certainly reflected contemporary fears rather than reality. More recent estimates have put the figure much lower – most recently and most authoritatively at a little more than 9,000. It is more difficult to estimate the proportion of native Irish, but there is little evidence to support an estimate higher than 2,000. Remarkably, some of these 2,000 deserted to the parliamentary cause, along with many of their Anglo-Irish colleagues.[32] With a downward revision of the estimated size of the army has come a consequent revision of the strategic benefit to the royalist cause of these soldiers.[33]

There is no disagreement about the propaganda effect, however, and fear of these armed papists threatened to introduce England to a fuller experience of wartime atrocity. On 23 October the first regiments arrived from Ireland and it quickly became clear that the terms of engagement with Irish troops were different. On 26 December, Byron's royalist forces had trapped a detachment of parliamentarians in Barthomley Church and put them all to the sword. When Byron's troops were defeated a month later at Nantwich, the parliamentary press made much of the fact that the 120 women captured had been carrying knives more than half a yard long, with a hook at the end, 'made not only to stab, but to tear the flesh from the very bones'. One newsbook recommended that they 'be put to the sword, or tied back to back and cast into the sea'.[34] This played on more general fears about the Irish: 'Do you imagine . . . the Irish rebels will be [any] more merciful to you, your wives and children than they were to the Protestants in Ireland?'[35] Attitudes like these informed a hostility to the Irish troops that was barely restrained.

In mid-December, following the capture of a minor royalist garrison at Beoley House in Worcestershire, all troops thought to be Irish had been put to the sword. One hundred and fifty troops intercepted en route from Ireland the following April by Vice-Admiral Richard Swanley were taken to Pembroke in triumph before, on St George's Day, being tied back to back and thrown into the sea. One newsbook reported with glee how they had been 'caused to use their natural art, and try whether they could tread the seas as lightly as their Irish bogs'.[36]

These atrocities invited responses, of course, and threatened that the war would lose all restraint. At Bolton in May 1644 parliamentary forces defending the town, having repulsed an attack, took a prisoner and 'hung him up as an Irish papist' in full view of his comrades. When the town fell many were slain out of hand in reprisal. At Lyme, Dorset, in June a royalist siege was abandoned. In the deserted royalist camp parliamentarian seamen found 'an old Irish woman', looking for her friends, who she had thought were still there. The seamen dragged her back to Lyme, 'drove her through the streets to the seaside, slashed and hewed her with their swords' before casting her corpse into the sea. Following the capture in Dorset of Irish troops, apparently native Irish who could not speak English, Essex had written to approve their execution: 'if the Irish he [the local commander] has taken prove to be absolute Irish, he may cause them to be executed: for he would not have quarter allowed to those'.[37]

By the autumn of 1644 this was near to official policy. On 24 October the English parliament passed an ordinance that no quarter should be offered to Irishmen or papists born in Ireland taken in arms against Parliament. They were to be exempt from all surrender agreements and, following any surrender, parliamentary officers were ordered 'forthwith to put every such person to death'. Officers failing to do so 'shall be reputed a favourer of that bloody rebellion of Ireland' and subject to such punishment as the Houses thought fit.[38] A similar order followed in Scotland, on 23 December 1645, that Irish prisoners should be executed without trial.[39] But the fear of reprisal seems to have restrained this escalation. Days after the execution of the Irish prisoners in Dorset twelve parliamentarian prisoners, civilians, were hanged 'upon the same tree' by Sir Francis Doddington. Following the passage of the ordinance of 1644 thirteen Irish prisoners had been hanged after Shrewsbury fell to the parliamentarians. Prince Rupert immediately hanged thirteen

Protestant English in retaliation, explaining that 'soldiers of [his] were barbarously murdered in cold blood, after quarter given to them'. '[L]et the authors of that massacre know, their own men must pay the price of such acts of inhumanity, and . . . be used as they used their brethren . . . in the same manner'.[40]

Hostility to the Irish threatened to change the terms of engagement, reflecting the power of the fear rather than actual size, composition and importance of the Irish armies. There were other groups who attracted similar, though by no means identical, hostility. The Cornish were talked about as if they were not English by their opponents, and hostile stereotypes of the Welsh were common in cheap print – as buffoons or near pagans. So relentless was this campaign that it informed attempts to propagate the gospel in Wales during the 1650s. Parallels were frequently drawn between the royalism of Cornwall and of Wales, resting it was said on ignorance and simplicity; the bumpkins were said to be dupes of the King. Covenanters on the other hand were presented as invaders, while Highlanders who fought against the Covenanters in 1645 were presented as barbarians in both England and Scotland.[41] But although these ethnic identities were clearly important to the paper battles, it was the Irish who were singled out as being beyond the reach of the laws of war, and that was related fairly specifically to the rising of 1641. Significantly, the ordinance denying them quarter in 1644 had applied the same judgement to 'papists', presumably independent of their ethnicity, and those who failed to kill them were deemed to be supporters of the rebellion.[42] Certainly, there seems to have been a qualitative difference between satirical accounts of cowardly Welsh bumpkins and Irish barbarians deserving only of death.[43]

From Edgehill in October 1642 until the arrival of Irish troops a year later, the English war had been exactly that: a war between English armies albeit one fought in the context of a wider crisis of the Stuart crowns. As a result of the Solemn League and Covenant and the Irish Cessation, however, England became the cockpit of a war of all three kingdoms. Henceforth ethnic identities had an impact on the conduct of war in England, and on its representation in print. When military victory was achieved in England, it did not resolve this wider military conflict. Moreover these alliances not only made the English war part of a war of three kingdoms, but also made it easier to claim it was a religious war, since there were, it was plausibly claimed, Catholics clearly engaged on one side. Royalists paid a high price for this alliance with popery.

In the short term, what saved Parliament's cause was not the Solemn League and Covenant, but the failure of the royalists to turn their position of strength into a decisive victory. The decision to move on Gloucester rather than London, and then to lay siege rather than storm it, had allowed Essex time to march to the relief of the city. There then followed a race as Essex sought to withdraw again to London, pursued by Rupert's army.

In the late afternoon of 19 September, Essex's quartermasters entered Newbury to arrange quarters and supplies for the main army. Not long after, however, Rupert's horse arrived, taking a number of prisoners and securing the town for the royalist army. This put the royal army between Essex and London, and on the following day a major battle was fought between armies numbering about 14,000 men each. Although the royalists had the advantage of taking Newbury, which afforded food and more comfortable quarters, they failed to secure the high ground on what became the battlefield. Confused fighting carried on into the night, but the parliamentary army managed to retain control of the Round Hill, thanks largely to the efforts of the London Trained Bands. The result was indecisive, rather than a clear parliamentarian victory, but the royalists withdrew and had suffered the loss of prominent officers. More importantly, if Essex's army had lost, the parliamentary cause would have been severely damaged: the north and west were secure for the royalists, Waller was in London and so, with central England under royalist domination, parliamentary armies would effectively have been confined to the immediate environs of London and East Anglia. Even with Covenanter troops promised this would have been a bleak prospect indeed. By not losing, Essex had achieved an important victory for the parliamentary cause. He was able to push on to Reading and London was again secure. The royalists, having chosen not to engage with Essex again on the day after the battle, withdrew to Oxford.[44] On his return to London, Essex received the thanks of the Commons and reviewed the Trained Bands. On 28 September the troops sent out to relieve Gloucester returned, also to a warm welcome.[45]

Further good news for Parliament followed in September and October, as royalist forces regrouped. Following a parliamentary victory at Gainsborough in July (notable for the importance and discipline of the cavalry under the command of Oliver Cromwell), the parliamentary troops had withdrawn from the town. But in the autumn they rallied again and, drawing troops from around the region, won another engagement at Winceby (11 October). Hull remained in parliamentary hands, an important limitation on royalist domination of the north, and the position of Hull was improved when the Earl of Manchester lifted a siege of Lynn (16 September). This freed troops for action elsewhere, and on 12 October the siege of Hull was also lifted. Newport Pagnell, an important garrison on the Great North Road, was abandoned by the royalists on 28 October and occupied by Essex two days later. Skirmishing in the west followed Ralph (now Lord) Hopton's return to the field, armed with a new commission, following recovery from wounds received when barrels of gunpowder exploded accidentally following the battle of Lansdown. Here, too, fortune no longer seemed to be so clearly favouring the royalists.[46]

Overall, the late summer and autumn saw a slight but significant shift in military fortune and this was of tremendous political significance. In particular, the lifting of the siege of Gloucester and the return of Essex via Newbury, bloodied but still intact, secured London for the winter and prevented an outright military victory. These victories, turning a tide of royalist success, were important for morale. On the day that Essex arrived back in London the Commons swore to the Covenant.

Over the winter there were no formal peace negotiations. Parliament had survived the campaign season, concluded its treaty with the Covenanters and put the finishing touches to its war effort. A South-Eastern Association was formed on 4 November 1643 under Waller's command and, on 4 December 1643, steps were taken to ensure the regular payment of Essex's troops from the receipts of the excise and assessment. This was in part a response to the difficulties that Waller faced in persuading his London levies to stick with the campaign as winter approached, and to the difficulties of supply that had hampered Essex earlier in the summer.[47] On 20 January the military effectiveness of the Eastern Association was improved by giving the Earl of Manchester control over the assessment revenues from the region, in place of the constituent county committees. Moreover, the assessment was increased to a massive £33,780 per month. Using this legislation he was able to establish central treasuries and supply departments in Cambridge which supported a formidable army the following year.[48] Pym had therefore masterminded a round of administrative reforms throughout 1643 designed to strengthen Parliament's military position. With a new military alliance in place, and with a firmer administrative structure taking shape, Parliament was not, over the winter 1643/4, committed to peace negotiations.

Neither were the royalists. They too had new military allies and during the autumn of 1643, despite the reverses at Gloucester and Newbury, their prospects still looked good. Irish troops were arriving and the news from minor engagements was not all bad: the royalists took Reading (3 October), Dartmouth (6 October) and Arundel (6 December) and its castle (9 December). Foreign diplomacy and the encouragement of the Ogle and Brooke plots offered more hopeful means of securing Charles's war aims.[49]

Parliament was on the defensive, but by the autumn a storm had been weathered and troops from Scotland could be expected for the campaigns of the spring. However, in seeking internal political commitment and Scottish aid, Parliament was increasingly identifying its cause as the promotion of further reformation in the English church. This had not been a consensual aim in 1642 and it was not clear now what further reformation entailed, or how much further there was to go. The royalist strategy, by contrast, seemed settled on exploiting weaknesses in the parliamentary coalition and seeking military support from any and every quarter. This had the disadvantage of trying to forge an alliance from completely incompatible religious aspirations, and that might reflect a lack of sincerity on Charles's part in giving commitments to any or all of these partners. The involvement of Irish troops introduced a new kind of ethnic hostility into the English war, and threatened to push codes of conduct further towards the extremes of seventeenth-century behaviour. Escalation of all kinds was changing the nature and purpose of the war. By the end of 1643 the military balance was still in the King's favour, but not decisively so; and both sides had entered military alliances which promised new strength the following year. If anything, though, it was becoming less rather than more clear what kind of political settlement could possibly satisfy the parties now involved.

Marston Moor

The Victory of the Covenant?

By the time of John Pym's death from disease in early December 1643 much of the architecture of Parliament's eventual victory was in place, and he must take a large share of the credit for that. A military alliance with the Covenanters, in the service of yet another covenant, this time between the two kingdoms, was underpinned by novel forms of taxation which would provide the basis for public revenues for over a century (assessment, excise and customs). These were reinforced by penal taxation and seizure from those who opposed the aims of the Covenant. Parliamentary committees, proliferating like mushrooms, allowed Parliament to act as an executive body, albeit a rather poorly co-ordinated one.

Pym's contribution to sustaining the political will to implement these measures was considerable, but not necessarily popular, even among those who had been riveted by his compelling speeches in May and November 1640.[1] Although his influence grew out of those influential speeches, what he had in the end championed was quite different from a defence of parliamentary liberties and the Church of England. A week or so before Pym's death, Parliament took a further highly significant step. In early November, Parliament had authorized the use of a new Great Seal, the highest symbol of sovereignty, and on 30 November it was entrusted to six parliamentary commissioners. It represented an escalation of the argument that the King enjoyed his powers in trusteeship, exercised in partnership with Parliament. When the King was absent or in danger of wrecking the kingdom, so the argument had gone, then Parliament could assume trust in his place. Now, it was said, those using the Great Seal were enemies of the state, which was not currently entrusted to the King. The new seal made the implications of this plain: it did not include the King's image but that of the House of Commons, and the arms of England and Ireland. As one commentator put it, there was consternation among 'all the People' who had 'reason to believe that, at last, the divisions between the King and Parliament would become irreparable, and that there would be no hopes left of their being reconciled to one another, the breach made in his Majesty's authority being so great, that it portended nothing less than the ruin of the state and the dissolution of the monarchy'.[2] In all these ways, defence of parliamentary liberty was clearly no longer the same as defence of the ancient constitution.

Pym's death also coincided with a reorganization of parliamentary military command. The formal alliance with the Covenanters called into being the Committee of Both Kingdoms, which took over from the Committee of Safety in February 1644. It was the first body to have responsibilities in both kingdoms. In one sense it filled the gap of a single executive body, acting as a kind of parliamentary Privy Council. But it was also a highly political body, on which opponents of the Earl of Essex were prominent, men anxious for a clearer military victory in order to secure a peace on demanding terms. Holles, for example, was not on the committee, but Cromwell was, and its terms of reference compromised the powers granted to Essex in his commission. Pym, man of the moment in 1640, died at a point when the parliamentary cause had plainly moved a long way from the aims set out at the meeting of the Long Parliament – it was now a military alliance with the Covenanters, more or less on condition that the English church be reformed along the lines of the kirk, in the hands of a parliamentary committee acting as an independent executive and likely to seek a decisive military victory over their King.[3] National subscription to the Solemn League and Covenant was promoted from 5 February, underpinning these aims.[4]

In this context, the fate of William Laud has an obvious significance – putting the issues of 1640 back in the forefront of people's minds, and paying an easy price to the Covenanters for their military support. Laud had been impeached on 19 October 1643, the first step on what proved a long path to his execution, and it is difficult to avoid the conclusion that this was a narrowly calculating political act, another way of promoting Protestant unity without raising difficulties about church government, and an easy way to curry favour with the Covenanters. It also perhaps reflected how Laud was the personification of the dangers of Catholic conspiracy, all too evident following the Cessation. One newsbook argued that 'the sparing of him hath been a provocation to Heaven, for it is a sign that we have not been so careful to give the Church a sacrifice as the State'. Strafford had died for the latter, but now revenge was sought on Canterbury in the cause of God: 'he having corrupted our religion, banished the godly, introduced superstitions, and embrewed both kingdoms at first in tincture of blood'. But there was a more prosaic reason – while he lived on as Archbishop of Canterbury he had to approve ecclesiastical appointments and, though he did his best to comply, some appointments made demands on him that he could not in conscience approve. In any case there can have been little to justify the prosecution of an ageing bishop, or the 'rancorous hatred' with which his prison cell was searched for incriminating evidence.[5] The hostility perhaps bears testimony as much to the difficulties of 1643 as to the certainties of 1640. It offered the same comforts as the bonfire of 'pictures and popish trinkets' staged on the site of Cheapside Cross in January 1644 to mark the defeat of the Brooke plot.[6] Even so, it was another year before the trial was concluded.

Pym had died at more or less the pivotal moment in the fighting. By not losing ín 1643, when military fortunes had favoured the royalists, Parliament had put its armies in a position to win, particularly in alliance with the Covenanters. This was not simply because of the intervention of the Covenanters, since the royalist momentum had already been halted, particularly by the victories at Newbury and Winceby. The first major engagement of the spring was at Cheriton (29 March), on the approaches to Winchester. A decisive victory that owed nothing to the Covenanters, it led to a royalist withdrawal and the recapture of Winchester. This not only halted royalist advances in the west but signalled, like Winceby, that the parliamentary cavalry was becoming a match for the royalists. It was followed within ten days by the fall of Salisbury, Andover and Christchurch (although Winchester Castle held out) and, by early April, Waller was on the verges of Dorset. Clarendon felt that the impact of the defeat at Cheriton on the royalist cause was 'doleful'.[7]

When the Covenanters arrived, then, it can plausibly be argued that the momentum was already with Parliament and that some of the further progress of parliamentary arms did not depend on their presence. On the other hand, this was also partly an illusion caused by royalist strategy. The King's forces now dispersed, seeking to re-establish control in the regions, a necessary preliminary to building strength for a renewed offensive, and that continued to be a reasonably hopeful strategy.[8] In any case, the Covenanters' army was undoubtedly significant in shifting the balance further in favour of Parliament, opening a new front in the north and introducing a new field army. In late spring there were five parliamentary armies in England. The Covenanters and the Fairfaxes in the north put pressure on Newcastle's position, Manchester was besieging Lincoln, Waller was the dominant force in the west and Essex was preparing to take the field. Against this, Rupert's army was in the north-west and potentially able to offer some support to Newcastle, but Charles had sustained a presence in the centre only by amalgamating his army with the remnants of Hopton's. Prince Maurice was laying siege to Lyme, with a small force, and there was no army available to confront Manchester.[9] The Covenanters did not turn the tide, but they did contribute significantly to the problem of over-stretch faced by the royalist forces.

Commitment to dispersal, and the demands of the overall situation, undoubtedly affected the movements of Rupert's army during the spring. He had left Oxford for Chester in March, where he was lobbied to pursue the relief of Lathom House, but the chief priority was the relief of Newark, which was achieved on 21 March. It was a significant victory, not least because the besieging forces surrendered siege artillery, 3,000-4,000 muskets and large numbers of pikes. But there was an immediate demand for Rupert's aid in the south. Many of his troops came from Wales and he set off there for replenishment and supply, but was recalled to Oxford on 3 April. The order was countermanded the following day, but it is evidence of the stretch that was now felt in the royalist ranks. Newcastle's pleas for support in Yorkshire continued to go unheard and the royalists had also been defeated at Nantwich. On 11 April, Selby fell to the Fairfaxes and Newcastle withdrew to York. This allowed the Covenanters and the Fairfaxes to join forces at Tadcaster a week later, threatening the extinction of the royal cause in the north.[10]

In this situation a parliamentary advance on Oxford, where morale was flagging, was quite possible. On 16 April the Oxford parliament was prorogued following an address imploring Charles to guarantee the safety of the Protestant religion; the failure of another political initiative and the death of what Charles was later known to have called his 'mongrel parliament'. For Parliament, Oxford and York were the two key military objectives, and the royalist forces were stretched to cover both. While Charles sought to strengthen the position around Oxford with garrisons at Reading, Wallingford, Abingdon and Banbury, Rupert left once more for the north. The Committee of Both Kingdoms was also interested in both objectives, and as the Earl of Manchester took control of Lincolnshire he was sent to York rather than Oxford. Nonetheless, parliamentary advances in May put such pressure on the royalist position in Oxford that the King decided to leave. Charles left Oxford on 3 June with 7,500 men, leaving 3,500 to defend the town, armed with all his heavy artillery, and marched west via Burford, Bourton and Evesham. By the time he reached Evesham it was known that Tewkesbury had fallen to Massey and he opted to take up quarters at Worcester, arriving on 6 June. Three days later Sudeley Castle fell and he ordered a further withdrawal to Bewdley.[11]

These then were promising days for the parliamentary armies. The King had withdrawn from Oxford and York was under pressure. But the initiative was lost. Essex was sent to relieve Lyme rather than join Waller in a pursuit of the King. This crucial and controversial decision was taken at a council of war at Chipping Norton, at which both Waller and Essex were present. It was an odd one, perhaps intended as a prelude to moving into the west and cutting off the King's supply. Historians have subsequently blamed Essex and Waller for a crucial error, and at the time the Committee of Both Kingdoms was shocked by the decision and ordered Essex to return, something he notoriously failed to do, on 14 June. Having decided to take this course, and to ignore a direct order from the Committee of Both Kingdoms, it was of course important for Essex to succeed, and at first he did. He lifted the siege of Lyme on 14 June and took Weymouth the next day. He now resolved to push on into the west. It is more than possible that this reflects in part personal frictions between Waller and Essex, who had been at odds before and seem to have squabbled during this campaign. But this disagreement was probably exaggerated retrospectively by Waller and his supporters – he initially supported the decision. Essex challenged Parliament to relieve him of his command and got his way – on 25 June he was ordered to move west in accordance with his wishes.[12] This order allowed him to continue the march he had already commenced in defiance of his previous orders.

Meanwhile, Waller pursued the royal army, which was moving back via Woodstock and Buckingham. He found it difficult to engage the army, and its very mobility was a problem, since it might suggest a move either on York or on London. Waller therefore had to have the defence of London in mind. This rested on a small and hastily assembled force under Major-General Browne and it appeared vulnerable until Waller made it back to Brentford on 28 June. In the end the indecisive engagement at Cropredy Bridge on 29 June was the only fruit of these manoeuvrings, and this must surely count as a lost opportunity for Parliament. After the battle the royal army was able to march off in pursuit of Essex in better spirits than the parliamentarians.[13]

In the north, however, the parliamentary campaign was decisive. York had been under siege by Leven and Fairfax since 22 April and the only hope of relief lay with Rupert. In May and June he won a string of victories in Lancashire. These mobile campaigns were frustrating parliamentary armies in the south, but the position in York looked bleak. On 13 June the Earl of Newcastle had been invited to negotiate its surrender and it was thought that the city could only hold out for another six days.[14]

On 14 June, Charles wrote a fateful letter to Rupert. 'If York be lost I shall esteem my crown little less, unless supported by your sudden march to me, and a miraculous conquest in the South, before the effects of the Northern power can be found here; but if York be relieved, *and you beat the rebels' armies of both kingdoms which were before it*, then, but other ways not, I may possibly make a shift upon the defensive to spin out time until you come to assist me'. The loss of York would be a catastrophe except in the very unlikely event that Rupert was able to get away and secure victories in the south before the parliamentarian armies got there. On the other hand, if York was relieved and the northern army defeated, Charles might avoid defeat long enough for Rupert to come to his aid. Relief of York and defeat of the northern army were the best hope for the royalist cause.[15]

This was a realistic view, but it conflated the relief of York and the defeat of the rebels: as it was to turn out it was possible to relieve York without defeating the Scottish and parliamentarian forces. Charles had not known this of course. His command to Rupert was:

all new enterprises laid aside, you immediately march according to your first intention, with all your force, to the relief of York; but if that be either lost or have freed themselves from the besiegers, or that for want of powder you cannot undertake that work, that you immediately march with your whole strength directly to Worcester, to assist me and my army, without which, or your having relieved York *by beating the Scots*, all the successes you can afterwards have most infallibly will be useless to me.[16]

Again, the possibility was not recognized here that York might be relieved without defeating the besieging army.

On 28 June it was clear that Rupert was coming. Besiegers were too exposed between the walls of a defended city and an army able to line up in one place, rather than as an encircling force, and on 1 July the siege had been broken up. The parliamentary forces withdrew to Tadcaster and York had been saved. But Rupert seems, not unreasonably, to have interpreted the letter to mean not simply that he should relieve York but that he should engage and destroy the besieging army. He therefore decided to seek battle despite the clearly expressed view of the Earl of Newcastle that it should be avoided. Most subsequent commentators have taken Newcastle's side: with the relief of York the King's position had been rendered more stable and there was no good reason for risking an engagement with the besieging army. In fact Rupert had received numerous letters in the weeks before Marston Moor containing more or less the same message, and urging haste, and so he was not unjustified in seeing his orders in this way. It seems that other royalist commanders feared that Rupert, left to his own devices, would have given priority to establishing full control of Lancashire. But he was also aggressive by instinct and that he interpreted his order in that way would not have surprised Colepeper: when he heard that the letter had been sent he said to Charles, 'Before God, you are undone, for upon this peremptory order he will fight, whatever comes on't'.[17]

For those interested in contingencies then, the moment at which Charles drafted that clause, or the moment when Rupert read it, was crucial to the course of the war in England. With York relieved, the King in what turned out to be a successful pursuit of Essex, and Oxford secure, honours might have been said to be even. But Rupert chose to engage numerically superior forces, with catastrophic results for the royalist cause.

Battle was joined at Marston Moor on 2 July. Rupert's forces were considerably outnumbered, particularly the cavalry. His relieving army and the force garrisoning York numbered about 18,000. The parliamentarians, by contrast, probably had around 28,000 men, the result of the confluence of forces under the command of Leven, Sir Thomas Fairfax and Manchester. The bulk of the parliamentary forces, about 16,000, were Scottish and Leven was in overall command both as the ranking officer and as a man of formidable experience in the European wars. His forces were drawn up with the infantry in the centre, cavalry on the right under Fairfax and on the left under Cromwell and Leslie. Opposite Cromwell were Rupert's cavalry, commanded by Byron, and Fairfax was opposed by Goring. Infantry numbers were fairly equal – around 11,000 on either side – but the parliamentary advantage in horse was considerable. This was not a guarantee of success, however, because the ground on which the battle was fought did not favour horse riders – furze, gorse, ditches and rabbit holes broke up the ground, making rapid advances difficult. Byron, in particular, was protected by rough ground.[18]

The initial deployment was not complete until late afternoon, and several hours of inconclusive skirmishing had achieved little by 7 p.m. At that point Rupert thought the battle would be postponed until the next day, and Newcastle was repairing to his coach to enjoy a pipe of tobacco. But as a thunderstorm broke, the parliamentary infantry began to advance. The rain interfered with the matchlocks of the royalist advance guard and the parliamentarians' infantry successfully engaged with the main body of the royalist infantry. But the royalist riposte was very successful. Goring advanced on the parliamentary cavalry ranged against him, and his men began to inflict heavy losses. Byron, perhaps encouraged by the sight, advanced on Cromwell, but in doing so had to tackle the difficult ground himself. Perhaps that contributed to the ensuing rout, in which Cromwell's cavalry were triumphant. But with Fairfax's cavalry now defeated and Goring's men inflicting heavy losses on the infantry it seemed as if Rupert's decision might be vindicated. Many Scottish troops fled and at one stage all three parliamentarian generals appeared to be in flight, thinking that a royalist victory was in the offing.

It was the discipline of Cromwell's cavalry that transformed this position. Fairfax made his way behind royalist lines to tell Cromwell what had happened on the opposite flank. Cromwell was able not only to rally his cavalry but to lead them back behind the royalist lines before leading a devastating charge on Goring's forces from the rear. This was utterly decisive – the royalist infantry were now completely exposed, and outnumbered. Most surrendered, and the parliamentary victory was total. It is likely that the royalists lost at least 4,000 men, probably many more, and a further 1,500 were captured. Rupert left York the next morning with only 6,000 men and Newcastle refused to make a fist of the defence of York, preferring exile, he said, to 'the laughter of the court'. York surrendered two weeks later and the parliamentary forces in the field now easily outnumbered the royalists. This was the worst case that Charles's letter had sought to avoid: the loss of both York and his field army.

Marston Moor was certainly a massive blow to royalist morale, and decisive for the war in the north, but Parliament was robbed of an outright victory in England by a combination of poor military judgement and political hesitancy. The military adventure launched by the Earl of Essex and the reluctance of the Earl of Manchester to pursue a complete victory allowed the King to recover his position in the west and enter winter quarters in Oxford in triumph.

In mid-June, having lifted the siege of Lyme and captured Weymouth, Essex set off into the west. Waller could not offer support partly because of the reluctance of the London Trained Bands to serve for long away from home. Nonetheless, supported by the navy under Warwick's command, Essex initially enjoyed considerable success. By early to mid-July he was threatening Exeter, where Henrietta Maria was recovering from the birth of her daughter, Henrietta Anne, on 16 June. Essex refused her safe conduct to Bath and offered instead personally to escort her to London. Given what subsequently happened, this would have been a considerable boon to the parliamentary cause, but Henrietta Maria refused – as both she and Essex knew she faced impeachment in London. Instead she fled to France, on 14 July, and never saw her husband again.[19]

Influenced by the threat of the northern army moving south, and also perhaps by this threat to his wife's safety, Charles moved decisively after Essex. On 26 July he reached Exeter and rendezvoused with Prince Maurice, who was at the head of 4,600 men, at Crediton the following day. Essex, meanwhile, was further west at Tavistock, where he had been received triumphantly – Plymouth had been secured. Cut off by a royal army and having secured Plymouth this might have been the moment for discretion, but instead Essex resolved to push on. On 26 July he decided to go on into Cornwall, arriving at Lostwithiel on 3 August. The King had pursued him, arriving at Liskeard the previous day.[20]

Now bottled up, with the King's army behind him, Essex had put himself in a desperate position. On 30 August he prepared to withdraw. The following night his cavalry were able to ride away, itself something of a puzzle since the King had been forewarned and yet apparently failed to cover the likely route of escape. The infantry fought a retreat to Fowey but were cut off by the arrival of a force under Goring, which commanded the road. That night Essex instructed Skippon to make such terms as he could while Essex himself slipped away on 1 September. The King offered surprisingly generous terms to Skippon, given the dire position in which Skippon found himself.[21]

This was a massive blow to morale. *Mercurius Aulicus* was withering in its scorn, asking 'why the rebels voted to live and die with the earl of Essex, since the earl of Essex hath declared he will not live and die with them'.[22] According to the terms of surrender negotiated by Skippon the army was to be allowed to march out with its colours, trumpets and drums, but without any weapons, horses or baggage apart from the officers' personal effects. They were offered convoy, the sick and the wounded were to be given protection, and permission was given to fetch provisions and money for the defeated troops from Plymouth. These could be claimed as honourable terms, but they did not stick, and the defeated army was subject to humiliations amounting to atrocity. The royalist convoy could not protect the unarmed soldiers from attack and local people, men and women, joined in the assault. They were stripped by the women, and left lying in the fields. Some were forced 'to march stark naked, and bare footed', and pillage and assault continued. One victim was a woman three days out of child bed, stripped to her smock, pulled by her hair and thrown into the river. She died shortly after. Ten days later the survivors, perhaps 1,000 of the 6,000 who surrendered, marched into Poole, 'insulted, stripped, beaten and starved'. Their numbers had been winnowed by desertion, but there were many who died on the road, after an honourable surrender.[23] If the propaganda effect was dire, the strategic importance could not be exaggerated: 'By that miscarriage we are brought a whole summer's travel back'.[24] Essex's adventure, for which he was solely responsible, had gone a long way towards grabbing stalemate from the jaws of victory.

Worse was to come, at least in political terms. Fairfax, Leven and

Manchester apparently felt that Marston Moor would force Charles to seek terms, and they did little to pursue an outright victory. In Manchester's case, at least, this reflected his belief that a lasting peace would be one recognized as honourable by all parties, and could not be delivered by total military victory. War was a means to peace, and had to be treated with caution.[25] This hesitancy allowed Charles to consolidate his position during September. Following his triumph over Essex, Charles moved eastwards again, arriving in Tavistock on 5 September. Having abandoned the attempt to retake Plymouth he sought to relieve garrisons further east and his forces established themselves at Chard, and both Barnstaple and Ilfracombe were retaken. His aim was to strengthen the garrisons at Basing House and Banbury to shore up the position of Oxford. This began to look like a potential threat to London and it finally spurred Manchester to bring his Eastern Association forces into the King's way. It proved difficult to co-ordinate and supply the parliamentary armies, and the Trained Bands contingents were reluctant to move too far, so Waller was forced to pull back from the west in early October, unable to gain support for his position in Sherborne. As Charles continued to advance Parliament began to consolidate forces, calling off the siege of Donnington on 18 October. The King's next objective was to lift the siege of Basing House, but Essex and Manchester joined forces there just in time, on 21 October, and the King was forced to withdraw to Newbury. Together with Waller's remaining forces, and levies from the London Trained Bands, the parliamentarians were finally able to bring a large force, perhaps of 18,000 men, to bear on a royal force which on some estimates was only half as strong.[26]

Despite this advantage in numbers the parliamentary forces did not win the second battle of Newbury (28 October). Not winning was in these circumstances almost as bad as losing. Explanations for the failure differ, but in essence the parliamentary battle plan was complicated and was not effectively executed. When night fell the outcome was still unclear and both sides had lost about 500 men, but the following morning the royalists decided not to renew the fight. They were allowed to because the parliamentary council of war decided not to follow them, at least not until it was too late. In the heated exchanges about this issue Manchester spoke in favour of restraint, and Waller, Haselrig and Cromwell urged more vigour. Posterity has on the whole blamed Manchester in particular. Moreover, the difficulty in executing the battle plan may have lain with Manchester, who was in command of one arm of a pincer movement. He moved too late to make it work, and his hesitancy during the battle had been damaging to the parliamentary cause, at least according to some accounts.[27]

Over the next ten days there were further manoeuvres, particularly concerned with Donnington Castle. It was summoned to surrender on 31 October and refused to do so. Charles and Rupert set out to relieve it on 7 November and succeeded two days later. Passing through Newbury once again the parliamentary forces refused battle, a decision that again lay with Manchester and enraged a number of men under his command. At a council of war, Manchester famously made the case for limited war: 'The king cares not how oft he fights but it concerns us to be wary, for in fighting we venture all to nothing'. By this he meant: 'If we beat the king ninety and nine times yet he is king still, and so will his posterity be after him; but if the King beat us once we shall all be hanged, and our posterity made slaves'. Cromwell spoke equally famously on the other side: 'My lord, if this be so, why did we take up arms at first? This is against fighting ever hereafter. If so, let us make peace, be it never so base'.[28]

After the Lostwithiel and Newbury campaigns Parliament's position was far worse than would have been predicted after the great victory at Marston Moor (see Map 3). Reasons were easy to enumerate: the Essex debacle; the immobility of Parliament's forces prior to the Newbury campaign; and also, perhaps, hesitations and misjudgements during and after the battle. Although parliamentary forces enjoyed some successes in some of the local struggles in the period after Newbury, overall strategic weaknesses had been revealed. Charles, by contrast, and despite a failed attempt to lift the siege of Basing House, was able to enter Oxford in triumph on 23 November. His position was much better than could have been hoped after Marston Moor. The royalists now set about a reconstruction of their forces, integrating the survivors of Marston Moor with the royal army under Charles's personal command, undertaking a recruitment drive and encouraging the formation of auxiliary regiments for local defence.[29]

His position had been further improved by the formation of an armed royalist party in Scotland, which served as a significant distraction for the Covenanting forces in England. An obvious response to the intervention of the Covenanters was to open up a front in Scotland, and this is what Charles chose to do. In March/April he switched his support away from those who had sought to promote a moderate royalist coalition in Scotland to the more confrontational policies advocated by Montrose and Antrim. All Scots who did not support the King were now regarded as his enemies and Montrose began to plan a war against Argyll using Irish soldiers. Antrim was sent to Ireland to negotiate for the service of Irish Catholics in Scotland. Montrose's scheme for an invasion of Scotland achieved little and on 6 May he was forced to retreat to England.[30]

Nonetheless, Montrose's view of Scottish affairs was to triumph, with very bloody results, later in the year. Shortly after Marston Moor, he met Rupert to discuss the continuing difficulty of securing a commission to promote a royalist rising in Scotland. As far as Montrose knew, troops were not arriving from Ulster, but he set off regardless, to try to open up a new front in Scotland. As it turned out, two days after his meeting with Rupert, men did arrive on the west coast of Scotland, and this allowed Montrose to raise forces among the Highlanders. It was the prelude to a dramatically successful campaign in the Highlands through the autumn of 1644 and into 1645.[31]

Montrose arrived in Perth on 22 August in disguise, with the aim of rousing Highland opponents of the Covenanters and of Argyll. By 1 September he had mustered sufficient strength of Irish and Highland troops to win a major victory at Tippermuir against the hastily assembled Covenanting force. The campaign was bloodier than the English wars, and Highland bands fought for plunder so that each victory was followed by what would in England have been considered atrocities. It has been estimated that nearly 15,000 men died in the fighting associated with Montrose's campaigns in 1644 and the following year: easily the lion's share of the deaths on Scottish soil in these years (see Map 5). From Tippermuir he marched on Aberdeen, many of the Highlanders returning home but his army augmented by troops from Angus. On 13 September he arrived before Aberdeen, whose capture was preceded by the murder of a drummer boy and followed by a massacre in a town not known for its Covenanting sympathies. Over the following winter Montrose led a successful march into the Highlands, aiming at the heart of Argyll power. This campaign culminated in a victory at Inverlochy over Argyll's army, close to his heartland. Although Leven had not removed troops from England in response to

Tippermuir and Aberdeen, he was forced to now. Inverlochy offered the prospect of breaking the power of the Covenanters and, hence, of reopening the war in the north of England. When the English campaigns recommenced in the spring, Leven's movements were influenced by the fact that he needed to remain in a position from which to go back to Scotland, if that proved necessary. In the event, Montrose was never able to find a way of keeping his Highlanders together in order to pursue a more sustained campaign outside the Highlands. The strategic significance of his campaigns was nonetheless considerable: the victory at Marston Moor had closed the northern front in England but Montrose had effectively opened a new northern front in Scotland, and that served to limit Parliament's operations in the south.[32]

It is often said that the intervention of the Covenanters made Parliament's victory inevitable, but that verdict is clearly questionable in two ways. Firstly, the best chance of catching the King in 1644 was in the early spring, and only indirectly a result of the presence of the Scots. It owed much more to the victories of Waller and the march of Essex the previous autumn. Secondly, in so far as the victory at Marston Moor was decisive, it can be said to have resulted from Rupert's error in seeking a battle and from the intervention of Cromwell's cavalry during the battle. The subsequent failure to take Oxford, or the King, similarly owed a lot to problems of command and, it is possible to argue, the shortcomings of Essex. Essex had launched an ultimately disastrous adventure in the west, the more damaging since it had involved him in disobeying direct orders from the Committee of Both Kingdoms. His adventure, ending in ignominy at Lostwithiel and the disappointments of the battle of Newbury, pointed up problems in the prosecution of the war. Leven and Manchester, having left the field in apparent defeat at Marston Moor, were presented with a resounding victory, but were then extremely reluctant to follow it up. These misjudgements and hesitations meant that the war was not concluded and Montrose was able to launch a fantastically successful campaign in Scotland.

Modern historians disagree about the blame for these failures and contemporaries certainly did. Since military mobilization was essentially political, it is hardly surprising that this was interpreted politically: military complaints raised political differences and the critics of Manchester and Leven, for example, tended also to be critics of their religious and political views. There was even a hint of resentment about aristocratic power in the parliamentary counsels.[33] Without the benefit of hindsight, and a certainty about the structural advantages on their side, many parliamentarians saw this as a political problem: in the sense both of who should be running the war, and of what those running the war ought to be trying to achieve. As in other wars involving coalitions, credit for victory was claimed by different parties with a view to making political capital from the victory; the blame for failure was rarely accepted.

These military frustrations coincided with signs of fracture over war aims, in particular the church settlement. In 1641 leading Puritan divines in London had met at the house of Edmund Calamy, a prominent London minister. There they agreed to avoid public controversy on the issue of church government in the interests of solidarity in the face of popery.[34] The shared ground of the anti-Laudian coalition was the attack on superstition, popery and idolatry, and these had been at the heart of the religious cause of the English parliament through 1643. A counter-polemic, about schism, heresy, ignorant preaching and error was mobilized by royalists, but was also important within the parliamentary alliance – these were threats recognized by all responsible Christians. Simonds D'Ewes, for example, in moving the second reading of the bill for the abolition of episcopacy had also suggested a companion bill to punish 'tradesmen and other ignorant persons who shall presume to preach'. Similarly, the Grand Remonstrance, while stringent on popery and bishops, had also disavowed any intention to 'loose the golden reins of discipline or government in the church', or of allowing 'private persons or particular congregations to take up what form of divine service they please'.[35] Attacks on episcopacy posed this question of religious decency with particular clarity.

Presbyterians favoured the persistence of the parish as the basis of religious decency – membership of a congregation was to be determined by place of residence. These parochial congregations would be integrated into a national church, and the dangers of errors, schism and heresy contained. To some advanced Protestants this looked little different from episcopacy. They favoured voluntary congregations, gathered churches, of like-minded Christians. These independent congregations could still be integrated into a national church through a Presbyterian system, but they would be independent of parochial discipline. Others favoured complete congregational independence as the guarantee of freedom of conscience. These were big issues, which raised fundamental questions about the nature of Christian community and its relationship to the national political community.[36]

The agreement reached in Calamy's house was respected, but it could only be temporary, and in early 1644 it came apart.[37] The Solemn League and Covenant, the ongoing deliberations of the Westminster Assembly and, after 1644, the increasing likelihood of a military victory that would force the King to agree a settlement all combined to make church government an immediate and pressing issue. Independency was routinely denounced as introductive of spiritual anarchy, or as the resurgence of a proven heresy, or both. And the challenges it posed ranged far beyond the merely doctrinal – sects were denounced in terms of the behavioural consequences of their teachings, and those consequences centred around inversions of decency. The double disadvantage was the difficulty of demonstrating that congregational independence could be squared with decency in public worship, and the influence of the Covenanters in Parliament and the assembly. On the other hand Presbyterianism might come to seem rather like another form of episcopacy, or even popery: coercive and an imposition on the individual conscience.

These developments led five leading Independents to break cover and seek to justify their beliefs publicly. *An Apologeticall Narration* was acquired by Thomason on 3 January 1644. The authors – Thomas Goodwin, Philip Nye, Sidrach Simpson, Jeremiah Burroughs and William Bridge – were respectable figures and the publication was approved by Charles Herle, one of twelve clergymen appointed by Parliament to license books.[38] He too was a thoroughly respectable figure and approved the publication for its 'peaceableness, modesty and candour'. Herle recognized the need for an explanation of the Independent position, answering claims that the Protestant party was incommunicable within itself and incompatible with magistracy and giving the lie to misrepresentations of Independency. Thus, although 'for mine own part I have appeared on and do still incline to the Presbyterial way of Church Government, yet do I think it is every way fit for the press'.[39] The authors themselves apologized for publishing, saying that they would have preferred their actions to prove their case over a long period of time, but were forced to an apology by the climate of opinion against them.

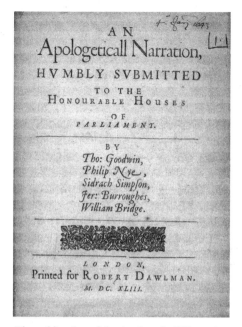

A N
Apologeticall Narration, [1]
HVMBLY SVBMITTED
TO THE
HONOURABLE HOUSES
OF
PARLIAMENT.

BY
Tho: Goodwin,
Philip Nye,
Sidrach Simpson,
Jer: Burroughes,
William Bridge.

LONDON,
Printed for ROBERT DAWLMAN.
M. DC. XLIII.

The publication of the *Apologeticall Narration*
sparked fierce controversy in the parliamentary alliance

They had all been exiled during the 1630s[40] and were apparently willing both to gather churches and to hold livings within a liberated Church of England. In essence, they argued for congregational independence within a national framework subordinated to civil authorities: churches should gather themselves, but recognize an external discipline. As with the deliberations in Parliament in 1640–42, so with the Westminster Assembly – it proved impossible for some to resist resorting to mobilization of opinion outside the assembly, and once that had been done an escalating pamphlet war took off.

An Apologeticall Narration was a very respectable publication, apparently produced in a spirit of brotherhood, but this spirit of brotherhood did not last, or at least was not unanimously adhered to. Their position on church government was subtle, and to many observers incoherent, and the publicists for a Presbyterian revival were very happy to point that out. But in doing so they clearly fuelled the suspicion that the Protestant party, the parliamentary alliance, was not in communion. This was to mark the beginning of a long and increasingly fractious public debate. In that debate anti-sectarian polemic was of course attractive to royalists, but was becoming as important to the argument within the parliamentary coalition.

These exchanges took on a new and shriller edge in the aftermath of Marston Moor. It was then that Thomas Edwards's *Antapologia* appeared, an intemperate response to the *Apologeticall Narration*. Edwards had participated in the sectarian scare in 1641, crossing swords with Henry Burton, the former martyr to Laudian persecution, and, with John Taylor, heating up the discussion of the dangers of spiritual indiscipline. He now found the times suitable to his purposes and temperament. *Antapologia* was ten times as long as the pamphlet that it attacked, a sprawling denunciation of sectarianism and error, championing a Presbyterian settlement as the guarantor of 'beauty, order [and] strength'. Presbyterian ministers in London quickly established Edwards in a weekly lectureship at Christ Church, Newgate, and from that pulpit he became a notorious preacher against the sects and vociferous opponent of toleration.[41]

Roger Williams's *Bloudy Tenent of Persecution* was also published about the time of Marston Moor, and seemed to offer a summary of where the more advanced critique of church government was leading. Williams had emigrated to Boston in 1631, probably in his mid- or late twenties, where he was invited to take up a position in the church. He declined the invitation, however, because the congregation was making a virtue of its refusal to separate from the Church of England, and had declared his opposition to the use of secular power to punish Sabbath breaking. As a result of these views Williams became perceived in Massachusetts as a threat to the New England way, of congregational independence within an overall discipline. Unable to find a teaching post in Massachusetts he moved to Plymouth plantation, but continued to attract controversy and returned to Massachusetts, only to be banished in 1636. He fled southwards and established a settlement at Providence based on the principle of the separation of civil and religious authority. There he attracted a number of other refugees, including Anne Hutchinson, and had a brief flirtation with the Baptist church. Returning to London in 1643–4, he obtained a charter for Providence and a number of settlements nearby. But he also caused uproar with his intervention in the English debate about church government.

Three pamphlets – *Queries of Highest Consideration*, his reply to *Mr Cotton's Letter Lately Printed* and the *Bloudy Tenent* – ridiculed the contortions caused by the state control of religion, exposed the illogicalities of non-separating Congregationalism and defended the Baptist argument for toleration. The 'bloody tenet' that he attacked was the belief that governments could impose a particular form of worship, a belief that led to the mutilation and even death of men and women seeking their own way to God. It was better to bear persecution by ungodly men than to seek to persecute others. It was said that, in Providence, Williams had first fallen off from his ministry, then from church fellowship, baptism, communion and eventually from all the current ordinances of the church. He was waiting for new apostles, ready to raise a new church from among the ruins of anti-Christian apostasy. The contemporary label for this was 'seeker', a description which Williams explicitly rejected, but there is some truth to the claim that he became 'what the opponents of Separatism had always prophesied would be its *reductio ad absurdum*, the one-man church'.[42] On 9 August, Parliament ordered the *Bloudy Tenent* to be publicly burned.

Pamphlets engaged with one another, in an escalating debate of increasing and immense vitality and creativity.[43] Freedom of religious assembly was closely related to the issue of freedom of expression, and John Milton, who had introduced Williams to his publisher, also got into trouble on this issue.[44] Milton married a woman half his age in May 1643 after a month of courtship. After a month of marriage he was convinced that it was a mistake: his seventeen-year-old wife was not bookish, resented the restraints of his style of life and was uninterested by his intellectual pursuits. In fact, she found his views detestable and profane. She deserted him for her parental home and Milton published *The doctrine and discipline of Divorce* in August 1643. It signalled a shift in Milton's career, at least on his own retrospective gloss, from a concern with religious liberty towards 'domestic' liberty – marriage, freedom of speech and education. This has a half-appeal to the modern reader, or perhaps an appeal to half of modern readers: he argued that marriage should be a union of soul and intellect, and in the absence of that men had a right to divorce. To seventeenth-century readers this was less than half-acceptable, of course, and attracted criticism. In the course of 1644 this put Milton on course to an argument for freedom of expression. He published an enlarged edition in February. In July he published a pamphlet citing the respectable reformer Martin Bucer in support of his views. Shortly after, he published his important tract *Of Education*, which laid out an extremely demanding intellectual training for the young citizen, another signal contribution to his arguments for domestic liberty; it made no mention, however, of the training girls would receive in order to make them appreciative of the conversation of their husbands.[45]

The hostile response to his tracts on divorce persuaded Parliament to consider prosecution – he had not sought a licence for their publication. It was this that led him to denounce prior restraint of publications, in the justly famous *Areopagitica*, which appeared without licence in

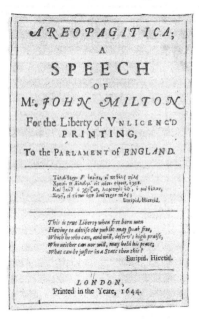

John Milton's *Areopagitica* argued against pre-publication censorship

November. It is often glossed as advocating a free market in expression, in which bad opinions would be driven out by good ones, individuals would be free to develop their views, and knowledge would increase. In fact, as with the divorce tracts, there are ambiguities: he did not raise any objection to the suppression of royalist opinions in time of war and excluded Roman Catholics from these freedoms, for example. These exceptions reflected the purpose of free speech – the promotion of virtue in society. Milton retained an attachment to the virtue and power of an educated elite. His tract *Of Education* was a manual for leaders in a mixed government, of Lords and Commons, and his defence of free speech was directed primarily at them.[46]

Milton's views are not quite as much our own as the more triumphant treatments suggest; but they bear testimony to the radicalizing effects of war, and the possibilities arising from the luxuriant political and religious debates. These were important domestic liberties, and not the ones at stake when Parliament had met in the aftermath of defeat in the second Bishops' War. Increasing freedom of worship and of expression offered opportunities which Williams and Milton felt were good in themselves. For others they were a temporary means to achieve other ends. For royalists these radical arguments, openly expressed in print, confirmed everything they had been saying since 1642, and this made it even more uncomfortable for those within the parliamentary alliance but worried by escalating radicalism.

On 4 January 1645 Parliament agreed to replace the Prayer Book with the Directory of Worship. Much of the Directory was very welcome to all parts of the parliamentary alliance – containing forms of worship free of popery, idolatry and superstition – but it was to be imposed through a national Presbyterian system. Congregational attempts to secure a different framework of church government had been derisively dismissed by the Commons (insisting that no more than 300 of their objections should be published) in December. On 6 January a proposal that voluntary congregations could exist alongside parochial ones, within a national church, was rejected by the Commons without a vote. A week later it was agreed that parochial congregations should be grouped under presbyteries, as the basis for national church government.[47]

Had he still had them, this would have been music to the ears of William Prynne – the former martyr to the Protestant cause. He had characterized Milton's views on marriage as 'divorce at pleasure'. In January 1645 he championed religious discipline in *Truth Triumphing*, which called for the establishment of a binding ecclesiastical discipline and the absolute suppression of all heresies and schisms, and cited tradition against novelty in favour of such discipline. This led him into conflict with John Lilburne, who had suffered alongside him in opposition to Laudianism in the 1630s. On 7 January Lilburne published his *Copie of a letter . . . To Mr. William Prinne Esq.*, in which he argued that no earthly power had authority over the kingdom of God and that persecution of individual consciences was the work of the Devil.[48]

These principles, once stated in detail and at length, were difficult to reconcile, but in practice it continued to be possible for people who differed on these issues to co-operate in the war effort. Sir Cheney Culpeper eventually came to denounce Scottish Presbyterians and their allies as miniature popes: 'I never shall make any difference between an imperial, national, provincial, presbyterial, parochial or congregational Pope'. In March 1648 he declared himself an ally of the Lilburnists, noting that 'the Scottish aristocratical interest both in church and state . . . having . . . [pulled] down the power of monarchy and episcopacy, do begin to find themselves to be part also of that Babylonish rubbish which must down'. For Culpeper the conscience was God's peculiar, a place beyond episcopal or any other jurisdiction, and all attempts to constrain conscience represented a form of bondage akin to the Babylonish captivity endured by the Israelites. But in November 1644 he admitted to having no hope 'but in our geud brethren the Scots'.[49] Many like him must have hoped that conflicts over discipline could be subordinated to the larger conflict – the form of church government was not, necessarily, one of the marks of a true church.[50]

It is difficult to know how many separatists there actually were in England in 1644. By then there were perhaps thirty-six Independent churches in London. They included seven congregations of Particular Baptists, who believed that the saved should undergo an adult baptism and who produced a collective confession of faith in 1644. There were also five congregations of General Baptists, who believed that all could be saved and were therefore in breach with Calvinist thinking about salvation. There were ten or so Independent churches under a learned minister, again rather diverse in their views. Around ten congregations gathered under lay ministers, many of them in 1643 and 1644, and represented no common denomination; they also tended to be ministers with a less respectable education in divinity. It was these groups, along with individual 'mechanic preachers', who created most anxiety. Among them were notorious mechanic men, like John Green and John Spencer, apprentices such as John Boggis and Thomas Webb, and women, such as Mrs Attaway and Katherine Chidley. Together these congregations, and the audiences for these preachers, can have represented only a tiny proportion of the London population, but this religious diversity fostered some very radical religious speculation. These forms of religious association were in themselves a threat to learned divinity and religious order, and their teaching threatened fundamentals of received doctrine – about sin, the soul, salvation, and the role of scripture in guiding Christian belief and practice. Millenarian views of the most exotic (and to many people frightening) kind were also preached.[51] This ferment prompted fears out of proportion to the size of the problem – but in matters of normative threat size is not everything. Moreover, there were serious questions about the implications of this for those excluded – the parochial basis of religion had the advantage of including everyone, after all. In 1644, for example, John Goodwin had established a gathered church in St Stephen's, Coleman Street, where he was the incumbent. Communion was refused to those considered to be ungodly, which amounted, effectively, to unchurching a large number of his parishioners.[52]

It is difficult to know about the numbers and size of Independent congregations outside London, although we should not dismiss the possibilities. In 1625, in much less helpful circumstances, there were five Baptist congregations, with a membership of at least 150.[53] In counties like Lincoln and Cornwall, where there was no strong tradition of pre-war separatism, sects were an established feature of local life by 1660. It is difficult to know exactly when these congregations took root, although it often seems from the surviving sources to have been a later, often post-war phenomenon. Certainly the Quakers did a lot to plant dissent in provincial life during the 1650s. But Thomas Edwards, writing in 1645 and 1646, certainly saw it as a national problem, and associated in particular with the armies.[54] On numerous occasions troops had been associated with iconoclasm, but that desire for purification says nothing about views on church government – Scottish Presbyterianism had a reputation for visual austerity, after all. It was easy to conflate this activism with Independency, though – preaching and worship in the army were, as in the sects, outside an established parish setting. Claims were frequently made for grossly transgressive behaviour by troopers, including the oft-repeated story of Captain Beaumont's men baptizing a horse in their urine in June 1644, or of the baptism of a calf in Lichfield Cathedral.[55]

This association between the army and a lack of religious discipline meant that the fractious debate between Independents and Presbyterians posed a double question about the meaning of a parliamentary military victory. What would it mean for religious order, and advocates of which position could claim the credit for military success? Norwich, shortly to see disarray in the parliamentary coalition, marked the victory at Marston Moor with an elaborate civic procession. Elsewhere, the strains were already becoming clear. Thomas Edwards's virulent attack on Independency in *Antapologia* resonated strongly with the outrage felt among his fellow travellers like Robert Baillie at the lack of credit offered to the Covenanters for the victory. Cromwell, on the other hand, no friend to Presbyterian discipline, had little doubt that the detail of the battle revealed a key role for men of his beliefs as the instruments of God's providence.[56]

Disputes about strategy and tactics within the army of the Eastern Association became inflected with these larger concerns about religious order. The Earl of Manchester was thought by many to be far too reluctant to seek out action following Marston Moor. On 10 August, Manchester refused an order to go against Rupert in Chester, where a significant force seemed to be mustering, something symptomatic of his military and political caution. Not until September did Manchester agree to take cavalry to the aid of Brereton in Cheshire. On 1 September the Committee of Both Kingdoms wrote the first of fourteen letters urging the army to move south to prevent the royal army, now returning from its victory over Essex at Lostwithiel, from regaining winter quarters in Oxford. Three orders from the Commons reinforced the message, and the need for haste, but by mid-October the army was still no further west than Reading.[57] Newbury and its aftermath confirmed this reluctance on Manchester's part. This perhaps reflected revulsion at what he had seen during the siege of York, and was certainly fuelled by a growing sense of the futility of the conflict.

Cromwell, his second-in-command, on the other hand, had no such hesitations, and was becoming embroiled in partisan struggle within the army. In particular Cromwell was in open conflict with Lawrence Crawford, a Scottish major-general. Crawford accused Cromwell of packing the army with Independents, which was probably true after York but not before. Cromwell had intervened to protect Independents from hostile Presbyterian officers, but this was probably in a spirit of brotherhood that he shared with his superior, Manchester. After

August 1644, though, there is evidence that he actively promoted sectarians in the army. He was motivated in this, it seems, by growing resentment of the persecuting spirit of Presbyterian officers, hostility to the increasingly obvious determination among them to impose a Presbyterian settlement on England and a feeling that victory at Marston Moor belonged to him, not them. When Cromwell became openly critical of Manchester's generalship in the autumn of 1644 it was inevitably inflected with these religious tensions. Although Manchester remained popular in the association, his command was increasingly difficult and, to many at Westminster, increasingly ineffective.[58]

The military advantages of an alliance with the Covenanting Scots were therefore offset by the political and religious complications that it created: many Protestants did not see Presbyterianism as liberation; nor was it what most opponents of Charles had been seeking in 1640. Potentially at least, Covenant politics were deeply problematic even for those committed to further reformation, particularly so on the issue of church government. In the autumn of 1644 Cheney Culpeper does not seem to have found the tensions irreconcilable, and he was clearly not alone. Similarly, William Dowsing, apparently more Independent than Presbyterian on matters of church government, was very active in 1644 extirpating popery and superstition in East Anglia, acting under warrant from the Presbyterian Earl of Manchester. On the other hand, his journal finishes in October.

Formal peace negotiations reopened at the end of 1644, with the parliamentary coalition in a strong military position but increasingly publicly divided over what kind of settlement to insist upon. There had been contacts between the two sides throughout 1644, with Essex a key figure on the parliamentarian side. The Oxford parliament had written to him in February, hoping that he could be an instrument of peace, and shortly before the surrender at Lostwithiel he had been contacted directly by Charles. On both occasions he said, as he always did, that he did not have the power to treat on his own behalf. Among the royalists there were significant divisions, and considerable personal hostility to Rupert. He secured a kind of agreement with Digby, who assured him that it was Newcastle rather than him who was held responsible for Marston Moor. But moderate royalists, in the Oxford parliament and at court, saw Rupert's influence as a primary obstacle; indeed, he was attacked as 'the only cause of war in this kingdom'.[59] It was hardly fair, but was an indication of a significant level of hostility.

Moderate counsels were not dominant, however. Charles himself seems to have been in combative mood: 'The settling of religion and the militia are the first to be treated on; and be confident that I will neither quit episcopacy nor that sword that God hath given into my hands'. He was also just as capable of self-righteousness as his Puritan opponents:

Nothing can be more evident than that Strafford's innocent blood hath been one of the great causes of God's just judgement upon this nation by a furious civil war, both sides hitherto being almost equally guilty, but now this last crying blood being totally theirs, I believe it is no presumption hereafter to hope that the hand of justice must be heavier upon them and lighter upon us, looking now upon our cause, having passed through our faults.

In pursuit of these ends his best hopes, as he well appreciated, lay in the divisions among his enemies:

I am put in very good hope – some hold it a certainty – that, if I could come to a fair treaty, the ringleading rebels could not hinder me from a good peace; first, because their own party are most weary of the war; and likewise for the great distractions which at this time most assuredly are amongst themselves, as Presbyterians against Independents in religion, and general against general in point of command.[60]

There was also the hope that Montrose's success in Scotland might further strengthen Charles's position. The Earl of Glamorgan was sent to Ireland in December to negotiate for military support, with powers to deal with the Pope to secure help from any other willing Catholic powers. Henrietta Maria was in France seeking aid from Mazarin.[61] Forces were balanced in Oxford, but the moderates were able to persuade the King that he might get a good deal, given the divisions on the parliamentary side.[62]

Charles could be persuaded to listen, therefore, but, as it turned out, what he heard was more or less out of the question for him, and he had reasonable hopes that he would not have to listen much longer. Parliamentary commissioners arrived in Oxford on 20 November 1644. The proposals included the demand that Charles swear the Solemn League and Covenant, abolish episcopacy, assent to reformation following the recommendations of the Westminster Assembly, pursue uniformity between England and Scotland and end the saying of Mass at court. He was also to agree to a number of specific pieces of legislation, to declare the Cessation void, and leave fifty-eight named supporters to justice. On the militia the terms were equally stringent: all military officers were to be 'persons of known integrity, and such as both kingdoms may confide in for their faithfulness to religion and peace of the kingdoms'. This was to be monitored by a joint Anglo-Scottish committee, and appointments to numerous offices of state were to be nominated by both Houses of Parliament. These were more stringent terms than had been offered in early 1643, and probably reflected the influence of the Scottish members of the Committee of Both Kingdoms.[63]

After some informal discussions in Oxford it was agreed that negotiations would open at Uxbridge on 30 January 1645. These Uxbridge proposals came after a year of bloody fighting and it is clear that around the country considerable hope was invested in them, at least if the reaction to their failure is anything to go by. But this was never a hopeful basis for settlement. Charles was presented with terms he would not accept and which he was actively seeking to avoid. This was suspected at the time, and publicly confirmed the next year when his private correspondence was captured and published. Along with other revelations this did unquestioned damage to his reputation, but his position was not necessarily unprincipled – he could not accept the terms offered, which were being urged on the basis of military success, and so it was reasonable enough that he should be seeking to find ways of undermining his opponents and inducing them to offer more realistic terms.

While some parliamentarians sought to get Charles to accept terms he surely would not accept, others at Westminster turned towards overcoming the strategic weaknesses of the previous campaign. In the complex recriminations that ensued it is possible to distinguish two problems. The southern army had been hampered by the reluctance of the Trained Bands to move, which contributed to Waller's immobility, and by the destruction of Essex's army at Lostwithiel, which was perhaps a reflection of problems in the direction of the war. The problems in the Eastern Association were more narrowly political – an escalating conflict between Independents and Presbyterians, which affected war aims. Reforms tackling the logistical problems in the southern army were made against the background of the political problems manifest in the Eastern Association army.

In late November, as what became the Uxbridge negotiations were being launched, Waller and Cromwell reported to the House of Commons on the recent campaigns, in response to an invitation from the Committee of the Army. Waller complained of Manchester's failure to come to his support at Shaftesbury, and Cromwell joined in the criticism. Cromwell in particular exceeded the bounds of politeness in his public criticism of Manchester. Despite the fact that he was a commoner speaking of an earl, and a second-in-command speaking of his superior, he did not hesitate to blame the failures of the campaigns on Manchester, and in particular on his reluctance to fight. The earl's response, made a week later in the other House, was withering. It was a reasonably effective defence of his military record and a clear attack on Cromwell's politics and religion, quoting Cromwell to the effect that he would rather fight the Scots than the King, that he wanted only Independents in his own army, and reporting comments from Cromwell that implied the levelling of social distinctions between aristocracy and commoners.[64]

These tensions should not be underestimated. The Covenanters were hopeful that they could charge Cromwell with being an incendiary between the two kingdoms – something in breach of the Solemn League and Covenant – and Essex and Holles were apparently willing to go along with it. One night in early December some of Cromwell's leading political opponents were invited to the Earl of Essex's house to discuss a plan to impeach him on these grounds.[65] Cromwell, it should be remembered, had only signed the Covenant when it was imposed nationally, and these events can only have confirmed the suspicions that he and others felt about that particular deal. On 4 December, Holles reported Manchester's accusations against Cromwell to the House, to which Cromwell issued a long and forceful denial.[66]

It was from this debate that the proposal for Self-Denial arose. On 9 December the Committee of the Army endorsed the criticisms of Manchester. During the ensuing debate, in what was no doubt a co-ordinated move, Cromwell made a speech which included an important assertion. Parliament's enemies, and even some of those who had initially been its friends, had become hostile to the vested interests created by the war: 'that the members of both Houses have got great places and commands' and 'will perpetually continue themselves in grandeur and not permit the war to speedily end, lest their own power should determine with it'. He called for the army to be put into another method, and the war more 'vigorously prosecuted'. The alternative, he suggested, was that 'the people can bear the war no longer, and will enforce you to a dishonourable peace'.[67]

Careers and fortunes were indeed being made on the back of the war, and Cromwell was prescient too: in the spring and summer of the following year locally organized armed groups began to intervene in the war, seeking to limit its effects on their localities. For him, rapid victory was the way forward, and that required reorganization. In early July, exasperated by the refusal of local levies to march onward, Waller had written to Parliament: 'till you have an army merely your own, that you may command, it is in a manner impossible to do anything of importance'.[68] This was to become the logic of the New Model Army.

Zouch Tate, the chair of the committee, stood up and in response to Cromwell's speech proposed the Self-Denying Ordinance and a reorganization of the war effort. Tate was in fact a strict Presbyterian, but he had no doubt that Cromwell was right about the need to prosecute the war vigorously, and about the kind of administrative reforms that would allow that. The northern armies could continue in alliance with the Covenanters, and measures were taken to secure more regular supply for them, but in the south there was an obvious need to rebuild and remodel.[69] It was not possible, however, to reorganize the southern armies without dismissing the existing command, and that was not easy to do directly. Self-Denial was a neat political solution to this difficulty: it disbarred all Members of Parliament from all civil and military office. In effect it barred all peers (not just Essex and Manchester) from command, since they were all, of course, members of the Lords: it would bring an end to the Earl of Warwick's command of the navy as well. There were other advantages too. It answered the charge that there were vested interests at Westminster whose profits depended on a prolongation of the conflict, and offered an expiation of the sins which had led to God's judgements at the end of 1644. In September the Westminster Assembly had considered the causes of the military failures, finding them in the sins of the assembly, Parliament, the army and the people. Self-Denial had psychological and religious appeal for those of a Puritan outlook.[70] There was an obvious disadvantage though, in that it would bring to an end a number of highly successful military careers against which no complaint was currently being raised – those of Cromwell, Fairfax senior and Waller, for example.

Self-Denial and New Modelling were closely related and considered responses to the logistical and political failures of the campaigns of 1643. Neither found an easy passage through the Lords, however. Self-Denial would remove noble influence from all civil and military office, both locally and nationally. Criticism of members of the Lords lay behind both measures and one of the obvious effects of the formation of the New Model would be to take the leading military command away from the Earl of Essex.[71] Resistance to the Self-Denying Ordinance could be overcome, however, by pressing on with the New Model Ordinance. This consisted of three principal proposals: the creation of a national army, free of regional loyalties and obligations; that this army would be professional, dedicated to the prosecution of the war without any allied political purpose; and that it was to have first call on parliamentary funds. The logic of all these measures was plain, and clearly reflected sensible thinking about the problems of previous campaign seasons. Pressure was applied to the Lords by including in the ordinance the names of the commanders, which achieved the same end without the need for the Self-Denying Ordinance. It was also made known that the Commons would not allow the Uxbridge negotiations to go forward without first seeing these reforms.[72]

As on previous occasions, then, peace negotiations ran in parallel with attempts to bolster the war effort, so that from late November until early January there were contradictory currents in parliamentary politics. At Westminster the progress of Self-Denial and New Modelling was tied to the development of the Uxbridge treaty. Through January the Lords seem to have resisted Self-Denial, and to have wanted to protect Manchester, but the pressure to create the New Model pushed them in that direction. Pressure for New Modelling, in turn, owed something to the fate of the Uxbridge negotiations.

In the event, this was the shortest formal peace negotiation of the war. Discussion opened on 30 January and was over in three weeks. The three principal topics were religion, the militia and Ireland, to be discussed for three days each in rotation. There was no progress on any of them. The prospects of agreement, of course, were nil – the bargaining position on religion was Presbyterianism, something to which Charles could not, in conscience, agree.[73] Charles wrote in a private letter on 6 February: 'I should think if in your private discourses ... with the London commissioners you would put them in mind that they were arrant rebels, and that their end must be damnation, ruin, and infamy except they repented and found some way to free themselves from the damnable way they are in ... it might do good'.[74] At the eleventh, or perhaps thirteenth, hour, the King made an offer of places to some of the leading parliamentarians (but not at the expense of current, honest incumbents) and to come to London on condition that the armies disbanded. He may have been encouraged to play for time in this way by news of another victory for Montrose in Scotland. The suggestion that he might come to London, extremely unlikely to be accepted at Westminster, was strongly opposed by Henrietta Maria.[75]

The failure of the negotiations, recognized on 22 February, considerably weakened moderate royalism, and in the following years hardliners such as Digby and Henrietta Maria were very prominent in the King's counsels, despite the latter's exile, at least if the letters between husband and wife are to be believed. A royalist Western Association was formed to stiffen the sinews of the English war effort, to which Hyde and Sir John Colepeper were sent as advisers to the Prince of Wales in early March. This effectively exiled two principal moderates from the court without giving them much influence in the Western Association.[76] As the negotiations faltered militant parliamentarianism had also prospered: on 13 February the Lords finally accepted the New Model Ordinance and it was passed two days later. There were subsequent delays over naming commands, and the Self-Denying Ordinance was not passed until April, but vigorous military action was once again in hand.[77]

The formation of the New Model Army and the passage of the Self-Denying Ordinance served military purposes but have been invested with a more than military significance. A national standing army had been created from which aristocratic command had been excluded. It was to be the New Model Army which carried through a coup in 1648 leading directly to the trial and execution of the King. Disappointment at the failure to follow up the victory at Marston Moor was expressed by some in criticism of aristocratic leadership. It seems clear that the greater mobility of the King's forces and the more decisive leadership that was offered had allowed him to recover a seemingly desperate situation between July and October. These things – concern about the commitment of Essex and Manchester, the lack of mobility and co-ordination in the parliamentary forces – came together in the New

Modelling of the Parliamentary army over the winter of 1644–5. But they were also, of course, connected with religious and political positions. Vigorous prosecution of the war by Parliament was not simply a matter of logistics and organization but also one of political commitment.

What these negotiations demonstrate, above all, is how politicized the war effort had become. Presbyterianism was associated with order and with a desire for an early settlement. This was partly because many prominent Presbyterians, concerned about what they perceived to be an escalating threat from Independency, did indeed want a quick settlement, but the match between Presbyterian beliefs and political moderation was not exact. It fitted with the polemical construction of the sects, however, and as the Uxbridge negotiations foundered the controversy over the war effort reinforced these incipient divisions.

In January 1645 a significant battle was won when Parliament passed the ordinance replacing the Prayer Book with the Directory of Worship – defence of the doctrine but not the discipline of the Church of England – but the controversy persisted. There was already a polemical link between Independency and anarchy, both social and religious, and a link between these things and the soldiery, encouraged not least by Bruno Ryves in his *Mercurius Rusticus*. It was also now clear that the New Modelling, and the vigorous prosecution of the war, was associated with Independency: with Cromwell's politics rather than Manchester's. It is easy to see why, therefore, the New Model was quickly reputed to be an instrument of the sectaries and a threat to religious and social order.

This was the third significant transformation of the parliamentary war effort: after the escalations of 1643 and the military alliance with the Covenanters. Each had changed the parliamentary cause, and how it was regarded. The royalists had also paid a price for escalation – particularly for the Cessation and for the behaviour of some commanders – but in the face of the ramifying threat of a parliamentary victory, that does not seem to have had such an impact on royalist solidarity in 1644 and 1645. What emerged from the Self-Denying and New Model ordinances was thought by many contemporaries to be a new social formation: an institution with massive political influence which was recruited more or less independently of social status. Modern scholarship has revealed that these perceptions were exaggerated, but the perception was very important. Moreover, although the New Model delivered military victory in the Midlands and the West Country during 1645, victories which more or less ended the war, it did so before any agreement had emerged on the parliamentary side about what an acceptable peace would look like. Escalation of warfare was not accompanied by any greater clarity as to what, precisely, the fighting was for.

12

A Man Not Famous But Notorious

Death and Its Meanings

Two prominent deaths more or less framed 1644 – those of John Pym
and William Laud. Pym died at about 7 p.m. on 8 December 1643
and the details and meaning of his death were immediately contested.
Mercurius Aulicus, the scurrilous royalist newsbook which had opened
up earlier in the year, was in no doubt about its significance: 'This I
cannot say famous, but notorious man, loaded with other diseases, died
this very day, chiefly of the *Herodian* visitation, so as he was certainly a
most loathsome and foul carcase'. The 'Herodian disease' was 'Phthiriasis or other loathsome skin disease', recalling the death of Herod
Agrippa in Acts xii, 23, a tyrant struck down by a hideous death. Clearly
this had significance – a preacher in Warwick was reported to have
prayed that Pym should not die of this disease 'lest the Cavaliers should
cry it up as God's judgement'. This *Aulicus* did, with a devastatingly
light touch. The judgement on Pym was part of a larger picture, now
becoming clear. He was the 'most eminent' of the five members 'so
justly' accused of treason in January 1642 and experience had vindicated
the King: 'the fruits whereof have been and are yet so visible to this
distressed kingdom'. Noting that it was remarkable how Pym had died,
he also observed that Hampden had died at Chalgrove 'where he first
appeared in arms to exercise that unjust and mischievous Ordinance of
the *Militia*'; that Lord Brooke, 'who loved not our Church, was slain
[by a shot from the roof of] one'; and how 'strange, if not wonderful'
that the two Hothams, 'seeds' of the present troubles, and Nathaniel
Fiennes, 'active and fruitful to this faction', were now all 'at their own
bar . . . attending the sentence upon their lives [for treason]'.[1]

That Pym's death was a divine punishment was a politically significant
charge. The analogy between the health of the individual body and of
the body politic was a popular one, and Pym himself had used the image

in 1641, following the revelation of the Irish rising and the suspicion that it was promoted from within Charles's circle of advisers: 'diseases which proceed from the inward parts, as the liver, the heart or the brains, the more noble parts, it is a hard thing to apply cure to such diseases'.[2] His own death naturally invited comment from his enemies. It was also common to make a connection between the physical sufferings of particular individuals and the judgements of God upon them. Judgements on individuals often took the form of a loss of mental faculties, and hideous outward afflictions – flesh falling away from the fingers, disfigurements of the skin, or the efflux of excrements from the wrong parts of the body.[3]

Parliamentarian newsbooks, at a disadvantage because of the timing of their editions, were on the defensive. *The Parliament Scout* noted that Pym's enemies had been quick to 'tell bad lies of him' and *Remarkeable Passages* reported that those who could not blemish Pym 'all his life, would have spotted his corpse now he is dead; but that 1000 are eye witnesses how clear a Coarse [*sic*] he is, to the shame of those that raise such wicked inventions'. *The Weekly Account* was more sober: 'It is reported that he died of that loathsome disease which the Greeks call Ptheriasis . . . but the dead body exposed to the view of above a thousand witnesses did sufficiently convince the truth and malice of the report'. *An Answer to Mercurius Aulicus* put the figure at 'many hundreds'.[4]

But the most remarkable riposte took the form of a short pamphlet collected by Thomason about three weeks after Pym's death. It reported the verdict of experts, rather than an unidentifiable mass of eyewitnesses: Theodor Mayerne, the most famous physician of the day, and the President of the College of Physicians; four others who were present at the dissection of his body (including the next President); two of those who had been attending Pym during his illness; a chyrurgion (surgeon) and an apothecary, with their servants. Together they testified that his skin was free of any roughness, scabs or scarring, 'much less *Phthiriasis* or lousy disease, as was reported'. There was no sign of poisoning and 'he had his intellectuals and senses very entire to the last', enjoying sufficient and quiet sleep for the most part. No raving death, then. His heart and lungs were fine and his lower organs also sound except for some discolouration, and his spleen seemed small. There was, however, such a large 'abscess or impostume' in his lower belly that it could be felt from the outside, and once opened could accommodate a fist. This affected the surrounding parts, and made it difficult for him to eat, so that he suffered loss of appetite and nausea. After a long languishment the abscess broke and he died.[5]

Pym's supporters also marked his death with eulogy. The parliamentarian champion against *Aulicus* was *Mercurius Britanicus*, which devoted much of its weekly content to a detailed refutation of *Aulicus's* reports, as did *An Answer to Mercurius Aulicus*, which contained a line-by-line refutation. The week of Pym's funeral, however, *Britanicus* broke off from this feud, and limited its reporting of other events in order to make space for an elegy to Pym, which was commended by *Remarkeable Passages*. All the parliamentarian papers did the same, emphasizing Pym's selfless service in the cause (even to the neglect of his own household, which Parliament was now taking measures to support). His ceremonial burial in Westminister Abbey on 15 December was crucial to this effort:

The Parliament so highly honours the memory of Master *Pym*, that they have ordered a monument to be erected in the *Abbey* at *Westminster*, where he is to be interred; and the House of Commons have appointed themselves to accompany the *corpse* to the *grave*, so highly do they value and esteem the merits and deservings of so good, so excellent a *patriot*, and commonwealths-man.[6]

Such ceremonies were also controversial of course and Bruno Ryves included this in his list of desecrations of the Abbey 'not to be passed over in silence': 'the carcass of *John Pym* (as much as the lice left of it)' was buried among dignitaries and with 'usurped Ensigns of honour displayed over him'.

Twas pity, that he, that in his life had been the author of so much bloodshed, and those many calamities, under which this Kingdom yet groans, and therefore deserved, not only to have his death with the transgressors, and wicked, but afterward *to be buried with the burial of an ass, drawn, and cast forth beyond the gates of the city* [Jer 22 19] should after his death, make his *sepulchre amongst the honourable*, and mingle his *vulgar, lousy* ashes with those of *Kings, Princes,* and *Nobles*.

Ryves's view was vindicated in the long run, of course: after the Restoration Pym's remains were dug up and flung into a ditch.[7] Outside academic circles he is now a more or less completely forgotten figure.

This public exchange reflected in microcosm the larger problem – the meaning of events, and the increasing numbers of deaths, was important but elusive; and more-elaborate efforts now had to be made to establish the pertinent facts. The subtitle of *An Answer to Mercurius Aulicus* is revealing in this context: *His Communicated Intelligence from The Court to the rest of the Kingdom Faithfully trased through, to undeceive those who love the Truth*. The week before Pym's death *The Parliament Scout* had commented that 'If there was ever need of making news, it is this week, for it hath afforded so little, that some have taken allowance to print more than is true'. His advice was sensible, but not that helpful: '*Caveat Emptor*'. *A Perfect Diurnall* was candid about the problem facing even the well-intentioned:

notwithstanding the most special care I ever had, and shall have in these relations to avoid untruths: yet considering, that from all parts of the Kingdom (where any act of hostility hath been) the many several relations are sent, as well to the Parliament as City, it is impossible but in some weeks some of those many relations may in some particulars fail.

All he could do was promise to correct them as they came to light.[8] Confused and contradictory reports made the political scene even more difficult to interpret – firm grounds for judgements about the truth of reports and the meaning of the conflict were hard to establish. In the week of Pym's death three of Thomas Case's sermons had been published as *The Quarell of the Covenant* – an indication that all in the parliamentary alliance was not as well as Pym's obsequies might suggest.

Laud's death provided a similar rallying point a year later, when the parliamentary cause was much more openly fractious. Laud's trial had opened in March 1644 but had dragged on until 11 October, partly because hearings were so infrequent. Accusations of treason and the promotion of popery were manifestly untrue and the prosecution sustained its case by unfair means: interfering with witnesses, failing to detail in advance the evidence which would be used to sustain the charges and giving Laud only a limited time to prepare answers before each hearing. Prynne, given access to voluminous private papers and driven by vengeance, was unable to substantiate the charges. Laud was not always straightforward in his answers, though: he was innocent as charged but less than candid in answer.[9]

With unpromising prospects of conviction the Commons resolved to proceed by attainder in an echo of the treatment of Strafford. An ordinance of attainder was moved on 31 October, which the Lords were reluctant to approve. A number of speakers revived the memory of the crowds that had bayed for Strafford's blood, hoping that the fear of disorder would bring waverers onside. It was the Earl of Essex who posed the embarrassing question: 'Is this the liberty that we promised to maintain with our blood? Shall posterity say that to save them from the yoke of the King we have placed them under the yoke of the populace?' The Lords fought a losing battle to stay the execution, which was finally agreed in the first week of January. On 10 January, Laud was executed, having initially been refused the mercy of being beheaded rather than hanged.[10] Laud's death, three weeks before the Uxbridge negotiations opened, can have done little to make Charles interested in peace.

Public executions were intended to be instructive and convicted felons were expected to make good deaths. In scaffold speeches the condemned admitted the justice of their fate, turning their deaths into useful lessons for others. Strafford had refused to do this, as some plebeian criminals are known to have done, and so did Laud.[11] But Laud embraced more fully the alternative – accepting his fate as a martyr to persecution. With pathos, the old man, now in his early seventies, asked for listeners' patience as he read his text, fearing that his failing memory would let him down: 'Let us run with patience that race that is set before us, looking unto Jesus the author and finisher of our faith, who for the joy that was set before him, endured the Cross, despising the shame, and is set down at the right hand of the Throne of God'. He accepted his Cross, despised the shame and hoped for salvation.

I was born and baptized in the bosom of the Church of England in that profession I have ever since lived, and in that I come now to die ... What clamours and slanders I have endured for the labouring to keep an uniformity in the external service of God according to the doctrine and discipline of the Church all men know, and I have abundantly felt.

In his commitment to the doctrine and discipline Laud was making appeal to the rhetoric of the defenders of the Prayer Book in 1641 and 1642: 'the Pope never had a harvest in England since the Reformation, as he hath now upon the sects and divisions that are amongst us'.[12]

He also prayed that God would give grace of repentance to the bloodthirsty people of the nation, or defeat them in:

their devices . . . contrary to the glory of Thy great name, the truth and sincerity of religion, the establishment of the King and his posterity after him in their just rights and privileges, the honour and conservation of Parliaments in their just power, the preservation of this poor Church in her truth, peace, and patrimony, and the settlement of this distracted people under their ancient laws, and in their native liberty.

Here again, the echoes of 1642 were strong, in the paper-thin differences between the proclaimed positions of the 'two sides'. Laud professed himself a champion of parliaments, although critical of some particulars, but 'There is no corruption in the world so bad as that which is of the best thing in itself, for the better the thing is in nature, the worse it is corrupted'. This threat to Parliament lay in popularity, particularly in the City of London, not royal tyranny:

[in] this great and popular City, which God bless, here hath been of late a fashion taken up to gather hands, and then go to the honourable and great court of the Kingdom, the Parliament, and clamour for justice, as if that great and wise court (before whom come the causes which are unknown to many) could not, or would not do justice, but at their call and appointment; a way which may endanger many an innocent man, and pluck innocent blood upon their own heads, and perhaps upon this City also, which God forbid. And this has lately been practiced against myself.

Laud, on his own account, was a martyr to the cause of 1642 – security of the Church of England and the liberties of Parliament under the crown – something Charles himself was to embrace four years later. Clearly this was contentious, and even among sympathizers accounts of what he had said differed.[13]

Laud enjoyed one of the only advantages of execution by getting in first with the interpretation of the meaning of his own death: martyrdom to a cause defined clearly in 1642. The polemical counterpart of a claim to martyrdom was, of course, hypocrisy, a charge which was duly levied in a flurry of pamphlets. Laud had not moved in his opinion about the policies of the 1630s, and neither had his critics.[14] Pym's legacy was perhaps more ambiguous, since he had ended his life as champion of a cause changed by military escalation and formal military alliance with the Covenanters. A year later, at the time of Laud's death, Parliament was in a strengthening military position, with further administrative improvements in hand. But this escalation was closely related to divisions within the coalition, which suggested that the political position was not improving as quickly as military fortunes did. What kind of military victory to pursue was a divisive issue, as was the nature of the post-Laudian settlement which the victory would allow to be imposed.

A week before Laud was executed, and apparently in the same spirit of vengeance, Carew and the two Hothams also lost their lives, unprotected from the workings of martial law against them for having considered handing over their military charges to the King. What did these deaths

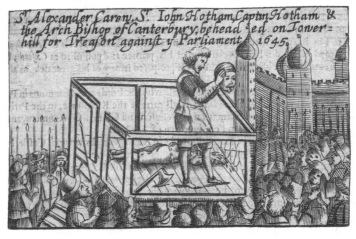

The executions of January 1645

mean? These men died traitors' deaths, having abandoned what they thought was the cause of 1642 and having been left to the mercy of martial law.[15] But had they really acted dishonourably? No-one wanted to lose the war, but it was not becoming any clearer, even to the central characters, what winning it would mean.

Death was of course at the heart of war. Every death is a means of appreciating the significance of a life, and the questions raised by the high-profile deaths of Pym, Laud, Carew and the Hothams could be asked about all the victims of the slaughter in 1644. Marston Moor was the largest battle of the war and may have been the largest battle ever fought on English soil. Those responsible for burying them thought that 4,150 royalist soldiers had died on the field; many others died of their wounds subsequently.[16] According to the most authoritative estimate, 1644 saw the largest number of military engagements of the war. A massive research effort has enumerated 645 separate 'incidents' of armed conflict in England and Wales between 1642 and 1660, ranging from the large pitched battles such as Marston Moor to minor skirmishes which do not rate a mention in most military histories of the war. The vast bulk of these incidents, 555, took place between 1642 and 1646, and the two most eventful years were 1643 (156) and 1644 (191), and 1644 was also a particularly bloody year of the war. It has been estimated that around 62,000 men died in fighting between 1642 and 1646. Of these perhaps 23,000 men died in 1643 and 22,000 the following year. Together this is probably more than half of the total number of deaths in the wars of the whole period 1642–60.[17] On 11 January 1645, the day after the execution of Laud, Charles ordered an attack on Abingdon, in which many men lost their lives: it was the harbinger of another very bloody year of fighting.[18]

These incidents, and the loss of life, were reported in a confused and partisan way, and newsbooks did not locate them in a larger strategic context. This makes the statistics unreliable in detail, although the larger picture is probably reasonably accurate. Contemporaries, of course, confronted the same problem: the war was reported day by day, as it happened, with all the chance and contingency that such coverage applies. 'The war is like a football play, where one side doth give the other a kind of overthrow, and strikes up another's heels, but presently they rise up and give the other as great a blow again', reported *Mercurius Cambro-Britannicus*.[19] Newsbook readers were left to make sense of this as best they could, and it is clear that it was the fortunes of individual commanders that were easiest to follow, not the overall condition of the war. It seems likely that the political mood changed quickly, as a run of victories or defeats was reported, but the overall direction of the war would have been difficult to divine. Accompanying these uncertainties was an increasingly fractious public dispute among parliamentarians about the purpose of the war. What was it for, what did it mean and how would it end?

Such uncertainties were opportunities, of course, for people with a message to sell, metaphorically or literally. On 3 April 1644 'Sir R' had a consultation with the astrologer William Lilly in order to ask 'whether best to adhere to King or Parliament'.[20] This was one of a rapidly growing flow of clients, which soon reached a peak near 2,000 per annum.[21] From the brief note it is not clear what Sir R meant by 'best', but many of Lilly's clients were concerned about personal and material well-being – illnesses, love, business ventures, fears of bewitchment or of evil spirits. These perennial concerns were regularly interspersed with enquiries about military affairs: 'if good for son to go to war, and if return safe'; 'A commander of his success into North Wales'; 'the success between Sir William Waller and Hopton being then supposed to be in fight'; or 'When will Essex advance on Oxford?'[22]

Lilly made precise observations of the heavens at the precise date, time and place of meetings in the course of the Uxbridge negotiations, and much of the business brought by his clients was topical: 'by what death [Laud] should die, and when?'; 'if any design to massacre parliament/if take effect/if near maturity'.[23] But the personal and the military intertwined. A question about the outcome of the siege of Pontefract, for example, seems to have been connected to concern about rents due from lands in the area.[24] A woman asked 'if her husband was alive in the wars'; Mrs Poole if 'her husband be dead or no?' Other questions were less fraught: Lady Holborne asked 'if best her husband come to parliament', an anonymous client 'if he should obtain what he desired of the committee?'[25]

Wartime uncertainties impinged on many areas of personal life, and Lilly was clearly meeting a significant demand. His real triumph was in print, however. In *Supernaturall sights . . . seen in London*, written the week after Marston Moor and published in August 1644, he made some bold predictions. Called into Somerset Yard, in London, he observed in the sky above London 'a long yellowish apparition in form and shape almost like to be a serpent'. It appeared over south-west Kent and north-east Surrey and lasted much of the night, in which time it had moved past London and into the Midland counties: that is, probably, to Oxford. Unlike other reports of supernatural phenomena during the 1640s, Lilly's pamphlet made a claim to a science (actually more an art) of interpretation. Based on precise observation of the location Lilly was able, as with his personal clients, to offer some firm opinions about the trend of events. In this case he claimed that this was a sign of a dissolution of a mischievous plot against the state and commonwealth, 'A renting in pieces or mutinous disturbance of some Monarchy near at hand'.[26] If this rather hedged his bets a predicted eclipse on 21 August foretold of Prince Rupert's death or ruin. This was, in fact, the first year of the most successful publishing career of the decade.

Lilly's art was an elaborate but imprecise one. Seventeenth-century astronomy was capable of discerning movement in seven celestial bodies, the sun, the moon and a number of planets of the solar system. These seven bodies seemed to move against an unchanging backdrop, which was divided into the twelve signs of the zodiac. The heavenly bodies, with their predictable movements, were thought to exercise an influence over the much more mutable and unpredictable 'sublunary' world, where change and decay were permanent features of existence. Astrology was the science by which these effects could be understood, and the art by which they could, perhaps, be predicted. All sublunary bodies were composed of combinations of the four elements – earth, air, fire and water – and these elements were emitted in different ways by the celestial bodies, effecting changes in the observable natural world. This reflects a common habit of thought in seventeenth-century Europe – seeking out the correspondences and sympathies which linked the various levels of the physical world together.[27]

Judicial astrology sought to make predictions about these influences – on the health of particular human bodies, on the weather and the fate of nations. There were four main areas of such predictions. General predictions, based on the movements of the heavens, related to effects on whole nations – the weather, the state of the crops, mortality and epidemics, war and politics. More immediate and personal predictions were possible in a number of ways. Nativities might enable predictions about the fate of individuals, based on a map of the heavens at the time of their birth. Elections offered advice about when best to undertake a particular project or action, in the light of the state of the heavens. Finally, astrologers might answer a particular question based on the exact time at which it was put to them – horary questions. This final category was very appealing to individuals, of course, and in dealing with horary questions astrologers gave advice about health, love and misfortune, including the likely identity of thieves and so forth. Its claims were considerable: 'Astrology is more certain than physic, for it reasons from the cause to the effect'.[28]

Although astrology was a practice of very long standing, with an impressive technical literature and complex procedures, it was inevitably imprecise. Even if the heavens were mapped very precisely for any particular prediction, each planet and each sign had many different qualities. In interpreting the effects of the heavens on any particular sublunary body or enterprise, the astrologer had resort to elaborate rules of interpretation and accumulated practice, but in the last resort every reading depended on judgement, with the result that the more precise the prediction 'the less likely it was to command unanimous assent'.[29] The result was that astrologers in general, and some in particular, acquired a reputation for quackery, and they were armed with a battery of excuses, but they amounted to the same thing: as John Booker put it, 'I confess that many superstitious and gross absurdities are practiced by the ignorant under colour of this most excellent art but this must not be charged on the art, but the artist'.[30]

Lilly was accused of quackery by many contemporaries, and he himself said that he had trained in seven weeks and that his move to London had been made for commercial reasons. Sceptical modern historians have also pointed to the commercially significant marriages that Lilly made. But Lilly also claimed that he worked for twelve, fifteen or eighteen hours a day, and his notebooks suggest that this may have been true.[31] If the role of individual judgement invited accusations of quackery, it also made for the development of particular reputations: Lilly, for example, was clearly the parliamentary astrologer. We know that he had been sympathetic to the London crowds in 1640–42.[32] He was persistently supportive of the parliamentary cause, during the 1640s, but was also a monarchist sceptical perhaps of Charles I as a king, sympathetic to him as an individual and very willing to predict the downfall of Prince Rupert. Part of his phenomenal success depended on what appeared to be an accurate prediction of the great parliamentary victory at Naseby in 1645.[33] This was an immediate contrast with George Wharton, who had emerged as the royalist competition but made a notoriously inaccurate prediction about the same royal march in 1645. He was ridiculed by Booker for his poor Latin and his partial prediction, advising Wharton to get his 'fellow liar Aulicus to English it [translate it] and then give your judgement upon another march'.[34] Even as it offered certainties, astrology was politicized and its authority undermined.

Lilly did not normally make his own observations, and *Supernaturall sights* is in that sense unusual. Much of his published work took the form of almanacs, making general predictions for the year. But in pub-

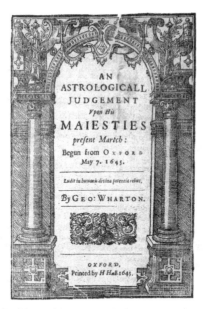

Political astrology: George Wharton's notoriously
inaccurate prediction in May 1645

lishing with as much success as he did, Lilly changed the market for
astrology. These were English astrology's halcyon days.[35] The long tradition in which Lilly stood had enjoyed currency in aristocratic and
royal circles since the fifteenth century at least. What was really remarkable about Lilly was his commercial success and the related claim that
he democratized astrology. Earlier in 1644 he had published the first of
a phenomenally successful series, *Merlinus Anglicus Junior*. It sold out
in a week and the print runs in subsequent years were phenomenal:
13,500 in 1646, 17,000 in 1647 and 18,500 in 1648. His success was
sustained throughout the following decade and in 1659, it was said, he
was selling 30,000 copies. This was very big business, even at 2d per
copy for cheap editions, and in a population of 5 million, with a relatively
low literacy rate, this represents an amazing market penetration.[36]

Although Lilly was the most successful astrologer of the 1640s, he
was by no means alone. He and Wharton enjoyed good sales and their
contemporary, John Booker, while less successful in print, had around
1,000 private consultations per year from 1648 to 1665.[37] Lilly led the

way in making astrology available to a wider market and was the most successful of a golden generation of astrologers. He also made another very distinctive contribution. In 1647 he published the methods of judicial astrology, in the first substantial English language text book, *Christian astrology*. It has been in use ever since. According to Lilly, the stars are divine signs, not physical causes, a position which allowed him to square astrology with Christianity, and explain failures: 'we predict nothing but with this limitation, the hand of the Almighty God considered or not impeding or preventing nature, for in his alone breast is all learning, science, knowledge, power and dominion'.[38]

Lilly also published prophecies, which offered similar reassurances; indeed, many of his early titles gesture towards prophecy, or Merlin. A prophecy of Merlin had circulated with approval among Covenanting soldiers in 1640, and it is not hard to see the attraction of prophecy in wartime. Prophecy was potentially subversive since it was so obviously political, and in more normal times was regarded with considerable suspicion, but in the 1640s the brakes were off. Mother Shipton was said to be a contemporary of Cardinal Wolsey's and her prophecies date from long before the war, but her career took off in 1641. It was then that her prophecies were first published, and they were published at least nineteen more times by 1700.[39] There was a minor publishing war, with escalating numbers of ancient prophecies set out for the public. Lilly also dealt with *Supernaturall sights and apparitions*, and these too continued to get aired in print. But astrology offered a more consistent set of observations, with stricter rules of interpretation – it was continuous and more systematic about interpretation, and, crucially, offered predictions, for both individuals and nations.

Lilly's success bears testimony both to the power of print and to the anxieties which the political crisis had fostered. Almanac sales, the flood of private consultations and the appetite to understand the method speak of a massive public appetite for certainty; some firm basis on which to judge what the future might hold. In *Merlinus Anglicus Junior* (1644) Lilly had gestured at this source of appeal in his predictions: Mercury 'the father of lies and untruths, and scandalous pamphlets' would be in a common sign during the coming year, 'as if he intended all this whole year to vex us with flying reports, continual fears, false alarums, untoward speeches, contradictory news, lying messengers, and cozening Accomptants, Receivers, Treasurers, and the like'.[40] But judicial astrology was an inexact and (in the 1640s, at least) partisan science. Uncertainty arose not just from the complexity of current events, but from the morass of conflicting claims in print about what it all meant, and that was an invitation to others to go to press with their certainties. But that was a source of further uncertainty. Print was a symptom, a cause and an opportunity; and it fed off itself.

Anxiety may have produced paralysis, but also creativity and activism. Lilly, Edwards, Williams and Milton all spoke to this uncertainty in creative ways. Many more were silent – undecided, passive or immobilized by doubt or circumstance. Efforts to convince and mobilize that silent body of opinion not only pedalled particular views, but made claims about authenticity. Expert, detailed witnessing helped to establish what had happened, as in the published autopsy of John Pym; on that basis it was possible also to try to establish a clear interpretation of the meaning and direction of events. Lilly did it with a science, Laud with a martyr's death. The meaning of all the deaths was central to understanding the meaning of the war; and it created both anxiety and creativity.

13

Naseby and the End of the War

The Triumph of the New Model Army

Uncertainties about what the war was for were reflected in the politics surrounding the formation of the New Model. Negotiations over the enabling legislation had been fraught, but also pragmatic. The army was created in response to a crisis in Parliament's southern forces – the surrender at Lostwithiel, dissensions within the Eastern Association and problems of supply and mobility in Waller's army. Tense parliamentary consideration of reform had been closely connected with the future of Essex's command, and the increasingly open religious conflict within the Eastern Association army. But these were not the reasons, or at least not the only reasons, for the creation of the army – although Essex, moderates and Presbyterians had the worst of the exchanges everyone had recognized the need for reform of the southern army. The New Model was not the armed wing of Independency, either in its original inception or in its actual formation.[1]

Pragmatism and statesmanship, as well as partisan struggle, were also evident in putting together the new army. Wherever possible, existing regiments were kept intact and some care was taken to balance commands between men of differing religious and political views. Nonetheless, there was an exodus of Scottish officers, which had an effect on the complexion of the army. The tense to-ing and fro-ing between the Houses over the officer list looks like House of Lords intervention against known radicals and in favour of a continuing role for the peers in overseeing the war effort.[2]

Sensitivities concerning these issues had re-emerged over the question of Fairfax's commission and Oliver Cromwell's eventual exemption from the Self-Denying Ordinance. There had been immediate difficulties in naming commanders for the new army since nearly all of the experienced and successful parliamentary commanders then in the field were excluded. Candidates for the overall command were therefore in short supply. Massey and Skippon were eligible since they were not MPs, but Massey's allegiance was not completely certain. He had been a royalist in 1642 and in 1643 had been rumoured to be ready to hand Gloucester over to the King. The choice eventually fell on Sir Thomas Fairfax, only thirty-two years old but with a dashing military reputation and unaffected by Self-Denial. His appointment as Lord-General had been one way of achieving Self-Denial without getting the measure passed – simply to form a new army which did not include the existing command. It was, therefore, a not-so-oblique approach to the difficulty of displacing Essex. Fairfax was later known as a moderate Presbyterian, but he was also known to favour vigorous prosecution of the war in order to force the King to reasonable terms. A measure of the political charge these decisions carried is that the vote was passed only by 101 to 69, and that the tellers for Fairfax were Cromwell and Sir Henry Vane (a rising star who favoured vigorous prosecution of the war and liberty for the sects), those against Denzil Holles and Sir Philip Stapleton (who were to lead attempts to achieve a Presbyterian settlement in 1647).[3]

Such political difficulties had slowed down the formation of the new army. The New Model Ordinance had passed on 15 February and a new Self-Denying Ordinance was prepared on 25 February; the list of officers was not finally agreed until 18 March, and not without considerable to-ing and fro-ing between the Houses. Some of the consequent wounds were reopened when Fairfax's commission was considered on 24 March. It gave him more power than Essex had enjoyed: he was to have control not just of his army but over all forts, castles, towns and garrisons within territory he controlled. More importantly, it did not commission him to preserve the safety of the King's person, as all previous parliamentary commanders had been commissioned. This caused more resistance in the Lords, but was justified on the grounds that it would serve as too much of a military limitation and that the King was not defending 'the true protestant religion'. The Solemn Vow and Covenant had not bound those taking it to preserve the King's safety, but this change in the terms of service for the Lord General still amounted to a formal change in war aims. The failure of the Uxbridge treaty and the imminence of a new campaign created pressure to fall in with the more militant prosecution of the war, but these measures caused considerable unease.[4]

Consideration of Fairfax's commission had begun on the same day that the Commons considered the second Self-Denying Ordinance. As eventually passed it required officers to resign their position within forty days, but re-employment was not debarred. Part of the price of the legislation was the requirement that all officers take the Solemn League and Covenant, which led John Lilburne to resign from the army. He was acting partly from sympathy with Independency – that consciences should be free from secular restraint – but also on the grounds that this oath cut across others which had previously been demanded. This was an example of parliamentarian tyranny, and he was fighting not for Parliament so much as against tyranny.[5] There were others like him.

In early April, however, the measures were finally passed: Essex, Manchester and Denbigh lost their commands, and Warwick resigned his (replaced by Batten). These were all men who favoured a moderate approach to the war, and were on the whole of Presbyterian sympathies. Oliver Cromwell, on the other hand, did not lose his command and was in fact to achieve higher command in the New Model. This led to a persistent suspicion that he had successfully manipulated the process to his own advantage; an example of how his high-minded rhetoric contrasted with a deep personal hypocrisy. Modern scholarship has tended to exonerate him from this charge, both at this moment and others, but it is an example of the ambiguities that surround the biography of 'God's Englishman'. What we do know is that he was in active service at the time when the Self-Denying Ordinance was passed, and was therefore given short-term exemption. This allowed him to fight at Naseby, where his contribution made it all but impossible to dismiss him – two days later his command was renewed for a further three months.[6]

In military terms the new army was remarkably successful. Its supply and provisioning were superior and this proved an advantage in recruitment too. By late April it was nearly at full strength and the cavalry units had been filled very easily. The infantry included many conscripts, who were not always easily secured, but also attracted deserters from other, less well-supplied, armies. There was a constant problem of desertion from the infantry, but its military success clearly rested on the relative attractiveness of service in the new army.[7] And while keeping the infantry at full strength required conscription, it should not be forgotten that there were many who served through choice.

We will never know much about what motivated common soldiers in the war, but there is evidence that ideas were significant in all the armies for at least some of the men. They marched behind colours that were protected with pride and bravery, and the messages on those colours suggest differences in what the men might have been fighting for. On the parliamentary side they emphasized the religious cause; on the royalist side there was more emphasis on personal honour and loyalty.[8]

Both sides produced catechisms, short pamphlets explaining how fighting for one cause or another could be reconciled with a good Christian conscience. This was by 1645 apparently a successful publishing venture, with rival versions for sale in London. Parliamentarians were, for example, armed against the 'base and absurd objection' that they were in arms against the King: they sought 'to rescue the King out of the hands of his and the Kingdom's enemies'. Royalists, by contrast, were assured that their opponents 'were rebels, and I fear (without God's great mercy and their own repentance) they shall be tormented by the Devil and his Angels'. Of course, they may not have been produced primarily, or only, for the edification of the rank and file, to offer guidance on matters of conscience, but for propaganda effect. The behaviour of troops was a significant factor in the political battle, and the reputation of some royalist commanders for failing to restrain their troops cost the King some support.[9] Either way, this was seen as a significant exercise – an extremely plausible-looking 'eighth edition' of the parliamentary catechism was produced, which completely subverted the message of the real catechism. It was so inflammatory that it was ordered to be burned by the common hangman.[10] Once in the New Model Army, conscripted or not, those who stayed long were given a clear message about the godliness of their calling – the army was full of hot Protestant preaching, and it seems clear that it bolstered morale.[11]

This was not then the Leveller army of later legend. Self-Denial had been in one sense an attack on aristocratic influence, but the officer corps was initially well-leavened with the sons of the gentry and aristocracy. Formation of the army had been a victory for those anxious for a more vigorous prosecution of the war, and a defeat for supporters of Manchester and Essex in particular. It had led to the exodus of Scottish Presbyterians, and there is some evidence that Independents were over-represented among its chaplains.[12] But it was not an army of Independents. Moreover, although it was the best-equipped and best-supplied army in the field, and played a crucial role in winning the war, it accounted for only half of the parliamentary soldiers in England. Massey and Brereton retained their regional commands and the Northern Association's forces were put under the command of Sydenham Poyntz, a man later known for his Presbyterian sympathies. Besides these armies there were numerous local garrisons and the London Trained Bands, all of which retained their autonomy. It is necessary to say all this because the New Model Army, having won the war, was eventually to dictate the peace, purging Parliament and underwriting the trial and execution of Charles I. This intervention was not on the horizon in the summer of 1645.[13]

Within months of taking the field the New Model had won the most significant single victory of the war, at Naseby in Leicestershire. As always, however, there was a measure of chance about it – both in the field and that the battle was joined at all. Indeed, it is not easy to explain what had brought the two armies together in the Midlands. For Parliament the twin objectives of the spring were Oxford and Taunton, which had become significant to the whole of the West Country. The Prince of Wales had been sent to Bristol to forge a new western command, with an obvious threat to Parliament (although, on the other hand, this new command created a power base from which Goring and others could resist Rupert's influence and therefore further complicated royalist politics). Taunton, currently in parliamentary hands, was under siege; if it fell it would facilitate the raising of forces by this new association, which could provide the basis for a new offensive. The Committee of Both Kingdoms was also worried about a possible royalist assault on the Eastern Association, and Cromwell took up position east of Oxford from where he could prevent forces picking up artillery en route from Wales to the parliamentary heartlands of East Anglia. Fairfax had in the meantime advanced to Reading.[14]

In response to these deployments near Oxford and at Reading, Goring was recalled from the West Country and, after a victory at Radcot Bridge, pushed Cromwell back. This also led to a recall of Fairfax, to support Cromwell rather than Taunton. On 8 May the royalist council of war met at Stow. An advance on the Eastern Association was ruled out and it was decided to split the armies between the relief of Chester and Taunton. Rupert advocated a decisive commitment to joining Montrose's forces in the north, with the hope then of bringing in Irish forces. Cheshire, and more particularly Chester, was crucial to both elements of this plan, providing a corridor between north and south and an entry point for troops from Ireland. On the other hand, the chance of capturing Taunton could not easily be ignored. Backing a northward march would have been a defeat for Rupert's enemies, similarly a westward march would have offered support to his rivals. Doing both was understandable, but not perhaps the shrewdest decision.[15]

Nonetheless, Goring was despatched to the west once more while the rest of the royalist forces were to move northwards. Those marching northwards were shadowed by Cromwell. As they approached Chester, Brereton called off the siege and asked Leven to cross the Pennines to help him confront the royalist army. This Leven refused to do, with an eye on Scotland, preferring instead to move to the northern side of the Lake District. In Scotland, Montrose had continued to enjoy military success, associated closely with plunder and excess. On 4 April, Dundee fell to him and atrocities ensued. His forces withdrew shortly after, the closest thing to good news for Parliament from Scotland, and marked with a day of thanksgiving in the mistaken belief that this was a victory. Chased by a superior force led by William Baillie he successfully avoided battle and reached the hills by Arbroath, where the superiority of the cavalry facing him was rendered ineffective. On 9 May he had the better of the battle of Auldearn, a cavalry engagement. Montrose's military reputation could hardly be higher following these victories and this record certainly gave Leven pause for thought in undertaking manoeuvres in England. In taking up position north of the Lakes he was covering any attempt by the royalists to join forces in Scotland. Parliament's force shadowing the royalist march was now broken up – part moving north to support Leven and part moving south to join Fairfax in laying siege to Oxford.[16]

The decision to besiege Oxford has been much criticized, but again there was a clear logic. It would force a response from the royalists and bring an end to the frustrating manoeuvres of the campaign to date. It would also stop any further advance to the north. But the response was devastating for parliamentary morale. On 31 May, Leicester was stormed by the royalists, following effective resistance. The victors then 'miserably sacked the whole town, without any distinction of persons or places'. The sack of Leicester caused consternation in London: after a month of campaigning Parliament's military reorganization had brought no dividend at all, and now a defeat that was catastrophic for morale. It prompted decisive action though. The siege of Oxford was broken up and the parliamentary army moved into the Midlands in search of a battle.[17]

As a result of these manoeuvres the two sides had ended up in positions that they had not initially anticipated. In early June the King was at Leicester, with Fairfax not far off, and Goring moving back towards Oxford. Having taken Leicester the royalists abandoned their northern march, much to the chagrin of the northern contingents in the army, and moved instead towards Market Harborough – a feint intended to draw Fairfax away from Oxford. Rupert remained committed to marching northwards, thinking (probably rightly) that this would draw the parliamentary army away from Oxford without risking a battle. But after Fairfax left Oxford on 5 June, Rupert's counsels were disregarded. The royalist army took up position at Daventry, intending to resupply Oxford with food and to receive munitions from there. It was with complete surprise that they learned of Fairfax's advance, but once it was discovered how close Fairfax was it might have been prudent to avoid battle. However, the open country northwards was unpromising for an armed retreat and there may have been hopes that Goring would arrive. In fact, he had good reasons to stay where he was, which he had set out in a letter to the King. In any case, by the time he was summoned by the King he was too far away to have arrived in time for the battle at Naseby.[18]

On 14 June 1645, after this frustrating and inconclusive manoeuvring, the New Model finally engaged the main royal army at Naseby in Leicestershire. Fairfax had a significant numerical advantage: he commanded between 14,500 and 17,000 men against the 9,000 or 10,000 led by the King. Parliament also had the advantage of the ground. After jockeying that began at 3 a.m., Fairfax took up position on a small hill, behind the brow of which the army formed up in order to conceal their numbers from the royalists. Charles's army would have to advance across wet ground and uphill.[19]

Despite these disadvantages, the royalists nearly won. The parliamentary infantry in the centre were commanded by Sir Philip Skippon, the cavalry on the right by Cromwell. Those on the left were commanded by Henry Ireton, a close associate of Cromwell and a rising star in the army who was soon to be a major political player, as well as being Cromwell's son-in-law. Ireton was faced by Prince Rupert, Cromwell by Langdale and Skippon by Byron. Battle was joined at 11 a.m., follow-

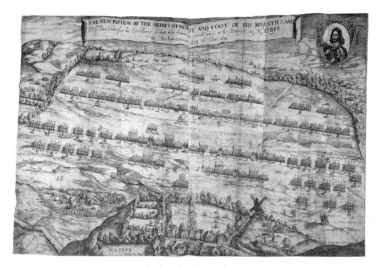

The battle of Naseby

ing a short and largely ineffective exchange of artillery fire. Rupert charged and Ireton advanced to meet him, but Ireton's line broke up and he also sent a detachment to protect the infantry, which appeared to be beleaguered. Rupert's charge was decisive and Ireton was seriously wounded and captured. The parliamentary infantry were also in retreat, and Skippon also wounded – so badly that it was a year before he was fit to fight again. Although Skippon was still on the field, Parliament had lost one of its cavalry commanders and its infantry commander.

It was decisive command from Cromwell and Fairfax that turned the day. While Ireton's cavalry had fallen before Rupert's charge Cromwell had led a successful charge on the other side of the field, exposing the flank of the royalist infantry. Rupert, rather than come to Langdale's aid, had gone after the parliamentary artillery train near the village of Naseby, but found unexpectedly fierce resistance. His decision was not the result of indiscipline, but a coherent choice, albeit one that has been criticized subsequently. It allowed Cromwell to cross the field and rally Ireton's cavalry. Fairfax took command of Cromwell's cavalry and they co-ordinated assaults on both wings of the royalist infantry. This allowed Parliament's forces to recover their ground and regroup. By that time Rupert's divisions were back on the field but, once in battle order and on the advance, Parliament's superiority in numbers was decisive – the royalist infantry fled, pursued by Cromwell for thirteen or fourteen miles, nearly to the gates of Leicester. The battle was marked by one of the most notorious atrocities of the war. Hundreds of women camp followers were attacked by the triumphant parliamentarians. One hundred of them were murdered – perhaps mainly Welsh women mistakenly identified as Irish, whose long knives were to be used for food preparation rather than the human butchery of which Irish women were thought to be capable. Many others were marked as whores by having their noses slit or their faces slashed.[20]

Although many fewer men were involved than at Marston Moor, and fewer died, this proved to be a more decisive battle for the course of the war. Fairfax lost 150 men, the King around 1,000. But the royalist infantry were destroyed and 4,000 prisoners captured, and 2,000 horses, the artillery train, arms for 8,000 men and forty barrels of gunpowder were also taken.[21] There was an immediate effect on parliamentary morale: a day of thanksgiving was appointed on 19 June, marked by a sumptuous banquet hosted by the City for the two Houses. Two days later 3,000 royalist prisoners were led through streets thronged with a triumphant multitude.[22]

Whatever each side had been trying to achieve, it is difficult to see why the royalists ended up fighting a pitched battle against a larger army in the Midlands. Behind the various shifts of the spring and summer lay divisions and rivalries but also distinct strategic views, and the mutually paralysing effect of successful manoeuvring by the two sides. The fall of Leicester, the culmination of a month of apparently aimless activity, was blamed on the continuing influence of the old generals who now sat on the Committee of Both Kingdoms every day (an unfair charge). Goring's reluctance to rejoin the main royalist army has been blamed on personal rivalries and his vanity, although there were sound military reasons for him to stay, or in favour of a march northwards by a united royalist army. The campaign had been shapeless, but not purposeless, and decisions which in retrospect seem misjudged had at the time something to commend them. Moreover, if Cromwell and Fairfax had not rallied the parliamentary cavalry and turned the battle at Naseby all this would seem rather different now. However, although the battle might have gone the other way, it would have been better to have stuck to the plan – it was not really clear what the royalists had to gain from seeking an engagement in Leicestershire. Before the battle, with Montrose's success inducing caution in Leven's army, the New Model detained by an ill-advised siege of Oxford and a successful assault on Leicester having been carried out, Charles was in a reasonably strong position. As at Marston Moor, the decision to join in battle with numerically superior forces had been avoidable, and had backfired.

Naseby did not end the war, but it began the end of the war and had important political implications too. It was a victory for the New Model, not the Anglo-Scottish alliance, and that increased the temperature of discussions about the post-war settlement. Thomas Edwards complained that the sectaries 'especially in this last year since the victory at Naseby [have] abused (in most insolent and unheard of manner, and that all kind of ways) all sorts and ranks of men even to the highest'.[23] For the same reason it was a blow to those who hoped for a rapid settlement, strengthening the hand of those keen to extract maximum advantage from the military victory. Revelation of the King's private calculations about his public negotiations was used to reinforce the point. It was bad news for the royalists, but also for Presbyterians and those seeking relatively limited concessions from the King. It was certainly a blow for traditionalists: a ballad of the following year complained that Naseby had killed Christmas.[24]

There could be no doubt that this victory belonged to the New Model, and many contemporaries assumed that it was therefore a victory for Independency and sectarianism. Whatever the truth of that, this was certainly not a victory for the Presbyterian interest. Cromwell wrote to Speaker Lenthall after the battle that 'Honest men served you faithfully in this action. Sir, they are trusty; I beseech you, in the name of God, not to discourage them . . . He that ventures his life for the liberty of his country, I wish he trust God for the liberty of his conscience, and you for the liberty he fights for'. The letter, as authorized for publication by the Commons, had these sentences cut – the thought that the war might be for freedom of conscience was not at all consensual among parliamentarians. Oddly, however, the Lords authorized its publication with these sentences included.[25] The royalist newsbooks simply failed to mention the defeat, but news of the victory caused frictions among rivals in the parliamentarian alliance.[26]

Hopes of a quick settlement along Presbyterian lines were also dealt a blow by the capture of the King's personal correspondence. A remarkable feature of the battle had been the discipline of the parliamentarian troops once the royalists had broken ranks and begun to flee. As the horse followed in ruthless pursuit, forbidden on pain of death to dismount for plunder, the rich pickings of the field were left to the foot. Among the prizes were arms, ammunition and more or less the entire baggage train, including the King's own coach, which contained his correspondence. It revealed in detail the wide gap between many of his public statements and his private convictions: for parliamentarians, in other words, the depth of his untrustworthiness. The letters were read to the two Houses and then at a Common Hall in the City. Selections were published as *The Kings Cabinet opened*, and those anxious to verify their accuracy and genuineness were invited to examine the originals.[27] Publication was justified as religious duty: 'It were a great sin against the mercies of God, to conceal these evidences of truth, which he so graciously (and almost miraculously) by surprisal of these papers, hath put into our hands'. But it was also a means to enlighten 'our seduced brethren . . . that they may see their errors, and return into the right way'. Others, of course, were wilful and beyond reason. Rather than revile them, and following the example of the Apostle St Jude, the editors merely confronted them with the truth: 'They may see here in his private letters what affection the King bears to his people, what language and titles he bestows upon his Great Council; which we return not again, but consider with sorrow, that it comes from a Prince seduced out of his proper sphere'.[28]

Here, from the hand of God, was proof positive of the justice of the parliamentarian cause. Anyone 'well affected to that cause of liberty and religion' maintained by the English and Scottish parliaments 'against a combination of all the Papists in Europe almost, especially the bloody tigers of Ireland, and some of the prelatical and court faction in England' will be 'abundantly satisfied . . . how the court has been Cajoled . . . by the Papists, and we the more believing sort of Protestants, by the Court'. 'Cajole' ('To prevail upon or get one's way with (a person) by delusive flattery, specious promises, or any false means of persuasion') was another new word thrown up by conditions of civil war. Apparently imported from the French, it was 'the new authentic word now amongst our Cabalistic adversaries'.[29] Again it bears testimony, both in its meaning and the context of its appearance in the language, to the increasing difficulty of arriving at the truth of matters, despite the massive increase in the flow of printed information. In private spaces – the cabinet and the closet – truth resided, and could be revealed: '[the closet is] the most secret place in the house appropriate unto our own private studies, and wherein we repose and deliberate by deep consideration of all our weightiest affairs'. It was 'a place where our readings of importance are shut up, a room proper and peculiar to ourselves'.[30] The revelation of private letters, the breaching of closets and the opening of cabinets, was a common literary form; revelation of these private statements gave the lie to a dissembling or dextrous public front.[31]

The main body of the pamphlet consists of transcripts of thirty-nine letters and papers, almost all of them individually witnessed as accurate by Zouch Tate, Miles Corbett or Edmund Prideaux and one by P.W. The cumulative effect is damning, including for example a letter written to Ormond during the Uxbridge negotiations telling him to secure peace or at least a cessation in Ireland, and to offer military support against the Scottish forces and even, if necessary, the Earl of Inchiquin, a prominent and vigorous defender of the Protestant interest.[32] The letters reveal a manifestly half-hearted commitment to the Uxbridge negotiations, and a complete unwillingness to give ground on episcopacy and the militia (two issues identified in the preface as core parts of the parliamentary cause from the Nineteen Propositions onwards). Many other letters demonstrate how willing he was to pursue alternative and incompatible policies at the same time as negotiating for peace. Here was vindication for those who had been reluctant to see the Uxbridge treaty go forward. As the *City Alarum* put it: 'it hath unlocked the mystery of former treaties, so I hope it will lock up our minds from thoughts of future'.[33]

Following the transcripts were four pages of annotations which made great play of the influence of Henrietta Maria: 'the Kings Counsels are wholly managed by the Queen, though she be of the weaker sex, born an alien, bred up in a contrary religion'; her advice had the effect of commands, and the 'King professes to prefer her health before the exigence and importance of his own public affairs'; and she was 'as harsh, and imperious towards the King . . . as she is implacable to our religion, nation, and government'.[34] Examples of counsel hostile to English interest illustrated this latter point, such as suggestions for a trade embargo and the dissolution of Parliament. Fears that, like Laud and Strafford, her head might well be on the block were clearly well-founded.

But the King too was guilty, and not just of being under the thumb:

'in many things', in fact, he exceeded 'the Queen for acts of hostility and covering them over with deeper and darker secrecy'.[35] There followed a devastating catalogue of his 'dextrous' dealings against national interests, the international Protestant cause, English parliaments and religion. 'The King will declare nothing in favour of his parliament, so long as he can find a party to maintain him in this opposition; nor perform any thing which he hath declared so long as he can find a sufficient party to excuse him from it'.[36] This was a longstanding weakness, as a brief history of his reign made clear. Finally the pamphlet compared six important public statements with his private views as revealed by the correspondence. All six were juxtaposed with 'distinctions' that might make apparently contradictory statements reconcilable. The presentation of these letters has had a devastating effect on subsequent views of Charles.

Despite the political damage, however, and the ruthlessly effective exploitation of this windfall, there were those who felt that these letters should not have been published. *The Kings Cabinet* had tried to forestall objections. Enemies to 'parliaments and reformation . . . made wilful in their enmity' could be expected to 'deny these papers to have been written by the King's own hand, or else that we make just constructions and inferences out of them'. Or deny that, although accurately recorded and interpreted, 'they are blameable, or unjustifiable against such rebels as we are'. In fact the replies did not contest the authenticity, but rather the construction placed on them or how reprehensible the King had been. 'The letters are not unworthy [of] a Prince *Defender of the Faith*, against whom so dangerous and causeless a *Rebellion* was then in its height, threatening both to his government, and to the Protestant profession of the Christian religion in this Kingdom, an utter ruin', went one response.[37] Another complained that 'They will not let him loath a rebel, nay, they will not let him love a wife; they will not let him use his sword, nay, they will not let him use his pen, but they will expose him for it'.[38] A plausible line of defence was that in order to make peace in such a complex situation, Charles needed to keep his own counsels, and that concessions for that purpose were not only carefully considered, but noble. Suspending punishment of Catholics might be a good deal in order to secure the established church, for example. And why shouldn't he bring in foreign forces, if his own subjects had deserted him?

This was a hard battle to win, not least because it required such close attention from readers. The author of *A Key To the Kings cabinet*, for example, did a clever job of reconciling a secret promise to abrogate the laws against popery with a public declaration to put them into execution: a promise to execute them is not a promise not to repeal them; a promise to abrogate the statutes clearly implies that he will do it with parliamentary consent.[39] But really this was in many places very unpromising material for Charles's defenders.

Others concentrated on the issue of seemliness, however: something at the heart of controversies over publication during the 1640s. As one pamphlet's response to the speeches at Common Hall put it: 'Men indeed, whose religion will allow them to ransack God's cabinet, no marvel, if they quickly find reason not to spare the King's'.[40] Here was the obverse of the revelation of private truths for public purposes – a kind of violation. Bruno Ryves, in his accounts of the spoliation of parliamentary troops, made much mention of the invasion of private spaces, especially ladies' closets.[41] The publication of the letters robbed the King of his dignity, something essential to the negotiation of a peace, and in revealing the depth of his dependence on Henrietta Maria they had violated his privacy.[42]

Reading these responses it is easy to see Charles's point of view: he was being asked to agree to things that were, in his view, absolutely wrong; and that was a much more serious thing for a king than for one of his subjects. Moreover, he was being pushed into them by armed subjects, unable to recognize their duties to him as the anointed monarch, and to justify himself to all his subjects in a world of printed propaganda. Since these things were unacceptable, and since the war was not going his way, what option did he have but to play for time and seek other sources of support? And, in any case, Parliament routinely prepared for war while negotiating for peace – this was in the nature of the crisis since 1642. Nonetheless, after the revelation of these letters no-one who did a deal with him could be comfortable that it would stick. Their revelation did no favours to the moderates at Westminster, and they immediately scuppered proposals for a peace treaty floated in the Lords, with the support of the Covenanters, in the week after Naseby.[43]

By any normal standards Naseby was terrible enough: one eyewitness reported that 'I saw the field so bestrewed with carcasses of horses and men, the bodies lay slain about four miles in length but most thick on the hill where the king stood'.[44] It was politically very significant, but not immediately seen as strategically so. Most of the King's cavalry got away and Goring's army, by virtue of its absence, was still intact. Two further developments served to turn Naseby into the decisive battle of the war – the triumphant march of the New Model through the West Country and the defeat of Montrose.

Following Naseby, Charles headed for the Welsh hills, arriving at Hereford on 19 June. On the previous day he had renewed his appeal to Ormond for Irish troops and such were his hopes of success that Langdale was made governor of north Wales in preparation for their arrival. On 27 June preparations were made to receive them in Cornwall too. Fairfax followed up the victory at Naseby first by laying siege to Leicester, which surrendered on 18 June. Further moves were made cautiously, given the presence of Goring's force in the west, and the mustering of the King's forces in the Marches. But from late June the New Model fought an apparently irresistible campaign in Dorset and Somerset. The siege of Taunton had been lifted on 29 June, probably in fear of Fairfax's approach.[45] But the march to relieve the siege was hampered by a 'third force': armed bodies of local people referred to as 'clubmen'. It was the second significant occasion when the field armies had been confronted in this way: a similar force had severely hampered royalist operations at Hereford earlier in the spring.[46]

Goring's orders were to fall back towards the Bristol Channel to await the arrival of regiments from Wales, but Fairfax managed to meet up with Goring's forces near Crewkerne and outmanoeuvred him, bringing them to battle at Langport on 10 July. Goring had sent his baggage train on ahead to Bridgewater and was intending to manage a retreat there. At Langport, outnumbered, he took up position on a hill overlooking a stream swollen with recent rain, and posted musketeers among the hedges that lined the fields and lanes from the ford up to his position. From this position Goring apparently thought he would not be attacked. But an artillery bombardment from the parliamentarians forced Goring's cavalry off the hillside, leaving the musketeers without support. Fairfax then sent 1,500 musketeers across the stream, under Colonel Rainborough, who advanced with considerable courage against entrenched opponents. When the moment seemed right 200 cavalrymen charged up a lane defended by Major Christopher Bethell, a charge which again required considerable courage. When they reached the top of the hill they were outnumbered perhaps six or eight to one, and there was close battle at sword point. But parliamentary support began to arrive and the royalist forces began to scatter. In the aftermath of the battle, as the royalists made for Bridgewater, Fairfax captured 1,400 prisoners, 2,000 horses, 4,000 arms, two cannon and three wagonloads of ammunition.[47] The last royalist field army in England had been routed.

Siege was laid to Bridgewater on 16 July and it fell on 23 July, completing a chain of parliamentary strongpoints which cut off the west – from Lyme through Langport and Bridgewater with Taunton an advanced point.[48] Rather than march into Cornwall like Essex had the previous year, Fairfax chose to operate elsewhere, knowing that royalist forces were bottled up in the peninsula. Goring's retreat into Devon was marked by assaults by clubmen, and royalists fleeing from Langport were also hunted.[49]

With Goring's army broken, the remaining objectives in the west were the main royalist garrisons, particularly at Bristol and Exeter. Fairfax's advance on Bristol was hampered by his own difficulties with armed locals, the clubmen. Fairfax negotiated with them on 3 July, having executed a soldier for plundering. His attitude hardened, however, and he arrested their leaders at Shaftesbury on 2 August and two days later Cromwell dispersed a large assembly at Hambledon Hill in a brief and largely bloodless rout. Fairfax had continued to enjoy the advantage through July, taking the surrender of Bath on 29 July (with the support of Somerset clubmen), and laying siege to Sherborne Castle on 2 August. On 11 August the siege train arrived at Sherborne and the castle fell four days later. Bristol now became the priority and siege was laid there in late August.[50]

As his fortunes waned in the west, England was largely lost to Charles (see Map 4). Naseby had been decisive for the Midlands and, therefore, the north. Royalist hopes flickered briefly in Wales, where Charles Gerrard fought a successful campaign against the parliamentary commander, Rowland Laugharne. In early July, Charles was in south Wales trying to raise troops to compensate for his losses in England, but there and in Hereford he was finding it difficult to press men. These hopes were extinguished by a parliamentary victory at Colby Moor (1 August), where successful co-ordination of operations on sea and land enabled Major-General Laugharne to rout the royalists under Sir Edward Stradling. It seemed that here too the royalist cause was crumbling, and Haverfordwest Castle fell on 5 August.[51]

The King's own army was now faced by both Fairfax and Leven, who had moved south during June, reassured that the King was not intending an invasion of Scotland. A week after Naseby he was at Mansfield and he was soon to lay siege to Hereford. Charles was finding it hard to get men, but he drew strength from news of Montrose's continued successes. In May, Montrose had headed north from Blair Athol, away from the numerically superior Covenanting forces. In June fresh levies were made in the Highlands and by the end of the month he was sufficiently confident to offer battle to Baillie at Keith. This was declined but on 1 July battle was joined at Alford, where Montrose won another great, and bloody, victory. Charles now set his hopes on getting to Yorkshire, raising men there and, on the basis of garrisons at Pontefract and Scarborough, making some connection with Montrose. To join Montrose from the crumbling position in Wales was a tall order, however. Charles set off on a meandering and ultimately unsuccessful march, leaving Hereford only to return, via Doncaster, Huntingdon and Oxford, a month later. It was in Huntingdon that Charles heard of Montrose's crushing victory over the Covenanters at Kilsyth. The most that could be said for his own march, however, was that Charles had avoided Leven's army. The King entered Hereford on 4 September, having seen Leven's siege of the city lifted, and spirits were a little higher.[52]

Once in Hereford, however, Charles received flurries of bad news. Fairfax summoned Bristol to surrender on 4 September. Whereas the King had not been able to recruit in south Wales again in early September, Fairfax's army was reinforced by 5,000 local people. Rupert recognized the desperate straits he was in and on 5 September asked for permission to communicate with the King. This was refused and he then spun out negotiations. On 10 September Fairfax lost patience and Bristol was stormed. Rupert surrendered and on the following day Bristol was evacuated. Charles blamed Rupert and, effectively, banished him.[53]

Only Montrose's campaign in Scotland offered the royalists any immediate comfort and, with his position in England deteriorating still further, Charles sought once again to join him. Marching from Hereford via Chirk he entered Chester with the intention of raising the siege. Langdale arrived to attack the besieging army from the rear, but was badly defeated at Rowton Heath. The parliamentary victory threatened the future of Chester, the only remaining port of importance for Ireland, and cut off the hope of a march northwards to Scotland through

Lancashire. The final blow for this particular strategy was the catastrophic defeat of Montrose at Philiphaugh on 13 September (see Map 5). On 6 September, Leslie returned to Scotland with troops and three days later prominent supporters of Montrose among the Lowland aristocracy were imprisoned. Met in battle on 13 September, Montrose's scanty cavalry were quickly disposed of and the foot destroyed. Two hundred and fifty Irish troops were killed and fifty or more surrendered on the promise of quarter. Most of them were subsequently shot on the pretence that the offer of quarter had applied only to officers, and a notorious massacre of Irish women and other camp followers then took place, which Leslie failed to stop. Charles had retreated to Denbigh, where, on 27 September, he heard the news from Philiphaugh and that Chester could not last much longer.[54]

Charles had no remaining options. His field armies in Scotland and England were defeated and important garrisons were falling like dominoes. Cromwell marched triumphantly through the south, capturing Devizes (23 September) and Winchester (28 September), and arriving before Basing House a few days later. This was the seat of the Catholic Marquess of Winchester, and had successfully withstood two previous sieges, but it was to become the twentieth garrison to fall to the New Model Army since June. It had been under siege since August and Cromwell arrived on 8 October anxious to get the job done. Two great holes were blown in the walls by his heavy artillery, but still the defenders refused to surrender. As the infantry advanced in the ensuing storm they shouted, 'Down with papists', and many within were put to the sword despite pleas for mercy. Among the dead were six Catholic priests and a young woman who had tried to protect her father. Women were roughly handled, and partially stripped, although there were no rapes. The house was pillaged without restraint and the sudden release of food stores onto the local market temporarily depressed prices.[55]

Basing held considerable symbolic significance: it had been besieged three times and was emblematic of loyalty and, to the King's opponents, popery. The marquess, standing bareheaded in defeat among the ruins of his house, responded to taunts by saying, 'If the King had no more ground in England than Basing I would venture as I did ... Basing is called loyalty'. He added, perhaps pathetically or just unnecessarily, 'I hope that the king may have a day again'.[56] Among those humiliated by the conquerors was Inigo Jones, architect of the Banqueting House and designer of the court masques of the 1630s in which the majesty of the King had served to reconcile the competing passions of his people in order to bring peace.

Just as the war had started with a series of whimpers rather than a bang, so it petered out. Abandoning his northward march, Charles went initially to Newark, one of his remaining strongholds, where he was rejoined by Rupert, who was forgiven by a council of war on 26 October, and the King set out again for Oxford. In November 1645 Goring left for France, in part because of his health and partly in hope of a high command in the continental forces expected to be mustered the following spring. His command had passed to Lord Wentworth, who suffered heavy losses to Cromwell's forces at Bovey Tracey on 9 January. Other garrisons surrendered in quick succession. Exeter was besieged and at Torrington, on 16/17 February, Hopton's army was destroyed. The Prince of Wales fled to the Isles of Scilly, and Hopton to Cornwall, where he surrendered on 12 March. His army was disbanded over the coming weeks. Exeter fell a month later, leaving Pendennis Castle standing alone in the west, but even after the New Model Army had swept through the west the war twitched on. Hereford fell on 17 December and by then Chester and Newark were very strictly blocked up. Hopton's had been the last force of any size in England, and Exeter the last significant stronghold aside from Oxford and Newark. Lord Astley had 3,000 men with him in Worcester and was ordered to try to cut his way through to Oxford, but the parliamentarians caught them at Stow-on-the-Wold, and Astley was forced to surrender on 20 March. In Wales, Raglan and Harlech held out, but without waiting for the fall of Oxford Charles could not really have been expected to delay surrender much longer than he did. He left Oxford in disguise on 27 April, surrendering to the Covenanters at Southwell on 5 May. As part of his surrender terms he delivered Newark on 8 May. When Oxford surrendered on 24 June, Prince Rupert and Prince Maurice left England for France and the Netherlands respectively. The last redoubts were Pendennis, which surrendered on 16 August, Raglan, which followed suit three days later, and Harlech, which held out until March 1647.[57] It was a feeble end to the military campaign, but in surrendering to the Covenanters, Charles had shown some astuteness about the coming political campaign to win the peace.

14

Winners and Losers

The Costs and Benefits of Civil War

England had paid a huge cost for this parliamentary victory, in lives and property. In 1640 the Shropshire village of Myddle had a population of less than 600, possibly much less. If Myddle was typical in age and sex ratios then there would have been no more than 175 adult men in the village, 55 aged between 15 and 24 and 120 between 25 and 59. It is therefore quite startling to learn that 21 of the young men of the village went to war: 40 per cent of the men under 25, 12 per cent of the men under 60. This was a rich recruiting ground for the royalist armies and, unsurprisingly, all but one of them went to fight for the King. Thirteen did not return. One died at Edgehill and two others, Reece Vaughan and John Arthur, died at the siege of Hopton Castle, where the parliamentary defenders were eventually butchered and dumped in a ditch. Three Preece brothers died, two of them in fighting at Ercall and one hanged for horse theft. Nat Owen met his end at the siege of Bridgenorth in 1645. He had been wounded earlier, in a fight with a comrade over plunder, and was unable to move, his comrades unable to help him. He died in the flames. The only parliamentarian, Thomas Mould, was shot in the leg while fighting in the parliamentarian cavalry. A neighbour recalled that his leg healed 'but was very crooked so long as he lived'.[1]

Villages all over England must have had similar tales to tell and similar wounds to heal. The most systematic estimates of war deaths put the total at 62,000 between 1642 and 1646, probably the equivalent to the population of the four largest cities in the country, London aside. Nearly 80,000 more were taken prisoner.[2] These deaths were widely spread across the country, although East Anglia and Wales saw many fewer than the regions where field armies were frequently in action. On the other hand, these figures are derived from incidents large enough to have been reported, but there were probably many other deaths which went unrecorded. Richard Gough recalled seeing, as a schoolboy in Myddle during the war, a clash between parliamentary and royalist garrison soldiers happening upon each other in the village. A man was badly wounded. Gough had gone with the minister to pray for him and saw the man lying on a bed 'with much blood running along the floor'. He died the next day.[3] Such memories lasted a lifetime, but they were not the stuff of press reports. Between April 1644 and December 1645 Guy Carleton, vicar of Bucklesbury, Berkshire, buried four soldiers, all of whom died individually and probably not in any recorded incident.[4]

Others died accidentally. Ralph Hopton was severely wounded when a casually placed tobacco pipe ignited barrels of gunpowder and two other soldiers in his army died from the accidental discharge of muskets. Edward Morton was blown up, along with his four children and his house, while mixing gunpowder for the royal army. His wife's escape was said to be providential, since she had tried to dissuade him from doing this work for the royalists.[5] Another judgement was visited on Captain Starker, inspecting the loot taken from the capture of Houghton Tower in Lancashire. One of the company lit a pipe, which ignited the powder, killing himself, his captain and sixty of his comrades.[6] The consequent burn and shatter wounds were horrifying. Richard Wiseman, a surgeon in the royal army, reported such an accident at the battle of Worcester in 1651: 'A soldier ... hastily fetched his bonnet full of gunpowder, and whilst he was filling his Bandoliers, another soldier carelessly bestrides it to make a shot at one of the enemies ... In firing his musket, a spark flew out of the pan and gave fire to the powder underneath him'. The man filling the bandoliers was 'grievously burned in the hands, arms, breast, neck and face', but the careless soldier suffered more fearfully. He was 'burned and scorched in all the upper part of his thighs, *scrotum*, muscles of the *abdomen* and the coats of the testicles ... And indeed it was to be feared, that when the Escar should cast off from his belly, his bowels would have tumbled out'. In this case the outcome was happier. After the town fell Wiseman's assistant saw the former soldier escape and the latter was 'cured'.[7]

Not all were so lucky: many of the fallen died of their wounds, often in pain and some time after the battle. John Hampden took six days to die of wounds received at the battle of Chalgrove Field, six agonizing days. Care of the wounded was taken seriously but was limited by both resources and expertise. Wiseman, seeking to learn from his battlefield experiences, seems to have made a diagnostic distinction between those who died howling like dogs and those who died screaming. His later *Treatise of Wounds* reflected a serious and hopeful attempt to save more lives, but it is also a catalogue of horrors. Wounds tended to be burns, slashing cuts, the effects of fragmentation agents or gunshots. For the latter there was little in civilian life to prepare a surgeon for his battlefield experience, and Wiseman devoted considerable space to trying to pass on what he had learned about them. Shattered bones and the threat of infection were the principal dangers. As Wiseman noted, an undressed wound was within days full of maggots. Amputation was often done immediately, while the wounded men were still in shock, since their courage might fail them later, but Wiseman was keen to try to save limbs as well. Those who survived initially had a good chance of surviving in the long term, however. The maimed could expect some care following their initial treatment, either in hospitals or quartered with people willing to care for them in return for payment.[8]

Of course, the impact of the war depended only in part on the quantity of the suffering – it was enough to see the effects of one gunshot in the face for the price of victory to be clear. Following battles many commentators noted the horror of corpses strewn widely and uncared for. After Naseby hastily dug graves proved to be too shallow, so 'that the bodies, in a short time became very offensive'. In general both sides sought to provide decent burial, at least for their own fallen, but bodies were often stripped and looted despite these attempts to preserve Christian decency. Mutual humanity survived these traumas, but many people saw shocking sights all the same.[9]

Although narratives of the war follow the movements of the field armies, it was the presence of garrisons and the ubiquity of skirmishing which characterized the experience of war most of the time. In June 1645 Charles had 40,000 troops at his command. One quarter of them were at Naseby, slightly more in the western army, but nearly half in garrisons in Wales, the west and the Midlands. Most of the recorded deaths in combat took place in minor skirmishes and sieges, in fact, not in the largest battles that dominate the military narrative.[10] Garrisons gave access to wealth and resources, control of trade networks and the economic hinterlands of the towns in which they were situated. Mansions and castles also gave control of agricultural hinterlands, and since almost every locality was of divided and questionable loyalty it was essential to maintain a military presence in order to maintain political and economic control. Sieges were also of political significance – both sides making great play of fortitude, loyalty and courage in the face of hardship, or of the triumphant seizure of strongpoints.[11]

This form of warfare made immense demands on the civilian population. Fortifications were mammoth construction projects which involved widespread destruction of suburban property. Buildings were cleared to make way for earthworks, to deny the enemy cover and to provide clear lines of fire. Besieging forces also destroyed buildings in order to protect themselves, or for the materials.[12] Work on London's fortifications had started in the autumn of 1642, but the real initiative came in the spring of 1643 in a massive programme of public works. By April 1643 there were twenty-eight 'works' (forts or sconces), along with two outworks covering the Mile End Road. The Venetian ambassador

One of the twenty-eight 'works' around London's civil war fortifications

reported the following month that they were impressive, and that earthworks linking them would be complete within weeks. These earthworks, which marked the 'lines of communication', were ramparts fronted by a ditch three yards wide. From the bottom of the ditch to the top of the rampart may have been as much as six yards. Eleven miles of wall along with the forts, sconces and outworks (designed with the advice of Dutch expertise) seem to have been built in less than a year, much of it in not much more than three months. Nonetheless, the apparent enthusiasm for this work was remarkable. One contemporary observer claimed that 100,000 citizens set their hands to the work; the Venetian ambassador estimated more modestly that 20,000 worked without pay each day, even on Sunday, normally 'so strictly observed by the Puritans'. The great and the good joined 'all sorts of Londoners', marching to the works 'with all alacrity'. One reason may have been that the very fact of fortification increased anxiety in the City, of course. If much of the work was voluntary, however, this was still a huge financial commitment, paid for by the City, some of it remitted from the tax bill, but some raised by special extra taxes. This was clearly a pay day, albeit one made much in arrears, for victuallers, bricklayers, masons and carpenters as well as for the soldiers and military suppliers.[13]

Much smaller places had to find the resources for large-scale works too: particularly well-studied are those at Exeter, where £4,400 was spent between November 1642 and August 1643, and to good effect too. Oxford and Newark (and Colchester in 1648) were made defensible in the face of increasingly heavy artillery bombardment.[14] Fortified country houses and castles became the focus for protracted sieges too: Basing House resisted parliamentary sieges repeatedly before its bloody fall in 1645. Lathom House was similarly celebrated for the heroism of its defenders, and tied up significant numbers of parliamentary troops in the north-west.[15]

Garrison towns were fortified and defended, or seized, at massive cost to the local population. Bombardment and the storming of defended towns could be extremely destructive. Estimating the extent of property destruction is no less fraught with difficulty than arriving at estimates of casualties, but it seems that at least 150 towns and fifty villages sustained some damage. Reliable sources for estimating the scale of this damage are available for a sample of these places – twenty-seven towns and seven villages. If the loss in these places is representative of the experience more generally, then across the whole country 10,000 town houses, 1,000 houses in villages and 200 mansions or country houses were lost. This suggests that the war might have made 55,000 people homeless – 2 per cent of the population; that is the equivalent of the entire population of Norwich, Bristol and York combined.[16] Obviously such a figure is only indicative of a general order of destruction, but in market towns sieges and associated property destruction were common, and much of it seems to have been concentrated in 1643.

As with the battlefield deaths it is perhaps better to talk of specific experiences than aggregated statistics. The siege of Gloucester was said to have resulted in the loss of properties worth £22,400, of personal goods worth £4,500 and another £2,000 through the deliberate flooding of surrounding fields for defensive purposes. The city had been assessed at £500 for the much-reviled ship money levies, although in 1638 that had been reduced to £180.[17] Exeter may have lost one fifth of its houses. Leicester, stormed by royalists on 31 May 1645 and retaken by Parliament only a few weeks later, was said to have lost 120 houses, besides other property damage and plunder.[18] It was not just the cities, of course: smaller communities, with fewer resources, might suffer too. Holt and Farndon, small towns either side of the Dee a few miles south of Chester, also suffered substantial damage. The castle at Holt commanded an important bridge over the Dee but the town itself was indefensible. Much property was destroyed, particularly, it was said, by the garrison as a preventive measure. After the Restoration it was claimed that 103 houses had been lost. In Farndon, similarly, houses were destroyed when Brereton forced a crossing of the river in November 1643, and then again in February 1645, following a parliamentary withdrawal when the garrison at Holt carried out further preventive destruction.[19] Repair of the damage in many places did not begin until the 1650s, and lasted in some places into the 1670s and beyond. The repair of communal resources – hospitals, schools and almshouses – could take much longer and the damage inflicted on churches and other monuments might be irreparable. The memory of sufferings often lasted longer than the physical loss.[20]

Prolonged sieges also bred disease. All civil war armies were prey to typhus, dysentery, plague and fevers, and these were frequently passed on to the civilian population too. The royalist occupation of Exeter in 1643 was followed by the worst outbreak of plague since the great plague of 1625. In the last weeks of the preceding siege the mortality rate had risen steadily. In June 31 burials are recorded. That figure rose to 45 in July and 60 in August but the peak came following the occupation: 95 in October. This was almost certainly 'war typhus', a disease which had killed one fifth of the population of Oxford earlier in the year. Under siege once more in late 1645, this time by Fairfax's triumphant New Model, it was again threatened by disease. Fairfax's army had already lost men 'killed by laying out' and now was ravaged by a mysterious sickness that convinced him of the need to find them healthy quarters. Nonetheless, common soldiers continued to rest in cramped quarters where the 'New Disease' claimed dozens of lives each week. During the siege of Plymouth 2,845 people died from disease.[21]

Overall, it has been estimated, 100,000 deaths from disease can be added to the tally of casualties in battle, and numerous local examples confirm the general point. According to one calculation 11,817 people died in Devon between 1643 and 1645, 4,193 of them as a result of the war: that is, the war contributed more than one third of the deaths in the county. It seems that only 1,634 of those deaths can be attributed to battle, so that the lion's share of these 'war deaths' arose from indirect causes.[22] Nationally burials during 1643/4 were 29 per cent above average, serious enough, but below the level of years of 'natural crisis' in 1558/9, 1597/8 or 1625/6. This was, nonetheless, one of the worst years of crisis mortality in the period 1641–1871. In Berkshire, however, the picture was almost unimaginably worse: burials rose 120 per cent higher than their average level. This mortality was concentrated in areas close to garrisons and concentrations of soldiers. Essex's army, hanging around near Reading for much of 1643, was a grievance in Westminster, but apparently a major health hazard too. The army was grievously afflicted with disease throughout the year, and in parishes across Berkshire there is widespread evidence of the presence of 'war typhus', plague, dysentery and other fevers.[23]

Despite the scale of the operations, and these horrors, England did not endure the horrors of the Thirty Years War and 'turn Germany': codes of conduct on the battlefield and in sieges were adhered to, and atrocities were limited. There were, of course, well-attested exceptions – at Barthomley Church, Milford Haven, Naseby and Lostwithiel, for example. Once again, it was not necessarily the engagements of greatest national significance which bred the most shocking behaviour. At Hopton Castle a parliamentary force which had recently taken control was summoned to surrender by a party of royalists early in 1644. The summons was refused and an assault was repulsed, as was another two weeks later, but on 13 March a mine destroyed much of the walls and made the castle indefensible. The defenders now offered to surrender, on condition that they could march away with their arms and ammunition. This was rejected and they asked for quarter, which was also refused. When the castle was taken all the defenders except the governor and his second-in-command were stripped and hog-tied back to back before having their throats cut. Their bodies were thrown into a ditch. Two maidservants were forced to watch this murder before they too were beaten. An old man of eighty, emerging from the cellars after the slaughter of the others, was tied to a chair before his throat too was slashed and his corpse tossed into the ditch with the others. One of the maidservants was said to have lost her wits as a result of this trauma. This fell within the codes of conduct, since the defenders had initially refused a summons and so were expected to pay the price, but it was an unusually brutal interpretation of the rules of war. Elsewhere, it seems, the codes kept behaviour within the bounds of recognized decency, although it was sometimes touch and go.[24] Rape, for example, does not seem to have been used systematically as a means of fighting the war, and when terms of surrender were granted they were almost always honoured. England did not turn Germany, but it saw plenty of horrors, and restraint was not always secure.[25]

Levels of formal taxation were by pre-war standards extraordinarily high. The proportion of national wealth taxed and spent by the government seems to have doubled. Many of the means by which governments had tapped wealth before the war had now gone, or went uncollected (wardship, monopolies, forest fines, impositions, ship money and so on), and so formal taxation loomed particularly large. By the late 1620s one subsidy produced about £55,000. The parliamentary assessment reached that as a monthly figure.[26] In particular counties, towns and villages this transformation was dramatic. Sussex paid a total of about £16,000 for parliamentary subsidies during the 1620s, and ship money had come to about £4,600 per annum for six years. The county seems to have paid £36,000 per annum for seventeen years, for the assessment alone: seven times as much as for ship money and vastly more than had been paid in the 1620s. To that burden would have to be added the excise and, for some people, sequestration (£9,500 was raised in Chichester rape in 1643 alone). John Everenden, a minor gentleman who had paid £3 for five subsidies in 1628, had to stump up £163 between 1643 and 1652. The 308 taxpayers in Rye in 1644 included all but the poorest. Formal national taxation was hugely more significant than in the years before 1640.[27]

Where military control was weak the picture might be even worse. Taxes might be claimed by both sides. Where a garrison could not feed itself from formal taxation soldiers might be forced, or choose, to live off the land, plundering or claiming free quarter from the local population. In the Midlands, an area with a patchwork of garrisons, and field armies regularly passing through, these problems of double taxation and informal exaction were very pronounced.[28] In Cheshire, a county which saw constant military activity and insecure control over territory, plunder and free quarter imposed greater costs than taxation. Chits given in return for free quarter could only be redeemed from victors, of course, and frequently went unpaid. Certainly there is ample qualitative evidence of the incidence of both plunder and free quarter.[29] In Warwickshire quarter and plunder was rarely less than half the level of formal taxation.[30] These experiences varied over time as well as between regions. South Warwickshire saw the battle of Edgehill, grave pits and horrors, but this gave way to more routine irritations – horse theft, quarter, taxation, the demands of garrisons or of royalist convoys moving through on their way to the west.[31]

For those on the receiving end these were terrible costs, but there were clear incentives for armies to be restrained. John Fettiplace, acting for the parliamentary garrison at Cirencester in 1642, where the soldiers 'were driven to exceeding straits, and ready to mutiny for want of pay', seems to have secured contributions by negotiation, albeit through agreements that broke down subsequently. Such disputes could be pursued at law several years later.[32] In general royalist armies subsisted, and were not defeated because they were less well-fed or less well-supplied, but they do seem to have resorted more often to informal exactions. Those with a bad record of payment could hope for little voluntary help. Goring's cavalry troops were active throughout the winter of 1644–5 because they were well-fed, but it was at the expense of ruthless plunder and widespread resentment, for which they paid a considerable price the following year. Certainly, the reputation of Prince Rupert as 'Prince Robber' did the royalist cause no good at all.[33]

Of course, these costs of the war borne by many were certainly benefits to some others. All the money being raised was spent in the country: the war machine was also a customer, not simply a burden. Supplying the material to the army – weapons, gunpowder, horses, clothing and food – provided opportunities, as did the need for transport. Large contractors could make huge fortunes, particularly if their services or political connections were good enough to secure payment in full, and for craftsmen in key trades the war was a source of steady demand.

When the war broke out the arms trade in England was small, and inadequate to supply the armies, but by the end of the decade, when huge expeditions were mounted to Scotland and Ireland, almost all the supplies were domestically produced. Weapons were made by skilled craftsmen working in small shops, and production could not be rapidly expanded. The long peace from the mid-1620s onwards had led to the further atrophy of an already limited industry. Massive orders to consortia of tradesmen stimulated development – blacksmiths, gunsmiths, turners and edgesmiths all did excellent business if they were able to adapt their skills to produce these goods. By the middle of the war the royalists had effectively created an arms industry in Oxford and, after it was taken in late 1643, Bristol. Parliament had the advantage of building on the existing trade in London, but stimulated a massive expansion, as well as the development of trades in Manchester and Birmingham. When the New Model Army was supplied in 1645 it was almost all done from domestic suppliers.[34]

This could provide steady work for large numbers of craftsmen. Partial data for London reveal that between August 1642 and September 1651 at least 30,000 pikes, 102,000 swords and 111,000 firearms were produced there. Two cutlers had received an order for 22,503 swords for the Bishops' Wars. Such contractors clearly flourished, but so too might the craftsmen who did the work. In Nottingham a gunsmith could earn between 1s and 1s 6d per day, a pike header 1s 2d.[35] The meaning of a wage in seventeenth-century England is difficult to determine: a figure might include costs of materials or subcontractors, and might omit payments in kind. It is equally difficult to know how many days' work any individual could get – clearly relevant to the value of a wage. Skilled craftsmen in these trades, however, were likely to be getting steady work. If they were keeping most of this wage for themselves, then they were not doing too badly.[36] Given the stories of accidents and mishaps, it is unlikely that many soldiers would want to cut costs or corners in these matters.

A similar story can be told of the development of heavy ordnance production. Although it was necessarily a much more capital-intensive business in the hands of fewer producers, both sides were able to find domestic sources of heavy ordnance. The demand for gunpowder led to the establishment of mills, to supply the parliamentary armies, in the lower Lea Valley on the edge of London, Manchester, Gloucester, Leicester, Nottingham, Stafford and Coventry; and to supply the royalists in Oxford, Chester, Shrewsbury, Worcester and Bristol.[37] The importance of these trades to the war effort further reinforced the strategic significance of garrison towns, of course.

Clothing and equipment was ordered from prominent merchants – haberdashers, woollen merchants, tailors, shoemakers – and provided employment for large numbers of craftsmen in urban and rural areas. In 1646, for example, 8,000 pairs of shoes were ordered from thirteen shoemakers.[38] The demand for horses stimulated an interest in breeding which was of long-term significance and speeded the decline of local horse markets and fairs. Smithfield prospered, since it was immune from attack and an established national market, but even it was increasingly dominated by a small group of dealers acting on contracts from the army. Elsewhere it was increasingly common to buy through dealers rather than at fairs.[39]

Carrying trades were also in high demand. Parliamentary control of the navy was significant, but the navy was too small to protect all parliamentary shipping or to stop all royalist shipments. Where possible, supplies were moved by sea, therefore, and when the royalists lost their western ports in 1645 it was a serious blow to their war effort. Carters and carriers also did very well though, since land transport had to be used eventually. In May 1643 Charles had 122 carts in his artillery train and at Newbury, later in the summer, had 400 draught horses and oxen. Thomas Bateman, a master wheelwright, did a very good business with the parliamentary armies throughout the 1640s: he supplied 10 wagons to the Earl of Essex early in the war, and was one of twenty-one artificers contracted to supply 120 wagons, one cart, 20 carriages for boats, 20 pontoon boats, 46 grapnells for the boats and 20 harnesses. In the spring of 1645 he was paid £13 each for 21 closed wagons for the New Model, £12 each for 6 open wagons and £5 each for a further 5. We do not know about his margins, of course, but this was big money for a craftsman – an order for £370, which would count as a pretty respectable annual income for a gentleman. He continued this work into the late 1640s and also made gun carriages. Carters were employed for particular purposes too, sometimes in lieu of tax payments, but sometimes for cash: a carter, cart and horse were charged at 2s 6d per day per horse, higher early in the war when supply was short.[40]

Armies waxed and waned in size, but it has been estimated that up to one in ten adult men were in arms during the 1640s.[41] The economic effects of this were likely to have been considerable, although very little is known about it. A brief consideration of some of the known facts is suggestive, however. Numbers in the New Model in the last two years of the war ranged from 24,800 in late May 1645 to a low of 13,400 in January of 1646. The number of horse remained fairly constant, around 5,000 to 6,500, so that the number of infantry in the New Model during this period ranged from perhaps 18,000 down to 7,000. The New Model was only about half of the total parliamentary strength, and the royalists had similar numbers in service in 1645, so that it may be that the total number of infantry ranged from 30,000 to 55,000 in these years.[42] The former is equivalent to the second largest city in the country, the latter is the equivalent of the three largest cities in the country, London excepted.

The infantry were recruited primarily from the lower orders, with labourers predominating. Their wages were continually in arrears, but not necessarily derisory. And no soldiers starved. Between April 1645 and June 1647 the New Model infantry received 76 per cent of their wage. Put the other way, they received 8d per day, as a minimum, 76 per cent of the time, in addition to being clothed and equipped.[43] Agricultural labourers had a better daily wage, but probably fewer days of employment, and are unlikely to have been clothed. Not only did soldiers' wages, even with this level of arrears, make these men more likely to be consumers than recipients of poor relief, but they also made them consumers rather than producers. The other armies were less reliably paid (in fact the New Model drew deserters seeking better conditions), but they add considerably to these figures. Conscription was a less reliable means of filling the armies than pay.[44]

In all this represents a considerable redistribution of wealth. The New Model wage bill was expected to be about £45,000 per month, much of that on the more expensive higher ranks, but much of it was actually paid, and much of it to men of low social status. This was £540,000 per year, in addition to clothing, and to that we would have to add the wages of the other armies. A 'cautious minimum figure' of the total yield of poor relief in 1650 puts it at £100,000: formal taxation paid to labouring men in the army was almost certainly a more significant economic transfer than poor relief, and free quarter would have to be added to that as well. Some of these men, and their dependants, would in more normal times have formed part of the harvest-sensitive population – those whose subsistence was threatened by rising prices and falling wages during a harvest failure. This may be one factor in an explanation for the absence of recorded famine deaths in the later 1640s: the first years of sustained dearth in which England had slipped the shadow of famine.[45] That and, of course, the huge death toll of the years immediately preceding it.

This demand for men must have affected the labour market as a whole. Given that the armies were drawn disproportionately from the labouring population, this is likely to have pushed wages up more generally by withdrawing a measurable proportion of the labouring population from the labour market. In September 1645, for example, there were 18,600 men in the New Model; following the harvest 2,000 men, mainly infantry, were recruited to an army whose overall size we do not know, although in December it contained 14,000 men. The New Model at 14,000 men represented 3 per cent of the male population between 15 and 24, and a little more than 1 per cent of the male population between 16 and 64.[46] To these figures for the New Model in 1645 would have to be added about the same number of parliamentary soldiers in other armies, and similar numbers serving in the royalist armies: in May of that year Charles had 40,000 men in arms, about half of them in garrisons.[47] After the war, the military establishments were more stable, paid more regularly and less exposed to traumatic loss. In May 1647 there were 21,480 in the army, 14,000 of them infantry. Infantry numbers then rose to 16,000 in February 1648, 20,200 in May 1649 and 24,000 the following spring. These infantry figures represent between 3 and 5 per cent of the male population aged 15–24, 1 and 1.5 per cent of the male population between 15 and 59.[48] The effects of this must have been particularly felt at harvest-time, pushing wages up and augmenting the market for food by increasing the non-agricultural population. At Myddle Hill, in Shropshire, in September 1642, Sir Paul Harris was offering a very generous 4s 4d per week to soldiers, with likely consequences for the supply of harvest labour.[49]

Again this might be relevant to the dearth of the late 1640s since, it seems, most famine in this period arose not from an absolute failure of food supply, but from a failure of exchange entitlements:[50] soldiers and agricultural labourers may have had better exchange entitlements as a result of a significant transfer of wealth via national taxation, with benefits to their dependants, resulting in a smaller harvest-sensitive population.

As we have seen, construction work on fortifications was not always achieved by forced or voluntary labour. Men from Upton, Nottinghamshire, seem to have been paid both to construct the massive earthworks at Newark in 1644 and, two years later, to take them down. In the

The Queen's Sconce, part of the civil war defences of Newark

spring of 1644 they were paid 8d per day, comparable with the pay of a foot soldier or for a day mowing hay in Lincolnshire during the 1620s.[51] Thomas Catrowe seems to have had employment as a carpenter in the 'service of the commonwealth' for at least eleven years after 1643, employing 'under him several workmen', particularly in the maintenance of Tilbury Fort. Quarter, as distinct from free quarter, might have been a useful income, another transfer from the taxpayer to the relatively poor. Joane Johnson quartered Col. Thomas Lanes for 'a long time' around 1644 and his case for payment of arrears of pay rested in part on what he owed to her: on this argument he secured £16 of the £20 owing to him (although he subsequently sued her to recover the money for his own use).[52]

Wounded soldiers were often quartered, and the burden and difficulty of dealing with severely wounded men was regarded with alarm. Soldiers' pay was supposed to cover these costs, but of course that was not reliable. Nonetheless, caring for the wounded was also a significant source of income for poor women – the records of the parliamentary army in East Anglia are full of fairly small payments to people of humble means. Cleaning, clothing, repairs, laundry and food provision all provided employments associated with care for the wounded.[53] It goes without saying that many of these people would surely have swapped these steady little earners for peace, but it is important to remember that the war brought benefits alongside the appalling costs. Taxes were raised and spent in the country, and the flow must have been a source of employment for many people. War was not simply a burden.

Some contractors in arms and clothing industries clearly did well, and the benefits of this business seem to have spread to craftsmen in those industries. There were also men of very modest means who signed up, whose pay was usually in arrears, but who were employed, fed and clothed; and there were other employments associated with servicing this massive military effort. But the real money lay in the world of public finance. There is some evidence from earlier in the century that men with liquid capital were particularly attractive as tax collectors, since they could advance sums to the government while recouping it in the localities (in return for a 'poundage' or cut of the proceeds). They could also transfer money using their own personal credit rather than hauling sacks of cash around. Certainly, later in the century, control of the flow of tax money was a source of profit – allowing men to use the balances to underwrite their own business, or even to act as bankers. More lucrative, potentially at least, was to contract for revenue collection – to farm taxes. Some men were able to build significant commercial careers because they were in a position to advance credit to the regime. Governments sold the right to collect customs, and, in the 1650s, the excise, to individual merchants who had the expertise to ensure collection. In return for a guaranteed income, paid on a particular date, the government gave up a slice of the pie. Men like Martin Noell and Thomas Povey grew rich in this way during the 1650s, diversifying into the emerging colonial trades.[54]

During the civil wars many of the services being paid for were secured locally, so that much of the money never left the county in which it was raised. In Worcester during the royalist occupation the monthly tax was about half as much as the entire subsidy of 1641. But the money was spent in the city, as it must have been in most fortified garrison towns. The ongoing work of building and maintaining the defences was paid at what appears to be a standard rate of 8d per day.[55] Almost all of the New Model's supplies, arms aside, came from the locality in which it found itself. In 1645 and 1646 the New Model resorted to free quarter, but this was the last year of the war. Thereafter, it depended on orderly supply and payment. John Cory, a Norwich merchant, both collected and disbursed tax revenue. Between 29 April and 20 November 1644 he paid out £480 to twenty local tradesmen for waistcoats, shirts, breeches, stockings and shoes, and another £313 for cloth.[56] This was a good position to be in – both collecting and spending government money.

Although the roots of this kind of relationship to government go deeper than the 1640s, the opportunities were greatly increased by the massive contracts now required to support the war effort. In these ways the war effort fostered a connection between merchants and government around the public finances. Spending often preceded the receipt of the revenue, and the gap was bridged by borrowing not from the money markets, but from individual suppliers or those handling the revenues. The need for credit and supplies stimulated improvements in the provision of both. There is some evidence that the need to find cash for tax payments accelerated the monetization of local economies, and caused frictions between landlord and tenant over rent levels and tax liabilities, as in the case of the farmers in Surrey who complained to Fairfax about their landlords, not the army: 'your petitioners all rack rented' had borne the charge of free quarter for six years, 'and that freely, without any deduction of rent'. Worse, they now faced rent increases. They sought parliamentary enforcement of a contribution from the landlords. This was a common dispute – the tax legislation imposed the burden on the landlord where the rent was racked (set, that is, at the full market rate) and on the tenant where it was not (being set at a customary or easy rent).[57]

There were winners clearly, but overall the benefits accrued to individuals rather than social classes – there is no evidence of significant structural social change. While some prospered, others were ruined. Ironically, sequestration caused acute difficulties even for Sir Cheney Culpeper, who was unhesitatingly parliamentarian. Taken ill in the early

1640s he had made over his lands to his father in anticipation of his death. He survived but before he could recover the lands war broke out and his royalist father was subject to sequestration, imposed on what were really Sir Cheney's lands.[58] Others paid a high price for royalism, either directly, or in spending their fortune in the service of the King. On the other hand, seized goods and lands enriched others: Oliver Cromwell for example. He had been born into the junior branch of a gentry family, and his personal fortunes had reached a nadir during the 1630s, when he may have been worth only £90 per annum. Rescued by his family, and then by an inheritance, he recovered a secure gentry status with an income of around £300 p.a. At the end of the war, in October 1646, he was granted a pension of £2,500 p.a. from estates confiscated from the Marquess of Winchester.[59]

These contrasting fortunes really represented a redistribution of wealth within the existing social structure, rather than a social revolution, however. Sequestration did not lead to redistribution between social classes, even where it was harshly enforced. In Cornwall, for example, royalist control during the war gave way to parliamentary rule thereafter, and sequestration was severely imposed, but it did not ruin the pre-war gentry class. Across the country as a whole many were allowed to compound at a relatively mild rate – compared to what might have been possible under the legislation – or to repurchase. Even where this did not happen the estates were not taken up by mechanic preachers or shoeless infantrymen.[60] The verdict on the effects of the sale of crown lands is broadly similar.[61]

The same is true of officeholding – purges or exclusions were a disaster for some, an opportunity for others – and there are signs of a slight downward shift in the status of JPs during the 1640s. The King relinquished control of appointments reluctantly as his military position deteriorated. From 1644 onwards Parliament took control of the commissions in the south and east. In Sussex this led to the displacement of twenty-seven men and the induction of twenty-four. There and in Hertfordshire a core of parliamentary activists provided continuity, recruiting friends and relatives as the need arose. But in other counties the changes were more dramatic. In Devon and Warwickshire there were more thorough clear-outs – in Warwickshire fifty-seven men were drafted in following the defeat of the royalist armies. There was a similarly wholesale change of personnel in Wales following the royalist defeat. This did result in a shift towards men of lower gentry status, and dissolved the cousinages that had dominated commissions before the war, but even in the 1650s, when changes were more dramatic, JPs remained gentry figures almost everywhere.[62] In Warwickshire and Cheshire the absence of the greater gentry from wartime administration gave authority to lesser men, who demonstrated that the leading gentry figures were not essential to the maintenance of local government.[63] Elsewhere, however, it was the political complexion rather than the social composition of the local officeholding population that changed – in Somerset, for example, it was political radicalism rather than humble roots that attracted adverse comment.[64]

Justices had rivals, however, in the military administrations and, particularly in parliamentary areas, the proliferating committees. Many places saw the routine of local administration – quarter sessions and assizes – disrupted, and in Somerset, in fact, the county committee was the only effective authority.[65] Junior military commands, committee positions or commissions such as that to William Dowsing to purify churches in East Anglia undoubtedly delivered considerable power to relatively obscure men. There was widespread friction between excise officers – salaried functionaries – and the established local officeholding population, a tension frequently expressed in accusations of corruption.[66]

Many wartime frictions arose from the new-found power of otherwise marginal or dependent men. Among those who left Myddle to fight was Thomas Formaston, 'A very hopeful young man', but there were also a number of men whose prospects in the village did not appear so rosy: Nathaniel Owen, whose 'father was hanged before the wars and the son deserved it in the wars'; Richard Chaloner, bastard son of the blacksmith who had been partly maintained by the parish; William Preece 'of the cave', also known as Scoggan of Goblin Hole; and 'an idle fellow' whose name escaped Richard Gough when he came to write his history of the parish. Preece had served in the Low Countries and as a sergeant in the Trained Bands, but was lame as a result of falling out of a pear tree while trying to commit a robbery.[67] Terrible as it was, military service may have been empowering for men such as these, as well as a way of making a living.

The existence of large armies may have been a help to apprentices, too. A Lambeth apprentice who ran away in June 1645 turned out to have gone via Kingston and Guildford to the army, returning in August with 'our regiment of dragoons'. His master had gone to William Lilly to try to find him, and there was, perhaps, some relief behind the laconic note that he had returned 'of his own accord'.[68] There is certainly evidence that other apprentices had an advantage on their masters, for once. Matthew Inglesbye, apprenticed as a weaver for two years then 'went forth a soldier for the parliament', serving five and a half years. On his return he served his master for another ten months but, he complained, 'the full term of his apprenticeship being now expired, and more' he was denied his freedom. Thomas Sheppard left the service of William King, a baker in Northamptonshire, 'taking notice of several ordinances and Acts of parliament to encourage masters to permit their apprentices to serve the parliament in arms'. In this case, having signed up, he was sued as a runaway, and he may not have been alone in seeing the armies as a way out. William Jennifer, in a similar dispute having left for service in Ireland in the later 1640s, was able to employ the language of national politics to his own advantage: he had served because of 'his good affection to the parliament' and also because he was aware of 'a want of supplies for Ireland against those bloody, barbarous and cruel enemies'.[69]

Apprentices, it seems, could take the chance to escape their masters and even, having served in the wars, to claim their military service against their apprenticeship term. This was not the only means by which they were empowered, of course. There can be little doubt that the surging crowds of 1642, and those to come in 1647, gave power and licence to young men formally subject to strict patriarchal discipline. The term 'roundhead' referred to the enforced hairstyle of the dependent young man; there must have been an appeal in the opportunities offered by war: as in the 'London Prentices' who had humiliated the minister of Marsworth in the summer of 1640, 'triumphing in contempt and derision'. These were perhaps moments when differences were submerged in a shared adolescent identity and licence.[70]

But this was not a faceless war. Soldiers were not simply an alien force having an impact on society, but were often known to the people among whom they lived, particularly garrison soldiers, of course. Nathaniel Owen's 'common practice' during the war 'was to come by night with a party of horse to some neighbour's house and break open the doors, take what they pleased, and if the man of the house was found, they carried him to prison, from whence he could not be released without ransom in money'. But it was Owen who was left to die in the flames by his fellows at Bridgenorth, and who in Gough's opinion deserved to hang.[71] William Preece, Scoggan of Goblin Hole, also worked off a pre-war grudge. He was made governor of a garrison at Abright, and when a group of parliamentary soldiers arrived in town he recognized an old adversary, Phillip Bunny. He broke off from his old soldier's tricks (he had stood in a window shouting, 'Let such a number go to such a place, and so many to such a place; and let twenty come with me', although he had only eight men at his command) to take up a grudge. Taking up a fowling gun he shouted, 'Bunny, have at thee!', and shot him through the leg, killing the horse. Following the war many royalist activists were 'troubled by the Parliament party', but not Scoggan: 'he that sits on the ground can fall no lower'.[72] War turned Scoggan, one of a kind normally invisible to history, into a local character, whose doings were remembered fifty years later.

As in other wars, some women also had new opportunities. Women petitioners in London had pushed at the boundaries of respectable female behaviour, claiming a traditional voice as defenders of their children but using it to make specific policy recommendations to the House of Lords. Some had voted in the elections to the Long Parliament, and others took public oaths – the Protestation or the Solemn League and Covenant. Women lent money, paid taxes, followed the armies and treated the sick. Their lives were no more insulated from the war than those of men; they too had felt the burdens but saw some of the opportunities. Elizabeth Alkin, 'Parliament Joan', was active in the news business, like a number of others – the new freedom of the press offering an opportunity to find a voice, and to serve the public good. Women were also employed as emissaries, their female skills and status allowing them to feel out the possibilities for more formal contacts, and a number of women played very significant military roles. Henrietta Maria, like Lady Macbeth, was reviled for her undue influence over her husband, particularly after the revelation of their letters in the *Kings Cabinet opened*. When a cannonade forced her from her lodgings at Bridlington in February 1643 it was thought to be ungentlemanly, but she was subsequently known as the she-generalissima. This gender ambiguity was evident elsewhere – in the career of Lucy Hutchinson or of the Countess of Derby. Lucy, however, always presented herself as the loyal wife, her views no more than an expression of her devotion to her husband.[73]

These public and martial roles posed a kind of challenge to patriarchy – at least in principle. The King's cause had suffered when 120 women were reported to have been taken in arms at Nantwich, in January 1644, and from the persistent accusation that he was in thrall to his wife.[74] It is not too fanciful to see in these gender troubles a reason for the acute anxieties aroused by John Milton's pamphlet on divorce. It was one of the publications that prompted Ephraim Pagitt to go into print with his denunciation of numerous schisms, heresies and errors of the 1640s. In contemporary polemic these gender troubles were a manifestation of the problem of order, of civil chaos, which seemed an important feature of the war. Political disorder was reflected both in sexual licence – a particular form of gender disorder – and in the intrusion of the feminine into the public arena. The world was governed by opinion (female) rather than knowledge (male), and by a parliament of women.[75]

Above all, though, it was in the sectarian scare that these anxieties about gender roles were most evident. Women preachers were a kind of *reductio ad absurdum* of the claims of the uneducated to preach – as in *A discoverie of Six women preachers*, which ridiculed the pretensions of middling-sort women to religious insight. Their 'manners, life, and doctrine [were] pleasant to be read, but horrid to be judged of', and the key scriptural text was I Corinthians xiv, 34–5:

Let your women keep silence in the Churches, for it is not permitted unto them to speak, but they are commanded to be under obedience, as also saith the Law. And if they will learn anything, let them ask their husbands at home: for it is a shame for women to speak in the Church.[76]

A common theme in stories about the corrosive effects of sectarianism was how virtuous women were led astray from the patriarchal authority of the godly household by false prophets, and this fear resonated widely. Alarmed by what he saw around him in Lincolnshire in 1646, Colonel King demanded that the Grand Jury in Lincolnshire present all 'Papists, Anabaptists, Brownists, Separatists, Antinomians and Heretics, who take upon them boldness to creep into houses, and lead captive silly women to sins'.[77]

These fears about female independence were not groundless; but neither were they proportionate. Women were prominent in the sects during the 1640s – the dependence on direct revelation cancelling contemporary assumptions about the inferiority of female reason and learning. The reformation of the spirit, with its relative distrust of the scripture and learned divinity, was easily satirized as a licence for ignorant women to preach, and it did certainly give a voice to some women. During the 1640s there was a steady flow of prophetic pamphlets. Some of them retold apparently ancient prophecies: the publisher Richard Harper fought something of a paper war, with a constantly escalating number of visions offering to give meaning and direction to the current confusion. But the 1640s also boasted an unusual number of living prophets, many of them women. John Thomas, founder of the newsbook and ally of Pym's in the world of print, had spent time and money in November 1641 printing a pamphlet retailing the visions of a maidservant from Worksop.[78] Sarah Wight was to become briefly famous in 1647, when despair and illness drove her to suicide attempts and fasting. In the midst of these travails she began to experience trances in which she spoke from scriptures, and ministers came to take down notes. By September she had recovered, but she had achieved celebrity. She entered into print, too, her story one of rebirth which was of more general relevance to Puritan piety, but this presence in print was mediated by male divines and authors. Little is known about her besides this: female prophecy was a fleeting, mediated, kind of power.[79]

This filled a role rather like astrology, but was a distinctively feminine realm, or at least a sphere in which women had easier access to public authority. But, for that very reason, sects were regarded with suspicion, as potentially subversive of stable patriarchal order. Prophecy was dangerously subversive in other ways – an authentic personal revelation overrode the claims of law, custom, status and tradition. As a licence for change it was very alluring; but it was an authority to be urged with caution. The validation and interpretation of visions were highly problematic.[80]

There were others too – Elizabeth Poole, who prophesied to the General Council of the Army, and Mary Cary. And women wrote theology as well as uttering prophecy. One of Thomas Edwards's chief interlocutors in his role as hammer of the sects was Katherine Chidley; in fact she was one of the only writers to respond to Edwards in 1641 – a source of irritation to him in itself. She had a long career as proselytizer in the Independent churches in London, as a pamphleteer and, later, Leveller petitioner. Lady Eleanor Davies, for further example, published at least thirty-seven tracts between 1641 and 1652.[81]

But while these women found a voice, and some of them found considerable influence, they often sought to present themselves in ways that conformed to convention – the relative independence of these women did not necessarily lead them to call for, or enact, radical action or social transformation. Within the Independent churches men often continued to claim a spiritual superiority, and the Levellers did not seek to extend the parliamentary franchise to women; their claim was for a spiritual rather than civic equality. For the Levellers, the cornerstone of political decency was the household, and their view of that institution was in many ways conventional. This was more generally true of women's writing during the period, which claimed a voice for women without, on the whole, repudiating male authority. Much the same has been said of the women who petitioned and demonstrated, notably Elizabeth Lilburne, wife of John. Women active in print, and politics more widely, often worked for 'less spectacular, all-consuming goals, such as sustaining businesses, households, and families'.[82]

John Taylor famously claimed that the world was being turned upside down and many of his readers may have believed him. We know that there were even some people who actually did want to see the world turned upside down. There is also little doubt about the practical disruption of the routines of local life: the absence of quarter sessions and assizes, the absence of established governors, the disruptions caused by tax demands and troop movements. In many ways, however, the routines of social life survived. In 1645 clubmen movements were to claim a voice for the rural middling sort, and even some of their poor neighbours, but in a respectable political idiom. The same was true of many of the women who emerged into public view, and may have been true of most men too. Established habits survived in a more profound sense too: in the persistence of familiar languages and metaphors of political life. Cheap print is full of the same stock of ideas which had served to make sense of the world before 1642: that no new languages had been found which could deal with the new circumstances was in fact an important part of the problem. Honour codes had emerged and survived, albeit under strain; order had been imposed, more or less, on the exaction of resources to support the war. We will never have any quantitative certainty about these things, but it seems likely that the fears were much worse than the reality.

That is not the main, or only, point, however: anxieties were probably of more political significance than realities, and fuelled a desire to protect these fundamental values. Moreover, our difficulty in assessing how seriously to take the fears expressed in these pamphlets mirrors a widespread contemporary uncertainty about the trustworthiness of cheap print. Lack of certainty is no reassurance in the face of anxiety; and anxiety, however unjustified by actual conditions, is a potent political force.

By 1645 there were no signs of a social revolution, despite contemporary fears and satirical attacks on upstart governors. Clearly, military, economic and governmental opportunities arose for relatively humble men and some women. Some eminent men lost their shirts, or their offices. The New Model Army officer corps included men of middling status, but continued to be leavened by the sons of the gentry and aristocracy,[83] local government and Parliament were still peopled by the landed classes. There were mechanic preachers, of course, but they were heavily outnumbered by Oxbridge graduates in possession of church livings. Nonetheless there were clearly benefits as well as costs, and Self-Denial was not a confected political issue: fortunes were being made and opportunities taken up as others suffered dreadfully.

15

Remaking the Local Community

The Politics of Parishes at War

Speaking on 9 December 1644 about the previous summer's campaigns, Oliver Cromwell had warned that 'the people can bear the war no longer'. His point was that it was important to win the war before that point was reached, although others might well have drawn a different conclusion from the same observation.[1] About the temper of the times, however, he seems to have been absolutely right. Nine days later, at Wem, in Shropshire, 1,200 clubmen gathered to defend their communities from the consequences of the war.[2] In fact, at a number of points during 1645 the garrisons and field armies of both sides encountered local forces of this kind. Hereford had been besieged by 5,000 clubmen in March, while another group had effectively assisted the parliamentary army following Langport: capturing royalist horses, arms and fleeing soldiers, blocking the roads to Bristol and joining in the siege of Bridgewater. On other occasions in the western campaigns, however, Fairfax and Cromwell had met less friendly clubmen, particularly in Dorset, where the claimed neutrality of some clubmen was rightly suspected to be a cover for royalism.[3]

Although they differed from locality to locality and over time (after September 1645 it was clear that Parliament was going to win, and so a neutralist stance had a different meaning), this was recognizably a general phenomenon. Such mobilizations have been identified in four broad groups: in Shropshire, Worcestershire and Herefordshire, between January and March; in Wiltshire, Dorset and Somerset between May and September; in Berkshire, Hampshire and Sussex in September and October; and in south Wales and the border between August and November.[4] In the end they posed little threat to the garrisons and field armies, and both royalists and parliamentarians asserted military control over them at different points, but fighting a war with such movements in train would clearly become complicated.

Comparatively little is known about the clubmen. In Shropshire the movement seems to have been prompted by the ill-discipline and depredations of royalist troops under Vangerris. Elsewhere there was a similar relationship between the activities of a particular commander and the organization of resistance – in Herefordshire it was Barnabas Scudamore's troops and in Somerset it was Goring's.[5] More generally, of course, it was in counties which saw the most active campaigning by field armies that the clubmen were located: the counties enumerated above were all prominent in the campaigns of the previous two and a half years. But there are some puzzles. There were no clubmen in the counties of the east Midlands, Cheshire or Lancashire, where there was a lot of military activity, and in Worcestershire the clubmen originated from the area of the county least affected by the fighting.[6]

The initiative in Shropshire found echoes in meetings in Worcestershire in March 1645 at Woodbury Hill and Malvern, the same month that clubmen had laid siege to Hereford.[7] By that time men were also being mobilized in Dorset and in May large numbers of men from Dorset and Wiltshire assembled at Gussage Corner, near Wimborne St Giles (Dorset). On 2 June there was another large meeting, at Castle Cary, Somerset.[8] The Sussex movement arose from a meeting in September, but was over as an effective protest four days later.[9] The numbers involved were impressive. In Berkshire it was claimed that 16,000 people had joined and in Wiltshire and Dorset it was claimed (and not denied) that 20,000 men could be raised within forty-eight hours.[10] If remotely true, this compares favourably with the military mobilizations of the two field armies, which took much longer and did not reach numbers significantly beyond this.

Some of the movements seem to have had identifiable preferences between the two sides – those in mid-Somerset were probably pro-parliamentarian, as were those in the cheese-producing country of Wiltshire, while those on the Dorset downlands and in Worcestershire were fairly clearly royalist.[11] Information about how the movements were mobilized is patchy, and there were undoubtedly differences among them. But, despite these differences, there were some underlying similarities in the ways that these movements harnessed traditions of communal self-government and applied them creatively to the new conditions of massive military mobilization.

In Somerset the clubmen were drawn from among the ranks of the yeomanry, and the most significant leader was of a status just below that of the gentry. Four leading figures in the Shropshire movement, who can be tentatively identified, were village notables and a minor clergyman. In Herefordshire the leadership seems to have come from among the ranks of the village worthies, too.[12] In a number of other cases, however, gentlemen and clergy joined the movements, and that may have changed their aims. Nonetheless, the clubman associations bear testimony to the traditions of village self-government that remained very important during the 1640s. They expressed their politics in demonstrative forms which were also familiar from a longer tradition. The Somerset men wore ribbons calling for peace and truth, and everywhere they generated petitions, delegations and declarations. In the south-west they often convened at the sites of ancient hill forts, places used for other such communal gatherings.[13] It may be, in fact, that the clubman associations took root most strongly where gentry influence was weak – in areas with extensive smallholdings and a correspondingly more limited gentry presence – since when a gentry leadership existed these energies were likely to be channelled in other directions.[14] There is some evidence of mutual awareness – the Somerset clubmen clearly acted in the light of what had happened to their fellows in Dorset, for example; there were connections between the Herefordshire and Shropshire movements, and between the events in Shropshire and rumours of a rising in Monmouthshire.[15]

A central concern of the surviving manifestos seems to have been the regulation of soldiers' behaviour and of garrisons. In Herefordshire the intention was to 'have the governor and soldiers out of [the garrison at Hereford]' but in Wiltshire the demand was more limited: that each side reduce the number of garrisons, and that those which were really necessary be maintained at local charge and put into the hands of 'the . . . county', unless command was transferred by order of both King and Parliament.[16] In fact the Herefordshire demands seem more anti-war than the more formal positions stated elsewhere, but it might be significant that they are often reported from a letter from a semi-hostile observer, Colonel Massey, the parliamentary governor of Gloucester. In fact, it might be that clubmen were strong where military command was weak – where there was no authority with which to negotiate the demands of war.[17]

In Dorset and Sussex, where fairly full manifestos survive, clubmen do not seem to have been against formal taxation either.[18] The Dorset association was mobilized to 'preserve ourselves from plunder and all other unlawful violence'. This was to be done through local men of note: 'the ablest men for wisdom, valour, and estate, inhabitants of the same' were to be appointed for each town, tithing, parish and great hamlet. They would set watches, disarm soldiers caught 'plundering or doing any other unlawful violence'. Searches would be undertaken only by local officeholders – the constables and tithingmen. In Sussex too a principal complaint, and motive for the movement, was that 'by free quarter and plunder of soldiers our purses have been exhausted'. They also complained of

insufferable, insolent, arbitrary power that hath been used amongst us, contrary to all our ancient known laws, or ordinances of parliament . . . by some particular persons stepped into authority who have delegated their power to men of sordid condition whose wills have been laws and commands over our bodies and estates.

But this was not opposition to formal, warranted exactions. They distinguished between known ancient laws and ordinances, but the complaint was about completely unwarranted and arbitrary actions – they did not denounce constitutional innovation, but lawlessness, and they did not denounce the cost of the armies, but its unregulated impact. In Dorset the *quid pro quo* of local regulation of unlawful violence and plunder was that 'the weekly contribution money and all other provision and necessary maintenance for armies, if it be demanded by a lawful warrant directed to an officer of the place, be not denied, but every man as he is able in some reasonable proportion forthwith to contribute'. Quarter would be provided if by Order Martial, 'the soldier is to be friendly entertained, he behaving himself fairly'. In Sussex a catalogue of maladministration and illegality in the raising and spending of money was a prelude for a demand that 'five or six gentlemen' be appointed by the county's MPs to take accounts there. Sequestration was not denounced, but those subject to sequestration were to be given a speedy and fair hearing according to the processes laid out, and those who had complied with royal authority during the time of its pre-eminence should not be punished. They also called for local participation in the division of the burden of taxation – again the point is to regularize the impact of the war.

What we know of the Worcestershire movement confirms this impression. The Worcestershire Grand Jury in October 1644 had petitioned the Governor of Worcester that 'whensoever any soldiers . . . shall commit any robbery or violence, the county may rise upon them and bring them to justice', and petitioned in similar terms in January 1645.[19] This disposition seems to have been reflected in the subsequent clubman movement, which has been characterized as anti-disorder, not anti-tax: the Woodbury league committed itself to support a royalist declaration laying down orders for the assessment; they did not denounce the tax in itself. The royalists gave commitments to submit the demands of the war to control by legitimate local officers – for example, Grand Jury approval had been sought for a new military association in the west. But it was in part the formation of this association which prompted the Shropshire movement, which sought to reassert the authority of local notables and established local institutions.[20] These various local initiatives had in common a desire to regulate the war by the means local communities had traditionally used to deal with the demands of national government. In general they did not oppose taxation or garrisons *per se*, but plunder, free quarter and crime: these were movements for the better regulation of the war as much as for an immediate end to it.

Implied in these manifestos is a sense that the war was something external to local life – like bad weather it was something to be dealt with rather than abolished. In Dorset, for example, those raising an outcry or assembly for or against either side would no longer enjoy the protection of the association and in Sussex their proposals were predicated on their own defence of the county's frontiers.[21] But there are clear signs that the national political debate that caused the war was not external to local discussions. The Wiltshire movement called for a settlement on the basis of the Protestation and the treaty of Uxbridge, demanding that once a negotiation was opened the King (not both sides) should enter a cessation.[22] Many clubmen referred to the recent failure of the Uxbridge negotiations, suggesting that their patience was worn out by the failure of negotiations. In Shropshire, in fact, they may have been responding directly to a royal proclamation from the late summer of 1644, calling for the raising of provincial forces under commanders of their own choosing, to march on London and force Parliament to seek peace. Both the Somerset and Shropshire gentry had subsequently petitioned for peace.[23] Like the clubmen in Wiltshire those in Somerset and Worcestershire echoed the language of the Protestation, while in Worcestershire their demands were also permeated by the language of moderate royalism. In Worcestershire, however, this moderate royalism was compounded with the virulent anti-popery more easily reconciled with the parliamentary cause. In Dorset, only Protestants, and those not in arms for either party, would enjoy the protection of the association.[24] In a number of cases, too, attachment to the Prayer Book, as distinct from the Directory of Worship, seems to have played a significant part. In Sussex they complained of 'the want of church government, whereby our churches are decayed, God's ordinances neglected, orthodox ministers cast out without cause and never heard, mechanicks and unknown persons thrust in'.[25]

These national arguments were refracted through the prism of local concerns for the regulation of religious and civil life. The clubmen were not anti-government, or apolitical, but they were focused on immediate local realities. They have been dismissed as apathetic and untouched by the great issues of the war, or celebrated as the moderating voice of the local community. In general, however, they were not turning their backs on the war and its practical needs, nor on the issues: they were clearly engaged with national politics at the same time that they sought local regulation of the demands of the war. Their demands were publicized in print, as were denunciations of them by their opponents. Their local campaigns were prompted by, and fed back into, developments in national politics.[26]

These movements were a creative adaptation of traditions of self-government at the King's command, an attempt to accommodate new realities, and pressing political concerns. They combined formal and informal aspects of village authority – patterns of government and of collective action. It is quite likely that they wanted an end to war, armies and taxes, but they did not say so: these local initiatives sought an accommodation with national politics, not immunity from them.

Although there is hardly any evidence about the identity of individual clubmen, their habits and activities in Dorset and Wiltshire bore close resemblance to those of enclosure rioters. In April 1643 men from Mere in Wiltshire had issued a proclamation summoning the inhabitants to assemble at White Hill on market day. From there they were to march, with drums and muskets, to throw down enclosures in the forests. Over the next couple of months groups of up to 300 assembled to do this work – a forceful, organized demonstration akin to the later clubman mobilization, rather than a spontaneous riot indiscriminate in its targets. Those rioters who can be identified in these years (not many of the total number involved) come from the ranks of artisans and smallholders, like those who can be identified among the clubmen.[27] The connections were even closer in May 1645, when men from Gillingham and Motcombe, en route for a general rendezvous of clubmen near Shaftesbury, tore up hedges and other enclosures. On the way home they did the same, beating a servant of Thomas Brunker (agent to the Earl of Elgin, a major local encloser) and leaving him for dead. As with many other civil war mobilizations, then, the clubmen movement was probably a coalition, and it afforded opportunities to pursue other agendas. Brunker himself said as much: 'The club army which I feared would put boldness into them concerning our forest business, hath brought them to this insolency, before they stood in some awe of commanders and soldiers, now they respect no man nor will give any obedience to any but contemn all superiors whatsoever and do what they please'.[28] The clubman leaders, in fact, may have been rather unusual figures.[29]

As in the first two years of the Long Parliament the war years provided opportunities for those with other grievances – these were political issues, for sure, but not very directly related to the partisan political issues over which the war was being fought. Over the previous three years the absence of effective quarter sessions and assizes had made it difficult to pursue and punish rioters in the forests of Dorset and Wiltshire.[30] The interruption of court activity elsewhere offered similar opportunities to reopen local disputes over resources – in fens and forests those seeking to assert traditional common rights against improvers and enclosers had another chance to stake their claims. The disputes in Waltham and Windsor extended into 1643 and there were other disputes in Duffield, Derbyshire, and in Neroche and Frome Selwood in Somerset. Forest rights were not at issue in the national dispute – attacks on prerogative courts had rendered forest jurisdictions relatively toothless, but the policy of enclosure and improvement, although contested, was not at issue between King and Parliament. John Pym, for example, had been an agent of crown forest policy in the south-west.[31]

The same was true in the Fens, where parliamentary policy soon came to favour agricultural improvement over established common rights and where Cromwell was no more a champion of the commoners than were the Earl of Manchester or Charles I. But in 1645 sluices were opened on the Isle of Axholme and the houses of French and Dutch settlers attacked. Here the action was explicitly linked to the interruption of effective legal authority. Rioters contemptuously dismissed a Lords order of 10 December 1645 calling for an end to the riots, saying 'they did not care a fart for the order which was made by the Lords and published in the Churches', insisting they would go on with their work. These events were a prelude to a sustained attack on the enclosures in the Isle. Elsewhere in the Fens rioting was more limited, but at Whittlesey and Ramsay commoners were clearly aware that an opportunity had come their way.[32]

Such events were made emblematic of more general problems, of course. All sides sought to mobilize opinion behind their projects, but were also quick to denounce the dangers being courted when their opponents did so. In Kent in 1643, for example, two blacksmiths were at the head of twenty men plundering the house of a parliamentarian gentleman. Parry the Smith was reported as saying, 'we have sped well here. Let us go to Hadlow and Peckham and plunder there, for they are rich rogues, and so we will go away into the woods'. Smale objected: 'But we must plunder none but Roundheads', eliciting a 'great oath' from Smith and the riposte that 'We will make every man a Roundhead that hath anything to lose. This is the time we look for'.[33] Royalists in Kent could not be complacent about these attempts to mobilize the men without shirts.

In fact, much of what we know about demonstrations against enclosures confirms that they were disciplined, a form of communal politics familiar from before the war. They were demonstrative – summoned and processing to the accompaniment of drums and carrying arms which were, on the whole, not used against people. They represented a statement of intent. The published version of the demands of the Dorset clubmen made similar reference to the force which underlay the movement – but the point was usually forceful demonstration rather than planned violence.[34] The violence which did occur was targeted primarily against property, not persons, and that against persons was not indiscriminate. Similarly, the organization was sophisticated – for example, those throwing down enclosures gathered in groups of two, since that evaded the legal definition of a riot. And they were tactically astute. In Gillingham the rioters apparently aimed at depriving the Earl of Elgin of all profits from the forest, by threats, backed up 'where necessary' with assault, destruction of property and seizure of cattle for ransom. Unpleasant this undoubtedly was, but it was not random or apolitical.[35] It was nonetheless true that civil war was making all forms of politics potentially more lethal: those opposing the rioters during the 1640s seem more often to have been armed, and that contributed to an escalation of the violence.[36]

Clubmen evidently mobilized in ways that drew upon these traditions of popular protest, and those forms of protest clearly persisted. In that sense, clubman leaders were trying to inflect a more traditional form of communal demonstration as a contribution to the politics of the civil war. Whatever their actual politics, in relation to the civil war and more immediate local issues, the clubmen were an unwelcome addition to the political scene. Colonel Massey had been bemused and suspicious of the Herefordshire clubmen, noting that they had resisted his invitation to 'join with me in observing the parliament's commands'.[37] Here was the rub – they were mobilizing without warrant, while at the same time claiming to uphold lawful regulation of violence and financial exaction. Their warrant, we might assume, derived from the local community – a claim with rather radical implications, if spelt out clearly, which it was not. Few English people relished the thought of armies being raised at the initiative of village worthies, without gentry or aristocratic leadership. It was a parliamentarian newsbook which expressed the fear that 'They will have an army without a king, a lord or a gentleman almost'.[38] It was also a practical issue, of course – Massey had noted that the Herefordshire clubmen wanted his help, '(for they dare trust me), but they will not yet declare themselves for Parliament but they conceive themselves able to keep off both the Parliament's forces and the King's also from contribution and quarter in their county'.[39] Neutralism was usually interpreted negatively by partisans, as covert sympathy for the other side. In Herefordshire, when the opportunity arose, the royalists crushed the clubmen, and the New Model also dispatched those considered hostile with little ceremony. The parliamentary coverage of the movements varied between relish of their anti-royalism in Herefordshire, and contempt for their illegitimacy in Sussex and Hampshire (both movements that took off in the face of an incipient parliamentary victory). Charles, on the other hand, made reassuring noises, but could not restrain the excesses of his commanders which fed the movements.[40]

*

Derbyshire did not see clubmen, but Sir John Gell, the parliamentary commander in Derby, did meet with a similar expression of communal politics in the summer of 1645, in the form of protests against the excisemen. The excise was a particularly unpopular tax – resented for the fact that it fell on goods regarded as necessities such as meat and salt, and for the fact that it was in the hands of outsiders, not local officeholders. Worse still, those excises that fell on inland commodities were often raised in marketplaces. The arrival of commissioners, and their intrusion into the marketplace, created a potential confrontation, and in that confrontation the poor might have allies among local officeholders.[41]

In May 1645 the Derby Committee had written to the Speaker of the House of Commons complaining that the excise was a burden on the countrymen and the soldiers.[42] This coincided with the organized demonstration encountered in Derby by John Flatchett, an excise sub-commissioner, on 23 May 1645, a market day.[43] It may be that the committee invited the protest; they certainly did little to help Flatchett face it down. Flatchett and his men had been at work for five or six days prior to that, but on market day two women went 'up and down the town' beating drums and proclaiming that anyone unwilling to pay the excise should join them and beat the commissioners out of town. Beating a drum was a means of summoning people to work – as on the roads in Blackheath in 1640 – as well as the work of communal protest – as in the enclosure riots in Wiltshire in 1645.[44] Commissioners in Haverfordwest had a similar experience the previous September, beaten out of the marketplace by angry women from whom the authorities were apparently unable to protect them. Women were prominent in market disputes because it was they who handled the day-to-day transactions of the marketplace.[45]

Seeking help from the mayor, the excisemen were told that they had brought it on themselves and could expect little help. Clearly, they could expect no sympathy either. The mayor did, however, take the excisemen to see the Recorder (the city's legal officer), Lieutenant-Colonel Thomas Gell. He said that one of the women beating the drums was married to a soldier and that he dared not interfere for fear of causing a mutiny. In any case, the mayor said that he had not heard any drums, although the effect of that intervention was rather spoiled when one of the women beat her drum on the market cross, underneath his window. The mayor did then go out to speak to her, and the drumming stopped, but it turned out that he had promised that the excise would not be collected until a reply was received to the letter sent to Parliament. Admitting defeat, the excisemen left it at that.[46]

Six weeks later they returned, and again there were no problems until market day. On that day, however, 4 July, Edward Burrow, a soldier who had been assisting the excisemen in delivering warrants and distraining goods for non-payment, was chained to the bullring by protesters from 4 a.m. to 2 p.m. It is this detail that suggests that the hostility was here directed against the excises on meat. The drumming was also heard again, but when the excisemen went to Colonel Sir John Gell, one of whose troopers it was who was chained to the bullring, they got no help in collecting the excise (or, as they put it, upholding Parliament's ordinance and authority). Gell, asked either to punish the women or to take them into custody, replied instead that 'he did not use to meddle with women unless they were handsome'.[47]

This disturbance was clearly more than an uprising of the dispossessed, unable to bear the burdens of the war any longer. The tensions between the excisemen and the local authorities were not uncommon. Neither was the apparent sympathy of local governors, who were perhaps accepting their much-stated obligations to protect their poorer neighbours or entering into an unusual alliance in order to protect their own authority from encroachment.[48] At the same time the intertwining of military and civil authority was not necessarily easy, but the ambiguity also meant that soldiers were not necessarily the enemies of the people, or anonymous outsiders. Although the armies depended on the excise for their pay, soldiers were sometimes associated with resistance to its collection, and in 1647 the attitude of a radicalized army to the proposed abolition of the excise was ambiguous.[49] In Derby there was at least a four-way tension: between army, excisemen, local civil authority and the local population. Again this may not have been unusual, and in these multi-dimensional local conflicts appeal to authority was common. It was Parliament that should reply, the presence of their representatives should ensure collection and refusal to pay was an affront to Parliament's authority. As with the fen and forest disturbances, there was order within the disorder – the protest was organized, targeted and employed a symbolism that communicated a specific grievance.

Authority in English villages was exercised personally and its effectiveness rested as much on local reputation as formal warrant. The civil war created new offices, staffed by people who did not have the qualities of a natural governor, or the local reputation and influence to mediate conflicts. Arbitrariness was often a personal quality as much as a formal one – as the clubmen's petitions had made clear. Here the poor and disaffected could find common cause with their social superiors whose own pre-eminence was challenged by these new offices. Excisemen were denounced in terms of a biblical plague – caterpillars devouring local crops to feed their own insatiable appetites. Behind this hostility lay a brute fact – they were earning a living through the collection of taxes rather than collecting taxes as part of the obligations of a prominent local man.

The proliferating committees of Parliament's local administration also prompted this kind of hostility. Rancorous conflicts between established local gentlemen and committeemen, or between committees and sub-committees, have been documented in Cheshire, Staffordshire, Kent, Cheshire, Sussex, Somerset and elsewhere. They all resonated more deeply, with a more humble objection to these forms of authority and the burdens they imposed. In fact, in most counties there was no dramatic difference in the status of the county's governors, but there was a proliferation of offices, complicating the relationships between them and fostering jurisdictional disputes and rivalries. These arguments were not only about the personal qualities of this emergent group of governors – there were clear worries too about how their powers might be formally limited, an important concern in discussions about excisemen too.[50]

It seems that 1645 was an important year for the development of these disputes, as a campaign to abolish the committees built up a head of steam, creating common cause among partisans with quite different views on what the national settlement should look like.[51] It is again striking how the new conditions of the 1640s also offered opportunities for new kinds of mobilization – in print, for example. Humphrey Willis, the clubman leader of whom we know most, published a pamphlet denouncing the Somerset county committee in 1647, and many of these county disputes were retailed for a national audience. As with the exemplary stories of providential judgements, local political battles were retold to a national audience through the London presses. Local battles in the parliamentary administration were pursued at Westminster, and used there as emblematic of the larger issues in the conflict.[52] The basis of

Times Whirligig, by a former clubman leader,
satirized Somerset's new low-born governors

local order was experienced as a local issue, but was of national significance, and had significance for the national political battle.

In Warwickshire, however, these disputes had an ideological dimension – they resembled a local version of the national debate about what
costs were acceptable to secure a victory. The county committee was
dominated by militants and their defence of their powers against the
Earl of Denbigh's association early in the war was in their eyes a defence
of the county's capacity to fight the royalists. Similarly, their defence of
themselves against the sub-committee of accounts, which was dominated
by Denbigh's supporters, was a defence of their capacity to fight the
war. Taking accounts in that context was a more loaded political statement, and both moderates and militants could identify their local cause
as part of the larger national argument. As John Bryan argued in a
sermon in 1646, people should not resent or murmur at the impositions
of Parliament, 'seeing we enjoy our lives, liberties, privileges, estates and
religion (all which were at stake and almost lost)'. The great difference

between these taxes and 'those which formerly our taskmasters laid upon us' was that 'Those were in design to ruin and enslave us to arbitrary power, these are to preserve us from it'.[53] Willingness to pay could be a test of commitment: as two Lancashire constables complained to the Justices, they had collected a rate and paid it to the benefit of the 'public', but could not collect it in full because some refused and also 'withdrew others (honestly affected) from co-operation'.[54] During the war, both nationally and locally, a desire to take accounts was often closely linked with a criticism of policy – it was how the money was being spent which was at stake.[55]

These disputes were not necessarily localist in the sense of inhabiting a narrowly bounded political world, oblivious to the larger battles being fought out in London and Oxford and on the battlefields. They might also reflect a habit of seeing the big issues in terms of local arrangements. This was a habit of thought familiar to all those who had heard a local sermon or read any seventeenth-century legal writing – small transgressions threatened the gravest sins or contraventions of the most fundamental principles. As with any other political argument in the 1640s, the attack on committeemen might be a vehicle for a number of purposes.

These local movements to defend or attack the powers of individuals or institutions were not a retreat into an apolitical bucolic idyll, but a resort to forms of solidarity and authority common before the war. A community, however, was a political body, whose institutions, obligations and membership might be contested. Community politics were not necessarily harmonious, and values such as tradition and deference might be means to attack those in power as well as to cow those without it. Certainly, local communities in early modern England were not the happy organic bodies of later nostalgic myth. New forms of authority, and new languages of politics, provided new kinds of local political order, and the resistance to these new orders drew on tradition and the new opportunities for the pursuit of local grievances thrown up by the war. Clubmen, excise rioters and attacks on committeemen were print phenomena too, publicized for a national audience. Others engaged with the national political scene more opportunistically – in the fen and forest disturbances, for example. But even here the disputes were not separate from, or unaware of, national politics, and they too might be played out for a national audience.

*

Close to the centre of these communal politics was the self-governing parish, which was under threat. The spiritual role of the parish was also threatened by the development of other forms of communion and by the loud polemical battle over the identity of English Protestantism. In some respects the ties of community might blunt the edge of religious zeal so that, for example, the abstract threat of popery was not always identified closely with actual Catholics living near by. Similarly, a frequent complaint of the godly was that the ties of neighbourliness blinded people to the dangers of religious error: that a kind of 'popular pelagianism' existed, in which it was thought that agreeable fellows would be saved, that a good neighbour must be a good Christian. Worse, it was said, countrymen mistook forms of idleness and sin for a virtuous good fellowship. All this said, however, it is very striking that the embrace of neighbourliness and community was provisional. Scolding women, disobedient servants, and the disreputable or vagrant poor – those who fell outside the boundaries of locally acceptable behaviour – could expect little charity or fellowship.[56]

On the other hand, successive attempts at purgation had corroded the legitimacy of some of the institutions through which Christian community had previously been fostered, notably the parish as a unified religious body. Partisan religious contest robbed the church, or particular incumbents, of the claim legitimately to embody the local Christian community. Ministers were ejected at the petition of their parishioners; others intruded into their places might face 'much opposition from disaffected persons'.[57] This was at the heart of the controversy over Independency, of course, and differences about the essence, and expression, of Christian community had been expressed through ejections of scandalous ministers and iconoclasm. County committees were frequently divided over what should replace bishops and parishes – to what extent membership of a congregation should be voluntary or geographically determined.[58] The counterpart to that, of course, was the extent to which the parish remained a spiritual community. Church courts, previously reasonably attractive institutions through which to police local spiritual life, had ceased to function in 1642.[59]

This was not simply a theoretical question: at the same time that these established forms were disrupted, divisive attempts at reformation and purgation were taking place across England. The history of Suffolk was once written as an exemplification of the view that English counties were in general autonomous gentry-led political communities, and that national administrative initiatives were an unwelcome and intermittently effective intrusion. But Suffolk had seen many ejections of scandalous ministers under the authority of a parliamentary committee, and had shared in William Dowsing's iconoclasm during 1643 and 1644. These attempts at purification of the Christian community were of much more than local significance: in each case the local was understood as the expression of transcendent issues in microcosm.[60] Activists could be found everywhere, taking advantage of the times to press their own vision of godly Protestantism.

One of the most dramatic forms of purgation for the Christian community was the prosecution of witches and in 1645 East Anglia saw the largest witch-hunt in English history. At the Essex assizes held on 17 July 1645, three days after Naseby, thirty-six witches were put on trial. Nineteen were executed, nine died in prison and a further six were still in gaol in 1648. Only one was acquitted. Not only was this an unusually large number of trials in such a short space of time; it was also a prelude to a much wider prosecution across East Anglia. In Norfolk forty trials probably led to twenty executions. There were trials in Huntingdonshire, Cambridgeshire, the Isle of Ely and some boroughs (Yarmouth, Kings Lynn, Stowmarket and Aldeburgh). One contemporary observer, who was close to events, thought that perhaps 200 had been executed; probably an exaggerated, but not completely incredible, estimate: it is likely that 250 people were tried and that at least 100 were executed. A significant proportion of all executions for witchcraft in English history came during this single summer.[61]

Of course, many more people died in battle – even in Essex, where 800 died in the siege of Colchester in 1648[62] – but the real significance of witch trials lies in the social tensions that they reveal. The Essex prosecutions are particularly well-documented, and many of the patterns they reveal are familiar from the longer history of witchcraft prosecutions. Nearly 90 per cent of the accused were women, predominantly of lower social status. Their crimes were ones familiar from many other witchcraft trials – causing illness in adults, children and livestock, or blighting crops or other foodstuffs. An influential interpretation of such prosecutions is that they were a means of dealing with misfortune. An explanation for misfortune was found in the behaviour of individuals thought difficult by their neighbours – the stereotype is of an older woman, spinster or widow, of relatively low status, who was unwilling to accept her place in life with due humility. Rather than blame bad luck, or accept a providential judgement on their own lives, the argument goes, substantial villagers found it easier to blame the malice of the poor and marginal. But other tensions were also clearly present, about the proper role of women, something which women themselves were keen to police: women frequently appeared as accusers and witnesses, establishing their own authority as respectable women by denouncing others.[63]

It is usually presumed that witches did not commit the crimes of which they were accused: although witchcraft can be effective on believers, it seems to modern observers unlikely that witches can successfully harm infants, animals or foodstuffs. Some witches did apparently think that they had done these things, and there is no real reason to doubt the sincerity of the accusations. It does, however, seem likely that these things tell us more about the anxieties of village life than about the actual behaviour of witches. The East Anglian witches seem to fit this pattern – witnessed against by their neighbours, for minor acts of malice achieved by terrifying means, they were denounced by neighbours with whom they had fallen out.[64]

Prior to the civil war the trend of prosecutions in Essex had been falling, and the great peak of 1645 can make it seem as if Matthew Hopkins and John Stearne, energetic 'witchfinders', were wholly responsible. But although these trials took place in an area of the country which saw relatively little military action, it is still tempting to see here the effects of the civil war: it may be the war, rather than these men, that was really to blame. Anxieties were increased, and the authorities more receptive to prosecutions, with the result that longstanding tensions were openly expressed. Most immediately, the war created the opportunity for Matthew Hopkins to exercise an authority that in less disrupted times would have been denied to him. He was the younger son of a provincial clergyman, probably in his twenties, and probably lacking legal training. In the winter of 1644–5 his concerns about the activities of a number of local witches were acute, and when they were arrested in March 1645 he gave detailed evidence against a number of them. In other times this would probably not have launched a career. Like William Dowsing, he was a man who before the war would have had little prospect of overseeing such important business. Moreover, there was an overlap between the areas in which Dowsing had been active and those in which Hopkins's activities resonated.[65] It is not fanciful to see these two efforts at purgation as somehow related.

Hopkins clearly played a leading role in promoting the prosecutions, and earned money from them. Hopkins and Stearne resorted to methods which, while legal, were unusual in England. Suspects were stripped naked and searched for the witches' mark – the unusual teat from which their familiar spirits would feed. In Essex a number of women searchers clearly did this work on the basis of some expertise – their names recur in the trial records. The accused were then placed on a stool in the middle of a room, with their feet off the ground, and watched for up to three days without food or sleep. It was hoped that in this time their familiars might come to them. At the end of this 'watching' they might be asked leading questions by Hopkins or Stearne, and were also interrogated by other interested parties.[66]

This process – torture, watching and leading questions – undoubtedly made the accused suggestible. Escalation followed, as networks of witches were 'revealed'. Although this allowed Hopkins to inflect the prosecutions with his own views, he clearly also drew on the beliefs and participation of many others. At the initial trials, in fact, he was just one of ninety-two witnesses. This is not to deny the importance of the role of the witchfinders, but to suggest that local communities, galvanized by debate about Christian purity, and subject to providential stories of the moral message of fortune and misfortune in this world, were plainly primed for the purging of witches from their midst.[67] There was a similar outbreak in Kent in the same years, perhaps significantly in the quarter sessions, a lower court without full-time judges, in the absence of assizes.[68] The restraining hand of county administration was absent or limited. Arthur Wilson, star witness of the Stour Valley riots in 1642, was also a sceptical observer at the Essex assizes, and such scepticism seems to have restrained prosecutions in Lancashire in 1633.[69] But in 1645 Hopkins and Stearne went out to look for witches and, apparently shocked by what they found, provided a service taken up with some enthusiasm by local authorities (the boroughs of the Suffolk coast paid £20 for witch prosecutions in these months) and the neighbours of suspects.[70]

Accepting that the accused witches were not guilty as charged, the stories told about them (since they were not actually true) attract psychological analysis – what anxieties were being expressed in these fantasies? The stories about witches in the 1640s reflect anxieties common to other periods of witch-hunting, but also anxieties arising from the war. One pamphlet told how soldiers searching for food on the eve of the battle of Newbury came across an old woman who was able to make a boat move against the current in a way that clearly suggested supernatural power. They tried to kill her, placing a carbine against her chest, but the bullet just bounced off. Another soldier, enraged, tried to run her through, but the sword could not penetrate her body. Only once they had taken a traditional remedy against the power of the Devil – letting blood from the veins crossing her temples – did she become vulnerable. At that point her fate seems to have been connected with anxiety about the war: 'is it come to pass that I must die indeed? Why then his excellency the earl of Essex shall be fortunate and win the field'. The Devil's side would lose. But there was another less obvious anxiety here too, about male potency and combat. Enraged by the failure of their weapons the men were mocked by the woman, 'though speechless, yet in a most contemptible way of scorn, still laughing at them [as they tried to kill her] which did the more exhaust their fury against her life'.[71]

There was an established connection for contemporaries between witchcraft and rebellion (modern readers need think only of *Macbeth*, although contemporaries might have read it too in Lucan's *Pharsalia*). *Signes and wonders from Heaven* interpreted the witch-hunt in East Anglia as another sign of God's anger at the divisions in civil government: alongside reports of the witchcraft prosecutions it related the story of two monstrous births – one human and one feline. 'It is said, that pestilence, the sword and famine are the searchers, wherewith the Lord draws blood of sinners' and since there is no-one who has not 'felt the smart of one, if not all of those forenamed scourges: no, no, there is none alive but hath smarted in one degree or another, even from the King to the beggar. *Ergo*, we are all sinners'. Wonders and marvels were further evidence of God's anger, 'strange comets, seen in the air, prodigies, sights on the seas, marvellous tempests and storms on the land . . . Have not nature altered her course so much, that women framed of pure flesh and blood, bring forth ugly and deformed monsters; and contrariwise beasts bring forth human shapes contrary to their kind'. It was in punishment for these sins that 'the Lord suffered the devil to ramble about like a roaring lion see[k]ing to devour us', not least in East

Anglia, where 'a crew of wicked witches, together with the devil's assistance [have] done many mischiefs'.[72]

In East Anglia, under torture, the accused produced stories that probably reflected an amalgam of educated and vernacular wisdom about witches. There was more mention of the Devil than in most previous English trials, and that may have been the result of the accused answering leading questions after torture and harsh treatment. It was a fundamental belief of the learned that witches enjoyed their power from the Devil. But the details of the confessions – the forms taken by the familiars, the names that they were given – do not seem to belong to the world of the learned demonologist.[73] It is more than possible that the particular anxiety about the Devil, about meetings where books were read, and about a familiar called 'Newes', reflect the particular tensions of civil war England. The preaching of hotter Protestants, anxious about the work of the Devil in this world, was common in East Anglia. In national political debate the relationship between the visible and invisible church

Matthew Hopkins 'watching' two witches, whose
familiars include one called 'Newes'

was of central importance, and the presses continually harped on the spread of the sects. Essex, like Suffolk, had seen campaigns to purge malignant clergy and enjoyed the attentions of William Dowsing. There had also been many examples of relatively spontaneous popular icono-clasm between 1640 and 1642.[74]

There were more direct connections with the war too. *Signes and wonders* claimed that the Norfolk witches 'have prophesied of the downfall of the King and his army, and that Prince Robert shall be no longer shot-free: with many strange and unheard of things that shall come to pass'.[75] Rupert, we should remember, was held by many to be the main obstacle to a negotiated peace at this point. There was an association between Rupert and witchcraft: his pet dog was repre-sented as a familiar and he himself referred to both as an incubus and as a devil.[76] It was not the first time that the power of an evil adviser of a monarch had been associated with witchcraft. Strafford, on the scaf-fold, had apparently answered a charge that he had been prey to the 'witchcraft of authority', an echo perhaps of a Puritan argument that worldly glory was one of the Devil's snares, tempting the sinner to forget the larger glory of the heavenly kingdom. As William Perkins had it, 'the power of this Prince of Darkness manifests itself herein by works of wonder, transcendent in regard of ordinary capacity ... to pur-chase himself the admiration, fear, and faith of the credulous world'. Parliamentarian propaganda made a general association between the popish plot and the Devil's wiles, and Charles himself was touched by these charges of diabolism. Cavalierism in general became a species of demonic activity. Royalists, on the other hand, charged that witchcraft was closely tied to the sin of rebellion.[77] The East Anglian witch-hunt was quickly invested with these meanings too. John Hammond, who printed *Signes and wonders*, saw it as a judgement on the whole people – he published a number of wonder pamphlets in these months with the message that everyone should look to their own sins in order to avoid similar judgements in the future. That it took place in parliamen-tary territory was, of course, fuel for the royalists, but *The parliaments post* turned this into a gender issue: 'There is an infection in wickedness; and the spirit of the Cavaliers because it could not prevail with our men, hath met with some of our women, and it hath turned them into witches'.[78]

The fight against witches was a godly work, and one described in martial language, requiring personal valour and other masculine values. As one writer had it in 1648:

The late lamentable wars began, yet God was good to us in discovering many secret treacheries . . . And many superstitious relics were abolished, which neither we nor our godly fathers (as ye have heard) were able to bear. Since which time, ye knew, many witches have been discovered by their own confessions, and executed; many glorious victories obtained (beyond any man's expectation) and places of strength yielded.

Once again, it seems, there might be a connection between the work of Dowsing and Hopkins. Dowsing, for example, thought that a victory for Fairfax at Nantwich owed something to his own successful destruction of images at Orford, Snape and Saxmundham on the same day. Hopkins and Stearne's evidence, and their account of themselves, can plausibly be seen as a means of dealing with social and spiritual chaos through an assertion of masculine control. That control rested in part in a physical violence which recalls accounts of male violence against women during the wars: a way of maintaining masculine identity in the face of violent and chaotic uncertainties.[79] Although the physical safety of women was usually respected, and stories of rape are rare, there were atrocities involving women near the fighting. At Naseby the massacre and mutilation of women camp followers was apparently an ethnic as well as a gender crime – this was an unusual story, but might be read as a masculine response to disorder, fear and female potency.[80]

Although not all the witches were women, the bulk of them were and a wider anxiety about the stability of patriarchal order is an important context for these trials, or at least for their representation in print.[81] *The parliaments post* had made a standard observation about the greater vulnerability of women to spiritual error, linking it to witchcraft in a way which was common to contemporary thinking about witches. It was also a common theme in writing about the dangers of sectarianism, a form of diabolical temptation. There was a common association between the Devil and over-zealous godliness, with sectarian excess the obvious fruit of the Devil's work.[82] These associations between the Devil and unbridled zeal, and between them both and sectarianism, were clearly close to witchcraft fantasies. Conventicles and covens were imagined in similar ways, with women prominent in both.

In numerous ways the women who petitioned, published or prophesied tried to present themselves within the bounds of conventional gender roles, but the pamphlet literature of the 1640s is full of anxieties about uppity women. Looking at the witchcraft prosecutions in Tudor and Stuart England as a whole, it seems clear that men and women saw in witches a threat to orderly gender relations.[83] We cannot put Hopkins on the couch to prove that the prosecutions were a response to these anxieties: this may not have motivated him or any of the other partici-pants in the witch-hunt. Even so, we can be fairly sure that the hunt acquired larger meanings in the world of print, and that these anxieties about masculinity and patriarchy were among them.

Before the war the local community had not been understood only in terms of neighbourliness and mutual support but also in terms of good government. Local notables held offices in the church and state, and used their authority and discretion to bring order and harmony to their parish. Constables, churchwardens, overseers of the poor were effectively arbiters of local decency. Parish communities formed around strongly held notions of order, hierarchy and authority, and membership of the community was policed. Local officeholders and village worthies might exercise a close and oppressive control over local sociability and sexual life. The village greybeards exacted deference in return for a fatherly care – it was by no means a bucolic paradise, but a very stable reconciliation of social status and political authority. Parish community was also marked ritually – the agricultural cycle, the devotional calendar and the life-cycle of the individual were marked out by public cere-monies. In towns the civic year was also marked, and strong corporate structures integrated individuals into a social body. These practices resolved conflict – communities were not marked by the absence of conflict so much as by collectively acceptable means to reconcile and live with it.[84] By the end of the war many of the established routines of village and county government were still in place, or had been re-established. Crimes were punished and social policies implemented. In some cases these activities were hampered or complicated by military authorities, or the administrative structures erected to fight the wars, but much had survived.[85]

Nonetheless, during 1645 there is plenty of evidence that the experi-ence and perception of disruption, and the publicity given to advocates of other forms of social compact, called forth an active attempt to refurbish older forms of community for the new world created by the war. The material costs were difficult to bear, and the new forms of authority and political mobilization presented a challenge to the ideals and institutions of local government. In a sense this was a crisis in community – the formal and informal sources of authority through which local conflicts had been reconciled, order established and protection provided. Established patterns of authority and ritual were also challenged by the threat to the territorial basis of religious community. Was communion for those of a like mind, or all those living together? And what forms of ritual life could bring people together in a shared community?

Drawing on traditions of self-government in these challenging times, there were active and creative responses to these problems during the latter stages of the war. For, just as with the financial balance sheet, there were opportunities as well as burdens. By 1646 the war had provided opportunities to work off grudges, to redress local wrongs, to further a particular view of reformation, to promote pet projects, to make money, to assume local office. The war created the problems addressed by clubmen, excise rioters and witch-hunters, but also created the opportunities for obscure people to promote their own solutions. It had unleashed energies and arguments that went beyond the issues at the heart of peace negotiations. That affected formal negotiation – inducing both caution and urgency – but also provided the basis for activists to pursue purposes quite different from the formal war aims of the military parties. Anxiety, opportunism and creative adaptation were symbiotically linked; and they resonated deeply in English society.

Revolution, 1646–1649

16

Post-War Politics

Print, Polemic and Mobilization

Certainties were easier to find on the battlefield than at the negotiating table: there was a limited number of outcomes, quickly apparent, which had a more or less obvious significance. The experience of battle was in that sense appealing to those looking for God's hand in this world. At Langport, Major Thomas Harrison, watching the Cavalier army crumble before the heroic attack of the New Model across a river and up a narrow lane lined with musketeers, 'with a loud voice [broke] forth into the praises of God with fluent expressions as if he had been in a rapture'. Oliver Cromwell seems to have been particularly persuaded by such signs. At Marston Moor, he exulted that God had made the enemy 'as stubble to our swords', and of the great victory at Naseby he wrote: 'this is none other than the hand of God, and to Him alone belongs the glory'. Like Harrison he was equally certain about Langport: 'Thus you see what the Lord hath wrought for us . . . Thus you have [Langport] mercy added to Naseby mercy. And to see this, is it not to see the face of God?'[1]

By the time final victory came, however, it was not at all clear what it meant, either in the limited sense of what the parliamentary coalition had ended up fighting for or in the deeper sense of what cause God had smiled upon. As a practical problem this was more difficult for the victors – it was clear that the royalists would now be negotiating a rearguard action. But in three stages Parliament had taken measures which put its cause in a different light: the administrative and financial escalations of 1643; the military alliance with the Covenanters; and the formation of the New Model, with all that was taken to imply. What was the peace that all this was intended to achieve? Following victory there were plenty of ideas about that question, and attempts to make victory a vehicle for them, but that made the peace no easier to win than the war had been. In the world of print, where these conflicting visions were promoted among overlapping publics, there had been another, less easily quantified, set of costs and benefits. Lost coherence in contemporary debate, a crisis of common sense, created the opportunity to fly kites and make creative arguments; as those opportunities were taken up, so the world of public debate seemed more and more anarchic.

On 19 July 1645, just over a month after Naseby, William Walwyn and a deputation of religious and political radicals were at Westminster, accusing the Speaker of sustaining correspondence with the royalists and with the King. Walwyn was by that time in his mid-forties, the second son of a landed gentleman, a member of the Merchant Adventurers and a medical practitioner of some substance. A conversion experience moved Walwyn from a relatively orthodox predestinarian Calvinism to belief in free grace, accepting love and inner peace. This led him to advocate freedom of conscience, arguing that as long as knowledge was imperfect, men would differ. As a result such differences should be tolerated. Since the world was not divided between the elect and the reprobate, and redemption was available to all, everyone should be free to follow God's promptings: there should be no human constraint on the conscience. He advocated this position in seven pamphlets published anonymously between 1641 and January 1646. Here was a man for whom the parliamentary cause was the pursuit of full reformation, and for whom, presumably, compromise with the King, which jeopardized freedom of conscience, was an ungodly act.[2]

While at Westminster on that day in July 1645, Walwyn met John Lilburne, who was there to answer charges about the publication of illicit political tracts. Lilburne had reached his twenties during the Laudian domination of the church, and that had radicalized him. An associate of Henry Burton, he was already a significant figure in radical Puritan circles by 1640 – released from the Fleet prison at the petition of Oliver Cromwell in November and the subject of an upmarket engraving by George Glover in 1641. He was part of the coalition of disaffected Protestants that dominated London's street politics in the first two years of the Long Parliament. He signed up for the parliamentary army in 1642 and by 1644 had a distinguished military record. By 1645, however, his militancy was leading him away from the military struggle and back to the world of print and polemic. He was worried by Presbyterian plans for the national church and the political influence Presbyterian leaders were apparently able to muster, and irritated both by military differences with his (Presbyterian) commanders and by what he perceived as inadequate recognition by them of his achievements. As a result he began a pamphlet assault on Presbyterian leaders, and the institutions which allowed them influence, which led to the expression of radical political principles.[3]

Pamphlets by, or attributed to, Richard Overton follow a similar trajectory, which began to intersect with Lilburne's in 1645. We know much less about Overton: he may have been born around 1600 or around 1615, he may or may not have matriculated at Queens' College, Cambridge (suggesting a relatively high-status background, perhaps), he may or may not have been married to Mary between 1642 and 1644. Unlike Lilburne there is no evidence to connect him with active politics: we do not know if he was in the crowds which shaped political events between 1640 and 1642, and there is nothing to suggest that he undertook any military service. Perhaps this is a difference in generation, or of education. His pamphlets support the view that he had received a relatively advanced education. Although his background and circumstances are obscure, the intellectual journey reflected in the 150 pamphlets and writings attributed to him is relatively clear. Between 1640 and 1642 he contributed to the vast output of anti-Laudian and anti-popish pamphlets. Taking up his pen again in 1644, however, he had moved in a more radical direction, arguing for the mortality of the soul, a publication which got him into trouble alongside Milton. Orthodox soteriology (theological argument about salvation) depended on the continued existence of the soul after physical death – it was the basis of beliefs about heaven and hell (and, for Catholics, purgatory). Overton's prominence in the world of illegal printing had probably brought him into contact with Lilburne the previous winter, if not before.[4]

Prior to the chance meeting on 19 July Walwyn and Lilburne had become fellow travellers in the fight against what they saw as Presbyterian intolerance. Lilburne had once been imprisoned for publicizing Henry Burton's views and, along with Burton, Bastwick and Prynne, had suffered at the hands of the Laudian regime. By January 1645, however, he and Prynne were separated on the issue of Church government. On 2 January, Prynne's *Truth Triumphing over Falsehood* had championed, intemperately, the Presbyterian cause. Both Lilburne and

Walwyn were prompted to reply, as were Burton and Thomas Goodwin, a leading Independent minister and one of the authors of the *Apologeticall Narration*. Lilburne's reply appeared within five days, testimony to the immediacy of the print polemic by this stage in the conflict. It was followed less than a month later by Walwyn's *A Helpe to the right understanding*, which argued for freedom of conscience. Richard Overton added his own counterblasts from April onwards, his the more withering and satirical contributions. In April *The Araignement of Mr Persecution* put Prynne on trial before the Grand Jury of virtuous principles, and this was followed by three pamphlets copying a notorious Elizabethan pamphleteering campaign by Martin Marprelate. In both cases the associations are interesting – laying claim to religious freedom in a traditional institution of English liberties and laying claim to a longer tradition of reformation polemic. A fourth pamphlet, *The Nativity of Sir John Presbyter*, assumed the form of a horoscope cast by 'Christopher Scale-Sky, Mathematition in chief to the Assembly of Divines'.[5]

The trajectories of these three – Overton, Walwyn and Lilburne – were crossing in the summer of 1645 in response to the Presbyterian campaign to take charge of the parliamentary cause. What cemented this incipient alliance was the political martyrdom of John Lilburne. Although Prynne had ignored Lilburne in the spring, he was prompted into action by a meeting at the Windmill Tavern in the summer. On one account this was convened to discuss the implications of Parliament's defeat at Leicester, immediately prior to Naseby. At the time of the loss of Leicester, however, the New Model had not been able to engage the royal army, another spring was slipping away and now the royalists had scored a significant military blow. According to Overton's *Martin's Eccho* this was one of the signs of God's wrath against the persecuting spirit in the parliamentary cause. The meeting recommended adjourning Parliament for a month, to allow members to reacquaint themselves with the temper of those they represented. The Westminster Assembly was to take a similar break. To Prynne this seemed to be an Independent attack on the assembly and the Presbyterian interest in Parliament. This provocation, and the pamphlet attacks on him, provoked *A Fresh Discovery of some Prodigious New Wandring-Blasing Stars*.[6]

A new bout of pamphlet jousting between Prynne and his opponents coincided with a print campaign in defence of Lilburne. He had been denounced by Bastwick (another man whom Lilburne had supported in the resistance to Laudianism) on the basis of a conversation overheard on 19 July. Bastwick claimed that in the course of that conversation Lilburne had said that Lenthall had sent £60,000 to the enemy at Oxford. Lilburne was brought before the Committee of Examinations the following week, where, rather than dispute the charge, he questioned the authority of the tribunal and asserted his rights as a free-born Englishman. And, of course, he launched into print, with *England's Birth-Right Justified* (10 October 1645). In this he was supported directly by Walwyn, whose pamphlet *England's Lamentable Slaverie* appeared the following day, and engaged in a public dialogue with Lilburne.[7]

One of Lilburne's gifts was for seeing in his own troubles principles of general significance, and it was this that facilitated the translation of religious freedom into the civic sphere: his serial oppressions at the hands of various civil bodies became the basis for arguments about the illegitimacy of their authority. Walwyn's view of free grace was the basis of a radical view of the constitution. Secular power ought to be so arranged as to guarantee freedom of conscience, since there could be no free moral agent without civil liberty. These were very clearly practical questions, in the light of Lilburne's experience. It was an anti-Calvinist position, and one based not on the ancient constitution but on ancient *rights*. In Lilburne's hands these ancient rights became the basis for political settlement, a uniform set of rights due to all Englishmen by birth.[8]

Measured against the flood of pamphlets in these months, this was a fairly insignificant set of exchanges. It is not clear that the arguments for religious toleration made by Walwyn were of more importance to contemporaries than those made by Burton and Williams the previous year, but an earlier generation of historians saw here the germ of a modern, and admirable, politics for in this convergence among London radicals lie the origins of the Levellers. 'To our generation fell the good fortune of re-discovering the Levellers', wrote H. N. Brailsford in 1958. For Brailsford it was the Levellers who came to champion popular sovereignty expressed in a democratically accountable House of Commons. In *The Araignement*, for example, Walwyn had appealed to human reason as a source of authority, combining it with the maxim that *salus populi suprema lex* (the good or safety of the people is the supreme law).[9] As we have seen, Overton had Presbyterian persecution arraigned before a Grand Jury, the voice of the local community. From these ideas, discernible in 1645, sprang a campaign that the army championed, carrying through a political revolution which was of significance to the history of the west as a whole – a people's army championing ideals resembling the secular democratic values of the nineteenth- and twentieth-century West. The practical significance of their ideas, according to this view, derived from their influence over the army: it was from the Levellers, and not from their commanders, that the New Model Army derived its political ideas and 'democratic drive'.[10] Here, too, the exchanges of 1645 offer some support – as well as arguing for the abolition of tithes and for religious toleration, Overton's *Martin's Eccho* argued for the payment of the soldiers' arrears. This was the basis of a political alliance, since refusal to pay up was another sign, so Overton thought, of the sin of Presbyterian half-heartedness in prosecution of the war effort.[11]

Both claims – about the relationship between Leveller ideas and democracy, and about the influence of the Levellers over the New Model Army – are now contested.[12] The rediscovery of the Levellers may have resulted in an exaggeration of their modernity and practical significance to the events of the 1640s. Lilburne, Overton and Walwyn's convergence in 1645 probably reveals more about the networks and mechanics of 1640s polemics than it does about the motive force of practical politics during these crucial years. Nonetheless, by the summer of 1645 the Stationers' Company was trying to shut Overton down.[13]

Polemicists in this highly competitive environment were forced to assert the authority of their views. Lilburne's first defence of himself employed a full 'apparatus of erudition': margins stuffed with textual references, a text interspersed with Latin phrases and constant scriptural allusions. His textual authorities included well-established touchstones of constitutional thinking – Magna Carta, the Petition of Right and Coke's *Institutes* – but also Husbands' *Exact Collection*. The latter was itself a confection from the plethora of publications in the first years of the Long Parliament and Lilburne's deployment of it reflects the ways in which this print culture fed off itself.[14] Indeed, the Levellers were themselves a print phenomenon long before they were a 'movement' – comrades in arms in the paper war before they had actually met, and sympathetic pamphleteers long before they could have been claimed to have been a party.[15]

It is now difficult to know what to make of this coalescence therefore: whether it was just paper talk or the expression of the views of a larger constituency. It is possible to see in 1645 traces of radical religious networks with roots in sectarian congregations, mobilizing to secure a complete military victory in order to safeguard the gains made for reformation since the collapse of Laudianism. The convergence of these three polemicists bears testimony to the ways that print had become a source of authority and community in itself. Even if it was just paper talk, in other words, it is still significant. For the generation of the 1950s and 1960s democracy mattered; for that of the early twenty-first century so does paper talk, even if it's not true.

As the war drew to a close, and victory approached, Thomas Edwards became the leading figure in Presbyterian polemics against these views. A relatively hot Calvinist, he had run into trouble during the 1630s, partly because of his beliefs and partly because of his combative personal style. Naturally sympathetic to the anti-Laudian politics of the period 1640–42 he had, nonetheless, been quick to identify the dangers of Independency – the attack on Laud, and then on episcopacy, was welcome, but beyond that had to lie a comprehensive and reformed national church. In 1641 he had published an attack on Independency which had elicited only one response – from Katherine Chidley. A principal reason for this relative silence was the agreement reached in November 1641 among leading Puritans not to engage in public controversy on the issue of church government. During 1644, however, as the Westminster Assembly leaned increasingly towards a strict Presbyterian settlement, that agreement broke down. The *Apologeticall Narration*, despite its moderate tone, had set off a heated argument.[16]

Edwards's own contribution to the ensuing exchanges did not at the time elicit much by way of direct response. *Antapologia*, however, did wonders for his career as a hammer of the sectaries, for that is what this campaign meant to Edwards: his critique of Independency concentrated almost exclusively on the sectarian consequences of the dissolution of a national church. *Antapologia* probably helped to secure him a lectureship at Christ Church, in the heart of the City, where his lectures became major public events (at least, if he is to be believed). People flocked to hear him speak about the dangers of the sects, among them his opponents, who heckled and scuffled as he spoke. This notoriety seems also to have put him at the centre of a network of correspondents shocked by the proliferating problems of maintaining religious order and decency and anxious to give publicity to the excesses of the sects.[17]

During 1646, exploiting this position, Edwards launched a massive publishing venture – *Gangraena*. Three parts were eventually produced,

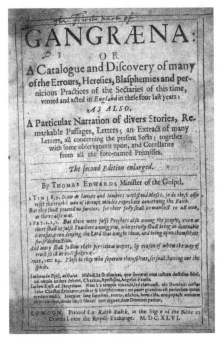

Thomas Edwards's *Gangraena*

totalling over 800 pages, forming an ill-disciplined catalogue of errors, schism and heresy, lavishly and sensationally illustrated with reports of religious excess from around the country. The first instalment, produced in January and February, invited readers to write in with more material, and that helped to stuff the further instalments in May and December with more lurid stories. The timings were significant and each edition was apparently being added to up to the point of publication. This was a calculated appeal for public support for the Presbyterian cause: the first at a moment when renewal of the Solemn League and Covenant was being sought; the second coincided with the promotion of a remonstrance in London, very hostile to the sects, and in favour of the Solemn League and Covenant and a rapid peace settlement on Presbyterian terms; the third when hostility to the army was renewed. This mode of operation, Edwards's own intemperance and the need to get the books out quickly contributed to their sprawling character. But that also helped to make their point – their very form communicated the sprawling, spiralling danger of the sects.[18]

This campaign was more or less purely negative. Edwards nowhere defended or described the correct form of Presbyterian discipline as he saw it. His only concern was with the monstrous profusion of sects, the deadly disease of the Christian body. In this he has been fabulously successful, mined for examples and evidence by his contemporary fellow travellers and by historians seeking to understand and evoke the chaotic profusion of religious experiments in this period. By the same token, however, the question of whether to believe Edwards has been equally persistent. He was immediately labelled as a liar, and his reputation has declined among historians in recent years, suspicious of his purposes and unable to verify his sources.

Edwards probably did not make things up,[19] but in any case counting sectaries does not really get at the heart of the problem of order – the issue was not a quantitative one. What was really new and radical about this was that fundamental questions were being debated before a public audience. It had become necessary to argue for, and defend, institutions which had previously been thought to be fundamental to spiritual and social order – learned ministry, a national church. In effect, public approval was being garnered for their place in a settlement even by those who, as a matter of principle, believed that their authority (and political settlement) did not depend on consent. Moreover, this was an escalating difficulty – those who sought to intervene were bound to try to establish the legitimacy of their intervention before a large public. Whatever their beliefs about public opinion, therefore, they courted it, and gave particular political arguments a public function. Radical reformation was now entrenched, cultural legitimacy had been eroded: English people confronted a world of competing certainties in which fundamental truths were no longer easily available.

Gangraena was published as a catalogue, and has some value as such, but it was also a political intervention, offering a window onto the fraught politics of the fracturing parliamentary coalition in 1646. It was a publishing sensation – part one was reprinted three times before the appearance of part two. There were at least twenty direct replies (Walwyn was prominent among the critics) and it was incidentally mentioned in many more. The author became known to contemporaries as Gangraena Edwards, or simply as Gangraena, and he was immortalized by Milton as 'Shallow Edwards'.[20]

Like William Lilly, whose career had also been launched in 1644 and took off in 1646, Edwards was tapping into a large market, one characterized by anxiety. As in 1640–42, the future of a church liberated from episcopal control was easily expressed in terms of a problem of order, and discussion of that problem clearly sold well. Gangraena's sprawling denunciation publicized the dangers, and in its very form demonstrated disorder, but it also offered some comforts. The desire to catalogue, count and categorize was an effort at rhetorical control – capturing the threat but also, by historicizing, taxonomizing and enumerating it, to make it more bounded and limited. It is a relief, in a way, to know that the festering affliction of the body that appears so worrying has a name, even if that name is gangrene.

In the polemical world inhabited by Edwards and his antagonists, an argument which had been postponed in 1641 was now in full spate. Where could the limits of decency be set once episcopacy had gone, and how could they be policed? In Scotland, when the shell of episcopal authority had cracked, there was a fully developed Presbyterian system ready to emerge – wanting only the abolition of bishops and the recognition of the authority of the General Assembly. In England nothing so complete had been growing within: what emerged was not formed and was, to Presbyterian eyes, monstrous. The world portrayed by Edwards, of dissolving limits and unpoliced religious experimentation, a world turned upside down, held appeal for the radicals of the 1960s.[21] For contemporaries it was more or less inseparably connected with anxiety.

In these pamphlet debates about war aims, and peace projects, standard metaphors and images were used for partisan purposes but in ways that became controversial, incomprehensible or straightforwardly incredible.[22] The 1640s saw remarkable rhetorical creativity, the innovative use of familiar arguments and languages, as much as in more formal conceptual innovation.[23] For example, resistance to Charles's policies was couched in terms of loyalty to the monarch, even when that entailed raising an army through Parliament but without the King's consent. Opponents claimed that they were protecting Charles from his evil advisers or from himself or, eventually, protecting the office from its present incumbent. By 1646 treason had been creatively reinterpreted to embrace, effectively, advising the King wrongly (Strafford, Laud) and surrendering a city to the royal army (Nathaniel Fiennes). In 1649 it was used to kill the King himself. Political battles were fought out on the scaffolds, where these novel claims were asserted and resisted, Laud and then Charles embracing martyrdom rather than the justice of their end. 'Strained readings' is a polite term for the often bizarre, incomprehensible or incredible uses to which standard terms were put. Many people had taken sides reluctantly and conditionally, and a number of people lapsed from activism into inactivity, or changed sides altogether, leading to public argument about what was more honourable – following an initial commitment to a cause, or the shifting dictates of the individual conscience.

Unsurprisingly this was a great age of satire but there was also a very evident desire to uncover the truth. This operated at several levels: most fundamental of all, a desire to know what was actually going on. Newspapers and pamphlets offered true relations and authentic versions at the same time as they denounced the lies of others. It also prompted stylistic innovation. Denunciations of the sensationalist accounts of the Irish rebellion may have given an extra emphasis to the development of a more sober style. Men like John Thomas and W.B. had been keen to maximize fear of the dangers of armed popery, but in response to the charge of sensationalism Thomas at least seems to have adopted a plain style in his pamphlet on Derbyshire, which 'performed' reliability and authenticity on its title page, even though it was probably untrue.[24] But contemporary chronicling was unashamedly polemical even as it performed this simple reportage. For example, Josiah Ricraft's account of *England's Champions*, written towards the end of hostilities, reviewed the military history of Parliament's campaigns from a shamelessly partisan angle. His purpose was to promote the reputation of those within the parliamentary coalition who were faithful to the Solemn League and Covenant, interpreted by him as a commitment to Presbyterianism. His account therefore rested on a clear view of which programme of political and religious reform God had favoured by delivering victories in battle. In seeking to establish his political and religious case Ricraft wrote a military history in which the heroes were Leslie, Manchester and Essex. In a manuscript version eighteen senior commanders were celebrated individually, a further twenty-seven given an important supporting role. Oliver Cromwell does not merit individual treatment and he appears in the chronology of Parliament's military history only for his victory at Stamford and his seizure of Basing House in 1645. According to Ricraft the truth about the second battle of Newbury, so controversial in the parliamentary coalition, was simple: Manchester, 'this noble General utterly routed [the royalists]'. When it appeared in print in 1647 Cromwell and others had been added, although the judgement on Newbury had remained unaltered.[25]

Newsbooks also pilloried strained readings of the standard terms of contemporary political discourse: most notably perhaps in Bruno Ryves's reporting on the actions of parliamentarian soldiers, crowds and religious radicals, which juxtaposed their behaviour with their claim to be acting to preserve religion and liberty. Political conflict in the 1640s was, in that sense, a battle over key words – treason, honour, allegiance, reformation, custom, popery, law – and over the relationship between political claims and real actions. These were closely related problems – definition of terms, accurate description of what was going on and authoritative interpretation of its meaning. For example, one of the texts published by Ryves in 1647 was the *Micro-chronicon*, a narrative of the battles of the civil war akin to that published by Ricraft. In this case, however, the text probably originated with George Wharton, on whose earlier publication Ryves's version seems to have rested. Wharton, as we have seen, was better known as the royalist astrologer, the main political opponent of William Lilly.[26] Given the bizarre interpretations of standard terms it is not surprising to find a pervasive and more practical concern to understand what important people were really up to, whatever they had said in public: private letters were often published in order to reveal underlying truths; cabinets were opened, and plots discovered.

Even if the facts of the case could be agreed there was plenty of room for disagreement about what they meant. This was particularly true of providential stories – it was often clear that an event carried meaning, but it was not at all clear what that meaning was. For example, an established genre of writing, the warning piece, was put to work. A sinner told the sorry tale of their sin and punishment, which they accepted as just, in the hope that their sad experience would serve to discourage others from taking the same path. These warning pieces were now made partisan – recounting, for example, the punishments consequent on disobeying a royal order to lay down arms, or divine judgements against popish plotters.[27] The language of providence, and of monstrosity and wonders, was ubiquitous, but if God's judgements were plain, the identity of the culprit and the nature of the sin were far less so. In reporting the signs of God's will in this world there was a double problem: to establish the truth of the phenomenon and then to come to an uncontested interpretation of its meaning. An effect of public discussion of these issues was to make the reading public arbiters of these fundamental questions.[28]

Perhaps the most profound element of this crisis of authority was the collapse of spiritual authority. As early as October 1642 Thomas Case had attributed conflict to this question of truth: 'And what is this quarrel all this while, is it not religion, and the truth of God? The truth of Doctrine?, the truth of discipline, the truth of worship?'[29] Criticism of tradition and learned divinity made scripture ever more clearly the bedrock of religious knowledge, but scriptural texts were often opaque, ambiguous or apparently contradictory. These were in fact the reasons why unguided access to scripture was regarded as dangerous. Appeals to scripture were made for quite contrary purposes. The injunction in Psalm 105.15, for example, 'Touch not mine anointed and do my prophets no harm', became unstable in its meaning. The royalists claimed, on the basis of long practice, that the King was God's anointed, and that this clearly ruled out the possibility of legitimate resistance. Prynne argued that the anointed were all God's chosen ones, and that the injunction was directed at kings – more than a counter-blast since it in fact indicted Charles of already having breached the injunction.[30] A veritable Babel of conflicting interpretations emerged, and was intimately connected to the debate about church government, since religious sects claimed spiritual warrant for their practices either from scripture or from personal revelation, liberated (to varying degrees) from tradition and learned divinity.

On the other hand, religious pluralism was denounced in terms of well-established idioms – as a disease or a rupture in the divine order – but exactly which forms of belief were pathogens, or threatened the organic moral order? There seemed to be no agreement as to how to answer this question. Those who took on these questions seemed to John Milton, and presumably to others, to be 'in wandering mazes lost'. Many polemicists, rather than reasoning high 'Of providence, foreknowledge, will and fate, / Fixed fate, free will, foreknowledge absolute',[31] simply cut to the chase: the boundaries of acceptable belief could surely be established on the basis of the behavioural consequences of a prophet's teaching, rather than on the basis of scripture or authority. If there was a definitive text here it was Matthew vii, 20: 'by their fruits ye shall know them'. False prophets led the flock to sin. Another response to the sectarian scare was taxonomical, and these taxonomies were also, frequently, historical in content, equating current errors with others in Christian history.[32] This process of numbering and taxonomizing both captured the escalating threat and promised, by labelling and counting, to contain it. Ephraim Pagitt's *Heresiography* of 1645 promised a *description of the Heretickes and Sectaries of these latter times*: numbering and historicizing at the same time.[33]

This was not a war of religion in the sense that the two sides were members of a different church. Neither anti-popery nor anti-sectarianism marked the boundary between royalist and parliamentarian: people on all sides deployed both for polemical purposes. In fact the most vituperative exchanges about the church settlement were within the parliamentary coalition, not between royalists and parliamentarians. It was a war about the identity of a single church, of which all should be members, and which should be organically linked to the political order. Preaching the Word and administering the sacraments were at the core; but episcopal discipline had been broken before a replacement was in place. Church government, so divisive within the parliamentary alliance, and a non-negotiable for the King, was absent. No authoritative source of authority now existed to interpret scripture, and God's signs in the world. John Benbrigge's *Gods Fury*, in its attempt to convince by pre-war means, was a symptom as much as a cure.[34]

Political cultures are probably best understood as 'common sense systems'. Certainly, early Stuart political culture was not a coherent philosophical system but 'a relatively organised body of considered thought' consisting of heterogeneous, unsystematic, 'down-to-earth, colloquial wisdom', something more than 'mere matter-of-fact apprehension of reality' but something less than a fully coherent, consciously articulated world view.[35] The crisis during the 1640s made plain some of the contradictions in Stuart common sense: for example, between law, custom, providence, prerogative, scripture and reason as sources of authority. Events were forcing people to choose between authorities which had not previously been seen to be in tension. In these circumstances it was clearly tempting to turn to established metaphors and languages as a means of making sense of the times. The language of tyranny, derived from learned works, was deployed by low-born balladeers to explain current affairs,[36] but who was the tyrant? The literature of monstrosity spoke of the ills of the body politic; that of heresiography spoke of the plague of sectarianism. Providentialism – the belief that the active hand of God was manifest in the world, and that it could offer direction in human affairs – was another staple element of contemporary thought which now provided a means to make sense of civil and religious Babel. Anti-popery, already an elastic term, was made to embrace ever wider areas of religious practice, both Catholic and Protestant. But the collapse of spiritual authority made all other forms of authority difficult to negotiate – this was the fundamental challenge posed by the crisis of Reformation politics.

Just as political disruption was both crisis and opportunity, so too was this polemical morass. This intellectual crisis might offer new vistas onto the wilder shores of Reformation thought – the late 1640s in England seem to have been a time of creative and exhilarating religious experimentation. Others went beyond Reformation politics, seeking workable truths on other bases. For example, indeterminacy and uncertainty were the context for more fundamental reflection about language. Elsewhere in Europe, an active response to this indeterminacy of meaning was to seek a new, transparent language that did not occlude our access to key ideas. In Spinoza this was a disdain for the 'language of men', in Descartes an aspiration for a mathematical philosophy and in Hobbes a careful definition of terms. Many reformers were attracted to the study of Chinese and Arabic. Chinese was attractive as a pictographic language, which communicated ideas, not sounds, and which was comprehensible to those whose spoken languages were quite different. Arabic, while not pictographic, was also a written language shared by people whose spoken languages were quite different. Babel in England gave rise to an interest in universal languages. Josiah Ricraft, the partisan historian, may have shared this interest.[37] There were more practically oriented responses too. William Lilly's demotic astrology offered hope in the face of uncertainty – identifiable and verifiable things to look out for that would offer a guide as to what was going on, and where it would all end. By 1645 others saw more-bracing possibilities, to take charge of events, and sought to make the approaching parliamentary victory a means to realize their own visions.

One such was Samuel Hartlib, a Protestant refugee from central Europe. Hartlib combined an interest in Baconian science – that is, knowledge based on verifiable experience, and located within a coherent intellectual system which is often regarded as the forerunner of modern natural science – with an interest in the educational ideas of Comenius (Jan Komensky) and John Dury's interest in the promotion of Protestant unity. Here the key issue was sound knowledge – of nature and of scripture – organized and taught in a coherent way, to produce an educated, properly Christian population. These ideas were presented in *Macaria* in 1641 and it was at Hartlib's invitation in 1644 that John Milton wrote *Of Education*, an outline of an education suitable for a better world, training boys to govern, cultivate and defend their commonwealth.[38]

A central element of these ideals was the communication of knowledge and experience, and Hartlib was himself a tireless letter writer and, when funds permitted, publisher. Accurate knowledge, and a method to understand its meaning, was also associated with the creation of institutions to validate truth: a college of experience in the utopian tract *Macaria* (and another college to consider doctrinal matters); the Office of Address in a later and more limited proposal. These hopes had a millenarian aspect too. Hartlib and many of his correspondents believed that in the Garden of Eden, before the Fall, Adam had enjoyed a perfect knowledge of creation. Through an active use of the resources around him, Adam was never hungry, or ill, and was at one with God's Word. Restoration of this knowledge would help to prepare the way for the return of Christ and the saints. This was an active and practical millenarianism, continuously concerned to make productive use of the environment.[39]

This desire to read the book of nature in order to come closer to God was akin to the interest in astrology, which promised to read in the heavens signs of God's intentions: the book of nature provided a means to supplement our knowledge of God's purposes derived from the often inscrutable book of scriptures. Clearly the conditions of the 1640s made that an enticing prospect. According to one modern authority, 'Astrology was probably the most ambitious attempt ever made to reduce the baffling diversity of human affairs to some sort of intelligible order', and the millenarian Baconianism of the Hartlib circle was scarcely less ambitious. Astrology fostered its own college too: the Society of Astrologers.[40]

In Samuel Hartlib's case, intellectual creativity was married to attempts at practical mobilization. He had visited England in 1626 and settled there in 1628, pursuing an ambitious programme of educational reform throughout the 1630s. In 1641 and 1642 it looked like his moment had come: convinced that the English were under a special dispensation from God, he was able to secure visits from Comenius and Dury and was clearly building a significant amount of support in Parliament. Although this moment passed – interest in *Macaria* gave way to a more immediate fear of armed popery – he was tireless in mobilizing support for projects throughout the 1640s and 1650s. A crucial element of many of them was the more effective use of God's bounty: the chemical manufacture of saltpetre (an essential ingredient of gunpowder, but also a powerful fertilizer); setting the poor to productive work, making idle hands useful to the commonwealth; or promoting Atlantic trade, which would maximize use of natural resources, increase knowledge and strengthen the commonwealth. Other projects included sponsorship of a woollen tank and testing torpedoes in the Thames, an interest in jam-making, bee-keeping and the cultivation of silk worms in Virginia. Behind these projects lay a single vision, of making full use of natural resources and political opportunities to edge the world back to a prelapsarian harmony with nature. Like astrology, this offered to lend meaning to the current confusion, and to provide a guide to the truth in conditions which made that an elusive commodity. As a series of practical proposals, it was given impetus and public appeal by the political circumstances of the 1640s, and in 1646 it seemed as if his time had come again.[41]

In 1644, the year of Marston Moor and the first signs of serious fracture in the alliance with the Covenanters, Hartlib had published two pamphlets enjoining correspondency among the Protestant churches. In August 1646, with a parliamentary victory looming, he published *The Parliaments Reformation*, a characteristic attempt to take advantage of a moment to push forward his larger agenda. His interest in saltpetre had reflected the difficulty of acquiring this crucial ingredient of gunpowder, and had concentrated on artificial manufacture rather than digging up pigeon lofts for the material in the nitrogen-rich droppings. It was a practical project, helping to meet a practical need while at the same time removing a common grievance. It would also push forward chemical knowledge and employ the poor. This latter concern was at the forefront of his concerns in the 1646 pamphlet – an injunction to use Parliament's power to force men to be good:

because the major part of the people do never move to any good work willingly before they are commanded; and the command must be upon a penalty too, else they will do little; now consider, who can impose a command on the subject for the carrying on of a good work, and to lay a punishment upon the neglecters of the command, but a parliament's power.

The pamphlet laid out practical proposals to house the poor, and employ them working on hemp and flax. He anticipated concerns about the effects on trade and the interests of clothiers, and made detailed suggestions about funding (including, for example, the use of fines on sins such as drinking, swearing, Sabbath-breaking and adultery to help meet the costs of the scheme). Overall, it was a plan for 'such a godly and politic government; that the godly and laborious poor may be countenanced and cherished, and the idle, and wicked poor be suppressed'. Full reformation would come through the education and employment of the children of the poor – orphans, those with careless parents, or those with godly but indigent parents. These, he thought, were 'the greatest part of the children in the kingdom, and most of them are like to become wicked members to the Commonwealth without this government'.[42]

This was clearly at an angle to the main political business of 1646, but it was a creative response to a widely remarked problem – poverty – and a new possibility – that Parliament might use its political muscle to promote reformation in the fullest sense. Behind it lay a distinctive vision of how to establish social, economic and political truths. With his eyes on this larger game, Hartlib was non-committal on the details of practical settlement in church and state:

I conclude with my prayers to God for the prosperity of this work; and that God will unite King and Parliament, to carry on this holy, godly and charitable work, that the poor children unborn may praise God, for the Parliament's preservation, and the Kingdom's reformation, for which we owe to God praise, and prayers, and all spiritual service.

In June, Hartlib had been granted £100 by a parliamentary committee dominated by Independents, but in August advertised this project as a concern for the new Presbyterian church.[43]

Hartlib enjoyed such minor but significant patronage from successive parliamentary regimes, and associates of his occupied important places in, for example, the drafting of the navigation laws (which governed the English and then British empire for a hundred years) and the survey of Ireland following the English conquest during the 1650s.[44] He was at the centre of a network of correspondents and fellow travellers, and promoted their shared vision in print. In those respects his efforts were like those of many other pamphleteers, mobilizing and galvanizing opinion, taking advantage of the press and political opportunities, to promote a particular agenda. In his case the aim was not a constitutional settlement of a particular kind, but the promotion of full reformation – one embracing all social problems and not just doctrine, church government and forms of worship.

Hartlib had close personal connections with Oliver St John and John Pym and was, we can presume, sympathetic to the more radical wing of the parliamentary cause, committed to the use of Parliament's power to transform, not merely defend. Cheney Culpeper, one of his regular correspondents, certainly was.[45] But Hartlib maintained correspondence with people of widely differing religious and political opinions: at the heart of his correspondence was a willingness to suspend differences about issues which were beyond human certainty in order to further human knowledge. Searching for a means to more secure knowledge in the future seems to have entailed for Hartlib and his associates a willingness to live with uncertainties in the present. It allowed for toleration of differences in spiritual matters, and for co-operation with those of differing opinions and temperament.

Hartlib's circle were important to the promotion of knowledge of the natural world and saw this as closely connected to the political crisis in England. Others also took advantage of the practical opportunities to pursue intellectual enquiry. Richard Wiseman, for example, gleaned much important surgical knowledge from his wartime experience and it is possible that the supply of corpses allowed for increased anatomical observation in wartime Oxford. It has often been claimed that there was a connection between Puritanism and science, and the Hartlib circle have been central to that discussion; in any case, it is clear that there was a connection between these wartime conditions and science. It was in part a matter of free intellectual expression, and the more or less inviting possibilities of the changed print market. But it was also a matter of practicalities – the great Thomas Hobbes, for example, was drawn into a debate about the mechanics of the sword stroke, something of immediate interest but long-term significance to the science of mechanics.[46]

Hartlib's circle are well-known because of the riches that survive in his papers, but there were clearly many such networks in this period. One with which his interests eventually intersected was a group of London merchants, with interests in New World trade and associated with the Independent congregations in London. Bound together by their hostility to the great merchants of the monopolistic Chartered Companies, men like Maurice Thomson, William Barkley and Owen Rowe can be seen at the cutting edge of the radicalization of the parliamentary cause throughout the 1640s. Their time was to come in 1651, when their influence can be seen at work in the transformation of state regulation of overseas trade.[47]

Another set of transatlantic ties was also crucial – that between the exiled godly and those who had stayed at home. Hugh Peter returned to put fire into the belly of God's soldiers, and Roger Williams came back in search of a charter for his godly community, pausing to reignite the divisions among the London godly over the correct form of church government. The diversity of these networks, and their intersecting, overlapping and sometimes conflicting visions, contributed to the confusion of post-war politics. In the next three years Lilburne, Walwyn and Overton would unite as 'Levellers', championing popular sovereignty as the basis of political order. Thomas Hobbes, already on a rather singular route, may have started work on his classic *Leviathan* in 1646, refiguring the classical heritage accessible to early modern gentlemen (Hobbes was a tutor in an aristocratic household) to argue for a new political world.[48] Milton, in *Areopagitica* (1644), had already made a case for (qualified) freedom of speech as the best means to arrive at truth; an argument of second nature to Western liberals in the twenty-first century. Such intellectual creativity, and the fluidity of political alliances, prompted attempts at a fundamental rethinking of politics.

*

Creativity was manifest in the content of arguments, in the forms in which they were expressed and the means by which they were disseminated. It was a product of the fluidity of the two coalitions and doubts about what would constitute a successful peace; and of escalating war efforts which had made both things more rather than less complex, and which sought to mobilize opinion and support among wide and overlapping publics. The resulting polemical morass exposed fundamental elements of political culture to sustained critical observation; and that public debate was far less socially bounded than was considered decent before 1640.

It was not the novelty of the problems which made this crisis remarkable. The problems of, for example, the origins of religious and other truths, the nature of the Christian community, and the relationship between religious and secular authority had all generated traditions of learned argument. What was remarkable about England in the 1640s was the depth and extent of their public discussion, the urgency with which they imposed themselves, and the creativity of some responses to them. Polemical fury had created a world of competing certainties: about the personal honour of particular individuals such as Nathaniel Fiennes, the trustworthiness of the King or the impropriety of revealing his private correspondence. Rival claims and rival accounts of the same event created a problem of authority: the authority of truth-claims. Expert testimony from physicians was a means of fixing the meaning of Pym's death; Laud's equally contested death was discussed in terms of martyrdom and hypocrisy. Print accelerated, generalized and amplified particular causes. Pamphlet debates articulated anxieties and uncertainty even as they laid claim to the truth, and in the course of the controversies some authors responded very creatively to these opportunities. Print was a means to mobilize, and the forum in which anxiety was amplified and creativity flourished.

One response to this effect of print was, of course, repressive. The lapse of licensing in 1641 had been unintentional, and a series of press-licensing measures followed, often in periods of acute political tension. Book-burnings were in a sense more than measures of censorship: they declared particular publications anathema to civil, Christian society. Whether an act of censorship or a statement of repugnance it was not only the content of the argument that attracted repression – it was often the form of expression. The 1643 Licensing Ordinance, for example, had cited 'seditious' texts as a problem, but in a longer list which was primarily concerned with civility: 'false, forged, scandalous, seditious [and] libellous' publications. Free speech in Parliament required that people have the freedom to speak – denunciation, misrepresentation, dishonourable satire all made the free exchange of views impossible. Secrecy about public proceedings, in Parliament and village bodies, was designed not simply to exclude the vulgar, therefore, but to allow political elites to discuss freely without the danger of their divisions becoming public, or the fear of public censure preventing them from making an important argument.[49]

With the spectacular growth of print these questions had become much more pressing. Some burnings – for example, those of Roger Williams's *Bloudy Tenent* or of the *Book of Sports* – reflected a deep hostility to what they contained. Others seem more particularly a response to tone and form. Dering's collection of speeches, burned in February 1642, had been scandalous to the proceedings of the House, rather than particularly offensive in their opinions. In early 1646 a collection of declarations published by the Scots was nearly burned, at a moment of tension in the military alliance – although in the end only the preface suffered this fate, presumably on similar grounds to Dering's.[50] Another case may have been the spoof of the parliamentary *Souldiers Catechisme*. Both armies were provided with catechisms, capturing the justness of their (conflicting) causes in apposite scriptural citation. The parliamentary catechism was issued seven times and there was a fake eighth edition, satirizing the use of biblical language in such an obviously godless enterprise.[51] Questioning the religious basis of the parliamentary cause was hardly unusual – but executing such a dangerously false and counterfeit text as a way of making the case was clearly offensive. Of course, these values were interpreted politically – satire in a good cause was unlikely to be proposed for burning – and so what was burned at any particular point reflected the influence of particular opinions. The general principles seem to have been fairly consistent, however: John Milton (whose pamphlet had been burned along with Overton's in August 1644) was unusual in arguing that there should be no prior restraint. Licensing, on any grounds, ran the risk of suppressing truth as well as error, and it was better to allow error than to suppress truth.[52] Most contemporaries were less excited about expanding truth than they were anxious about proliferating error and the corrosion of political decencies, however.

Polemic and mobilization, along with the attendant anxiety and crea-tivity, were not only a matter for pamphlet readers, however. Soldiers and civilians of humble status were confronted by the material costs of the fighting. If they could not avoid these realities of war it is also unlikely that they could avoid the political principles that the war raised. The circulation of rival proclamations (something taken very seriously by both sides), the raising of armies and of money, and the elaboration of local bureaucracies to achieve this: all these things forced an engage-ment with the arguments and costs of the war. So, too, did the many independent mobilizations – petitioning campaigns, the clubmen move-ments and the religious ginger groups anxious to impose their view of an appropriate settlement. The presence of garrisons and passage of field armies, perhaps even service in them, all fostered political education, and engagement.

Before the war the middling and poorer sort had on occasion deployed the language of authority in order to legitimate their own claims. These opportunities were increased during the 1640s, by the greater variety of political languages available. Partisanship became a common feature of local disputes – disputes in Warwickshire over the legality of soldiers' actions, for example, reveal how deeply the languages of national politics had penetrated; elsewhere malignant contested with well-affected, and scandalous ministers were denounced.[53] Thomas Miles was prosecuted at sessions in late 1648 for saying 'that the parliament men were rogues and traitors, and that he would be one of the first to cut their throats and that the Lord General [Fairfax] would die like a rogue and rot limb from limb'. He counter-sued that the witness against him, Anne Smith, had scandalized the Queen. Smith not only denied this but claimed in her petition: 'it is dubious . . . whether any suit can justly be commenced against [her] in the name of the Queen, so long as she is declared traitor by both Houses of Parliament'.[54] Others claimed to be of 'approved fidelity', or to have suffered for upholding order against those who 'did give out very opprobrious and railing speeches against the parliament', or suffered 'opprobrious words against the parliament' while carrying out its commands: partisan identities were self-consciously adopted throughout England.[55] People with reputations for malignancy were not good friends to have. William Flacke was anxious to dissociate himself from Richard Filch, 'a person disaffected to the parliament and an enemy to the present government'. Flacke was present at a particularly violent outburst, but was anxious to point out that he had been 'incidentally in his company'.[56]

Memories of actions during the war clearly persisted long after. Francis Smith, of Bury St Edmunds, Suffolk, was sued in 1651 for the price of a prayer book ordered while he was churchwarden 'about the beginning of the late troubles'. It was a replacement for one taken by soldiers and was itself destroyed. Smith claimed he had counselled against ordering a replacement, but had been overruled by the minister, Mr Jewell, 'one not well-affected to the proceedings of the parliament'.[57] Richard Harrymon, a butcher from Beverley, was known five years after the war as 'a notorious delinquent who has been in actual arms against the parliament and a great plunderer of the goods of divers persons that were well-affected'. Disputes over actions during the war might persist for years: men were prosecuted for taking horses seven or eight years later, and such law suits could be a considerable expense.[58] After the war, ordinances excluded malignants from office, and this gave scope to those like the 'well-affected inhabitants' of St Ives, Cornwall, to invoke central authorities against local officeholders. They claimed to lie 'under a heavy burden and great oppression by reason of the insolency of these magistrates who now bear office ... who for the most part were in actual rebellion against the parliament'.[59]

Larger principles could be made relevant to particular issues as easily in the Lincolnshire fens or the forests of the West Country as by politicians in Parliament. Iconoclasm offered a practical means of demonstrating the progress of reformation, but also threatened the triumph of ignorant zeal; the clubmen mobilized in order to mediate the new realities with more established institutions of local politics. Both had significance in every village and town, and both were almost immediately contested print phenomena. Pamphlets were an adjunct to these campaigns, and a response to these practical problems, not a separate world.

Print contributed to the mobilizations which rendered institutional politics unstable and, feeding off itself, fostered a lush and confusing world of comment and polemic. In that world there was an intertwining political and cultural crisis with implications for the practical order of local communities. And this was an accelerating problem because the cacophony of opinion fostered tremendous intellectual creativity which in turn became the basis for further practical political mobilization. Presbyterians, religious independents, political mavericks, astrologers, witch-hunters and natural philosophers all found a voice in a freer intellectual environment – robbed of its commonsensical certainties and the practical means to choke off dangerous public debate. At the same time it placed a premium on establishing fundamental truths. Sceptical commentators forced Hopkins and Stearne to defend themselves; Hartlib encouraged communication among natural philosophers in order to speed up the improvement of human understanding; innumerable authors theorized on the nature of the Christian community. Those with a solution to peddle could look to the world of print, and to support from the churches, the Covenanters, Parliament, and the City, or from wider publics. The excitement is impossible to separate from the trauma and anxiety from which it resulted, and to which it contributed.

In the months before and after Naseby, clubmen movements had creatively interpreted traditional forms of authority in differing though related ways, while others had pursued old material grievances or grudges against the committeemen. In East Anglia, in the summer of the New Model's victories, witches were purged from local communities in unprecedented numbers. By the end of the war Samuel Hartlib thought he could see the opportunity to promote his vision of universal reform through practical proposals leading towards full reformation. Those with more-concrete constitutional and religious demands were by then sharpening their quills, or rather their moveable type. For it was not just the content of the argument that rendered politics unstable; it was the use of these ideas to mobilize opinion among competing and overlapping publics.

Edwards, Prynne, Lilburne, Walwyn and Overton inhabited a world in which arguments escalated: rapid, fixed and detailed responses called for endless responses, in which the polemical edge was honed and fundamentals were outlined.[60] Print was crucial both to the practical complexities of politics and to the creation of the sense of chaos and confusion on which Lilly and others were trading. The explosion in the number of titles being produced, from a rapidly increasing number of presses, was dominated by down-market, ephemeral and time-sensitive publications – tomorrow's 'bum fodder', often with the same value as testaments of truth.[61] The use of print, petition and demonstration for all these purposes created a sense of disorder, and in the ensuing arguments individuals adopted increasingly polarized positions. Civil war – both the real one and the paper combats – was throwing up new forms of authority, and new sources of solidarity: gathered churches and textual communities, excisemen and garrison commanders, magistrates, witchfinders and clubman leaders.

As with the material impact of the fighting, however, these obvious costs were to some extent offset by the opportunities presented; taking up those opportunities further accentuated the problem. Some of the creative responses to these problems were bracingly radical – in secular politics, on issues of church government and, at a more fundamental level, on the possibilities of harnessing human reason in order to come close to God and achieve a secular millennium. Public discussion ranged far more widely than the formal peace negotiations – war had spawned arguments more profound and open-ended than who could have a negative voice in relation to legislation, or control of the militia.

Even if Charles had been inclined to be helpful on these narrower issues (which he does not seem to have been), it was not clear what he should be asked to agree to, or even whom he should try to settle with. Edwards and Cromwell were supposed to be on the same side after all and both had taken the Solemn League and Covenant. Initiatives for settlement, in these conditions, did not arise only from Parliament and the court, and ranged far beyond the issues of 1642 – one of the complexities of the post-war position was to be the rise of new sources of authority, new promoters of settlement. It was this practice of mobilizing opinion which had destabilized the Long Parliament, and it was no less significant following the war. Some were relatively opportunistic, some direct contributions to the debates about church government. All of them were a product of the war, and were organized in ways that took advantage of the practical conditions of life in wartime England.

A very common reaction to these conditions was a desire to resume normal politics but none of the partisans – constitutional or militant royalists, Presbyterian or Independent parliamentarians – could claim that desire as their natural territory. All had, in one way or another, violated these principles and practices. And no group on the parliamentary side could command sufficient support to force Charles to deal with them.

17

Military Defeat and Political Survival

Attempts at Settlement from Newcastle to Newmarket

Charles had surrendered to the Covenanters at Southwell in May 1646 and from there he was taken to Newcastle, arriving on 13 May. It was not until 13 July, fully two months later, that formal peace proposals were sent north from Parliament, and when they arrived there was more than an air of familiarity about them. Charles was to swear the Solemn League and Covenant, accept reformation according to its provisions and seek 'the nearest conjunction and uniformity in matters of religion between England and Scotland'. On secular matters, the terms were also stringent. For twenty years the militia was to be in the hands of men approved by both Houses. During the same period the Houses were to have absolute control over all armed forces, and the power to suppress any forces raised against them. Subject to the assent of the Scottish parliament, the same provisions would apply there, and the forces of the two kingdoms would act together, when necessary. New arrangements would be devised at the end of the twenty years and, if necessary, implemented against the King's will. This twenty-year limitation was therefore a compromise only in one sense, since it was a fairly clear statement of distrust of this particular monarch – in twenty years' time, all being well, Charles would be six feet under. In the unhappy event that he was not, or that his heirs were no more reliable, then the Houses had reserved to themselves the right to make the crown submit once more. While his posterity might be kings in the sense which he understood, he never would be again. Charles had gone to war, effectively, to avoid relinquishing control of the militia and the form of reformation in his kingdoms and was now, following defeat, being asked to submit on both issues.[1]

On the issues arising since 1642 the terms were equally stringent. There was to be a general pardon for those who had fought for the

King, but there were eleven qualifying clauses which exempted, in all, fifty-eight royalists from the pardon. One third of the lands of the bishops and clergy were to be sold and the number of offices of state to be nominated by Parliament now expanded to include the Mastership of the Rolls. All grants made under the King's Great Seal since 22 May 1642 were declared invalid.[2] The men carrying the propositions were not empowered to negotiate; they were simply to report Charles's answer: as Charles contemptuously put it, 'an honest trumpeter might have done as much'. Their orders had been to secure consent within ten days, or to return.[3]

Behind these uncompromising terms, however, lay serious potential divisions among the victors, particularly of course over church government. English Presbyterians saw in the Covenanters potential allies, even if they did not want a completely 'Scottified' English church. They tended also to be rather suspicious of the New Model, which had won the war but not on behalf of Presbyterianism, and had in any case been created partly as a means of ousting the earls of Essex and Manchester. Many others saw in this Presbyterianism the threat of a new intolerance, and were anxious to secure freedoms alongside any future Presbyterian settlement. There was also resentment at Scottish influence in England: it seemed worthwhile on 14 August, for example, to pass an ordinance imposing punishment on libellers of the Scots kingdom or army, but significantly, perhaps, it passed only by a majority of 130 to 102. For those thinking this way the New Model was more likely to seem an ally than a threat: it was not Scottish, and not Presbyterian. There were differences on secular issues too, or at least the extent to which Charles's hands should be tied or the powers of monarchs in general restrained, and whether or not it was worth pushing these issues once the future of the church had been decided. The costs of the war, and the new forms of authority and the institutions of government that it had spawned, were also unpopular – the excise, the committeemen and, above all, the expensive armies. These issues were not yet being addressed: indeed, in October it was agreed without any division that the New Model Army should stay in being for another six months.[4]

It was for his perceptiveness about these divisions that Jacob Astley is best remembered. A senior royalist commander, with a distinguished military record, both in the European wars and in the English civil war, such fame as he enjoys comes instead from his surrender in the last months of the war. On 21 March he was on the move from the Welsh borders with 3,000 men, with the rather desperate hope of meeting French troops arriving on the east coast. Near Stow-on-the-Wold he was met by parliamentary forces and defeated. His soldiers surrendered in crowds and Astley, recognizing the finality of the defeat, said to the parliamentarian victors, 'You have now done your work and may go play, unless you will fall out among yourselves'.[5] In 1640 Charles's problem in England had been the plurality of responses to the Scottish crisis. In 1646 the much more marked and explicit plurality of responses to the civil war was his opportunity.

Faith in the division of his enemies was a central plank of Charles's response to the Newcastle Propositions: on the whole he waited for something better to turn up. His private correspondence reveals that royalist counsels were divided about how much of the Newcastle Propositions could safely be accepted, and also that Charles personally hated the whole package. On the other hand, he did not want to antagonize the Covenanters to the extent that they might retire to Scotland and hand him over to Parliament. Before he officially received the propositions, he knew enough of their contents to know that he would not accept them, but that delay was the key to eventual success. On 1 July he wrote to Henrietta Maria that 'a flat denial' was to be 'delayed as long as may be'. Nonetheless, over the summer the balance of forces seemed to be pushing him towards a concession, although Henrietta Maria continued to advise against it, and he continued to write letters reassuring her on that point. He could never have agreed to the propositions with conviction, however, and as long as other possibilities presented themselves there was little hope of his submitting.[6]

Charles was strongly opposed to a Presbyterian settlement, believing it to be as destructive of monarchical government as resignation of control of the militia. The previous September he had challenged Colepeper, Ashburnham and Jermyn to 'show me any precedent where ever a Presbyterial government and regal was together without perpetual rebellions . . . the ground of their doctrine is anti-monarchical'.[7] There was some possibility of an alliance with Independents against this pressure for a Presbyterian settlement. In the autumn he proposed settling for Presbyterianism for three years, in which time an assembly consisting of 20 Presbyterians, 20 Independents and 20 of his own nominees should discuss a permanent settlement. But this concession was difficult to square with his conscience: on 21 September, in rejecting advice to make more-permanent concessions on Presbyterianism in order to woo the Covenanters, he had argued that it was a lesser evil to submit to one pope than to many. He thus made a connection with the rhetoric of Independents like Cheney Culpeper, and he was, indeed, receiving fresh approaches from Independents at that time.[8] But Independency was hardly more attractive to the King than Presbyterianism. Both the Directory of Worship and the threat of sectarian chaos were unpopular with many people and there were large numbers of Protestants who were attached to the Prayer Book, not least as a bulwark against sectarianism.[9] This was the most plausible ground on which to stand.

Charles was advised by some counsellors (including Henrietta Maria, who did not make strong distinctions among the various Protestant heresies) to make concessions on the church in order to save the militia. Hyde was not among them, though, since he thought a Presbyterian settlement completely unacceptable. In July he wrote:

It is not the change of Church Government which is chiefly aimed at (though that were too much) but it is by that pretext to take away the dependency of the Church from the Crown, which, let me tell you, I hold to be of equal consequence to that of the Militia, for people are governed by pulpits more than the sword, in times of peace.

In the end both the militia and the church were non-negotiable for Charles, as they had been in 1642, in fact. Counsellors who advised compromise on one in order to save the other made no headway; instead, it was another line of advice from Henrietta Maria that won out – to be resolved and constant until they could 'again be masters'.[10]

For Charles, of course, this was not simply an English matter, and while he waited and hoped for the dissolution of the English parliamentary alliance he continued to look for allies outside his metropolitan kingdom. In fact, the thread of consistency running through his actions from 1637 onwards may have been an unwillingness to 'deal' with rebels, and his preferred option in 1646 was probably to renew the war so that he could punish them. He was also consistently willing to make tactical concessions to draw people into negotiation which he had no intention of conceding in the end – he had a clear sense of 'grounds', fundamentals of his view of kingship, which could and should be protected by whatever 'means' were effective.[11]

In any case, throughout these treaty negotiations he pursued covert diplomacy which made and makes him appear shifty. The possibility of renewing the war with French help had been actively considered as the last strongholds of English royalism fell, and in the first months of his captivity he cast around for help in Ireland and Scotland too. In Ireland things did not look particularly good for him. There the Confederation of Catholic forces formed in the rising of 1641 was fighting on several fronts, while in more or less continuous negotiation for a peace with the King. They faced an army raised by the Dublin administration, under the command of the Marquess of Ormond, and a force sent from Scotland under Monro. Ormond was the King's representative – his appointment to the Dublin administration was no business of the English parliament – and remained loyal to Charles, but was also committed to the defence of Irish Protestantism. These Protestant armies, including Ormond's, enjoyed considerable support in England and Scotland. But it was not easy for Ormond to hold the ring in Confederate circles, as both a royalist and a Protestant. At several critical moments in the complex and protracted negotiations he stood out against crucial concessions to Irish Catholics. This fed opposition to him on the clericalist wing of the Confederate coalition, which began to make a common cause with opposition to the leadership, which seemed both high-handed and ineffective at securing an acceptable peace.[12]

This situation was made more complicated by the arrival in 1645 of the Earl of Glamorgan, a Catholic who arrived directly from the King's side and who, in the aftermath of Naseby and the deteriorating royalist position in England, was able to offer more substantial concessions. He had been negotiating directly with the Confederates on the King's behalf for military aid, a reflection of the pressing military needs in England, but something which undermined the authority of the King's official representative, Ormond. In August 1645 Glamorgan signed a treaty promising dramatic concessions – more than Ormond would have been comfortable to offer – in return for further military aid. It is not clear whether or not the King had approved these concessions, although Glamorgan did sign a defeasance exempting the King from anything that he did not like – this probably tells the story it seems to. Distrust in Ireland delayed agreement, and when the nature of the negotiations became public late in 1645 Glamorgan's efforts collapsed.[13]

This left Ormond unrivalled as the King's representative in Ireland,

and he negotiated a peace with the Confederates which was signed at the end of March 1646. In return for important concessions on religion, he secured the promise of troops to support Chester: too late, however, since it had fallen on 3 February. Not only did this fail to produce military aid, but it also divided the Irish Confederates. The clericalist wing, now led by a papal nuncio called Rinuccini, rejected the terms as too soft. Rinuccini had arrived in October 1645, with money and arms, intent on securing freedom of worship for Catholics in Ireland and willing to exploit divisions among the Confederates to avoid a peace that fell short of that. By comparison, he was relatively casual about the need to restore Charles's authority: an alliance with the royalists was not his priority. The Ormond peace offered almost no guarantees about the future of Catholicism and was not acceptable to an important slice of Confederate opinion. In the meantime, the war with Monro's army continued, and through June and July 1646 the Confederate army enjoyed considerable military success, including a significant victory at Benburb (5 June) and the capture of castles at Roscommon and Bunratty in the first half of July. This allowed preparations for an attack on Dublin.[14]

Ormond faced other difficulties too. On 4 July, Digby had arrived in Ireland with the news that, during the King's captivity, Ormond was to take instructions from Henrietta Maria and the Prince of Wales. At the end of the month, however, Digby told the Irish privy council that his own authority was sufficient for him to act in the King's name, and that the Ormond peace should be published. This was duly done the following day, 30 July. Not only did this breach a confidentiality agreement, but it prompted Rinuccini into open opposition. He convened a meeting of the Irish clergy at Waterford, which denounced the peace on 12 August. They then threatened an interdiction on any town that proclaimed the peace, and the effect seems to have been fatal to Ormond's authority. He summoned a meeting of the Irish nobility at Cashel, but was refused admission to the town and by mid-September his ruin was complete. Leading figures of the Supreme Council of the Confederacy were arrested when Rinuccini arrived at Kilkenny at the head of an armed force, and the Ormond peace was denounced. A purged Confederate leadership was in place, with Owen Roe O'Neill at the head of its forces, and was very unfriendly to a peace in Ireland that was no more than a capitulation. Faced with the triumph of this wing of the Confederacy, Ormond decided to surrender Dublin to the English parliament rather than risk a Catholic capture. In response Rinuccini recognized the Earl of Glamorgan as the King's lieutenant, in place of Ormond. Parliament accepted Ormond's resignation in the middle of October.[15] By September 1646, then, the King could at least be clear that the Irish were not his salvation. The Irish Confederates were, like the English parliamentarians, seeking to extract concessions at this moment of weakness and concessions to the English parliament and the Irish Confederates were likely to be mutually unacceptable.

In Scotland the prospects for Charles looked no less bleak. It had been clear for some time that the English parliament was not necessarily reliable from the point of view of the Covenanters, and they had been negotiating with the King directly since the middle of 1645, although they denied it publicly. Early in 1646 papers presented by the Covenanters to the English parliament were published, prefaced by an outline of how the terms for negotiation had been softened since the Uxbridge negotiations. The Commons ordered that they should be burnt, although the Lords modified the measure to mean that only the preface, not official papers produced by formal allies, would be publicly burnt.[16] Clearly there were possibilities here for Charles.

But what the Covenanters wanted from the English parliament – chiefly a strict Presbyterian settlement – was no more acceptable to Charles. Henrietta Maria and the French consistently urged compromise on the church settlement in order to secure military help, but Charles was never willing to pursue this line, and French help never arrived. In April the Covenanter terms for a settlement became clear and Charles soon discovered, following his surrender, that there was little room for manoeuvre. He agreed to receive instruction on Presbyterian government (no easy thing to agree to, one might think) and that encouraged hopes that he might throw in his lot with them. At Newcastle, however, it quickly became clear that he was not really learning from Alexander Henderson's instruction. His hopes rested on divisions in Scotland, between the relative hardliners like Argyll and a group led by Hamilton which sought security both for the kirk and for monarchical authority, and which might be persuaded to help restore Charles to effective rule with weaker demands about the church settlement in England. But the Hamiltonians had little leverage in these months.[17]

In the late summer of 1645, Charles received a special envoy from

France, Jean de Montreuil, who had been sent to broker a deal between Charles and the Covenanters. This would allow for an invasion of England, with French support; one of the final schemes of the first war. Behind this lay a French plan to annexe the Spanish Netherlands. They now offered Charles the prospect of military support in the hope that it would ensure there was no English intervention in the Netherlands. The French remained interested (at least apparently) in pursuing this following Charles's surrender in 1646 and the scheme was picked up again the following spring.[18]

Charles then had many options, and that was bound to make him seem flirtatious to the many parties with which he was apparently willing to deal. It was quite reasonable for a man of his convictions to play the field in this way – the most important thing was to preserve the monarchy, not pander to the opinions of his subjects. On the other hand, to those with whom he was dealing he must have seemed actively deceitful, rather than open to offers from any potentially helpful source. For example, on 11 June he wrote a letter to the long-suffering Ormond telling him to treat no further with the Irish, and allowed the Scots around him to see the letter. This was clearly intended to foster the impression that his dealings with the Confederates were over and that the Covenanters could be reassured about dealing with him. In a letter to the Queen, however, he explained that he meant no *further* negotiation – what had already been agreed was not to be undone. An unfortunate feature of this minor conceit was that Ormond did not understand this distinction. Later in the year Charles offered to Parliament management of the war in Ireland, boasting to the Queen that it was the management that was offered – if he chose to make peace then his engagement with Parliament would be ended. Most of us would think, perhaps, that Charles should have backed only one of these horses – opted for a deal with Covenanters and English Presbyterians or with English Independents, and probably not (for domestic reasons) a deal with the Irish Catholics or the French. But instead he was always interested by all options, and in November toyed with encouraging a general rising against the English parliament.[19]

For all these reasons, nothing much happened in relation to the English peace treaty between July and December. Charles's initial response to the Newcastle Propositions was to play for time. His first reply, on 1 August, asked for the opportunity to come to London personally to 'raise a mutual confidence between him and his people' and satisfy his conscience in full discussion since the propositions 'do import so great alterations' in church and state.[20] This call for a return to London had recurred throughout the 1640s, but was completely unacceptable to the Westminster leadership, who feared that it would lead to an unravelling of their position. William Sancroft, writing in May 1646, said that the dominant Westminster faction 'fear nothing more than' the King's arrival in London: 'they know not what to do with him if he comes . . . his presence will attract hearts and animate many of the members to appear for him with open face who now mask under a visor'.[21] It was probably a well-grounded fear, which Charles played on again, in his second formal response to the propositions in late December. It was only the following May that he gave a substantive answer to the specific proposals, and then the purpose was largely disruptive.[22]

From the late summer onwards the Covenanters had been preparing to go home. Charles's intransigence made it seem that there was little hope of reaching a deal with him, while the revelation of their negotiations with him made the English parliament increasingly hostile. Open trading had started in mid-August, when the Commons voted £100,000 to cover the Scots' costs. In retaliation they estimated those costs at £2,000,000, but said that they were willing to accept £500,000. Two weeks of haggling produced a settlement at £400,000, half to be paid before they left and the rest to be paid in instalments thereafter. The security for the loans raised in the City was the sale of bishops' lands and the excise. The quid pro quo was that the English parliament claimed power over the King's person and this became the deal – payment of reparations to the Covenanters in return for control of the King. The details were worked out by the end of December: this was the context of Charles's second plea to come to London and be heard ('the which if refused to a subject by a King, he would be thought a tyrant for it'). Parliament again felt unmoved by the attractions of this plan and it was decided to hold the King at Holmby, Northamptonshire. The alternative had been Newmarket – a favourite royal stamping ground before the war but in the now-Presbyterian Eastern Association. In January the Committee of Both Kingdoms was superseded as the crucial political body by the Committee for Irish Affairs at Derby House. Payments to the Covenanters began and at the end of January parliamentary commissioners arrived in Newcastle to take the King south. The Covenanters marched north on 30 January, having received the first £100,000, and the second instalment arrived a few days later: to many royalists then and since this has looked rather like the Scots selling their king. Charles himself embellished the story by noting that it was 'at too cheap a rate'.[23]

A fixed point in these negotiations was the centrality of the King to any settlement. The surrender of Charles had not settled much and had clearly not ruled out the possibility of renewed fighting. The idea of deposition, or of some kind of 'temporary abdication', was in the air, but this was plainly hampered by the fact that none of the alternative claimants to the throne was willing to deal with Parliament. The heir, in fact, had prudently been sent abroad. Martyrdom was in any case preferable for Charles, as he was keen to let everyone know.[24] The military defeat of the King was by no means a political defeat for monarchy since there was every prospect of a dissolution of the parliamentary coalition. Prevarication worked in his favour because of this essential fact, which reflected the cultural prestige of monarchy. Charles I and his policies were in general less popular than the idea of monarchy, and he was at his most effective when he presented himself as the embodiment of the latter. From 1647 onwards he increasingly presented himself as such, and as a monarch suffering in the service of that sacred office. In a way he was preparing himself for the martyrdom which he did indeed ultimately embrace – it was certainly a turn away from the austere image of a distant figure, seeking the welfare but not the approval of his people, that had been presented by Van Dyke in the 1630s.

En route from Newcastle to Holmby, Charles was greeted by enthusiastic crowds, which provide vivid testimony to the continuing cultural power not just of the idea of monarchy, but even the appeal of this particular monarch. Many of those who attended hoped to be healed by the royal touch. At Ripon on 7 February he touched for the King's Evil.[25] The King's Evil was scrofula, a tubercular infection which manifested itself in swellings in the neck and in skin conditions. It was claimed that by his sacred touch an English king could cure this disease, and there is plenty of contemporary testimony that it worked. Richard Wiseman, the royalist surgeon, devoted a whole book of his *Chirurgicall Treatises* to medical treatments of the disease but noted in advance that the royal touch was the most effective cure, as testified in 'our chronicles' and by 'the personal experiences of many thousands now living'.[26] Given the symbolic force of the royal touch, and his own immediate interests, Wiseman could hardly have been expected to say anything else, of course. His book was dedicated 'To the most sacred majesty of Charles II': the royal touch was a crucial demonstration of that sacred majesty which attached to kings.[27] Wiseman's professional and political interests could be resolved, however: those unable or unwilling to attend the King were missing the simplest and most effective cure, but there were medical alternatives 'since it is not necessary that a disease which is cured by miracle, should be remediable by no rules of art'.[28] Wiseman was certainly not alone in thinking that the royal cure worked. Those who came to be touched were issued with 'touch-pieces' and these too acquired supernatural qualities.[29]

Charles had touched for the Evil throughout the 1630s, although, characteristically, he had also issued numerous proclamations attempting to bring order to the procedure.[30] The 1635 edition of the Prayer Book had been bound with directions for the touching ceremony: this came close to integrating the enactment of sacred monarchy into the liturgy of the national church, of which, of course, he was head.[31] In that sense, touching was a powerful demonstration of exactly the image of monarchy and church that Charles had consistently defended. It is, perhaps, no surprise that he had touched at Edinburgh during his coronation visit in 1633 and at York on the eve of his ill-fated campaign in the second Bishops' War.[32] He was certainly assiduous about touching in the spring of 1647 and afterwards: it made his point that someone with these powers could not reasonably be asked to submit to the terms of the Newcastle Propositions and suggested that there were many others who might agree.[33]

Only the French and English kings claimed the power to touch, the English claiming that since the time of Edward the Confessor their monarchs had been endowed with this power. In fact, it seems, the ceremony was of more recent origin and some of the evidence cited that there was an unbroken tradition from the time of the Confessor comes from seventeenth-century claims to that effect.[34] Indeed, Charles and his son seem to have been among the most enthusiastic touchers in English history,[35] and it may be their propaganda that fooled historians subsequently.

Not only did the rite chime with Charles I's sense of church and state, but it made a powerful political point at a moment when monarchy was being demystified. The relationship between the sacred office and the royal body was here very direct. At Hull in 1642 Sir John Hotham had refused the King entry, claiming that the King's authority was expressed through Parliament, and that in obeying an order of Parliament he was not disobeying the King. Charles had nailed this argument of convenience with a neat debating point – he was familiar with the argument that his authority could be where his body was not, but not that his body could be where his authority was not. In 1643 some poor petitioners had sought permission from the King to go from London to Oxford to receive the touch. This miraculous cure, they noted, 'is one of the greatest of his Majesty's prerogatives, which no force can deprive your highness of'.[36] Touching demonstrated the particular powers that resided in the King's actual body, while at the same time demonstrating the seamlessness of his political vision.

It was not just those with scrofula who were drawn to the King. Outside Leeds the road was crowded for two miles with onlookers and everywhere he went the bells were rung. On 13 February, Fairfax rode out from Nottingham to meet him and there was an honourable exchange between the two former enemies. In Northamptonshire hundreds of gentry came to escort him and in Northampton bells were again rung and guns fired in his honour. Wherever he went, apparently, he was greeted with shouts of 'God bless your majesty!' and he arrived at Holmby, unsurprisingly, in very good spirits.[37] In April 1647, as crowds continued to flock to Holmby for the healing touch, Henry Marten jokingly suggested in the Commons that 'the parliament's Great Seal might do it if there was an ordinance for it'. He was responding to preparations to send the Newcastle Propositions to the King once more, and his barb was linked to his description of the King as a 'man': 'The man to whom these propositions shall be sent ought rather to come to the bar himself than to be sent to any more'. But like many of his jokes, this was uncomfortably close to the bone – neither the new Great Seal nor the recent expedient of an ordinance claimed sacred sanction dating back 600 years. Many evidently felt that a powerful and divinely sanctioned authority really was embodied in the King, that he was not a man just like any other. A week later the Commons denounced the practice of touching as superstitious,[38] further evidence that Charles's touching was a powerful demonstration of a significant political fact.

*

Given the cultural attractions of monarchy, the beliefs of this particular king and his negotiating habits, the best way forward in securing a settlement was probably for a single English party to achieve primacy. This would enable it to deal effectively with Charles, and force him to recognize that it was his only plausible option. From February onwards a Presbyterian party in Parliament, with allies in the City of London, sought exactly this, although probably driven more by a fear of the alternative.

Through the autumn the prospects of toleration around a Presbyterian settlement had receded, but the position of the New Model had remained strong. The abolition of the bishops was accepted by the Lords on 9 October – and the sale of their lands provided an important resource with which to pay off the Covenanters. While strides were made towards settling a Presbyterian church in England, steps were also taken to rein in more radical reformation: on 2 September an ordinance against blasphemy and heresy was proposed, including the death penalty for denial of the Trinity or incarnation. Against this, the political influence of Independents was still plain. The blasphemy ordinance did not make it onto the statute book, and when a measure was passed in February 1647 it did not inflict physical punishments for false belief but called instead for a day of public humiliation 'for that great reproach and contempt which hath been cast upon his name and saving truths'. What those truths were, and what the falsehoods were, was not defined. Meanwhile, on 10 October, Cromwell was granted his pension from the estate of the Marquess of Winchester – a very public and generous reward for a leading Independent. At the same time, the surrender of fortresses and the departure of the Covenanters meant that the continued need for an army was questionable, but it was the forces of the Presbyterian-sympathizer Edward Massey that were disbanded, a couple of weeks after the life of the New Model had been extended for six months (a vote passed without division). The disbanded soldiers – Reformadoes – were subsequently very visible on the streets of London, petitioning for relief, a symbol of what many Presbyterians regarded as a disreputable Independent manoeuvre.[39]

With these tensions in the background Parliament had, in the autumn of 1646, indulged in some political theatre of its own. On 14 September the Earl of Essex died, four days after suffering a stroke while out hunting. He was buried with full chivalric honours, in a ceremony modelled on that of Charles I's elder brother, Prince Henry. Henry's death in 1612, at the age of eighteen, had been the occasion of massive public mourning. On this occasion £5,000 was voted by Parliament 'towards the discharging of his debts and defraying the expenses of his funeral': a statement of the debt owed in return for his service to the parliamentary cause. The route from Essex House, just downriver from Somerset House, was lined by five regiments of the Trained Bands. Ahead of the main procession rode the marshal of the City of London and twenty others dressed in black cassocks. The procession itself was led by sixty-eight poor men, then servants of the gentry, four regiments of the Trained Bands, the pikemen trailing their pikes. They marched from Covent Garden, via Essex House, where they were joined by fifemen, drummers and trumpeters, all wearing the Devereux arms. Five chaplains followed, then more musicians, officers of the Trained Bands, and musicians with other heraldic arms to which the earl had claim. A riderless horse, led by a groom, and an effigy of the earl preceded the coffin, which was borne by prominent Presbyterians. There followed eminent mourners, then members of both Houses, the Recorder and Aldermen of London, the Assembly of Divines and fifty or sixty cavalrymen. In all, over 1,000 processed, and up to 10,000 soldiers had either processed or guarded the route. As a result there was a problem of fitting everyone into Westminster Abbey, even though the Lords had ordered that the multitude and all women 'of whatsoever quality' were barred (chivalric funerals were in any case, by custom, all-male affairs). An eloquent sermon by Richard Vines was heard by those fortunate enough to cram in, before they processed back to Essex House for a funeral banquet. That evening, five hours after the procession had begun, the bell at St Margaret's, Westminster, tolled twice. A signal was then given to the Stone Fort at Southwark to fire its great cannon, and each of the forts around the eleven-mile defences fired its great cannon in turn. This was done three times.[40]

But this was a more ambiguous affair than this ritual suggested. Controversially, it had been ordered that those who had been in arms for the King should not attend and almost all the chief mourners were prominent Presbyterians: Fairfax, Cromwell and Ireton were all absent. The effigy, which had become an important site for those wishing to reflect on the contribution of Essex to a noble cause, was attacked on the night of 26/27 November. John White, using an axe acquired from a Ludgate ironmonger, wrecked the elaborate catafalque erected in the abbey in the earl's honour, hacked the head off the effigy, with seven or eight blows, ripped off the buff coat the earl had worn at Edgehill, slashed his breeches and boots, and stole his golden sword. In his excitement he also took the nose off an image of Sir William Camden, a relatively blameless antiquarian, whose tomb was nearby. White claimed that an angel had directed him 'to cut all the said image, hearse and all that was about it in pieces, and to beat down the rest of the images in the said church'. In his defence he said it was a dishonour to Christ to introduce the effigy of a man into a sacred building. The repaired image was placed behind glass, and lasted to the Restoration, when the effigy was destroyed at the command of Charles II, although the corpse was left undisturbed.[41]

Dubbed by the press a disaffected Cavalier, White expressed a line of argument that might not have been so far from that of some members of the parliamentary coalition – there were those on Essex's side, after all, who had smashed funerary monuments and supported his replacement at the head of the parliamentary army. Even if they would not have desecrated this particular tomb, the point can hardly have been lost on contemporaries. This appeal to a grand chivalric tradition appears elegiac – the Self-Denying Ordinance, which had ended Essex's martial career, had also diluted the importance of baronial and aristocratic images in the promotion of the parliamentary cause; the unity it proclaimed, if it had ever existed, belonged more to the beginning than the end of Essex's career. Certainly, if Cavaliers could turn the language of reformation against the images of parliamentary virtue then this was a more contested vision than that of Charles healing the sick.

While the politicians wrangled there had been no peace dividend and, on the evidence of the Newcastle negotiations, military victory had not produced a political breakthrough. Worse, there had been numerous disorders in the provincial armies. Anti-war and anti-army feelings were of prime political importance during 1647: to those who wanted to reduce taxation, re-establish legal and constitutional forms of politics and to set clear limits to further reformation, it seemed obvious that the armies had to be disbanded.[42] At the same time, it became increasingly clear to radicals that the pursuit of their aims depended on the continued influence of the New Model and, by the same token, that if the New

Model was to receive just treatment, it should seek the protection of radically minded politicians.

These intersecting political and religious concerns came together in a Presbyterian 'counter-revolution' as partisans on the parliamentary side battled for control of the sources of political power – the streets of London, Parliament, the City and the New Model. Those that had little hope of bringing the New Model along with them sought to abolish it as an obstacle to their will and a burden on the people which cost them support. In resisting these moves the New Model became an independent political actor, resisting elements of the Protestant coalition in Parliament and the City in defence of its own interests.

Crowds, particularly in London, came to play a key role in the complex politics of 1647, just as they had in 1640–42. At Holmby, Charles was playing to the gallery and thereby discomfiting his captors, who came jokingly to refer to him as 'the stroker'. The funeral of the Earl of Essex attempted a moment of public unity celebrating a hero of the parliamentary cause, identifying it with a Presbyterian church settlement. As in 1641 there was also a battle for the control of the political and administrative institutions of the City, and the future of English and Scottish politics were once more closely entwined. But these battles were now within the parliamentary coalition, rather than between emergent royalist and parliamentary parties – the King was a (presumably rather gratified) spectator in all this. In the end it was to be an alliance between Independents and the New Model that established control of London's streets, and of Parliament, but as this battle was fought out it is easy to see why the King's position might appear to be strengthening.

In the autumn, a priority at Westminster was to begin to reduce public expenses. For the Presbyterians this came to focus on the New Model, which was both the largest force and one that was regarded as politically suspect. There had been previous Presbyterian campaigns which had seemed to identify enemies within as much as outside the parliamentary coalition – starting in November 1644, then in 1645 and as the war ended in 1646. But that which opened in December 1646 was the most concerted and the most confrontational. Thomas Edwards had been critical of the New Model in the first two parts of *Gangraena*, but the third part, published as part of this Presbyterian campaign in the City and at Westminster, devoted much of its energy to a denunciation of its role in promoting heresy. Presbyterians around Sion College co-operated

with Covenanters and members of the Westminster Assembly to achieve
dominance in the City and Parliament. Their aim was a Presbyterian
church settlement and a rapid peace, which led them to contemplate
pretty easy terms on many secular issues. Following the death of the
Earl of Essex these views were championed in Parliament by the old
peace-party man Denzil Holles and Sir Philip Stapleton.[43]

In December 1646 a petition circulated in London which called for a
high-Presbyterian settlement and the disbandment of the army since it
was an encouragement to heresy. The Lords took the opportunity to
command Fairfax to impose the Solemn League and Covenant on all
the men under his command. The petition was sufficiently inflammatory
for the Commons to have the three promoters arrested, but the City
accepted the petition. At Common Council elections on 21 December a
large Presbyterian majority was returned, and the petition had been
something of a manifesto for them. Those who resisted the petition were,
on the whole, unsuccessful. Alongside a strict Presbyterian settlement the
new Common Council called for disbandment of the New Model Army,
elections to a free parliament, reform of county committees and dissolution of the committee of Haberdashers' Hall.[44]

These aims were pursued pretty consistently through 1647, on the
basis of the influence of Holles and Stapleton in the Commons, and of
their allies in the City. On the key issues before the King they were
willing to concede a settlement that established presbytery for only
three years, and control of the militia only for ten. This did not produce a
breakthrough, of course, and in February more confrontational measures
were taken – communion plate from the royal chapel was melted down to
make a dinner service for Charles, and his household was disestablished
until he came to terms with Parliament.[45] Although the negotiation
with Charles appeared unpromising, many MPs now swung against the
Independents, more concerned with order and peace than with the more
relaxed religious settlement they offered.

Pressure on Parliament in the last week of December coincided with
the resurgence of crowds around the Houses, and the crowd on
31 December was particularly menacing. Street politics were not easy to
control or subsume, however. If the crowds at Holmby in February
reflected a resurgent royalism, this was a natural ally of those seeking to
restore central elements of the pre-civil war world. These were not
necessarily the Presbyterians. For example, there is evidence of increasing

hostility to the new Puritan calendar. From September 1641 onwards there were measures designed to secure more godly observation of the Sabbath – a reaction against the Caroline *Book of Sports* and its associated indulgences. But this became connected to a more fundamental assault on the ritual calendar – Easter, Whitsun, 'Christ's birthday' and saints' days – a campaign associated particularly with the Solemn League and Covenant. This had culminated in the issue of the Directory of Worship in January 1645. The Directory banned holy days, reinforcing earlier measures against May Day, and contained explicit injunctions against Shrove Tuesday rituals of misrule. In place of this ritual year stood fast days on the last Wednesday of every month, and other days of national thanksgiving from time to time. In 1644, when the monthly fast fell on Christmas Day, an ordinance had called for 'the more solemn humiliation' on the fast, since Christmas celebrations had turned into a 'liberty to carnal and sensual delights'. Christmas too was abolished, and the unpopularity of that measure was evident during 1646.[46]

These rituals had a more than religious significance – they were moments at which local differences were submerged in a celebration of shared faith, or identity, or in which tensions were released in rituals of misrule and inversion. On the other hand, it was precisely because they had a more than religious significance that Puritans were opposed to them and favoured instead celebrations of national triumph or delivery – such as 5 November, for example.[47] In this they were not necessarily in tune with the streets.

On 9 February, London apprentices petitioned Parliament for a monthly 'playday' to replace the lost saints' days. It may not be coincidence that this came one day after the Lords had voted that anyone not taking the Covenant should be barred from office, a measure taken in response to Presbyterian pressure from the City. Shrove Tuesday (9 March), a day traditionally associated with apprentice disorder, seems to have passed without incident, but apprentices gathered again on 20 April. This was two days after Easter and three days before St George's Day, both important dates in the now defunct ritual year. The crowd waited patiently until 5 p.m. but eventually dispersed peacefully, without receiving an answer. On St George's Day itself, 23 April, crowds pressed round the Houses again, awaiting a reply. This campaign, although one with resonances on the streets of London, clearly held little appeal for Presbyterians: perhaps they shared the view of the *Moderate Intelli-*

gencer, that it was unwise to give scholars and apprentices too much leisure.[48]

Agitation against the excise also revealed a limit to Presbyterian populism. For the relatively poor, particularly in London, the early months of 1647 were very hard. The 1646 harvest was poor, signalling the start of what may have been the worst run of bad harvests between the early seventeenth century and the middle of the eighteenth.[49] This pushed up the price of food grains while at the same time depressing activity in the economy, so that wage earners were doubly squeezed – steep inflation in the costs of necessities and declining opportunities to find work. Towns and industrial districts had high concentrations of wage-earners and were dependent on the market for food supplies, and so were particularly vulnerable to dearth and disorder. Grain riots in such places were not spontaneous and randomly violent responses to hunger, or the weather – they were targeted against human agents of hardship, such as profiteers or governors who failed to intervene to protect the needy. Hard times often triggered responses from governors aimed at ameliorating the difficulties – prompted no doubt by a mixture of concern for the welfare of the poor, and concern for social order. In London, in January 1647, a number of such measures were visible – a petition from the City to Parliament for relief of the poor and punishment of vagabonds, and measures to prevent the consumption of meat, exports of fish, the slaughter of calves and lambs, and the use of food grains in brewing. In February there was great relief when 'many ships . . . laden with corn in great abundance' arrived.[50]

High levels of taxation and, in particular, the excise did not help. The excises on meat and salt put an inflationary pressure on staple food items and served as a focus for hostility to the burdens of war, and the officials who administered them. The excise probably produced less money than the assessment, but it was more regressive (since payment was made by everyone who used salt and meat, or drank beer, regardless of their income), was not time-limited, and was in the hands of professional collectors rather than local officeholders. In November and December there were serious disorders in Norwich, Beccles (where rioters were said to have been encouraged by the failure to punish the Norwich rioters) and Worcester.[51] As with the disturbance at Derby in 1645, and grain riots, these were identifiably political demonstrations, led by butchers (those best placed to understand the burdens of the excise on meat) and joined by brewers in late December. There is some suggestion that the Presbyterians who dominated Norwich at that point were in sympathy with the rioters – the excise was, after all, a principal support of the New Model Army.[52] There was also a wider reaction against the burdens of war and the abuses of power associated with committee government, although what counted as an abuse was a political question – what the situation demanded appeared differently to people of different political opinions. Excise disturbances were the popular edge of what could seem a wider phenomenon and for that reason may have enjoyed some sympathy from partisan local governors.[53]

A week after the initial demonstration in favour of recreation days, London saw its only major excise disorder, at Smithfield. In late January the Commons heard a report dealing with 'obstructions' to the excise and in the first week of February this seems to have been high on the agenda. The author of *London's Account*, an indictment of the entire financial edifice erected by Parliament which compared the whole lot unfavourably with ship money, was brought to the bar of the House, and the commissioners for the excise appeared in person with a petition for help in facing the difficulties of collection. When the issue was finally discussed, on 8 February, the House was unsympathetic to opponents of the excise. It ordered that an exemplary declaration should be prepared, and that abuses by minor officials and the impact on trade should be investigated. On the whole, however, the intention was, thought the *Weekly Account*, to 'manifest that the House intend to continue the [excise] for a time longer for the satisfying of the public debts of the kingdom'.[54]

Disappointment at this outcome was probably part of the reason for the riot at Smithfield a week later. On 15 February a buyer refused to pay excise and tried to remove his livestock. When he was stopped a crowd gathered in his defence. It was dispersed but another crowd gathered later, burning down the excise house, and £80 or £100 was 'scattered and purloined'. The later crowd was led by butchers, one of whom said that they would 'bear down the excise by force'. There certainly was force – 'many of the officers of the excise were beaten' – but it was limited and focused. At least some of the money was scattered, not stolen, and it was the officers and their house that were attacked. The rioters also took the trouble to spoil the records kept by the officers. Clearly there was method in the violence.[55]

The official response was again unyielding – measures were taken to punish the ringleaders and to police the market more effectively. Ordinances followed and included some measures to protect the poor – the excise was not to be levied on those receiving alms, or by poll except by consent, and local officeholders were given some powers to examine sub-commissioners suspected of abuse or corruption. But the main message was clear: Parliament would listen to complaints, but in the meantime 'expect all persons whatsoever shall duly pay all sums imposed . . . by way of excise'. The excise house was rebuilt as a private dwelling so that future damage could be prosecuted as a felony. Newsbooks echoed the message – the excise was unavoidable until the army was disbanded. The *Moderate Intelligencer* went further:

[the rioters] have made a rod for themselves; for had they been quiet, and paid excise, the soldiery might have been nulled and the cause taken away . . . whereas now, its probable the Parliament will be necessitated to keep an army to preserve themselves, those they employ and pay the debts of the kingdom.[56]

As with the recreation days, therefore, there was no initial concession. Just as the Puritan calendar was crucial to the cultural aims of the Presbyterians, the excise was no less essential to their position, and preferable to a land tax. On 4 March it was the assessment that the Lords, an assembly of landholders, refused to renew.[57] The winter of 1646/7 saw a resurgent royalism, associated with an attachment to tradition and hostility to the military and the administrative measures necessary to support it. This was not necessarily territory that belonged to Presbyterians. Nonetheless, their immediate prospects looked good. On 11 March one of William Lilly's clients wanted to know 'If Presbytery will continue any long time'.[58]

The Smithfield riot may have had an indirect effect on parliamentary politics, galvanizing the campaign to disband the army. On the day of the riot a petition had been received from Suffolk calling for a Presbyterian settlement, the suppression of toleration and the disbandment of the army, and it was Presbyterians in Parliament who proposed, four days later, cuts in the number of horse and the disbandment of all infantry units not in garrisons. These moves to disband the army were quickly connected with the mobilization of new forces for service in Ireland. On 20 February a letter arrived from Dublin in which Ormond detailed his woes, including the refusal of the Dublin population to continue to support his troops. He was finally and unequivocally a discredited political force, and Dublin was now very vulnerable.[59] With the Confederates in the ascendant a military response was imperative. Disbandment of the English forces became a means of releasing troops for Ireland, and easing the burdens on the English taxpayer.

Although this was a virtuous circle it was being proposed by politicians hostile to the New Model Army. Within the New Model it was feared that arrears of pay would not be honoured, and a movement developed within the army to demand that soldiers would not be pressed to serve in Ireland without first receiving arrears for service already given, and that soldiers should be given indemnity from prosecution for actions taken in the service of Parliament. Indemnity was a serious issue – there is evidence from Yorkshire of a serious effort to bring soldiers to court after the war and that the prosecution rate for soldiers was considerably higher than for civilians. During the war many horses were taken and if this could be prosecuted as theft it might result in the death penalty – horse theft was one of the more serious crimes in rural England, and some of these cases rumbled on for years.[60] Fears that indemnity and arrears would not be granted were well-grounded: the Presbyterian desire to disband, and to export, the army was at least in part politically motivated. It was certainly helpful that it achieved so many good things at once.[61]

Discontent in the army in March 1647 prompted direct political intervention. It is clear that by March there were petitions circulating in the army which linked its material grievances to the political conflict. One even ranked the extirpation of ungodliness and the liberty of the subject above the preservation of the privileges of Parliament. At the same time divisions were emerging in London between the Presbyterian petitioning campaign and one launched by radical Independents – prominent among them Lilburne, Walwyn and Overton. During 1646, in the course of tussles with Colonel King, the Earl of Manchester, the court of Common Pleas and the House of Lords, Lilburne had appealed in print to fundamental principles: he should be tried by his peers; the House of Lords had no jurisdiction over him. This was a form of tyranny and his struggle became, in his own eyes and in the pamphlets of his supporters, the struggle of the English people for their liberties. In pamphlets stuffed with legal citations and precedents he launched an attack on the judicial authority of the House of Lords and appealed to the Commons for protection. He was in prison from August 1646 until the autumn of 1647 by the authority of the Lords, and for much of the time his appeal to the Commons was pending. In July 1646 Overton and Walwyn's pamphlet *A Remonstrance of Many Thousand Citizens* had taken up Lilburne's case as an example of a more general political problem, producing something resembling a political platform. It was in March 1647, however, that this process was completed, with the publication of the *Large Petition*. This made a strong case for popular sovereignty as a restraint on arbitrary power, the means by which Parliament could be called to account: Parliament 'having its foundation in the free choice of the People' and the end of all government being 'the safety and freedom of the governed'. Contrasting the reforms of 1640–42 with recent threats to liberty, it blamed the latter on the authority of the Lords – a not very coded assertion of which House was the supreme authority. The petition was addressed to the Commons, and called on them to 'be exceeding careful to preserve your just Authority from all prejudices of a Negative voice in any person or persons whatsoever, that may disable you, from making that happy return to your people which they justly expect'.[62]

Here were some of the arguments of 1642 – the supremacy of the representative of the people and the refusal to allow a Negative Voice against that representative – taken to a new, and more socially levelling, conclusion. This was not resistance of Parliament to the King, but of citizens to an aristocratic 'interest'. Similarly, this represented an escalation of the practice of petitioning. During the period 1640–42 pressure had been applied to Parliament by people petitioning on behalf of counties, boroughs or particular interest groups. The Levellers were developing the habit of petitioning on behalf of people of a particular opinion: 'many thousands, earnestly desiring the glory of God, the freedom of the common-wealth and the peace of all men'. Ultimately, they were to petition on behalf of 'the people': a significant, and radical, escalation in the rhetoric of petitions.[63]

Parliament was extremely hostile to the *Large Petition*. On 15 March, as the work of circulating and collecting signatures had begun, it was turned over to the Commons. It was voted a 'seditious paper' and two days later the Lord Mayor of London asked the Lords to suppress it. In response a paper was submitted to the Committee for the Suppression of Unlicensed Printing, arguing that it was a genuine petition. As this was heard, Nicholas Tew spoke out strongly in favour of being allowed to petition, and was arrested. This resulted in a violent altercation and the committee ordered the room to be cleared. When its order was disobeyed Sir Philip Stapleton grabbed Major Tulidah by the throat and threw him out. The following day, 19 March, the House approved the committal of Tew and sent Tulidah to join him. On 20 March, Walwyn petitioned again, for the release of Tulidah and Tew, and for recognition of the right to petition Parliament as an essential freedom. Tulidah was released on bail about a week later, but Tew remained in prison. Finally, on 20 May, Walwyn submitted a third petition, this time for the release of Tew and for the right to present the *Large Petition*. In response Parliament ordered the burning of all three petitions.[64] The possibility of an alliance therefore emerged between the increasingly politicized army and radical Independents in the City: refusal of the right to petition and a bullying response to political opposition no doubt cemented the connection.[65]

But the organization of the army's campaign came from within the army – it was not a creature of any civilian movement.[66] The officers massaged the initiatives within the army into a politically acceptable form and on 21 March received a parliamentary deputation at Saffron Walden. Rather than simply accede to disbandment the commanders also wanted clarification about which regiments would stay in England and so forth and, in particular, what guarantees were on offer in relation to arrears and indemnity. There were divisions – not all officers endorsed all the questions that were put to the delegation – but it was clearly an exercise in assertiveness. There were hardliners among the officers, such as Robert and Thomas Hammond, Robert Lilburne (John's brother), John Okey, Thomas Pride and Henry Ireton. It is clear though that others in the army were more conciliatory, willing to trust Parliament, and were amenable when the parliamentary commissioners expressed concern about a petition. It is certainly true that there is very little sign of incipient mutiny in March. But the parliamentary commissioners got hold of a copy of the petition, as well as piles of an inflammatory tract (*A Warning for all the Counties of England*) published clandestinely in London, and they returned to London unnerved.[67]

Even the five moderate demands put by the army caused outrage at Westminster and on 27 March anti-army measures were taken. Money must have been part of the reason for their reluctance, but not all. In any case, refusal to pay up set them on a collision course. The revelation on 29 March of letters which showed that the agitation within the army was continuing led to parliamentary attacks on Cromwell and a declaration, sneaked through while the Independents were out of the House, which condemned the 'mutiny', and referred to the army as 'enemies of the state and disturbers of the peace'. Hurriedly penned by Holles, late in the evening, this was the notorious 'declaration of dislike' which acted as a permanent impediment to building trust between the New Model and Parliament. Army officers were summoned to the House to explain events at Saffron Walden and denied having secured signatures to the petition by force. In the course of the arguments Holles challenged Ireton to a duel.[68]

By the time another parliamentary delegation was despatched to discuss disbandment on 12 April the army had been enraged by a petitioning campaign in Essex for disbandment. Promoted through the pulpits, it was the second such campaign and it prompted a printed reply. *A New Found Strategem ... to destroy the Army*, which Thomason noted had been 'scattered abroad in the army when the commissioners were sent from Parliament to disband them', floated the idea that the army, not Parliament, was the safeguard of liberty and property. In this there was clearly the possibility of common cause with John Lilburne, whose prosecution and imprisonment by the Lords had led him to identify that institution as tyrannous. The pamphlet coincided with a revival of the condemned petition, at the initiative of men in Ireton's regiment, with the intention of sending it up with two members of every troop, despite the threat of imprisonment. This initiative may be the first sign of a new, formal, political organization in the army – the election of 'agitators'.[69]

Shortly afterwards eight cavalry regiments in East Anglia elected agitators to represent them in seeking redress, and a number of infantry regiments followed suit in May. There has been controversy about this term – it lacked some of its modern connotations and using that term rather than one of the contemporary alternatives (adjutator or agent) is perhaps misleading to the modern ear. In origin the agitators seem to have been representing the army's professional concerns, not acting as the armed wing of London Independency, or the incipient Leveller movement. There was a lot of suspicion about these connections at the time, and many historians have been tempted to see it that way subsequently, but there is no direct evidence of connections between the agitators and London radicals.[70] Important as it is to be clear about the limits of their role, however, it is also important to recognize the significance of this development. Formal consultation was taking place about the response of the army to its political masters. Whether it was primarily a consultation about immediate concerns rather than partisan political matters, the appointment (and recognition) of agitators was a significant step towards the creation of an independent political body. There was a risk, soon realized, that this might weaken the power of the military command, if agitators began to make decisions of their own.

By mid-April the army was alive with militancy. Troops were heard referring to their foes as tyrants and Lilburne's books were apparently quoted 'as statute law'. The possibility of an alliance with civilian radicals was openly mooted.[71] This reinforced the attractions of an agreement between the army and the King against Parliament, and between Independents and the King against Presbyterians. Later in the summer Jeremy Taylor, a former favourite of Laud's, published *The Liberty of Prophesying*, which argued for a latitudinarian church, in which there was freedom of expression for opinions which did not undermine religion or morality. Although he did not embrace sectarianism as a benefit to the discovery of truth, he believed that 'matters spiritual should not be restrained by punishments corporal'. The King did not approve, but the line was one that might promote an alliance against Presbyterian intolerance. David Jenkins, a Welsh judge, had been thrown into prison for publishing a pamphlet which argued that the rule of law was inseparable from the rule of the King. In prison in September he was apparently able to find common ground with John Lilburne, then much exercised about the issue of parliamentary tyranny, and impressed by the possibility that the King might be a protection against it.[72] In April this possible alliance lay behind an approach from the army to Charles to take refuge in its ranks so that he could be restored to his honour and power. It was repudiated at army headquarters but it had still been possible for the Earl of Pembroke to allege that the New Model contained 7,000 Cavaliers seeking to restore the King to his throne.[73] These were strange days, when the New Model saw hope in the King rather than its master, when the possibility of such an alliance became a reason for disbandment and when former darlings of Laudianism spoke in favour of freedom of religious expression.

Despite the growing ferment in the army and the City, Holles and Stapleton were able to press on with disbandment at Westminster. Plans were made for a force with infantry under the command of Philip Skippon and the horse under Edward Massey. From the start arrears of pay had been used as a bargaining counter – those who agreed to disband would be paid them, those who signed up for Ireland would be paid arrears and a month in advance. There had been some difficulty in getting officers to agree to serve, and it seems that many more men would have enlisted under Fairfax and Cromwell. Fairfax, in fact, did not obstruct the work of the commissioners who came to promote disbandment and enlistment, and the initiative was really defeated by the mood within the rank and file. At root it was a matter of trust – the Covenanters had been paid their money, but Parliament was using it as a bargaining counter in the case of its own army.[74]

A further element in the increasingly tense political atmosphere was a Presbyterian coup in the City of London, in which control of the militia was put in reliably Presbyterian hands. London's 'covenant-engaged' householders – those who held firm to a vision of a Presbyterian model for further reformation – sought to recruit the powers of government to their cause, which was best served by those trying to dissolve the armies, and this alliance lay behind a concerted attempt to take control of City institutions. In April the power to nominate to the militia was given back to the City authorities (it had been taken over by Parliament in 1643) and at the same time the militias of the relatively down-market and disorderly suburbs were integrated with the City militia. This was in return for a loan of £200,000 for the Irish expedition, but also cemented an alliance between Presbyterians in the City and Parliament, an alliance that was now, potentially, supported by 18,000 armed men. This had been an important part of the context for *A New Found Strategem*, and for the election of agitators.[75]

By late April a dangerous conjunction was approaching. The Presbyterians in Parliament were increasingly confident about denying arrears and calling men from the New Model to the bar for publishing, authoring or distributing inflammatory tracts. At the same time, within the New Model, agitators provided a ready means by which resentment at this treatment could be transformed into mobilization, and a form of mobilization that could put organized pressure on the officers. A kind of paper war was developing, akin to that in 1642. The army called for the retraction of charges made in the parliamentary declarations, not least the claim that they were 'enemies of the state and disturbers of the public peace', and in September compiled a *Book of Declarations*, rather like that assembled by Husbands in the spring of 1643.[76] Control of key institutions in the City had created a power base for a party and there was a renewal of Scottish interest in English affairs. The Covenanters' army had established complete control following the defeat of Alastair McColla in the Highlands, and was remodelled under the command of David Leslie, a supporter of Argyll. Amidst growing alarm at the rise of the New Model in England the possibility of renewed Scottish intervention was mooted.[77]

All this was encouraging for the King. In late April, the slightly amended Newcastle Propositions were urged on him and his reply was longer and a little more hopeful than on the first two occasions. He was willing to come to London and to grant Presbyterian government for three years pending discussions in the Westminster Assembly (with his nominations added), but he reserved his position on the Solemn League and Covenant. On the militia he was willing to give up control for ten years for the sake of peace, but on condition that it thereafter returned to the control of the crown.[78] His reply was voted sufficient by Parliament and the Scottish commissioners.[79] Standing above the fray, the King had little to lose from this increasingly fractious argument among his former enemies.

Through May this stand-off continued, but the political prospects of the New Model seemed to deteriorate. Another meeting was held at Saffron Walden church, on 7 May, where it was decided that deals could not be done without representation of the rank and file. Accordingly, each troop or company elected agitators. After a week of consultations with the agitators the officers met the parliamentary commissioners once more, on 15 May. The result was the *Declaration of the Army*, which bore the signatures of 223 commissioned officers. On 17 May, Cromwell offered reassurances that the Indemnity Ordinance had already passed the Commons and that arrears in addition to the six weeks' already offered would soon be promised. The commissioners were able to report back to Westminster that they found the army to have legitimate grievances.[80]

The promise of settlement with the King, however, seems to have made the Presbyterians in Parliament even less inclined to generosity towards the army. Rumours circulated in the New Model of a plan to pay off the privates and take revenge on the officers and that, once demobilized, the soldiers would be vulnerable to the press or prosecutions without indemnity: unless the parliamentary declaration that they were enemies of state and disturbers of the public peace was stricken from the record they had little hope of protection under the law. Presbyterians in the Lords invited the King closer to London, to Oatlands (near Weybridge in Surrey), further fuelling distrust of Parliament's intentions. It was on that day that the *Large Petition* and its two sequels were ordered to be burnt by the public hangman. On 25 May the Presbyterians decided to proceed with disbandment, not indemnity, and their scheme was adopted by the Lords two days later. They had also taken a number of measures of defence – for better securing the King and bringing arms from Oxford to London, and Sydenham Poyntz was sent to York with orders to prepare for battle with Fairfax. On 28 May, Parliament offered security for the arrears, and redress of grievances *after* disbandment.[81] During May the City loan to pay off the arrears of the New Model was put in the hands of Presbyterian treasurers and one of their centres of operation was Christ Church, Newgate, Thomas Edwards's church. Here they cashiered, recruited and preached – a nerve centre of a pretty comprehensive assault on the power base of their opponents.[82]

For the army two matters were now coming to a head – the defence of their collective interests and the control of the King. Their treatment at the hands of Parliament, and their resistance to a strict Presbyterian settlement, was increasingly cementing an alliance with radicals in the City. Against this alliance was arrayed a Presbyterian mobilization which had secured control of Parliament, had a firm base in London's pulpits and presses, and had the possibility of military support from the London militia and even the Covenanters. Fears about these military forces prompted a move to take control of arms in Oxford and, in a related initiative, of the person of the King.

On 31 May the Presbyterian Committee for Irish Affairs ordered control to be taken of the artillery, and at a meeting at Cromwell's house the same day Cromwell approved a plan put to him by George Joyce to replace the guards around the King with men of proven loyalty. Their intention was to block the removal of the King. Remarkably, Joyce and the agitators had already put together a force of 1,000 horse – this was a political intervention taking force from the rank and file, not dictated by the officers. These men had already ridden to Oxford on 29 May to secure the artillery. Joyce then sent a detachment north before going to London, presumably to seek Cromwell's approval. He caught up with the rest of his troops on 1 June, and when they arrived at Holmby they were not resisted by the guards there, or the parliamentary commissioners; and Graves, the parliamentary commander, fled. After a tense day, Joyce wrote to London for further instructions – to whom is not known, although it was claimed that Cromwell or Haselrig was the intended recipient. As news of the action spread in London, Holles and Stapleton resolved to arrest Cromwell, but he fled to the New Model. Late on the evening of 2 June, Joyce decided to take the King with him to a safer location. He forced entry to the King's chamber and told him that he would be leaving in the morning.[83]

At daybreak one of the more remarkable conversations of the 1640s took place. The King was acquiescent, but demanded to know by what authority Joyce was acting. If the account given above is accurate, that was a particularly tricky question. The change of guard was at the command of the army, not Parliament, and therefore of debatable propriety; but the evidence suggests that removing the King was Joyce's idea. His rank was Cornet – hardly the level of the army at which such decisions should be made. But his response was even more interesting – he claimed the authority of 'the soldiery of the army'. Charles then pressed him to know if he had anything in writing from Fairfax, a question which Joyce evaded. Scenting blood, perhaps, Charles pressed him again: 'I pray Mr Joyce, deal ingeniously with me, and tell me what commission you have?' Joyce replied, 'Here is my commission'. 'Where?' said the King. 'Behind me', said Joyce, pointing at the mounted soldiers. The King smiled and said, 'it is as fair a commission, and as well written as he had seen a commission in his life; and a company of handsome proper gentlemen as he had seen a great while'.[84] When Charles asked where he was to be taken Joyce suggested Oxford – the nearest reliable garrison – but Charles objected and Joyce suggested Cambridge instead. They compromised on Newmarket – coincidentally or not, the site of a planned general rendezvous of the army the following day.[85]

Here were respectable fears made manifest – a former tailor giving orders to the King. It is not clear what Joyce meant when he gestured over his shoulder at his troops – that his authority rested in force, or in the will of the soldiers or of the common man (hence Charles's gentle teasing about gentlemen).[86] But it might be a little clearer what Charles's smile meant – this was no commission, not even from Fairfax. If he had fears for his personal safety then he almost certainly had some pleasure at the evident desperation of his enemies. He sent a message to Parliament with the Earl of Dunfermline that he had travelled against his will and that he expected Parliament to uphold its own honour and the laws of the land.[87] It is not hard to imagine a smile playing on his lips as he composed that message, either.

While these extraordinary scenes were unfolding, the main body of the New Model came into open conflict with Parliament and in the process articulated an independent political vision. On 31 May commissioners arrived at Chelmsford to begin the disbandment of Fairfax's regiment but they faced mutiny. The troops marched off to Newmarket, the place appointed for the general rendezvous. Addressed again at Braintree they were disrespectful and marched off again, and on 2 June the parliamentary commissioners were recalled. Fairfax arrived at Newmarket on 5 June, where he was met enthusiastically and received a 'Humble Representation of the Dissatisfactions of the Army', drawn up by the agitators. A rather more outspoken *Solemn Engagement of the Army* was produced that day, read and assented to by the men and officers of every regiment.[88]

As well as systematizing the complaints of the army the *Solemn Engagement* called forth the institution which became known as the General Council of the Army, empowered to accept offers made to the army. This may have been an attempt to rein in the agitators, by bringing them into contact with the officers. Although it recognized the role of agitators, it did not necessarily recognize the agitators so far elected. Nonetheless, it institutionalized and legitimated the role of agitators in the larger political decisions facing the army. Fairfax, meanwhile, had ordered Whalley to join the King to protect him from insult and then ordered that he be returned to Holmby. The latter order was frustrated by Charles, however, now seemingly enjoying himself. He continued to his house at Newmarket by back lanes. Villagers strewed green boughs and rushes before him and an entry to Cambridge was ruled out in case he was greeted too enthusiastically by the townspeople – he did not see, therefore, the hundreds of bonfires lit for him in the city.[89]

As the army published its manifestos and took control of the King, Parliament seems to have tried to take control of the streets of London. A parliamentary Committee of Safety was established to operate in tandem with the City militia committee. On 6 June, Massey rode through the City calling on citizens to defend themselves against the madmen in the army whose intention was to behead the best men in Parliament and the City. On five successive days from 4 June onwards Reformadoes (recently disbanded soldiers) thronged the Houses pressing for payment of their arrears, and promises were made. It was also the pretext for granting to the City the power to raise troops of horse, although this was also pretty plainly a means to raise a Presbyterian force, which might well include Reformadoes among its recruits. Payments for service in Ireland were made to reliably Presbyterian officers and £10,000 was earmarked for the pay of officers and soldiers who deserted the New Model to join the new force.[90]

At the same time, measures were taken to win support among the apprentices and opponents of the excise. On 8 June, five months after the initial petition, and long after two further petitions had been ignored, an ordinance was passed appointing the second Tuesday of every month a recreation day. Apprentices were to be given as much time as their masters 'could conveniently spare from their extraordinary and necessary services'. A subsequent ordinance sought to restrict masters' discretion on this point, and empowered JPs to investigate complaints. This was only a partially populist move, but still pretty clearly an attempt to win support since the same ordinance gave legislative force to the abolition of holy days, including Christmas – in part in response to a very widely discussed proclamation from Charles in favour of the celebration of Easter.[91]

This desire to curry favour on the streets, in the face of a looming confrontation with the army, seems also to have prompted the abolition of the excise duties on meat and salt three days later. These were the two most regressive excises, and the ones that had produced the most significant disorders, which were often led by butchers or salt workers. The day after it took effect the newly erected excise house was demolished and the materials given to the waiting crowd. There were bonfires of celebration this time. There do not appear to have been any significant disturbances since February, when Parliament had issued an explanation rather than an apology. Neither is there any record of prior discussion, or explanation in the legislation itself. But since nothing had happened to shift the financial position, it seems pretty clear that this was a populist, anti-army measure, passed for short-term advantage.[92]

This bid for control of the streets was only partially successful. In June, Presbyterian belligerence did not resonate on the streets: on 12 June the Lord Mayor summoned the Trained Bands on pain of death, but most of the men stayed at home. Those out drumming to call them out were jeered by small boys, and most shops stayed open.[93] The first apprentices' playday, 13 July, however, was marked by the presentation of a petition for the suppression of conventicles, the restoration of the King and the disbandment of the army.[94]

From mid-June until early August a new war seemed possible. The army moved slowly on London, making increasingly political demands, while Presbyterians struggled to hold their nerve. On 13 June, Fairfax was met at St Albans by a delegation from the City. There a *Declaration* of the army was handed over, laying out a more political programme, and it was published the following day. They were, they said, no 'mere mercenary army, hired to serve any arbitrary power of a State, but called forth and conjured by the several declarations of parliament to the defence of our own and the people's just rights and liberties'. They were making their demands as Englishmen, not soldiers, and they had a right to that even though they were soldiers. Drawing explicit comparison not only with the Covenanters, but with contemporary rebels in Portugal and the Netherlands, they said they could ground their actions in the defence of the fundamental laws of the kingdom, without 'visible form either of parliament or king to countenance them'. They called for a purge of corrupt members of the House and constitutional reforms to ensure that it remained a true representative of the people: regular but limited meetings, no dissolution without its own consent and the right of the people to petition. In line with the interests of the people, they also called for restraint of the powers of military officers in the localities, full account of all the monies raised to fight the wars and public justice on the main delinquents responsible for the bloodshed. It was with this political programme in mind that the army would now move closer to London.[95] This was not a completely unanimous display. Hardly any of the soldiery left the army during the early summer, but many officers did, and this tended to further reduce the social status of the command.[96]

The *Declaration* was received on 15 June, along with charges against eleven Members of Parliament, including Holles, Stapleton and Massey. When the charges were drawn up they were detailed and difficult to prove, but revolved around negotiations with the royalists: for example, dealing with the Queen's party in France to restore the King on their terms, enlisting forces to prepare for a new war, and inviting the Covenanters to invade England in their support. It did not take a particularly hostile witness to compare this with the King's charges against the Five Members, although they were not yet backed up by direct force. On 23 June, Parliament refused to discuss the constitutional proposals and demanded to see the evidence about the eleven members. On that day the *Humble Remonstrance* was issued. As the conflict escalated Fairfax refused an order to retire forty miles from London and the Houses issued defiant declarations. In the last week of June, though, they gave way. The army withdrew to Uxbridge, from where it was in a position to cut off supplies to London, and on 26 June the eleven members withdrew from the House. Two days later the minimum demands from the army were forwarded to Parliament.[97] The Presbyterians, it seems, had blinked.

With the army hovering outside London at Uxbridge and then Reading, the pressure at Westminster and in the City was intense. And things were apparently moving against the Presbyterians. The Northern Association army was under the control of Poyntz, a man of reliable Presbyterian convictions, alarmed at the subversion being fostered by the agitators and almost certainly willing to co-operate with an intervention by the Covenanters if ordered to do so. But agitators in his army were co-operating with those in the New Model. At a council of war held at York on 2 July agitators demanded that some of the colonels there should sign a representation from the army to Parliament. Poyntz decided to resign his commission, since the army was no longer under his command and a dispute ensued about the command of the York garrison and the stronghold, Clifford Tower. It culminated with Poyntz being dragged from his bed and, still in his slippers, being taken under guard to Fairfax's headquarters.[98]

This military blow to Presbyterianism coincided with another shift towards conciliation. On 6 July the army presented articles of impeachment against the eleven members. No impeachment had been moved from outside the House before, and it is clear that the agitators were fully involved in the drawing up of the (unprovable) charges. Central to the final charges was the issue of the corruption of the parliamentary process – the New Model was intervening to purge Parliament of corruption. Drawing up these charges had raised a fundamental question, which the army's internal political organization had been asked explicitly: could the army act on behalf of the nation, particularly in opposition to the will of Parliament? Put another way, the issue was whether the army could plausibly act on behalf of the people against the body which was formally considered to be the people's representative.[99] There were good reasons for feeling queasy about this. On the following day the articles against the eleven members were read. An ordinance expelling the Reformadoes was passed on 9 July. This, and very powerful rumours of an impending Scottish invasion, prompted the agitators to press for a march on London. But parliamentary events were moving in their favour – all the armies in pay in England and Wales were placed under Fairfax's command (effectively recognizing the agitators' coup in Poyntz's army), and all those who had deserted his army were to be disbanded (19 July).[100]

Military power seemed to have delivered political dominance to the army. There was a further extraordinary consequence of this: an independently generated platform for national political settlement, the *Heads of Proposals*, was presented to the King. The *Heads* arose from the first meeting of the General Council, at Reading on 16 July. The decision to convene the council was apparently a response to pressure from the agitators, increasingly impatient with the hesitation about entering London. Their 'Humble Petition and Representation' was discussed until midnight and on the following day the draft of the *Heads of Proposals* was discussed.[101] They were more generous than anything previously offered to the King, concerned as much to limit parliamentary tyranny as to constrain the King. They called for the repeal of the Triennial Act, establishing biennial parliaments sitting for between 120 and 240 days, and redistributing seats to make the Commons 'an equal representative of the whole'. Control of the militia would be relinquished only for ten years, and those in arms against Parliament would be barred from office for only five. But the terms were particularly generous on religion. Bishops and all ecclesiastical officers would be retained, albeit stripped of 'all coercive power, authority, and jurisdiction'. Although this posed the question that Charles asked about the monarchy in relation to the militia – what kind of bishop had no coercive powers? – this was the first peace settlement which did not presume the abolition of episcopacy. Moreover, the Prayer Book could be used on a voluntary basis, no Presbyterian structures were to be imposed and the Covenant was not to be forced on anyone. With these safeguards against intolerance and parliamentary tyranny in place, the army would see the King restored to his regal powers, including his legislative veto. Finally, only five royalists would be exempt from a general Act of Oblivion.[102] These proposals were put to the army council, of 100 officers and agitators, before they had been communicated to either the King or Parliament, or even the parliamentary commissioners at headquarters.[103]

That the army, the servant of Parliament, should act independently, propose and frame impeachments, and now generate its own peace terms demonstrated that politics had entered another completely new realm. The position of the army was a tolerant one, however, and concerned with healing and settling – religious toleration alongside a restored Anglican church and a relative forgiveness about actions during the war was clearly a less partisan position than that championed by Presbyterians. Moreover, they were outlines of proposals, not propositions – a basis for discussion rather than an ultimatum.

As things moved against them, in mid-July, Presbyterian confidence evaporated. On 20 July, Holles and others sought permission to travel abroad for six months to prepare their defence, which they were granted. But the whiff of defeat also called forth powerful demonstrations in the city. On 20 July demonstrators swarmed around Westminster in such a tumultuous way that the Commons ordered 100 halberds be brought in for their defence. The following day, in the City, crowds of militiamen, watermen, Reformadoes and sailors assembled around Skinners' Hall. They were there to sign a 'Solemn Engagement' (presumably titled in imitation of the army's own declaration) pledging to do their best to bring the King to Westminster for a personal treaty on the basis of his third reply to the Newcastle Propositions, of the previous May. It was framed as a recommitment to the Solemn League and Covenant, and of the Oath of Allegiance. The following day two or three thousand Reformadoes were at St James's Field, intending to request the Corporation to join their petition to Parliament to bring the King home. But these City Presbyterians were on their own. The old Militia Commission was restored on 22 and 23 July, and on the 24th both Houses denounced the City's 'Solemn Engagement'. The previous day the *Heads of Proposals* had been shown to the King – there can be little doubt that the senior officers wanted to secure the basis for a negotiated settlement before any march on London. Lord Wharton had read a version in the Lords on 19 July, and there was a fear among Presbyterians that a deal was in the offing.[104]

This seems to have been part of the explanation for a final, counter-productive and desperate attempt at mobilization in the city. On 26 July, Holles, Clotworthy and Waller met at the Bull Tavern in Westminster Street. It seems likely that they were co-ordinating the presentation of a petition against the Militia Act. They probably did not plan a coup against Parliament, but the petition was accompanied by a crowd which subsequently invaded the Houses. Terrified members were kept sitting until 9 p.m. and in that time first the Lords and then the Commons were forced to reinstate the Presbyterian Militia Commission and to retract their denunciation of the 'Solemn Engagement'. The Commons was also forced to issue an immediate invitation to the King. Over the next few days a reduced and intimidated Parliament passed a series of measures helpful to the Presbyterian cause, but this naked intimidation of Parliament provided a final, very good, reason for the New Model to march on London. On 30 July the Speaker and fifty-seven members fled, many of them to the army, taking the mace with them, and it seemed that Parliament might not be able to sit. However, borrowing a mace from the City, business was resumed by the small number of members still willing to sit. A letter was sent to Fairfax forbidding him to approach within thirty miles, and the Committee of Safety was re-established. Fairfax's control of the Trained Bands was denied and Massey placed in control of the forces directly under Parliament's control. This firm line was initially supported by the City authorities, which issued a similar injunction to the New Model.[105]

In the first week of August, London seemed on the brink of serious disorder. Reformadoes were rumoured to be planning to plunder the City. On 2 August the City Militia Committee and Common Council sat in an agony of indecision, waiting on tenterhooks for news of the army's movements. Political will was crumbling, however. The Westminster Assembly urged negotiation with the army. On 3 August the City sent a deputation to Fairfax disavowing any intention of starting a new war. Authorities in Southwark implored his help. The King also wrote, on

4 August, disavowing any attempt to make a new war (although not disowning the Presbyterian attempt to). By the time that peace protestors at the Guildhall were cut down by troops under the command of Poyntz (now returned from the north and vigorously committed to the Presbyterian cause), leaving some of the petitioners mortally wounded, the Presbyterian image problem was becoming acutely difficult.[106]

Fairfax was able to enter the City unopposed on 6 August, after Southwark had been delivered to an advance guard. It was a triumphant procession rather than an occupation and the warmth of the reception bears testimony to the fact that London was not solidly Presbyterian. The fugitive members and the Speakers were escorted back to the Palace of Westminster by troops with laurel leaves in their hats, and the church bells pealed out. Fairfax was made constable of the Tower. On the following day 18,000 troops marched through London. The Lifeguard and train of artillery, as well as twenty regiments, assembled in Hyde Park. Accompanied by flying colours, drums and trumpets they marched to Cheapside in the heart of the City before fanning out to walk through every street from 11 a.m. to 8 p.m. Their behaviour was exemplary and, having made their point, Fairfax led them across London Bridge to quarters in Kent and Surrey. A force remained behind to protect the Houses from crowds. This, it was thought by Fairfax and the other officers, was but a preliminary to an accommodation with the King. Fairfax was shown the Magna Carta and records of kingdom: 'This is that which we have fought for, and by God's help we must maintain', he said.[107]

There followed a struggle for control in Parliament and on 14 August the agitators called for a purge. This seems to have convinced six of the eleven impeached members to flee two days later. On 20 August an ordinance was prepared declaring null all the actions taken by the Houses in the absence of the Speakers and those who were present while forced votes were taken were exempted from indemnity. Although Fairfax had prevented a purge these tactics ensured that many of those who would have been purged stayed away. The Independent majority was re-established. Similar measures were taken in the City, and London's defences were ordered to be destroyed. The work was completed by the end of September.[108] The defeat of political Presbyterianism seemed complete – there was no attempt to rescue the programme, or to protect its promoters. Thereafter Presbyterian ambition was limited to energizing reformation through the existing church structures, rather than the establishment of new national discipline. Thomas Edwards, spokesman for the more militant view, joined the exodus, eventually dying in a bitter and disappointed exile.[109]

There had been more than a little familiarity about the Newcastle Propositions. What was being offered, and refused, was similar to what had been offered and refused in 1642: the war, it seems, had not really changed the terms of the argument. Worse still, it had not really changed the balance of power. A royal military victory would have broken the deadlock, but a parliamentary one apparently had not. To that extent Manchester had been right in his famous exchange with Cromwell: 'If we beat the king ninety and nine times yet he is king still, and so will his posterity be after him; but if the King beat us once we shall all be hanged, and our posterity made slaves'. But it also gave continuing relevance to Cromwell's riposte: 'if this be so, why did we take up arms at first?'[110] Worst of all, perhaps, the war had not only failed to change the political negotiation very much, but it had created further difficulties. These mobilizations took place against the background of continued publicity about the details of political negotiation in newsbooks, pamphlets, declarations and leaks. The public did not have to work hard to be informed.[111]

For those interested in history's ironies, there were plenty here. In 1642 Parliament had armed itself against the King and contested control of the country's military resources. In the ensuing paper war arguments had sharpened and constitutionally radical arguments had been made. One of the triggers for the breakdown of normal politics was the attempt to exclude five members from the House. In 1647 it was the army, and it was eleven members, but the claim against Parliament was similar – it was no longer a real parliament. To some extent that was true – there does seem to have been a new ruthlessness with which Holles and Stapleton dominated the House of Commons in pretty close co-operation with the City and crowds. In the intervening five years the techniques by which support was mobilized among wider publics had also become more sophisticated – particularly in the co-ordinated use of print – and in the *Large Petition* a new and more radical discourse had inflected a petitioning campaign.

Alliances could form around these various appeals – for arrears of pay, religious decency, toleration, opposition to the Negative Voice of the House of Lords, for recreation days or the abolition of the excise – and there were now more players. In addition to the City, Parliament and the King, the New Model became an independent actor, with a conscious political organization. Apprentices, excise rioters, Presbyterians, Covenanters, royalists and London radicals were all mobilizing in a more sophisticated political environment and appealing to different institutions. But, as in 1642, the resulting alliances did not necessarily bind very closely. The Presbyterians took control of London's government and militia, but their appeal to the anti-excise and pro-recreation day crowds was of more measured success. And such loose alliances did not necessarily withstand the pressure to go to war – perhaps even less so in the immediate aftermath of the one just fought. When it came to the crunch, the Presbyterians could not deliver an armed and determined capital, or a northern army, with which to defeat the New Model.

In the face of all this Charles had little reason to do anything other than look on. As these divisions widened, his prospects improved by leaps and bounds: as the *Heads of Proposals* seemed to demonstrate. This was a contest about whom he should deal with, and none of the parties spoke for the people as a whole, or championed a settlement that would obviously satisfy all shades of opinion. These various interests were all to some extent disposable, except perhaps the King. The Covenanters could be bought off, the army disbanded and Parliament dissolved, but few thought there could be a king other than Charles and very few, if any, thought that there need be no king at all.

Spring and summer passed as Presbyterians and Independents fought for control of Parliament, the City and military force. There were no formal peace proposals after Newcastle and before the late autumn. But there is little sign that this battle resonated strongly outside London and the armies: no record of provincial mobilization for Presbyterian or Independent reaches us, except perhaps in Norwich. Elsewhere there is plenty of evidence of anti-army and anti-sectarian feeling, but it is difficult to document a powerful Presbyterian movement and, outside London and Lancashire, there is not much evidence of concerted attempts to establish a national Presbyterian church.[112]

In the provinces the clearest message seems to have been a desire for settlement, and demilitarization, without much sense of commitment to the precise political measures that would allow this. In September 1647 pamphlet readers were treated to another story of monstrous birth, this one from Scotland. The child was born with two heads, one female and one male, its other features described with parallels in classical mythology: Midas, Polyphemus, Satyrs and a Gorgon. At its birth 'nature seemed to be disquieted and troubled; in so much that the heavens proclaimed its entrance into the world with a loud peal of thunder, seconded with such frequent flashes of lightning that it was credibly believed of all . . . that the latter now was now come upon them'. At the height of the storm the monster announced with 'a hoarse but loud voice . . . I am thus deformed for the sins of my parents'.[113]

The lesson was a familiar one – the repentant mother admitted how she had been 'seduced by heretical factious fellows', and as a result had ignored the 'laws and ancient customs of England and Scotland' and had 'vehemently desire[d] . . . to see the utter ruin and subversion of all church and state-government'. The editorial line was also predictable: this should be a lesson not just for those labouring with similar births, but for all people 'whose outsides though they appear not so horrid to the eye as this misshapen monster, I fear their insides are hung round with all sorts of crying sins'.[114] The symbolism and the visual image echoed John Taylor's famous pamphlet of 1647, *The World turn'd*

Images of political monstrosity

upside down.[115] While partisans fought for the right to deal with the King, or slugged it out in rural churchyards,[116] others looked on in horror. In fact, the line taken on this Scottish birth could have been in print in 1642, as the first edition of *The World turn'd upside down* had been.

The confrontation between Presbyterian and Independent seems to have been primarily a difference among activists on one side, seeking with little success to assimilate other issues, and to take control of Parliament and the City. It is not easy to see the Presbyterians as the 'moderates' in the parliamentary coalition – they were more a party of religious law and order. Their support for iconoclasm, reform of the calendar and intolerance, their willingness to use force and act beyond the constitution, and their polemical bitterness all speak against the view that they were the voice of common sense. Among the activists, in any case, there was a clear winner: the New Model. Its peace terms turned out to be relatively generous, but Charles still seemed to feel he could do better. He was probably wrong, but the mistake was pardonable in the circumstances.

18

The Army, the People and the Scots

Putney, the Engagement and the Vote of No Addresses

Defeat of the Presbyterian mobilization in 1647 seemed dangerously like a defeat for Parliament. Two extra-parliamentary forces had dominated the politics of the victorious coalition – the Presbyterian alliance of City, Covenanters and London divines on one hand, and a developing alliance between City radicals and the New Model on the other. They had fought for control of the political complexion of Parliament and as the conflict reached crisis point the army had shifted decisively from a body petitioning for redress to a political body seeking a particular form of settlement. A key moment in this transformation was the signing of the *Solemn Engagement* in early June, which had also established a new consultative body, the General Council of the Army. When the army published its *Declaration* on 14 June a dangerous political transformation was under way. Within the army there was now a mechanism for political mobilization and the army as a whole was lining up behind the idea that Parliament was no longer the true representative of the people. During the ensuing stand-off, as the army hovered outside London, it had presented a settlement to the King apparently on its own authority: the *Heads of Proposals*.

By the time of the occupation of London in August there was no escaping the fact that this was a political body, but these developments were not necessarily comfortable for the officers. The role of the agitators was a potential threat to the normal chain of military command – hence, for example, Fairfax's discomfiture when Charles pitched up at Newmarket in June. Moreover, as the army began openly to pursue a settlement, acting independently, it offered possibilities to Independent activists, who might make it a vehicle for their view of settlement. In particular, the call for a free parliament intersected with a gathering campaign by Lilburne, Walwyn and Overton: a spectrum of opinion from Charles I to John Lilburne and army agitators could now agree that the body sitting in Westminster was not a true parliament. The precise connections between the New Model agitators and these City radicals is unclear; so too that between Walwyn, Lilburne and Overton. These three did not become 'the Levellers' until labelled as such by royalists (and perhaps army officers) in November. Before that date five regiments had appointed 'new agents', alongside the agitators, who met daily in London in late September and early October. Their status is also unclear, and their connections with the London radicals are largely suppositious, but their purpose was plain: to galvanize the army into the pursuit of more-ambitious political ends.[1]

This complicated conjunction between the 'Lilburnists' and elements within the army reflected the potential of the army as an independent political actor. But what would the army do with this role? The parliamentary cause had been sustained, in part, by the myth of loyal rebellion: to fight the King was in some circumstances to protect him. Implausible as this may seem to modern eyes, it did at least have the virtue of expressing what was happening in terms which were respectable to contemporaries. There was no such easy resort for the army. Created as a servant of Parliament, in its service of the King, the army was now turning on its master and claiming a say in the settlement. What could possibly justify its posture in repudiating the authority of its master and creator? One seductive strategy, adopted during the summer of 1647, was to adopt the royalist line on Parliament – that it did not represent the people any more – to argue that the army was intervening to restore the people's liberty. This line of argument potentially led in very radical directions.

The affluent London suburb of Putney is not now associated with the clash of great ideas, but in October 1647 it was the scene of some of the most remarkable exchanges in English history. These large questions about the army's political role, and hence about the sources of political legitimacy, were addressed at meetings of the General Council of the Army held in Putney church each Thursday from 9 September onwards. These meetings have attracted their fair share of attention and controversy. With the rediscovery of the Levellers in the 1950s came an emphasis on their influence in the army so that the exchanges at Putney came almost to be viewed as meetings of the Leveller party. In fact, the origins of the meetings lie in the army's campaign for arrears and indemnity in March, and the politicization of that campaign in June and July. The meetings at Putney were not inspired or led by the Levellers, but were instead attempts to reconcile established army demands with the aspirations of more-radical spirits.[2]

Of course, a meeting of the army General Council in Putney church to discuss England's constitution is scarcely less startling than a meeting of Levellers. At the time of the first meeting the constitutional questions were framed by the *Heads of Proposals*, which were, at least formally, still being considered by Charles. On the eve of the march on London in late July, Ireton had ridden from Reading to Woburn, hoping to get the King to accept the *Heads of Proposals*. As we have seen, these were in some crucial respects the best terms he had been offered so far; but they were also the most radical in implication, since they rested on the power of the army, not the authority of Parliament. This may have been Charles's best chance – agreement to settle on the basis of the proposals might have allowed the army to march into London to restore both Parliament and the King. But it was not to be. A three-hour discussion ensued, at which the King secured further concessions, but in the end no agreement was reached and he did not issue a formal response until 9 September.[3]

Charles was quick to adjust to the changed conditions following the army's occupation of London. Early in August he reopened contacts, praising the *Heads* and denouncing the Presbyterian demonstrations in London. In the meantime he had been moved to Hampton Court, where he was necessarily less closely watched and quite comfortable. By that point, the King had hopes of a Scottish alliance and there had been very public support in London for his suggestion of a personal treaty. With the army at loggerheads with Parliament, hopes of a Covenanter army and evidence of a desire to settle on something like his terms, his calculation was that he did not need to do this deal. Rather against the advice of Sir John Berkeley, he told Ireton, 'You cannot be without me, you will fall to ruin if I do not sustain you'.[4] As the negotiations dragged on, the Independent-dominated parliament was persuaded to re-present the Newcastle Propositions: facing a choice between the two he might come to see the advantages of the *Heads of Proposals*. The King's response on 9 September was that the propositions were largely the same as the ones to which he had repeatedly said that he could not, in conscience, agree. The proposals of the army, on the other hand, 'much more conduce to the satisfaction of all interests, and may be a fitter foundation for a lasting peace, than the Propositions which at this time are tendered to him'. He commended them to Parliament as the basis of a personal treaty, to which commissioners from the army might also be admitted.[5]

But the moment had passed: when this was reported to the Commons on 21 September it was perceived as a rebuff, and there was some talk of imprisoning the King. In July, Ireton and others in the army had washed their hands of negotiation with the King and now Henry Marten proposed a vote that no further addresses should be made to Charles. It was defeated 84–34, with Cromwell acting as a teller against. Cromwell was trying to act as a mediator between the King and Parliament, without losing the support of the army, but Charles did not help him. Another sign of the mood in Parliament is that on the following day the Lord Mayor and five aldermen were impeached for raising forces in the City to oppose the army.[6]

Through September the army was also keen to get its message out. On 24 September the *Heads* were republished, with annotations by the army's General Council, clearly an appeal to public opinion. By 27 September a *Book of Declarations* had been prepared, collating (and editing slightly) the remonstrances and declarations of the New Model since March.[7] It was a move reminiscent of Husbands in 1643, defining the cause which was now being pursued. Attacks in the press had led, on 20 September, to suggestions for stronger gagging measures, proposals made by Fairfax but representing the general feeling on the army's General Council. On 28 September, Parliament imposed new press restrictions. The concern, as usual, was as much with civility as what was being said: it was not just 'seditious' but 'false and scandalous' publications which attracted attention, which served 'to the great abuse and prejudice of the people, and insufferable reproach of the proceedings of the Parliament and their army'.[8] Thomason's collection for the previous week or so contained a large number of verse satires, and some virulent prose pamphlets.

Just as Parliament's *Book of Declarations* was an attempt to clarify and fix the cause of a divided body, subject to external influence, so too was the army's *Book*. Given this wider context, of tense negotiation and public appeal, it is no surprise that as soon as the General Council began regular meetings at the beginning of September its proceedings were canvassed to a wider public. The woodcut on the front, however, showing Fairfax in council with his officers, is reminiscent of contemporary representations of Parliament, similarly artificially insulated from the outside world.[9]

The manner of His Excellency Sir *Thomas Fairfax*, and the Officers of His Armie sitting in COVNCELL.

Sir Thomas Fairfax presiding over the General Council of the army

At the first meeting of the General Council, on 9 September, Major White, an agitator from Fairfax's own regiment of foot, argued that there was now no power in the land but the sword – the way stood open for a new and just settlement based on first principles rather than custom, tradition and established interests. This was pretty clearly meant as a repudiation of the *Heads of Proposals* as a basis for settlement, and in particular of a discussion of the rights of the King and his heirs. The debate immediately became a public one: White was expelled from the General Council and a declaration was published announcing this, and the unequivocal support of the army for the fundamental laws and government of the kingdom. White responded by publishing an open letter to Fairfax, prompting speculation in the royalist press that the agitators were contesting Fairfax's right of veto. But Fairfax won – the next meeting considered more directly the *Heads of Proposals* and, through to the middle of October, discussion followed this less radical line. The redress of grievances was to be pursued alongside settlement framed on the assumption of monarchical rule – the question before the General Council was not whether Charles should be reinstated but on what terms. White, in December, made his submission to the General Council and was readmitted.[10]

What precipitated the famous debates of late October, however, was not so much the failure of the *Heads of Proposals* as the production of *The Case of the Armie Truly Stated* signed by the new agents. It seems to have been a composite and the product of more than one hand, but most experts agree that John Wildman and Edward Sexby were involved in the drafting.[11] Wildman was a civilian, a London radical, unlike Sexby, who was an army agitator. Disagreement about the extent of their influence therefore follows a contemporary question about the extent to which the army was acting independently, and pursuing its own grievances, and how far it was being successfully infiltrated and manipulated by City radicals. What is clear, and perhaps most significant about this, is that the General Council, no less than any other public institution during the 1640s, was the focus for mobilization – its proceedings were not hermetically sealed, and its agenda was not entirely its own. Networks of personal and religious connection, reinforced by the resort to print to appeal to wider publics, exerted a pressure on the army's definition of its cause and purposes. The call for new agents, for example, had been made by Lilburne from the Tower, at a time of tense relations with Cromwell, and it is not even clear how many of them were actually present at the debates at Putney.[12] But the agenda was not set by the officers, whatever the woodcut at the front of the army's official publication seemed to suggest.

The Case of the Armie was drawn up at Guildford on 9 October and presented to Fairfax nine days later. It is a sprawling document but the main thrust is plain: it opened with a complaint at the failure to do anything 'effectually, either for the Army or the poor oppressed people of this nation'. The fault, it argued, lay not only in Parliament but in the attitude of the officers, who had put obstacles in the way of the agitators. Throughout, it made careful reference to public declarations and engagements, holding the officers to account for failing to live up to the stated aspirations of the army. It also called for the dissolution of Parliament within nine or ten months to allow for settlement and then free elections. Here the argument reached fundamentals: 'all power is originally and essentially in the whole body of the people of this Nation, and . . . their free choice or consent by their representatives is the only original or foundation of all just government'. The Commons is the supreme authority, and the will of the people is the guarantee of freedom and the only proper restraint on tyranny. At the moment the army was the safeguard of these rights: 'In case the union of the Army should be broken (which the enemy wait for) ruin and destruction will break in upon us like a roaring sea'. It was an exhortation to the army to take up this task: 'we expect that the same impulsion of judgement and conscience that we have all professed, did command us forth at first for the people's freedom, will be again so effectual, that all will unanimously concur with us, so that a demand of the people's and Army's rights shall be made by the whole Army as one man'. Appended was a letter to Fairfax from Hemel Hempstead, written on 15 October, justifying both their argument and their action on the basis of the interest of the people: 'the safety of the people is above all forms, customs, &c., and the equity of popular safety is the thing which justifies all forms, or the change of forms for the accomplishment thereof; and no forms are lawful longer than they preserve or accomplish the same'. With the failure of the relatively moderate course represented by the negotiations over the *Heads of Proposals*, more radical counsels were doubly empowered: the alternative had failed, and they had predicted this some time ago. Throughout, however, these fundamental claims are mixed in with more immediate concerns – about financial burdens, the costs and corruptions of financial administration, indemnity for the soldiers and so on.[13]

Poorly structured it may have been, but the political challenge presented by this tract was immediately apparent. Following its presentation to Fairfax on 18 October and a debate on 21 October, a committee of the General Council was established to consider a response. Working while it was sold from London bookstalls, the committee produced a list of objections. This was sent to the signatories of *The Case of the Armie*, along with a polite invitation to debate the issues at the next meeting of the council on 28 October. The signatories arrived instead with a new document, agreed the previous day, called *The Agreement of the People*. Like *The Case of the Armie* this was published over the names of the agents of the five regiments. The respective titles suggest, as does close analysis of the texts, that the *Agreement* was not simply a cleaned-up version of *The Case of the Armie*, but a new and more radical programme, addressing more clearly the settlement of the kingdom, not the cause of the army. On one reading, therefore, the ensuing debate revolved around the *The Case of the Armie* as the basis for consensus within the army in the face of this pressure to adopt a broader and more radical cause.[14]

Certainly, the radicalism of the *Agreement* was bracing.

Having by our late labours and hazards made it appear to the world at how high rate we value our just freedom, and God having so far owned our cause as to deliver the enemies thereof into our hands, we do now hold ourselves bound in mutual duty to each other to take the best care we can ... to avoid both the danger of returning into a slavish condition and the chargeable remedy of another war.

Four demands followed – for parliamentary representation on an equal basis; dissolution of the current parliament on 30 September 1648; biennial parliaments thereafter; and that the power of the representatives of the people should be considered 'inferior only to those who choose them'. This last clause implied limitations on the legislation – for example, religious regulation could not interfere with conscience (although the parliament might establish a public form of religious instruction) and the people could not be liable to impressment by their representatives.[15] It presumed a clean slate in which the claims of law and tradition had been dissolved and a settlement could be established on the basis of principles of freedom and justice, and made little reference (beyond the abolition of impressments) to the immediate grievances of the army. Pamphleteers had been edging towards arguments about popular sovereignty since 1642. Now, however, they were proposed not to the court of public opinion but as suggestions for adoption by the most powerful actor in English politics. The *Agreement* was in print by 3 November at the latest, although it may not have taken its final form until 27 October.[16]

Debate about the *Agreement* opened on 28 October with some sharp exchanges. Cromwell and other officers were accused of having lost honour by dealing with the King and a degenerate Parliament. A settlement should instead be grounded in rational principles, reflecting the good of the people and the judgement of God. Revolution, in other words, was in the air. The response of the army leadership was not confrontational, however. Cromwell had indeed been seeking ways to negotiate a settlement, and had acted as a teller against a Vote of No Addresses, for example. On 20 October he delivered a three-hour speech in defence of the monarchy, disavowing any connection between him, Fairfax or any of the chief officers and the *Agreement*, and claiming that his intention throughout the war had been to strengthen, not weaken, it.[17] Of course, the fact that he had to say it was in itself a source of unease.

Despite the porousness of the army organization, and the fact that its cause was pursued in print, the ensuing debates were barely noted in the newsbooks. However, evidence that they were recognized to be of momentous significance lies in the careful record made of them by William Clarke.[18] Despite the radicalism of the ideas being touted, though, the exchanges reflect some more familiar habits of thought. In particular it seems clear that the meetings were run with the intent of securing consensus – debate was intended to persuade, not to conquer. At Putney, it seems, the army tried to live by the standards that it wished on public debate.

On 28 October debate centred around the status of the *Agreement* – Cromwell argued that it might have reason in it, but had not been subscribed by all the people, and so might not be more reasonable than a document produced by another group of people.[19] He also raised the objection that it might not be consistent with previous declarations and engagements of the army. Many historians have been tempted to see that as merely expedient, but Cromwell had been accused of betraying the army by dealing with the King and the degenerate Parliament. Honour was important to army figures and they had just published a compendium of their public statements; and *The Case of the Armie* had made great play of the fact that the officers had failed to live up to them. Moreover, Charles was (and is) consistently criticized for not following his declared intentions – trust and credibility depended on matching deeds with words, a principle Bruno Ryves had been anxious to establish in his anti-parliamentarian writings. Sympathy with the cause of the *Agreement* should not blind us to the sincerity of those who opposed it. And the arguments of those who wanted simply to break former agreements in order to establish a new order did have a problem to answer. As Ireton was quick to point out: this argument suggests that 'if he that makes an engagement (be it what it will be) have further light that this engagement was not good or honest, then he is free from it'.

Such a view eroded all authority: 'men of this principle would think themselves as little as may be obliged by any law if in their apprehensions it be not a good law'.[20] This question, of whether the *Agreement* should be discussed at all, particularly in the light of the army's previous statements about itself, took up the first day of debate. The outcome was a committee established to sift all the army declarations published since June.

The following morning was given over to prayer as the participants in the debate sought guidance. This was no doubt sincere, but it also allowed those who spoke later to clear themselves of charges of insincerity – Cromwell and others felt with some justice that they were the victims of hostile briefing and leaks. In his third intervention he said:

I hope that there is not such an evil amongst us as that we could or would exercise our wits, or our cunning, to veil over any doubleness of heart that may possibly be in us. I hope, having been in such a presence as we have been in this day, we do not admit such a thought as this into our hearts.[21]

Common prayer had both the spiritual and practical effect of establishing trust among men of differing judgements.

Radicals arrived at the prayer meeting in the afternoon and, seeing that a large number of the participants were present, demanded an immediate debate. Cromwell, who was chairing the council, was reluctant to concede this, but lost. Discussion turned at once to the issue of representation – Ireton asked whether an equal distribution of representation implied an equal voice for all inhabitants. It was in the ensuing discussion that the famous exchange between principles of democracy and property took place. There followed some confused moments, in which a number of people spoke over one another, but Maximilian Petty made himself heard: 'We judge that all inhabitants that have not lost their birthright should have an equal voice in elections'. It is Thomas Rainborough's interjection which has resonated more loudly, however: 'really I think that the poorest he that is in England hath a life to live, as the greatest he; and therefore truly, sir, I think it's clear, that every man that is to live under a government ought first by his own consent to put himself under that government'. Ireton's response is equally famous: 'I think that no person hath a right to an interest or share in the disposing of the affairs of the kingdom, and in determining or choosing those that shall determine what laws we shall be ruled by here

– no person hath a right to this, that hath not a permanent fixed interest in the kingdom'. In other words, those in whose hands lay the land and trade of the nation were those who had an interest in the government.[22]

These few minutes of discussion have been central to much controversy about the political theory of the civil war and revolution. It seems that the subsequent debate concluded that only foreigners and those too dependent to make a free choice – beggars and servants – should be excluded from the vote. The significance of these exchanges is not diminished by an appreciation of the context they were uttered in – here was a confrontation over fundamentals of political society, a debate cut loose from the moorings of the controversies of 1642. Who were the people and how were they to be represented? Did this discussion affect women? Issues lurking at the edges, or below the surface, of the paper war in 1642 were here being discussed in the governing council of one of the most important power brokers of the post-war settlement.[23]

Concentration on this issue took attention away from potentially shared ground, and may have reflected the fact that the debate was sprung on Cromwell and Ireton – had they had more leisure they might have started discussion at another point. Meanwhile, in a manner now familiar, partisans launched into print as Leveller sympathizers published denunciations of the leadership. *A Call to All the Soldiers of the Army by the Free People of England*, almost certainly the work of Wildman, was circulating among the regiments on 29 October. It called on the army to act to establish a free parliament and to throw out the usurpers.[24] This may well have captured the mood of the army more completely than the more moderate line of the officers.

On 30 October a committee met to discuss the June proposals and the *Agreement*. What emerged owed much to the *Heads of Proposals*. After a day of prayer the council met again on 1 November, in the last meeting recorded by Clarke. Cromwell, again in the chair, asked those present what answers God had vouchsafed to them in their prayers. Some of the answers were disturbing, or exhilarating. Goffe, for example, claimed that the voice of heaven had spoken against 'tampering' with God's enemies. Captain Bishop, 'after many enquiries in' his 'spirit', concluded that the root of their sufferings was 'a compliance to preserve that man of blood, and those principles of tyranny which God from heaven, by His many successes, hath manifestly declared against'. This was dangerous language – that the blood on the King's hands made him as culpable as any other man. It implied that justice should be sought against a man of blood if further judgements from God were to be avoided. This Old Testament view had been expressed in the aftermath of Edgehill amidst fears of a peace no better than capitulation, but gathered force through the war. One preacher was later remembered to have argued during 1645 that 'the King was a man of blood, and that it was a vain thing to hope for the blessing of God upon any peace to be made with him, till satisfaction should be made for the blood that had been shed'.[25]

In the face of these inflammatory arguments Cromwell and others questioned whether divine purposes for the detail of political life could be accurately interpreted in this way. Cromwell himself, however, was conciliatory, acknowledging that God might want these things but professing uncertainty that the army was His instrument in this matter. He was more comfortable with the argument that they owed their life to Parliament so either it was a parliament and they should obey it or it was not a parliament, in which case the army had no legitimate existence either. A long and unhelpful wrangle developed which did not clarify what proposals to back, but it was agreed to continue to meet each day until all proposals had been considered.

In the face of these divisions Cromwell and Fairfax seem to have been concerned above all to preserve army unity. In this they were ultimately successful. There were five more meetings of the General Council before 8 November, in which there was an increasingly obvious hostility to Charles and to monarchy. There were signs of similar impatience, at least with the man Charles Stuart, in Parliament and on 6 November it was declared that he should assent to measures propounded by Parliament: in other words he should accept the settlement offered, not seek to negotiate.[26] But there were also signs of hostility to the officers, including a threat of impeachment against Cromwell, which Rainborough and Marten claimed would be supported by 20,000 citizens. There were increasing concerns too that Charles was close to an agreement with Scottish commissioners and that he intended to bolt from Hampton Court (which he did indeed do, on 11 November). Control of the General Council debates was increasingly tenuous, although on 8 November a letter was sent to the Speaker that the army had no intention of vetoing further approaches to Charles.

Control was ultimately asserted by the officers in a more straightforward way. Early in the debates Rainborough had called for a general rendezvous at which the position of the army could be cleared before all the soldiers. In the event the army was assembled in three separate rendezvous where Fairfax asserted his own authority, and successfully promoted a new declaration. At Ware on 15 November, the first of the rendezvous, the opposition seemed less impressive than the desire for unity. Some regiments attended without orders to do so, and some were wearing the *Agreement* in their hats: radicals hoped to get the *Agreement* adopted by acclamation in place of a new *Remonstrance* being promoted by Fairfax. At one point armed confrontation threatened, and in the end nine ringleaders were court-martialled. Three were sentenced to death and drew lots for their lives. This assertion of army discipline seems to have worked – there were no difficulties at the subsequent rendezvous at Ruislip Heath and Kingston.[27]

Not only was army discipline restored, but a new platform was adopted and the attempt by outside forces to manipulate army counsels was denounced. The *Remonstrance* denounced the role of the new agents, 'who . . . have . . . taken upon them to act as a divided Party from the . . . Council and Army'. Their claims about the betrayals of the officers were scandalous, and so were their methods. The problems in the army arose from 'divers private persons that are not of the Army, [who] have endeavoured, by various falsehoods and scandals, raised and divulged in print, and otherwise, against the General, the General Officers and Council, to possess the Army and the Kingdom with jealousies of them'. Wildman, the civilian who had spoken more than most at Putney, and who had briefed against the officers in the press, was obviously one such. The demands returned to more moderate realms: redress of the army's professional grievances over pay, impressment, freedom for apprentices who had served in the war, and indemnity. Appended to these was a call for a date to be named for an end to the present parliament, for free and equal elections to the next one, to render the 'House of Commons (as near as may be) an equal representative of the people that are to elect'.[28] There was no formal equality, and no statement about the franchise; but this did nonetheless give ground to the radicals while at the same time asserting the organic unity of the army against their malign influences. The vision of the army's *Book of Declarations* had been reaffirmed.

*

Scottish commissioners – the earls of Lanark, Loudoun and Lauderdale – had been holding out the possibility of military support for the King since June. It was not clear that they would actually be able to deliver it, but, by late October, Charles was certainly interested. On 22 October the Scottish commissioners had been with the King at Hampton Court and encouraged him to escape with them. In fact, fifty armed men arrived to escort him, but Charles refused, saying that he had given his word not to. Unfortunately, news of the plan leaked out even as he refused to go along with it – the worst of both worlds. As a result, on 31 October, the guard on him was strengthened and the following day his attendants were removed. In the first week of November, Ashburnham and the Scottish commissioners were clearly encouraging him to consider flight. By 9 November he was being convinced that his life was in danger and it may indeed have been: Cromwell ordered extra guards because an assassination would look bad.[29]

Charles therefore had two main options: a deal with the army on toleration; or a deal with the Covenanters on Presbyterianism. These were clearly incompatible. Growing certainty in the army and at Parliament that he was not negotiating with any serious intent was used by his friends to urge him to settle quickly, but also to take flight for Scotland. He could not do both: flight would confirm the suspicions that he did not intend a settlement; settlement on the army's terms would cost him Scottish support. Although the *Heads of Proposals* were the best offer yet, the army was not a body with which he was likely to want to deal. If, however, he chose to escape, it was not exactly clear where he would go unless, that is, he was sincere in his commitment to Scotland. The Covenanters now saw that Parliament and the City did not offer much security for their cherished Britannic Presbyterianism, and there was a danger that their king might be assassinated or deposed by an English army. But they continued to demand that Charles take the Solemn League and Covenant.[30] That Charles was in negotiation with the Covenanters and that they were willing to help him escape was well-known. It was also feared that this might lead to a renewal of hostilities. Once he had escaped there was apparently talk in the army of bringing Charles to trial in order to prove that he, not the army, was responsible for a renewal of fighting.[31]

On 11 November, Charles chose to escape, and rode off with Berkeley and Ashburnham into the night, heading south rather than north, apparently because he did not trust the Covenanters. He ended up on the Isle of Wight, having searched in vain for a ship to take him to France. This was something of an embarrassment to the island's new governor, Colonel Robert Hammond, who took his commission from Parliament seriously, and was less than delighted to have this new guest. The King seems to have become keen on going straight to France, but the expected boat never arrived and he was escorted to Carisbrooke Castle on 14 November.[32]

Having escaped, and seen the restoration of army discipline, Charles seems to have decided to deal with the army. But having flirted with the Covenanters, and escaped from Hampton Court, he had a real credibility problem. On 16 November he sent a letter to the House of Lords, following up a message that he had left for them at Hampton Court on the day of his escape, which seemed to offer a compromise between his own position and the *Heads of Proposals*. He declared his conscientious objection to the abolition of bishops and the alienation of church lands, but also his willingness to see the Presbyterian church currently established persist for three years, in order to avoid further disorder. But that church was to have no power to coerce men of his mind, or any others. Here was potentially shared ground on the issue of toleration – some royalists had been making a case against coercion in matters of conscience, notably Jeremy Taylor.[33] Papists, and public professions of atheism or blasphemy, were excluded from this toleration. This was a strange alliance, however: toleration being urged as a way of safeguarding episcopacy. Charles again proposed a conference in the Westminster Assembly, with divines of his choosing added to the body. He also offered to give up the militia during his lifetime, to put down disturbances of the peace and resist invasion. Thereafter, control would revert to the crown. He also gave commitments about arrears of pay, disposing of the great offices of state during his lifetime, an Act of Oblivion to prevent reopening of these conflicts, and offers on Ireland and the status of measures taken by rival authorities during the war. Settling all these things, he declared, would be a prelude to reforming parliaments in the way suggested by the *Heads of Proposals*.[34]

All this was, of course, unacceptable to the Covenanters, to whom Charles cheerfully explained that it was only a lure to start negotiations – he had no intention of entering into a final agreement along these lines. To those trying to deal with the King this approach was maddening, and it is hard to believe that it did not occur to the Scots that he was toying with their affections too. But there was for Charles a stable core of principle here – in order to preserve essentials it might be necessary to concede ground tactically, and while he would not break an explicit promise (such as not to escape), offering something as an inducement to negotiate with no intention of actually conceding it was not dishonest, merely politic.[35]

The offer he had made was in itself skilfully judged, offering to forge a royalist–Independent coalition against strict Presbyterianism, and to answer the demands of the army in relation to Parliament. On the other hand, it also established Presbyterianism, and so made a large concession to that lobby too. But it was too late in the day to seem sincere or serious and it was answered with an ultimatum. After letting it lie for nine days the Houses came up with four counter-propositions, which were converted into bills for the royal assent on 14 December. They would grant Parliament control of the militia for twenty years and concede the need for parliamentary consent before the militia could be exercised; revoke declarations against the Houses; revoke peerages created since 1642 (which affected the composition of the Lords, of course); and give the existing Houses the right to adjourn to any location where they felt safe. Other pieces of legislation were offered as propositions and a number of qualifications were added. The deal was that once they had received royal assent then Charles could be admitted to a personal treaty.[36] In one sense this was a return to more normal politics – the use of Acts rather than ordinances would at least signal a return to legislative normality. But they were really a test of honesty rather than a gesture of loyalty, and they turned negotiating points into preconditions. Even so, it seems that some people in the army and in Parliament had given up on him completely.[37]

It was not until 24 December that a delegation arrived at Carisbrooke to present the Four Bills to Charles formally. The Scottish commissioners followed after the delegation, ostensibly to express their opposition to the bills, but really to present an alternative: the Engagement. The Four Bills gave no guarantees about the Solemn League and Covenant: either on religion or on the closer political union of the two kingdoms, and the prospects for this seemed to be diminishing. Henry Marten had published a pamphlet expressing English hostility to these 'extra-national' demands of the Covenanters, and the mood seems to have been a more general one. Fearing this development, the Covenanters became a soft touch for Charles. In the gap between the arrival of the Four Bills and the Scottish commissioners Charles successfully gave the impression that he was interested in a deal with Parliament, and this probably helped him to secure more concessions from the Scottish commissioners when they did arrive.[38]

On 26 December, probably in consummation of his plans for the last eighteen months or more, Charles signed an agreement that allowed him to resume the fighting: the Engagement.[39] Under its terms he offered to confirm the Solemn League and Covenant by Act of Parliament, provided that no-one (including him) was forced to take it. He would establish Presbyterian church government and the Directory of Worship for three years (although exempting himself and his household), to be followed by a free debate at the Westminster Assembly. There would also be legislation against schism and heresy. In return for this, the Scots would provide an army:

for preservation and establishment of religion, for defence of His Majesty's person and authority, and restoring him to his government, to the just rights of the Crown and his full revenues, for defence of the privileges of Parliament and liberties of the subject, for making a firm union between the kingdoms, under His Majesty and his posterity, and settling a lasting peace.[40]

Duly signed, it was wrapped in lead and buried in the garden of the castle until the opportunity arose to take it off the island.[41]

Two days later Charles rejected the Four Bills. Proposals which had already been denounced by the Scottish commissioners could clearly not be the basis for peace, he argued, and the form of the approach foreclosed negotiation – not least because he would have to assent to actions taken under a Great Seal created without his authority. He had asked for a personal treaty and they 'in manner propose the very subject matter of the most essential parts thereof to be first granted, a thing which will be hardly credible to posterity'.[42] This was not an unreasonable position, at least if it had been taken up by someone who had not just entered an agreement to start another war.

Although the Engagement was not public knowledge until February 1648, when it was discussed in the Edinburgh parliament, Charles's preference for Scottish military intervention as an alternative to settlement with Parliament was widely suspected. The Four Bills had been an ultimatum which had in the end met a brisk and wounding rejection. The result was the Vote of No Addresses. The Houses declared they would make no more approaches, and declared that no-one should make an application without their approval on pain of prosecution for treason. They would also receive no further approaches from the King, and no-one else was to either. A similar measure had been floated three months previously, and the Four Bills had been a means to forestall a similar measure as rumours about Charles and the Scots spread.[43]

It is not clear how this particular deadlock could be broken, although it does seem to have been a measure attractive to those thinking about solutions which did not include Charles – abdication in favour of a more suitable monarch, for example. Cromwell appears to have experienced a conversion to this view, arguing in favour of the measure, referring to the King as a dissembler and quoting scripture: 'thou shalt not suffer a hypocrite to reign'. But for that very reason it was not immediately acceptable even to an Independent-dominated House of Lords (the impeached Presbyterian Lords still being absent): it was reasonable to fear that those casual of the authority of monarchy in these terms were unlikely to be more friendly towards the authority of the Lords. The General Council of the Army approved a statement ending with the promise to stand by Parliament 'in what shall be further necessary for prosecution [of the Four Bills], and for settling and securing of the parliament and kingdom, *without the King* and *against him*, or any other that shall partake with him'.[44]

The Lords did not pass the Vote of No Addresses until 17 January, under pressure from the army, which was brought into London following disorders. In the meantime measures of defence had been taken and the powers previously vested in the Committee of Both Kingdoms were now to be exercised by an all-English Committee of Safety (soon to become known as the Derby House Committee). The Scottish commissioners left London on 24 January having completed arrangements for risings to coincide with an invasion. Their general intentions were no secret, even if the details were as yet not public. Parliament reduced the King's household at Carisbrooke and set about preparing a declaration in defence of the Vote of No Addresses.[45]

Both the Engagement and the *Declaration* explaining the Vote of No Addresses justified their positions on the basis of histories. The Engagement passed over the moment at which the Covenanters had sold their monarch, and instead took up the story with the King's involuntary departure from Holmby in the hands of the army. Forced to flee to the Isle of Wight, he had been pressed by the Scottish commissioners to go to London to enter into a personal treaty but this too had been thwarted by the army. They had driven members out of the House and occupied London. Moreover, using their influence they had made propositions to the King without consulting the Scots, in contravention of the Solemn League and Covenant. Not only was this in breach of the treaty, but it was dangerous to religion. It was this – the malign influence of the army – which justified the military intervention now being planned.[46]

The *Declaration*, drawn up between 5 and 11 February, was published for the service of Parliament and members of the Commons were ordered to disseminate the pamphlet. It ran to thirty-seven pages: a long denunciation of Charles's negotiating tactics was followed by a history of Charles's untrustworthiness. Despite opposition in the Commons, it raked up an old canard that Charles had colluded with his friend Buckingham in his father's murder and went on from there: it was a case that had been made not only in the Grand Remonstrance but also following the capture of the King's letters at Naseby. But the now-familiar view of Charles was here used to clinch a more or less final view of him: there could be no more addresses since the King could not be trusted, and so no agreement with him was possible. It was passed 80–50.[47]

Most modern historians have been more persuaded by the *Declaration* than the Engagement. In early 1647 Charles had been the natural rallying point of those opposed to war; by the end of the year it was dangerously easy to present him as a warmonger, bringing further bloodshed on his suffering people. A (more or less) uninvited Scottish occupation in 1640 had been followed by one in 1643 at the instigation of Parliament. Now it was the King's turn.

Two powerful images of Charles compete for attention during 1647. He had spent the year under more or less undignified restraint. 'Sold' by the Covenanters at Newcastle he was moved to Holmby, where he had been able to hunt and to entertain, and to attract crowds of subjects anxious to be healed. Removed from Holmby by a tailor with a dubious commission he was kept under guard in his house at Hampton Court. Escaping from there he took off for the Isle of Wight and Carisbrooke Castle, where he was placed under increasingly close guard. In late

Behold your King

THE
ILE
OF WAIT

Charles I in captivity at Carisbrooke Castle

December an escape by sea from Carisbrooke was thwarted by the direction of the wind, leading to a doubling of his guard. But perhaps most emblematic of these indignities was his attempted escape from Carisbrooke in March the following year. He had planned to climb through his window and jump onto a lawn, where he would meet Sir Henry Firebrace. Firebrace would then hand over a rope which would allow him to drop down from the castle walls, to meet Richard Osborne and Henry Worsley, who would take him to a fishing boat anchored discreetly nearby. Advised to remove the bars from his window, Charles did not, and as a consequence nearly became stuck fast when he tried to climb out. The attempt was abandoned.[48] There was an attempt on the part of royalists to turn this to advantage, by portraying the King as a martyr, suffering at the hands of his errant subjects. The image projected by the monarch during the 1630s was the austere and distant patriarch of the Van Dyke portraits. He was now becoming the sacred monarch whose persecution was testament to his faith: in June a parody of George Herbert's poem 'Sacrifice' likened Charles's sufferings to those of Christ in a style which was to become quite commonplace in royal propaganda.[49] His public declarations made a similar case: a well-intentioned monarch, anxious to do good to all parties, was consistently thwarted by errant subjects.

Although Charles was in the end to suffer, and even embrace, martyrdom, he apparently still harboured hopes of a political triumph. And this is the second powerful image from 1647: these stories of indignity and suffering contrast sharply with Charles's interest in theatrical displays of regality. In the early months of 1647 Charles had been enthusiastic in touching for the King's Evil; and many of his people had responded equally enthusiastically. Over the following winter he turned his attention towards the construction of a spectacular royal palace at Whitehall. The plans he eventually approved incorporated the Banqueting House in the river frontage of a huge palace set back from the river and constructed on lines that at least echoed the best royal architecture in Europe. The Banqueting House now fronts onto Whitehall, but this would have become the internal face of a large courtyard in a palace with a long river frontage, 800 or 900 feet (around 250 metres), which stretched 1,100 feet (more than 330 metres) back across St James's Park. It would have been twice the size of the Escorial, seat of the Spanish monarchy, the most powerful in Europe. It is possible, but not likely, that these drawings represented a rebirth for Inigo Jones. The mastermind of the austere royal masques of the 1630s had been at Basing House, symbol of both loyalty and popery, and had shared fully in the humiliations that followed its capture. In fact, it was almost certainly Jones's pupil, John Webb, who made the design.[50]

At first glance these plans seem delusional, but the political prospects for the monarch might have appeared good. The dissolution of the parliamentary alliance was more or less complete, and the Covenanters now identified the King as the best hope for Presbyterianism, as did many English Presbyterians (although few were willing to fight for him in the following year). As the winter and spring were to demonstrate, tradition had as great a claim on the English people as did their self-proclaimed champions, the Levellers and the army. Armed intervention, the evident attachment of many English people to the idea of monarchy and the disarray of his former English opponents must all have encouraged Charles in the hope that he would soon be restored to his regality. The army, the people and the Scots all seemed less attractive sources of political authority than the crown. Of course, he could not have afforded

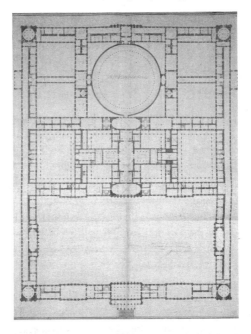

Plans for a new Whitehall Palace approved by Charles during his captivity at Carisbrooke Castle; they incorporate the Banqueting House into the middle of the right-hand side of the frontage as seen in this elevation

a palace on this scale, and the importance of the plan was presumably psychological – an imagined future to warm the heart at this moment of indignity. Webb, and this style, were to prosper after the Restoration, but not before and not on this scale. While not perhaps a plan for the real world, then, this was not a mark of incipient madness. In the winter of 1647/8 it still seemed overwhelmingly more likely that a king restored to his regality would construct a sumptuous palace around the Banqueting House than that he would be publicly executed in front of it.

19

To Preserve That Which God Hath Manifestly Declared Against

Charles, the Scots and the Second Civil War

When the Scottish commissioners left England there had been some preliminary discussion about co-ordinating an invasion with provincial risings in England, but there was no clear plan in place. Their report on the Engagement to the Committee of Estates was well-received, but no further measures were taken prior to the meeting of the Scottish parliament on 2 March. This delay proved fatal to the enterprise, since events in England were moving more quickly. Moreover, the Scottish commitment to the Engagement was not unanimous. Once back in Scotland the commissioners had begun to whip up support for the King, but there were serious concerns that the Engagement was a betrayal. Hamilton, Loudon and others felt that the King had given ample commitments. However, Argyll and others were bitterly opposed and were supported by leading figures in the kirk (the 'kirkmen'), who felt that Charles, having failed to agree to take the Solemn League and Covenant, had given insufficient commitments on religion. This was after all the same King that had brought Scotland the new Prayer Book, prompting armed resistance. When it met, opinion in Parliament was similarly divided over renewing war in England and the divisions became bitter – in fact, a series of duels were offered. Englishmen keen to renew the conflict travelled to Edinburgh to try to encourage the laggardly Scots, among them notable Cavaliers like Sir Philip Musgrave, Sir Thomas Glemham, Sir Marmaduke Langdale and Sir Charles Lucas. Royalist newsbooks reported that whole districts of England were ripe for revolt, but the Scottish clergy, and the women of Edinburgh and Leith, were said to have 'cried out' against a renewal of war. Petitioning campaigns against the invasion were organized by the kirkmen, and this worsened the divisions.[1]

There had been hopes of help from Ireland, but they came to nothing.

In the summer of 1647 the Confederates had been in a strong military position, although under Rinuccini's influence they were not particularly eager to intervene in England to support a heretic king. The upshot of the English debate about Ireland during the spring and summer was the landing of an English force under Michael Jones which quickly pushed back the Confederates. The Confederates were defeated at Dungan's Hill on 8 August, a battle which changed the balance of power, and, on 10 August, Jones entered Dublin in triumph. Inchiquin, commander of parliamentary forces in Munster, also won major and bloody victories during September, eventually reaching the walls of Kilkenny. George Monck had been put in command of the parliamentary forces in Ulster. He had fought for the King in England and, following capture at Nantwich, had preferred imprisonment to changing sides. Following the King's final defeat in 1646, however, Monck felt free of personal obligation, took the Covenant, and accepted service in Ireland. On 2 October 1647 Jones set out from Dublin to meet Monck, and Inchiquin won another major victory at Mallow on 13 November.

All this put the Confederates on the defensive by the winter of 1647. But they were not the only potential royalists. Ormond, strongly opposed to the Confederate programme and Rinuccini's influence, was nonetheless loyal to the King. For that reason he was willing to pursue peace with the Confederates, and he was joined by Inchiquin, commander of the parliamentary forces in Ireland, who 'changed sides' in March 1648. He was upset by the Vote of No Addresses and drawn towards the Scottish/royalist coalition in favour of Presbyterianism and a relatively powerful monarchy. Although Inchiquin was sufficiently disillusioned with the parliamentary regime to throw in his lot with Ormond, however, he did not take all his men with him. Rinuccini, meanwhile, was extremely hostile to the compromises necessary to forge this proto-alliance and pronounced excommunication on all those who co-operated with Ormond and Inchiquin. For a time though, in the spring of 1648, a menacing royalist alliance of Irish and Scottish forces had seemed to be taking shape.[2]

In England royalist hopes rested on an apparently rising tide of hostility to the parliamentary regime. The failure to settle, the continuing burden of the army, and fear of social and religious radicalism all fed impatience with those in control in London. These were hard times: a second bad harvest in succession made for a 'sad, dear time' for the poor in Essex, where 'money [was] almost out of the country'. In Wiltshire there were food riots and attacks on soldiers and excisemen at Chippenham on New Year's Eve.[3] These miscellaneous discontents were the basis for mobilizing support, as in 1642; but, as in 1642, it was not clear that any of the national platforms really addressed them.

The festive calendar was a powerful focus for political mobilization. In Kent there was opposition to the reformed liturgy and in many places worship continued according to the Prayer Book. During 1647 the county committee heard reports of 'sundry seditious sermons' and 'dangerous speeches . . . darkly implying threats against the parliament and a course to be taken with the Roundheads about Christmas'. As a result they took a hard line, publishing an order throughout the county underlining the prohibition of Christmas celebrations. This proved badly misjudged. One minister's sermon was protected by armed men at the door of the church, and when the mayor of Canterbury ordered that the market should stay open only twelve shopkeepers complied. They were told to shut up again 'by the multitude', and when they did not their goods were 'thrown up and down'. In the ensuing melee the sheriff was 'stoutly resisted' and the mayor knocked down. Despite his torn and dirty gown the mayor commanded everyone to go home, and those who resisted were briefly imprisoned. But only briefly – they soon broke out and were jeering at the aldermen. Shortly afterwards some of the leaders, along with some soldiers, appeared on the high street with two footballs. Joined by large crowds the football game quickly became a tumultuous demonstration, surging through the streets to cries of 'Conquest'. Holly bushes were set up at doorways and free entertainment offered. The gaol was opened, aldermen chased and beaten into their houses and Richard Culmer, the Puritan minister, pelted with mud.[4]

Over the weekend Canterbury became the focus for a wider protest as people from surrounding parishes flocked into the town. On Monday a heated argument with 'a busy prating' Puritan led to pistol shots and cries of 'Murder'. Crowds surged through the town, calling out 'For God, King Charles, and Kent'. The sheriff, trying to keep the peace, was knocked down, receiving a serious head injury in the process. Windows were broken in the houses of the mayor and other prominent men, and some of the godly ministers and members of the accounts committee were assaulted, imprisoned and 'laid in irons'. Worse, the city magazine was seized, and there were reports of similar, smaller riots elsewhere in the county. This was quickly becoming a pro-royalist rising: when news arrived of the King's attempted escape from Carisbrooke on 29 December a number of gentry were reported to have openly declared their willingness to support the King and the Engagers. Their aim, they said, was to 'release the King's Majesty out of thraldom and misery, . . . restore him to his just rights, . . . and . . . endeavour the preservation of the honourable constitution of parliament . . . and all the just privileges thereof'.[5]

In the event the county committee was able to muster sufficient support to re-establish control in Canterbury. Elsewhere, however, festive pastimes became a means of expressing political dissent. A hurling match between the men of Devon and Cornwall was thought to be a pretext for anti-army action. In Bury St Edmunds on May Day a crowd gathered around a maypole or May bush as a troop of Fairfax's cavalry rode into town. The soldiers were attacked to cries of 'For God and King Charles', before the gates were shut, streets barricaded and the magazine secured. There followed attacks on parliamentarians by a crowd containing 600 armed men and another hundred on horseback. The rising was contained by a ring of five troops of horse around the town, but it did not stop other protesters gathering at Newmarket 'under pretence of horseracing'.[6] The anniversary of Charles's accession, 27 March, was another focus for discontent. In Norwich the mayor permitted bonfires and feasting to mark the occasion, and refused a summons to attend Parliament to explain himself. On 24 April a crowd gathered in his support seized the headquarters of the Norfolk county committee, which was also the county magazine. When troops arrived to take back the building the magazine blew up, killing more than a hundred people.[7]

London was not immune. On 17 July 1647, a week before the Presbyterian assault on London, with tensions reaching a crisis point, the theatres had been closed down, reviving an ordinance of 1642 passed in similar circumstances. The measure lapsed on 1 January 1648, probably by oversight, and theatre owners and patrons took full advantage. On 27 January 120 coaches were said to have delivered customers to the Fortune Theatre alone. On 11 February the theatres were closed once more – a traditional measure of crowd control and probably therefore a sign more of security concerns than of Puritan hostility to pleasure. On the anniversary of Charles's accession bonfires were lit across the City and those passing along the streets in coaches were compelled to drink the King's health. There were shouts both for the King and against Hammond, his keeper. Butchers were apparently saying that if they caught Hammond 'they would chop him as small as ever they chopped any of their meat'. On Sunday, 9 April, during afternoon service, the Lord Mayor sent a party of Trained Band members to stop boys playing tip-cat (a relatively harmless bat and ball game) in Moorfields. A crowd of apprentices intervened, pelting the men with stones and disarming them. Now armed they marched along Fleet Street and the Strand, attracting a crowd of 3,000 or 4,000, raising shouts of 'Now for King Charles'. Their target was a regiment in Whitehall, but they happened to pass Cromwell and Ireton at the head of cavalry regiments. Cromwell led a charge along the Strand in which two of the crowd either were killed or were nearly so. During the following night apprentices secured the gates at Newgate and Ludgate, and attacked the house of the Lord Mayor. By 8 a.m. they controlled the City, and were only finally subdued when a regiment of foot and four troops of horse were let into the City at Moorgate. Onlookers appeared more sympathetic to the rioters than to the troops sent to restore order.[8]

Mixed in with these disputes were hostility to the burdens of taxation and the tyrannies of parliamentary administration, and positive commitment to royalism and Prayer Book religion, and to the forms of local government that had existed prior to the war. There were rival petitioning campaigns once more as activists sought to harness these multiple grievances to drive forward their programme. Through 1647 there were sporadic petitions for settlement, and an end to military occupation. October, for example, had seen a petition promoted at Somerset quarter sessions against the persistence of free quarter. But following the Vote of No Addresses a number of Independent MPs promoted petitions in support of their position: in Warwickshire, Essex, Somerset and the northern counties. In Essex, Sir Henry Mildmay did get a packed Grand Jury to approve his petition, but a meeting of freeholders at Romford expressed strong opposition. In Buckinghamshire 5,000 signatures were gathered and in Somerset a packed Grand Jury at the March assizes also approved a petition which had enjoyed some success in parts of the county. It commended the Vote of No Addresses, was critical of local malignants holding office, and drew attention to the material hardships of the times: just as in 1642 complaints about material hardships were not necessarily the home ground of the royalists.[9]

This Independent mobilization did not go unanswered. A ring of counties from Essex to Hampshire produced petitions against military government and centralization. In Essex, the failure of the petition in favour of the Vote of No Addresses was followed by the adoption of a petition calling for a personal treaty with Charles, which was accepted by the Grand Jury at the Chelmsford assizes in March. It linked this call for a personal treaty with a denunciation of free quarter and high taxation, and a call for the disbandment of the army. Two thousand men came to London to present the petition. The key point in the 'moderate' campaign, therefore, was the call for a personal treaty, and opposition to the Vote of No Addresses: it was intended to forestall a Scottish invasion, and secure a rapid settlement by bringing Parliament back to the table. Similar petitions were produced in Sussex and Hampshire, and calls for restraint of the county committees, local control of the militia, and restraint of the military and of sectaries were heard around the country throughout the summer.[10] But while that might offer a means to resolve disparate problems it was not clear that those who joined in these campaigns were royalists, or in favour of a return to the religion of bishops and the Prayer Book.

Naturally, these disparate issues also got an airing in print. During March there were attacks on sectarianism and protestations in favour of the calendar and promoting the image of a royalist London. *A true and perfect picture of our present reformation* was yet another catalogue of sectarian errors, arranged thematically (scripture, God, Trinity and so on). Its diagnosis was plainly stated on the title page: 'the Christian's Prospective to take a short view of the new lights that have brake forth since Bishops went down', 'Printed in the first year of King Charles His Imprisonment'. Heading the list of authors in whose works these new views could be found was Thomas Edwards, rubbing shoulders with some of the pantheon of religious enthusiasts – Roger Williams, Laurence Clarkson, Richard Overton, John Lilburne, John Milton and others. The current parliament was denounced as mother to this monstrosity in *Mistris Parliament Brought to Bed of a Monstrous Childe of Reformation*, while another pamphlet announced the *Last will and testament* of that 'monstrous, bloody, tyrannical, cruel and abominable' parliament, which was 'desperately sick in every part of its ungodly members, as well committees, sequestrators, agitators, solicitors, promoters, clerks, door keepers and all her other untrue and unlawful adherents'.[11]

The tide was not all in one direction, of course. Along with calls for parliamentarian unity, vindications of Independents and celebrations of the conversion of Indians in the New World came a translation of the *Vindiciae, Contra Tyrannos*, the leading work in favour of the right of subjects to resist their monarch in early modern Europe. The man often named as the translator, William Walker of Darnall (near Sheffield), was later credited with cutting the King's head off, although it is more likely that his credit lay in the inspiration than in the physical act. More ambiguously, Edward Husbands republished Elizabeth I's speech to her last parliament, made on 30 November 1601.[12] Here, in miniature, lay one of the crucial weaknesses of the royalist mobilization in 1648: did attachment to this view of harmonious relations between monarch and Parliament necessarily support a second civil war? Proponents of this vision might be in favour of the Vote of No Addresses and bringing the King to see reason, for example – would a weak peace of the kind threatened by the Treaty of Newport really restore this vanished world?

It was not, however, completely unreasonable to think that these grievances might support pro-royalist risings all over England. Henry Firebrace had a plan for the King's escape from Carisbrooke, rumours of which reached the Committee of Derby House on 7 February and of another one on 13 March. The following week came the attempt foiled by the failure of the King's physical body to fit through the window. If he had got out, though, he would have had a welcome – there is evidence of individuals seeking with some success to mobilize arms from many areas of the north, north Wales, the Marches, East Anglia, Hertfordshire, Herefordshire and the east Midlands as well as Bristol, Bath and Tavistock. Many people seem to have gone from, or through, London to join the risings in Essex and Kent.[13]

There were strong parallels with 1642 – the end of parliamentary attempts to come to terms, against a backdrop of more or less spontaneous expressions of miscellaneous grievances, led activists to mobilize support. Petitions, promoted at quarter sessions and assizes, and pamphleteering publicized grievances, while activists sought to forge from them coherent political campaigns – to renounce the Vote of No Addresses and enter into a personal treaty with the King, for example. In June 1648 in Hampshire a petition was organized, despite pressure from the county committee, which denounced the continued restraint of the King, high taxation, 'arbitrary power' and 'those that think they have monopolised all truth and would therefore square our religion according to their own confused models'. The King was to be restored to his 'indubitable right' and 'the true reformed Protestant religion professed in the reigns of Queen Elizabeth, and King James of blessed memory', with some 'ease to tender consciences'.[14] This was more comforting for the King than Parliament, for sure, but it was not particularly happy reading for many of his allies among Presbyterians and Engagers.

As in 1642 this attempt was only partially successful, for there were two essential difficulties in forging an alliance from these very disparate forces: it was going to require people to start a new war, aimed in part against the consequences of the last one; and that people persuade themselves that the King, who was what held the alliance for a personal treaty together, was worth fighting for. Hostility to the army, the sects, the parliamentary regime might all fuel resentments, but they did not necessarily lead to support for the aims of the Engagers. The Scottish kirk, after all, was not a known supporter of Christmas festivities, or games of tip-cat during divine service. Formal Scottish demands, received in Parliament on 3 May, included the suppression of heresies and schisms, including the Prayer Book, and the extirpation of episcopacy.[15] The previous summer the Presbyterians had made concessions to anti-excise feeling largely because they had to, and had sought to insulate apprentices from the consequences of their reform of the calendar. But they were no more the people's friends than the army, which, its material burden aside, offered a potentially attractive alliance of tolerant Independents and indulgent Anglicans. Being against the Vote of No Addresses was not the same as being in favour of the Engagement; indeed, it might mean quite the opposite – talk not silence might be the best way to keep the Engagers out.

With hindsight it is possible to see that the story of the second civil war is the story of a dog that didn't bark. As in 1642 there were plenty of grievances but a relatively small number of activists willing to resort to arms. And in 1648, it turned out, there were more-effective forces of suppression, including auxiliary forces raised by hawkish parliamentarians, which prevented activists from rallying effective support.[16] It may also be that the disparateness of the movement, and recent experience of the costs of warfare, served as another disincentive: for how many of these grievances was warfare likely to be an effective solution? In Scotland, as in 1640, the decision to invade England was controversial, particularly since it was in defence of a king who was so palpably unreliable on religion. An alliance of Charles with Presbyterians against Parliament was, in the end, a peculiar sight, in both kingdoms. Enthusiasm for renewed warfare was limited, in both England and Scotland, but quite what forms of negotiation might forestall it was impossible to say.[17]

Last-minute attempts to square the Vote of No Addresses with the pursuit of a settlement were less impressive than the preparations for war. The obvious solution was to try to secure a deposition or forced abdication in favour of one of his elder sons. Charles, Prince of Wales, now seventeen years old, had fled to the Isles of Scilly in March 1646 and from there to Jersey, before taking up an offer of refuge in France following his father's surrender. There he was beyond reach or persuasion. His younger brother James, Duke of York, now in his fifteenth year, had been in Oxford during the war. When it ended he was placed under the guardianship of the Earl of Northumberland at St James's Palace in London. He was not willing to countenance a deal of the kind being proposed and was to escape, at the third attempt, in April 1648, in the course of a specially arranged game of hide-and-seek. Colonel Bampfield was waiting for him, and spirited him away to the Netherlands. Replacing the King was therefore not an option, however attractive it might have been as a way out of the impasse. Henry Marten had made overtures to the Scottish commissioners to try to avert an invasion, but they were rebuffed. Meanwhile men rushed north to sign up for the Engagers' army and both Berwick and Carlisle were quickly occupied in the last days of April. For a time, the prospects for armed royalism looked quite good. In late April the Scottish parliament announced that the Solemn League and Covenant had been broken, called for the establishment of Presbyterianism in England and named its officers. On 4 May the Scottish parliament ordered the raising of an army.[18] But it would not arrive for some time, until after England and Wales had been pacified, in fact.[19]

In the meantime the situation in many areas of England and Wales was tense – the disorders of March, April and May and the rival petitioning campaigns spoke of serious problems for the parliamentary position. On a number of occasions there had been moves to take hold of local magazines and to resist the army, but only two of these movements actually resulted in armed risings against the parliamentary regime: in south Wales in April and May; and in Kent and Essex in June.

Politics in south Wales displayed continuities from 1642, a history which illustrates the uneasy relationship between local grievances and national political platforms. In Glamorganshire in 1642 prompt action by the Marquess of Hertford had secured royalist control, but in 1645, faced with increasing military burdens, a 'Peaceable Army' was formed, committed to a programme rather like that of the English clubmen. The King went along with their demands, but when he seemed to be about to renege on the deal the Peaceable Army made common cause with the parliamentarians in neighbouring Pembrokeshire. By February 1646, however, there was open resistance to parliamentary government on more or less the same grounds – the intrusion of new men and the suppression of the rites and traditions of the Anglican church prominent among the grievances. A similar revolt took place in June 1647, defeated by force. In 1648, however, there was a military ally. Colonel John Poyer, the mayor of Pembroke in 1642, had taken military control of the county under cover of a fabricated popish plot. In alliance with Rowland Laugharne he had established military domination in an area where there was little sign of enthusiasm for either side. By 1648 Poyer and Laugharne had many local enemies, however, and Poyer had become very vulnerable should he lose command of Pembroke Castle – his power base. When the armies were rationalized late in 1647 this happened and he was required to hand over the castle to a detachment from the New Model.[20] The resulting mutiny became a vehicle for a pro-royalist rising, drawing on the kinds of grievance visible in many other areas.

Although Poyer never accepted a commission from the King, he did put his mutinous troops behind a rising of the Glamorgan gentry. The aim of the movement was to bring the King to a personal treaty, along with demands that:

the just prerogative of the King, privileges of the Parliament, laws of the land, liberties of the people, may be maintained, and preserved in their proper bounds, and the Protestant religion, as it now stands established by the law of the land, restored throughout the kingdom with such regard to tender consciences as shall be allowed by Act of Parliament.[21]

In a sense this was the programme of the Prayer Book petitions of 1642, but without the anti-sectarian bite – liberty to tender consciences had become a currency of 'moderate' politics. But here, in essence, was the problem of the second war – a movement in favour of the Book of Common Prayer was hardly an easy bedfellow of a Covenanting army and it seems unlikely that ease of tender consciences would extend very far in the direction of the Irish Catholics also being wooed by royalists. The secular concerns about the balance between the prerogative, law and the people's liberty was the kind of mother and apple pie declaration that all sides had been making since 1642. Little had changed to promise agreement about what that meant in practice.

At St Fagan's on 8 May a small force under Colonel Horton, who had been sent to disband Laugharne's force, engaged them instead. Many of Laugharne's troops wore papers in their hats saying 'we long to see our king'. The battle was a small one, and Parliament's forces were victorious, but elsewhere in south Wales the picture was less good. In late April, Colonel Fleming had led 120 horse too far into rebel territory and was forced to surrender. He died by a shot from his own pistol, although whether it was suicide or an accident was not clear. In the meantime Cromwell had been ordered to march into south Wales to retake Pembroke Castle.[22] His campaign was quickly successful. Chepstow fell on 25 May and Tenby a few days later, so that he soon arrived before Pembroke.[23]

What proved to be the only substantial English rising was by then under way in Kent. There were plenty of signs of hostility to Parliament elsewhere in England, however: May saw the riots at Bury St Edmunds, and a petition from Surrey, approved by a meeting of freeholders, in imitation of one from Essex that had claimed 20,000 signatures. The petition called for restoration of the King, disbandment of the army and restoration of known laws – all very well, but offering little guidance about the religious or constitutional settlement. It had a cool reception at Westminster, leading to serious disorder. In London the Essex petitioners had been cheered through the streets.[24] News of the raising of the Scottish army reached Westminster as an army prayer meeting was taking place at Windsor, and there was very evident discontent around the country about taxation, the army and the end of negotiation. Awareness of all this prompted the suspension of the Vote of No Addresses in late April, so that members could consider how to settle the kingdom.[25]

The Kentish rising had grown out of the Christmas disturbances.

Leading figures in the Canterbury Christmas riots were put on trial at the assizes starting on 10 May in Canterbury. Two trials were organized, one for the city and one for the county, and the Grand Juries were carefully filled with the well-affected. However, Sergeant Wilde, one of the judges sent down to ensure a clear outcome, delivered a misjudged address, which seems to have inflamed opinion and the Grand Juries proved less tame than hoped. They refused to support the prosecution and rumours immediately circulated that they would be prosecuted, or even hanged. In the heated atmosphere a petition was drawn up and approved by the Jurymen, calling for a personal treaty with the King to settle the just rights of King and Parliament; disbandment of the army; government by known laws; and defence of property according to the Petition of Right against illegal taxes and impositions. When the county committee drew up an order declaring the petition to be seditious, however, the campaign took off. Two hundred gentlemen signed the petition in Canterbury and then sent copies all over the county to be signed more widely. In fact all but ten members of the county committee signed, and the copies returned from the county were collated on 29 May. Anyone who wanted to accompany the petition was called to assemble at Blackheath the following day.[26]

Annexed to the petition was an engagement to defend the petition by force of arms, if necessary, and a remonstrance declaring the necessity of this provocative step. More than 27,000 people were said to have signed this declaration – more or less equivalent to the total adult male population in the county. Helped by defections many of the county's strongpoints and magazines fell into the hands of those promoting the petition, although Dover held out. Crucial too was the mutiny of the navy. The displacement of the Earl of Warwick as admiral by the Self-Denying Ordinance, and of Sir William Batten on partisan grounds in September 1646, had been unpopular; so, too, was the appointment of his replacement, Thomas Rainborough. Many of the crews were from Kent, and in May there was an open mutiny, which included Rainborough's own ship.[27] Swift military action was taken, Fairfax abandoning his march north in order to relieve Dartford. In order to forestall what seemed like an imminent general mutiny in the fleet Rainborough was moved aside in favour of Warwick.[28] The origins of the Kentish rising can be traced to numerous discontents, but it is again clear that its political programme did not sit particularly easily with any of the main players on the national stage, and there were significant divisions within the county about what this movement was for.[29]

With superior resources and the advantage of a singular purpose, the New Model was able to contain the military threat in Kent very easily. Fairfax occupied Blackheath, the place set aside for the mustering of the Kentish army, on 30 May and the following day moved on through Gravesend towards Rochester. Unable to cross the Medway he moved south along the river reaching Malling on 1 June. The royalist forces, around 11,000 men, were concentrated in and around Maidstone under the command of Goring's father, the Earl of Norwich, who had filled in a blank commission for himself. But he was no military commander. Fairfax marched into Maidstone without significant trouble and there followed a major engagement in which the parliamentary forces were completely victorious. As a consequence Norwich pulled his forces out, heading first for Blackheath and then Bow Bridge, but the way into London was blocked by Skippon. By now reduced to only 3,000 men, and with Fairfax's army doing efficient work of putting down resistance in Kent, Norwich crossed the Thames, hoping to make political capital out of discontent in Essex.[30]

There, a demonstration against the county committee on 4 June quickly threatened to become a rising. Norwich arrived at Chelmsford on 7 June and Sir Charles Lucas was able to induce the Essex men to rally to his support, arranging a rendezvous at Brentwood on 8 June. The following day a substantial royalist force was established at Chelmsford, but the county magazine was seized by Sir Thomas Honeywood on behalf of Parliament. Edward Whalley, a parliamentary colonel at the head of only 1,000 cavalry, was content to shadow their movements, rather than engage them. They marched through Essex via Leighs (the Earl of Warwick's house, where they took what arms they could) and Braintree before heading for Colchester. There, Lucas hoped, he would be able to get recruits. On 12 June they were admitted to the town.[31]

Fairfax had crossed from Gravesend to Tilbury the previous day, meeting with Honeywood and Whalley at Coggeshall and on 12 June parliamentary forces began to gather outside Colchester. The town was not easily defensible and Fairfax ordered a swift attack, hoping for another quick success, as at Maidstone. The fighting, however, was intense. By 19 June an attempt to bring supplies for the defenders up the river from the sea had been repulsed and the besiegers had settled down to building fortifications – it looked as if it would be a long stay. Norwich and Lucas settled in for a long resistance, hopeful, no doubt, that events elsewhere would go their way.[32]

They did not. Kent had quickly given way and risings elsewhere did not amount to much. Efforts to raise royalists in Devon and Cornwall in June were headed off, and preparations in Herefordshire to rise in support of a Scottish invasion also came to little. The minutes of the Derby House Committee betray a sense of panic, and there were signs of at least some trouble in Nottingham, Lincoln, Huntingdon, Rutland, Leicester, Hertford, Cambridge, Sussex, Dorset, Hampshire, Surrey, Worcester and Warwick.[33] But this was not the same as a co-ordinated war effort. The Earl of Holland, charged with co-ordinating the English royalist effort, was arranging for the removal of horses from London two or three at a time, but the organization was extremely leaky and the Derby House Committee well-informed about the operation. On 4 July he took the field and the following day appeared at Kingston to try to raise men. He sought recruits at a horse race on Banstead Downs and in Reigate, but was eventually chased out by Colonel Michael Livesay. He gave up on 8 July and headed north with 200 horse, arriving at St Neots on the evening of the following day. There, however, he was surprised and captured. The debacle was a great morale-booster for the Derby House Committee and they signalled their new confidence by taking a sterner tone with the City, calling on the Lord Mayor to keep better order in London.[34]

In the north of England the seizure of Pontefract Castle on 1 June and the desertion of the garrison at Scarborough at the end of July were the sum of royalist successes. Many fortifications in England had been 'slighted' (rendered indefensible) the previous year, and that drew the teeth of these risings. Pontefract Castle was not among them and illustrates the danger – taken by John Morris, a former officer in Ireland who had returned to fight for the King, before defecting to Parliament, and now fought on the other side. His control of Pontefract effectively tied up a considerable body of John Lambert's forces.[35] The failure of co-ordination, the successful suppression of those risings that did occur, the containment of naval mutiny and the failure of discontent in many places to support risings meant that by early June the situation was far less threatening than it once might have appeared. When Pembroke

Castle surrendered on 11 June, the threat in England and Wales had been contained – Colchester, Pontefract, Scarborough, Carlisle and Berwick aside.[36]

To that extent the second civil war in England was more or less over by the time the Scots invaded. They crossed the Tweed on 8 July, only days before resistance in south Wales gave out and Cromwell was freed to march north against them. With risings elsewhere either abortive or snuffed out this left Colchester very isolated and gave Fairfax no particular reason to risk troops in more assaults. Naval mutiny, although not suppressed, had been contained. Attempts to put the Prince of Wales at the head of an army, with Dutch support, also came to little. With the navy in mutiny, and support for the rising in East Anglia, a landing on the east coast might have posed serious problems to the parliamentary forces. But his blockade of the Thames eventually came to nothing.[37] There were defections from Parliament – notably of Scarborough and Batten, who took with him one of the best of the parliamentary ships. But when the Engagers arrived the main strategic hope had already been lost – parliamentary forces were not divided amongst numerous threats but confronted only two: Colchester and the Engagers. Parliamentary control of the seas was not entirely secure, but help from Ireland or the continent was not going to arrive.

Hamilton had raised only 9,000 of the projected force of 30,000 men. His march through the north of England, however, was opposed only by Lambert, commanding the remnants of the Northern Association army. Some of Lambert's men had been despatched to lay siege to Pontefract and this left him with only 3,000 men, not enough to engage Hamilton. Cromwell was able to leave Pembroke on 14 July with 3,000 foot and 1,200 horse and so Lambert merely shadowed Hamilton, awaiting Cromwell's arrival.[38] Both Cromwell and Lambert expected Hamilton to march to the eastern side of the Pennines, to take the faster route south to relieve Pontefract then Colchester. As a result they stayed to the east, while Hamilton took a relatively slow march southwards on the western side of the Pennines, arriving at Hornby Castle, north of Lancaster, on 9 August. It was only then, at an argumentative council of war, that Hamilton finally committed to a continued march via Lancaster rather than to cross the Pennines.[39]

By the time this decision was taken Cromwell was in position to join

The Scottish invasion, 1648 (with an exaggerated estimate of
the size of the army)

Lambert, having taken on supplies in the Midlands. On 9 August, Henry
Lilburne, brother of John and Robert, turned Tynemouth Castle over
to the royalists but died in its defence against Haselrig the following day.
Cromwell and Lambert joined forces at Ripon, to create an army of 8,600
men, which set off across the Pennines. Hamilton probably had 10,000
men by this time, and was supported by Langdale's 3,600 men and, potentially, troops from Ulster. But Cromwell was able to catch this larger army
in the flank, with devastating effect. Hamilton had allowed his cavalry to
advance sixteen miles beyond the main body of infantry, which was near
Preston, when Cromwell's forces arrived from the east on 17 August.
The Engagers' army was north of the river Ribble, with the cavalry far
to the south. Cromwell faced a choice of seeking battle on either bank,
and chose the northern side, cutting off the retreat and separating the
army from potential reinforcements. It was the more confident move,
since if he had lost the march to the south would have been unopposed.[40]

Cromwell's approach was resisted by Langdale's forces on Ribbleton
Moor, and it took hard fighting to advance, by which time most of
Hamilton's infantry had crossed the Ribble to the south. This made the
Ribble Bridge vital, and it was defended tenaciously, but by nightfall it
had fallen to Cromwell. So had the wagon train, 4,000 arms and perhaps
as many prisoners. Hamilton decided to head southwards to meet his
cavalry as they came north under Middleton, but they took different

roads and Middleton's forces were turned back by Cromwell before they met the infantry. There followed a pursuit in which the Engagers' resistance was hampered by the loss of supplies at Preston, and by the fact that powder flasks had been soaked in heavy rain. It was a dispiriting retreat, in which they suffered heavy losses, ending in a last stand at Winwick, near Warrington. A thousand men died there, and 2,000 more were captured. William Baillie made what terms he could for the remaining infantry while Hamilton rode off with the remnants of the cavalry. Hamilton was later caught at Uttoxeter and Langdale in Northamptonshire.[41]

This campaign was nothing less than a disaster for the Engagers. Cromwell and Lambert had lost fewer than a hundred men, although there were of course many wounded. In return they had crushed the armies of Langdale and Hamilton, taking nearly 10,000 prisoners. Those among the prisoners who had served voluntarily were bound for servile labour in the New World, and when there was no more demand there, for service under the republic in Venice.[42] These victories confirmed Lambert's rise: he had been given command of the northern forces in place of Poyntz the previous year and was increasingly well-known as a champion of a robust version of the army's political programme. The defeat at Preston was also a fatal blow to the Prince of Wales's plans, which had come to focus on a landing in the north in order to join forces with Hamilton. The death of that plan was a mortal blow to royalist hopes in general. The Prince of Wales, forced to sail up the Thames by mutinous sailors at the end of August, tried to engage Warwick but was separated by a storm. Shortage of supplies forced him to return to Holland on 3 September.[43]

Colchester, isolated since mid-July, was by mid-August completely alone and the county of Essex, which had previously been spared the horrors of war, was now to experience them in full. The siege lasted eleven weeks and by the end conditions were appalling. Food quickly ran short and it was said that at the time of the surrender there were no cats or dogs and few horses left alive. Water supplies had been cut or spoiled and both sides had destroyed property by fire in order to deny cover to the enemy. There had been heavy bombardments, which had also caused extensive damage. Houses, property and livelihoods had been consumed. Desperate inhabitants, led by starving women, demanded surrender, but

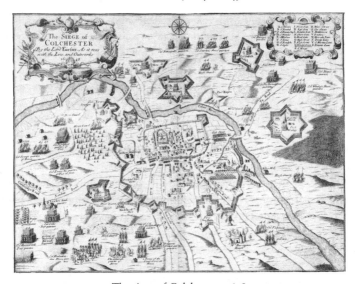

The siege of Colchester, 1648

Norwich refused. Instead he sent the women and children out of the town, but the besiegers would not let them pass. Caught between the two armies they were eventually readmitted to the town. Contemporaries were shocked by conditions in the town after its fall.

How sad a spectacle it is to see goodly buildings, well furnished houses, and whole streets, to be nothing but ruinous heaps of ashes, and both poor and rich brought almost to the same woeful state, to see such people scarce able to stand upon their legs, . . . to see poor and rich men, late of good quality, now equal to the meanest, toiling and sweating in carrying some mean bed or other away, or some inconsiderable household stuffs out of the burning, all of them with wailing weeping ghastly countenances and meagre thin faces, shifting and flying in distraction of mind they scarce know wither.

Another witness remarked on the 'sad spectacle to see so many fair houses burnt to ashes and so many inhabitants made feeble and weak with living upon horseflesh and dogs, many glad to eat the draught and grains for preservation of life'.[44] One comparison that came to mind was with Magdeburg, the town which suffered most notoriously in the Thirty Years War.[45] Here, in Colchester, was a moment when England threatened to turn Germany.

The horrors inflicted on Colchester were within the laws of war, but only just, and both sides accused the other of a lack of decency. Fairfax, in refusing passage to the women and children, had denied their often-claimed right to special protection, but he did so in order to keep up pressure on Norwich to bring an end to an increasingly futile resistance. If Norwich thought their suffering was too great then he should accept the offer of a treaty to end the siege. The defenders were also accused of having used poisoned bullets and there were rumours of cannibalism. Norwich's decision to hold the city was increasingly difficult to justify in military terms, and his refusal to surrender threatened to waste human lives. To the besieging parliamentarians it was this stubborn and unjustifiable denial of military realities that was the root cause of the enormities.[46]

When capitulation came, the defenders could therefore hope for little sympathy. Their resistance had persisted well beyond the point dictated by common sense. They chose to surrender only under pressure of civilian rebellion and news of the defeat at Preston. Norwich made some show of being involved in a negotiation, but was forced to a humiliating capitulation on 27 August, ten days after Hamilton's army had been crushed. All officers above the rank of captain surrendered at mercy rather than quarter – that is to say that their fate depended on the discretion of their captors and there were no guarantees. In this case, it meant 'without certain assurance of quarter so as the Lord General may be free to put some immediately to the sword if he see cause'. Junior officers were offered quarter 'for their lives' – which guaranteed them freedom from physical harm, warm clothes and food. It was explained though that in this case this meant only that they would have 'their skins whole, though stripped of all their outward apparel'. The only point of negotiation was whether the senior officers were to surrender to the mercy of Parliament and the Lord General or to the Lord General alone. The latter was preferred by the defenders since it meant that they remained subject to military rather than civil law. But it made little difference that this was granted since the codicil to the treaty added by Fairfax stated that he had summary power in the short term and that he could hand over the generality to the mercy of Parliament.[47]

Thorough prosecution of the siege and unforgiving terms had the advantage of discouraging others – the logic of the laws of war in this case was that they discouraged unnecessary loss of life by making adventurous souls aware of the costs of their ambition, and of defeat.

The royalists having plunged the country into renewed war, there was some justification for seeing these as appropriate responses. But Fairfax went further and actually executed two of the royalist commanders, reprieving a third at the last moment. Appropriately enough the officers had taken refuge at the King's Head, from where Lucas, Sir George Lisle, Sir Bernard Gascoigne and Colonel Farr were summoned. Farr escaped but the others were condemned by a court martial. So too were Norwich and Capel, but their fate was left to Parliament to decide. Loughborough, the other senior officer, also escaped.[48]

Lucas, Lisle and Gascoigne all faced immediate death, however, and despite their pleas that they needed more time to prepare to meet their end. Lucas was a senior officer, responsible for the royalist presence in Colchester in the first place. He was also, arguably, in breach of a previous parole – having surrendered before and received quarter on condition that he did not take up arms again. There were other *post facto* justifications too, and it may have been significant that he was a local man, brother of Sir John Lucas, who had been the principal target of the rioters in 1642. Lisle was a less clear-cut case, though. He was less senior, but was held responsible for orders to destroy many properties and was a close ally of Lucas. In reality, whatever the arguments in favour of these particular executions, these were in Fairfax's words 'Persons pitched upon for this example'. These lives were taken, Fairfax explained, 'for some satisfaction to military justice, and in part of [*sic*] avenge for the innocent blood they have caused to be spilt, and the trouble, damage, and mischief they have brought upon the town'. Gascoigne was pardoned at the last minute, perhaps because he was Florentine, and it was feared that his death might lead to reprisals. Lisle and Lucas died, treated firmly and unsympathetically by Ireton.[49]

These two were memorialized as martyrs, but not necessarily with strong justification.[50] In October the parliamentary cause acquired its own martyr of dubious credentials. Pontefract and Scarborough had held out after the defeat of the other risings. Thomas Rainborough was sent north to help with the siege of Pontefract, despite the misgivings at Parliament and the hostility of the Yorkshire county committee, which did not want to find supplies for another 800 men. Based in Doncaster he dispersed his men in order to limit the burden, but this left him vulnerable. On 29 October a party of royalists from Doncaster surprised him in his bed

– the guard, John Smith, had not reported for duty, owing either to illness (as he said) or to his being engaged in a local bawdy house (as a press report had it). Once captured Rainborough tried to escape, noting that he was held by only four men. One of his captors tried to drag him down, and Rainborough managed to grab a sword, his lieutenant grabbing a pistol. Rainborough was run through the throat but still resisted, receiving another wound in the body, this time a fatal one. His lieutenant also died. This was not, therefore, cold-blooded murder, but Rainborough was immortalized as a martyr, and the army lined up behind the demand for vengeance. Rainborough was given a hero's burial in London – fifty or sixty coaches of women and men on horseback, numbering around 3,000, processed through the City, entering at Islington and then making their way via Smithfield, St Paul's, Cheapside and out to Wapping, where he was buried alongside his father. A cannon salute from the Tower marked his interment.[51]

Charles had turned an amalgam of discontents into a new war, resulting in more unnecessary deaths, and this helped to crystallize support for hardliners in the army. In late April, on his way to war, Cromwell attended a prayer meeting in Windsor. There he would have heard Goffe call again for justice on a king who would plunge his people into war once more. News of the death of Colonel Fleming in south Wales arrived on the third day of the meeting, and it was in this atmosphere of anger that 'Charles Stuart, that man of blood' was said to be liable to be called to account 'for that blood he had shed and mischief he had done to his utmost against the lord's cause and people in these poor nations'.[52]

These were more radical arguments than those of 1642/3, but they did not represent a consensus. Radical political demands were divisive within the army, and these divisions were exacerbated by renewed Leveller agitation. In April attempts to elect agitators were launched, and renewed campaigning behind the *Agreement of the People* enjoyed some success in Rich's regiment, but there is little evidence of success elsewhere, and it was headed off at a meeting in St Albans.[53] The call for justice should not be read forwards as a settled desire to kill the King, and the constitutional radicalism implied by Goffe was not necessarily representative of the whole army. But Goffe's views as stated in Windsor did reflect something of the mood in which this war was embarked upon – fearfully, and hesitantly, but also with a strong resentment at the profligacy with which the royalists were willing to spend human lives.

At Colchester later in the summer, the acrimony and recrimination brought England close to atrocities. That siege in particular suggested that at the end of the second civil war England was in danger of descent into the horrors experienced in Germany. Many in the army held Charles Stuart responsible for this, and the 'murder of Rainborough', having ignored God's judgement in the first war and deliberately precipitated another one. Determination to avoid a third war might well come to justify harsh, and previously unthinkable, measures: individual cruelties might be seen as necessary to prevent cruelties of a more general and terrible kind.

20

The Occasioner, Author, and Continuer of the Said Unnatural, Cruel and Bloody Wars

The Trial and Execution of Charles I

Military victory was in political terms no more decisive now than it had been in 1646: what had been defeated, and what that defeat meant for the future, was in the eye of the beholder, and the certainties of the executions at Colchester were hardly the basis for political settlement. Failure to support armed royalism was an indication neither of support for those views, nor of any great love for matters as they stood. Some former parliamentarians had been prominent in their support for the risings, and for the Engagers, and there were significant divisions in the parliamentary alliance. The opinions voiced in print by the Levellers and by Goffe at the Windsor prayer meeting threatened the kind of settlement so strenuously opposed by Edwards and others towards the end of the first war.

Parliamentary attitudes towards the Engagers and the provincial risings in England had been surprisingly equivocal. On 28 April, with invasion plans well in hand, Parliament had voted to reopen negotiations with the King on the basis of the Hampton Court proposals, and on 6 May the Lords and Commons passed a resolution 'for the speedy settlement of the peace of both kingdoms, and preservation of the union, according to the [Solemn League and] Covenant and treaties'.[1] In one sense this was quite reasonable since a settlement was clearly going to have to involve the King and could not be dictated by either a Scottish Presbyterian or the New Model army, certainly not if it was going to be a settlement for all three kingdoms. Parliament was also responding to sympathy for the risings, not least in London. But it was equally easy to see why that would enrage the New Model. At the time these votes were made public, military preparations in Scotland were under way, mutineers in Wales and the navy were supporting provincial risings, and more risings threatened elsewhere. In July, with the battle in England largely won, but Hamilton's invasion under way, there was a clash between Lords and Commons over whether or not Hamilton's army were enemies to the kingdom and putting the Duke of Gloucester on the throne was almost certainly mooted as a way out of the impasse. On 31 July Charles helpfully declared himself not to be bound by the Engagers' manifesto, which declared against toleration of sects or those using the Prayer Book.[2]

Given these political ambiguities, it was reasonable for the soldiers of the New Model Army to feel that their risks and sacrifices had been made in the service of people who did not support them. The authorities in London, while committed enough to its defence, had certainly sent mixed messages in July and August; sufficiently mixed that they were regarded with suspicion by many of the firmer spirits in the army. Parliamentary moves during the summer to try to create the possibility for further negotiation involved political moves that were unacceptable to the army. The eleven members impeached at the command of the army the previous summer were readmitted, and quickly resumed their seats. Another breach was in the offing, between the New Model and a significant body of opinion in Parliament committed to keeping Charles and the Scots on board.[3] Military victory ruled out the possibility of forcing such a treaty using the Engagers' army, but did not settle much else.

The royalist cause had been severely handicapped during 1648. Charles had been forced to sit out the war, in close confinement on the Isle of Wight. It was the Queen and the Prince of Wales who had failed to provide the military co-ordination. But the royalist cause in 1648 had been at least equally an alliance of convenience. Personal loyalty to Charles, or at least a commitment to keeping him on the throne with some regal dignity intact, united people with very different aspirations – Engagers, English constitutionalists and Confederate Irishmen had all been courted by the King. In one view, of course, this was entirely appropriate – he was king to all these people, and had to find some way of reconciling all these people to a peaceful life under his rule. But in the conditions that now prevailed the practical future of such an alliance was far from clear – what kind of settlement could the Engagers, Poyer's troops, the Confederates and the Kentish royalists all support? The *Heads of Proposals* probably came closest, but they were a product of the army that now confronted them. In this fundamental sense the war had settled none of the questions of 1642, and had been the more futile for being the second attempt to resolve them by arms. Calls for a deal with the King had tended to predominate in provincial petitions during the spring and summer, merging with violent resistance to the parliamentary regime. But once new talks about a settlement opened following the second civil war, it was petitions against a deal that predominated.[4] For his critics, Charles appeared not as a monarch acting for all his people, but as a man, Charles Stuart, willing to do deals with anyone, however mutually contradictory those deals might seem. What could a further attempt at treaty possibly produce from a man such as this?[5]

Parliamentary politics seemed to be moving towards a reopening of negotiations with the King. On 24 August, on news of the victory at Preston, the Vote of No Addresses was repealed: something that had been mooted earlier in the summer. There was an alliance here in favour of negotiation to avoid further conflict, a contrast with the view that only complete military dominance would secure a respectable peace. The best hope for this more moderate position was to get the King to agree to parliamentary control of the militia for twenty years and appointments of officers of state and the abolition of episcopacy in favour of Presbyterianism for at least three years.[6] This was familiar territory, of course. Nothing had changed since the exasperated Vote of No Addresses except that Charles had started, and lost, another war. We can presume it was the losing rather than the starting that mattered; Charles was no more worth dealing with but was, perhaps, closer to being backed against a wall.

But perhaps not. Division and disarray continued to characterize his opponents (or potential allies). Defeat for the Engagers' army in England led to their political eclipse in Scotland, as kirk and Covenant risings in the west of Scotland, and the Whiggamore raid (a march on Edinburgh of several thousand supporters of the Covenant from south-west Scotland), drove them out of the centres of power.[7] But these groups had little in common with the army and Independents in England beyond their mutual hostility to the Engagers. Scotland was not ripe for further military intervention in England, but it was not lined up behind the New Model, either. The decision to reopen negotiations with the King was contentious in army circles and there was more Leveller activity, calling for the long-delayed harvest of the fruits of the people's sacrifice. The *Humble Petition of Thousands of Well-Affected Persons* was presented to Parliament on 11 September, urging settlement on the basis of the *Agreement of the People*, and an end to the Negative Voice of the King and the Lords. Two days of silence followed, prompting the presentation of another petition saying the same thing. Amidst the ensuing disturbance demonstrators were heard to say 'that they knew no use of a King or Lords any longer; and that such distinctions were the devices of men, God having made all alike'. Some members commended the message: 'the House must yield to them, or else it might be too hot to hold such as opposed it'. For others, like Sir Roger Burgoyne, this radicalism was a reason to persist in negotiation, demonstrating 'what we are to look for from such a kind of men ... if the Treaty should not proceed'.[8]

Belief in the guilt of those who had prompted another war also led militants to demand an end to negotiation. According to his later, and possibly self-serving, recollections, Edmund Ludlow had met Fairfax earlier in September, hoping to get him to halt negotiations. Frustrated he went on to see Ireton, who agreed that the only peace likely to emerge would be a betrayal of the cause, but did not agree that now was the moment to intervene.[9] From mid-September onwards such militants were mobilizing petitions. On 10 October the Commons received petitions against the treaty from Oxfordshire (a Leveller petition), Newcastle, Yorkshire and Somerset. That from Somerset had, in the now customary manner, been organized at the assizes, courtesy of a packed Grand Jury: it argued that the treaty would be the 'ruin of God's people'. Those in favour of negotiation, although slower off the mark to get petitions going, were more influential in Parliament.[10]

Against the background of these divisions formal negotiations opened at Newport on 18 September. Charles had declared the impending negotiation a 'mock-treaty' on 2 August, and his only purpose in entertaining the proposals was to buy time. For example, on 9 October a breakthrough was apparently made – Charles agreed to hand control of the militia to Parliament for twenty years. He wrote the same day to a confidant: 'The great concession I made this day, was merely in order to my escape, ... for my only hope is, that now they believe I dare deny them nothing, and so be less careful of their guards'.[11]

These doomed discussions were initially limited to forty days, but the deadline was allowed to pass as a settlement was sought. Charles had insisted on a stipulation that no concession was valid until all points had been agreed, so the concession of control of the militia was even more worthless than our knowledge of his intentions suggests. There were divisions among the commissioners: Denzil Holles (who had only just had the threat of impeachment lifted from him by those on 'his side') and Harbottle Grimston wanted Presbyterianism but were relatively easy on political terms; Viscount Saye and Sele and Henry Vane wanted more constitutional safeguards but were willing to see a religious settlement along the lines of the *Heads of Proposals*. Negotiation on Presbyterianism was encouraged by Vane in particular, anxious for toleration. Locked into a familiar negotiation, with no clear new way out, Charles planned another escape on 7 October, aiming to spin out negotiations as long as possible to facilitate it. In the following days he accepted proposition after proposition until, on 17 October, they ran into the buffers on the treatment of delinquents. Proposals were batted backward and forward between the negotiators and Parliament throughout late October.[12]

All the while Henrietta Maria, with the knowledge of her husband, was making plans for a renewal of the war with continental and Irish help. Ormond had been in Kilkenny since early October, trying to secure a peace in Ireland, which might allow a third war in England. On 1 November, Charles gave an evasive answer to Parliament's demand that he disavow Ormond and this confirmed the suspicions about Charles that he had some such plan up his sleeve (the negotiations were not at this point public knowledge).[13] Nonetheless, and although there was more than a little familiarity about all this, Charles did seem more willing to make concessions – not only on control of the armed forces and the government of Ireland for twenty years, but also his right to appoint his chief officials. By mid-November he had accepted much greater restrictions on his power than would have been necessary a year earlier, but the key sticking point remained – the fate of episcopacy.

Charles's own view of his best hope, as he revealed in a letter to Ormond, was to bring peace to Ireland in the hope of renewing war in England.[14] As the treaty negotiations progressed, but those in Kilkenny were not called off, and as the risks of a peace that gave too much away increased, radical opinion in the army hardened.[15]

A key figure in this was Ireton. He had probably given up on Charles as early as the autumn of 1647, at the time of his escape from Hampton

Court. Regimental petitions echoing Leveller and county opposition to treaty gave Ireton support in his efforts to get the army to bring an end to the Newport negotiations. In October, Ireton's regiment had been prominent in calling for justice irrespective of persons, a not very coded call to put the King on trial. With Cromwell at that time in Scotland, far away from the action, and Fairfax apparently indecisive, Ireton seized the initiative and drafted *The Remonstrance of the Army*. In its final form the *Remonstrance* called for an end to the treaty at Newport and for the King to be put on trial, promising 'exemplary justice . . . in capital punishment upon the principal author and some prime instruments in our late wars'.[16]

The demand for justice on the King was of course dramatic: it figured prominently in a shorter digest of the *Remonstrance*, and was echoed in the charges against the King when he was put on trial. But did 'justice' in this case necessarily mean execution? In the many calls for justice in the autumn of 1648 unequivocal demands for the King's death were rare, and this righteous desire for vengeance did not lead directly to the killing of the King. The *Remonstrance*, one of the most straight-talking texts, also left room for manoeuvre. For example, in the passages about the necessity of justice much is made of Charles's failure to show any remorse for his sins. If he were remorseful 'his offence being first judged according to righteousness, his person might be capable of pity, mercy and pardon, and an accommodation with him, with a full and free yielding on his part . . . might in charitable construction be just (possibly) safe and beneficial'.[17] This was hard to sell to men who believed that Charles was a man of blood on whom God demanded judgement,[18] but that was not the opinion of the whole army. Equally problematically, there was little in his character or record to encourage the hope that he would be contrite. Nonetheless, the possibility was raised: killing him was not the main point. The real problem the army was addressing was how to get a just, safe and beneficial settlement. As things stood – the King unrepentant and still bent on conflict when he could manage it – there was no possibility of such a settlement by personal treaty. If he repented, or submitted to judgement, that might become possible – in particular, if he pleaded guilty, he need not die.

Putting the King on trial was also a means of demonstrating that his interests were subject to the authority of the representative of the people. The army's political intervention was justified, it was argued, because they were acting on behalf of the people: pursuit of their own rights had thus been transformed into a defence of English freedoms. The *Remonstrance* opens with an appeal to the principle of *salus populi*, acknowledging that the principle is easily abused, but asking whether that is best served by a personal treaty with the King. It goes on to argue that in order to avoid future wars the people's good must be at the centre of government, and that there must be a permanent safeguard against the use of government to pursue personal or private interests. Only a true representative of the people, with power over all persons, could guarantee this. Constitutional reform and the submission of the King to the power of the people's representative were the two crucial elements of this constitutional settlement. The authority of this representative lay in reason and the law of nations, not custom or tradition, so that 'if they [the people's representative] find the offence, though not particularly provided against by particular laws, yet against the general law of reason or nations and the vindication of the public interest to require justice; . . . in such case no person whatsoever may be exempt from such account or punishment'.[19] Clearly this aims at the King, who was throughout the *Remonstrance* and at his trial accused of pursuing a personal interest in upholding and extending his prerogative power against the interest of the people. But it goes on to say that no-one should 'have power to protect others from their judgment or (without [the people's representative's] consent) to pardon whom they have judged'. The authority of the representative of the people was asserted by making the King answerable, and unable to excuse his friends.[20]

The *Remonstrance*, though, sought to base the constitutional settlement not in custom, law or tradition, but in popular sovereignty: in that context the purpose of a trial would be to establish the ultimate source of authority by demonstrating that the King was answerable to the people. Another lengthy section lays out the need to limit the life of each parliament, since perpetual parliaments are open to manipulation and corruption, not least by the King. A regular succession of parliaments, with rules for election, is argued to be the only means to safeguard settlement, again suggesting that restoring him to his throne is one of the possible outcomes. Such a constitutional settlement, however, would not be safe so long as he was considered 'above any human justice, and not accountable to, or not punishable by any power on earth, what ever he does': the King must be admitted to trial and judgement as an example to his successors.[21] Popular sovereignty restrained the will and interest of the King and was the guarantor of good government.[22] An equal franchise would be introduced, but those who had engaged against Parliament would be excluded for a period of time, and those who did not subscribe to 'a general contract or Agreement of the People' would be excluded from its benefits.

The most immediate concern was not regicide but the danger of a settlement by personal treaty with Charles, which would be unjust, unsafe and not consistent with the *salus populi*. Regicide was countenanced as a means to avoid that, but was not the main business. History proved that the King was unreliable but, as they frankly acknowledged, 'The king comes in with the reputation (among the people) of having long graciously sought peace'.[23] The text is dominated by fears that an expedient settlement will be tempting but ultimately disastrous. The digested version appended petitions from Rainborough's and Overton's regiments in which fears about an unsafe treaty were more prominent than calls for execution of the King.[24] The threat was clearly there, more clearly than in most other discussions from these weeks, but it is part of a complicated text, nearly seventy pages long. A trial, alongside the adoption of a written constitution for the people's representative, would be the basis for a settlement. It would show who was boss, tie the hands of the monarch for ever and make expiation for the blood spilt. 'That exemplary justice being done in capital punishment upon the principal author and some prime instruments of our late wars, and thereby the blood thereof expiated, and others deterred from future attempts of the like in either capacity', the others can be pardoned, and fined, and excluded from public office, having shown proper 'submission and rendering of themselves to justice'.[25]

In principle, this might mean that the King, if he was not the capital author, could be pardoned and readmitted to government on these new terms. His death was clearly compassed, but not necessarily demanded – there was a little distance between the demand for justice and the demand for his head. Shocked responses, while acknowledging the threat of regicide, tended to concentrate instead on the dangers of the power of the sword – a threat to all liberty and law, which made claims about the *salus populi* plainly hypocritical – and the army's own record of inconsistency and betrayal.[26] The life of the King was clearly at stake, but it was being transformed into a symbolic battle over the origins of political power; if that battle came out in a particular way, the man

Charles Stuart need not die. His death might be desirable, but was not an inevitable outcome: having pleaded it did not matter so much if he was convicted, or pardoned.

This position had been thrashed out over a couple of weeks and, at the final moment, had involved active participation by Lilburne, Wildman and other London radicals. Fairfax called a meeting of the General Council – officers only – at St Albans on 7 November, and Ireton's draft was considered on 10 November. Fairfax declared himself against it, which was effectively to block it since his soldiers could not confront King and Parliament without the support of their commander. The continuing flow of petitions from the army, however, and Charles's refusal to abandon the negotiations at Kilkenny, told against more moderate views. So too did news of Rainborough's 'murder' at Pontefract. The compromise was to agree to accept the outcome of the Treaty of Newport but also to put minimal demands before the King which, if he accepted them, would then be put to Parliament. This was, as Ireton surely knew, bound to ensure the failure of the negotiation. In fact, the increasingly obvious danger of a peace which fell short of a full reward for their service and sacrifices stiffened resolve in the army. The final draft of the *Remonstrance* was agreed as the manifesto of a coalition of army and London radicals, united by their desire to prevent Parliament making a hasty peace with the King. Part of the price for this unity was a committee to draft a new *Agreement of the People* as the basis of the new constitution – composed of representatives of the Levellers, army, 'honest party' in Parliament and London Independents.[27]

This was undoubtedly a dangerous conjunction for the King – a revolutionary constitution, the proposal for a court of justice and the backing of the Council of Officers – but he seemed intent on avoiding a settlement reached in these circumstances. By mid-November, Charles was considering escape and on 12 November he had been enquiring about the tides with that in mind. The newsbooks quite correctly guessed what Charles was up to – that if at liberty he would put himself at the head of Ormond's army and reopen the conflict with foreign help, and Hammond was once again told of the importance of not allowing Charles out. The *Remonstrance* was presented to the Commons on 20 November, the day before the extension of the Treaty of Newport expired. It took four hours to read and was greeted in silence by members, who must have heard in it the death knell of this parliament.

Consideration of the *Remonstrance* was postponed for a week while a final response was sought from Charles. During that week Charles had been stubborn about negotiation, in this case about the treatment of his supporters, on which issue he had been offered concessions, but not enough to tempt him. Parliament was reluctant to shut the door on him, and voted a final extension, but the key question was now clear: what would the army do to implement its *Remonstrance*?[28]

Through November the army had been gathering ominously: headquarters were moved from St Albans to Windsor on 22 November and representatives of each regiment were summoned to a General Council. In the meantime every unit was invited to declare its support for the *Remonstrance*. Intervention seemed increasingly likely, but there was disagreement over what was intended – whether to dissolve or purge Parliament, and what kind of constitution would be put in place afterwards. On 28 November it was agreed to move to quarters in or around London, and that a declaration justifying the imminent intervention should be prepared. When it was published, two days later, it protested against the refusal to discuss the *Remonstrance*, and appealed to 'the common judgements of indifferent and uncorrupted men'.[29] Meanwhile pressure was being applied to Hammond to agree to arrest the King. Eventually he was induced to go to Windsor with Ewer to talk things over with the army commanders personally. There developed a tussle between officers sent by Fairfax and those left in command by Hammond. It became fairly public knowledge that Charles was to be removed to Hurst Castle, across the Solent from the Isle of Wight, but he refused to escape and was duly moved on 1 December. There his room was so gloomy as to require candles at midday.[30]

Over the following days London was the scene of tense discussion. Parliament began debate on the King's responses at Newport on 1 December and continued as the army established its headquarters in Whitehall on 2 December. Two days later news of the seizure of the King reached London; a week earlier there had been bonfires celebrating rumours that a deal had been reached at Newport. There followed a mammoth debate in the House of Commons, lasting until 8 a.m. the following morning. It is not well-recorded, but seems to have centred on whether the King's answers could be trusted, and it was finally agreed that Charles's position at Newport offered a viable basis for further negotiation. Prynne, recently elected for the first time, thought this reasonable and that the King would see further sense once he came to London.[31] This can only have been, for most of those present, because it was a more palatable way forward than the *Remonstrance*. At a meeting of figures from Parliament and army later the same day Ireton had argued for a dissolution, but was out-voted. Instead a purge was agreed upon, using two criteria: those who found the King's response to the Newport treaty a sound basis for further negotiation; and those who had resisted the declaration in August that the Scottish invaders were enemies, traitors and rebels. Between eighty and ninety MPs were listed for arrest on this basis.[32]

So it was that members arriving on the cold, dry, blustery morning of 6 December were met on the stairs of the palace by Colonel Pride. The City Trained Bands had been turned back from their duties defending the House and a regiment of foot and one of horse deployed in and around the palace. Two others patrolled the neighbouring streets. Pride, initially helped by a doorman in identifying those on his list, was joined by Lord Groby. Together they arrested forty-one MPs, and more the next day. Others were excluded but not arrested, while many stayed away from fear or disapproval. The best estimate is that the purge actively excluded no more than 110 members in all, but that because so many stayed away voluntarily, the House was reduced by about 270 of its 470 members. On the other hand, many others attended, in the full knowledge of what was going on outside – some with approval, many more apparently simply conforming. What was in the minds of those conducting the purge is not clear but what most of those included had in common was a record of hostility towards the army or, more recently, a favourable attitude towards the Newport treaty.[33] The latter point, in particular, suggests that the purge had a relatively restricted rationale – to avoid settlement on the terms proposed at Newport. It was in favour of the Vote of No Addresses rather than regicide. The purge did not make the death of the King inevitable; there were some who wanted that, but others who supported the purge with other purposes in mind.

The first step of those who had escaped the purge, naturally enough, was to call for the liberation of the prisoners, something which had no effect (they were eventually freed on 7 December in return for undertakings not to try to resume their seats). Cromwell arrived on 6 December, claiming to have had no knowledge of proceedings, 'yet since it was done, he was glad of it, and would endeavour to maintain it'. As was often the case, Cromwell had been absent at the crucial moment, and his attitudes hard to discern. He had a record of trying to preserve the possibility of a monarchical settlement which included Charles, but his absence in these crucial weeks was probably not the result of hesitation. He had serious military business in the north, and there is evidence that he kept in contact with radicals during this time. Once back in London he made several visits to the Duke of Hamilton, who following capture at Uttoxeter was being held prisoner in Windsor Castle. Cromwell was at pains to get from Hamilton an admission that he had invaded at the invitation of Charles I: this would have established who the 'principal author' of the late war had been, and provided damning evidence for any trial of the King. Cromwell, it seems, was quite willing to see a trial and condemnation.[34]

The purged House was weak – clearly a creature of the military, its meetings were thinly attended in the following days. This was an important part of the post-purge calculations – anything done by Parliament needed as much support as possible. Money was sought for army arrears, recent votes were repealed (including the revocation of the Vote of No Addresses and those authorizing the Treaty of Newport for example). Although the purged parliament had secured the release of the excluded members from prison, there was little hope of their readmission to Parliament. A request for a formal explanation of the grounds for their exclusion was made on 14 December with no effect, and on the following day the House actually branded as scandalous a protestation drawn up by Waller on behalf of the excluded members. There was little resistance in the City, and in the House dissent was expressed mainly in absence. The brute fact of the purge seems rapidly to have been accepted, but it left a real problem of legitimacy for those who had engineered it.[35] In the counties it seems that it was now the 'honest radicals' who had the upper hand in mobilizing petitions.[36]

England was now in the hands of men willing to put Charles on trial for his life and to change the basis of the constitution, even if their views were hardly consensual. But it was another five weeks before legislation passed to enable the King's trial, and another fortnight after that before public sessions began. Throughout that time the leaders of the coup were in negotiation, a key aim of which was to prevent another war. The King had slender hopes of raising an army in England, or Scotland.

Following the defeat of Hamilton's army Scotland was in the hands of the kirk party – not likely to co-operate with the English army, but not likely to take up arms for the King in the near future. That left Ormond. While the King pursued that option he could still hope, and his opponents could still feel that they did not quite have him completely over the barrel. It also emerged in December that the Confederates had concluded a commercial treaty with the Dutch which would have made their naval strength very formidable indeed. With their own fleet, that of the Prince of Wales and Dutch maritime strength behind them, they could mount an effective trade blockade.[37] The King had been militarily defeated in England and Scotland, but not Ireland, and previous form suggested that he would be willing to engage in a third war – thus ran the charge, and it was correct.

Moves towards the trial of the King went in tandem with attempts at negotiation, which probably reflected the desire to avoid this third war as much as anything else. Those who promoted the purge had been united by a desire to prevent the progress of the Treaty of Newport, probably in the face of this menacing international situation, rather than to execute the King and abolish monarchy. In the face of the growing naval threat, the allegiance of the navy was crucial. The experience of 1648 had been that the navy was not four square behind the most radical army programmes, and the arrival of the Earl of Warwick back in London seems also to have had a restraining influence on the course of political action: it is plausible that he wanted prominent royalists tried, not the King, and it is unlikely that he supported regicide at this point. Those opposing the treaty at Newport feared that this treaty would give too much ground to the King, and that delay was simply offering him the opportunity to re-gather his strength. On the other hand, killing the King was not a particularly attractive alternative. With peace on the cards in Ireland, and Scotland divided but hardly supportive of the army programme, it could plausibly be said that the best way to start a third war would be for the English to execute Charles, who was after all the King of Ireland and Scotland too. With the legitimate claimant beyond the seas and out of reach, there was more than enough reason to think that regicide would precipitate further armed conflict. And this line of thinking was vindicated after the fact too – following the King's execution the army was indeed forced into battle again, in both Scotland and Ireland, against armed supporters of the Prince of Wales.[38]

This is the context for another attempt to engage the King, the 'Denbigh mission' of late December. The details of the offer are unclear, but seem to have been that the King should accept the alienation of the bishops' lands (and hence, by implication, the perpetual abolition of episcopacy), abandon his Negative Voice and renounce any role for the Scots in the settlement of English affairs. Denbigh was also keen in these months to secure a disavowal of Ormond from the King. Such a deal would have allowed Charles to keep his life and throne.[39] Charles met the approach with a rebuff – Denbigh was not admitted to the presence. Another approach made by the Earl of Richmond, on 11 January, is even more obscure in its details, but it too bears testimony to the continuing desire to negotiate a settlement. Even during the trial there were apparently attempts to get the King to abdicate in favour of the Duke of Gloucester.[40]

Purge, and even trial, did not lead directly to regicide. Throughout the period from the purge on 6 and 7 December 1648 until the eve of the King's execution there were hesitations and delays. The best explanation for this is that at least some of those organizing the trial and passing judgement – those at the heart of the action – were seeking ways to achieve a settlement that included the King, or at least had his acquiescence. In fact, these initiatives probably show that important players were actually trying to avoid having to kill the King, not just trying to seem to want to avoid it. An acquiescent king was more useful than a definitely dead one, as the execution was to prove. That he knew this probably explains something of Charles's attitude towards these proceedings – the almost unflinching confidence with which he resisted the political demands being made of him. On the other side, the trial seems to have been almost a threat, intended to demonstrate that they really meant business this time. In this sense Charles called that threat as a bluff, and only at that point realized that there were a sufficient number of his opponents, in sufficient authority, who were willing to have the bluff called.

Certainly, for a number of the key players the main purpose of the trial seems to have been settlement, not regicide. For over a year the army's politics had been as much anti-parliamentarian as anti-monarchical – the intervention of the army had been against a corrupt representative, which was acting against the interests of the people. Regular elections and franchise reform had been designed to restrain

Parliament, and secure the good of the people; implied in that was a new role for the crown, but there was nothing in these arguments to suggest that popular sovereignty was incompatible with monarchical rule. The army was the instrument by which popular sovereignty would be restored: this was not a position that required the execution of Charles, let alone the abolition of monarchy. If time had been on their side, then those like Ireton calling for dissolution, rather than purge, might have made the case more clearly. Central to post-purge politics was a need to define the nature of the new regime, and to secure the King's recognition of its legitimacy. With these fundamentals in place a settlement might then have been achieved. It is for this reason that the central drama of the trial seems to have been to get the King to plead.

Crucial to the political claims of the putative new order being pursued by men of these views was a revised *Agreement of the People*. Responsibility for drafting this had been given to a committee of Levellers, and was quickly produced. But Lilburne was apparently disappointed to learn that it was not to be simply accepted – the Council of Officers not only looked it over, but also amended it, prior to publication. The initial draft seems to have presumed the abolition of the monarchy and House of Lords, dissolution of the current parliament and elections according to a new, equal, franchise. The electorate would include adult males who paid poor rates, were not royalists, servants or wage-earners, and had signed the *Agreement*. The demand that the representative of the people would have no power to command in matters of religion gave rise to extensive and fundamental discussion about freedom of conscience, the most extensive discussions of the whole series of debates. The issue they addressed had been thrashed out in polemics since 1641 – where was the boundary between freedom of conscience and religious anarchy, error and schism? These discussions took from 10 to 21 December at Whitehall, debates recorded in detail by William Clarke. This seems to have been a very serious attempt to thrash out the basis for a new political order, not simply a sop to radicals while the serious business of executing the King was transacted.[41]

There were, indeed, attempts to forestall the trial, which was strongly opposed by Lilburne and of course many others with less radical views. A plan seems to have emerged whereby the trial would be a means to pressure the King into making minimal but fundamental concessions. Proceedings against Hamilton might bring the King to see reason, or a trial of the King might lead him to accept deposition; excluded members might be readmitted in order to smooth the way to a compromise. Since the purge, thin attendances had meant that Parliament offered barely a fig leaf of respectability for army power – certainly dissolution would have been a more respectable policy for those acting in the name of popular sovereignty. But the argument against dissolution was tied up with an urgent desire to see justice done, and to forestall another war.[42]

Despite the importance of popular sovereignty in these arguments, these were days for the Saints, as much as the people. With Common Council elections due in London the purged parliament had passed legislation excluding all those who had sided with the King in the wars, or who had signed an engagement calling for a personal treaty the previous summer. This secured the City for the army – radical militia committees and financial support were quickly in place, and the chorus of opposition to the purge from City Presbyterians was robbed of institutional power. This might have been the effect of the exclusions from the franchise in the latest *Agreement of the People*: 'a dictatorship of the godly [rather] than a golden age of democracy'.[43] Such were the discomforts of the army's position: an instrument of the people, but suspicious of the people's attachment to monarchy, and to this particular king; committed to freedom of conscience, but forced to exclude from power those whose consciences dictated unpalatable policies.

Even the hand of providence was unclear. A desire for guidance led to the extraordinary spectacle of the Council of Officers listening solemnly to the visions of Elizabeth Poole, a woman of humble background from Abingdon, expelled from a Baptist congregation for her beliefs. Although many people thought miracles had ceased, it was quite common to accept the possibility of direct, personal revelation, and dreams were often interpreted in this light. But for women prophets this authority was ambiguous – it depended on their being empty vessels. There was an acute suspicion of female prophets and their motives.[44]

These were the resonances of Elizabeth Poole's appearance before the General Council of the Army at Whitehall on 29 December, at the height of tense discussion about how to proceed. To be heard in such circumstances she had to act as a kind of spiritual consultant – answering questions put to her, but not affiliating herself with a partisan position.[45] What she offered though was in a sense a reconciliation of the politics of Reformation and of Enlightenment, 'declaring the presence of God with the army, and desiring that they would go forward and stand up for the liberty of the people as it was their liberty and God had opened the way to them'. Her vision had been of a man, representing the army, being a means to cure the weak and distressed land, personified of course as a woman. But she also warned that 'the business was committed to their trust, but there was a great snare before them'. Colonel Rich was moved: 'I cannot but give you that impression that is upon my spirit in conjunction with that testimony which God hath manifested here by an unexpected providence'. Poole was engaged in conversation by Harrison and Ireton, the latter declaring, 'I see nothing in her but those things that are the fruits of the spirit of God'.[46]

So powerful was the impression that she was called back on 5 January. There she made a direct political intervention, in relation to the *Agreement of the People*. She warned the army that the kingly power had fallen into their hands, but only as 'stewards, and so stewards of the gifts of God in and upon this nation'. As stewards their duty was to improve upon this gift, without fear of the great, but without overbearing their own position either: 'I know it hath been the panges [?] of some of you that the King betrayed his trust and the parliament theirs; wherefore this is the great thing I must present to you: Betray not your trust'. She then handed over a paper against the King's execution. This was very powerful, and very serious. But now she was closely questioned about the genuineness of her vision, and the preciseness with which she had been told to deliver a paper. Asked if she was told to speak against his trial or against his execution, she replied, 'That he is to be judged I believe, and that you may bind his hands and hold him fast under'. The printed account is clearer: 'Bring him to trial, that he may be convicted in his conscience, but touch not his person'.[47] The seriousness of these encounters – they are carefully recorded – suggests a desire for guidance on the part of men unsure what God had called them to. Prophecy offered the means to resolve doubt, but was not easy to authenticate or interpret.

Providence, like the will of the people but for different reasons, was an unreliable guide for the detail of political life. In the aftermath of the second civil war there was undoubtedly a righteous anger about the King's actions, a belief that he was a 'man of blood' who might now face Old Testament justice.[48] This made a relatively easy bedfellow with ecstatic revelation, so that the trial of the King might reflect the culmination of a strand of millenarian speculation evident from early in the crisis. Trial and even regicide, in other words, might be a remote descendant of the Reformation politics of the Prayer Book rebellion. But the power of these views made contemporaries take them seriously, though they regarded them with caution too. Moreover, to modern eyes at least, they were not the natural partner of the more secular, contractarian thinking of the *Agreement of the People*, which underpinned the political legitimacy of the purge and trial. Those arguments seem to belong more to the world of the Enlightenment. Indeed the *Agreement* was to be literally a social contract, actually taken by members of the political community prior to their admission – a kind of secularized covenant.

Despite the certainty implied by the purge there had been subsequent indecision: the need for legitimacy was in tension with pressure, within the army and honest radical circles, for justice on the King, and a settlement which reflected the will of God. There were a variety of arguments in favour of trial, and for regicide, and a similar range of reasons for opposing, or failing to oppose, each of these things.[49] By the end of December, however, a trial had been settled upon. Just before Christmas the army published an indictment of the King and called for his trial. This triggered a debate in Parliament about whether the King would stand trial for his life. Cromwell, a strong believer in providence, was not clear: 'If any man whatsoever had carried on this design of deposing the King, and disinheriting his posterity or if any man had yet such a design, he should be the greatest traitor and rebel in the world. But since the Providence of God hath cast this upon us, I cannot but submit to Providence, though I am not yet provided to give you my advice'. In the meantime Charles was brought to Windsor under heavy guard. On 28 December the Commons approved charges against the King which more or less echoed those of the army a few days earlier.[50]

From the start, the trial was as much about political legitimacy as about the King's crimes. On 4 January the Commons declared 'That the people are, under God, the original of all just power: that the Commons of England, in Parliament assembled, being chosen by and representing the people, have the supreme power in this nation; that whatsoever is enacted or declared for law by the Commons in Parliament assembled, hath the force of law, and all the people of this nation are concluded thereby, although the consent and concurrence of King or House of

Peers be not had thereunto'. Three days earlier an ordinance establishing a High Court of Justice had been sent to the Lords, which rejected it; this declaration of popular sovereignty, represented in the Commons, was to be the political basis of the trial of the King, and of the new political order.[51]

On 6 January the House of Commons passed an Act without the assent of the House of Lords or the King – that setting up the court to try the King. This was the first time that one House had legislated on its own, without the assent of the other and of the King, and referred to that as an Act. It was a practical assertion of Commons supremacy, based on the sovereignty of the people, which could not be overborne by the Negative Voice, or veto, of the Lords or the King. This was a practical, or functional, radicalization which overbore opposition to the policies now being pursued; but it was also an important principle that was being declared. Moreover, if Charles agreed to undergo trial on the basis of this legislation, or to participate in the trial, he would be assenting to the underlying constitutional claims. By the same token, of course, refusal to stand trial made an obvious and pretty mainstream repudiation of the army's proceedings in a simple and effective way. The text of the Act, naturally enough, passed over these constitutional and legal difficulties, concentrating instead on the supposed crimes. A clause limiting the authority of the Act to one month gave some guarantee of an eventual return to constitutional government. Its effect, however, was to subordinate Parliament to the military – to drive a wedge, in fact, between the army and its remaining legal credibility. Even among the trial commissioners – 135 were appointed – there were significant divisions over this claim to popular sovereignty. Many of the tensions, ambiguities and hesitations of the following month derived from this particular contest about the origins of legitimate political power.[52]

Among those staging the trial were those who felt it was important that the proceedings should reflect their view that the regime was founded in popular sovereignty. For example, one possible site for the trial was Windsor, which would have protected the proceedings from the view of the world, and made it easier to deal with the King, and to protect his dignity. Others preferred to try the King publicly, as an open statement about the nature of the regime, and their views prevailed: the trial was held in the Great Hall at Westminster, home of the central courts of the English legal system. The publicity attending the trial was magnified by official and semi-official reporting. Daily accounts of proceedings by licensed journalists documented the trial – one royalist, one official parliamentarian account and several independent but broadly parliamentarian. It seems clear that those in the post-purge regime most committed to demonstrating the importance of popular sovereignty had a significant hand in these arrangements. At the same time, however, there was clearly a desire to demonstrate that this sovereignty could be expressed through established forms of government. Holding the trial in the Great Hall laid claim to legal authority, and for three days of the proceedings the royal arms appear to have hung over proceedings.[53] Even at this stage the assertion of popular sovereignty did not necessarily imply the end of monarchy, or of Charles I.

The court met for the first time on 8 January, and consisted of commissioners who would be both judge and jury. Only 52 of the 135

The trial of Charles I

named commissioners attended and the civilian members in particular seem to have stayed away. The Lords made a last-minute counter-proposal but the Commons were increasingly willing to do without the

Lords – a new Great Seal was being made which disavowed any role in government for the Lords. The president was to be John Bradshaw, a Cheshire lawyer of gentry stock, who had built up a prosperous practice before the war and who had made his way in the legal service of the parliamentary cause thereafter with the backing of Independents. A second key decision about the trial was the nature of the charges. It took ten days to draw them up, starting on 9 January, and the controversy was essentially about whether to draw the charges narrowly or broadly. The chief prosecutor, John Cook, lost out in these discussions – he had drafted a very wide-ranging charge reminiscent of the Grand Remonstrance. Instead, what was charged was the shedding of his people's blood since 1642, in England and Ireland but not in Scotland. As drawn up the charges were easy to beat and many amounted to little more than pointing out that he had been present at some of the battles of the first civil war. It was clearly difficult to prove, in court, that his presence on those occasions had been 'carried on for the advancement and upholding of a personal interest of will, power, and pretended prerogative to himself and his family, against the public interest, common right, liberty, justice, and peace of the people of this nation, by and from whom he was entrusted'. Still less did it clinch the argument that he was 'the occasioner, author, and continuer of the said unnatural, cruel and bloody wars; and therein guilty of all the treasons, murders, rapines, burnings, spoils, desolations, damages and mischiefs to this nation, acted and committed in the said wars, or occasioned thereby'.[54]

This latter phrase, which concludes the charge, is a more or less direct quotation from the army *Remonstrance* which preceded the purge, but its insistence on Charles as the sole author of the troubles made it unlikely to stick. It might in fact have been an invitation to get the King, having pleaded, to allow others to be executed instead of him. The army, in fact, had said as much: if this cannot be proved, 'let him then be acquitted in judgement and the guilt and blame be laid where else it is due'.[55] In any case, few people can have thought that this was the set of charges most likely to secure a conviction, and it may be that they were deliberately enfeebled – the obvious weakness of the charges might have served as a bait to get the King to plead. If this is right it suggests once more that the real point of the trial was to get the King to recognize the court, not to secure his conviction. If the King could be tempted to answer the charges he would, implicitly, have recognized the jurisdiction of the court, and the claims about the constitution that it implied. Once he had pleaded a number of outcomes were possible – restoration as a monarch fettered by the principle of popular sovereignty, or deposition in favour of the Duke of Gloucester among them. Just as importantly, a number of very unappealing outcomes would have been foreclosed.[56] These were desperate calculations, made in dire political circumstances, and this is not a point that one would want to start from in constructing a settlement. But this was where things stood, and this was one way out, well short of regicide.

For Charles there was plenty of reason to believe that he could embarrass his prosecutors, by refusing to plead – he had good principled and practical reasons to deny the implied claims about popular sovereignty – and thereby confronting them with the divisive question of what to do next. Sure enough, when the King appeared, on 20 January, he demanded to hear proof of the jurisdiction of the court. On 22 January, Charles, 'discoursing with those about him', apparently 'spoke very much against the court, as no true judicature, and that he did not believe the major part of the commissioners were of that opinion'.[57] And there was the rub. This was to be Charles's main contribution to the drama – his refusal to recognize the legitimacy of the tribunal – and one significant source of encouragement to him in pursuing this line was that he did not believe his accusers were convinced about it either, and he was not completely wrong. He was certainly in a position to know that there were divisions even among those arranging the trial about what it was supposed to achieve, and he played on those divisions very successfully. He did not doff his hat to the officers of the court, and appeared in the garb of a Knight of the Garter, an expression of his respect for the aristocratic traditions of the English monarchy. He denied that this was a parliamentary court since he could not see any Lords, and he seemed willing to stand at the mention of the Lords but not in honour of the court as it was actually constituted. Charles apparently laughed at the charge of treason, and when he was told that his trial represented the will of the people, he replied that he was king by inheritance not election and so to answer would be in contravention of his coronation oath. As court room drama, the key issue was the nature of legitimate political authority, and both sides sought to make their case demonstratively.[58]

Before the formal proceedings began the use of the contempt clause was foreclosed – predicting that the King would refuse to plead, the trial organizers were anxious that this should not lead to an immediate condemnation. The first session of the court, on 20 January, had taken place on a Saturday. Bradshaw, apparently provoked by the King's performance but unable to invoke the contempt clause, warned Charles to answer at his next appearance, on Monday, 22 January. A prayer meeting on the intervening Sunday was the occasion for further attempts to find a basis for compromise – Hugh Peter arguing for a distinction between *salus populi* (the good of the people) and *vox populi* (the voice of the people) as the governing principles of political legitimacy. Here, from a firebrand Independent preacher, was an olive branch to the King, who might in conscience subscribe to the first but not the second of these principles: indeed it is something he might himself have said in the late 1620s or during the Personal Rule. When proceedings resumed, the King refused once again to answer and was warned that the next time would be his last chance. In fact it was not. On the following day he refused again, and began to read a prepared statement about his grounds for refusing to answer. He now claimed, with some plausibility, to be the more credible defender of the people's rights than this 'court', and stuck to his claim that he would answer for his conduct to a properly constituted parliament.[59]

After three formal sessions no progress had been made. The court took two days to consider the evidence that had been prepared to support the charges. This was hardly necessary since those who had prepared the charges and gathered the evidence were also those who were now hearing it. On 25 January it was resolved that the King was guilty and that his punishment might extend to death, but that this resolution was not binding on the court. After further debate the following day the court assembled again on 27 January and the King was given another chance to plead. He refused, and requested instead a conference with the two Houses. There was some concession here, however, since the terms in which he made this request did not presume the illegitimacy of the court before which he currently stood. This was in turn refused and he was offered two further chances to plead – these were the sixth and seventh opportunities since he was first offered his last chance. It is easy to see why the King might have remained confident that it was a bluff. Continued refusal to plead, and the ambiguity of the concession he had made to the authority of the court, had really backed the commissioners into a corner.[60]

At this dramatic moment, the will of the commissioners held – Charles was condemned. He seems to have been genuinely shocked by this – the patent hesitation and reluctance of his pretended judges had perhaps made it impossible for him to believe that they would actually go through with it. In any case, he now tried to speak to the charges. Now that he was no longer disputing jurisdiction, he evidently wanted to rebut these claims against him, but since the court had determined its judgement, and since he had not recognized its jurisdiction, there was little reason to let him. Bradshaw rather wearily silenced him.[61]

Judgement had come on 27 January, another Saturday, and over the rest of the weekend there were further delays in getting the death warrant signed. Here, too, there may have been attempts to pull back from the brink. Comparing the order of the signatures on the warrant with attendance records at the hearings reveals some anomalies – some of those present on 27 January did not sign, and some of those whose names appear high on the list of signatories were not, apparently, present for the condemnation on that day. There has been some technical discussion of this, and the anomalies may reflect the unreliability of the court's attendance lists, but the simplest explanation may well be the correct one – that the death warrant was not drawn up until after the condemnation, and that signatures were collected on 29 January, the day before the King's execution. If correct this gives plausibility to the story that the King was approached for a final time, between his condemnation and execution. The story goes that he was approached with a 'paper book' prepared by the army grandees, and that if he had been willing to sign it, he could have had his 'life and some shadow of regality'. This story is usually discounted but it might be true – it was set down after the execution, when it was wistful rather than wishful thinking. It is certainly the case that the King had been approached between 27 and 29 January, since he was aware of the chosen place of execution.[62]

Whatever the truth of the claims about a last-minute attempt to negotiate, it is clear that some of those present for the condemnation did not sign the death warrant and that others agreed to sign the warrant only after being tracked down. Thirteen of those who signed were apparently present when the King was condemned, but not at the meeting in the Painted Chamber on 29 January when the warrant was presented. They must have been pursued for their signature subsequently. Condemnation was in all early modern proceedings a different thing from the execution of the sentence. It is reasonably likely that condemnation on 27 January, without naming the time and place of execution, had left room for a final attempt to avoid king-killing: to speak to the King with an axe to his neck, in the hope that some crucial concession might be secured in return for a pardon. When this failed too, a number of those who had been persuaded to go along with the condemnation became much less willing to see the sentence actually carried out: only fifty-nine of those present for the condemnation actually signed the death warrant.[63]

Much of this is guesswork, and it may be that there was more intent behind these proceedings than has been suggested here. But it is difficult to read all this as the proceedings of a military faction bent on a show-trial to be followed in short order by an execution. They seem more likely to have been elements of a negotiation, signs of a willingness to take drastic action in order to demonstrate that there was indeed a real threat to the King, despite the many reservations and hesitations among the parliamentarians, and that there was therefore some reason to try to reach a settlement.

But the pressure was certainly applied. It was later said that when the King heard that he was going to be moved from Hurst Castle to Windsor accompanied by Colonel Thomas Harrison, he feared that he would be killed at some lonely spot – it had not escaped his ears that Harrison had favoured assassination at an earlier point in negotiations. Harrison, the godly soldier who had experienced rapture at Langport, reassured the King that in fact all he had said was that justice should have no respect of persons, great or small. Harrison was a willing regicide, but not a murderer.[64]

At Windsor, Charles had touched for the King's Evil, until his captors had stopped him doing so. From there he was taken to St James on the eve of formal proceedings and his conditions seem to have been much worse. Writing much later, Clarendon dwelt on the petty humiliations. No-one other than his guards had access to him, but he was never free from his guards, 'some of whom sat up always in his bedchamber, and drank and took tobacco ... nor was he suffered to go into any other room, either to say his prayers or to receive the ordinary benefits of nature, but was obliged to do both in their presence and before them'. Such 'rudeness' and 'barbarity' represented a kind of 'monstrous duty' and soldiers were apparently only asked to do it once. Charles's refusal to plead in the formal proceedings, and his refusal to show the proper deference in his gestures and demeanour, was echoed by his prosecutors. In particular Bradshaw was castigated by posterity for his arrogance and insolence – he 'insolently reprehended the King for not having stirred his hat' and his manner was marked by 'great sauciness and impudence of talk'. But this was political theatre of course. The court could not show deference to this man, Charles Stuart, who stood before it, denying its jurisdiction over him: Bradshaw's point, even on a hostile reading, was that the King had not shown 'more respect to that high tribunal'.[65]

Publicity was part of the trial, and it was political theatre for all parties, but it was not all choreographed. Here again there was a relatively even battle. For example, when proceedings opened and the roll of the names of the commissioners was called silence greeted Fairfax's name. When it was called a second time his wife called out from the gallery that 'he has more wit than to be here'. Her voice rang out again when the impeachment was read in the name of 'the good people of England': 'It is a lie, not half, nor a quarter of the people of England. Oliver Cromwell is a traitor'. Exasperated, Daniel Axtell, who was commanding the guard in the court, ordered shot to be fired into the box, but wiser counsels prevailed.[66] Although this rather intemperate order was not obeyed, Axtell remained sufficiently prominent in proceedings that he could incite the soldiers to chant 'justice, justice' as Charles was led away at the end of proceedings.[67] Clarendon claimed that Axtell's brutality was matched by others present: although in the course of the trial 'there was in many persons present . . . a real duty and compassion for the King, so there was in others so barbarous and brutal a behaviour towards him, that they called him *Tyrant* and *Murderer*, and one spit in his face; which his majesty, without expressing any trouble, wiped off with a handkerchief'. Another reasonably well-attested story is that Charles tried to interrupt Cook as he read the charge by touching him on the sleeve with his cane. As he reached over the silver tip of the cane came off and there was a momentary pause as Charles waited for someone to retrieve it, before doing so himself.[68]

These stories of cruelties and indignities suffered silently and patiently in the name of larger ideas formed the bedrock of Charles's martyrdom: by the time Clarendon wrote he felt that 'the saint-like behaviour of that blessed martyr, and his Christian courage and patience at his death, are

... so well known' that there was no need to enlarge upon them.[69] This martyrdom he willingly embraced on the scaffold, and in the subsequent propaganda battle both sides had reason to play down the ambiguities and tensions of the trial. Charles, in Clarendon's and subsequent accounts, was the patiently suffering martyr in the trial who died a good death on the scaffold. His judges were later portrayed by their partisans as implacably pursuing justice on that man – both sides found a simpler version of the trial as a foregone conclusion, or an unavoidable act of justice, useful to their self-image.

All this is not to deny that Charles did indeed conduct himself bravely both during the trial – where he apparently shed a life-long stutter in delivering a commanding performance – and on the scaffold. In preparation for his execution, Charles burned his papers and was visited by his two youngest children, Henry and Mary, on 29 January. Sentence was carried out on 30 January in Whitehall, probably because it was more easily policed than Tyburn or the Tower. Again there is significance to this choice of site, and irony too. Charles was led to the scaffold through the Banqueting House, Inigo Jones's masterpiece which he had once dreamed of turning into part of the frontage of a massive new palace on the Thames. The ceiling under which he passed was decorated with Rubens's *Apotheosis of James I* – a giant portrait of his father and a powerful representation of Stuart aspirations for the English monarchy. There were fears that he would make a scene on the scaffold and his execution was delayed to allow the Houses to pass an ordinance forbidding the naming of a successor. In anticipation that he might not co-operate the scaffold had been prepared to allow for the King to be roped down, but they need not have worried. Charles gave, literally, the performance of his life. Dressed in an extra shirt in order to avoid shivering and thereby giving the appearance of fear, he finally delivered his answer to the charges laid against him in the high court. Predictably, given the weakness of the charges, his response was ringing and effective. Two days earlier it would have saved his neck, but not perhaps the monarchy in a form he could accept. Unusually, his executioners were disguised and, equally unusually, he did not forgive them for what they were about to do.[70]

The response of the crowd was horrified, and two troops of horse were set to patrol the streets in anticipation of trouble. The fatal blow was said to have been greeted with a groan: 'such a groan as I never heard before, and desire I may never hear again', remembered one witness who was seventeen on the day that the axe fell.[71] But quite what the groan meant is not clear – regret at the cruel necessity which Cromwell was later said to bemoan? Shock at the rupture of the divine order or more prosaic fears for the future? A late outpouring of love and loyalty to the monarch? The most famous image of the execution, complete with swooning woman in the foreground, was produced in Holland two years after the fact and has to be distrusted – such images were clearly of political importance at that point, and may have been intended as political interventions. Nonetheless, shock at the execution

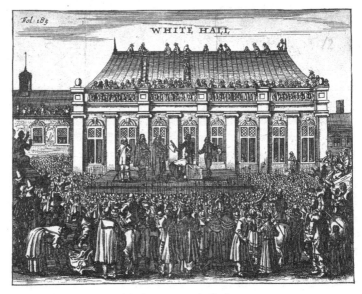

The execution of Charles I

clearly did resonate, and is easy to reconcile with the reservations of those who actually orchestrated these events.

Royalists of course were clear what the groan had meant: 'None of the Kings, no not one, . . . ever left the world with more sorrow: women miscarried, men fell into melancholy, some with consternations expired; men women and children then, and yet unborn, suffering in him and for him'. But a provincial Puritan who noted the shock at news of the execution – 'There was such a consternation among the common people throughout the nation, that one neighbour durst scarcely speak to another when they met in the streets' – thought it did not denote disapproval – 'not from any abhorrence at the action, but in surprise at the rarity and infrequency of it'.[72] William Simpson, drinking in the Dolphin at Bishopsgate, London, in March 1649, 'drank a health to Charles II and confusion to the parliament', but was denounced to a parliamentary committee a month later as 'a malignant spirit' who had 'several times vented his malice against the parliament by evil speaking'. In Stratford-upon-Avon around the same time Thomas Sharpe, a parliamentary soldier with seven years' service behind him, was assaulted by William Greene, an 'inveterate malignant who has several times raised the rabble people of the said town against the parliament soldiers'. Hearing that Sharpe had arrived in town he came out of his house 'with a great club in his hand and unexpectedly . . . without any provocation' attacked Sharpe. Opinion in the provinces was probably no less complex and divided about the regicide than about any of the other major political turning points of the decade.[73]

Ralph Josselin, an Essex Puritan who set much store by providence, had in August interpreted another impending harvest failure as a judgement on the divisions among the righteous: 'the nations sins are many and sad, Lord let public ones be pardoned', he wrote, noting as causes of the Lord's anger 'the war in the nation, the divisions among ourselves; our cryings out after peace on any terms to save our skins, and estates whatsoever become of others'. Here was a Puritan opposed to an easy settlement, and the Engagers' cause, but he was not reassured by the regicide a few months later: 'I was much troubled with the black providence of putting the King to death, my tears were not restrained at the passages about his death, the lord in mercy lay it not as sin to the charge of the kingdom, but in mercy do us good by the same'. His diary is not clear, but his tears for Charles seem to have been personal sympathy as much as settled hostility to the act: 'the death of the king talked much of, very many men of the weaker sort of Christians in divers places passionate concerning it, but so ungroundedly, that it would make any to bleed to observe it'. Even for those anxious about the Treaty of Newport and an easy settlement the regicide did not appear an easy answer; but neither did the immediate hostility of the ungodly to the act, either. In the face of these difficulties Josselin was in the hands of God: 'the lord has some great thing to do, fear and tremble at it oh England'.[74]

Some at least clearly approved. When soldiers in Yorkshire mistook a relative of Fairfax for his wife, Lady Fairfax, the vociferous dissenter at the trial, they held a pistol at her breast in her coach.[75] Samuel Pepys, then fifteen and at school at St Paul's, remembered celebrating the execution – if invited to preach on that day his text would have been 'And the memory of the wicked shall rot'.[76] This transgressive thrill was also felt by others. The identity of the executioners was not known – later rumours suggested that it might have been Cromwell and Fairfax, William Walker or Hugh Peter – suggesting fear of reprisal. But after the Restoration, when a concerted effort was made to identify them, it emerged that pretending to have been an executioner had been a promising way for one Phineas Payne to impress countrymen in London shops on the day of the execution. A number of others got in trouble for such boasting eleven years later.[77]

Charles was buried on 8 February at Windsor, not Westminster, and the ceremony was conducted in silence because the military governor had refused permission to use the Book of Common Prayer.[78]

The purged parliamentary regime and its friends in the army had been unsure about regicide, and most reactions to the execution suggest that they were not political winners as a result of having carried it out. Charles, on the other hand, clearly did secure a political victory, for the day of his death was also the day of his rebirth, or at least reinvention. During the 1630s two dominant images of Charles had been projected – the austere and distant patriarch of the Van Dyck portraits and the dispeller of discord celebrated in court masques. From the mid-1640s these were increasingly abandoned in favour of the suffering king, protecting sacred monarchy from the passions of malicious spirits. An identity was created between the sufferings of the King and of his subjects. This transformation was epitomized in the *Eikon Basilike*, the supposedly autobiographical account of his travails and martyrdom. Charles had probably approved the text at Newport, during his close captivity. In any case the book, advance copies of which were available on the morning of the execution, was an instant publishing success, enjoying thirty-five editions in 1649 alone. Over the following decade it was translated into Latin, French, German, Dutch and Danish. It was also set in verse and to music. It created, in the words of one historian, 'the King Charles experience'. It was by far the greatest propaganda

The frontispiece of *Eikon Basilike* portraying Charles I, the royal martyr

success following the regicide, calling forth anxious, and ineffective, rival histories. Those facing execution, as we have seen, could accept their death but deny the justice of it by appealing to the ideal of martyrdom. This Charles did with tremendous, and immediate, effect. His opponents were irritated by this success and by the partiality of the account – after his cabinet was opened at Naseby, Charles can hardly have hoped to be so read, or so believed. As history the *Eikon* is clearly flawed, but the poetic meaning obviously spoke to many readers: this truth about Charles's martyrdom was powerful, more powerful than the man when alive. Following his death a handkerchief stained with his blood was said to have in it the power to heal scrofula. Those of his supporters who had, in the months around the trial, seemed to favour his execution were vindicated by the power of this image of Anglican royalism. The resonance was with Christ, but in one sense it was a more remarkable event – Charles rose again, effectively, on the very same day.[79]

21

Epilogue

England's Freedom

The use of history, and the just rules for composure of it, have been so well and fully described heretofore by judicious writers, that it were lost labour and a needless extension of the present work to insist by way of introduction, upon either of them.

So wrote Thomas May in the preface to his *The history of the parliament Of England, which began November the third, MDCXL*, published 'by authority' in May 1647. John Langley, who had licensed it for publication, pronounced it 'an impartial truth; and judge it fit for public view by the printing'. Authority lay in this official licence, but also in the claims of a truthful discourse. 'I will only profess', wrote May reassuringly, 'to follow that one rule, truth, to which all the rest (like the rest of the moral virtues to that of justice) may be reduced'.[1]

It was an impossible task. May was writing against the background of the increasingly public collapse of the parliamentary coalition, splintering under the enormous pressure of making peace. By the time his book was complete, and available in a handsome folio edition, the New Model was close to rebellion against its political master and was becoming the champion of a programme for which no-one had been fighting at Edgehill. A history of the still-sitting parliament could not be anything but contested in those circumstances.

May knew this as well as anyone:

The subject of this work is a civil war, a war indeed as much *more than civil*, and as full of miracle, both in the causes and effects of it, as was ever observed in any age; a war as cruel as unnatural; that has produced as much rage of swords, as much bitterness of pens, both public and private, as was ever known; and divided the understandings of men, as well as their affections, in so high a degree, that scarce could any virtue gain due applause, any reason give satisfaction, or any relation obtain credit, unless among men of the same side.[2]

Tacitus himself had faced such difficulties, and certainly those of us labouring in the area of seventeenth-century studies have good reason to share May's unease. May's appeal was to the court of public opinion, 'to the memory of any English man, whose years have been enough to make him know the actions that were done; and whose conversation has been enough public to let him hear the common voice, and discourses of people upon those actions, . . . whether such actions were not done, and such judgments made upon them, as are here related'.[3] Like many of his contemporaries, and without much greater success, May sought to rise above the polemic and broadcast the truth, appealing to the 'people' and the 'common voice' as the arbiters of it.

May was writing for a society accustomed to viewing its present condition against much longer histories: mapping contemporary experience onto received accounts of classical history (May had translated Lucan); or against the universal Christian history. Contemporaries continually found parallels for their condition in the annals of Greek and Roman civilization, and in the Bible: precedents and examples which lent meaning to the current chaos. Political conflict arose from the disputed meanings of current affairs, understood against a historical backdrop. Meaning, politics and history were closely intertwined.

In the polemical battles of the 1640s, for this very reason, history had been much abused:

there are many ways besides plain falsehood, whereby a writer may offend. Some historians, who seem to abhor direct falsehood, have notwithstanding dressed truth in such improper vestments, as if they brought her forth to act the same part that falsehood would; and taught her by rhetorical disguises, partial concealments, and invective expressions, instead of informing, to seduce a reader, and carry the judgement of posterity after that bias which themselves have made.[4]

Bruno Ryves's chronicles of parliamentarian excess were sourced, but hardly unbiased; Ricraft and Wharton's chronologies of battles selective, though not invented.

Histories pretending to impartiality rested on another common contemporary practice – of collecting. In fact May's history was published by Moses Bell for George Thomason, the greatest collector of them all.

Collecting was not necessarily more neutral an activity than chronicling. Thomason's politics are almost invisible to us – almost but not quite.[5] Other collections had a more or less directly political purpose: Husbands's collation of parliamentary declarations in the spring of 1643, perhaps, or the army's book of (edited) declarations four years later. They were certainly put to use, immediately. Lilburne held Parliament to account using Husbands and at Putney the agitators and radicals held the army grandees to account using their own *Book of Declarations*, while the *Agreement of the People* was in turn measured against those declarations. Each cause was defined by public statements which were collected: historicizing and fixing, offering a point of reference in a wild polemical world. Clarendon, writing against May, also collected his papers; John Rushworth, subject of suspicion in 1640 because of his command of shorthand, collated important documents in his *Historical Collections* (the first part was also published by Thomason); Clarke took careful notes of the meetings at Putney. Without these histories, and these collections, we would have much poorer access to the experiences of the 1640s, but all of them are flawed, and partial. Many of the authors collected by Thomason were more deliberately so.

In these conditions, of partial or even false reporting, trust was essential to claims about truth – truthfulness was a social or rhetorical quality, something performed as much as demonstrated. May favoured a plain style which found applause among a Victorian audience, although his impartiality is less credited now.[6] An unvarnished style, with copious factual support, was a common writing device during the 1640s. Tales of plots, wonders, miracles and prodigies were buttressed in these ways, and by external sources of authority: credible witnesses of social status, the origin of the information in a private (and therefore more reliable) communication, or in the revelation of a private collection – cabinet or closet. Truth was at a premium, and contemporaries were creative in their approaches to claiming access to it: trust was the crucial quality, and a very difficult one to foster.

In May we hear the voice of many contemporary anxieties: about the direction of current events, measured historically, and the related difficulty of agreeing what had happened and what it meant. In his anxiety to foster trust, as a necessary preliminary to promoting belief, he shares much with our own politicians – the projection of a reliable image was crucial to the arts of political, or historical, persuasion.

Much contemporary polemic focused on these questions – the persistent whispering campaign, sometimes a shouting campaign, about Charles's untrustworthiness, scurrilous accusations about Cromwell's private life. In Thomas May's appeal to a truth outside the subjective view of an individual historian we can also hear the voice of modern professional history in its hubristic pomp: in its claims to be able to arrive at a definitive account. If we ever really did have confidence in the possibility of such a definitive account, we have lost it now. Ours is in some ways a less historically conscious society than May's, or the Victorians'. History is more often a diversion or entertainment than a guide to action, or to justice – a stock of stories to divert rather than experiences in which we can find ourselves reflected, informed, or even corrected. Remote events such as the English civil war are very unlikely to be recruited as a detailed guide to action in current political affairs. That may be a mistake; but it may be one reason why the current generation is more comfortable with a plurality of meanings, or parallel realities and alternative values.

Thomas May certainly saw some advantage in this multiple perspective: 'If those that write on the other side will use the same candour, there is no fear but that posterity may receive a full information concerning the unhappy distractions of these Kingdoms'.[7] Milton, surprised, offended but not cowed by the hostile response to his arguments about divorce, went further: he embraced this clash of opinion as the best route to the truth. Our generation is more sceptical about the possibility of such final truths, and more likely to find more than one meaning in the events of the 1640s. Emphasizing this indeterminacy has contemporary warrant too, since those who lived through the wars certainly did. It was a conflict fought with pens as well as swords, and which 'divided the understandings of men, as well as their affections'. In fact, in a sense, it was what the war was about.

Killing the King did not settle the arguments. For most people, even many of those most responsible for carrying it out, the execution of Charles had not been the main business of civil war politics, the abolition of monarchy even less so. Those who carried through this revolution subsequently declared England to be a 'Commonwealth and Free State', to be governed by the supreme authority, 'the representatives of the people in Parliament, and by such as they shall appoint and constitute as officers and ministers under them for the good of the people'. These ideals were neatly expressed in the new Great Seal: '1649 in the First Year of Freedome by Gods Blessing Restored'. The central image was not a head of state, but the representative of the people, the expression of their sovereignty. In practical terms, however, this vision proved more difficult to realize than simply by maintaining government 'without any King or House of Lords'. Throughout the 1640s the strength of the parliamentary alliance had been as a negative force – anti-Laudian, anti-episcopalian and, eventually, explicitly anti-Caroline. As a movement for a positive and defined end it had been liable to fissure, and this continued to be the case.

In the regicide we might see the consummation of a number of revolutionary impulses: the army purged the Commons of its corrupting elements, hoping thereby to create a body more nearly representative of the people; the purged Commons shed an inhibition and passed an Act without the consent of the Lords or the King; the King was held to be a man, answerable like all others to the representative of the people, his interest subordinate to the *salus populi*, and capable of treason against the state erected to defend it; the children executed their father. But this was, even in the last days, a reluctant consummation. In these final weeks the party who most wanted Charles dead may have been Charles himself: in his martyrdom lay the best hope for monarchy as he understood it, more attractive by far than the various emasculations being proposed to him. It was probably personally appealing too. Unable to 'deal' with rebels, it was better to call their bluff, to let them paint themselves into a corner and be forced to commit this final, monstrous, barbarity.

If we can be reasonably sure what the regicide meant to Charles, then, its wider meaning was more complex. Although this was clearly not a popular act, there were at least two Londoners who were actively thrilled by these events: Phineas Payne, the boastful man about town, intent on impressing countrymen; and Samuel Pepys, the equally boastful schoolboy.[8] Moreover, consternation at the regicide did not necessarily imply support for Charles Stuart's politics or behaviour, or a commitment to the brand of royalism that he had championed. But it remains the case that Charles's killers did not have a message with the clarity of Charles's royal martyrdom. John Milton identified the main point, titling his response *Eikonoklastes*: the transformation of Charles's life and death into an ornament of the church called forth the demand for further breaking of images. Milton's work appears to have enjoyed far less success than its target: there seem to have been only two editions in England before 1690, in 1649 and 1650, and one French one in 1652.[9] It was not just the textual image of the King that was attacked. In 1649 and 1650 Parliament issued a series of orders against Stuart images and it was these, increasingly, that were to be cleansed, rather than the churches themselves. Statues of James I and Charles I at the west end of St Paul's were demolished and the inscriptions erased. The statue of Charles at the Royal Exchange was beheaded, its sceptre removed and the legend inscribed: 'Death of the last royal tyrant in the first year of England's liberty restored, 1648'. Two weeks later the remnants of the statue were removed, leaving only the inscription.[10] This was a political erasure rather than a revolution in aesthetics: the people responsible for this cleansing were quite willing to buy items from the King's art collection, and images of Cromwell during the 1650s owed a lot to the same iconography from which the Stuart monarchs had drawn.[11]

The erasure was only partially successful. There was a market for some of the more impressive portraits, which were sold rather than destroyed. A large bronze equestrian statue of Charles I, commissioned by the Earl of Portland before the troubles broke out, was acquired by residents of Covent Garden in 1644. It was by then inadvisable to erect a new monument and the statue was put in the churchyard of Covent Garden for the time being. Despite an instruction 'to break the said statue in pieces to the end that nothing might remain in memory of [Charles I]' the statue survived, buried in the ground, until the Restoration. It now stands in Whitehall, on the site of Charing Cross, close to the spot where Charles was executed. The greater success was in attempts after the Restoration to erase the memory of the republic. Cromwell, who came to embody the authority of the new regime, adopted monarchical trappings, but had to wait until 1899 for a public statue outside Parliament.[12]

Many of the most important legacies of the 1650s were unintended or at least unforeseen consequences of the conflicts, or means to some other end. The defence and security of the new regime were established using the machine created in civil war. Decisive campaigns against pro-Stuart forces in Ireland (1649) and Scotland (1650–51) were marked by crushing, perhaps pitiless, victories at Rathmines, Drogheda and

The equestrian statue of Charles I at Charing Cross, pictured soon after
it was erected

Wexford (1649) and at Dunbar (1650). Defeat of a final Scottish in-
cursion into England at Worcester in 1651 effectively ended the cycle
of wars in the three kingdoms (see Map 5). There followed successful
naval campaigns against the Dutch and in the Caribbean. Forced to
defend themselves against internal and external threats, the nation's
governors created military resources unprecedented in English history,
achieving military dominance within Britain and Ireland and laying the
foundations of a powerful maritime empire. And although *Eikon
Basilike* was more successful than its rebuttals, the 1650s were a lean
time for active royalism – defeated in arms, and reduced to a rump of
ineffectual plotters for most of the decade. In exile the heir to the throne
enjoyed a thin time of it, he and his court frequently an embarrassment
to their hosts. Barbados and Virginia were made to submit to the authority of the Free State, and the military means created to achieve this
became also the means to regulate and direct the trade of the colonies.
The foundation of the navigation system was the foundation too of the
first English (later British) empire, and it contained the central contradic-
tion of later imperial life – the forcible imposition of English liberties,
and their costs. By the mid-1650s this ambition was translated into
armed conquest in the Caribbean, and the Commonwealth was recog-

The Cromwell statue in Parliament Square,
pictured soon after it was erected

nized and wooed by the major European powers. Cromwellian England
was a nascent global power and secure against domestic opposition.

These partial and ultimately outmatched efforts at destruction, and
the achievement of security at home and abroad, were not the sum of
the republican achievement, however. Anxiety, confusion and discord
continued to spur intellectual, rhetorical and communicative creativity.[13]
In an important sense 1649 was a moment of opportunity, at which
definition could be given to the people, their representative, their religion
and the purposes of government. For this reason it was the opening of
'the epic years of the English political intellect'.[14] The opportunities were
so plural, however, that any practical solution would simultaneously be
a rejection and a limitation. There followed successive attempts to set
limits and boundaries, to give definition to the new dispensation, and
this created new victims and martyrs beyond the ranks of the defeated
royalists. This fertile legacy of political argument, however, far outlived
the failures and compromises of the 1650s.

*

In a way, the failure of monarchy, Parliament or local government to contain and resolve conflict in 1640–42 represented the dissolution of political community. This posed a profound challenge, and gave rise to an enormously destructive civil war, but it was for some an exhilarating experience, rich in reflection on what it meant to belong to a political community. It was prompted by a religious protest in Scotland which fractured the English peace. Rival, plural mobilizations gave rise to loose coalitions, held together by fear. Print accelerated, generalized and amplified the resultant argument. During the war further escalation resulted in further acceleration. Pamphlets engaged with one another, sharpening, refining, escalating and radicalizing arguments. This became a political crisis with great social depth, not just or even principally in print, but in all the practical attempts to mobilize – pamphleteers, armies, iconoclasts, witch-hunters, clubmen, Levellers, protesters and petitioners. The social depth of the crisis was important not just in itself, but because it was part of the crisis. Intellectual coherence was challenged by multiple mobilizations around common-sense values – Protestantism, law, honour, treason, loyalty – for partisan purposes among overlapping publics. This process of mobilization fractured a common-sense system, making manifest contradictions and encouraging the development of new ways of imagining the world. If killing the King did not end the arguments then neither did the declaration of the first year of England's freedom: it set off another round of paper combats over what that was.

In particular, further reformation had opened up the boundary problem – the attack on the authority of bishops removed the umpire of questions of theological error and decency in worship. The ensuing debate operated on both levels – where were those limits (fought out using popery and sectarianism) and, more fundamentally, who should decide, and how? The two archetypes which drove polemic during 1640–42 – anti-popery and anti-Puritanism – were well-established world views, religious in tone, but embracing visions of social and political relationships too. But they expressed fears about the edges of the reformed faith rather than certainties about its core.

Regicide did not answer this uncertainty and the 1650s saw an unresolved debate about the nature of the Christian community. On what basis should Christians be gathered into communities, and who should decide the boundaries of acceptable belief and practice? Here the regime was minimalist – allowing latitude but marking the outer limits with draconian measures. Acts against adultery and blasphemy set the fundamental limits of decency: unquestioned sins were markers of unacceptable belief and practice. The question of authority and conscience settled on the issue of toleration – what could be tolerated? When James Naylor rode into Bristol on a donkey, his followers laying leaves before him, he was performing his belief – that each of us has the spark of the divine within us. For many others, though, this was a demonstration of the dangers of toleration: the claim to be Christ himself. Naylor was prosecuted for 'horrid blasphemy' and Parliament spent some time discussing which physical punishments might fit this awful crime. Toleration, in a post-Laudian world, still did not mean freedom of belief and expression; nor does it now.

Redress of secular grievances about the limits of the prerogative was transformed into quite novel claims for the powers of Parliament over armed force, and the composition of the executive. In a kind of analogy with the religious arguments a practical boundary question – about the powers of the monarch – gave way to a more fundamental question about how to decide the issue. The claims of custom, law and tradition gave way before arguments about sovereignty (of parliaments and even the people); claims for sacred or divine kingship were challenged by arguments about a providential mandate for a clean slate. An escalating public debate about the meaning of key words, and about fundamentals, gave rise to considerable creativity.

Some of the most exotic products of the creative chaos belong on the wilder shores of Reformation thought, and some were constructive attempts to apply traditions of communal demonstrative politics to the new situation. But some belong with the Enlightenment rather than the Reformation – dealing with the relationship between the individual and the state, rather than with the proper relationship between traditional powers and liberties. The Levellers and Thomas Hobbes (whose masterpiece, *Leviathan*, was first published in 1651) were not typical voices, and nor were their arguments the ones that were necessarily at stake, but they indicate the beginnings of a passage from the world of reformation to the world of enlightenment. Going into the 1640s the political crisis was being driven by the politics of reformation; by 1649 something like enlightenment politics can be observed close to the centres of power. It was this, rather than the constitutional experiments of the 1650s, that was the really revolutionary product of the crisis of the 1640s.

Much of this was faltering, anxious and, for many, reluctant – amidst the trauma of war those with creative solutions to sell were not all pursuing these forward-looking arguments, and those doing so were often regarded as beyond the pale. The pursuit of a settlement was a practical question, but it had to be tackled against the background of these anxious, creative, chaotic politics; and support had to be mobilized among diverse and often incompatible constituencies. Nonetheless intellectual ferment was at least as visible as a creative power.

On these questions the civil war and regicide spawned arguments which rumbled on for generations. Sovereignty and toleration were at the heart of argument into the nineteenth century, and no workable settlement was achieved, arguably, before 1715. Cromwell, it is often said, was torn between an inspirational, exhilarated godliness, which spurred him to imagine new worlds, and a more pragmatic desire for healing and settlement. He is often accused of abandoning or betraying the dream, but others certainly did not, not in the 1650s and not under Charles II either. And their legacy was important in the wider British Atlantic world and beyond, long after England's eleven-year interregnum had been legally annulled. This revolution, the challenge of new visions of the good (Christian) political community, was a long one, resonating in our own time. How to reconcile groups with conflicting transcendent visions within a single political community is a question which has not lost its edge. The Covenanters had an answer for a united society confronted with an ungodly ruler; the English grasped for answers in more plural conditions.

Nathaniel Butter and Nicholas Bourne, editorializing on a report of a spectacular volcanic eruption in the Azores in July 1638, wrote: 'Let the speculative ponder, and the philosopher search out the cause of so portentous an effect, in as much as the mathematician seeks rects for his judgement, and the historian knowledges for his discourse'.[15] It was no easy task to discover the meaning of meaningful events.

For those who lived through the civil wars it was no easier, and many continued to feel betrayed by the cause they had felt they were fighting for. At the same time, opportunities were taken up by networks of activists, creating effects that were not at first thought of, or aimed at. Experiences of these portentous events were confused and diverse: startling creativity arose alongside great trauma. It had no single voice and no single significance; it transcended the immediate practical problems of political settlement, and was not definitively expressed in any of the subsequent constitutional solutions. This story, of creative confusion, was relevant not only to the 1640s and not only to the English – it inflected the revolutions in America and France, fostered the rise of a great power, was significant to the history of European republicanism and to the roots of the Enlightenment. Experiences of these conflicts were plural, ambiguous, divided and contrasting; their potential meanings equally diverse. In the end, events so portentous as the sufferings of the 1640s, and the multiple responses to them, deserve to be remembered not for a single voice or consequence, but because they provide many 'knowledges for our discourse.'

Acknowledgements

In a profession marked by generosity and collegiality it is not possible to acknowledge all debts, but it is important to try. How this book is written owes a lot to Peter Lake, whose mark is on both the overall approach and much of the detail; Ann Hughes, a generous colleague whose work in this field exercises a much greater influence on my approach than is evident simply from the footnotes; John Walter, once teacher and now colleague, whose example and advice have informed and improved everything that I have written, particularly on popular politics; John Morrill, under whose supervision I first studied this period; and Mark Greengrass, with whom I taught and thought about the Hartlib circle for several years.

Karen Harvey, as booster and helpful critic, has no equal and she has read or talked about almost everything in this book. Ann Hughes, Tom Leng, Anthony Milton and Simon Winder all read the manuscript, which was much improved as a result. For their generosity with advice, references and their own work in progress I am particularly grateful to Alastair Bellany, Katherine Braddick, Dan Beaver, Bill Bulman, Ann Carmichael, Justin Champion, Tom Cogswell, David Como, David Cressy, Brian Cummings, Richard Cust, Barbara Donagan, Carol Gluck, Julian Goodare, Genevieve Guenther, Ariel Hessayon, Steve Hindle, Andrew Hopper, Sean Kelsey, Linda Kirk, Mark Kishlansky, Irving Lavin, Tom Leng, Keith Lindley, Jason McGelligot, Anthony Milton, John Morrill, Marcus Nevitt, Jason Peacey, Jill Pritchard, Joad Raymond, Steve Renshaw, Gary Rivett, Mary Robertson, Quentin Skinner, Nigel Smith, Laura Stewart, Alex Walsham, John Walter, Laura Weigert and Phil Withington. Some of my central arguments were first trailed as papers or lectures at the universities of Leicester, Pennsylvania, Princeton, Sheffield and Yale, at University College London, the School of East European Studies, University of London, the European University Institute in Florence, the Seminário de História do Instituto de Ciências Sociais, Universidade de Lisboa, the Université Paris IV, Sorbonne, and the Institute for Advanced Study in Princeton. I am very grateful for those opportunities to try to clarify my thoughts and for the many helpful questions and suggestions that I received on those occasions. That I wrote this book at all is due to Felicity Bryan and I am very grateful to Simon Winder, whose advice and enthusiasm have been invaluable throughout.

It would not have been possible to write this book without the award of a Major Research Fellowship from the Leverhulme Trust, for which I am profoundly grateful. During the academic year 2005–6 I held an Elizabeth and J. Richardson Dilworth Fellowship as a Member of the School of Historical Studies at the Institute for Advanced Study, Princeton, and an Andrew W. Mellon Foundation Fellowship at the Huntington Library, San Marino. My work benefited immeasurably from the opportunities provided in those admirable institutions. I am also grateful to my department at the University of Sheffield for the long period of special leave which allowed me to take up these fellowships. The shifting population of that excellent department, both staff and students, has continually stimulated my thoughts on this and all other historical subjects and for that I am also very grateful. Throughout the time I have worked on this book my research has been admirably supported by the staff of the Sheffield University Library.

The dedication of this book is a poor recompense to my family. They have, it is true, given me some insight into the creative potential of chaos, but the daily and abiding lesson has been (mercifully) in the virtues of harmony, co-operation and civil order. For that, and everything else, I am more grateful than I can say.

Picture Credits

The following images are published with permission of ProQuest; further reproduction is prohibited without permission: 1, 16, 19, 39, 47 (Copyright © British Library Board, all rights reserved. Wing T2705, TT, E.116[49], E.173[13], E.388[2], Wing T2705; images produced by Pro-Quest as part of Early English Books Online. Inquiries may be made to info@il.proquest.com); the following items are reproduced by permission of the Huntington Library, San Marino, California: 2, 5, 9, 10, 25, 26, 27, 28, 33 (John Vicars, *True information of the beginning* (1648)), 18 (Anon., *A damnable treason* (1641)), 31 (Thomas Goodwin *et al.*, *An Apologeticall Narration* (1644)), 32 (John Milton, *Areopagitica* (1644)), 34 (George Wharton, *An Astrologicall Judgement* (1645)), 38 (Humphrey Willis, *Times whirligig* (1647)), 40 (Thomas Edwards, *The first and second part of Gangraena* (1646)), 41 (Anon., *Strange newes from Scotland* (1647)), 42 (John Taylor, *The world turn'd upside down* (1647)), 43 (*A declaration of the engagements* (1647)); the following items are reproduced by permission of The Royal Collection: 3, 4 (Copyright © 2007 Her Majesty Queen Elizabeth II); the following items are reproduced by permission of Guildhall Library and Art Gallery, City of London: 6, 11, 12, 13, 14, 50, 52 (Collage image numbers 7221, 31774, 20680, 24830, 1902, 29448, 22112); the following item is reproduced by permission of the National Portrait Gallery, London: 7; the following items are reproduced by permission of the Bridgeman Art Library: 8 (Copyright © Museum of London, UK/The Bridgeman Art Library, image number MOL226448), 29, 30, 36 (Copyright © British Library Board, all rights reserved. TT, 669.f.8 [22]/The Bridgeman Art Library, image number BAL242575 [details]), 49 (Copyright © Private Collection/The Bridgeman Art Library, image number XJF97556); the following items are reproduced by permission of the

Abbreviations

A&O	C. H. Firth and R. S. Rait (eds.), *Acts and Ordinances of the Interregnum, 1642–60*, 3 vols. (London, 1911)
AHR	*American Historical Review*
BL	British Library
Bod. L	Bodleian Library, Oxford
CJ	*Journals of the House of Commons*
Clarendon	W. Dunn Macray (ed.), *The History of the Rebellion and Civil Wars in England by Edward, Earl of Clarendon*, 6 vols. (Oxford, 1969 edn)
CSPD	*Calendar of State Papers, Domestic Series*
Culpeper Letters	Michael J. Braddick and Mark Greengrass (eds.), 'The Letters of Sir Cheney Culpeper, 1641–1657', *Camden Miscellany xxxiii: Seventeenth-Century Political and Financial Papers*, Camden 5th series, 7, Royal Historical Society (Cambridge, 1996), pp. 105–402
EEBO	Early English Books Online (http://eebo.chadwyck.com/home)
EcHR	*Economic History Review*
EHR	*English Historical Review*
ESTC	English Short Title Catalogue (http://estc.bl.uk/)
Gardiner	S. R. Gardiner, *History of the Great Civil War*, 4 vols. (Moreton-in-Marsh, 1991 edn)
Gardiner, *CD*	S. R. Gardiner (ed.), *The Constitutional Documents of the Puritan Revolution 1625–1660*, 3rd edn (Oxford, 1906)
Gough, *Myddle*	David Hey (ed.), Richard Gough, *The History of Myddle* (Harmondsworth, 1981)
HEH	Henry E. Huntington Library, San Marino

HJ	*Historical Journal*
HLQ	*Huntington Library Quarterly*
HR	*Historical Research*
JBS	*Journal of British Studies*
LJ	*Journals of the House of Lords*
ODNB	H. C. G. Matthews and B. Harrison (eds.), *Oxford Dictionary of National Biography*, 61 vols. (Oxford, 2004) (available online at http://www.oxforddnb.com/)
OED	*The Oxford English Dictionary*
PP	*Past and Present*
TNA	The National Archives
TRHS	*Transactions of the Royal Historical Society*
TT	Thomason Tracts

More and more primary sources are available online without subscription, some of them as this book was going to press. As I write *A&O*, *CJ* and *LJ* are available at http://www.british-history.ac.uk/ and Gardiner, *CD*, at http://www.constitution.org/.

Note on Authorship and Dating of Pamphlets

Most pamphlets have a place and date (year) of publication. Using the bibliographical data of ESTC or EEBO, searchers can trace shifts in the numbers of titles each year with a narrow margin of error. Pamphlets from the largest individual collection, that assembled by George Thomason, can usually be dated much more precisely. Thomason often noted a precise date on the covers of pamphlets: this has been noted below as the 'Thomason date'. Where no Thomason date exists, I have relied on the 'Fortescue date' derived from G. K. Fortescue (ed), *Catalogue of the Pamphlets, Books, Newspapers, and Manuscripts Relating to the Civil War, the Commonwealth and the Restoration, Collected by George Thomason, 1640–1661*, 2 vols. (London, 1908). In general Thomason's collection was bound in date order, although in several different series according to format. Thus, an undated pamphlet with no date appended by Thomason can be given an approximate date by reference to pamphlets bound with it that are dated. Fortescue catalogued the entire collection chronologically largely on this basis, although he did not follow Thomason's binding precisely, often dating a pamphlet according to the events it describes. In neither case is the date absolutely precise, therefore – the Thomason date might indicate a date of publication, acquisition or cataloguing, for example; and Fortescue dates may relate to the events that they refer to, rather than publication date. Dates for individual pamphlets are not entirely reliable, therefore, although aggregate numbers of titles per month are likely to be broadly accurate. For the problems of dating pamphlets see Stephen J. Greenberg, 'Dating Civil War Pamphlets, 1641–1644', *Albion*, 20 (1988), 387–401; and Michael Mendle, 'The Thomason Collection: A Reply to Stephen J. Greenberg' and Greenberg,

'The Thomason Collection: Rebuttal to Michael Mendle', *Albion*, 22 (1990), 85–98.

I have in general followed the attribution of authorship in EEBO and ESTC.

Note on Dates and Quotations

Dates are given old style but with the New Year beginning on 1 January. Spelling and punctuation have been modernized where that aids comprehension.

Notes and References

Preface

1. For the Reformation and the problem of reliable knowledge see Richard Popkin, *The History of Scepticism from Savonarola to Bayle*, rev. edn (Oxford, 2003), esp. ch. 1. Benbrigge was a Sussex minister of no great fame or distinction. He may have been a relative of Joseph Benbrigge, the Puritan mayor of Rye in 1629: Anthony Fletcher, *A County Community in Peace and War: Sussex 1600–1660* (London, 1975), p. 239. Sussex, too, had an unexceptional experience of warfare – neither spared nor ravaged. The pamphlet was dedicated to Captain Thomas Collines, another obscure figure, a relatively unknown member of Parliament's county committee. Benbrigge's pamphlet has attracted little, if any, attention from modern historians, although he is discussed by J. Sears McGee, *The Godly Man in Stuart England: Anglicans, Puritans, and the Two Tables, 1620–1670* (Yale, 1976), esp. p. 22n. Benbrigge's parliamentary sympathies are clear: he thought those labelled Puritan or Roundhead were 'the flower of [god's] people', 'howsoever the world despises them'. See also J. Sears McGee, 'Conversion and the Imitation of Christ in Anglican and Puritan Writing', *JBS*, 15:2 (1976), 21–39, at p. 25. Benbrigge had an unspectacular publishing career, which seems to have lasted less than a year. In October 1645 he had published a sermon, *Christ above all exalted, as in justification so in sanctification. Wherein severall passages in Dr Crisps sermons are answered*, a response to Tobias Crispe, *Christ alone exalted* (London, 1643, and subsequent editions). In September 1646 Benbrigge published a pamphlet about the regulation of usury, his third and final publication.
2. Speaking in Parliament in 1625: quoted in Jacqueline Eales, *Puritans and Roundheads: The Harleys of Brampton Bryan and the Outbreak of the English Civil War* (Cambridge, 1990), pp. xi–xii.

1. From the Bowels of the Whore of Babel

1. HEH, EL 7852, Castle to Bridgewater, 22 August 1640.
2. Quoted in Edward J. Cowan, *Montrose: For Covenant and King* (London, 1977), p. 41.
3. Jenny Wormald, *Court, Kirk and Community: Scotland, 1470–1625* (Edinburgh, 1997), pp. 6–7.
4. For an overview of the government of the Borders, and further references, see Michael J. Braddick, *State Formation in Early Modern England c. 1550–1700* (Cambridge, 2000), esp. pp. 344–6, 371–8.
5. David Cressy, *England on Edge: Crisis and Revolution 1640–1642* (Oxford, 2006), p. 94.
6. HEH, EL 7852, Castle to Bridgewater, 22 August 1640.
7. Conrad Russell, *The Fall of the British Monarchies 1637–1642* (Oxford, 1991),

pp. 68–70. It is likely that this letter refers to papers prepared following the decision, taken on 3 August, to cross the Tweed: David Stevenson, *The Scottish Revolution, 1637–44: The Triumph of the Covenanters* (Edinburgh, 2003), p. 206. The Covenanters had directed arguments to English audiences over the previous two years: Peter Donald, *An Uncounselled King: Charles I and the Scottish Troubles, 1637–41* (Cambridge, 1990), esp. pp. 85–6, 128–32, 161, 178–9, 186–93, 223–5, 228–30; Russell, *Fall*, esp. pp. 61–2, 122–3. For the Covenanters' use of the press from 1637 onwards see Joad Raymond, *Pamphlets and Pamphleteering in Early Modern Britain* (Cambridge, 2003), pp. 172–87, esp. pp. 177–81; Joseph Black, ' "Pikes and Protestations": Scottish Texts in England, 1639–40', *Publishing History*, 42 (1997), 5–19; Cressy, *England on Edge*, pp. 72, 286–7, 388–90.

8. The Venetian ambassador's reports back home suggest that the picture at the English court was pretty bleak: Peter Razzell and Edward Razzell (eds.), *The English Civil War: A Contemporary Account*, vol. 2: *1640–42* (London, 1996), esp. pp. 21–30.

9. HEH, EL 7852, Castle to Bridgewater, 22 August 1640. For the proclamation see J. F. Larkin (ed.), *Stuart Royal Proclamations* (Oxford, 1983), vol. II, pp. 726–8. The Venetian ambassador thought it a 'labour lost' on an already pro-Scottish public: Razzell and Razzell (eds.), *A Contemporary Account*, vol. 2, p. 27. The Castle letter apparently summarizes it inaccurately, adding the claim that failure to support the war effort strenuously was treasonous. For another example of the inaccurate circulation of information in provincial copies see Walter Yonge's copy of an inaccurate version of a Covenanters' petition in 1637: Donald, *Uncounselled King*, pp. 176–7.

10. Stevenson, *Scottish Revolution*, p. 208.

11. HEH, EL 7859, Castle to Bridgewater, 8 September 1640. Other copies of this letter survive, see below, ch. 3, n. 98.

12. Donald, *Uncounselled King*, pp. 244–51; Peter Donald, 'New Light on the Anglo-Scottish Contacts of 1640', *HR*, 148 (1989), 121–9; Russell, *Fall*, pp. 151–3; Stevenson, *Scottish Revolution*, pp. 205–6; David Scott, ' "Hannibal at our gates": Loyalists and Fifth-Columnists during the Bishops' Wars – the Case of Yorkshire', *HR*, 70 (1997), 269–93. For Castle's suspicion about collusion see EL 7847, Castle to Bridgewater, 8 August 1640.

13. For the litmus test see Russell, *Fall*, pp. 154; see also Stevenson, *Scottish Revolution*, p. 214. For the politics of the label 'rebel' see also the Commons rebuke of a speaker for referring to them as rebels: *CJ*, ii, p. 25. There is also evidence of problems in publishing the proclamation: Larkin (ed.), *Royal Proclamations*, p. 727 n. 2. For collusion see John Adamson, *The Noble Revolt: The Overthrow of Charles I* (London, 2007), esp. ch. 1.

14. Stevenson, *Scottish Revolution*, p. 43.

15. For excellent introductions and overviews see Diarmaid MacCulloch, *Reformation: Europe's House Divided 1490–1700* (London, 2003), pp. 106–27, 241–4; Euan Cameron, *The European Reformation* (Oxford, 1991), ch. 8. For precise summaries with a view to the political implications see Quentin Skinner, *The Foundations of Modern Political Thought*, vol. 2: *The Age of Reformation* (Cambridge, 1978), pp. 3–12; Francis Oakley, 'Christian Obedience and Authority, 1520–1550', in J. H. Burns, with the assistance of Mark Goldie (eds.), *The Cambridge History of Political Thought 1450–1700* (Cambridge, 1991), pp. 159–92, esp. pp. 163–75.

16. MacCulloch, *Reformation*, pp. 126–32; Cameron, *European Reformation*, chs. 9–11.

17. For the role of the priesthood see Cameron, *European Reformation*, pp. 148–51. For Münster and the Peasants' War see ibid., pp. 202–9, 324–5; MacCulloch, *Reformation*, pp. 157–63, 204–7.

18. See especially Peter Lake, 'Anti-Popery: The Structure of a Prejudice', in Richard Cust and Ann Hughes (eds.), *Conflict in Early Stuart England* (Harlow, 1989), pp. 72–106; Paul Christianson, *Reformers and Babylon: English Apocalyptic Visions from the Reformation to the Eve of the Civil War* (Toronto, 1978).

19. MacCulloch, *Reformation*, pp. 237–41; Cameron, *European Reformation*, pp. 151–5;

Gordon Donaldson, 'The Scottish Church, 1567–1625', in A. G. R. Smith (ed.), *The Reign of James VI and I* (London, 1972), pp. 40–56, at pp. 44–5. For the wider political background see Oakley, 'Christian Obedience', and Robert M. Kingdom, 'Calvinist Resistance Theory, 1550–1580', in Burns with Goldie (eds.), *History of Political Thought*, pp. 193–218.

20. MacCulloch, *Reformation*, p. 238.

21. Cameron, *European Reformation*, pp. 145–8; Gordon Donaldson, *The Scottish Reformation* (Cambridge, 1960), pp. 76–80, 107–8.

22. The Book of Discipline that Knox produced for the kirk was almost certainly completed after the end of the parliamentary session, and the parliament had clearly worked with a draft version: Donaldson, *Scottish Reformation*, pp. 61–2. For the sceptical view of the heroic view of an irresistible and popular pressure for reformation, and the inevitability of its Presbyterian temper, see, in addition to Donaldson, Alec Ryrie, *The Origins of the Scottish Reformation* (Manchester, 2006); Alec Ryrie, 'Congregations, Conventicles and the Nature of Early Scottish Protestantism', *PP*, 191 (2006), 45–76.

23. Donaldson, *Scottish Reformation*, ch. 5.

24. Ibid., pp. 135–6, 139–44.

25. Ibid., ch. 4; Ryrie, 'Congregations'; Margo Todd, *The Culture of Protestantism in Early Modern Scotland* (New Haven, Conn., 2002), passim, esp. pp. 405–8; Walter Makey, *The Church of the Covenant, 1637–1651: Revolution and Social Change in Scotland* (Edinburgh, 1979), pp. 6–12; Michael F. Graham, *The Uses of Reform: 'Godly discipline' and Popular Behaviour in Scotland and Beyond* (Leiden, 1996); Julian Goodare, *State and Society in Early Modern Scotland* (Oxford, 1999), ch. 6, esp. pp. 177–80, 205–11.

26. Donaldson, *Scottish Reformation*, pp. 204–8.

27. Ibid., pp. 67, 144–6.

28. Ibid., ch. 8.

29. Ibid.

30. Ibid., pp. 208–9; Goodare, *State and Society*, pp. 193–4.

31. Donaldson, *Scottish Reformation*, ch. 9; Donaldson, 'Scottish Church' (which offers a convenient summary, and takes the story beyond 1592); Goodare, *State and Society*, pp. 194–6.

32. Donaldson, *Scottish Reformation*, ch. 9; Goodare, *State and Society*, pp. 195–200.

33. Donaldson, *Scottish Reformation*, ch. 9; for English views that Presbyters were simply popes in miniature see above, p. 344.

34. Donaldson, 'Scottish Church', pp. 51–3.

35. For discipline as a mark of the true church see Goodare, *State and Society*, p. 175; Donaldson, *Scottish Reformation*, pp. 78–9; Graham, *Uses*, p. 39; for kirk sessions above, n. 25.

36. Gordon Donaldson, *The Making of the Scottish Prayer Book* (Edinburgh, 1954), pp. 3–40; Goodare, *State and Society*, pp. 197–8. Donaldson emphasizes the closeness of formal liturgical positions, but the situation in practice was more complicated: Todd, *Culture of Protestantism*, passim.

37. Goodare, *State and Society*, pp. 198–205, 211–13; for the abolition of Yule see MacCulloch, *Reformation*, pp. 379–80. The practice was more complicated: Todd, *Culture of Protestantism*, pp. 183–90; for self-determination and Scottish Protestant identity see ibid., passim.

38. MacCulloch, *Reformation*, ch. 11; Richard Bonney, *The European Dynastic States 1494–1660* (Oxford, 1991), pp. 188–205.

39. Allan I. Macinnes, *The British Revolution, 1629–1660* (Basingstoke, 2005), pp. 52–4.

40. MacCulloch, *Reformation*, pp. 373–8.

41. For the faltering nature of the official reformation and its sequels see Christopher Haigh, *English Reformations: Religion, Politics and Society under the Tudors* (Oxford, 1993); for the subsequent Protestantization of England see Patrick Collinson, *The Birthpangs of Protestant England: Religious and Cultural Change in the Sixteenth and Seventeenth*

Centuries (Basingstoke, 1988); for an overview see Peter Marshall, *Reformation England 1480–1642* (London, 2003).

42. *Culpeper Letters*, pp. 273–4.

43. The fundamental works are Nicholas Tyacke, 'Puritanism, Arminianism and Counter-Revolution', reprinted in Nicholas Tyacke, *Aspects of English Protestantism, c. 1530–1700* (Manchester, 2001), pp. 132–59 (see also chs. 6–9); and Nicholas Tyacke, *Anti-Calvinists: The Rise of English Arminianism c. 1590–1640* (Oxford, 1987). Peter White, *Predestination, Policy and Polemic: Conflict and Consensus in the English Church from the Reformation to the Civil War* (Cambridge, 1992), gives a strong counter-case. For the debate see Kenneth Fincham (ed.), *The Early Stuart Church, 1603–1642* (Basingstoke, 1993); Marshall, *Reformation England*, pp. 126–35.

44. Marshall, *Reformation England*, p. 134; Anthony Milton, *Catholic and Reformed: Roman and Protestant Churches in English Protestant Thought, 1600–1640* (Cambridge, 1994), chs. 2, 3, 9 and conclusion; Anthony Milton, 'The Church of England, Rome and the True Church: The Demise of a Jacobean Consensus', in Fincham (ed.), *Early Stuart Church*, pp. 187–210.

45. P. G. Lake, 'Calvinism and the English Church, 1570–1635', *PP*, 114 (1987), 32–76; Marshall, *Reformation England*, pp. 129–30; Patrick Collinson, *The Religion of Protestants: The Church in English Society 1559–1625* (Oxford, 1982), ch. 6.

46. Patrick Collinson, *The Elizabethan Puritan Movement* (London, 1967); Nicholas Tyacke, 'The Fortunes of English Puritanism, 1603–40', reprinted in Tyacke, *Aspects*, pp. 111–31. For a clear narrative see Diarmaid MacCulloch, *The Later Reformation in England, 1547–1603* (Basingstoke, 1990), chs. 3–4; John Spurr, *English Puritanism 1603–1689* (Basingstoke, 1998), chs. 4–6.

47. Tyacke, *Aspects*, chs. 5–9; Tyacke, *Anti-Calvinists*; Lake, 'Calvinism'; Peter Lake, 'The Laudian Style: Order Uniformity and the Pursuit of Holiness in the 1630s', in Fincham (ed.), *Early Stuart Church*, pp. 161–85; Kenneth Fincham and Peter Lake, 'The Ecclesiastical Policies of James I and Charles I', in ibid., pp. 23–49. The debate is summarized in Marshall, *Reformation England*, pp. 194–205.

48. Lake, 'Anti-Popery', pp. 81–2, 87–92. This was indeed the analysis presented in the Grand Remonstrance: see above, pp. 169–70. For court Catholicism see above, p. 73. For conspiracy theories as a product of a system in which personal influence was crucial, and competing world views contended for influence, see Peter Lake, 'The Monarchical Republic of Elizabeth I Revisited (by Its Victims) as a Conspiracy', in Barry Coward and Julian Swann (eds.), *Conspiracies and Conspiracy Theory in Early Modern Europe: From the Waldensians to the French Revolution* (Aldershot, 2004), pp. 87–111; and Peter Lake, 'Anti-Puritanism: The Structure of a Prejudice', in Kenneth Fincham and Peter Lake (eds.), *Religious Politics in post-Reformation England: Essays in Honour of Nicholas Tyacke* (Woodbridge, 2006), pp. 80–97.

49. Stevenson, *Scottish Revolution*, pp. 43–6; John Morrill, 'The National Covenant in Its British Context', in John Morrill (ed.), *The Scottish National Covenant in Its British Context 1638–51* (Edinburgh, 1990), pp. 1–30, esp. pp. 7–11. These conflicts may have been anticipated well in advance by those planning the ceremonies: Dougal Shaw, 'St Giles' Church and Charles I's Coronation Visit to Scotland', *HR*, 77 (2004), 481–502.

50. Russell, *Fall*, pp. 37–42. For the importance of religious unity see Patrick Collinson, 'William Shakespeare's Religious Inheritance and Environment', reprinted in Patrick Collinson, *Elizabethan Essays* (London, 1994), pp. 219–52; Conrad Russell, 'Arguments for Religious Unity in England, 1530–1650', reprinted in Conrad Russell, *Unrevolutionary England 1603–1642* (London, 1990), pp. 179–204; and the summary in Braddick, *State Formation*, pp. 56–60.

51. For the dissemination of this image see Christopher Brown and Hans Vlieghe (eds.), *Van Dyke, 1599–1641* (London, 1999), p. 304.

52. For influential views of Charles I see Conrad Russell, *The Causes of the English Civil War* (Oxford, 1990), ch. 8; Richard Cust, *Charles I: A Political Life* (Harlow, 2005);

Richard Cust, 'Charles I and Popularity', in Thomas Cogswell, Richard Cust and Peter Lake (eds.), *Politics, Religion and Popularity in Early Stuart Britain: Essays in Honour of Conrad Russell* (Cambridge, 2002), pp. 235–58; Richard Cust, 'Charles I and Providence', in Fincham and Lake (eds.), *Religious Politics*, pp. 193–208. An elegant statement of the standard view is Alan Cromartie, *The Constitutionalist Revolution: An Essay on the History of England, 1450–1642* (Cambridge, 2006), pp. 234–5. Charles now has a powerful advocate in Mark Kishlansky, 'Charles I: A Case of Mistaken Identity?', *PP*, 189 (2005), 41–80.

53. Allan I. Macinnes, *Charles I and the Making of the Covenanting Movement, 1625–1641* (Edinburgh, 1991), chs. 3–4; Maurice Lee, Jr, *The Road to Revolution: Scotland under Charles I, 1625–37* (Urbana, Ill., 1985), ch. 2. For crisp summaries see Macinnes, *British Revolution*, pp. 86–93; Keith M. Brown, *Kingdom or Province? Scotland and the Regal Union, 1603–1715* (Basingstoke, 1992), pp. 101–3; Cromartie, *Constitutionalist Revolution*, p. 235. For a defence of Charles's position see Kishlansky, 'Charles I', 71–2; Lee suggests, contrary to much conventional wisdom, that some of the heat had in fact gone out of the conflict quite quickly: Lee, *Road to Revolution*, pp. 66–71.

54. See, especially, David Stevenson, 'The English Devil of Keeping State: Élite Manners and the Downfall of Charles I in Scotland', in Roger Mason and Nicholas Macdougall (eds.), *People and Power in Scotland: Essays in Honour of T. C. Smout* (Edinburgh, 1992), pp. 126–44; Keith M. Brown, 'Aristocratic Finances and the Origins of the Scottish Revolution', *EHR*, 104 (1989), 46–87. For a summary and further references see Braddick, *State Formation*, at pp. 367–8.

55. Kevin Sharpe, *The Personal Rule of Charles I* (New Haven, Conn., 1992), pp. 778–83; for Charles's lack of empathy with Scottish sensibilities see Morrill, 'National Covenant', pp. 6–9. For Kishlansky's defence see 'Charles I', p. 70.

56. Stevenson, *Scottish Revolution*, pp. 43–4.

57. For the drawing up of the book and the variations introduced in deference to Scottish opinion see Donaldson, *Making of the Scottish Prayer Book*, esp. pp. 41–71; Donald, *Uncounselled King*, pp. 34–7. Kishlansky's defence of Charles's role in drawing up the book is contested: Kishlansky, 'Charles I', pp. 72–3; Julian Goodare, 'Charles I: Comment', *PP* (forthcoming).

58. Stevenson, *Scottish Revolution*, pp. 46–7: 'The fact that many of those who protested at the prayer book had never read or even seen it is thus no evidence that their opposition concealed non-religious and less worthy motives than they pretended', p. 47.

59. Stevenson, *Scottish Revolution*, pp. 58–61.

60. Ibid., pp. 61–2; Sharpe, *Personal Rule*, p. 788. For the claim about the bishop's accident. see 'the Bishop was redacted ... to such a point of backside necessity, that (as may be supposed) he never in his life got such a laxative purgation ... [I]t was constantly affirmed, that when he come out of the coach, he apprehended such danger (notwithstanding of the guards that was about him) that no man could endure the flewre nor stinking smell of his fat carcage': 'A breefe and true Relatione of the Broyle', in John Leslie, *A relation of the proceedings concerning the kirk of Scotland ... by John Earl of Rothes*, Bannatyne Club (Edinburgh, 1830), pp. 198–200, at p. 200.

61. HEH, EL 7809, Castle to Bridgewater, 24 October 1639.

62. J. R. M. Sizer, 'Stewart, John, First Earl of Traquair (c.1599–1659)', *ODNB*, 52, pp. 718–20. For tensions with bishops see Stevenson, *Scottish Revolution*, esp. pp. 53, 54–5 and the index entry on his 'duplicity', p. 415, sn Stewart, James, 1st Earl of Traquair. See also Donald, *Uncounselled King*, chs. 1–2 passim.

63. Donald, *Uncounselled King*, pp. 45–8; Stevenson, *Scottish Revolution*, pp. 64–6.

64. Donald, *Uncounselled King*, pp. 48–58; Stevenson, *Scottish Revolution*, pp. 66–79. For the October protests see Makey, *Church of the Covenant*, p. 21.

65. Donald, *Uncounselled King*, chs. 1–2. For Traquair's permission to travel see pp. 61–2; for the anti-episcopal tone of the petitions see pp. 53–7. See also Stevenson's verdict: 'on the eve of the troubles in Scotland the administration was in no condition to meet the

crisis thrust upon it by a king who refused to recognise the difficulties involved in imposing his policies': *Scottish Revolution*, p. 55.

66. Makey, *Church of the Covenant*, pp. 1–6.

67. For a full discussion of the material grievances which may have lain behind the alienation of the political nation see Macinnes, *Charles I*, ch. 5.

68. Ibid., chs. 2–4, Lee, *Road to Revolution*, ch. 7.

69. Todd, *Culture of Protestantism*, conclusion.

70. For early signs of awareness in Scotland of the possibility of a common cause with the godly in England see Donald, *Uncounselled King*, p. 37; Russell, *Fall*, pp. 60–61.

71. Macinnes, *British Revolution*, p. 114; Macinnes, *Charles I*, pp. 163–73; Makey, *Church of the Covenant*, identifies the social significance of this organization slightly differently: pp. 22–5. For Henderson see John Coffey, 'Henderson, Alexander (*c.*1583–1646)', *ODNB*, 26, pp. 288–93; and for Johnston see John Coffey, 'Johnston, Sir Archibald, Lord Wariston (*bap.* 1611, *d.* 1663)', *ODNB*, 30, pp. 338–46.

72. 'The Scottish National Covenant', reprinted in Gardiner, *CD*, pp. 124–34, quotations at pp. 125, 131.

73. Ibid., p. 132.

74. Ibid.

75. Skinner, *Foundations*, ch. 7.

76. Macinnes, *Charles I*, esp. p. 177; Macinnes, *British Revolution*, pp. 114–16. See also Edward J. Cowan, 'The Making of the National Covenant', in Morrill, *Scottish National Covenant*, pp. 68–89.

77. Stevenson, *Scottish Revolution*, pp. 83–7, 97.

78. For this reading of the text see ibid., pp. 84–6; Morrill also finds it an ambivalent document: 'National Covenant', pp. 11–12, reflecting a genuine failure to realize the full implications of their position. Stevenson's view of its practical significance is similar to that of Macinnes.

79. Macinnes, *British Revolution*, p. 116.

80. Stevenson, *Scottish Revolution*, p. 87.

81. John J. Scally, 'Hamilton, James, First Duke of Hamilton (1606–1649)', *ODNB*, 24, pp. 839–46; see also Stevenson, *Scottish Revolution*, p. 94.

82. For the limits on Hamilton's powers see Donald, *Scottish Revolution*, pp. 72–5, 78–9; Makey, *Church of the Covenant*, pp. 32–4.

83. Stevenson, *Scottish Revolution*, pp. 88–95; Donald, *Uncounselled King*, pp. 79–87.

84. Stevenson, *Scottish Revolution*, p. 96.

85. Ibid., pp. 18, 24; population estimate Laura Stewart, personal communication.

86. Quoted in Scally, 'Hamilton'.

87. Stevenson, *Scottish Revolution*, pp. 100–101.

88. Ibid., pp. 104–9.

89. Ibid., pp. 109–12; Donald, *Uncounselled King*, ch. 3, narrates Hamilton's mission in greater detail and with more attention to the possibilities for settlement.

90. Stevenson, *Scottish Revolution*, pp. 116–26; Donald, *Uncounselled King*, pp. 109–12.

2. Self-Government at the King's Command

1. The most detailed account of the murder is contained in the letter from Dudley Carlton to the Queen, reprinted in Henry Ellis (ed.), *Original Letters Illustrative of English History*, 3 vols. (London, 1824), III, pp. 254–60. For some additional material see Frederick W. Fairholt (ed.), *Poems and Songs Relating to George Villiers, Duke of Buckingham: and his assassination by John Felton, August 23, 1628*, Percy Society, Vol. 29, No. 40 (London, 1850), pp. i–xxxi. Much of this material is also gathered in Isaac D'Israeli, *Curiosities of Literature*, 12th edn (London, 1841), pp. 307–10. It is discussed in James Holstun, *Ehud's Dagger: Class Struggle in the English Revolution* (London, 2000); Alastair Bellany, ' "Rayling Rymes and Vaunting Verse": Libellous Politics in Early Stuart England,

1603–1628', in Kevin Sharpe and Peter Lake (eds.), *Culture and Politics in Early Stuart England* (Basingstoke, 1994), pp. 285–310, esp. pp. 304–9. For a brief description of the assassination in the context of problematic military mobilization see Thomas G. Barnes, 'Deputies not Principals, Lieutenants not Captains: The Institutional Failure of Lieutenancy in the 1620s', in Mark Charles Fissel (ed.), *War and Government in Britain, 1598–1650* (Manchester, 1991), pp. 58–86, esp. pp. 82–3.

2. Fairholt, *Poems and Songs*, p. xxi. For other versions see Ellis, *Original Letters*, pp. 259–60.

3. Ellis, *Original Letters*, pp. 257–8. See also *CSPD*, 1628–9, pp. 268, 271.

4. Ellis, *Original Letters*, p. 258; for the grievances about pay and place see *CSPD*, 1628–9, pp. 274, 277–8. For the relationship between Felton's personal frustrations and the broader hostility to Buckingham see Thomas Cogswell, 'John Felton, Popular Political Culture, and the Assassination of the Duke of Buckingham', *HJ*, 49 (2006), 357–83.

5. Fairholt, *Poems and Songs*, p. xxviii.

6. John Rushworth, *Historical Collections of Private Passages of State . . .*, 8 vols. (London, 1721 edn), vol. I, p. 641; Fairholt, *Poems and Songs*, p. xxvii.

7. Rushworth, *Historical Collections*, I, p. 638; *CSPD*, 1628–9, p. 321.

8. For the preparations before his examination see *CSPD*, 1628–9, pp. 321, 340. Once, having 'received an injury from a gentleman, he cut off a piece of his little finger, and sent it with a challenge to the gentleman to fight with him, thereby to let him know that he valued not the exposing of his whole body to hazard so he might but have an opportunity to be revenged': Rushworth, *Historical Collections*, I, p. 638. A number of those examined afterwards commented that he was a melancholy and angry man, and his family seem to have been pained and bewildered by his actions: *CSPD*, 1628–9, pp. 274, 277–8, 343, 349.

9. Rushworth, *Historical Collections*, I, p. 638. According to one account it was Dorset who had threatened him with the rack, and it was to him that Felton made the threat in return: Fairholt, *Poems and Songs*, p. xxvii. Suspicion that leading parliamentarians were connected with the murder was not confined to the council: Kevin Sharpe, *The Personal Rule of Charles I* (New Haven, Conn., 1992), p. 48. For Laud and the Puritan plot see Jason Peacey, 'The Paranoid Prelate: Archbishop Laud and the Puritan Plot', in Barry Coward and Julian Swann (eds.), *Conspiracies and Conspiracy Theory in Early Modern Europe: From the Waldensians to the French Revolution* (Aldershot, 2004), pp. 113–34.

10. Rushworth, *Historical Collections*, I, pp. 638–9. Fairholt, *Poems and Songs*, also suggests that legal niceties did not always prevent the use of the rack: p. xxvin.

11. Rushworth, *Historical Collections*, I, pp. 640–41. See also Ellis, *Original Letters*, pp. 279–81.

12. James A. Sharpe, ' "Last dying speeches": Religion, Ideology and Public Execution in Seventeenth-Century England', *PP*, 107 (1985), 144–67.

13. Anon., *The Prayer and Confession of Mr Felton, word for word as hee it spake immediatly before his Execution, Novem 29 1628*, ESTC 19762. It was published anonymously and bears no place and date of publication, or the publisher, as if it had been published clandestinely. Although this was a publication likely to play well with the crown, the subject matter was rather sensitive, of course. As a matter of general policy Charles and his advisers had turned their backs on propaganda in 1627, reversing a policy which Charles and Buckingham had pursued in 1623: Thomas Cogswell, 'The Politics of Propaganda: Charles I and the People in the 1620s', *JBS*, 29:3 (1990), 187–215; see also Richard Cust, 'Charles I and Popularity', in Thomas Cogswell, Richard Cust and Peter Lake (eds.), *Politics, Religion and Popularity in Early Stuart Britain: Essays in Honour of Conrad Russell* (Cambridge, 2002), pp. 235–58.

14. Sir Thomas Barrington reported that Felton 'condemned and bewailed his fate, died penitently and disavowed all justification of the deed, desired all the people to pray for him and so ended his days', Arthur Searle (ed.), *Barrington Family Letters 1628–1632*, Royal Historical Society, Camden Society, 4th ser., 28 (London, 1983), p. 39. See also Ellis, *Original Letters*, pp. 281–2.

15. Thomas Laqueur, 'Crowds, Carnival and the State in English Executions, 1604–1868', in A. L. Beier, David Cannadine and James M. Rosenheim (eds.), *The First Modern Society: Essays in English History in Honour of Lawrence Stone* (Cambridge, 1989), pp. 305–55; Peter Lake and Michael C. Questier, 'Agency, Appropriation and Rhetoric under the Gallows: Puritans, Romanists and the State in Early Modern England', *PP*, 153 (1996), 64–107.

16. Anon., *Prayer and Confession*.

17. *CSPD*, 1628–9, p. 277; Ellis, *Original Letters*, pp. 260–61.

18. Ibid., pp. 278–9. For an example of an execution rearranged in order to 'avoid a crowd of people' see Donald Woodward, ' "Here comes a chopper to chop off his head": The Execution of Three Priests at Newcastle and Gateshead, 1592–1594', *Recusant History*, 22 (1994), 1–6, at p. 1.

19. Ellis, *Original Letters*, p. 281.

20. Fairholt, *Poems and Songs*, pp. xxix–xxx. See also Holstun, *Ehud's Dagger*, pp. 186–91; Christopher Hill, *Milton and the English Revolution* (New York, 1977), p. 28.

21. Fairholt, *Poems and Songs*, passim. Some of this material is discussed in David Norbrook, *Writing the English Republic: Poetry, Rhetoric and Politics, 1627–1660* (Cambridge, 1999), pp. 53–8; David Norbrook, *Poetry and Politics in the English Renaissance*, rev. edn (Oxford, 2002), pp. 211, 312–12; Sharpe, *Personal Rule*, pp. 48–9; Bellany, ' "Rayling Rymes and Vaunting Verse" ', esp. pp. 304–9.

22. Christopher Hill, *A Turbulent, Seditious and Factious People: John Bunyan and His Church 1628–1688* (Oxford, 1988), p. 4 and n.

23. For a clear overview of the order of events see Roger Lockyer, *The Early Stuarts: A Political History 1603–1642* (London, 1989). Conrad Russell, *Parliaments and English Politics 1621–1629* (Oxford, 1979), offers a detailed outline of the parliamentary politics, but is now criticized for underplaying the importance of ideological conflict and its resonances in the localities. For important studies which re-emphasize these things see Richard Cust, *The Forced Loan and English Politics 1626–1628* (Oxford, 1987); Thomas Cogswell, *The Blessed Revolution: English Politics and the Coming of War, 1621–1624* (Cambridge, 1989); Thomas Cogswell, 'England and the Spanish Match', in Richard Cust and Ann Hughes (eds.), *Conflict in Early Stuart England: Studies in Religion and Politics 1603–1642* (Harlow, 1989), pp. 107–33; Thomas Cogswell, 'Phaeton's Chariot: The Parliament Men and the Continental Crisis in 1621', in J. F. Merritt (ed.), *The Political World of Thomas Wentworth, Earl of Strafford, 1621–1641* (Cambridge, 1996), pp. 24–46; Richard Cust, 'Politics and the Electorate in the 1620s', in ibid., pp. 134–67; Johann Sommerville, 'Ideology, Property and the Constitution', in ibid., pp. 47–71. For Russell's response on foreign policy see Conrad Russell, 'Sir Thomas Wentworth and anti-Spanish Sentiment, 1621–1624', in Merritt (ed.), *Political World*, pp. 47–62. For the interconnection of threats to civil and religious liberties see Alan Cromartie, *The Constitutionalist Revolution: An Essay on the History of England, 1450–1642* (Cambridge, 2006), esp. intr. and ch. 8. Thomas Cogswell, 'A Low Road to Extinction? Supply and Redress of Grievances in the Parliaments of the 1620s', *HJ*, 33 (1990), 283–303, argues that Parliament was effective both in securing redress and in granting supplies during the 1620s; for the royal perception that parliaments would not grant *enough* money see Cust, *Forced Loan*, pp. 30–31. For Arminianism see above, ch. 1, n. 43.

24. Richard W. Stewart, 'Arms and Expeditions: The Ordnance Office and the Assaults on Cadiz (1625) and the Isle of Rhé (1627)', in Fissel (ed.), *War and Government*, pp. 112–32; Cogswell, 'John Felton', pp. 362–4; Cust, *Forced Loan*, esp. pp. 58–62; Russell, *Parliaments and English Politics*, pp. 334–76; John Guy, 'The Origins of the Petition of Right Reconsidered', *HJ*, 25 (1982), 289–312, esp. pp. 294–9. The reliability of the accusations on which Guy's article is based is contested by Mark Kishlansky, 'Tyranny Denied: Charles I, Attorney General Heath, and the Five Knights' Case', *HJ*, 42 (1999), 53–83. The point here is that they were made, and what that indicates about the political atmosphere of the late 1620s.

25. Stewart, 'Arms and Expeditions'.

26. Barnes, 'Deputies not Principals'; Thomas Cogswell, 'War and the Liberties of the Subject', in J. H. Hexter (ed.), *Parliament and Liberty from the Reign of Elizabeth to the English Civil War* (Stanford, Calif., 1992), pp. 225–51.

27. Russell, *Parliaments and English Politics*, ch. 8, esp. pp. 377–84, and for the subsequent dispute over publication, pp. 401–2. For the printing and legal status see L. J. Reeve, *Charles I and the Road to Personal Rule* (Cambridge, 1989), esp. pp. 90–91; L. J. Reeve, 'The Legal Status of the Petition of Right', *HJ*, 29 (1986), 257–77, esp. pp. 261–3; E. R. Foster, 'Printing the Petition of Right', *HLQ*, 38 (1974–5), 81–3. The totemic significance of the Petition of Right for those anxious about English liberties is clear in Reeve, *Charles I*, esp. ch. 5.

28. Russell, *Parliaments and English Politics*, pp. 391–2; Alastair Bellany, 'Basting the Lambe: Witchcraft, Court Scandal and the Lynching of the Duke's Devil, June 1628', *PP* (forthcoming).

29. Glenn Burgess, *The Politics of the Ancient Constitution: An Introduction to English Political Thought, 1603–1642* (Basingstoke, 1992); Clive Holmes, 'Parliament, Liberty, Taxation, and Property', in Hexter (ed.), *Parliament and Liberty*, pp. 122–54.

30. For fundamental disagreements in Stuart political thought see Johann Sommerville, *Royalists and Patriots: Politics and Ideology in England 1603–1640* (rev. edn London, 1999); Cromartie, *Constitutionalist Revolution*. For the articulation of a fundamental view of political liberty in the debates about the Petition of Right see Quentin Skinner, 'Rethinking Political Liberty', *History Workshop Journal*, 61:1 (2006), 156–70, esp. pp. 156, 158; Guy, 'Origins of the Petition of Right'; Cogswell, 'War and the Liberties of the Subject'.

31. For the rise of Arminianism see above, ch. 1, n. 43; and for a summary see Peter Marshall, *Reformation England, 1480–1642* (London, 2003), esp. pp. 195–7. For Maynwaring and Sibthorpe see, Cust, *Forced Loan*, esp. pp. 62–5; Sommerville, *Royalists and Patriots*, esp. pp. 119–24; Vivienne Larminie, 'Maynwaring, Roger (1589/90?–1653)', *ODNB*, 37, pp. 612–4. For Sibthorpe see also John Fielding, 'Sibthorpe, Robert (d. 1662)', *ODNB*, 50, pp. 500–501; Cromartie, *Constitutionalist Revolution*, esp. pp. 244–5.

32. Russell, *Parliaments and English Politics*, pp. 404–12.

33. Marshall, *Reformation England*, pp. 135, 196; Cromartie, *Constitutionalist Revolution*, pp. 172–4.

34. The classic discussion is Patrick Collinson, *The Birthpangs of Protestant England: Religious and Cultural Change in the Sixteenth and Seventeenth Centuries* (Basingstoke, 1988), ch. 1.

35. Cogswell, *Blessed Revolution*; Cogswell, 'England and the Spanish Match'.

36. The literature on this is very large. See, especially, Peter Lake, 'Defining Puritanism – Again?', in Francis J. Bremer (ed.), *Puritanism: Transatlantic Perspectives on a Seventeenth-Century Anglo-American Faith* (Boston, Mass., 1993), pp. 3–29. For the construction of Puritanism in public debate see, in particular, Peter Lake with Michael Questier, *The Antichrist's Lewd Hat: Protestants, Papists and Players in post-Reformation England* (New Haven, Conn., 2002); Peter Lake, 'Anti-Puritanism: The Structure of a Prejudice', in Kenneth Fincham and Peter Lake (eds.), *Religious Politics in post-Reformation England: Essays in Honour of Nicholas Tyacke* (Woodbridge, 2006), pp. 80–97; Patrick Collinson, 'The Theatre Constructs Puritanism', in David L. Smith, Richard Strier and David Bevington (eds.), *The Theatrical City: Culture, Theatre and Politics in London, 1576–1649* (Cambridge, 1995), pp. 157–69. Marshall, *Reformation England*, offers an excellent overview and further references: pp. 135–41.

37. Esther S. Cope and Willson H. Coates (eds.), *Proceedings of the Short Parliament of 1640*, Camden 4th ser., 19 (London, 1977), p. 147.

38. Cromartie, *Constitutionalist Revolution*, pp. 144–5; Marshall, *Reformation England*, pp. 194–5.

39. Tessa Watt, *Cheap Print and Popular Piety, 1550–1640* (Cambridge, 1991), p. 11. The figure for literacy is derived from David Cressy, *Literacy and the Social Order: Reading*

and Writing in Tudor and Stuart England (Cambridge, 1980), although most authorities agree that this is a minimum figure, and possibly much lower than the real size of the reading population. For a judicious review see Adam Fox, *Oral and Literate Culture in England 1500–1700* (Oxford, 2000), pp. 16–19.

40. Watt, *Cheap Print*, ch. 2; Angela McShane Jones, ' "Rime and Reason": The Political World of the English Broadside Ballad, 1640–1689', unpublished Ph.D. thesis, Warwick (2004), esp. ch. 6.

41. Ian M. Green, ' "For children in yeeres and children in understanding": The Emergence of the English Catechism under Elizabeth and the Early Stuarts', *Journal of Ecclesiastical History*, 37 (1986), 397–425, at p. 425; see also Ian Green, *The Christian's ABC: Catechisms and Catechizing in England c. 1530–1740* (Oxford, 1996); Ian Green, *Print and Protestantism in Early Modern England* (Oxford, 2000). For instructional material see also Tessa Watt, 'Piety in the Pedlar's Pack: Continuity and Change, 1578–1630', in Margaret Spufford (ed.), *The World of Rural Dissenters, 1520–1725* (Cambridge, 1995), pp. 235–72.

42. Watt, *Cheap Print*, chs. 4–8; work on chapbooks is much indebted to Margaret Spufford, *Small Books and Pleasant Histories: Popular Fiction and Its Readership in Seventeenth-Century England* (Athens, Ga., 1981).

43. Matthias Adam Shaaber, *Some Forerunners of the Newspaper in England, 1476–1622* (Philadelphia, Penn., 1929), esp. chs. 1, 4.

44. Alexandra Walsham, *Providence in Early Modern England* (Oxford, 2001 edn); Lake with Questier, *Antichrist's Lewd Hat*, chs. 1–5; Peter Lake, 'Popular Form, Puritan Content?: Two Puritan Appropriations of the Murder Pamphlet from mid-Seventeenth-Century London', in Anthony Fletcher and Peter Roberts (eds.), *Religion, Culture and Society in Early Modern Britain: Essays in Honour of Patrick Collinson* (Cambridge, 1994), pp. 313–34.

45. For public awareness of politics more generally see Richard Cust, 'News and Politics in Early Seventeenth-Century England', reprinted in Richard Cust and Ann Hughes (eds.), *The English Civil War* (London, 1997), pp. 233–60; Cogswell, 'Politics of Propaganda'; Thomas Cogswell, 'Underground Verse and the Transformation of Early Stuart Political Culture', in Susan D. Amussen and Mark A. Kishlansky (eds.), *Political Culture and Cultural Politics in Early Modern England: Essays Presented to David Underdown* (Manchester, 1995), pp. 277–300; Thomas Cogswell, ' "Published by Authoritie": Newsbooks and the Duke of Buckingham's Expedition to the Île de Ré', *HLQ*, 67:1 (2004), 1–25; Bellany, ' "Rayling Rymes and Vaunting Verse" '; Alastair Bellany, 'Libels in Action: Ritual, Subversion and the English Literary Underground, 1603–42', in Tim Harris (ed.), *The Politics of the Excluded, c. 1500–1850* (Basingstoke, 2001), pp. 99–124; Fox, *Oral and Literate*, esp. chs. 6–7 and the works cited there.

46. Fox, *Oral and Literate*, esp. chs. 6–7 and the works cited there.

47. For an overview of court politics see Kevin Sharpe, 'The Image of Virtue: The Court and Household of Charles I 1625–1642', in David Starkey and D. A. L. Morgan, John Murphy, Pam Wright, Neil Cuddy and Kevin Sharpe (eds.), *The English Court: From the Wars of the Roses to the Civil War* (London, 1987), pp. 226–60. For the politics of Buckingham's bridging of two reigns see Russell, *Parliaments and English Politics*, esp. pp. 107–8, 145–8, 202–3; Cust, *Forced Loan*, esp. pp. 27–35. For the rumours about the poisoning of James I, which persisted into the 1640s, see Cogswell, 'John Felton', pp. 366–8; Alastair Bellany, 'The Murder of James I: Mutations and Meanings of a Political Myth, c. 1625–1660' (unpublished paper).

48. Peter Lake and Steve Pincus, 'Rethinking the Public Sphere in Early Modern England', *JBS*, 45 (2006), 270–92; Peter Lake, 'Anti-Puritanism'; Peter Lake, ' "The monarchical republic of Elizabeth I" Revisited (by Its Victims) as a Conspiracy', in Coward and Swann (eds.), *Conspiracies*, pp. 87–111. For a similar analysis see Richard Cust, ' "Patriots" and "popular spirits": Narratives of Conflict in Early Stuart Politics', in Nicholas Tyacke (ed.), *The English Revolution c. 1590–1720* (Manchester, 2007), pp. 43–61.

49. *CSPD*, 1628–9, pp. 343, 363.
50. Ibid., p. 274. See also ibid., p. 359.
51. Cogswell, 'Politics of Propaganda'.
52. Cromartie, *Constitutionalist Revolution*, pp. 1–3, ch. 8.
53. See, in particular, Blair Worden, 'Classical Republicanism and the Puritan Revolution', in Hugh Lloyd-Jones, Valerie Pearl and Blair Worden (eds.), *History and Imagination: Essays in Honour of H. R. Trevor-Roper* (London, 1981), pp. 182–200; Markku Peltonen, *Classical Humanism and Republicanism in English Political Thought, 1570–1640* (Cambridge, 1995); Markku Peltonen, 'Citizenship and Republicanism in Elizabethan England', in Martin van Gelderen and Quentin Skinner (eds.), *Republicanism: A Shared European Heritage*, vol. 1: *Republicanism and Constitutionalism in Early Modern Europe* (Cambridge, 2002), pp. 85–106. For the practical importance of these ideas see Mark Goldie, 'The Unacknowledged Republic: Officeholding in Early Modern England', in Harris (ed.), *Politics of the Excluded*, pp. 153–94; Richard Cust, 'The "public man" in Late Tudor and Early Stuart England', in Peter Lake and Steven Pincus (eds.), *The Politics of the Public Sphere in Early Modern England* (Manchester, forthcoming); Richard Cust and Peter G. Lake, 'Sir Richard Grosvenor and the Rhetoric of Magistracy', *Bulletin of the Institute of Historical Research*, 54 (1981), 40–53; Philip Withington, *The Politics of Commonwealth: Citizens and Freemen in Early Modern England* (Cambridge, 2005), esp. chs. 3, 7, 8.
54. Quentin Skinner, 'Classical Liberty and the Coming of the English Civil War', in Van Gelderen and Skinner (eds.), *Republicanism*, vol. 2: *The Values of Republicanism in Early Modern Europe*, pp. 9–28.
55. Norbrook, *Writing the English Republic*, ch. 1; see also David Norbrook, 'Lucan, Thomas May, and the Creation of a Republican Literary Culture', in Sharpe and Lake (eds.), *Culture and Politics*, pp. 45–66. Republican values were not necessarily anti-monarchical: 'In general English republicanism defined itself in relation not to constitutional structures but moral principles': Jonathan Scott, *England's Troubles: Seventeenth-Century English Political Stability in European Context* (Cambridge, 2000), ch. 14, quotation at p. 317. See also Jonathan Scott, *Commonwealth Principles: Republican Writing of the English Revolution* (Cambridge, 2004). Significantly, perhaps, there was a strong imperial theme in representations of Charles during the Personal Rule: John Peacock, 'The Image of Charles I as a Roman Emperor', in Ian Atherton and Julie Sanders (eds.), *The 1630s: Interdisciplinary Essays on Culture and Politics in the Caroline Era* (Manchester, 2006), pp. 50–73.
56. Norbrook, *Writing the English Republic*, esp. pp. 54–5.
57. Russell, *Parliaments and English Politics*, ch. 7.
58. Quoted in Kevin Sharpe, 'The King's Writ: Royal Authors and Royal Authority in Early Modern England', in Sharpe and Lake (eds.), *Culture and Politics*, pp. 117–38, at p. 133.
59. The classic cutting-down-to-size of Stuart parliaments is Conrad Russell, 'Parliamentary History in Perspective, 1604–1629', reprinted in Conrad Russell, *Unrevolutionary England, 1603–1642* (London, 1990), pp. 31–57. See also Russell, *Parliaments and English Politics*, ch. 1. For the frequency of meetings see Michael A. R. Graves, *Tudor Parliaments: Crown, Lords and Commons, 1485–1603* (Harlow, 1985), p. 7; Cogswell, 'Low Road', p. 285. For a crisp overview see David L. Smith, *The Stuart Parliaments 1603–1689* (London, 1999), pt 1.
60. Much of the literature relating to this and the next paragraph is cited and summarized in Michael J. Braddick, *State Formation in Early Modern England, c. 1550–1700* (Cambridge, 2000), pp. 48–56, 104–7. For a fuller survey see Keith Wrightson, *Earthly Necessities: Economic Lives in Early Modern Britain* (New Haven, Conn., 2000), chs. 5–9; and for the lives of the poor, Steve Hindle, *On the Parish? The Micro-Politics of Poor Relief in Rural England, c. 1550–1750* (Oxford, 2004). For 1623 see Andrew B. Appleby, *Famine in Tudor and Stuart England* (Liverpool, 1978), chs. 8–9. For famine and the social practices which limited the effects of harvest failure see John Walter and Roger

Schofield, 'Famine, Disease and Crisis Mortality in Early Modern Society', in John Walter and Roger Schofield (eds.), *Famine, Disease and the Social Order in Early Modern Society* (Cambridge, 1989), pp. 1–73; and John Walter, 'The Social Economy of Dearth in Early Modern England', reprinted in John Walter, *Crowds and Popular Politics in Early Modern England* (Manchester, 2006), pp. 124–80.

61. The classic account is Keith Wrightson, 'Aspects of Social Differentiation in Rural England, c.1580–1660', *Journal of Peasant Studies*, 5:1 (1977), 33–47; see also Keith Wrightson, *English Society 1580–1680* (London, 1982), ch. 5.

62. Braddick, *State Formation*, ch. 3. Essential reading includes: Paul Slack, *Poverty and Policy in Tudor and Stuart England* (London, 1988); Paul Slack, *From Reformation to Improvement: Public Welfare in Early Modern England* (Oxford, 1998), chs. 1–2; Hindle, *On the Parish?*.

63. Michael J. Braddick, 'State Formation and Social Change: A Problem Stated and Approaches Suggested', *Social History*, 16:1 (1991), 1–17; Braddick, *State Formation*, pp. 27–38, 68–85, 101–35; Steve Hindle, *The State and Social Change in Early Modern England, c. 1550–1640* (Basingstoke, 2000), esp. chs. 2, 6.

64. Paul Slack, 'Books of Orders: The Making of English Social Policy, 1577–1631', *TRHS*, 5th ser., 30 (1980), 1–22; B. W. Quintrell, 'The Making of Charles I's Book of Orders', *EHR*, 95 (1980), 553–72; Sharpe, *Personal Rule*, pp. 456–87; Thomas G. Barnes, *Somerset 1625–1640: A County's Government during the 'Personal Rule'* (Chicago, 1961), ch. 7. In Kent there was no conflict, but compliance was not complete: Peter Clark, *English Provincial Society from the Reformation to the Revolution: Religion, Politics and Society in Kent, 1500–1640* (Hassocks, 1977), pp. 350–53; Henrik Langelüddecke, 'Law and Order in Seventeenth-Century England: The Organization of Local Administration during the Personal Rule of Charles I', *Law and History Review*, 15 (1997), 49–76; Henrik Langelüddecke, ' "Patchy and spasmodic"?: The Response of Justices of the Peace to Charles I's Book of Orders', *EHR*, 113 (1998), 1231–48. For Manchester see Conrad Russell, *The Fall of the British Monarchies 1637–1642* (Oxford, 1991), p. 6. For the 1640s see Anthony Fletcher, *Reform in the Provinces: The Government of Stuart England* (New Haven, Conn., 1986), esp. p. 187; Ann Hughes, *Politics, Society and Civil War in Warwickshire, 1620–1660* (Cambridge, 1987), pp. 51–8. Steve Hindle argues that the extent of rates has been overstated and that magistrates intervening in the grain market during the 1640s were not so much self-activating as prompted from below: Hindle, *On the Parish?*, pp. 253–4; Steve Hindle, 'Dearth and the English Revolution: The Harvest Crisis of 1647–50', *EcHR*, 61 (2008), pp. 64–98.

65. Mark Brayshay, Philip Harrison and Brian Chalkley, 'Knowledge, Nationhood and Governance: The Speed of the Royal Post in Early-Modern England', *Journal of Historical Geography*, 24 (1998), 265–88.

66. David Cressy, *England on Edge: Crisis and Revolution 1640–1642* (Oxford, 2006), p. 311; Jacqueline Eales, *Puritans and Roundheads: The Harleys of Brampton Bryan and the Outbreak of the English Civil War* (Cambridge, 1990), pp. 116–18; for the density of communication see Michael Frearson, 'Communications and the Continuity of Dissent in the Chiltern Hundreds during the Sixteenth and Seventeenth Centuries', in Spufford (ed.), *World of Rural Dissenters*, pp. 273–87.

67. Figures for population and age profile derived from E. A. Wrigley and R. S. Schofield, *The Population History of England 1541–1871: A Reconstruction* (Cambridge, 1981), table A3.1.

68. For studies of the officeholding population of particular villages see Joan R. Kent, *The English Village Constable, 1580–1642* (Oxford, 1986), ch. 4; Jan Pitman, 'Tradition and Exclusion: Parochial Officeholding in Early Modern England, a Case Study from North Norfolk, 1580–1640', *Rural History*, 15 (2004), 27–45. The point about influence over government is also made by Goldie, 'Unacknowledged'.

69. Withington, *Politics of Commonwealth*, for numbers see table 2.1; Goldie, 'Unacknowledged'; Pitman, 'Tradition and Exclusion', esp. pp. 38–40.

70. This was particularly true in the mid sixteenth century: Anthony Fletcher and Diarmaid MacCulloch, *Tudor Rebellions*, 5th edn (Harlow, 2004), pp. 12–13; Andrew McRae, *God Speed the Plough: The Representation of Agrarian England, 1500–1660* (Cambridge, 1996), esp. ch. 1. But the language persisted into the seventeenth century: John Walter, 'Public Transcripts, Popular Agency and the Politics of Subsistence in Early Modern England', reprinted in Walter, *Crowds*, pp. 196–222, esp. pp. 198–9.

71. For this approach see Quentin Skinner, 'Language and Social Action', reprinted in James Tully (ed.), *Meaning and Context: Quentin Skinner and His Critics* (Princeton, NJ, 1988), pp. 119–32.

72. John Walter and Keith Wrightson, 'Dearth and the Social Order in Early Modern England', reprinted in Paul Slack (ed.), *Rebellion, Popular Protest and the Social Order in Early Modern England* (Cambridge, 1984), pp. 108–28; Walter, 'Public Transcripts'; John Walter, 'A "rising of the people"?: The Oxfordshire Rising of 1596', in Walter, *Crowds*, pp. 73–123; Walter, 'Social Economy of Dearth', in ibid., pp. 124–80; Steve Hindle, 'Exhortation and Entitlement: Negotiating Inequality in English Rural Communities, 1550–1650', in Michael J. Braddick and John Walter (eds.), *Negotiating Power in Early Modern Society: Order, Hierarchy and Subordination in Britain and Ireland* (Cambridge, 2001), pp. 102–22.

73. Hindle, 'Dearth and the English Revolution'.

74. For a summary and further references see Braddick, *State Formation*, pp. 30–41, 137–40.

75. For a summary and further references see ibid. For some influential studies see Keith Wrightson, 'Two Concepts of Order: Justices, Constables and Jurymen in Seventeenth-Century England', in John Brewer and John Styles (eds.), *An Ungovernable People?: The English and Their Law in the Seventeenth and Eighteenth Centuries* (London, 1980), pp. 21–46; Cynthia Herrup, *The Common Peace: Participation and the Criminal Law in Seventeenth-Century England* (Cambridge, 1987); Hindle, *State and Social Change*, ch. 5.

76. Clive Holmes, 'The County Community in Stuart Historiography', *JBS*, 19:2 (1980), 54–73.

77. Patrick Collinson, *The Religion of Protestants: The Church in English Society 1559–1625* (Oxford, 1982), ch. 4.

78. Keith Wrightson and David Levine, *Poverty and Piety in an English Village: Terling 1525–1700*, rev. edn (Oxford, 1995); David Underdown, *Fire from Heaven: Life in an English Town in the Seventeenth Century* (London, 1992); Cust and Lake, 'Sir Richard Grosvenor'.

79. For more indulgent paternalism see David Underdown, *Revel, Riot, and Rebellion: Popular Politics and Culture in England 1603–1660* (Oxford, 1985), ch. 3. For social control without Puritanism see Margaret Spufford, 'Puritanism and Social Control', in Anthony Fletcher and John Stevenson (eds.), *Order and Disorder in Early Modern England* (Cambridge, 1985), pp. 41–57; Martin Ingram, 'Reformation of Manners in Early Modern England', in Paul Griffiths, Adam Fox and Steve Hindle (eds.), *The Experience of Authority in Early Modern England* (Basingstoke, 1996), pp. 47–88.

80. Sharpe, 'Image of Virtue'.

81. Braddick, *State Formation*, pp. 181–96.

82. Ibid., esp. pp. 181–4.

83. For summaries and further references see Sharpe, *Personal Rule*, pp. 487–505; Braddick, *State Formation*, pp. 187–8, 192–5.

84. For a full account see Michael J. Braddick, 'Administrative Performance: The Representation of Political Authority in Early Modern England', in Braddick and Walter (eds.), *Negotiating Power*, pp. 166–87. See also Esther Cope, 'Politics without Parliament: The Dispute about Muster Masters' Fees in Shropshire in the 1630s', *HLQ*, 45 (1982), 271–84; Sharpe, *Personal Rule*, pp. 495, 496–7.

85. The sense of occasion is evoked by A. H. Smith, *County and Court: Government and Politics in Norfolk, 1558–1603* (Oxford, 1974), pp. 87–8.

86. Braddick, 'Administrative Performance', p. 168. For Burton's attitude in the 1620s see ibid., p. 182; Sharpe, *Personal Rule*, p. 497.
87. For the abuse of tax collectors and the intersection with local reputation see Michael J. Braddick, *Parliamentary Taxation in Seventeenth-Century England: Local Administration and Response* (Woodbridge, 1994), esp. pp. 39–54, 117–24, 154–6; Michael J. Braddick, *The Nerves of State: Taxation and the Financing of the English State, 1558–1714* (Manchester, 1996), esp. pp. 196–7.
88. Braddick, 'Administrative Performance', quotations at pp. 170, 174.
89. Sharpe, *Personal Rule*, pp. 494–5.
90. Thomas Cogswell, *Home Divisions: Aristocracy, the State and Provincial Conflict* (Manchester, 1998), esp. ch. 11; see also Sharpe, *Personal Rule*, p. 499.
91. For the most sympathetic account of these fiscal policies see Sharpe, *Personal Rule*, ch. 3; and, for a longer-term perspective on their logic and politics, Braddick, *Nerves of State*, ch. 4, which also contains a guide to further reading. For the longer-term perspective see Holmes, 'Parliament, Liberty, Taxation, and Property'. For the burdens of these various devices in Leicestershire see Cogswell, *Home Divisions*, pp. 194–200, 230–36, 245–50, 255–60. For knighthood fines see Derek Hirst, *England in Conflict 1603–1660: Kingdom Community, Commonwealth* (London, 1999), pp. 140, 142.
92. Hirst, *England in Conflict*, quotation at p. 142.
93. For an overview see Sharpe, *Personal Rule*, ch. 9; A. A. M. Gill, 'Ship Money during the Personal Rule of Charles I: Politics, Ideology and Law 1634 to 1640', unpublished Ph.D. thesis, Sheffield (1990).
94. Kenneth Fincham, 'The Judges' Decision on Ship Money in February 1637: The Reaction of Kent', *Bulletin of the Institute of Historical Research*, 57:136 (1984), 230–37.
95. Sharpe, *Personal Rule*, p. 721.
96. For a clear account see ibid., pp. 721–5.
97. Ibid. For Bramston and Davenport see Conrad Russell, 'The Ship-Money Judgments of Bramston and Davenport', reprinted in Russell, *Unrevolutionary England*, pp. 137–44; Clarendon quoted in R. W. Ketton-Cremer, *Norfolk in the Civil War: A Portrait of a Society in Conflict* (London, 1969), p. 91.
98. Clarendon, I, p. 86. Sharpe, *Personal Rule*, pp. 727–9, points to the slight improvement over the summer of 1638, as those waiting for the verdict paid up; for places where receipts held up see C. A. Clifford, 'Ship Money in Hampshire: Collection and Collapse', *Southern History*, 4 (1982), 91–106, at p. 102; Clark, *Kent*, pp. 358–61; John T. Evans, *Seventeenth-Century Norwich: Politics, Religion and Government, 1620–1690* (Oxford, 1979), pp. 80–84. For those with worsening records of payment or difficulties in getting officials to serve from 1637 onwards see Barnes, *Somerset*, ch. 8, esp. pp. 228–33; M. A. Faraday, 'Shipmoney in Herefordshire', in *Woolhope Naturalists' Field Club*, 41 (1974), 219–29, esp. pp. 226–7; Clive Holmes, *Seventeenth-Century Lincolnshire* (Lincoln, 1980), p. 131; Ketton-Cremer, *Norfolk*, p. 94; Mark Stoyle, *Loyalty and Locality: Popular Allegiance in Devon during the English Civil War* (Exeter, 1994), pp. 172–6.
99. For the politics of Star Chamber see Sharpe, *Personal Rule*, esp. pp. 665–82; for its wider history see Hindle, *State and Social Change*, ch. 3 and the references therein.
100. Quoted in Marshall, *Reformation England*, p. 197.
101. For religious policies in the 1630s see ibid., ch. 8; Kenneth Fincham (ed.), *The Early Stuart Church, 1603–1642* (Basingstoke, 1993). Sharpe, *Personal Rule*, ch. 6, is, as always, full and informative and sympathetic to the views and aims of the regime.
102. Peter Lake, 'The Laudian Style: Order, Uniformity and the Pursuit of Holiness in the 1630s', in Fincham (ed.), *Early Stuart Church*, pp. 161–85, quotation at p. 167; Andrew Foster, 'The Clerical Estate Revitalised', in ibid., pp. 93–113; Holmes, *Lincolnshire*, pp. 112–21. For the argument that fears for the doctrine of predestination were not at the heart of the controversies, at least outside the universities, and that there had been other periods when it had been more threatened, see Peter White, *Predestination, Policy and Polemic: Conflict and Consensus in the English Church from the Reformation to the Civil*

War (Cambridge, 1992). For a good overview and further references see Cressy, *England on Edge*, pp. 133–41.

103. For the local appeal of Laudianism among Catholics and anti- or non-Puritans see Michael Questier, 'Arminianism, Catholicism and Puritanism in England during the 1630s', *HJ*, 49 (2006), 53–28; Alexandra Walsham, 'The Parochial Roots of Laudianism Revisited: Catholics, Anti-Calvinists and "Parish Anglicans" in Early Stuart England', *Journal of Ecclesiastical History*, 49 (1988), 620–51; and for the 'multiple realities' of parish life see Christopher Haigh, 'The Troubles of Thomas Pestell: Parish Squabbles and Ecclesiastical Politics in Caroline England', *JBS*, 41 (2002), 403–28. For a judicious overview of the academic debate about the origins and appeal of 'Laudianism' see Marshall, *Reformation England*, pp. 199–205, which contains the key references. For examples of local enforcement see Anthony Fletcher, *A County Community in Peace and War: Sussex 1600–1660* (London, 1975), ch. 4; Holmes, *Lincolnshire*, pp. 112–21; Evans, *Norwich*, pp. 84–104; Eales, *Puritans and Roundheads*, pp. 84–8; Hughes, *Warwickshire*, pp. 104–11; J. F. Merritt, *The Social World of Early Modern Westminster: Abbey, Court and Community, 1525–1640* (Manchester, 2005), pp. 343–51.

104. For the complexities see Anthony Milton, *Catholic and Reformed: Roman and Protestant Churches in English Protestant Thought, 1600–1640* (Cambridge, 1994), ch. 8, esp. pp. 187–209.

105. Caroline Hibbard, *Charles I and the Popish Plot* (Chapel Hill, NC, 1983), esp. chs. 2–3, quotation at p. 71; Caroline Hibbard, 'Henrietta Maria (1609–1669)', *ODNB*, 26, pp. 392–406. For a rounded view of the cultural and political role of Henrietta Maria's court see Caroline Hibbard, 'Henrietta Maria in the 1630s: Perspectives on the Role of Consort Queens in *Ancien Régime* Courts', in Atherton and Sanders (eds.), *The 1630s*, pp. 92–110.

106. For a summary and further references see Braddick, *State Formation*, esp. pp. 294–8, 309–10.

107. Ibid., pp. 298–301.

108. Quoted in Cogswell, *Home Divisions*, pp. 189–90 (the sermon was published in 1635).

109. See, for example, Claire S. Schen, 'Constructing the Poor in Early Seventeenth-Century London', *Albion*, 32:3 (2000), 450–63; Claire S. Schen, *Charity and Lay Piety in Reformation London 1500–1620* (Aldershot, 2002), p. 235. For Scots in the European wars see Allan I. Macinnes, *The British Revolution, 1629–1660* (Basingstoke, 2005), esp. pp. 50–54; for the English see David Trim, 'Calvinist Internationalism and the English Officer Corps, 1562–1642', *History Compass*, 4/6 (2006), 1024–48. Cromwell may have been one of them, although probably not: Barry Coward, *Oliver Cromwell* (Harlow, 1991), p. 8.

110. The best account of the ritual construction of community is Daniel C. Beaver, *Parish Communities and Religious Conflict in the Vale of Gloucester 1590–1690* (Cambridge, Mass., 1998), esp. intro., chs. 1–3. See also David Cressy, *Birth, Marriage and Death: Ritual, Religion, and the Life-Cycle in Tudor and Stuart England* (Oxford, 1997); for churching see esp. ch. 9. For an account of pewing emphasizing community against a general stress on hierarchy, and with full references to the literature it is attacking, see Christopher W. Marsh, ' "Common Prayer" in England 1560–1640: The View from the Pew', *PP*, 171 (2001), 66–94.

111. Sharpe, *Personal Rule*, pp. 751–7; for John Pym's flirtation with migration see Anthony Fletcher, *The Outbreak of the English Civil War* (London, 1981), p. xxi; for Lord Say and Sele and Lord Brooke see Russell, *Fall*, p. 1; for Cromwell's possible flirtation see Coward, *Cromwell*, p. 8. Eighty thousand left for the New World during the 1630s (Macinnes, *British Revolution*, p. 64), but only a fraction of this movement can be accounted for by religious exiles. Twenty thousand left England for New England: John Spurr, *English Puritanism 1603–1689* (Basingstoke, 1998), p. 91. For an excellent overview see Alison Games, 'Migration', in David Armitage and Michael J. Braddick (eds.), *The British Atlantic World, 1500–1800* (Basingstoke, 2002), pp. 31–50.

112. For the general problem see Spurr, *Puritanism*, pp. 90–93. For Puritan acquiescence, or silence, during the 1630s and the role of networks in sustaining the godly in their faith see Eales, *Puritans and Roundheads*, pp. 10–13 and ch. 3; Fletcher, *Sussex*, ch. 3; Cressy, *England on Edge*, pp. 141–6; Barnes, *Somerset*, pp. 21–3. Of course, this solidarity and mutual support might also serve to divide the godly from their neighbours.

113. For the complexities of Puritan attitudes in the 1630s see Peter Lake, ' "A Charitable Christian Hatred": The Godly and Their Enemies in the 1630s', in Christopher Durston and Jacqueline Eales (eds.), *The Culture of English Puritanism, 1560–1700* (Basingstoke, 1996), pp. 145–83; and for a case study see John Fielding, 'Opposition to the Personal Rule of Charles I: The Diary of Robert Woodford, 1637–1641', reprinted in Peter Gaunt (ed.), *The English Civil War* (Oxford, 2000), pp. 104–27.

114. Sharpe, *Personal Rule*, pp. 758–65, quotation at p. 763.

115. This case is eloquently stated by Cromartie, *Constitutionalist Revolution*, esp. pp. 254–6.

3. Drawing Swords in the King's Service

1. Andy Wood, *Riot, Rebellion and Popular Politics in Early Modern England* (Basingstoke, 2002), p. 127. Wood reads this incident differently. For impressment in 1639 see M. C. Fissel, *The Bishops' Wars: Charles I's Campaigns against Scotland 1638–1640* (Cambridge, 1994), pp. 224–41; for Cheshire and the war effort see map 1, and pp. 12–18.

2. All examples from Conrad Russell, *The Fall of the British Monarchies 1637–1642* (Oxford, 1991), pp. 85–7. For the circulation of Covenanter propaganda see Joseph Black, ' "Pikes and Protestations": Scottish Texts in England, 1639–40', *Publishing History*, 42 (1997), 5–19; Joad Raymond, *Pamphlets and Pamphleteering in Early Modern Britain* (Cambridge, 2003), pp. 181–7; Jacqueline Eales, *Puritans and Roundheads: The Harleys of Brampton Bryan and the Outbreak of the English Civil War* (Cambridge, 1990), pp. 91–5.

3. Russell, *Fall*, pp. 85–6: they had refused to remove their hats during the reading of the royal proclamation against the Scots. Two of them claimed that they had done so initially but then put them back on because the church was cold.

4. Fissel, *Bishops' Wars*, pp. 18–22; Russell, *Fall*, pp. 84–5. For Brooke see Ann Hughes, 'Greville, Robert, Second Baron Brooke of Beauchamps Court (1607–1643)', *ODNB*, 23, pp. 792–5; Ann Hughes, *Politics, Society and Civil War in Warwickshire, 1620–1660* (Cambridge, 1987), esp. pp. 120–26. For the Providence Island Company see Karen Ordahl Kupperman, *Providence Island 1630–1641: The Other Puritan Colony* (Cambridge, 1993).

5. Russell, *Fall*, pp. 82–3, 87–8.

6. Peter Donald, *An Uncounselled King: Charles I and the Scottish Troubles, 1637–1641* (Cambridge, 1990), pp. 81–2.

7. Ibid., p. 71; Russell, *Fall*, pp. 79–80.

8. Ronald G. Asch, 'Wentworth, Thomas, First Earl of Strafford (1593–1641)', *ODNB*, 58, pp. 142–57. See also J. F. Merritt (ed.), *The Political World of Thomas Wentworth, Earl of Strafford, 1621–1641* (Cambridge, 1996); G. C. F. Forster, 'Faction and County Government in Early Stuart Yorkshire', *Northern History*, 11 (1976 for 1975), 70–86.

9. Russell, *Fall*, p. 80.

10. 1639: Fissel, *Bishops' Wars*, p. 24 – this was roughly the same size as the army of the Covenanters; 1640: Austin Woolrych, *Britain in Revolution 1625–1660* (Oxford, 2002), p. 145; see also Fissel, *Bishops' Wars*, pp. 45–53.

11. Northumberland to Wentworth, 23 July 1638: William Knowler, *The Earl of Strafford's Letters and Dispatches*, 2 vols. (London, 1739), II, p. 186. Russell reports similar views from Northumberland in 1640: *Fall*, p. 131. See also David Cressy, *England on Edge: Crisis and Revolution 1640–1642* (Oxford, 2006), p. 80.

12. Fissel, *Bishops' Wars*, pp. 246–9.

13. For impressment in general see Michael J. Braddick, *State Formation in Early Modern England, c. 1550–1700* (Cambridge, 2000), pp. 196–9 and the references therein.

14. Fissel, *Bishops' Wars*, p. 237. A sidesman was a minor official in the church, responsible for greeting the congregation and seating them.

15. Ibid., pp. 232–6; Victor L. Stater, 'The Lord Lieutenancy on the Eve of the Civil Wars: The Impressment of George Plowright', *HJ*, 29 (1986), 279–96. For Sibthorpe, see above, p. 48. He was vocal too about divisions later in 1639: Russell, *Fall*, p. 85.

16. Fissel, *Bishops' Wars*, pp. 226–32.

17. For financial questions see ibid., pp. 124–37; for reluctant nobles and the officer corps see ibid., pp. 18–22, 78–80, 152–62. For the problems of arms supply see ibid., pp. 90–110; Richard Winship Stewart, *The English Ordnance Office 1585–1625: A Case Study in Bureaucracy* (Woodbridge, 1996).

18. For the weakness of the arms market see Fissel, *Bishops' Wars*, pp. 98–106. Some of the difficulties in the case of the officer corps were political, however: ibid., pp. 86–7.

19. Edward M. Furgol, 'Scotland Turned Sweden: The Scottish Covenanters and the Military Revolution', in John Morrill (ed.), *The Scottish National Covenant in Its British Context 1638–1651* (Edinburgh, 1990), pp. 134–54. Fissel argues that the Covenanters enjoyed considerable superiority in committee and command structure, officer corps and infantry, but that they might not have been able to sustain a campaign for very long: *Bishops' Wars*, pp. 38, 73–7, 81–2, 244–6; for the weaknesses of the Covenanters' army, which he sees as bluffing the King, see David Stevenson, *The Scottish Revolution, 1637–44: The Triumph of the Covenanters* (Edinburgh, 2003), esp. pp. 127–31, 141–51.

20. For doubts on the Covenanter side see Stevenson, *Scottish Revolution*, esp. pp. 145–6, 151, 154–5. For an evaluation of the relative strengths see Fissel, *Bishops' Wars*, pp. 31–2.

21. Fissel, *Bishops' Wars*, pp. 24–9; for Leslie's trick see pp. 28–9.

22. Russell, *Fall*, pp. 71–90.

23. Stevenson, *Scottish Revolution*, pp. 155–6; Russell, *Fall*, pp. 63–8.

24. Stevenson, *Scottish Revolution*, pp. 156–61.

25. Hamilton declined the offer, saying to the King that he would not be trusted in Scotland and would be required to give concessions that would make him unpopular with Charles: Stevenson, ibid., p. 160. Russell suggests that this was because Hamilton thought Charles was willing to see the abolition of episcopacy, and that in the light of Hamilton's posture on this question the previous year, this would leave him no personal credibility with the Covenanters: Russell, *Fall*, p. 67.

26. Stevenson, *Scottish Revolution*, pp. 162–76.

27. For the letter see ibid., pp. 180–81.

28. Russell, *Fall*, pp. 92–3; for the financial position see Fissel, *Bishops' Wars*, ch. 3.

29. HEH, EL 7830, Castle to Bridgewater, 9 April 1640; HEH EL 7831, Castle to Bridgewater, 11 April 1640. A window that would accommodate five or six people would cost no less than £5, another that would accommodate only three or four would cost £3 10s. Only a fiscal historian or a curmudgeon would point out that this was a large sum by comparison, for example, with a ship money assessment. For other examples of anticipation see David Underdown, *Somerset in the Civil War and Interregnum* (Newton Abbot, 1973), p. 24; Eales, *Puritans and Roundheads*, pp. 94–5; Cressy, *England on Edge*, p. 111 (where the promise of an election was a reason to postpone emigration); Hughes, *Warwickshire*, pp. 116–17; A. R. Warmington, *Civil War, Interregnum and Restoration in Gloucestershire 1640–1672* (Woodbridge, 1997), pp. 24–6, 27–8.

30. Woolrych, *Britain in Revolution*, pp. 130–31. For the elections see Derek Hirst, *The Representative of the People: Voters and Voting in England under the Early Stuarts* (Cambridge, 1975), pp. 147–53 and appendix 4; Richard Cust, ' "Patriots" and "Popular Spirits": Narratives of Conflict in Early Stuart Politics', in Nicholas Tyacke (ed.), *The English Revolution c. 1590–1720* (Manchester, 2007), 43–67. Conrad Russell suggested that these elections represented a significant departure as organized godly lobbying overcame the more general reluctance to see elections contested: Russell, *Fall*, pp. 94–8. See

also Anthony Fletcher, *A County Community in Peace and War: Sussex 1600–1660* (London, 1975), pp. 243–8.

31. Esther S. Cope and Willson H. Coates (eds.), *Proceedings of the Short Parliament of 1640*, Camden 4th ser., 19 (London, 1977), pp. 115–18, 122–3. For the text of the letter and its translation see *LJ*, iv, p. 48.

32. Russell finds this reading unconvincing (Russell, *Fall*, p. 103) and Woolrych's verdict is that it was 'absurd, and probably struck his hearers so': Woolrych, *Britain in Revolution*, p. 133.

33. Cope and Coates (eds.), *Proceedings*, p. 134; Stevenson, *Scottish Revolution*, pp. 183–4.

34. Cope and Coates (eds.), *Proceedings*, pp. 135–8. The image of a biblical plague was often deployed by those critical of revenue officers: Michael J. Braddick, *The Nerves of State: Taxation and the Financing of the English State, 1558–1714* (Manchester, 1996), pp. 170, 206–9, 220–22.

35. Cope and Coates (eds.), *Proceedings*, pp. 138–43.

36. The precise extent of the co-operation is not clear: Russell, *Fall*, pp. 122–3. For Charles's suspicions see also Stevenson, *Scottish Revolution*, p. 188. For a general account of the balance of opinion in the Short Parliament see Russell, *Fall*, pp. 90–123.

37. Russell, *Fall*, pp. 97–9.

38. Cope and Coates (eds.), *Proceedings*, pp. 148–57, quotations at pp. 149, 155; Russell, *Fall*, pp. 106–7. For Pym: Conrad Russell, 'Pym, John (1584–1643)', *ODNB*, 45, pp. 623–40.

39. The comparison is Russell's, *Fall*, p. 108.

40. Ibid., p. 110.

41. Keith Lindley, *Popular Politics and Religion in Civil War London* (Aldershot, 1997), pp. 4–6; HEH, EL 7833, Castle to Bridgewater, 12 May 1640. Castle saw this as the direct result of the 'two pasquils that were affixed to the pillars of the old Exchange the last week, [which] have brought forth this sour fruit'. The crowd is generally estimated to have comprised between 500 and 800 people, although the Venetian ambassador put the number at 2,000: Lindley, *Popular Politics*, p. 4n; Peter Razzell and Edward Razzell (eds.), *The English Civil War: A Contemporary Account*, vol. 2: *1640–1642* (London, 1996), p. 14. Laud thought it 500: Keith Lindley (ed.), *The English Civil War and Revolution: A Source Book* (London, 1998), p. 43. See also Cressy, *England on Edge*, pp. 118–22.

42. HEH, EL 7836, Castle to Bridgewater, 27 May 1640. The letter reports his anxious black humour about when to return.

43. Lindley, *Popular Politics*, pp. 4–6.

44. Ibid., pp. 26–35.

45. Ibid., pp. 5–6; HEH EL 7835, Castle to Bridgewater, 18 May 1640; EL 7837, Castle to Bridgewater, 9 June 1640. See also EL 7834, Castle to Bridgewater, 15 May 1640: the rioters aimed at 'the Fox [Laud], and the little bird [Matthew Wren, Bishop of Norwich]' as well as some at St James and 'the swarms of the French'. For Marie de Medici see Caroline Hibbard, *Charles I and the Popish Plot* (Chapel Hill, NC, 1983), esp. pp. 87–8, 151–2, 198–9.

46. Lindley, *Popular Politics*, pp. 7–8. For Charles's reaction, and the torture of Archer, see also Russell, *Fall*, p. 129. This may reflect the extent to which Charles was unnerved by the disturbances: Castle reported that precedents were being sought for recalling a parliament without new elections ('I hear they have not as yet found any'), HEH, EL 7834, Castle to Bridgewater, 15 May 1640.

47. For the text of the canons see the extract in J. P. Kenyon (ed.), *The Stuart Constitution: Documents and Commentary* (Cambridge, 1966), pp. 166–8; Julian Davies, *The Caroline Captivity of the English Church* (Oxford, 1992), ch. 7. For Convocation and the Royal Supremacy for Charles's role and intentions see Russell, *Fall*, pp. 15–16, 136–9.

48. Russell's verdict is that it would have been plausible to argue that the campaign should go without a parliament, or that Charles should hold a parliament in order to secure support and supply; what was not plausible policy was to hold a parliament after eleven

years without being willing to consult, discuss, secure consent and redress grievances: Russell, *Fall*, pp. 92–4.

49. Ibid., pp. 126–8; for an overview see Fissel, *Bishops' Wars*, pp. 39–44.

50. See Fissel, *Bishops' Wars*, esp. pp. 119–20, 162–6, 172–3; for the expedition of the King to Hamburg see also HEH, EL 7841, Castle to Bridgewater, 1 July 1640; for hopes of Spanish help see also Russell, *Fall*, p. 129.

51. Quoted in ibid., p. 123.

52. HEH, EL 7836, Castle to Bridgewater, 27 May 1640. These rumours were bad for credit, among other things: Fissel, *Bishops' Wars*, p. 123.

53. Russell, *Fall*, pp. 106 and 107n.

54. HEH, EL 7817, Castle to Bridgewater, 17 January 1640; EL 7819, Castle to Bridgewater, 28 January 1640; EL 7822, Castle to Bridgewater, 12 February 1640; EL 7845, Castle to Bridgewater, 1 August 1640; EL 7846, Castle to Bridgewater, 4 August 1640; EL 7848, Bridgewater to Castle, 10 August 1640.

55. Lindley, *Popular Politics*, pp. 8–10.

56. Ibid., p. 7.

57. Ibid., pp. 44–5; for provincial echoes of the riots see also Cressy, *England on Edge*, pp. 122–4.

58. Russell, *Fall*, pp. 93–4, 132–6; John Morrill, *Revolt in the Provinces: The People of England and the Tragedies of War 1630–1648*, 2nd edn (Harlow, 1999), pp. 44–5; Hughes, *Warwickshire*, pp. 114–18. As Hughes points out, it was only in relation to some controversial policies that government collapsed.

59. Fissel, *Bishops' Wars*, pp. 119–23. For the suggestion that the scheme was a bluff intended to lever money from the Corporation of London see HEH, EL 7844, Castle to Bridgewater, 25 July 1640. The proposal certainly did coincide with an approach to the City for money: Fissel, *Bishops' Wars*, p. 122.

60. Fissell, *Bishops' Wars*, chs. 5–6; Cressy, *England on Edge*, pp. 73–90.

61. HEH, EL 7835, Castle to Bridgewater, 18 May 1640.

62. Fissel, *Bishops' Wars*, pp. 272–3; Russell, *Fall*, p. 131; HEH, EL 7837, Castle to Bridgewater, 9 June 1640.

63. HEH, EL 7842, Castle to Bridgewater, 6 July 1640; EL 7838, Castle to Bridgewater, 23 June 1640.

64. Russell, *Fall*, pp. 130–31.

65. Fissel, *Bishops' Wars*, esp. pp. 270–72.

66. Ibid., pp. 285–6.

67. Ibid., p. 271.

68. Ibid., pp. 278–83. HEH, EL 7838, Castle to Bridgewater, 23 June 1640. The soldiers, like Castle, referred to him as Moon. See also Cressy, *England on Edge*, pp. 87, 88–9, 91–2; Mark Stoyle, *Loyalty and Locality: Popular Allegiance in Devon during the English Civil War* (Exeter, 1994), pp. 168–9, 178.

69. HEH EL 7765, Mr Roger Wilford minister his certificate, 16 August 1640. Nehemiah Wallington collected examples of these actions, which he clearly regarded as religious acts, albeit ones about which he felt ambivalent: BL Sloane MS 1457, fos. 60r–66v; BL Add MS 21935, fos. 88r–91r; R. Webb (ed.), *Historical Notices of Events Occurring Chiefly in the Reign of Charles I by Nehemiah Wallington*, 2 vols. (London, 1869), pp. 122–6.

70. John Walter, ' "Abolishing superstition with sedition"?: The Politics of Popular Iconoclasm in England, 1640–1642', *PP*, 183 (2004), 79–123; John Walter, 'Popular Iconoclasm and the Politics of the Parish in Eastern England, 1640–1642', *HJ*, 47 (2004), 261–90.

71. Cressy, *England on Edge*, pp. 90–91.

72. John Walter, ' "Affronts & insolencies": The Voices of Radwinter and Popular Opposition to Laudianism', *EHR*, 122 (2007), 35–60.

73. John Walter, 'Anti-Popery and the Stour Valley Riots of 1642', in David Chadd (ed.),

History of Religious Dissent in East Anglia, III (Norwich, 1996), pp. 121–40, at pp. 121–2. For the fear of fire see Keith Thomas, *Religion and the Decline of Magic: Studies in Popular Belief in Sixteenth- and Seventeenth-Century England* (Harmondsworth, 1991 edn), pp. 17–20.

74. HEH, EL 7860, Castle to Bridgewater, 24 September 1640. See also EL 7863, Castle to Bridgewater, 29 September 1640; Hibbard, *Popish Plot*, pp. 166–7.

75. The examples are from Russell, *Fall*, pp. 139, 142. Russell's judgement that 'It would seem that soldiers were capable of turning against anyone they could blame for their predicament' (p. 142) seems no more true of 'soldiers' than of, say, 'the aristocracy'.

76. HEH, EL 7847, Castle to Bridgewater, 8 August 1640.

77. Stevenson, *Scottish Revolution*, pp. 192–202.

78. Ibid., pp. 205–7; Russell, *Fall*, pp. 143–4; Cressy, *England on Edge*, pp. 93–4.

79. For the Covenanters' difficulties see Stevenson, *Scottish Revolution*, pp. 208–10. Russell emphasizes the fact that the English took the wrong ground: Russell, *Fall*, pp. 144–5. The battle is described in Fissel, *Bishops' Wars*, pp. 53–9..

80. Russell, *Fall*, pp. 149–64; Stevenson, *Scottish Revolution*, pp. 210–12.

81. John Adamson, *The Noble Revolt: The Overthrow of Charles I* (London, 2007). Adamson's important study was published as this book went to press, and I have been unable to take full account of its findings. For the peerage see also Brian Manning, 'The Aristocracy and the Downfall of Charles I', in Brian Manning (ed.), *Politics, Religion and the English Civil War* (London, 1973), pp. 37–80.

82. Eales, *Puritans and Roundheads*, pp. 98–9; for London see above, pp. 116–17.

83. Russell, *Fall*, pp. 157–64.

84. Holmes, *Lincolnshire*, p. 137.

85. Pauline Croft, 'Trading with the Enemy, 1585–1604', *HJ*, 32 (1989), 281–302; Michael J. Braddick, ' "Upon this instant extraordinarie occasion": Military Mobilisation in Yorkshire in the Armada Year and Thereafter', *HLQ*, 61 (2000 for 1998), 429–55.

86. The exchange is reported in Quentin Skinner, *The Foundations of Modern Political Thought*, vol. 2: *The Age of Reformation* (Cambridge, 1978), p. 189.

87. Stevenson, *Scottish Revolution*, pp. 133–7.

88. Russell, *Fall*, p. 86; *CSPD*, 1638–9, p. 167; 1639–40, p. 585.

89. See also David Smith: 'In many ways it makes sense to see the Short Parliament as a continuation, indeed a finale, of the Parliaments of the 1620s': *The Stuart Parliaments 1603–1689* (London, 1999), p. 120.

90. For the following see David Como, 'Secret Printing, the Crisis of 1640 and the Origins of Civil War Radicalism', *PP*, 196 (2007), 37–82.

91. Ibid. See Jonathan I. Israel, *Radical Enlightenment: Philosophy and the Making of Modernity 1650–1750* (Oxford, 2001).

92. Lindley, *Popular Politics*, p. 33.

93. BL, Add MS 21,935, fos. 12r–12v. This does not seem to have been reproduced in Webb (ed.), *Historical Notices*. For Wallington see Paul Seaver, *Wallington's World: A Puritan Artisan in 17th Century London* (London, 1985).

94. HEH, EL 7859, A letter from a gentleman of Newcastle to a friend in London, 8 September 1640. This letter circulated in manuscript copy: see below, n. 98. For the power of prophecy see Thomas, *Religion and the Decline of Magic*, ch. 13, esp. pp. 469–93. For influential studies see Ottavia Niccoli, *Prophecy and People in Renaissance Italy* (Princeton, NJ, 1990); Sharon Jansen, *Political Protest and Prophecy under Henry VIII* (Woodbridge, 1991); Ethan Howard Shagan, 'Rumours and Popular Politics in the Reign of Henry VIII', in Tim Harris (ed.), *The Politics of the Excluded, c. 1500–1850* (Basingstoke, 2001), pp. 30–66; Bertrand Taithe and Tim Thornton (eds.), *Prophecy: The Power of Inspired Language in History 1300–2000* (Stroud, 1997). Prophecy is placed in the broader context of the radical potential within popular politics by Krista J. Kesselring, 'Deference and Dissent in Tudor England: Reflections on Sixteenth-Century Protest', *History Compass*, 3:1 (2005).

95. HEH, EL 7831, Castle to Bridgewater, 11 April 1640; EL 7832, Castle to Bridgewater, 11 May 1640; EL 7842, Castle to Bridgewater, 6 July 1640; EL 7838, Castle to Bridgewater, 23 June 1640. For other examples see Cressy, *England on Edge*, pp. 30–36.

96. Fissel, *Bishops' Wars*, pp. 25–6. According to Robert Woodford's diary, the eclipse was observed in Northamptonshire between four and five o'clock in the afternoon, ibid., n. 82.

97. The phrase 'oligarchic centralism' is from Allan I. Macinnes, 'The Scottish Constitution, 1638–1651: The Rise and Fall of Oligarchic Centralism', in Morrill (ed.), *Scottish National Covenant*, pp. 106–33.

98. HEH, EL 7859, A letter from a gentleman of Newcastle to a friend in London, 8 September 1640. Howell notes four existing manuscript copies of this letter: Roger Howell, 'Newcastle and the Nation: The Seventeenth-Century Experience', in R. C. Richardson (ed.), *The English Civil Wars: Local Aspects* (Stroud, 1997), pp. 309–29, p. 326n. For sympathy with the Covenanters in Newcastle prior to their occupation, and diminishing sympathy thereafter, see Roger Howell, *Newcastle upon Tyne and the Puritan Revolution: A Study of Civil War in North England* (Oxford, 1967), esp. pp. 122–41. Following defeat, anxious measures were taken for defence against the Scots, particularly in the north: Cressy, *England on Edge*, pp. 39, 96. For the economic dislocation arising from the disruption of the coal trade and for the unpopularity of the royal army see ibid., pp. 57–9, 97–103; for the latter point see also Ronan Bennett, 'War and Disorder: Policing the Soldiery in Civil War Yorkshire', in Mark Charles Fissel (ed.), *War and Government in Britain, 1598–1650* (Manchester, 1991), pp. 248–73, at pp. 251–3.

4. We Dream Now of a Golden Age

1. I am using the term loosely to embrace not just the City of London, but Westminster and suburbs too. There is a huge literature on early modern London. For an overview and bibliography see Jeremy Boulton, 'London 1540–1700', in Peter Clark (ed.), *The Cambridge Urban History of Britain*, vol. 2: *1540–1840* (Cambridge, 2000), pp. 315–46; and the important essays collected in A. L. Beier and Roger Finlay (eds.), *London 1500–1700: The Making of the Metropolis* (London, 1986), and Paul Griffiths and Mark S. R. Jenner (eds.), *Londinopolis: Essays in the Cultural and Social History of Early Modern London* (Manchester, 2000). For its overseas trade see also Robert Brenner, *Merchants and Revolution: Commercial Change, Political Conflict and London's Overseas Traders, 1550–1653* (Cambridge, 1993), and Ben Coates, *The Impact of the English Civil War on the Economy of London, 1642–50* (Aldershot, 2004). For the increase in litigation see Christopher W. Brooks, *Pettyfoggers and Vipers of the Commonwealth: The 'Lower Branch' of the Legal Profession in Early Modern England* (Cambridge, 1986); Christopher Brooks, 'Interpersonal Conflict and Social Tension: Civil Litigation in England, 1640–1870', in A. L. Beier, David Cannadine and James M. Rosenheim (eds.), *The First Modern Society: Essays in English History in Honour of Lawrence Stone* (Cambridge, 1989), pp. 357–99. For Westminster see J. F. Merritt, *The Social World of Early Modern Westminster: Abbey, Court and Community, 1525–1640* (Manchester, 2005). For the national growth of consumption see Linda Levy Peck, *Consuming Splendor: Society and Culture in Seventeenth-Century England* (Cambridge, 2005).

2. For an overview and further reference see C. G. A. Clay, *Economic Expansion and Social Change. England 1500–1700*, 2 vols. 1: *People, Land and Towns* (Cambridge, 1984), esp. pp. 187–91; E. A. Wrigley, 'A Simple Model of London's Importance in Changing English Society and Economy, 1650–1750', reprinted in E. A. Wrigley, *People, Cities and Wealth: The Transformation of Traditional Society* (Oxford, 1987), pp. 133–56.

3. Valerie Pearl, *London and the Outbreak of the Puritan Revolution: City Government and National Politics 1625–1643* (Oxford, 1961), chs. 1–2; for the earlier period see Ian W. Archer, *The Pursuit of Stability: Social Relations in Elizabethan London* (Cambridge, 1991); for the religious diversity and the 'Puritan underground' see Peter Lake, *The*

Boxmaker's Revenge: 'Orthodoxy' and 'Heterodoxy' and the Politics of the Parish in Early Stuart London (Manchester, 2001); David R. Como, *Blown by the Spirit: Puritanism and the Emergence of an Antinomian Underground in pre-Civil-War England* (Stanford, 2004); David R. Como, 'Predestination and Political Conflict in Laud's London', *HJ*, 46 (2003), 263–94; David R. Como and Peter Lake, 'Puritans, Antinomians and Laudians in Caroline London: The Strange Case of Peter Shaw and its Contexts', *Journal of Ecclesiastical History*, 50 (1999), 684–715; Peter Lake and David R. Como, ' "Orthodoxy" and Its Discontents: Dispute Settlement and the Production of "Consensus" in the London (Puritan) "Underground" ', *JBS*, 39 (2000), 34–70.

4. Roger Finlay and Beatrice Shearer, 'Population Growth and Suburban Expansion', in Beier and Finlay (eds.), *London*, pp. 37–59; Jeremy Boulton, *Neighbourhood and Society: A London Suburb in the Seventeenth Century* (Cambridge, 1987).

5. For important overviews see Ian Archer, 'Popular Politics in the Sixteenth and Early Seventeenth Centuries', in Griffiths and Jenner (eds.), *Londinopolis*, pp. 26–46; and Keith Lindley, 'Riot Prevention and Control in Early Stuart London', *TRHS*, 5th ser., 33 (1983), 109–26. For the Protestant calendar see David Cressy, *Bonfires and Bells: National Memory and the Protestant Calendar in Elizabethan and Stuart England* (London, 1989); for 1623 see Thomas Cogswell, 'England and the Spanish Match', in Richard Cust and Ann Hughes (eds.), *Conflict in Early Stuart England: Studies in Religion and Politics 1603–1642* (London, 1989), pp. 107–33.

6. Keith Lindley, *Popular Politics and Religion in Civil War London* (Aldershot, 1997), p. 6. For evocations of talk on the streets of revolutionary London see Ann Hughes, *Gangraena and the Struggle for the English Revolution* (Oxford, 2004), ch. 3; Malcolm Gaskill, *Witchfinders: A Seventeenth-Century English Tragedy* (London, 2005), pp. 135–6.

7. Lindley, *Popular Politics*, pp. 8–9; see also David Cressy, *England on Edge: Crisis and Revolution 1640–1642* (Oxford, 2006), pp. 114–16.

8. Lindley, *Popular Politics*, pp. 10, 33; Pearl, *London and the Outbreak*, pp. 174–5.

9. Anthony Fletcher, *The Outbreak of the English Civil War* (London, 1981), pp. 1–2; David Underdown, *Somerset in the Civil War and Interregnum* (Newton Abbot, 1973), p. 25; Cressy, *England on Edge*, pp. 40–41.

10. Hugh Trevor-Roper, 'Three Foreigners: The Philosophers of the Puritan Revolution', reprinted in Hugh Trevor-Roper, *Religion, the Reformation, and Social Change, and Other Essays* (London, 1984), pp. 237–93; J. H. Elliott, 'The Year of the Three Ambassadors', in Hugh Lloyd-Jones, Valerie Pearl and Blair Worden (eds.), *History and Imagination: Essays in Honour of H. R. Trevor-Roper* (London, 1981), pp. 165–81.

11. Following the summary in Austin Woolrych, *Britain in Revolution 1625–1660* (Oxford, 2002), pp. 157–8. For the debate about the extent of popular participation in parliamentary elections prior to 1640 see Derek Hirst, *The Representative of the People: Voters and Voting in England under the Early Stuarts* (Cambridge, 1975); Mark A. Kishlansky, *Parliamentary Selection: Social and Political Choice in Early Modern England* (Cambridge, 1986); Richard Cust, 'Politics and the Electorate in the 1620s', in Cust and Hughes, *Conflict in Early Stuart England*, pp. 134–67. For some examples see Anthony Fletcher, *A County Community in Peace and War: Sussex 1600–1660* (London, 1975), pp. 248–51; Ann Hughes, *Politics, Society and Civil War in Warwickshire, 1620–1660* (Cambridge, 1987), pp. 119–30; A. R. Warmington, *Civil War, Interregnum and Restoration in Gloucestershire 1640–1672* (Woodbridge, 1997), pp. 26–8. Counties further from London may have had fewer ideological contests: Anthony Fletcher, 'National and Local Awareness in the County Communities', in Howard Tomlinson (ed.), *Before the English Civil War: Essays on Early Stuart Politics and Government* (London, 1983), pp. 151–74, at p. 173. For the petitions see also Fletcher, *Outbreak*, pp. xxv–xxvii.

12. John Rushworth, *Historical Collections: The Second Part* (London, 1686 edition), p. 1338. For another full transcript see Sheffield University Library, Hartlib Papers, 55/5/1a–4b. The denunciation of monopolists is quoted at greater length in Michael J. Braddick, *The Nerves of State: Taxation and Financing of the English State, 1558–1714*

(Manchester, 1996), pp. 208–9. It is possible that Colepeper did not actually deliver the speech, merely depositing a script with Rushworth, but this seems unlikely: Conrad Russell, *The Fall of the British Monarchies 1637–1642* (Oxford, 1991), p. 219n.

13. Woolrych, *Britain in Revolution*, p. 158.

14. Russell, *Fall*, pp. 214–21.

15. Ibid., pp. 221–2.

16. Brian Manning, *The English People and the English Revolution* (Harmondsworth, 1978), p. 14; see also EL 66705, Richard Kinge to Edward Parker, 12 December 1640. For the orchestration of this 'pageant of power', see John Adamson, *The Noble Revolt: The Overthrow of Charles I* (London, 2007), pp. 128–30.

17. Lindley, *Popular Politics*, p. 14.

18. Quoted in Manning, *English People*, p. 15; and Lindley, *Popular Politics*, p. 14. See also Russell, *Fall*, pp. 221–2.

19. Manning, *English People*, pp. 14–16. For Wallington see above, p. 109.

20. David L. Smith, *The Stuart Parliaments 1603–1689* (London, 1999), pp. 71–5; Fletcher, *Outbreak*, pp. 37–8; for the list of surviving select committees after the first purge see J. P. Kenyon, *The Stuart Constitution 1603–1688: Documents and Commentary* (Cambridge, 1966), pp. 216–17. For parliamentary procedure, and its predication on the importance of achieving consensus rather than decisions, see Mark A. Kishlansky, *The Rise of the New Model Army* (Cambridge, 1979), pp. 11–15, and on the Committee of the Whole House as a means to achieve that, Conrad Russell, *Parliaments and English Politics 1621–1629* (Oxford, 1979), pp. 38–42.

21. James S. Hart, *Justice upon Petition: The House of Lords and the Reformation of Justice 1621–1675* (London, 1991), pp. 3–4.

22. Russell, *Fall*, ch. 6, esp. pp. 164–205; David Stevenson, *The Scottish Revolution 1637–44: The Triumph of the Covenanters* (Edinburgh, 2003), pp. 214–23.

23. Fletcher, *Outbreak*, pp. 92–4; Russell, *Fall*, pp. 174–5. See, in general, Hugh Trevor-Roper, 'The Fast Sermons of the Long Parliament', reprinted in Trevor-Roper, *Religion, the Reformation, and Social Change*, pp. 297–344; and John Frederick Wilson, *Pulpit in Parliament: Puritanism during the English Civil Wars, 1640–8* (Princeton, NJ, 1969).

24. Russell, *Fall*, esp. pp. 164–7.

25. For their domination of the committees, and the influence that gave them over the flow and pace of business, see Adamson, *Noble Revolt*, esp. ch. 4.

26. For this and the following paragraphs see Conrad Russell, 'Pym, John (1584–1643)', *ODNB*, 45, pp. 624–40; Russell, *Fall*, chs. 5–6. Russell's position is challenged in Adamson, *Noble Revolt*, esp. ch. 5. Unfortunately this work appeared as the current book was going to press and I have been unable to take full account of its arguments.

27. See above, p. 92.

28. For the speech see Fletcher, *Outbreak*, pp. xix–xxv; Russell, *Fall*, pp. 216–17, quotation at p. 216.

29. For King Pym, see Jack H. Hexter, *The Reign of King Pym* (Cambridge, Mass., 1941). For more measured accounts of his role see Russell, 'Pym'; Russell, *Fall*; Woolrych, *Britain in Revolution*, pp. 164–7; John Morrill, 'The Unweariableness of Mr Pym: Influence and Eloquence in the Long Parliament', in Susan Dwyer Amussen and Mark A. Kishlansky (eds.), *Political Culture and Cultural Politics in Early Modern England: Essays Presented to David Underdown* (Manchester, 1995), pp. 19–54.

30. Conrad Russell, 'Russell, Francis, Fourth Earl of Bedford (*bap.* 1587, *d.* 1641)', *ODNB*, 48, pp. 241–50.

31. Russell, *Fall*, esp. pp. 238–58.

32. Ibid., ch. 6.

33. Lindley, *Popular Politics*, pp. 37–8, 51. Cressy, *England on Edge*, pp. 158–65, takes the most alarmed contemporary comment at face value; for the hopes of the godly see ibid., ch. 8.

34. Extracts reprinted in Kenyon, *Stuart Constitution*, pp. 171–5.

35. See above, pp. 5–6.
36. Lindley, pp. *Popular Politics*, pp. 14–16.
37. Fletcher, *Outbreak*, p. 92.
38. Ibid., p. 96; Hirst agrees that Dering was responding to constituency pressure, but feels that despite the moderation of the language Dering was probably seen as an advocate of the abolition of episcopacy: Derek Hirst, 'The Defection of Sir Edward Dering, 1640–1641', reprinted in Peter Gaunt (ed.), *The English Civil War* (Oxford, 2000), pp. 207–25, esp. pp. 216–17.
39. For the mobilization of other petitions see Fletcher, *Outbreak*, pp. 192–8; Anthony Fletcher, 'Petitioning and the Outbreak of the Civil War in Derbyshire', *Derbyshire Archaeological Journal*, 113 (1973), 34–8; David Zaret, *Origins of Democratic Culture: Printing, Petitions, and the Public Sphere in Early-Modern England* (Princeton, NJ, 2000), ch. 8. For detailed discussions of the local politics of petitions from the following autumn see John Walter, 'Confessional Politics in pre-Civil War Essex: Prayer Books, Profanations, and Petitions', *HJ*, 44 (2001), 677–701; Peter Lake, 'Puritans, Popularity and Petitions: Local Politics in National Context, Cheshire, 1641', in Thomas Cogswell, Richard Cust and Peter Lake (eds.), *Politics, Religion and Popularity in Early Stuart Britain: Essays in Honour of Conrad Russell* (Cambridge, 2002), pp. 259–89.
40. Compare the dates of delivery with the timings of important parliamentary debates: Fletcher, *Outbreak*, pp. 92, 98–103. For the development of the debates see also A. J. Fletcher, 'Concern for Renewal in the Root and Branch Debates of 1641', in Derek Baker (ed.), *Renaissance and Renewal in Christian History: Papers Read at the Fifteenth Summer Meeting and Sixteenth Winter Meeting of the Ecclesiastical History Society* (Studies in Church History, 14) (Oxford, 1977), pp. 279–86.
41. Fletcher, *Outbreak*, pp. 98–9.
42. Lindley, *Popular Politics*, pp. 17–18, quotation at p. 17. Such debates had a prehistory in early Stuart unease about 'popularity', and the ambivalent attitude towards the 'public sphere'. See above, pp. 48–53, 56 and the works cited there.
43. George Digby, *The third speech of the Lord George Digby* (London, 1641); Nathaniel Fiennes, *A speech of the honorable Nathanael Fiennes, (second son to the right honourable the Lord Say) in answere to the third speech of the Lord George Digby* (London, 1641).
44. Fletcher, *Outbreak*, pp. 99–107, quotations at pp. 99, 100.
45. Russell, *Fall*, pp. 223–4; for the text of the Act see Gardiner, *CD*, pp. 144–55, quotation at p. 144.
46. Fletcher, *Outbreak*, pp. 22–3.
47. Michael J. Braddick, *Parliamentary Taxation in Seventeenth-Century England: Local Administration and Response* (Woodbridge, 1994), ch. 2; for Henry Best see pp. 74–5.
48. Russell, *Fall*, pp. 234, 242.
49. Braddick, *Parliamentary Taxation*, pp. 81–3.
50. As a result of the financial difficulties of the Tudor and Stuart monarchies, this vision of the crown finances was increasingly unrealistic, but it remained widely held.
51. Braddick, *Nerves of State*, pp. 49–55, and, for the praetermitted custom, ibid., p. 133.
52. Ibid., pp. 52–3.
53. Russell, *Fall*, pp. 256–8, 346–50, 357–64, 436–7, and, for the 1641 Book of Rates, ibid., p. 256.
54. Ibid., p. 258.
55. Michael J. Braddick, 'Administrative Performance: The Representation of Political Authority in Early Modern England', in Michael J. Braddick and John Walter (eds.), *Negotiating Power in Early Modern Society: Order, Hierarchy and Subordination in Britain and Ireland* (Cambridge, 2001), pp. 166–87; Thomas Cogswell, *Home Divisions: Aristocracy, the State and Provincial Conflict* (Manchester, 1998); see above, pp. 65–7.
56. See above, p. 96. For a convincing reading of this crucial speech see Russell, *Fall*, pp. 125–9. For the impeachment see ibid., p. 211; Fletcher, *Outbreak*, pp. 3–4.
57. Russell, *Fall*, pp. 274–94; see also his important essays on 'The Theory of Treason in the

Trial of Strafford' and 'The First Army Plot of 1641', reprinted in Russell, *Unrevolutionary England, 1603–1642* (London, 1990), pp. 89–109 and 281–302; Fletcher, *Outbreak*, pp. 7–14, quotation at p. 14; Manning, *English People*, pp. 20–23. The account given here should be read in the light of John Adamson's important revision: Adamson, *Noble Revolt*, chs. 8–9.

58. Lindley, *Popular Politics*, pp. 21–2; HEH, EL 66707, John Blackburne to John Braddill, 4 May 1641; Manning, *English People*, pp. 23–5; Andrew Sharp, 'Lilburne, John (1615?–1657)', *ODNB*, 33, pp. 773–83.

59. Lindley, *Popular Politics*, p. 23; Manning, *English People*, p. 26; Tai Liu, 'Burges, Cornelius (d. 1665)', *ODNB*, 8, pp. 751–5.

60. Lindley, *Popular Politics*, p. 24; Manning, *English People*, pp. 26–8.

61. Lindley, *Popular Politics*, pp. 26–35; Pearl, *London and the Outbreak*, pp. 228–36.

62. Lindley, *Popular Politics*, pp. 25–6; Manning, *English People*, pp. 30–31; Terence Kilburn and Anthony Milton, 'The Public Context of the Trial and Execution of Strafford', in J. F. Merritt (ed.), *The Political World of Thomas Wentworth, Earl of Strafford, 1621–1641* (Cambridge, 1996), pp. 230–51, esp. pp. 242–51.

63. Lindley, *Popular Politics*, p. 26.

64. Fletcher, *Outbreak*, pp. 27–8; Russell, *Fall*, pp. 333, 340 (gelding); see also Manning, *English People*, p. 27; Cressy, *England on Edge*, p. 43.

65. There is a clear summary in Russell, 'Fall', pp. 248–9.

66. Smith, *Stuart Parliaments*, p. 124.

67. Fletcher, *Outbreak*, p. 167.

68. Braddick, *Parliamentary Taxation*, pp. 234–5. See also Fletcher, *Outbreak*, pp. 49–50.

69. For the negotiations see Russell, *Fall*, pp. 346–50, 357–64, 436–7. For the text see Gardiner, *CD*, pp. 159–62, quotations at pp. 160, 162.

70. For this calculation see Braddick, *Nerves of State*, pp. 9–12, and fig. 1.3.

71. David Stevenson, 'Graham, James, First Marquess of Montrose (1612–1650)', *ODNB*, 23, pp. 189–95.

72. For the text see Gardiner, *CD*, pp. 163–6. For the politics of this period see Fletcher, *Outbreak*, ch. 2; Russell, *Fall*, ch. 9.

73. Gardiner, *CD*, pp. 155–6. For a concise discussion of the introduction and contents of the Protestation see Fletcher, *Outbreak*, pp. 14–16; David Cressy, 'The Protestation Protested, 1641 and 1642', *HJ*, 45 (2002), 251–79, at pp. 253–6.

74. Fletcher, *Outbreak*, p. 113; for Baillie see Russell, *Fall*, pp. 294–5.

75. Fletcher, *Outbreak*, pp. 15–16; Edward Vallance, *Revolutionary England and the National Covenant: State Oaths, Protestantism and the Political Nation, 1553–1682* (Woodbridge, 2005), pp. 52–3; David Martin Jones, *Conscience and Allegiance in Seventeenth Century England: The Political Significance of Oaths and Engagements* (Woodbridge, 1999), esp. pp. 116–19, 273–4.

76. Fletcher, *Outbreak*, pp. 77–9; Russell, *Fall*, pp. 294–5.

77. Cressy, 'Protestation', p. 254.

78. Ibid., pp. 257–9.

79. John Walter, *Understanding Popular Violence in the English Revolution: The Colchester Plunderers* (Cambridge, 1999), pp. 292–4; Cressy, 'Protestation', pp. 267–8; Russell, *Fall*, p. 295.

80. Walter, *Understanding*, pp. 292–3; Cressy, 'Protestation', pp. 259–62.

81. Walter, *Understanding*, pp. 295–6.

82. John Morrill, *Cheshire 1630–1660: County Government and Society during the English Revolution* (Oxford, 1974), pp. 36–7.

83. John Walter, ' "Affronts & insolencies": The Voices of Radwinter and Popular Opposition to Laudianism', *EHR*, 122 (2007), 35–60, esp. p. 37; for other examples see Cressy, *England on Edge*, ch. 9.

84. Julie Spraggon, *Puritan Iconoclasm during the English Civil War* (Woodbridge, 2003), pp. 138–40, 221, 231.

85. *CJ*, ii, p. 72. Sir Edward Dering was among the members added to this committee; Russell, *Fall*, pp. 367–72.

86. David Cressy, *Agnes Bowker's Cat: Travesties and Transgressions in Tudor and Stuart England* (Oxford, 2000), pp. 234–43; for the longer history of the cross see Nicola Smith, *The Royal Image and the English People* (Aldershot, 2001), ch. 2.

87. See above, pp. 262–4, for its eventual fate.

88. *LJ*, iv, p. 134.

89. Hirst, 'Defection of Sir Edward Dering'. There were others too: Smith, *Stuart Parliaments*, p. 126; see also David L. Smith, *Constitutional Royalism and the Search for Settlement, c. 1640–1649* (Cambridge, 1994), ch. 4. Aston's attachment to religious decency thus defined had deep roots: Lake, 'Puritans, Popularity and Petitions', pp. 259–89.

90. See especially Margaret Aston, *England's Iconoclasts*, vol 1: *Laws against Images* (Oxford, 1988); Margaret Aston, 'Puritans and Iconoclasm, 1560–1660', in Christopher Durston and Jacqueline Eales (eds.), *The Culture of English Puritanism, 1560–1700* (Basingstoke, 1996), pp. 92–121; Margaret Aston, 'Iconoclasm in England: Official and Clandestine', reprinted in Peter Marshall (ed.), *The Impact of the English Reformation 1500–1640* (London, 1997), pp. 167–92.

91. Anon., *A Discovery of 29 Sects here in London* (1641); Anon., *A Nest of Serpents Discovered* (1641); Fortescue dates.

92. Cressy, *Agnes Bowker's Cat*, ch. 15, esp. pp. 259–61.

93. *Nest of Serpents*, p. 6.

94. Cressy, *Agnes Bowker's Cat*, p. 271.

95. Keith Lindley, *Popular Politics*, pp. 79–91; for the history of the sects in London see Murray Tolmie, *The Triumph of the Saints: The Separate Churches of London, 1616–1649* (Cambridge, 1977); and the works by Como and Lake cited above at n. 3.

96. Russell, *Fall*, pp. 368–70. See also Cressy, *England on Edge*, pp. 180–82.

97. Fletcher, *Outbreak*, p. 284; Walter, 'Confessional Politics', p. 699, quoting Judith Maltby, *Prayer Book and People in Elizabethan and Early Stuart England* (Cambridge, 1998), appendix 1, pp. 238–47.

98. Fletcher, *Outbreak*, pp. 284–9. For Aston's published collection see Sir Thomas Aston, *A collection of sundry petitions* (1642).

99. Fletcher, *Outbreak*, p. 290.

100. Ibid., pp. 289–91.

101. Walter, 'Confessional Politics'.

102. Lake, 'Puritans, Popularity and Petitions'.

103. Calculated from G. K. Fortescue (ed.), *Catalogue of the Pamphlets, Books, Newspapers, and Manuscripts Relating to the Civil War, the Commonwealth and the Restoration, Collected by George Thomason, 1640–1661*, 2 vols. (London, 1908). This assumes, of course, that these patterns reflect the market, rather than Thomason's collecting. For discussions of the explosion of print in these years see Joad Raymond, *Pamphlets and Pamphleteering in Early Modern Britain* (Cambridge, 2003), chs. 5–6; Cressy, *England on Edge*, ch. 12. Estimates of press output based on searches of the ESTC or EEBO include collections other than Thomason's (although his is the largest component) but do not allow for monthly (or weekly) calculations. There are difficulties with dating the Thomason Tracts, however (see above, pp. 600–601, note on dating).

104. Fletcher, *Outbreak*, p. 287.

5. Barbarous Catholics and Puritan Populists

1. [Gabriel Plattes], *A description of the famous kingdome of Macaria* (London, 1641), quotations at sig. A2r, pp. 2, 3. For background see Charles Webster, *Utopian Planning and the Puritan Revolution: Gabriel Plattes, Samuel Hartlib and 'Macaria'* (Oxford, 1979); Charles Webster, 'The Authorship and Significance of *Macaria*', *PP*, 56 (1972), 34–48;

J. C. Davis, *Utopia and the Ideal State: A Study of English Utopian Writing, 1516–1700* (Cambridge, 1981).

2. Hugh Trevor-Roper, 'Three Foreigners: The Philosophers of the Puritan Revolution', reprinted in Hugh Trevor-Roper, *Religion, the Reformation, and Social Change, and Other Essays* (London, 1984), pp. 237–93; G. H. Turnbull, *Samuel Hartlib: A Sketch of His Life and His Relations to J. A. Comenius* (London, 1920); G. H. Turnbull, *Hartlib, Dury and Comenius: Gleanings from Hartlib's Papers* (Liverpool, 1947); Charles Webster, *The Great Instauration: Science, Medicine and Reform, 1626–1660*, 2nd edn (Oxford, 2002); Mark Greengrass, 'Samuel Hartlib and International Calvinism', *Proceedings of the Huguenot Society*, 25 (1993), 464–75.

3. See in general Webster, *Great Instauration*; the essays collected in Mark Greengrass, Michael Leslie and Timothy Raylor (eds.), *Samuel Hartlib and the Universal Reformation: Studies in Intellectual Communication* (Cambridge, 1994), esp. Anthony Milton, ' "The unchanged peacemaker"?: John Dury and the Politics of Irenicism in England, 1628–1643', pp. 95–117. For the Hartlib circle see above, pp. 453–8.

4. Webster, 'Authorship and Significance of *Macaria*', p. 38.

5. Ibid., p. 39.

6. David Stevenson, *The Scottish Revolution, 1637–44: The Triumph of the Covenanters* (Edinburgh, 2003), pp. 233–4.

7. For a good brief account, see Austin Woolrych, *Britain in Revolution, 1625–1660* (Oxford, 2002), pp. 182–3, 189–92.

8. Stevenson, *Scottish Revolution*, pp. 238–9; John J. Scally, 'Hamilton, James, First Duke of Hamilton (1606–1649)', *ODNB*, 24, pp. 839–46.

9. *A damnable treason by a Contagious Plaster of a plague sore* ([London], 1641), quotations at sig A2r. See Paul Slack, *The Impact of the Plague in Tudor and Stuart England* (Oxford, 1985), p. 293; William G. Naphy, 'Plague-Spreading and Magisterially Controlled Fear', in William G. Naphy and Penny Roberts (eds.), *Fear in Early Modern Society* (Manchester, 1997), pp. 28–43. The pamphlet is discussed further above, pp. 174–5. For the plague in these months see also David Cressy, *England on Edge: Crisis and Revolution 1640–1642* (Oxford, 2006), pp. 60–67; John Adamson, *The Noble Revolt: The Overthrow of Charles I* (London, 2007), pp. 406–7.

10. Politicians, Pym included, were not above fostering Catholic panics for political purposes: Robin Clifton, 'The Popular Fear of Catholics during the English Revolution', *PP*, 52 (1971), 23–55, at pp. 39–40. There is, though, independent evidence that this incident actually occurred. D'Ewes records the incident: W. H. Coates (ed.), *The Journal of Sir Simonds D'Ewes from the First Recess of the Long Parliament* (New Haven, Conn., 1942), p. 37. Nehemiah Wallington recorded that it was verified – even he was at least a little suspicious of this particular example of popish plotting: 'There was a letter brought to Mr Pym with an odious plaster taken from a plague sore, saying if this will not doe, then a dagger shall and as I did hear very credibly one standing by him looking over his shoulder upon it took a conceit [look] at it and sickened and died presently', BL, Add MS 21,935, fo. 188v. George Mordant was examined the next day on suspicion of having delivered the letter but dismissed: *CJ*, ii, p. 295.

11. *CJ*, ii, p. 300.

12. The key recent work is Nicholas Canny, *Making Ireland British 1580–1650* (Oxford, 2001). For a summary and further references see Michael J. Braddick, *State Formation in Early Modern England c. 1500–1700* (Cambridge, 2000), pp. 379–97.

13. Aidan Clarke, 'Selling Royal Favours, 1624–32', in T. W. Moody, F. X. Martin and F. J. Byrne (eds.), *A New History of Ireland*, vol. 3: *Early Modern Ireland 1534–1691* (Oxford, 1976), pp. 233–42; Canny, *Making Ireland British*, esp. pp. 258–75.

14. Aidan Clarke with R. Dudley Edwards, 'Pacification, plantation and the Catholic Question', in Moody, Martin and Byrne, *New History of Ireland*, vol. 3, pp. 187–232; Clarke, 'Selling Royal Favours'; Canny, *Making Ireland British*, pp. 265–9; Conrad Russell, *The Fall of the British Monarchies 1637–1642* (Oxford, 1991), pp. 380–82; John Reeve,

'Secret Alliances and Protestant Agitation in Two Kingdoms: The Early Caroline Background to the Irish Rebellion', in Ian Gentles, John Morrill and Blair Worden (eds.), *Soldiers, Writers and Statesmen of the English Revolution* (Cambridge, 1998), pp. 19–35.

15. For an overview of Wentworth's policies in Ireland see Canny, *Making Ireland British*, pp. 275–98. See also Aidan Clarke, 'The Government of Wentworth, 1632–40', in Moody, Martin and Byrne (eds.), *New History of Ireland*, vol. 3, pp. 243–69.

16. Canny, *Making Ireland British*, pp. 275–98; Clarke, 'Government of Wentworth'.

17. Russell, *Fall*, pp. 382–8; for a concise discussion of the constitutional question see David Scott, *Politics and War in the Three Stuart Kingdoms, 1637–49* (Basingstoke, 2004), p. 30.

18. Russell, *Fall*, pp. 388–92; Aidan Clarke, 'The Breakdown of Authority, 1640–41', in Moody, Martin and Byrne (eds.), *New History of Ireland*, vol. 3, pp. 270–88.

19. Patrick J. Corish, 'The Rising of 1641 and the Catholic Confederacy, 1641–5', in Moody, Martin and Byrne (eds.), *New History of Ireland*, vol. 3, pp. 289–316, esp. pp. 289–93; Michael Perceval-Maxwell, *The Outbreak of the Irish Rebellion of 1641* (Dublin, 1994); Canny, *Making Ireland British*, ch. 8, emphasizes the extent to which this high political approach to the rebellion conceals the roots of the rebellion in Irish society at large; see also Micheàl Ó Siochrú, *Confederate Ireland, 1642–1649: A Constitutional and Political Analysis* (Dublin, 1999), esp. pp. 23–4. Jane H. Ohlmeyer, 'Introduction: A Failed Revolution?', in Jane Ohlmeyer (ed.), *Ireland from Independence to Occupation 1641–1660* (Cambridge, 1995), pp. 1–23, places the rebellion in a comparative perspective. For aristocratic rebellions in Tudor England see Anthony Fletcher and Diarmaid MacCulloch, *Tudor Rebellions*, 5th edn (Harlow, 2004), esp. pp. 122–7; Mervyn James, *Society, Politics and Culture: Studies in Early Modern England* (Cambridge, 1986), esp. chs. 8, 9.

20. Woolrych, *Britain in Revolution*, pp. 194–6. For the offer to try to call it off see Russell, *Fall*, pp. 396–8.

21. Canny, *Making Ireland British*, ch. 8.

22. Ibid. See also Nicholas Canny, 'What Really Happened in Ireland in 1641?', in Ohlmeyer (ed.), *Ireland from Independence to Occupation*, pp. 24–42. For the rapid formation of the Catholic Confederacy see Ó Siochrú, *Confederate Ireland*.

23. Thomas Partington, *VVorse and worse nevves from Ireland* (London, 1641), printed for Nathaniel Butter. Quoted from Keith Lindley, *The English Civil War and Revolution: A Source Book* (London, 1998), pp. 81–3. For an overview of this literature and its impact see Keith Lindley, 'The Impact of the 1641 Rebellion upon England and Wales, 1641–5', *Irish Historical Studies*, 18 (1972), 143–76. The most convincing reconstruction of events on the ground is Canny, *Making Ireland British*, ch. 8.

24. Reprinted in Lindley, *English Civil War and Revolution*, pp. 80–81.

25. Gardiner, *CD*, pp. 199–201, quotations at pp. 199, 200, 201; for the Ten Propositions see ibid., pp. 163–6, quotation at p. 164.

26. J. P. Kenyon, *The Stuart Constitution: Documents and Commentary* (Cambridge, 1966), p. 216; Anthony Fletcher, *The Outbreak of the English Civil War* (London, 1981), pp. 81–8.

27. Gardiner, *CD*, pp. 202–32, quotations at pp. 206–8.

28. See, for example, measures against English Catholics in Ireland, to control movement, discussion with the Lords about the Capuchins, and close scrutiny of household priests of Henrietta Maria and ambassadors: *CJ*, ii, 300–301.

29. Gardiner, *CD*, p. 204.

30. For a reading of the remonstrance as an attempt to find consensus see Fletcher, *Outbreak*, pp. 145–6.

31. Quoted from Joad Raymond, *The Invention of the Newspaper: English Newsbooks 1641–1649* (Oxford, 1996), p. 121.

32. Russell, *Fall*, pp. 424–9, 433; Keith Lindley, *Popular Politics and Religion in Civil War London* (Aldershot, 1997), pp. 94–5; Brian Manning, *The English People and the English*

Revolution (Harmondsworth, 1976), p. 86; *CJ*, p. 344. Dering quoted from Russell, *Fall*, p. 427. For partisanship see Fletcher, *Outbreak*, ch. 4.

33. Clifton, 'Popular Fear of Catholics', pp. 30–31, 49; for the chronology of such panics see Robin Clifton, 'Fear of Popery', in Conrad Russell (ed.), *The Origins of the English Civil War* (Basingstoke, 1973), pp. 144–67 at pp. 158–61; Fletcher, *Outbreak*, pp. 203–6; for an example see John Morrill, *Cheshire 1630–1660: County Government and Society during the English Revolution* (Oxford, 1974), p. 37.

34. See Lindley, 'Impact of the 1641 Rebellion'; for the general influence of pamphlet representations of Catholicism see Clifton, 'Popular Fear of Catholics', pp. 37–8.

35. Raymond, *Invention*, chs. 1–2, esp. pp. 20–21, 101, 104–5; for the manuscript circulation of news see Ian Atherton, ' "The itch grown a disease": Manuscript Transmission of News in the Seventeenth Century', in Joad Raymond (ed.), *News, Newspapers and Society in Early Modern Britain* (London, 1999), pp. 39–65.

36. Raymond, *Invention*, ch. 2; Cressy, *England on Edge*, pp. 298–302. Numbers of titles calculated from G. K. Fortescue (ed.), *Catalogue of the Pamphlets, Books, Newspapers, and Manuscripts Relating to the Civil War, the Commonwealth and the Restoration, Collected by George Thomason, 1640–1661*, 2 vols. (London, 1908).

37. Raymond, *Invention*, pp. 20–36, 108–25. The pamphlet is *The discovery Of a late and Bloody conspiracie At Edenburg, in Scotland* (London, 1641).

38. Title evidence derived from Fortescue, *Catalogue*. Newsbooks included material of this kind: Joad Raymond (ed.), *Making the News: An Anthology of the Newsbooks of Revolutionary England 1641–1660* (Moreton-in-Marsh, 1993), ch. 4.

39. Fees varied, as did the services offered or requested, but £20 is the annual charge made by John Pory to Viscount Scudamore: Atherton, ' "The itch grown a disease" ', p. 41. See also figures in Raymond, *Invention*. Bridgewater paid £20 to Castle, although it is not clear what period of service this 'token' was intended to cover: see HEH, EL 7808, Bridgewater to Castle, 13 January 1640; EL 7816, Castle to Bridgewater, 14 January 1640. For a concise discussion of the growing literature on the widening market for news see Ian Atherton, 'The Press and Popular Political Opinion', in Barry Coward (ed.), *A Companion to Stuart Britain* (Oxford, 2003), pp. 88–110. For the cultural and political significance of the birth of the newsbook see Raymond, *Invention*; Adam Fox, *Oral and Literate Culture in England, 1500–1700* (Oxford, 2000), ch. 7; Richard Cust, 'News and Politics in Early-Seventeenth-Century England', reprinted in Richard Cust and Ann Hughes (eds.), *The English Civil War* (London, 1997), pp. 233–60.

40. EL 7848, Bridgewater to Castle, 10 August 1640; see above p. 97. See also Cressy, *England on Edge*, pp. 297–8.

41. I am grateful to Marcus Nevitt and Jason Peacey for discussing this material with me.

42. The English Short Title Catalogue database covers the period 1475–1700. One twentieth of all titles containing the word 'plot' come from 1641 and 1642 (91 out of 1,733), i.e. in two out of 225 years. For 'conspiracy' the figure is nearly 4 per cent (21 out of 578) and for the more time-dependent spelling 'conspiracie' the figure is 32 per cent (32 out of 100). It was a fairly precisely defined peak, too: taking the three terms together there are five pamphlets advertised in this way from 1640, rising to 75 in 1641, and 69 in 1642, falling back to 31 in 1643, 14 in 1644 and 3 in 1645. All figures calculated on simple searches on 15 December 2005. These are, of course, limited indicators of the market, and it should be noted that even in 1641 and 1642 these pamphlets are a small part of the total.

43. Calculated from Fortescue, *Catalogue*.

44. Jane Ohlmeyer, 'The Civil Wars in Ireland', in John Kenyon and Jane Ohlmeyer (eds.), *The Civil Wars: A Military History of England, Scotland, and Ireland 1638–1660* (Oxford, 1998), pp. 73–102, at p. 74.

45. Derek Hirst, *England in Conflict, 1603–1660: Kingdom, Community, Commonwealth* (London, 1999), p. 183.

46. R. M. Smuts, 'Public Ceremony and Royal Charisma: The English Royal Entry in London, 1485–1642', in A. L. Beier, David Cannadine and James M. Rosenheim (eds.),

The First Modern Society: Essays in English History in Honour of Lawrence Stone (Cambridge, 1989), pp. 65–93, at pp. 89–93; Lindley, *Popular Politics*, pp. 95–6; Richard Cust, *Charles I: A Political Life* (Harlow, 2005), pp. 313–14.

47. Howell quoted in Raymond, *Invention*, pp. 121–2.
48. For the text see Gardiner, *CD*, pp. 233–6. The answer was published in several editions: much as he deplored it, the King had to engage with the world of print.
49. Russell, *Fall*, p. 437; Gardiner, *CD*, pp. 232–3.
50. Austin Woolrych, *Commonwealth to Protectorate* (Oxford, 1982), p. 224.
51. Clifton, 'Popular Fear of Catholics', p. 33.
52. Raymond, *Invention*, p. 114; see also Elizabeth Skerpan, *The Rhetoric of Politics in the English Revolution, 1642–1660* (London, 1992), pp. 60–80.
53. Quoted in Manning, *English People*, p. 42.
54. Lindley, *Popular Politics*, ch. 4; Valerie Pearl, *London and the Outbreak of the Puritan Revolution: City Government and National Politics 1625–1643* (Oxford, 1961), pp. 131–9; Manning, *English People*, pp. 86–7. Robert Brenner identifies a group with distinct social and economic interests at the heart of this City revolution: *Merchants and Revolution: Commercial Change, Political Conflict, and London's Overseas Traders, 1550–1653* (Cambridge, 1993), esp. pp. 396–400.
55. Clarendon also dates the emergence of these terms to this period: Raymond, *Invention*, p. 114. These tumultuous weeks are fully described and evoked by Lindley, *Popular Politics*, pp. 98–117; and Manning, *English People*, ch. 4. For their relationship to parliamentary politics see Russell, *Fall*, pp. 439–46.
56. Russell, *Fall*, pp. 445–53.
57. Gardiner, *CD*, pp. 236–7.
58. BL, Add MS 21,935, fos. 159v–160r. These running heads do not appear at the relevant pages in R. Webb (ed.), *Historical Notices of Events Occurring Chiefly in the Reign of Charles I by Nehemiah Wallington*, 2 vols. (London, 1869), I, pp. 278–9. I am grateful to Peter Lake, who first pointed this juxtaposition out to me.
59. See Russell, *Fall*, p. 448. For the ways in which Parliament men could 'mould and guide' opinion in the City see Pearl, *London and the Outbreak*, pp. 228–35. Russell's verdict is measured: Russell, *Fall*, pp. 432–3. The authoritative account is Lindley, *Popular Politics*, which supplies little evidence of manipulation or orchestration from within Parliament. Crowds were helpful to Pym and others though, and that made the accusations plausible: they were made from within Parliament too: Lindley, *Popular Politics*, p. 97.
60. Gardiner, *CD*, pp. 237–41, at p. 239. D'Ewes put the figure at 400 in his journal, correcting an initial estimate of 200, and made no mention of papists. The evocative passage is reprinted in Lindley, *Civil War and Revolution*, pp. 76–7. The whole episode is narrated from complementary perspectives by Lindley, *Popular Politics*, pp. 117–20; and Russell, *Fall*, pp. 445–53; see also Manning, *English People*, pp. 109–13.
61. Lindley, *Popular Politics*, pp. 120–21, 123–5.
62. Ibid., pp. 122, 125–6; Russell, *Fall*, p. 452; Fletcher, *Outbreak*, pp. 184–5.
63. Lindley, *Popular Politics*, p. 127.

6. Paper Combats

1. Many localities produced petitions for accommodation between King and Parliament, and the return of the King to Parliament was a common element of these petitions: Anthony Fletcher, *The Outbreak of the English Civil War* (London, 1981), ch. 8. It was a repeated demand during the war, both by the King himself and 'peace party' lobbyists. The City petition of January 1643, for example, caused controversy with this demand: *The humble petition of the major, aldermen, and commons of the City of London to His Majesty* (London, 1643); Keith Lindley, *Popular Politics and Religion in Civil War London* (Aldershot, 1997), pp. 345–7.
2. Samuel R. Gardiner, *History of England from the Accession of James I to the Outbreak*

of the Civil War 1603–1642, 10 vols. (London, 1884), X, pp. 152–7. See also Conrad Russell, *The Fall of the British Monarchies 1637–1642* (Oxford, 1991), pp. 457–8, 466; Fletcher, *Outbreak*, pp. 185–6.

3. Russell, *Fall*, p. 464. For the resultant promotion of the Protestation see above, pp. 200–201.

4. Michael Mendle, 'The Great Council of Parliament and the First Ordinances: The Constitutional Theory of the civil war', *JBS*, 31:2 (1992), 133–62, esp. pp. 139–50; see also Fletcher, *Outbreak*, pp. 76–7. For the longer history of the idea of the Great Council see David L. Smith, *The Stuart Parliaments 1603–1689* (London, 1999), pp. 43–8.

5. Mendle, 'Great Council', p. 140. For the change represented by the Ten Propositions see Fletcher, *Outbreak*, pp. 42–76.

6. Russell, *Fall*, pp. 464, 467–8.

7. Lindley, *Popular Politics*, pp. 130–37; Fletcher, *Outbreak*, pp. 188–9, 223–4; John Walter, *Understanding Popular Violence in the English Revolution: The Colchester Plunderers* (Cambridge, 1999), pp. 256–9; Robin Clifton, 'The Popular Fear of Catholics during the English Revolution', *PP*, 52 (1971), 23–55, at pp. 41–2; David Cressy, *England on Edge: Crisis and Revolution 1640–1642* (Oxford, 2006), pp. 56–9. For Pym's use of the petitions see Russell, *Fall*, pp. 468–9.

8. Lindley, *Popular Politics*, pp. 134–6; Patricia Higgins, 'The Reactions of Women, with Special Reference to Women Petitioners', in Brian Manning (ed.), *Politics, Religion and the English Civil War* (London, 1973), pp. 179–222, at pp. 184–5. For women in food riots see John Walter, 'Grain Riots and Popular Attitudes to the Law: Maldon and the Crisis of 1629', reprinted in John Walter, *Crowds and Popular Politics in Early Modern England* (Manchester, 2006), pp. 27–66, esp. pp. 40–41. The image of a parliament of women was a common one in contemporary satire.

9. Russell, *Fall*, pp. 457–8; Fletcher, *Outbreak*, pp. 228–9.

10. *LJ*, iv, pp. 523–4.

11. Russell, *Fall*, pp. 458–9, 464–7.

12. John Adamson, *The Noble Revolt: The Overthrow of Charles I* (London, 2007), esp. ch. 16.

13. For the exodus see Russell, *Fall*, pp. 470–71. Average numbers voting in Commons divisions fell from 276 in January to 159 in April: Smith, *Stuart Parliaments*, p. 128.

14. Russell, *Fall*, pp. 470–76, 479. For the Militia Ordinance see also Fletcher, *Outbreak*, pp. 244–6.

15. Mendle, 'Great Council', pp. 155–6; Russell, *Fall*, pp. 476–7.

16. Russell, *Fall*, pp. 478–87, for the metaphor of the matrimonial quarrel pp. 477–8; Fletcher, *Outbreak*, pp. 230–31.

17. Lewes quoted in William Cliftlands, 'The "Well-Affected" and the "Country": Politics and Religion in English Provincial Society, c. 1640–1654', unpublished Ph.D. thesis, Essex (1987), pp. 15–16. See Cressy, *England on Edge*, chs. 14–15 and pp. 405–8. For ballads see Angela McShane Jones, ' "Rime and Reason": The Political World of the English Broadside Ballad, 1640–1689', unpublished Ph.D. thesis, Warwick (2004).

18. Mendle, 'Great Council', pp. 152–9.

19. For this gloss, see Russell, *Fall*, esp. p. 487.

20. For this view of Pym's importance in this period see Fletcher, *Outbreak*, pp. 234–44.

21. Fletcher, *Outbreak*, pp. 231–2. For Hyde's role as the King's draughtsman see David L. Smith, *Constitutional Royalism and the Search for Settlement, c. 1640–1649* (Cambridge, 1994), pp. 88–91; Russell, *Fall*, pp. 480–85; Paul Seaward, 'Hyde, Edward, First Earl of Clarendon (1609–1674)', *ODNB*, 29, pp. 120–38. Hyde was knighted in February 1643 and was created Earl of Clarendon in April 1661. For Henrietta Maria's influence over policy from early 1642 see also Richard Cust, *Charles I: A Political Life* (Harlow, 2005), pp. 327–58; Michelle Anne White, *Henrietta Maria and the English Civil Wars* (Aldershot, 2006), esp. ch. 3.

22. Gardiner, *History of England*, X, pp. 191–3; Russell, *Fall*, pp. 503–4.

23. Russell, *Fall*, pp. 505–6.

24. See above, p. 182; Gardiner, *History of England*, X, pp. 154–6; Fletcher, *Outbreak*, pp. 185–6.

25. Bernard Capp, 'Naval Operations', in John Kenyon and Jane Ohlmeyer (eds.), *The Civil Wars: A Military History of England, Scotland and Ireland 1638–1660* (Oxford, 1998), pp. 156–91, at pp. 157–8. Malcolm Wanklyn and Frank Jones are more sceptical about the significance of parliamentary control of the navy to the overall course of the war: *A Military History of the English Civil War 1642–1646: Strategy and Tactics* (Harlow, 2005), pp. 12–13.

26. Russell, *Fall*, p. 505.

27. Cited in Smith, *Stuart Parliaments*, pp. 46–7.

28. Gardiner, *CD*, pp. 249–54. For an introduction to the controversy see David Wootton (ed.), *Divine Right and Democracy: An Anthology of Political Writing in Stuart England* (Harmondsworth, 1986), intr. and ch. 3; M. J. Mendle, 'Politics and Political Thought 1640–1642', in Conrad Russell (ed.), *The Origins of the English Civil War* (London, 1973), pp. 219–45. The key work is Michael Mendle, *Dangerous Positions: Mixed Government, the Estates of the Realm, and the Making of the Answer to the 19 Propositions* (Tuscaloosa, 1985).

29. Smith, *Constitutional Royalism*, pp. 90–91. See also Wootton, *Divine Right*, ch. 3.

30. Following the summary in Mendle, 'Great Council', p. 160. See also Mendle, *Dangerous Positions*; Michael Mendle, *Henry Parker and the English Civil War: The Political Thought of the Public's 'Privado'* (Cambridge, 1995); Michael Mendle, 'Parliamentary Sovereignty: A Very English Absolutism', in Nicholas T. Phillipson and Quentin Skinner (eds.), *Political Discourse in Early Modern Britain* (Cambridge, 1993), pp. 97–119; Michael Mendle, 'Henry Parker: The Public's Privado', in Gordon J. Schochet, P. E. Tatspaugh and Carol Brobeck (eds.), *Religion, Resistance and Civil War: Papers Presented at the Folger Institute Seminar 'Political Thought in Early Modern England, 1600–1660'* (Washington, DC, 1990), pp. 151–77; Michael Mendle, 'The Ship Money Case, *The case of shipmony*, and the Development of Henry Parker's Parliamentary Absolutism', *HJ*, 32 (1989), 513–36; Richard Tuck, *Philosophy and Government 1572–1651* (Cambridge, 1993), esp. pp. 221–33.

31. Quentin Skinner, 'Rethinking Political Liberty', *History Workshop Journal*, 61:1 (2006), 156–70; see, more generally, Quentin Skinner, 'Classical Liberty and the Coming of the English Civil War', in Martin Van Gelderen and Quentin Skinner (eds.), *Republicanism: A Shared European Heritage*, vol. 2: *The Values of Republicanism in Early Modern Europe* (Cambridge, 2002), pp. 9–28, esp. pp. 17–28.

32. For the declarations see Skinner, 'Rethinking Political Liberty', pp. 165–8; for Parker and the Committee of Safety see Jason Peacey, *Politicians and Pamphleteers: Propaganda during the English Civil Wars and Interregnum* (Aldershot, 2004), pp. 53–4.

33. For *Reasons*, see Skinner, 'Rethinking Political Liberty', pp. 167–8. For the output of Bishop and White see Jason Peacey, ' "Fiery Spirits" and Political Propaganda: Uncovering a Radical Press Campaign of 1642', *Publishing History*, 55 (2004), pp. 5–36. I am grateful to John Morrill for discussing this material with me.

34. For this general phenomenon see Peacey, *Politicians and Pamphleteers*.

35. See above, p. 172.

36. A. D. T. Cromartie, 'The Printing of Parliamentary Speeches November 1640–July 1642', *HJ*, 33 (1990), 23–44; John Morrill, 'The Unweariableness of Mr Pym: Influence and Eloquence in the Long Parliament', in Susan D. Amussen and Mark A. Kishlansky (eds.), *Political Culture and Cultural Politics in Early Modern England: Essays Presented to David Underdown* (Manchester, 1995), pp. 19–54, esp. pp. 36–43.

37. Fletcher, *Outbreak*, pp. 255–6. His comment on the Grand Remonstrance is quoted from Russell, *Fall*, p. 427. For his defection see above, p. 147. See also Derek Hirst, 'The Defection of Sir Edward Dering, 1640–1641', reprinted in Peter Gaunt (ed.), *The English Civil War* (Oxford, 2000), pp. 207–25; S. P. Salt, 'Dering, Sir Edward, First Baronet

(1598–1644)', *ODNB*, 15, pp. 874–80. Book-burning was as much a statement of anathema as of censorship, and it was frequently an expression of revulsion at the tone as much as the content of a publication: see above, pp. 277–81.

38. *A Seasonable Lecture, or A most learned Oration: Disburthened from Henry VValker, a most judicious Quondam Iron-monger, a late Pamphleteere and now (too late or too soone) a double diligent Preacher. As it might be delivered in Hatcham Barne the thirtieth day of March last, Stylo Novo. Taken in short writing by Thorny Ailo; and now printed in words at length, and not in figures* (London, 1642). Taylor used this pseudonym on a number of occasions. For Taylor's remarkable career see Bernard Capp, *The World of John Taylor the Water-Poet 1578–1653* (Oxford, 1994).

39. According to Fortescue, the lowest monthly total during 1642 was 117. Across the whole period 1640–1651 there were only twenty-seven months in which the total exceeded 100 titles. Sixteen of them were in a continuous run from January 1642 to April 1643: G. K. Fortescue (ed.), *Catalogue of the Pamphlets, Books, Newspapers, and Manuscripts Relating to the Civil War, the Commonwealth and the Restoration, Collected by George Thomason, 1640–1661*, 2 vols. (London, 1908).

40. For characterizations of the motives of activists in these terms see Fletcher, *Outbreak*, pp. 405–6; John Morrill, *Revolt in the Provinces: The People of England and the Tragedies of war 1630–1648*, 2nd edn (Harlow, 1999), pp. 68–9, and the reservations expressed at pp. 185–90.

41. Figures quoted or calculated from Keith J. Lindley, 'The Impact of the 1641 Rebellion upon England and Wales, 1641–5', *Irish Historical Studies*, 18:70 (1972), 143–76, at p. 144; Anon., *No pamphlet but a detestation Against all such pamphlets As are Printed, Concerning the Irish Rebellion, Plainely demonstrating the falshood of them* (London, 1642), quoted in Lindley, 'Impact', at p. 146. For the influence of the Foxean tradition, and its rival, see Ethan Howard Shagan, 'Constructing Discord: Ideology, Propaganda, and English Responses to the Irish Rebellion of 1641', *JBS* 36:1 (1997), 4–34.

42. Lindley, 'Impact', pp. 154–9. For the extent to which this fear of local Catholics was exaggerated see William Sheils, 'English Catholics at War and Peace', in Christopher Durston and Judith Maltby (eds.), *Religion in Revolutionary England* (Manchester, 2006), pp. 137–57, at pp. 138–42. After the Restoration Catholics made up about 1 or 1.5 per cent of the population, with estimates for particular places varying from 0.4 to 2 per cent or more. Most studies emphasize their political loyalty: Michael J. Braddick, *State Formation in Early Modern England, c. 1550–1700* (Cambridge, 2000), pp. 324–30; for numbers see p. 325, n. 132.

43. Anon., *A bloody plot, Practised by some Papists in Darbyshire* (London, 1642): the date of the plot is 18 January, but there is no Thomason date. The pamphlet is bound with others dealing with events in late January.

44. This was a recurring feature of the Catholic scares of these months: Clifton, 'Popular Fear of Catholics', pp. 29–31, 45; Fletcher, *Outbreak*, pp. 204–6; [John Davis], *A great discovery of a damnable plot at Rugland castle in Monmoth-shire in Wales related to the High Court of Parliament, by Iohn Davis, November the 12. 1641* (London, 1641); Anon., *Gods late mercy to England in discovering of three damnable plots by the treacherous Papists and Iesuits in England and Wales, and many other places, &c.* (London, 1641).

45. See above, p. 183.

46. Anon., *A bloody plot*, sig. A2r.

47. Braddick, *State Formation*, pp. 304–6, 324–30.

48. See above, pp. 171–2. Clifton, 'Popular Fear of Catholics', pp. 30–31; Robin Clifton, 'Fear of Popery', in Conrad Russell (ed.), *The Origins of the English Civil War* (London, 1973), pp. 144–67, at pp. 158–61; Cressy, *England on Edge*, pp. 46–9; Fletcher, *Outbreak*, pp. 203–6.

49. Fletcher, *Outbreak*, esp. p. 206. For the disturbances in Essex see above, pp. 230–31; Lindley, 'Impact', pp. 157–9.

50. Caroline Hibbard, *Charles I and the Popish Plot* (Chapel Hill, NC, 1983), pp. 219–20; Fletcher, *Outbreak*, pp. 59–60; Diane Purkiss, *The English Civil War: Papists, Gentlemen, Soldiers, and Witchfinders in the Birth of Modern Britain* (New York, 2006), pp. 137–9; Anon., *Arthur Browne, A Seminary Priest, His Confession* (London, 1642). For another cause célèbre see the revelations of John Browne: *The confession of John Brovvne a Iesuite* (London, 1641). For the King's attempt to save the lives of Catholic priests see Russell, *Fall*, pp. 258–62.

51. Fletcher, *Outbreak*, ch. 6. For the complex connections between these campaigns and national political developments see also John Walter, 'Confessional Politics in pre-Civil War Essex: Prayer Books, Profanations, and Petitions', *HJ*, 44 (2001), pp. 677–701, esp. pp. 699–701. The Somerset petition from these months, for example, called for the preservation of the Prayer Book and the liberties of Parliament, which was hardly a non-partisan set of priorities: David Underdown, *Somerset in the Civil War and Interregnum* (Newton Abbot, 1973), pp. 26–9

52. David Zaret, 'Petitions and the "Invention" of Public Opinion in the English Revolution', *American Journal of Sociology*, 101 (1996), 1497–1555; David Zaret, *Origins of Democratic Culture: Printing, Petitions, and the Public Sphere in Early-Modern England* (Princeton, NJ, 2000).

53. David Cressy, 'The Protestation Protested, 1641 and 1642', *HJ*, 45 (2002), pp. 251–79, esp. pp. 266–77. For the politics of the Protestation in Essex see Walter, 'Confessional Politics', and Walter, *Understanding Popular Violence*, ch. 8. For mental reservation see Edward Vallance, *Revolutionary England and the National Covenant: State Oaths, Protestantism and the Political Nation, 1553–1682* (Woodbridge, 2005), esp. pp. 103–7; David Martin Jones, *Conscience and Allegiance in Seventeenth Century England: The Political Significance of Oaths and Engagements* (Woodbridge, 1999). For the administration and importance of the returns as population listings see Anne Whiteman, 'The Protestation Returns of 1641–1642. Pt. 1: The General Organisation', *Local Population Studies*, 55 (1995), 14–26; Anne Whiteman and Vivian Russell, 'The Protestation Returns, 1641–1642. Pt. 2: Partial Census or Snapshot? – Some Evidence from Penwith Hundred, Cornwall', *Local Population Studies*, 56 (1996), 17–29; J. S. W. Gibson and A. Dell (eds.), *The Protestation Returns 1641–2 and Other Contemporary Listings* (Birmingham, 1995); David Cressy, *Literacy and the Social Order: Reading and Writing in Tudor and Stuart England* (Cambridge, 1980), passim.

54. Shagan, 'Constructing Discord', esp. pp. 17–23.

55. For the vote see above, pp. 185–6; and for its significance see Margaret Aston, 'Puritans and Iconoclasm, 1560–1660', in Christopher Durston and Jacqueline Eales (eds.), *The Culture of English Puritanism, 1560–1700* (Basingstoke, 1996), pp. 92–121, at pp. 114–17.

56. Anon., *Wonderfull Nevves: Or, a True Relation of a Churchwarden in the Towne of Tosceter* (London, 1642), quotations at sig. A2r, A2v, A3r. For the Lords order see above, pp. 146, 176. Wallington also noted judgements on those who destroyed good books, although his sense of what was a good book clearly differed: hence the importance and inscrutability of God's judgements: BL, Sloane MS, fo. 73r.

57. See, in this context, Edward Bowles as discussed in Philip Withington, *The Politics of Commonwealth: Citizens and Freemen in Early Modern England* (Cambridge, 2005), pp. 234–7.

58. John Locke, *A strange And Lamentable accident that happened lately at Mears Ashby* (London, 1642). Thomason date August [?] 1642. This pamphlet is also discussed in David Cressy, 'Lamentable, Strange, and Wonderful: Headless Monsters in the English Revolution', in Laura Lunger Knoppers and Joan B. Landes (eds.), *Monstrous Bodies/Political Monstrosities in Early Modern Europe* (Ithaca, 2004), pp. 40–63.

59. Walter, *Understanding Popular Violence*, pp. 295–6.

60. Locke, *Strange And Lamentable accident*, quotations at sig. A3r.

61. Ibid., quotations at sig. A3r, A2v, A4r.

62. Fletcher, *Outbreak*, pp. 370–71. For divisions in Northamptonshire see John Fielding, 'Arminianism in the Localities: Peterborough Diocese 1603–1642', in Kenneth Fincham (ed.), *The Early Stuart Church, 1603–1642* (Basingstoke, 1993), pp. 93–113.

63. John Taylor was a prominent exponent of these lines of polemic: Capp, *John Taylor*, esp. chs. 6, 8; Cressy, *England on Edge*, pp. 229–30.

64. The new name was given 'to those that strive to walk in the ways of God': BL, Sloane MS 1457, fos. 67–72v.

65. Ronald Hutton, *The Royalist War Effort 1642–1646*, 2nd edn (London, 1999), p. 4 for Croft and Hereford; Ronald Hutton, *The Rise and Fall of Merry England: The Ritual Year 1400–1700* (Oxford, 1994), p. 205 for Ludlow; Jacqueline Eales, *Puritans and Roundheads: The Harleys of Brampton Bryan and the Outbreak of the English Civil War* (Cambridge, 1990), p. 143–5.

66. Adamson, *Noble Revolt*, p. 387.

67. *CJ*, ii, p. 478. For hostility to the methods of Pym and his allies see Fletcher, *Outbreak*, pp. 127–30, 293–7; Cressy, *England on Edge*, pp. 338–46.

68. Walter, 'Confessional Politics', p. 699n; Peter Lake, 'Puritans, Popularity and Petitions: Local Politics in National Context, Cheshire, 1641', in Thomas Cogswell, Richard Cust and Peter Lake (eds.), *Politics, Religion and Popularity in Early Stuart Britain: Essays in Honour of Conrad Russell* (Cambridge, 2002), pp. 259–89. For a general account of these campaigns see also Fletcher, *Outbreak*, ch. 9; and, for a list of extant petitions, Judith Maltby, *Prayer Book and People in Elizabethan and Early Stuart England* (Cambridge, 1998), appendix 1, pp. 238–47. See also Cressy, *England on Edge*, ch. 11 (although it is not clear that this was necessarily Laudians fighting back).

69. Fletcher, *Outbreak*, pp. 307–10; Gardiner, X, pp. 179–82; Russell, *Fall*, pp. 498–500, quotation at p. 499; Alan Everitt, *The Community of Kent and the Great Rebellion 1640–60* (Leicester, 1966), pp. 95–107.

70. Joad Raymond, *The Invention of the Newspaper: English Newsbooks 1641–1649* (Oxford, 1996), p. 122.

71. Anon., *A Relation of a terrible Monster* (London, 1642), quotations at p. 3. For the reporting of wonders in newsbooks see Joad Raymond (ed.), *Making the News: An Anthology of the Newsbooks of Revolutionary England, 1641–1660* (Moreton-in-Marsh, 1993), ch. 4.

72. John Hare, *The Marine Mercury* ([London], 1642). The sailors are: Nicholas Treadcrow, Josias Otter, Humfrey Hearnshaw, Alexander Waterrat, Sim. Seamaule and Tim. Bywater. The ESTC identifies Hare as the author of later tracts critical of the lingering effects of the Norman conquest on the rights and liberties of Englishmen, which might suggest broadly parliamentarian sympathies.

73. Alexandra Walsham, *Providence in Early Modern England* (Oxford, 2001), p. 41.

74. HEH, EL 7846, Castle to Bridgewater, 4 August 1640.

75. Russell, *Fall*, p. 419.

76. Fletcher, *Outbreak*, p. 170.

77. Reprinted in John Morrill, *Revolt of the Provinces: Conservatives and Radicals in the English Civil War, 1630–1650*, 1st edn (Harlow, 1980), at p. 137 (these documents are not included in their entirety in the second edition).

7. Raising Forces

1. Bulstrode Whitelocke, *Memorials of the English Affairs*, 4 vols. (Oxford, 1853), I, p. 176.

2. John Morrill, 'Devereux, Robert, Third Earl of Essex (1591–1646)', *ODNB*, 15, pp. 960–69. See also John Adamson, *The Noble Revolt: The Overthrow of Charles I* (London, 2007).

3. Samuel R. Gardiner, *History of England from the Accession of James I to the Outbreak of the Civil War 1603–1642*, 10 vols. (London, 1884), X, pp. 196–20; for Parliament's order see Gardiner, *CD*, p. 261. For the navy see Bernard Capp, 'Naval Operations', in

John Kenyon and Jane Ohlmeyer (eds.), *The Civil Wars: A Military History of England, Scotland and Ireland* (Oxford, 1998), pp. 156–91.

4. Gardiner, *History of England*, X, pp. 199–202. Actually, the King's reception at Heyworth Moor was a little discouraging: Joyce Malcolm, 'A King in Search of Soldiers: Charles I in 1642', *HJ*, 21 (1978), 251–73, at pp. 257–8. For the Commission of Array see Ronald Hutton, *The Royalist War Effort 1642–1646*, 2nd edn (London, 1999), pp. 5–6.

5. John Morrill, *Revolt in the Provinces: The People of England and the Tragedies of War 1630–1648*, 2nd edn (Harlow, 1999), pp. 60–61.

6. For the Kentish petition see above, p. 205; for the role of assizes and quarter sessions see Anthony Fletcher, *The Outbreak of the English Civil War* (London, 1981), esp. p. 194. It was frustration at the conduct of a Grand Jury which seems to have prompted the Essex Prayer Book petition: John Walter, 'Confessional Politics in pre-Civil War Essex: Prayer Books, Profanations, and Petitions', *HJ*, 44 (2001), 677–701, at pp. 691–9.

7. Fletcher, *Outbreak*, pp. 298–300; for the correlations with subsequent success of the rival militia authorities compare maps 6, 7, 8.

8. Ibid., p. 300.

9. *The Declaration and Protestation agreed upon by the Grand Jury at the Assizes held for the County of Worcester* (York, 1642); this was the outcome of successful political manoeuvring: Hutton, *Royalist War Effort*, pp. 10–11; Fletcher, *Outbreak*, p. 358; Ian Roy, 'The Royalist Army in the First Civil War', unpublished D.Phil. thesis, Oxford (1963), pp. 18–22.

10. *The Declaration and Protestation of divers the Knights, Gentry and Freeholders* (London, 1642); *Declaration and Protestation agreed upon by the Grand Jury*. As elsewhere, the unanimity of this Lincolnshire declaration was the result of successful mobilization by one party, rather than representing the authentic 'voice of the county': see Clive Holmes, *Seventeenth-Century Lincolnshire* (Lincoln, 1980), ch. 9, esp. pp. 145–8.

11. Fletcher, *Outbreak*, pp. 300, 356, 359, and for other examples pp. 306, 362–3, 389, 395; Hutton, *Royalist War Effort*, pp. 10–11; John Walter, *Understanding Popular Violence in the English Revolution: The Colchester Plunderers* (Cambridge 1999), pp. 129–34; for Worcester see also Roy, 'Royalist Army', pp. 18–22; for the City of Worcester see Philip Styles, 'The City of Worcester during the Civil Wars, 1640–60', reprinted in R. C. Richardson (ed.), *The English Civil Wars: Local Aspects* (Stroud, 1997), pp. 187–238, at pp. 192–3.

12. Fletcher, *Outbreak*, pp. 347–56.

13. Ibid., p. 350.

14. Ibid., pp. 356–68; Ann Hughes, *Politics, Society and Civil War in Warwickshire, 1620–1660* (Cambridge, 1987), pp. 136–42.

15. Bernard Capp, 'Naval Operations', pp. 160–62.

16. Alan Everitt, *The Community of Kent and the Great Rebellion* (Leicester, 1966), pp. 111–16.

17. Peter Young and Richard Holmes, *The English Civil War: A Military History of the Three Civil Wars 1642–1651* (Ware, 2000), pp. 84–8; David Underdown, *Somerset in the Civil War and Interregnum* (Newton Abbot, 1973), pp. 31–8.

18. Malcolm Wanklyn and Frank Jones, *A Military History of the English Civil War, 1642–1646: Strategy and Tactics* (Harlow, 2005), pp. 42–3. For Portsmouth see John Webb, 'The Siege of Portsmouth in the Civil War', reprinted in Richardson (ed.), *Local Aspects*, pp. 63–90.

19. Young and Holmes, *English Civil War*, pp. 88–91. Cornwall was later a stronghold of royalism but the gentry were apparently united in their opposition to Laudianism and the abuse of the prerogative until the trial of Strafford, and were deeply divided by the Militia Ordinance and the Commission of Array: Mary Coate, *Cornwall in the Great Civil War and Interregnum 1642–1660: A Social and Political Study* (Oxford, 1933), ch. 4.

20. HEH, EL 7762, Relation of some passages at Manchester 15 July 1642. For the

pre-history, and rival versions, of these events see Ernest Broxap, *The Great Civil War in Lancashire (1642–51)*, 2nd edn (Manchester, 1973), pp. 12–19; Fletcher, *Outbreak*, pp. 360–61, 392–3.

21. HEH, EL 7762.

22. Ibid.

23. Quoted in Morrill, *Revolt in the Provinces*, 2nd edn, pp. 52–3.

24. Charles Carlton, *Going to the Wars: The Experience of the English Civil Wars 1638–1651* (London, 1992), pp. 64–5.

25. For the importance of a unified public front see Michael J. Braddick, 'Administrative Performance: The Representation of Political Authority in Early Modern England', in Michael J. Braddick and John Walter (eds.), *Negotiating Power in Early Modern Society: Order, Hierarchy and Subordination in Britain and Ireland* (Cambridge, 2001), pp. 166–87.

26. Fletcher, *Outbreak*, pp. 374–5; Hughes, *Warwickshire*, p. 130; Cressy, *England on Edge*, pp. 53–5 (1640–41).

27. Fletcher, *Outbreak*, pp. 370–71.

28. Ibid., pp. 381–5; D. H. Pennington and I. A. Roots (eds.), *The Committee at Stafford, 1643–1645: The Order Book of the Staffordshire County Committee*, Collections for a History of Staffordshire, 4th ser., 1 (Manchester, 1957), pp. xx, 341.

29. Ibid., p. xx.

30. Fletcher, *Outbreak*, p. 380.

31. The classic statements of the importance of neutralism were Alan Everitt, 'The Local Community and the Great Rebellion', reprinted in Richardson (ed.), *Local Aspects*, pp. 15–36; and John Morrill's. Both were more nuanced than is often claimed, although the hostage to fortune given by Everitt at p. 33 has been gleefully seized upon by critics. For Morrill's original position and his later thoughts about the problems of analysing 'neutralism' see Morrill, *Revolt in the Provinces*, 2nd edn, pp. 54–8, 185–90, 197–204. For influential revisions of Morrill's view see Fletcher, *Outbreak*, ch. 12; Ann Hughes, 'Local History and the Origins of the Civil War', in Richard Cust and Ann Hughes (eds.), *Conflict in Early Stuart England: Studies in Religion and Politics 1603–1642* (Harlow, 1989), pp. 224–53; Hughes, *Warwickshire*, esp. pp. 144–5, 158–67; Anthony Fletcher, 'National and Local Awareness in the County Communities', in Howard Tomlinson (ed.), *Before the English Civil War: Essays on Early Stuart Politics and Government* (London, 1983), pp. 151–74; and, for the war years, Ann Hughes, 'The King, the Parliament and the Localities during the English Civil War', *JBS*, 24 (1985), 236–63; Mark Stoyle, *Loyalty and Locality: Popular Allegiance in Devon during the English Civil War* (Exeter, 1994), ch. 6.

32. Fletcher, *Outbreak*, pp. 385–7; Morrill, *Revolt in the Provinces*, 2nd edn, pp. 55–6. Fletcher corrects the account of Cheshire's 'third force' given in J. S. Morrill, *Cheshire 1630–1660: County Government and Society during the English Revolution* (Oxford, 1974), pp. 57–8.

33. Holmes, *Lincolnshire*, ch. 9, quotation at p. 156.

34. For the mingling of national awareness and local ambition in Worcestershire see Fletcher, *Outbreak*, pp. 389–90. For the role of partisans in overriding these qualms see ibid., pp. 400–405. For Gloucestershire see A. R. Warmington, *Civil War, Interregnum and Restoration in Gloucestershire 1640–1672* (Woodbridge, 1997), ch. 2.

35. Fletcher, *Outbreak*, pp. 390–91; Morrill, *Revolt in the Provinces*, 2nd edn, p. 56; Andrew Hopper, *'Black Tom': Sir Thomas Fairfax and the English Revolution* (Manchester, 2007), pp. 12–20, 26–8.

36. Young and Holmes, *English Civil War*, pp. 99–100.

37. Fletcher, *Outbreak*, pp. 391–3.

38. Patrick McGrath, 'Bristol and the Civil War', reprinted in Richardson (ed.), *Local Aspects*, pp. 91–128, esp. pp. 91–101; see also David Harris Sacks, 'Bristol's "Wars of religion" ', in R. C. Richardson (ed.), *Town and Countryside in the English Revolution*

(Manchester, 1992), pp. 100–129; Styles, 'City of Worcester', pp. 192–6; David Scott, 'Politics and Government in York 1640–1662', in Richardson (ed.), *Town and Countryside*, pp. 46–68, esp. pp. 49–50; Ian Roy, 'The City of Oxford 1640–1660', in Richardson (ed.), *Town and Countryside*, pp. 130–68, esp. p. 140.

39. Fletcher, *Outbreak*, pp. 393–400; for Coventry see Ann Hughes, 'Coventry and the English Revolution', in Richardson (ed.), *Town and Countryside*, pp. 69–99, esp. pp. 77–80. For the earlier emphasis on neutralism in the towns see Morrill, *Revolt in the Provinces*, 2nd edn, pp. 57–8; Roger Howell, 'Newcastle and the Nation: The Seventeenth-Century Experience', reprinted in Richardson (ed.), *Local Aspects*, pp. 309–29; Roger Howell, 'Neutralism, Conservatism and Political Alignment in the English Revolution: The Case of the Towns, 1642–9', in John Morrill (ed.), *Reactions to the English Civil War 1642–1649* (Basingstoke, 1982), pp. 67–87. For a persuasive case that the political culture of incorporated towns sat most easily with the emerging parliamentarian programme see Philip Withington, *The Politics of Commonwealth: Citizens and Freemen in Early Modern England* (Cambridge, 2005), esp. pp. 41–4.

40. See Robert M. Bliss, *Revolution and Empire: English Politics and the American Colonies in the Seventeenth Century* (Manchester, 1990), esp. pp. 74–92; in many ways the conditions of the 1640s fostered the development of a more autonomous Atlantic community: Carla G. Pestana, *The English Atlantic in an Age of Revolution, 1640–1661* (Cambridge, Mass., 2004).

41. Clive Holmes, *The Eastern Association in the English Civil War* (Cambridge, 1974), pp. 33–62. For Norfolk see also R. W. Ketton-Cremer, *Norfolk in the Civil War: A Portrait of a Society in Conflict* (London, 1969), ch. 8.

42. Hutton, *Royalist War Effort*, esp. pp. 3–4. In Herefordshire partisanship erupted from January 1642, prompted by the departure of the King from Parliament and the use of ordinances in his absence, producing a battle between commitment to godly reformation and to constitutional royalism: Jacqueline Eales, *Puritans and Roundheads: The Harleys of Brampton Bryan and the Outbreak of the English Civil War* (Cambridge, 1990), ch. 6.

43. Fletcher, *Outbreak*, pp. 324–9.

44. Malcolm, 'A King in Search of Soldiers', pp. 259–71; Fletcher, *Outbreak*, pp. 329–33; Andrew Hopper, ' "The popish army of the north": Anti-Catholicism and Parliamentarian Allegiance in Civil War Yorkshire, 1642–46', *Recusant History*, 25:1 (2000), 12–28. For a judicious overview of the involvement of Catholics see William Sheils, 'English Catholics at War and Peace', in Christopher Durston and Judith Maltby (eds.), *Religion in Revolutionary England* (Manchester, 2006), pp. 137–57. For the disarming of the Trained Bands see also C. H. Firth, *Cromwell's Army: A History of the English Soldier during the Civil Wars, the Commonwealth and the Protectorate* (London, 1967 edn), pp. 16–17.

45. Fletcher, *Outbreak*, pp. 334–40.

46. Malcolm, 'A King in Search of Soldiers', p. 263; Astley quoted in Wanklyn and Jones, *English Civil War*, p. 43.

47. Roy, 'Royalist Army', ch. 1.

48. See, for example, Coleby's discussion of the Hampshire Grand Jury petition for accommodation in the summer of 1642: Andrew Coleby, *Central Government and the Localities: Hampshire 1649–1689* (Cambridge, 1987), pp. 6–7.

49. Barbara Donagan, 'Troubled Consciences: Choice and Allegiance in the English Civil War' (unpublished paper), pp. 22–6; see also Barbara Donagan, 'Casuistry and Allegiance in the English Civil War', in Derek Hirst and Richard Strier (eds.), *Writing and Political Engagement in Seventeenth-Century England* (Cambridge, 2000), pp. 89–111. For background on godly choice, and other examples, see Barbara Donagan, 'Godly Choice: Puritan Decision-Making in Seventeenth-Century England', *Harvard Theological Review*, 76 (1983), 307–34; Barbara Donagan, 'Understanding Providence: The Difficulties of Sir William and Lady Waller', *Journal of Ecclesiastical History*, 39:3 (1988), 433–44; Barbara Donagan, 'Providence, Chance and Explanation', *Journal of Religious History*, 11 (1981), 385–403.

50. Donagan, 'Troubled Consciences', p. 27.
51. Gardiner, I, p. 168.
52. Ibid., pp. 15–16.
53. David L. Smith, *Constitutional Royalism and the Search for Settlement, c. 1640–1649* (Cambridge, 1994), chs. 3–4. For Colepeper's speech see above, p. 119; for the Kentish petition see above, p. 205.
54. Roy, 'Royalist Army', pp. 80–83; Richard Cust, *Charles I: A Political Life* (Harlow, 2005), pp. 327–31, 360–26. On Digby see Ian Roy, 'George Digby, Royalist Intrigue and the Collapse of the Cause', in Ian Gentles, John Morrill and Blair Worden (eds.), *Soldiers, Writers and Statesmen of the English Revolution* (Cambridge, 1998), pp. 68–90; Adamson, *Noble Revolt*, esp. p. 312. For overviews of the range of royalist opinion see also Ronald Hutton, 'The Structure of the Royalist Party, 1642–1646', *HJ*, 24 (1981), 553–69; James Daly, 'The Implications of Royalist Politics 1642–1646', *HJ*, 27 (1984), 745–55.
55. Ian Roy, 'Rupert, Prince and Count Palatine of the Rhine and Duke of Cumberland (1619–1682)', *ODNB*, 48, pp. 141–54.
56. Sheils, 'English Catholics', p. 141.
57. John Morrill (ed.), *Oliver Cromwell and the English Revolution* (Harlow, 1990); Barry Coward, *Oliver Cromwell* (Harlow, 1991), intr. and ch. 1; Blair Worden, 'Oliver Cromwell and the Sin of Achan', in Derek Beales and Geoffrey Best (eds.), *History, Society and the Churches: Essays in Honour of Owen Chadwick* (Cambridge, 1985), pp. 125–45.
58. Holmes, *Eastern Association*, pp. 54–5.
59. Walter, *Understanding Popular Violence*.
60. For Somerset see above, pp. 215–16; Stoyle, *Loyalty and Locality*, pp. 39–40.
61. Stoyle, *Loyalty and Locality*, p. 143.
62. Morrill, *Cheshire*, pp. 78–9. Brian Manning, *The English People and the English Revolution* (Harmondsworth, 1976), chs. 7–8, argues for an independent middling sort parliamentarianism lined up against an aristocratic loyalism supported by deferential tenants. While valuable in emphasizing the potential of political commitments below the level of the gentry he is surely too dismissive of the possibility of a genuine popular royalism: see his position in *Aristocrats, Plebeians and Revolution in England, 1640–1660* (London, 1996), esp. pp. 56–8. This line is also detected by many commentators in Underdown, *Somerset*, and David Underdown, *Revel, Riot and Rebellion: Popular Politics and Culture in England 1603–1660* (Oxford, 1985). For a review and rebuttal see Buchanan Sharp, 'Rural Discontents and the English Revolution', in Richardson (ed.), *Town and Countryside*, pp. 251–72. On deference and independence more generally, see C. B. Phillips, 'Landlord–Tenant Relationships 1642–1660', in Richardson (ed.), *Town and Countryside*, esp. pp. 226–33; Morrill, *Revolt in the Provinces*, 2nd edn, pp. 185–9.
63. Hughes, *Warwickshire*, pp. 142–65; Warmington, *Gloucestershire*, pp. 33–7.
64. Underdown, *Revel, Riot and Rebellion* is the pioneering work of this kind, followed by Stoyle, *Loyalty and Locality*, see esp. here, ch. 7. For some searching but respectful criticism of Underdown see John Morrill, 'The Ecology of Allegiance', reprinted in John Morrill, *The Nature of the English Revolution* (Harlow, 1993), pp. 224–41. See also David Underdown, 'A Reply to John Morrill', *JBS*, 26 (1987), 468–79 and Morrill, *Revolt in the Provinces*, 2nd edn, pp. 186–7.
65. A case made very powerfully by Holmes, *Eastern Association*, ch. 3.
66. See David Underdown, 'The Problem of Popular Allegiance in the English Civil War', *TRHS*, 5th ser., 31 (1981), 69–94, at pp. 92–3 for some suggestive comments along these lines.
67. Andy Wood, 'Beyond Post-Revisionism?: The Civil War Allegiances of the Miners of the Derbyshire "Peak Country"', *HJ*, 40 (1997), 23–40.
68. An argument put most pungently by Manning, *Aristocrats, Plebeians and Revolution*, ch. 8.
69. Keith Lindley, *Fenland Riots and the English Revolution* (London, 1982); Clive Holmes,

'Drainers and Fenmen: The Problem of Popular Political Consciousness in the Seventeenth Century', in Anthony Fletcher and John Stevenson (eds.), *Order and Disorder in Early Modern England* (Cambridge, 1985), pp. 166–95, esp. pp. 168–9.

70. See above, p. 123.

71. Daniel C. Beaver, 'Sacrifice, Venison and the Social Order in Waltham Forest, 1608–1642' (unpublished paper). These disputes are discussed more fully in ch. 15.

72. Daniel C. Beaver, 'The Great Deer Massacre: Animals, Honor, and Communication in Early Modern England', *JBS*, 38 (1999), 187–216; see also Daniel C. Beaver, ' "Bragging and daring words": Honour, Property and the Symbolism of the Hunt in Stowe, 1590–1642', in Braddick and Walter (eds.), *Negotiating Power*, pp. 149–65. Purkiss surely misrepresents these events in assimilating them to the effects of hunger (the animals were for the most part not eaten) on soldiers enduring long, hard service (they were not soldiers and there was as yet no war): Diane Purkiss, *The English Civil War: Papists, Gentlemen, Soldiers, and Witchfinders in the Birth of Modern Britain* (New York, 2006), ch. 18.

73. For the dispute see Heather Falvey, 'Crown Policy and Local Economic Context in the Berkhamsted Common Enclosure Dispute, 1618–42', *Rural History*, 12 (2001), 123–58. For Edlyn's contribution see TNA, E.179/248/19; Andrew Hopper, 'The Wortley Park Poachers and the Outbreak of the English Civil War' *Northern History*, 44 (2007), 93–114.

74. See above, pp. 184–5. For a sensitive discussion of the issues see John Walter, 'The English People and the English Revolution Revisited', *History Workshop Journal*, 61 (2006), 171–182. For the ability of merchant networks to take advantage of the times see Robert Brenner, *Merchants and Revolution: Commercial Change, Political Conflict and London's Overseas Traders, 1550–1653* (Cambridge, 1993), esp. pt 3. This is my gloss on his argument; he emphasizes the potential of this analysis to support a broader interpretation of the conflict as grounded in class interests.

75. Walter, *Understanding Popular Violence*: John Morrill and John Walter, 'Order and Disorder in the English Revolution', in Fletcher and Stevenson (ed.), *Order and Disorder*, pp. 137–65; Fletcher, *Outbreak*, ch. 12. Manning put this fear of disorder at the heart of royalism: *English People*, chs. 3, 7, 8. See also Lady Sydenham above, pp. 227–8. For an overview of theories of allegiance see Underdown, *Revel, Riot and Rebellion*, ch. 1.

76. Ann Hughes, *The Causes of the English Civil War*, 2nd edn (Basingstoke, 1998), p. 168.

8. Armed Negotiation

1. Details of this and all military encounters are hard to agree and are much written about. For a general account of the difficulties see Malcolm Wanklyn, *Decisive Battles of the English Civil War: Myth and Reality* (Barnsley, 2006), chs. 1–2. Here and elsewhere I have relied upon Peter Young and Richard Holmes, *The English Civil War: A Military History of the Three Civil Wars, 1642–1651* (Ware, 2000 edn), pp. 69–71; Malcolm Wanklyn and Frank Jones, *A Military History of the English Civil War, 1642–1646: Strategy and Tactics* (Harlow, 2005), pp. 44–5. Austin Woolrych's fine political narrative *Britain in Revolution 1625–1660* (Oxford, 2002) is also informative about military matters: Woolrych wrote a number of important military histories. For the battle and subsequent desecration of the cathedral see Gardiner, I, pp. 30, 66.

2. Wanklyn and Jones, *Military History*, pp. 46–8; Young and Holmes, *English Civil War*, pp. 71–3. The King's infantry complement at Edgehill was probably larger than at any point later in the war, but was not at all well armed: Ian Roy, 'The Royalist Army in the First Civil War', unpublished D.Phil. thesis, Oxford (1963), pp. 50, 160–63.

3. M. C. Fissel, *English Warfare, 1511–1642* (London, 2001), offers a very good overview.

4. For the role of Scottish 'soldiers of fortune' see Mark Stoyle, *Soldiers and Strangers: An Ethnic History of the English Civil War* (New Haven, Conn., 2005), esp. pp. 77–9: being in pay is not always the same as being a mercenary in the more general sense, of course: see his index entry for 'mercenary' for the conflation.

5. David Trim, 'Calvinist Internationalism and the English Officer Corps, 1562–1642', *History Compass*, 4/6 (2006), 1024–48, at pp. 1024–5.

6. Barbara Donagan, 'Halcyon Days and the Literature of War: England's Military Education before 1642', *PP*, 147 (1995), 65–100. For the muster masters see also Lindsey O. Boynton, *The Elizabethan Militia, 1558–1638* (London, 1967), esp. pp. 224–7, 287–91; Kevin Sharpe, *The Personal Rule of Charles I* (New Haven, Conn., 1992), pp. 28–30, 487–500.

7. Donagan, 'Halcyon Days'. For the importance of the Trained Bands, and their stores of arms, see above, p. 223.

8. For this and the following two paragraphs I have relied on Young and Holmes, *English Civil War*, pp. 73–81, updated in the light of the account in Wanklyn and Jones, *Military History*, pp. 50–55. For a detailed account of the sources and the ambiguities of any narrative based on them see Wanklyn, *Decisive Battles*, chs. 4–5.

9. Charles Carlton, *Going to the Wars: The Experience of the English Civil Wars, 1638–1651* (London, 1992), pp. 134, 137–9.

10. Richard Wiseman, *Severall Chirurgicall Treatises* (London, 1676), pp. 348–9.

11. Oliver Lawson Dick (ed.), *Aubrey's Brief Lives* (Harmondsworth, 1972 edn) p. 287. For the stripping of corpses, see Carlton, *Going to the Wars*, p. 146.

12. Dick, *Aubrey's Brief Lives*, pp. 286–7.

13. Carlton, *Going to the Wars*, pp. 146–7, 227.

14. John Kenyon, *The Civil Wars of England* (London, 1989 edn), p. 57. Kenyon's is another political narrative firmly grounded in a knowledge of military affairs.

15. Wanklyn and Jones, *Military History*, p. 56; Young and Holmes, *English Civil War*, p. 80.

16. Young and Holmes, *English Civil War*, p. 79; Carlton, *Going to the Wars*, p. 50. For Verney's commitment to the royalist cause see above, p. 226.

17. Wanklyn and Jones suggest that Essex withdrew northwards expecting the King, who had suffered heavy losses of infantry, to retreat towards Wales. They also argue that the suggestion of a rapid advance on London by the royalists was probably not made until four days after the battle, when it had more chance of success, rather than the morning after, as is often maintained. In any case, they suggest, it probably had less hope of success than is often argued: *Military History*, pp. 56–60. For the likely strategic effect of the taking of London see Woolrych, *Britain in Revolution*, p. 242.

18. Carlton, *Going to the Wars*, pp. 230–31; see also Wanklyn, *Decisive Battles*, chs. 1–2.

19. Gardiner, I, pp. 53–7. For Brentford see *The humble petition of the inhabitants of the town of Old Braintford* (London, 27 November 1642). According to the *Oxford English Dictionary*, 'the word was much used in Germany during the Thirty Years War, in reference to which it was current in England from c. 1630; here word and thing became familiar on the outbreak of the Civil War in 1642, being especially associated with the proceedings of the forces under Prince Rupert' (accessed online 7 March 2006: http://dictionary.oed. com/). This may be to accept parliamentarian propaganda at face value. The word was also used prior to active hostilities in relation to parliamentarian crowds or mustering soldiers: it was applied retrospectively to the Stour Valley rioters by Bruno Ryves (writing in 1643), but also appears in a document describing the fears of Lady Goring: EL 7795. The document is undated, but clearly comes from mid-August 1642.

20. Young and Holmes, *English Civil War*, pp. 82–3. Wanklyn and Jones cast doubt on the usual claim that Skippon, a man of military experience, added to the parliamentarian advantage by taking better advantage of the ground: *Military History*, pp. 60–61.

21. For good examples see A. R. Warmington, *Civil War, Interregnum and Restoration in Gloucestershire 1640–1672* (Woodbridge, 1997), pp. 43–50; John T. Evans, *Seventeenth-Century Norwich: Politics, Religion and Government, 1620–1690* (Oxford, 1979), pp. 119–28. In Lincolnshire, as in many other counties, a 'snarling modus vivendi' had survived up until the eve of Edgehill: Clive Holmes, *Seventeenth-Century Lincolnshire* (Lincoln, 1980), p. 159. The Staffordshire neutrality pact was agreed after Edgehill, and parties crystallized slowly thereafter: D. H. Pennington and I. A. Roots (eds.), *The*

Committee at Stafford, 1643–1645: The Order Book of the Staffordshire County Committee, Collections for a History of Staffordshire, 4th ser., 1 (Manchester, 1957), pp. xx–xxi.

22. Gardiner, I, pp. 13–14; David L. Smith, *Constitutional Royalism and the Search for Settlement, c. 1640–1649* (Cambridge, 1994), pp. 109–10.

23. Gardiner, I, pp. 15–18.

24. Smith, *Constitutional Royalism*, pp. 110–11. For a general account of royalist politics see Richard Cust, *Charles I: A Political Life* (Harlow, 2005), ch. 6. Ronald Hutton's brief account has been very influential: 'The Structure of the Royalist Party, 1642–1646', *HJ*, 24 (1981), 553–69. For some revision see James Daly, 'The Implications of Royalist Politics, 1642–1646', *HJ*, 27 (1984), 745–55.

25. Gardiner, I, p. 18.

26. Smith, *Constitutional Royalism*, pp. 111–12.

27. For the proposal see Gardiner, I, p. 39.

28. Gardiner, I, p. 20. He took this issue seriously. For example, having accepted that he did not have this combination of powers, he refused to negotiate without parliamentary authority at Lostwithiel in 1644: Gardiner, II, p. 11. Essex's powers may have been recognized by contemporaries to have been more extensive: J. S. A. Adamson, 'The Baronial Context of the English Civil War', *TRHS*, 5th ser., 40 (1990), 93–120, esp. pp. 105–19. This is based on a closer analysis of protocol and ceremonial than of the practice of politics.

29. Gardiner, I, pp. 19, 37, 39, 64, 71–2.

30. Young and Holmes, *English Civil War*, pp. 89–90.

31. Ibid., pp. 100–102.

32. Ibid., pp. 83, 115; Gardiner, I, pp. 71–2.

33. Woolrych, *Britain in Revolution*, pp. 243–5.

34. Gardiner, I, p. 73.

35. John Morrill, 'Holles, Denzil, First Baron Holles (1598–1680)', *ODNB*, 27, pp. 708–14. See also Patricia Crawford, *Denzil Holles, 1598–1680: A Study of His Political Career* (London, 1979).

36. Conrad Russell, 'Pym, John (1584–1643)', *ODNB*, 45, pp. 624–40; Gardiner, I, p. 62.

37. Michael J. Braddick, *The Nerves of State: Taxation and the Financing of the English State, 1558–1714* (Manchester, 1996), pp. 95–9.

38. *CJ*, ii, p. 865, 26 Nov. 1642: 'Mr. *Pym*, Sir *H. Vane* senior, Mr. *Pierrepointe*, Sir *H. Vane* junior, Mr *Holles*, Mr *Rous*, Mr *Whitlock*, are appointed to consider of some propositions to be presented to this House, for the entering into a strict league with the States of the *United Provinces*: And are to meet when and where they please'.

39. Gardiner, I, p. 77. For the history of the Eastern Association see Clive Holmes, *The Eastern Association in the English Civil War* (Cambridge, 1974).

40. Gardiner, I, p. 63.

41. Keith Lindley, *Popular Politics and Religion in Civil War London* (Aldershot, 1997), pp. 236–55, 337–48; Gardiner, I, pp. 74–5; for the Committee of Both Houses for the Advance of Money see Gerald Aylmer, *The State's Servants: The Civil Service of the English Republic 1649–1660* (London, 1973), esp. p. 13.

42. For the measures see Gardiner, I, pp. 14–15, 75. Anon., *The actors remonstrance* (London, 24 January 1643), complained that the theatres had been closed but that bear-baiting continued.

43. Lindley, *Popular Politics*, pp. 344–5.

44. *The New Yeares wonder being a most cernaine* [sic] *and true Relation of the disturbed inhabitants of Kenton: And other neighbouring villages neere unto Edge-Hil* (London, 1643), printed for Robert Ellit, Thomason date 27 January 1643, quotations from title page, pp. 6, 7–8; *A great vvonder in Heaven: shewing the late Apparitions and prodigious noyses of War and Battels, seen on Edge-Hill neere Keinton in Northampton-shire* (London, 1643), printed for Thomas Jackson, pub. date 23 January 1643.

45. For special providences see Alexandra Walsham, *Providence in Early Modern England*

(Oxford, 1999). For some other examples of sky battles and similar atmospheric phenomena see *Irelands Amazement, or the Heavens armado* (London, 1641); *A Signe From Heaven* (London, 12 August 1642); *Severall apparitions Seene in the Ayre* (London, 1646), Thomason date 18 June; Wallington collected examples too: BL, Sloane MS 1457, fos. 5r, 56r–58r; and, more generally, Vladimir Jankovic, 'The Politics of Sky Battles in Early Hanoverian Britain', *JBS*, 41 (2002), 429–459, esp. pp. 432, 438, 452. Title searches are a crude measure, of course, but they do reflect the means by which a pamphlet was sold. The whole database of titles in Early English Books Online contains forty items with 'wonder' prominent in the title. They date mainly from before 1644, and fall particularly heavily in 1641 and 1642. For the ambiguous place of ghosts in reformed religion see Peter Marshall, *Beliefs and the Dead in Reformation England* (Oxford, 2002).

46. *The New Yeares wonder*, p. 8. For the complexity of attitudes towards these phenomena see Jankovic, 'Sky Battles', and more generally Walsham, *Providence*.

47. *A great vvonder*, p. 4. For an example from Austria during the Thirty Years War see Jankovic, 'Sky battles', p. 432.

48. *A great vvonder*, p. 4; *The New Yeares wonder*, p. 4.

49. *A great vvonder*, p. 4.

50. Ibid., p. 7.

51. Richard Williams, *Peace, and No Peace* (London, 1643), Thomason date 5 January 1643.

52. David Wootton, 'From Rebellion to Revolution: The Crisis of the Winter of 1642/3 and the Origins of Civil War Radicalism', reprinted in Richard Cust and Ann Hughes (eds.), *The English Civil War* (London, 1997), pp. 340–56. For Baxter's views see pp. 341–3, 347–8. For Baxter's career see N. H. Keeble, 'Baxter, Richard (1615–1691)', *ODNB*, 4, pp. 418–33.

53. Wootton, 'Rebellion to Revolution', pp. 345–6.

54. Ibid., p. 346.

55. Ibid., pp. 347–9.

56. Ibid., p. 351.

57. Quentin Skinner, 'Rethinking Political Liberty', *History Workshop Journal*, 61 (2006), 156–70; and more generally, Quentin Skinner, 'Classical Liberty and the Coming of the English Civil War', in Martin Van Gelderen and Quentin Skinner (eds.), *Republicanism: A Shared European Heritage*, vol. 2: *The Values of Republicanism in Early Modern Europe* (Cambridge, 2002), pp. 9–28.

58. Quoted in Patricia Crawford, 'Charles Stuart, That Man of Blood', reprinted in Peter Gaunt (ed.), *The English Civil War* (Oxford, 2000), pp. 303–23, at p. 310.

59. Gardiner, I, ch. 4; Smith, *Constitutional Royalism*, pp. 112–13. For the text see Gardiner, *CD*, pp. 262–7.

60. Smith, *Constitutional Royalism*, pp. 113–15.

61. Lindley, *Popular Politics*, pp. 177–9, 345–8; see also Gardiner, I, pp. 82–3.

62. Gardiner, I, pp. 98–103.

63. Wootton, 'Rebellion to Revolution', p. 353 n. 9, citing the distinction made by Skinner, between motives and intentions: Quentin Skinner, 'Motives, Intentions and the Interpretation of Texts', reprinted in James Tully (ed.), *Meaning and Context: Quentin Skinner and His Critics* (Princeton, NJ, 1988), pp. 68–78.

9. Military Escalation, Loyalty and Honour

1. David Cressy, *Agnes Bowker's Cat: Travesties and Transgressions in Tudor and Stuart England* (Oxford, 2000), ch. 14, quotations at pp. 247, 248. See also Julie Spraggon, *Puritan Iconoclasm in the English Civil War* (Woodbridge, 2003), pp. 42–6; Nicola Smith, *The Royal Image and the English People* (Aldershot, 2001), ch. 2; Margaret Aston, 'Iconoclasm in England: Official and Clandestine', reprinted in Peter Marshall (ed.), *The Impact of the English Reformation 1500–1640* (London, 1997), pp. 167–92, esp. pp. 183–5.

2. Cressy, *Agnes Bowker's Cat*, quotations at pp. 238, 239. For the social geography of Cheapside and the politics of its physical appearance see also Paul Griffiths, 'Politics Made Visible: Order, Residence and Uniformity in Cheapside, 1600–45', in Paul Griffiths and Mark S. R. Jenner (eds.), *Londinopolis: Essays in the Cultural and Social History of Early Modern London* (Manchester, 2000), pp. 176–96

3. Cressy, *Agnes Bowker's Cat*, quotation at p. 246. For the controversy in 1641 see above, p. 145.

4. Peter Young and Richard Holmes, *The English Civil War: A Military History of the Three Civil Wars 1642–1651* (Ware, 2000), pp. 91–4.

5. Quoted in ibid., p. 102.

6. Ibid., pp. 102–11, 122.

7. Ibid., pp. 113–14.

8. Ibid., pp. 115–22.

9. Gardiner, I, p. 67; Young and Holmes accepted the case: *English Civil War*, p. 98, and for the royalist command see pp. 54–7. For scepticism about royal strategy, and a more positive view of parliamentary strategy, see Ian Roy, 'The Royalist Army in the First Civil War', unpublished D.Phil. thesis, Oxford (1963), ch. 2, esp. p. 74; Malcolm Wanklyn and Frank Jones, *A Military History of the English Civil War, 1642–1646: Strategy and Tactics* (Harlow, 2005), pp. 23, 43, 82, 92–4.

10. Nigel Smith, *Literature and Revolution in England 1640–1660* (New Haven, Conn., 1994), p. 64. Bruno Ryves noted, apparently neutrally, that Brooke was shot in the eye on St Chad's Day. The cathedral is named for St Chad, the first holder of the see: [Bruno Ryves], *Micro-chronicon* (London, 1647), unpaginated, under the heading 21 April 1643.

11. Young and Holmes, *English Civil War*, p. 103.

12. See above, pp. 253–4.

13. Clive Holmes, *The Eastern Association in the English Civil War* (Cambridge, 1974), pp. 62–3; *A&O*, I, pp. 49–80, passim. See also Clive Holmes (ed.), *The Suffolk Committees for Scandalous Ministers 1644–1646*, Suffolk Records Society, XIII (Ipswich, 1970), pp. 20–21.

14. Holmes, *Eastern Association*, pp. 62–7, quotations at p. 63. See also J. H. Hexter, *The Reign of King Pym* (Cambridge, Mass., 1941), esp. pp. 28–9, and, for the measures discussed in this chapter more generally, ch. 1.

15. John Morrill, *Revolt in the Provinces: The People of England and the Tragedies of War 1630–1648*, 2nd edn (Harlow, 1999), pp. 102–4; Holmes, *Eastern Association*, esp. pp. 67–8.

16. *A&O*, I, pp. 73–4, 76–7, 104–5, 123–4.

17. See above, pp. 392–3.

18. For these forms of taxation in general see Michael J. Braddick, *Parliamentary Taxation in Seventeenth-Century England: Local Administration and Response* (Woodbridge, 1994), chs. 3, 4; Michael J. Braddick, *The Nerves of State: Taxation and the Financing of the English State, 1558–1714* (Manchester, 1996), ch. 5. For the Assessment Ordinance see *A&O*, I, pp. 85–100. For the excise proposal see Gardiner, I, pp. 101–2. For Hunstanton and Hanworth see Braddick, *Parliamentary Taxation*, p. 139. For influential studies of the escalating local burden of taxation see Alan Everitt, *The Community of Kent and the Great Rebellion 1640–60* (Leicester, 1966), esp. pp. 155–72; Holmes, *Eastern Association*, esp. ch. 7; Anthony Fletcher, *A County Community in Peace and War: Sussex 1600–1660* (London, 1975), esp. pp. 336–9; Ann Hughes, *Politics, Society and Civil War in Warwickshire, 1620–1660* (Cambridge, 1987), esp. pp. 255–71; J. S. Morrill, *Cheshire 1630–1660: County Government and Society during the English Revolution* (Oxford, 1974), ch. 3.

19. *A&O*, I, pp. 106–117.

20. Ibid., pp. 145–55 (7 May 1643).

21. For the development of this strand of opinion see Robert Ashton, 'From Cavalier to Roundhead Tyranny, 1642–9', in John Morrill (ed.), *Reactions to the English Civil War*

1642–1649 (Basingstoke, 1982), pp. 185–207; Robert Ashton, *Counter-Revolution: The Second Civil War and Its Origins, 1646–1648* (New Haven, Conn., 1994).

22. Morrill, *Revolt in the Provinces*, 2nd edn, pp. 79–80. For a general account see Gerald Aylmer, *The State's Servants: The Civil Service of the English Republic 1649–1660* (London, 1973), esp. pp. 9–24.

23. Morrill, *Revolt in the Provinces*, 2nd edn, pp. 83–4; Lotte Glow, 'The Committee of Safety', *EHR*, 80 (1965), 289–313; Wallace Notestein, 'The Establishment of the Committee of Both Kingdoms', *AHR*, 17 (1912), 477–95; John Adamson, 'The Triumph of Oligarchy: The Management of War and the Committee of Both Kingdoms, 1644–1645', in Chris R. Kyle and Jason Peacey (eds.), *Parliament at Work: Parliamentary Committees, Political Power and Public Access in Early Modern England* (Woodbridge, 2002), pp. 101–27.

24. Morrill, *Revolt in the Provinces*, 2nd edn, pp. 79–89. For the civilian committees see also Aylmer, *State's Servants*, pp. 8–29.

25. Edward Husbands, *An exact collection of all Remonstrances . . .* (London, 1643). On 5 August 1644 the Commons ordered Husbands to print 'all the Ordinances and Declarations that have passed since the Setting-forth the last Volume of Ordinances and Declarations, set forth by him: And, that he do take care diligently to compare his Copies with the Originals'. This latter provision suggests that he had met some criticism. He was once again given copyright: *CJ*, iii, p. 580. For the original order see *CJ*, iii, p. 16 (reproduced in Husbands, *Exact collection*, p. 956). Husbands also published as Husband – I have followed the spelling on this publication since it is the one which I have discussed in detail. I am grateful to Jason Peacey, on whose knowledge much of this paragraph is based, for discussing Husbands with me.

26. Quoted from Husbands, *Exact collection*, p. 932. See *A&O*, I, p. 85.

27. See above, p. 414.

28. Gardiner, I, pp. 100–102.

29. *CJ*, iii, p. 57; Spraggon, *Puritan Iconoclasm*, pp. 71–3.

30. Spraggon, *Puritan Iconoclasm*, pp. 73–5, 83–98; Keith Lindley, *Popular Politics and Religion in Civil War London* (Aldershot, 1997), esp. pp. 256–60; Cressy, *Agnes Bowker's Cat*, ch. 14; Gardiner, I, p. 132.

31. *Certaine informations* (24 April–1 May 1643), p. 119; Spraggon, *Puritan Iconoclasm*, pp. 83–5; for Harley see Jacqueline Eales, *Puritans and Roundheads: The Harleys of Brampton Bryan and the Outbreak of the English Civil War* (Cambridge, 1990), esp. pp. 56–60, 108–16.

32. For the administrative history see Holmes, *Suffolk Committees*, pp. 9–12. See also Ian Green, 'The Persecution of "Scandalous" and "Malignant" Parish Clergy during the English Civil War', *EHR*, 94 (1979), 507–31, esp. pp. 512–15.

33. Holmes, *Suffolk Committees*, pp. 9–12; Green, 'Persecution of "Scandalous" and "Malignant" Parish Clergy', esp. pp. 512–16; for an earlier example see David Cressy, *England on Edge: Crisis and Revolution 1640–1642* (Oxford, 2006), pp. 259–60.

34. Holmes, *Suffolk Committees*, pp. 9–10; *CJ*, ii, p. 54.

35. Holmes, *Suffolk Committees*, pp. 9–10, 115–19, quotation at p. 118.

36. *Certaine informations* (24 April–1 May 1643), p. 118.

37. David Cressy, 'Book Burning in Tudor and Stuart England', *Sixteenth Century Journal*, 36 (2005), 359–74, esp. pp. 361–8; Cyndia Clegg, 'Burning Books as Propaganda in Jacobean England', in Andrew Hadfield (ed.), *Literature and Censorship in Renaissance England* (Basingstoke, 2001), pp. 165–86.

38. Cressy, 'Book Burning', pp. 369–70; for Prynne and *Histrio-Mastix* see William Lamont, 'Prynne, William (1600–1669)', *ODNB*, 45, pp. 489–94.

39. Quoted in Cressy, 'Book Burning', pp. 370–71. I am also very grateful to Ariel Hessayon for allowing me to see his forthcoming paper 'Incendiary Texts: Radicalism and Book Burning in England, c. 1640–c. 1660'.

40. Cressy, 'Book Burning', p. 373. For Dering, the press and the wider public see also Jason

Peacey, 'Popularity and the Politician: An MP and His Public, 1640–1644' (forthcoming).

41. *Certaine informations* (24 April–1 May 1643), p. 118.

42. For the Somerset controversy see Thomas G. Barnes, 'County Politics and a Puritan *Cause Célèbre*: Somerset Church Ales, 1633', *TRHS*, 5th ser., 9 (1959), 103–22. For the *Book of Sports* and its local reception see Ronald Hutton, *The Rise and Fall of Merry England: The Ritual Year 1400–1700* (Oxford, 1994), pp. 196–8; Kevin Sharpe, *The Personal Rule of Charles I* (New Haven, Conn., 1992), pp. 353–9; Julian Davies, *The Caroline Captivity of the English Church* (Oxford, 1992), ch. 5.

43. Hutton, *Merry England*, pp. 200–201, 205–6; *A&O*, I, pp. 81–3, quotations at pp. 81, 82.

44. Cressy, *Agnes Bowker's Cat*, p. 249. For examples of maypoles and anti-Puritanism see David Underdown, *Revel, Riot and Rebellion: Popular Politics and Culture in England 1603–1660* (Oxford, 1985), esp. pp. 177, 269, 274–5; and see above, p. 204.

45. For this range of responses see Cressy, *Agnes Bowker's Cat*, p. 247. For concern about iconoclasm and disorder see John Walter, ' "Abolishing superstition with sedition"? The Politics of Popular Iconoclasm in England 1640–1642', *PP*, 183 (2004), 79–123.

46. See above, pp. 312–13.

47. William Cliftlands, 'The "Well-Affected" and the "Country": Politics and Religion in English Provincial Society, c. 1640–1654', unpublished Ph.D. thesis, Essex (1987), esp. chs. 2, 4.

48. Joad Raymond, *The Invention of the Newspaper: English Newsbooks 1641–1649* (Oxford, 1996), pp. 26–7.

49. The text has a relatively complicated history. Thomason collected several numbers as a serial up to December 1643. The ninth edition in Thomason's collection is numbered 18, suggesting a continuous weekly production, although it was interrupted in the autumn. These separate issues were included in an omnibus published in 1646, along with other material. This was largely reprinted in 1685 as a warning to a new generation. The 1685 edition is reset, with a new pagination, and seems to have introduced some errors. Another edition published as *Angliae Ruina* in 1648 has a completely new preface and includes some material not in the 1646 and 1685 editions, excluding some of the component parts. I have used and cited the 1685 edition, which is easily accessible, checking it where possible with the 1646 edition. For the publishing history see also Margaret Aston, *England's Iconoclasts*, vol. 1: *Laws Against Images* (Oxford, 1988), p. 71 n. 26.

50. *Mercurius Rusticus* (1685 edn), p. 70. Early orders had protected funerary monuments, but from August 1643 onwards they were included in the remit of the legislation: Spraggon, *Puritan Iconoclasm*, pp. 75–7. The legislation had sought to protect monuments, including coats of arms, of all those not 'commonly reputed or taken for' a saint. Wallington's notes record a kind of mirror-image version of a grossly transgressive Cavalierism: BL, Sloane MS 1457, esp. 27v ff., and Add MS 21935.

51. Young and Holmes, *English Civil War*, pp. 54–6; Wanklyn and Jones, *Military History*, p. 41; Morrill, *Revolt in the Provinces*, 2nd edn, pp. 77–9; Roy, 'Royalist Army', ch. 2, esp. pp. 51–85. For the conflict between military men and moderates see also Ronald Hutton, 'The Structure of the Royalist Party, 1642–1646', *HJ*, 24 (1981), 553–69.

52. Morrill, *Revolt in the Provinces*, 2nd edn, pp. 116–18; Richard Cust, *Charles I: A Political Life* (Harlow, 2005), pp. 384–5; Martyn Bennett, 'Between Scylla and Charybdis: The Creation of Rival Administrations at the Beginning of the English Civil War', reprinted in Peter Gaunt (ed.), *The English Civil War* (Oxford, 2000), pp. 167–83.

53. Roy, 'Royalist Army', pp. 220–47; Jens Engberg, 'Royalist Finances during the English Civil War, 1642–6', *Scandinavian Economic History Review*, 14:2 (1966), 73–96; Morrill, *Revolt in the Provinces*, 2nd edn, pp. 111–15, 116. For the Earl of Pembroke see Young and Holmes, *English Civil War*, p. 116.

54. Gardiner, I, pp. 132–3.

55. Ibid., pp. 57, 66, 107: at Birmingham the destruction occurred despite an order from Rupert. The general point is also made by Underdown, *Revel, Riot and Rebellion*, pp. 152–3.

56. Young and Holmes, *English Civil War*, pp. 113–14.
57. Barbara Donagan, 'Codes and Conduct in the English Civil War', *PP*, 118 (1988), pp. 65–95, esp. pp. 73–80.
58. Andrew Hopper, ' "Fitted for desperation": Honour and Treachery in Parliament's Yorkshire Command, 1642–1643', *History*, 86 (2001), 138–54, at pp. 140–41.
59. *Certaine informations* (24 April–1 May 1643), pp. 117–18. For the accepted view of royalist severity in dealing with civilians see Morrill, *Revolt in the Provinces*, 2nd edn, pp. 117–18.
60. Young and Holmes, *English Civil War*, p. 122.
61. Ibid., pp. 94–7, 122–4; Gardiner, I, pp. 155–6. For the Vow and Covenant see above, pp. 293–4. Hampden may have lost a hand when his pistol burst. Hampden's death is lyrically treated in Gardiner, I, pp. 152–5.
62. Young and Holmes, *English Civil War*, ch. 8, quotation at p. 137, and see also p. 142; Patrick McGrath, 'Bristol and the Civil War', reprinted in R. C. Richardson (ed.), *The English Civil Wars: Local Aspects* (Stroud, 1997), pp. 91–128, at pp. 101–11.
63. Young and Holmes, *English Civil War*, pp. 111–13.
64. Ibid., pp. 142–3, 151–4.
65. Gardiner, I, pp. 194–6, quotation at p. 195; Wanklyn and Jones, *Military History*, chs. 9–10. See also Cust, *Charles I*, pp. 378–81.
66. Young and Holmes, *English Civil War*, pp. 142–3; Gardiner, I, p. 207.
67. Austin Woolrych, *Britain in Revolution 1625–1660* (Oxford, 2002), pp. 257–8, quotation at p. 258; Lindley, *Popular Politics*, pp. 348–51; Gardiner, I, pp. 144–9.
68. Lindley, *Popular Politics*, pp. 304–19; Robert Brenner, *Merchants and Revolution: Commercial Change, Political Conflict and London's Overseas Traders, 1550–1653* (Cambridge, 1993), pp. 443–59; Valerie Pearl, *London and the Outbreak of the Puritan Revolution: City Government and National Politics 1625–1643* (Oxford, 1961), pp. 257–73.
69. Gardiner, I, pp. 183–8; Lindley, *Popular Politics*, pp. 351–2.
70. *LJ*, vi, pp. 86–7; Edward Vallance, 'Protestation, Vow, Covenant and Engagement: Swearing Allegiance in the English Civil War', *Historical Research*, 75 (2002), 408–424, esp. pp. 415–17. See also Edward Vallance, *Revolutionary England and the National Covenant: State Oaths, Protestantism and the Political Nation, 1553–1682* (Woodbridge, 2005), pp. 56–7, 69–70; David Martin Jones, *Conscience and Allegiance in Seventeenth Century England: The Political Significance of Oaths and Engagements* (Woodbridge, 1999), esp. pp. 119–25, 274–5.
71. *Culpeper Letters*, at pp. 176–7. The Scottish alliance is considered in detail above in ch. 10.
72. Lindley, *Popular Politics*, pp. 348–9.
73. Michael Mendle, 'De Facto Freedom, De Facto Authority: Press and Parliament, 1460–1643', *HJ*, 38 (1995), 307–332; *A&O*, I, pp. 184–6, quotation at p. 184.
74. Gardiner, I, p. 155. For the proclamation see *LJ*, vi, pp. 108–9.
75. Gardiner, I, pp. 199–202; Cust, *Charles I*, pp. 380–81; Hutton, 'Royalist Party', p. 558.
76. Hutton, 'Royalist Party', pp. 558–9. Hutton's analysis is criticized as too schematic by James Daly, 'The Implications of Royalist Politics, 1642–1646', *HJ*, 27 (1984), 745–55. See, in general, Cust, *Charles I*, pp. 358–419.
77. Braddick, *Parliamentary Taxation*, ch. 4; Braddick, *Nerves of State*, chs. 1, 2, 5; John Brewer, *The Sinews of Power: War, Money and the English State, 1688–1783* (London, 1989); for a full study of innovations in public finance in the 1640s and 1650s and their long-term significance see James Scott Wheeler, *The Making of a World Power: War and the Military Revolution in Seventeenth-Century England* (Stroud, 1999).
78. Saltmarsh was already on a journey which took him from an orthodox, perhaps relatively High Church, sensibility during the 1630s to the advocacy of free grace by the mid-1640s. Free grace built on the Reformation prioritization of grace over adherence to the law as

the key to salvation, but did not limit grace to the elect. Saltmarsh later became chaplain to Sir Thomas Fairfax and was identified as a major threat to religious order. For Saltmarsh see Roger Pooley, 'Saltmarsh, John (d. 1647)', *ODNB*, 48, pp. 770–71; Ann Hughes, *Gangraena and the Struggle for the English Revolution* (Oxford, 2004). For Henry Marten see Sarah Barber, 'Marten, Henry (1601/2–1680)', *ODNB*, 36, pp. 908–12.

79. Jack Binns, 'Cholmley, Sir Hugh, First Baronet (1600–1657)', *ODNB*, 11, pp. 504–5. Discussed alongside the Hothams and other Yorkshire side-changers in Hopper, ' "Fitted for desperation" '.

80. Hopper, ' "Fitted for desperation" '. See also Vallance, *Revolutionary England*, p. 68.

81. Gardiner, I, pp. 142, 159–61, II, pp. 103–4; David Scott, 'Hotham, Sir John, First Baronet (1589–1645)', *ODNB*, 28, pp. 257–9; David Scott, 'Hotham, John (1610–1645)', *ODNB*, 28, pp. 259–61.

82. Scott, 'Hotham, Sir John'; Scott, 'Hotham, John'; Nicholas quoted from Gardiner, I, p. 161.

83. History of Parliament Trust, London, unpublished article on Sir Matthew Boynton, Bart, for 1604–29 section by Simon Healey. I am grateful to the History of Parliament Trust for allowing me to see this article in draft. *History, Topography, and Directory of East Yorkshire (with Hull)* (Preston: T. Bulmer and sons, 1892), p. 152; Bulstrode Whitelocke, *Memorials of the English Affairs*, 4 vols. (Oxford, 1853), I, pp. 194, 206, 487.

84. Ashton, *Counter-Revolution*, p. 403.

85. Hopper suggests that, had these defections been co-ordinated, it might have changed the course of the entire war: ' "Fitted for desperation" '.

86. Young and Holmes, *English Civil War*, p. 141; for the pressure to surrender to avoid unnecessary loss of life see Donagan, 'Codes and Conduct', pp. 79–80.

87. For the Chudleighs, see Gardiner, I, p. 139; Mary Wolffe, 'Chudleigh, Sir George, Baronet (1582–1658)', *ODNB*, 11, pp. 570–71; Mary Wolffe, 'Chudleigh, James (1617–1643)', *ODNB*, 11, pp. 571–2. For Massey see Gardiner, I, pp. 198–9; Andrew Warmington, 'Massey, Sir Edward (d. 1674)', *ODNB*, 37, pp. 208–11. For Carew see Gardiner, I, pp. 207–8; Stephen Wright, 'Carew, Sir Alexander, Second Baronet (1609–1644)', *ODNB*, 10, pp. 40–41, quotation at p. 40.

88. Gardiner, I, 162–3; Young and Holmes, *English Civil War*, p. 113; Fletcher, *Sussex*, p. 289. For the intellectual and social context see Barbara Donagan, 'The Web of Honour: Soldiers, Christians, and Gentlemen in the English Civil War', *HJ*, 44 (2001), 363–89, esp. pp. 384–7.

89. Gardiner, I, pp. 164–5, 199.

90. Young and Holmes, *English Civil War*, p. 142; see also Charles Carlton, *Going to the Wars: The Experience of the English Civil Wars, 1638–1651* (London, 1992), pp. 218–19.

10. The War of the Three Kingdoms

1. The standard account of Confederate politics is Micheál Ó Siochrú, *Confederate Ireland, 1642–1649: A Constitutional and Political Analysis* (Dublin, 1999): see here esp. pp. 17–20. For a concise narrative see Patrick J. Corish, 'The Rising of 1641 and the Catholic Confederacy', in T. W. Moody, F. X. Martin and F. J. Byrne (eds.), *A New History of Ireland*, vol. 3: *Early Modern Ireland 1534–1691* (Oxford, 1976), pp. 289–316, quotation at p. 302. There is a useful summary in Austin Woolrych, *Britain in Revolution 1625–1660* (Oxford, 2002), pp. 268–73, and a fluent overview in Roy Foster, *Modern Ireland 1600–1972* (London, 1988), ch. 4. For analysis of the implications for Ireland's relationship with British authority, see Nicholas Canny, *Making Ireland British 1580–1650* (Oxford, 2001), ch. 9. For the armies in Ireland see James Scott Wheeler, 'Four Armies in Ireland', in Jane H. Ohlmeyer (ed.), *Ireland from Independence to Occupation 1641–1660* (Cambridge, 1995), pp. 43–65. This collection contains a number of other important essays on this period in Irish history. For Plunkett see also Tadhg Ó hAnnracháin, 'Plunkett, Sir Nicholas (1602–1680)', *ODNB*, 44, pp. 645–6.

2. For Ormond see Toby Barnard, 'Butler, James, first Duke of Ormond (1610–1688)', *ODNB*, 9, pp. 153–63. He was created First Duke of Ormond in 1661.

3. David Stevenson, *The Scottish Revolution, 1637–1644* (Newton Abbot, 1973), pp. 243–6; David Stevenson, *Revolution and Counter-Revolution in Scotland, 1644–1651* (London, 1977), pp. 1–2; David Stevenson, 'Monro, Sir George, of Culrain and Newmore (d. 1694)', *ODNB*, 38, pp. 649–50. See also Wheeler, 'Four Armies'. For the Irish adventurers see also Canny, *Making Ireland British*, pp. 553–6 and the references therein.

4. Ó Siochrú, *Confederate Ireland*, pp. 63–8; Corish, 'Rising of 1641', pp. 303–9; Woolrych, *Britain in Revolution*, pp. 272–3. For the impact of the Cessation on the political and military cause of the Confederates see Wheeler, 'Four Armies'. Gardiner, I, ch. 9 also contains interesting material.

5. Bulstrode Whitelocke, *Memorials of the English Affairs*, 4 vols. (Oxford, 1853), I, p. 238.

6. Corish, 'Rising of 1641', pp. 303–9; Stevenson, *Scottish Revolution*, pp. 265–75.

7. For the failure of moderate Scottish royalism see Stevenson, *Scottish Revolution*, ch. 8.

8. Stevenson, *Revolution and Counter-Revolution*, pp. 4–5.

9. Quoted in Gardiner, I, pp. 177–8.

10. For Charles's diplomacy see also Richard Cust, *Charles I: A Political Life* (Harlow, 2005), esp. pp. 373–4.

11. Stevenson, *Scottish Revolution*, ch. 9.

12. W. A. Shaw, *A History of the English Church during the Civil Wars and under the Commonwealth*, 2 vols. (London, 1900), vol. 1, ch. 2; Stevenson, *Scottish Revolution*, pp. 279–80, 285, 288–9.

13. Gardiner, I, p. 229; Stevenson, *Scottish Revolution*, pp. 283–4.

14. Stevenson, *Scottish Revolution*, pp. 284–9. For the text of the final version see Gardiner, *CD*, pp. 267–71.

15. David Martin Jones, *Conscience and Allegiance in Seventeenth Century England: The Political Significance of Oaths and Engagements* (Woodbridge, 1999), pp. 125–46; Edward Vallance, *Revolutionary England and the National Covenant: State Oaths, Protestantism and the Political Nation, 1553–1682* (Woodbridge, 2005), chs. 6–7.

16. Stevenson, *Scottish Revolution*, pp. 284–7.

17. Ibid., pp. 287–9.

18. Shaw, *History of the English Church*, I, pp. 145–7, quotation at p. 147.

19. Quoted in ibid., pp. 149–50.

20. Ibid., pp. 149–52.

21. Gardiner, *CD*, pp. 268–9.

22. Julie Spraggon, *Puritan Iconoclasm during the English Civil War* (Woodbridge, 2003), pp. 75–7; Margaret Aston, *England's Iconoclasts*, vol. 1: *Laws Against Images* (Oxford, 1988), chs. 1–2; Margaret Aston, 'Puritans and Iconoclasm, 1560–1660', in Christopher Durston and Jacqueline Eales (eds.), *The Culture of English Puritanism, 1560–1700* (Basingstoke, 1996), pp. 92–121, at pp. 117–19. The September order and the ordinance are reprinted in ibid., pp. 257–8, 259–60, but the latter appears to be misdated to 28 August: see *A&O*, I, pp. 265–6; *LJ*, vi, pp. 200–201. For Herring see also Keith Lindley, *Popular Politics and Religion in Civil War London* (Aldershot, 1997), esp. pp. 45–6. For the relationship between the purging of Norwich Cathedral and crystallization of parties see John T. Evans, *Seventeenth-Century Norwich: Politics, Religion and Government, 1620–1690* (Oxford, 1979), ch. 4, esp. pp. 128–9.

23. Trevor Cooper (ed.), *The Journal of William Dowsing: Iconoclasm in East Anglia during the English Civil War* (Woodbridge, 2001), pp. 156–301.

24. John Morrill, 'William Dowsing and the Administration of Iconoclasm in the Puritan Revolution', in Cooper (ed.), *Journal of William Dowsing*, pp. 1–28; John Morrill, 'Dowsing, William (bap. 1596, d. 1668)', *ODNB*, 16, pp. 817–19.

25. Spraggon, *Puritan Iconoclasm*, pp. 120–28, 225–31. Two commissions to Dowsing from Manchester are reprinted in ibid., pp. 264–5, and, with much other useful material,

in Cooper (ed.), *Journal of William Dowsing*. The essays collected there are invaluable. See also Aston, *England's Iconoclasts*, vol. 1, pp. 74–84.

26. Morrill, 'William Dowsing', pp. 8–9. Manchester took a personal interest in the visitation of Cambridge University over the winter 1643–4: J. D. Twigg, 'The Parliamentary Visitation of the University of Cambridge 1644–1645', *EHR*, 98 (1983), 513–28.

27. For the longer-term history see Aston, *England's Iconoclasts*, vol. 1; Aston, 'Puritans and Iconoclasm'; Patrick Collinson, 'From Iconoclasm to Iconophobia: The Cultural Impact of the Second English Reformation', reprinted in Peter Marshall (ed.), *The Impact of the English Reformation 1500–1640* (London, 1997), pp. 278–308.

28. Cust, *Charles I*, pp. 381–5. For attendance see also Gardiner, I, p. 300, who puts the figures higher, at 82 and 175 (including those who would have liked to attend but could not). For the Westminster figures see David L. Smith, *The Stuart Parliaments, 1603–1689* (London, 1999), p. 129.

29. Cust, *Charles I*, pp. 381–2.

30. Ibid., pp. 373–88; Gardiner, I, pp. 268–73. The Ogle plot is placed in the context of contacts between moderates on both sides by David L. Smith, *Constitutional Royalism and the Search for Settlement c. 1640–1649* (Cambridge, 1994), pp. 116–17.

31. Cust, *Charles I*, esp. ch. 6.

32. Joyce Lee Malcolm, 'All the King's Men: The Impact of the Crown's Irish Soldiers on the English Civil War', *Irish Historical Studies*, 21 (1979), 239–64, at pp. 251–5 (she puts the total at 21,000 at p. 263); Mark Stoyle, *Soldiers and Strangers: An Ethnic History of the English Civil War* (New Haven, Conn., 2005), pp. 56–61 and table at pp. 209–10. This agrees with John Barratt, *Cavaliers: The Royalist Army at War, 1642–1646* (Stroud, 2000), pp. 138–9; Malcolm Wanklyn and Frank Jones, *A Military History of the English Civil War, 1642–1646: Strategy and Tactics* (Harlow, 2005), p. 15. Woolrych, *Britain in Revolution*, p. 273, suggests only 5,000, mainly Protestants.

33. Malcolm, 'All the King's Men', argued for a very significant impact, esp. pp. 255–63. These claims are strongly criticized by Stoyle, *Soldiers and Strangers*, pp. 61–5; Wanklyn and Jones, *Military History*, pp. 15–16.

34. Gardiner, I, pp. 294–7. For Barthomley, see also Barbara Donagan, 'Atrocity, War Crime, and Treason in the English Civil War', *AHR*, 99 (1994), 1137–66, at pp. 1152–4.

35. Quoted in Stoyle, *Soldiers and Strangers*, p. 66.

36. Stoyle, *Soldiers and Strangers*, pp. 59–60. This may perhaps have been influenced by the suggestion made about the Irish women captured at Nantwich in January: ibid., pp. 67–8.

37. Ibid., pp. 68–9. For Bolton, 'the Geneva of the north', see also Ernest Broxap, *The Great Civil War in Lancashire (1642–51)*, 2nd edn (Manchester, 1973), pp. 3, 120–25.

38. *A&O*, I, pp. 554–5.

39. Gardiner, III, p. 26.

40. Stoyle, *Soldiers and Strangers*, p. 69; Donagan, 'Atrocity', pp. 1148–9. There seem to have been two other hangings at Wem: Richard Gough, *The History of Myddle*, ed. David Hey (Harmondsworth, 1981), pp. 74–5.

41. Stoyle, *Soldiers and Strangers*, chs. 1–4; Lloyd Bowen, 'Representations of Wales and the Welsh during the Civil Wars and Interregnum', *Historical Research*, 77 (2004), 358–76; Joad Raymond, *Pamphlets and Pamphleteering in Early Modern Britain* (Cambridge, 2003), pp. 220–22.

42. A&O, I, pp. 554–5.

43. A point also made by Bowen, 'Representations of Wales', p. 365; see also Barbara Donagan, 'Codes and Conduct in the English Civil War', *PP*, 118 (1988), 65–96, at pp. 93–4.

44. Peter Young and Richard Holmes, *The English Civil War: A Military History of the Three Civil Wars 1642–1651* (Ware, 2000), pp. 146–9; Malcolm Wanklyn, *Decisive Battles of the English Civil War: Myth and Reality* (Barnsley, 2006), chs. 6–7; Wanklyn and Jones, *Military History*, ch. 11.

45. Gardiner, I, p. 237.

46. For royalist strategy in this period see Wanklyn and Jones, *Military History*, ch. 12. For the fighting see also Young and Holmes, *English Civil War*, pp. 151–64; for Hopton's injury see ibid., pp. 130–31.

47. *A&O*, I, pp. 333–9; Gardiner, I, pp. 250–52.

48. Clive Holmes, *The Eastern Association in the English Civil War* (Cambridge, 1974), esp. chs. 5–8.

49. Gardiner, I, pp. 238, 253, 294; and see above, p. 316.

11. Marston Moor

1. For the speeches, see above, pp. 92, 125–6.

2. Gardiner, I, p. 250; D. E. Kennedy, *The English Revolution 1642–1649* (Basingstoke, 2000), p. 37.

3. Wallace Notestein, 'The Establishment of the Committee of Both Kingdoms', *AHR*, 17 (1912), 477–95; Lotte Glow, 'The Committee of Safety', *EHR*, 80 (1965), 289–313; John Adamson, 'The Triumph of Oligarchy: The Management of War and the Committee of Both Kingdoms, 1644–1645', in Chris R. Kyle and Jason Peacey (eds.), *Parliament at Work: Parliamentary Committees, Political Power and Public Access in Early Modern England* (Woodbridge, 2002), pp. 101–27.

4. Gardiner, I, pp. 301–2; Edward Vallance, 'Protestation, Vow, Covenant and Engagement: Swearing Allegiance in the English Civil War', *Historical Research*, 75 (2002), 408–24, at pp. 417–22.

5. Gardiner, I, pp. 246–7; Anthony Milton, 'Laud, William (1573–1645)', *ODNB*, 32, pp. 655–70.

6. Gardiner, I, pp. 273–4. For the Brooke plot see above, p. 316.

7. Peter Young and Richard Holmes, *The English Civil War: A Military History of the Three Civil Wars, 1642–1651* (Ware, 2000), pp. 167–71; Malcolm Wanklyn and Frank Jones, *A Military History of the English Civil War, 1642–1646: Strategy and Tactics* (Harlow, 2005), ch. 13; Malcolm Wanklyn, *Decisive Battles of the English Civil War: Myth and Reality* (Barnsley, 2006), chs. 8–9.

8. Wanklyn and Jones, *Military History*, ch. 13 and pp. 157–62.

9. Young and Holmes, *English Civil War*, p. 181.

10. Ibid., pp. 175–80.

11. Wanklyn and Jones, *Military History*, pp. 162–5; Young and Holmes, *English Civil War*, pp. 181–4; Gardiner, I, pp. 331, 352–3; for the Oxford parliament and its place in royalist politics see Richard Cust, *Charles I: A Political Life* (Harlow, 2005), pp. 381–4.

12. Wanklyn and Jones, *Military History*, pp. 165–6; Young and Holmes, *English Civil War*, pp. 184–5; Gardiner, I, pp. 358–62.

13. Wanklyn and Jones, *Military History*, pp. 166–9; Young and Holmes, *English Civil War*, pp. 185–9.

14. Wanklyn and Jones, *Military History*, ch. 15; Young and Holmes, *English Civil War*, pp. 190–91; Gardiner, I, p. 370.

15. Gardiner, I, p. 371, emphasis added.

16. Ibid., emphasis added.

17. Ibid.; Wanklyn and Jones, *Military History*, pp. 178–80.

18. For the following three paragraphs see Young and Holmes, *English Civil War*, pp. 193–203; Wanklyn and Jones, *Military History*, ch. 16; Wanklyn, *Decisive Battles*, chs. 10–11; Gardiner, I, pp. 374–82. For an account emphasizing the importance of Cromwell's actions, see Frank Kitson, *Old Ironsides: The Military Biography of Oliver Cromwell* (London, 2004), pp. 380–90. Wanklyn is sceptical about the influence on the course of the battle of the rabbit holes which marked parts of the field: *Decisive Battles*, p. 111 (see Kitson, *Old Ironsides*, p. 87).

19. Young and Holmes, *English Civil War*, p. 204; Wanklyn and Jones, *Military History*, pp. 190–91; Gardiner, II, pp. 6–8.

20. Young and Holmes, *English Civil War*, pp. 204–5; Wanklyn and Jones, *Military History*, pp. 190–96; Gardiner, II, pp. 8–11.

21. Young and Holmes, *English Civil War*, pp. 207–12; Wanklyn and Jones, *Military History*, pp. 196–7; Gardiner, II, pp. 12–19.

22. Gardiner, II, p. 18.

23. Barbara Donagan, 'Codes and Conduct in the English Civil War', *PP*, 118 (1988), pp. 65–95, at pp. 87–91.

24. Gardiner, II, p. 19.

25. Clive Holmes, *The Eastern Association in the English Civil War* (Cambridge, 1974), pp. 197–8. See also Gardiner, II, p. 3.

26. Gardiner, II, pp. 31–45; Young and Holmes, *English Civil War*, pp. 213–16; Wanklyn and Jones, *Military History*, pp. 197–202; for a downward revision of the customary estimate of the disparity in numerical strength see Wanklyn, *Decisive Battles*, p. 145.

27. Wanklyn, *Decisive Battles*, chs. 12–13; Young and Holmes, *English Civil War*, pp. 216–21; Wanklyn and Jones, *Military History*, ch. 18; Gardiner, II, pp. 44–53.

28. Gardiner, II, pp. 52–63, quotations at pp. 58–9; Young and Holmes, *English Civil War*, pp. 221–3; Wanklyn and Jones, *Military History*, p. 201; Austin Woolrych, *Britain in Revolution 1625–1660* (Oxford, 2002), quotation at p. 291.

29. Ian Roy, 'The Royalist Army in the First Civil War', unpublished D.Phil. thesis, Oxford (1963), pp. 115–16, 134–8, 185–99.

30. David Stevenson, *Revolution and Counter-Revolution in Scotland, 1644–1651* (London, 1977), pp. 4–9.

31. Woolrych, *Britain in Revolution*, p. 293.

32. Gardiner, II, ch. 26; Stevenson, *Revolution and Counter-Revolution*, pp. 19–29. Casualty figures quoted from Charles Carlton, *Going to the Wars: The Experience of the British Civil Wars 1638–1651* (London, 1992), p. 212. Large numbers of Scots were killed in England, Wales and Ireland, of course, just as English troops died in Scotland. Similarly, the death toll for England and Wales cited above includes Irish troops.

33. Cromwell's reported views tended in this direction: Gardiner, II, p. 24. In fact this does not appear to have been a significant factor in Cromwell's hostility to Manchester's command: Holmes, *Eastern Association*, pp. 199–205.

34. Ann Hughes, *Gangraena and the Struggle for the English Revolution* (Oxford, 2004), pp. 34–7; for the accord and larger context see also Elliot Curt Vernon, 'The Sion College Conclave and London Presbyterianism during the English Revolution', unpublished Ph.D. thesis, Cambridge (1999), esp. pp. 48–68.

35. Quoted in M. R. Watts, *The Dissenters*, vol. 1: *From the Reformation to the French Revolution* (Oxford, 1978), p. 83.

36. For these debates and the longer context see John Coffey, 'The Toleration Controversy during the English Revolution', in Christopher Durston and Judith Maltby (eds.), *Religion in Revolutionary England* (Manchester, 2006), pp. 42–68; John Spurr, *English Puritanism 1603–1689* (Basingstoke, 1998), ch. 12; Alexandra Walsham, *Charitable Hatred: Tolerance and Intolerance in England, 1500–1700* (Manchester, 2006).

37. Hughes, *Gangraena*, pp. 42–9; Vernon, 'Sion College', ch. 2; see also P. R. S. Baker, 'Edwards, Thomas (c.1599–1648)', *ODNB*, 17, pp. 965–8.

38. Reprinted in William Haller (ed.), *Tracts on Liberty in the Puritan Revolution, 1638–1647*, 3 vols. (New York, 1934), II, pp. 305–39; for Herle see p. 305.

39. Ibid., p. 306.

40. Watts, *Dissenters*, pp. 99–100.

41. Hughes, *Gangraena*, pp. 30, 42–54, 131–7; Baker, 'Edwards'.

42. Watts, *Dissenters*, pp. 103–5, quotation at p. 104; see also Francis J. Bremer, 'Williams, Roger (c.1606–1683)', *ODNB*, 59, pp. 293–7.

43. Ann Hughes, 'The Meanings of Religious Polemic', in Francis J. Bremer (ed.), *Puritanism: Transatlantic Perspectives on a Seventeenth-Century Anglo-American Faith* (Boston, Mass., 1993), pp. 201–29.

44. For Williams and Milton's publisher, see Bremer, 'Williams', p. 295.
45. The literature on Milton is vast. For the broad outline given here see Gardiner, II, pp. 69–72; Gordon Campbell, 'Milton, John (1608–1674)', *ODNB*, 38, pp. 333–49; David Norbrook, *Writing the English Republic: Poetry, Rhetoric and Politics, 1627–1660* (Cambridge, 1999), pp. 109–18; Joad Raymond, *Pamphlets and Pamphleteering in Early Modern Britain* (Cambridge, 2003), pp. 263–75.
46. Norbrook, *Writing the English Republic*, pp. 118–39; Campbell, 'Milton', p. 339.
47. Gardiner, II, pp. 108–9.
48. For his characterization of Milton on divorce see Gardiner, II, p. 72. William Prynne, *Truth triumphing over falshood, antiquity over novelty. Or, The first part of a just and seasonable vindication of the undoubted ecclesiasticall iurisdiction, right, legislative, coercive power of Christian emperors, kings, magistrates, parliaments, in all matters of religion, church-government, discipline, ceremonies, manners: summoning of, presiding, moderating in councells, synods; and ratifying their canons, determinations, decrees: as likewise of lay-mens right both to sit and vote in councells; . . . In refutation of Mr. Iohn Goodwins Innocencies Triumph: my deare brother Burtons Vindication of churches, commonly called Independent: and of all anti-monarchicall, anti-Parliamentall, anti-synodicall, and anarchicall paradoxes of papists, prelates, Anabaptists, Arminians, Socinians, Brownists, or Independents: whose old and new objections to the contrary, are here fully answered* (London, 1645); John Lilburne, *A copie of a letter, written by John Lilburne Leut. Collonell. To Mr. William Prinne Esq. (Upon the coming out of his last booke, intituled Truth triumphing over falshood, antiquity over novelty) in which he laies down five propositions, which he desires to discusse with the said Mr. Prinne* (London, 1645).
49. *Culpeper Letters*, pp. 137–50, quotations at pp. 144–5.
50. See above, pp. 10–12.
51. The standard work on these congregations is Murray Tolmie, *The Triumph of the Saints: The Separate Churches of London 1616–1649* (Cambridge, 1977). There is much useful additional material in Keith Lindley, *Popular Politics and Religion in Civil War London* (Aldershot, 1997), pp. 281–303. The classic evocation of the atmosphere of religious experimentation in this period is Christopher Hill, *The World Turned Upside Down: Radical Ideas during the English Revolution* (Harmondsworth, 1975).
52. Tolmie, *Triumph*, pp. 111–16.
53. Ibid., p. 71.
54. Clive Holmes, *Seventeenth-Century Lincolnshire* (Lincoln, 1980), pp. 41–6, 198–9; Mary Coate, *Cornwall in the Great Civil War and Interregnum 1642–1660: A Social and Political Study* (Oxford, 1933), ch. 15; David Underdown, *Revel, Riot and Rebellion: Popular Politics and Culture in England, 1603–1660* (Oxford, 1985), p. 247 (Baptists in the West Country from 1645 onwards); for Baptists see Mark Bell, 'Freedom to Form: The Development of Baptist Movements during the English Revolution', in Durston and Maltby (eds.), *Religion*, pp. 181–201; for a county study see Jacqueline Eales, ' "So many sects and schisms": Religious Diversity in Revolutionary Kent, 1640–60', in ibid., pp. 226–48.
55. For transgressions of baptismal rites see also David Cressy, *Agnes Bowker's Cat: Travesties and Transgressions in Tudor and Stuart England* (Oxford, 2000), ch. 11; for soldiers in cathedrals see Julie Spraggon, *Puritan Iconoclasm during the English Civil War* (Woodbridge, 2003), pp. 203–12.
56. John T. Evans, *Seventeenth-Century Norwich: Politics, Religion and Government, 1620–1690* (Oxford, 1979), pp. 131, 151–5; Holmes, *Eastern Association*, p. 204, for Baillie and Cromwell; Hughes, *Gangraena*, pp. 42–3, for Edwards and Baillie.
57. Holmes, *Eastern Association*, p. 195; Gardiner, II, pp. 25–6, 35–41.
58. Holmes, *Eastern Association*, pp. 195–205. See also Gardiner, II, ch. 20.
59. David L. Smith, *Constitutional Royalism and the Search for Settlement, c. 1640–1649* (Cambridge, 1994), pp. 117–20, quotation at p. 120.
60. Quoted from Gardiner, II, pp. 114–15.
61. For Glamorgan and Henrietta Maria see ibid., pp. 164–73.

62. Cust, *Charles I*, pp. 393–6; James Daly, 'The Implications of Royalist Politics 1642–1646', *HJ*, 27 (1984), 745–55, at p. 749. Hutton argued that this was a key period in the achievement of dominance by hardliners: Ronald Hutton, 'The Structure of the Royalist Party, 1642–1646', *HJ*, 24 (1981), 553–69, esp. pp. 563–4.

63. Summarized in Smith, *Constitutional Royalism*, pp. 120–21. For the proposals see Gardiner, *CD*, pp. 275–86. For the Scots and these proposals see also Lotte Glow, 'Peace Negotiations, Politics and the Committee of Both Kingdoms, 1644–1646', *HJ*, 12 (1969), 3–22, at pp. 9–13.

64. For the intersection of plans of reform with religious politics see Holmes, *Eastern Association*, pp. 206–10. See also Gardiner, II, p. 83; Mark A. Kishlansky, *The Rise of the New Model Army* (Cambridge, 1979), pp. 28–9; Ian Gentles, *The New Model Army in England, Ireland and Scotland, 1645–1653* (Oxford, 1992), pp. 4–5.

65. Gentles, *New Model Army*, p. 5; Gardiner, II, pp. 86–7.

66. Gentles, *New Model Army*, p. 5; Gardiner, II, p. 88.

67. Kishlansky, *Rise*, pp. 28–9, quotation at p. 29; Gentles, *New Model Army*, pp. 6–7, quotations at p. 6; Holmes, *Eastern Association*, pp. 210–12.

68. Gardiner, II, p. 5.

69. Kishlansky, *Rise*, pp. 35–6.

70. Ibid., pp. 26–7.

71. For Essex, see J. S. A. Adamson, 'The Baronial Context of the English Civil War', *TRHS*, 5th ser., 40 (1990), 93–120, esp. p. 113; Gentles, *New Model Army*, pp. 4–5, 8–9, 23–4; Kishlansky, *Rise*, pp. 40–41.

72. Gentles, *New Model Army*, pp. 10–25; Kishlansky, *Rise*, pp. 35–48.

73. Smith, *Constitutional Royalism*, pp. 121–4.

74. Quoted in Gardiner, II, p. 125.

75. Smith, *Constitutional Royalism*, pp. 123–4; Gardiner, II, p. 132.

76. Cust, *Charles I*, pp. 393–4, 396–7; Hutton, 'Structure of the Royalist Party', pp. 563–4.

77. *A&O*, I, pp. 614–26, 664–5.

12. A Man Not Famous But Notorious

1. *Mercurius Aulicus*, [week ending] 9 December 1643, p. 703; *OED*, 'Herodian disease'. For the death of Lord Brooke see above, pp. 265–6, and for Hampden, pp. 287–8.

2. See above, p. 207.

3. See above, pp. 201–3.

4. *Remarkeable Passages*, 8–15 December 1643, A2v; *The Parliament Scout*, 8–15 December 1643, p. 214; *The Weekly Account*, 13 December 1643, pp. 5–6; *An Answer to Mercurius Aulicus*, week ending 9 December 1643, p. 7.

5. *A narrative of the disease and Death Of that Noble Gentleman John Pym* (London, 1643), quotations at pp. 2–3. For Mayerne, see Hugh Trevor-Roper, *Europe's Physician: The Various Life of Sir Theodore de Mayerne* (New Haven, Conn., 2006).

6. *An Answer to Mercurius Aulicus*, week ending 9 December 1643, p. 7; *Mercurius Britanicus*, 7–14 December 1643, pp. 126, 127, 128; *Remarkeable Passages*, 8–15 December 1643, sig. A2v; *Kingdomes Weekly Intelligencer*, 5–13 December 1643, pp. 273–4. Three elegies were published separately and acquired by Thomason on 10, 15 and 18 December (TT: 669.f.8[40, 42, 43]); see also John Hammond, *A Short View of the life and actions of John Pim* (London, 1643).

7. Bruno Ryves, *Mercurius Rusticus* (London, 1685 edn), pp. 155–6; Conrad Russell, 'Pym, John (1584–1643)', *ODNB*, 45, pp. 624–40, at pp. 639–40, for the burial and disinterment.

8. *A Perfect Diurnall*, 11–18 December 1643, p. 161. He had also stopped publishing for a while, given the flood of news available, but had been persuaded to resume 'at the instigation of some friends'.

9. Following the judgements of Anthony Milton, 'Laud, William (1573–1645)', *ODNB*, 32, pp. 655–70.

10. Gardiner, II, pp. 99–106; Keith Lindley, *Popular Politics and Religion in Civil War London* (Aldershot, 1997), pp. 323–4.

11. J. A. Sharpe, ' "Last dying speeches": Religion, Ideology and Public Execution in Seventeenth-Century England', *PP*, 107 (1985), 144–67; Peter Lake and Michael C. Questier, 'Agency, Appropriation and Rhetoric under the Gallows: Puritans, Romanists and the State in Early Modern England', *PP*, 153 (1996), 64–107; Andrea McKenzie, 'Martyrs in Low Life? Dying "Game" in Augustan England', *JBS*, 42:2 (2003), 167–205; for Strafford see above, p. 138.

12. John Hinde, *The Archbishop of Canterbury's speech* (London, 1644), quotations at pp. 6, 10; Peter Heylyn, *Cyprianus Anglicus*, p. 527, quoted in Gardiner, II, p. 107.

13. Hinde, *Archbishop of Canterbury's speech*, quotations at pp. 11, 14; Heylyn, *Cyprianus Anglicus*, p. 527, quoted in Gardiner, II, p. 107. A 'corrected' version of the speech was published in Oxford, claiming that Hinde's text had been doctored to please the censors in the City: *A briefe relation of the death and sufferings of the most Reverend and renowned prelate the L. Archbishop of Canterbury* (Oxford, 1644), p. 23. It included a history of Laud's life. The passage quoted here about the popular clamour for Laud's execution contains an additional phrase: 'the Magistrates standing still and suffering them openly to proceed from Parish to Parish without check'.

14. For a flavour see William Starbuck, *A Briefe exposition, paraphrase or interpretation upon the Lord of Canterburies sermon* (London, 1645); Anon., *A Full and Satisfactorie ansvvere to the Arch-Bishop of Canterbvries speeh* [sic] (London, 1645); Anon., *The Life and Death of William Lawd, late Archbishop of Canterburie* (London, 1645). The last offers a history of the betrayal of the Reformation. J.B., *A Relation Of the Troubles Of the three forraign Churches in Kent* (London, 1645), does the same on the basis of the history of a particular policy.

15. David Scott, 'Hotham, Sir John, First Baronet (1589–1645)', *ODNB*, 28, pp. 257–9; David Scott, 'Hotham, John (1610–1645)', *ODNB*, 28, pp. 259–61; Stephen Wright, 'Carew, Sir Alexander, Second Baronet (1609–1644)', *ODNB*, 10, pp. 40–41.

16. Austin Woolrych, *Britain in Revolution 1625–1660* (Oxford, 2002), p. 288. The dubious honour of the largest battle on English soil is also claimed for the battle of Towton in 1461, on the basis of the claims in contemporary chronicles about numbers engaged.

17. Charles Carlton, *Going to the Wars: The Experience of the English Civil Wars, 1638–1651* (London, 1992), p. 204.

18. Gardiner, II, p. 113.

19. *Mercurius Cambro-Britannicus*, 27 November–5 December 1643, pp. 3–4.

20. Bod. L, Ashmolean MS 184, fo. 3r. For Lilly see also Patrick Curry, 'Lilly, William (1602–1681)', *ODNB*, 33, pp. 794–8. For astrology more generally see Keith Thomas, *Religion and the Decline of Magic: Studies in Popular Beliefs in Sixteenth- and Seventeenth-Century England* (Harmondsworth, 1991 edn), chs. 10–12; Patrick Curry, *Prophecy and Power: Astrology in Early Modern England* (Princeton, NJ, 1989), esp. chs. 1–2; Bernard Capp, *Astrology and the Popular Press: English Almanacs 1500–1800* (London, 1979). For a close understanding of Lilly and his art see Ann Geneva, *Astrology and the Seventeenth-Century Mind: William Lilly and the Language of the Stars* (Manchester, 1995).

21. Thomas, *Religion and the Decline of Magic*, p. 364.

22. Bod. L, Ashmolean MS 184, fos. 1r–2v, 'Quando Essex eius iterus ad Oxonium'. For other examples see fos. 83v, 102v, 160r; Ashmolean MS 178, fo. 63v.

23. Ashmolean MS 184, fos. 46v, 69v–70v; Ashmolean MS 178, fo. 174r.

24. Ashmolean MS 184, fo. 62v.

25. Ibid., fo. 36r (see also fos. 64r, 67r, 67v, 98v); Ashmolean MS 178, fo. 24r; Ashmolean MS 184, fo. 44r (see also Ashmolean MS 178, fos 16r, 63r).

26. Geneva, *Astrology and the Seventeenth-Century Mind*, pp. 81–3.

27. Thomas, *Religion and the Decline of Magic*, pp. 337–8.

28. Ibid., pp. 338–9; John Booker, *Mercurius Coelicus* (London, 1645), quotation at p. 33.

29. Thomas, *Religion and the Decline of Magic*, p. 340.

30. Booker, *Mercurius Coelicus*, p. 34.

31. Capp, *Astrology*, pp. 57–9; Curry, 'Lilly, William'.

32. Lindley, *Popular Politics*, p. 138.

33. William Lilly, *The starry messenger* (London, 1645): 'George, a stickling prophet, . . . pipes out nothing but victory for his Majesty: be it granted, that the storming of Leicester hath in part verified some part of his prediction, (and a little treason besides) yet I deny it was signified by this posture, or that the rest of this mans words shall have like success; Nay, by position of Mars, Lord of the fourth, in the twelve, his Majesty shall not keep that Town long, or any else that he may take in this prophetic march, without infinite loss on his party: Venus in her house, doth assuredly tell us we shall keep Evesham taken by plain valour, and were it not for that accursed Cauda in Aquarius we should seldom be losers, but be gainers, but Division and Treason have got an habit and live with us, and are your friends, yea your only friends. The figure doth at the beginning promise success, but the end of this march will be unlucky, and foreshow some wilful obstinate Commanders on his Majesty's side will afford us an absolute victory over you'. 'Keep Leicester if you can, July may give it to us again': postscript (unpaginated). Lilly reported this success with pride: *A collection of prophecies* (London, 1645), p. 55.

34. John Booker, *Mercurius Coelicus* (London, 1646), unpaginated, 'Of Harvest'.

35. Curry, *Prophecy and Power*, pp. 5–8, ch. 2.

36. Figures for sales and prices from Thomas, *Religion and the Decline of Magic*, ch. 10; for Lilly's sales see p. 348; for the price, p. 349; and for the income of leading astrologers, pp. 380–82. Curry, 'Lilly, William'; Curry, *Prophecy and Power*, ch. 2.

37. Thomas, *Religion and the Decline of Magic*, p. 364.

38. William Lilly, *Merlinus Anglicus Junior* (London, 1644), sig. A2v. Curry characterizes Lilly's astrology as 'democratic': *Prophecy and Power*, pp. 28–31. For the relationship with Christian orthodoxy see Thomas, *Religion and the Decline of Magic*, ch. 12. See also C. Scott Dixon, 'Popular Astrology and Lutheran Propaganda in Reformation Germany', *History* (1999), 403–18.

39. See above, p. 110; Thomas, *Religion and the Decline of Magic*, pp. 465 and n, 487. There is some useful material in Harry Rusche, 'Merlini Anglici: Astrology and Propaganda from 1644 to 1651', *EHR*, 80 (1965), 322–33; and Harry Rusche, 'Prophecies and Propaganda, 1641 to 1651', *EHR*, 84 (1969), 752–70.

40. Lilly, *Merlinus Anglicus Junior*, p. 4.

13. Naseby and the End of the War

1. Mark A. Kishlansky, *The Rise of the New Model Army* (Cambridge, 1979), ch. 2; Ian Gentles, *The New Model Army in England, Ireland and Scotland, 1645–1653* (Oxford, 1992), ch. 1; J. S. A. Adamson, 'The Baronial Context of the English Civil War', *TRHS*, 5th ser., 40 (1990), 93–120, esp. pp. 112–16.

2. Kishlansky, *Rise*, pp. 42–6; Gentles, *New Model Army*, pp. 10–16; Adamson, 'Baronial Context', pp. 113–19. I have followed Gentles, who differs from Kishlansky over the extent of political partisanship he discerns in the arguments over the officer list, but not over the revision of the view that it was an army of Independents, or that its origin was marked by political compromise.

3. Kishlansky, *Rise*, pp. 37–8; Gentles, *New Model Army*, pp. 11–12. Fairfax was not simply a cipher in these manoeuvres: Andrew Hopper, *'Black Tom': Sir Thomas Fairfax and the English Revolution* (Manchester, 2007), pp. 54–66.

4. Kishlansky, *Rise*, pp. 46–8; Gentles, *New Model Army*, pp. 21–4; Adamson, 'Baronial Context', pp. 117–18. For the Vow and Covenant, see above, p. 293.

5. For Lilburne and the Covenant see Edward Vallance, *Revolutionary England and the National Covenant: State Oaths, Protestantism and the Political Nation, 1553–1682*

(Woodbridge, 2005), pp. 154–5; David Martin Jones, *Conscience and Allegiance in Seventeenth Century England: The Political Significance of Oaths and Engagements* (Woodbridge, 1999), esp. pp. 140–41.

6. Gentles, *New Model Army*, pp. 24–7; Gardiner, II, p. 195.

7. Gentles, *New Model Army*, ch. 2.

8. Ian Gentles, 'The Iconography of Revolution: England 1642–1649', in Ian Gentles, John Morrill and Blair Worden (eds.), *Soldiers, Writers and Statesmen of the English Revolution* (Cambridge, 1998), pp. 91–132.

9. Ian Gentles, 'The Civil Wars in England', in John Kenyon and Jane Ohlmeyer (eds.), *The Civil Wars: A Military History of England, Scotland, and Ireland 1638–1660* (Oxford, 1998), pp. 103–55, at p. 114. Charles Carlton, *Going to the Wars: The Experience of the English Civil Wars* (London, 1992), pp. 86–7 (catechisms); for plunder see ibid., ch. 11, and the effects of royalist support, pp. 187–9, 268–9.

10. *The Kingdomes VVeekly Intelligencer*, no. 111, 29 July–6 August 1645, p. 887: it was condemned as a 'libellous, and scandalous pamphlet', suggesting once again that book-burning was as much about civility of discourse as the contents: it was hardly unusual to suggest that Parliament's cause was not in fact a godly one. For book-burnings see above, pp. 277–9. In this case the burning was associated with a concerted attempt to suppress the publication and dissemination of the pamphlet.

11. Gentles, *New Model Army*, ch. 4.

12. Anne Laurence, *Parliamentary Army Chaplains, 1642–1651* (Woodbridge, 1990), pp. 49–57.

13. Kishlansky, *Rise*, chs. 2–3; Gentles, 'Civil Wars in England', pp. 140–41.

14. Malcolm Wanklyn and Frank Jones, *A Military History of the English Civil War, 1642–1646: Strategy and Tactics* (Harlow, 2005), pp. 229–33; Peter Young and Richard Holmes, *The English Civil War: A Military History of the Three Civil Wars 1642–1651* (Ware, 2000), pp. 233–4. For the politics of the Committee of Both Kingdoms see John Adamson, 'The Triumph of Oligarchy: The Management of War and the Committee of Both Kingdoms, 1644–1645', in Chris R. Kyle and Jason Peacey (eds.), *Parliament at Work: Parliamentary Committees, Political Power and Public Access in Early Modern England* (Woodbridge, 2002), pp. 101–27.

15. Wanklyn and Jones argue persuasively that it was not in and of itself a disastrous decision: *Military History*, pp. 233–5. See also Young and Holmes, *English Civil War*, pp. 234–5.

16. Wanklyn and Jones, *Military History*, pp. 235–6; Young and Holmes, *English Civil War*, pp. 236–7. For Montrose see Gardiner, II, pp. 215–20; David Stevenson, *Revolution and Counter-Revolution in Scotland, 1644–1651* (London, 1977), pp. 28–9.

17. Wanklyn and Jones, *Military History*, pp. 236–40; Young and Holmes, *English Civil War*, pp. 236–8, quotation at p. 237; for the sack of Leicester see also Carlton, *Going to the Wars*, p. 177.

18. Wanklyn and Jones, *Military History*, pp. 240–43, which revises the conventional wisdom about Goring's behaviour.

19. For the best brief account of the battle see Gentles, *New Model Army*, pp. 55–60. See also Malcolm Wanklyn, *Decisive Battles of the English Civil War: Myth and Reality* (Barnsley, 2006), chs. 14–15; Wanklyn and Jones, *Military History*, ch. 21; Young and Holmes, *English Civil War*, pp. 239–250.

20. For this atrocity see Young and Holmes, *English Civil War*, pp. 249–50; C. V. Wedgwood, *The King's War 1641–1647* (London, 1958), p. 445. *Mercurius Belgicus* noted that 'Above all the rebels' cruelty was remarkable in killing upon cold blood at least 100 women, whereof some of quality, being commanders' wives, and this done under the pretence they were Irish women': *Mercurius Belgicus* (London, 1646), sig. E2v.

21. Figures vary in some degree for the army sizes, casualties and numbers of prisoners; I have followed Gentles's estimates here: *New Model Army*, p. 60.

22. Gardiner, II, pp. 256–7.

23. Thomas Edwards, *The Second Part of Gangraena* (London, 1646), p. 127.

24. David Underdown, *Revel, Riot and Rebellion: Popular Politics and Culture in England, 1603–1660* (Oxford, 1985), p. 258.

25. Gardiner, II, pp. 252–3.

26. For Baillie's mixed feelings about the victory see Ann Hughes, *Gangraena and the Struggle for the English Revolution* (Oxford, 2004), p. 323.

27. Derek Hirst, 'Reading the Royal Romance: Or, Intimacy in a King's Cabinet', *Seventeenth Century*, 18 (2003), 211–29, at pp. 212–13; R. E. Maddison, ' "The King's Cabinet opened": A Case Study in Pamphlet History', *Notes and Queries*, 211 (1966), 2–9; Joad Raymond, 'Popular Representations of Charles I', in Thomas N. Corns (ed.), *The Royal Image: Representations of Charles I* (Cambridge, 1999), pp. 47–73, at pp. 56–60.

28. *The Kings Cabinet opened* (London, 1645), sig. A3r. *Mercurius Britanicus* was less restrained, while taking essentially the same line: see Joad Raymond (ed.), *Making the News: An Anthology of the Newsbooks of Revolutionary England 1641–1660* (Moreton-in-Marsh, 1993), pp. 339–49.

29. *The Kings Cabinet opened*, sig. A3v. This is apparently the first use of the term in England: 'Cajole', *OED*, accessed online, 2 April 2007.

30. Philip Withington, *The Politics of Commonwealth: Citizens and Freemen in Early Modern England* (Cambridge, 2005), p. 155.

31. See, for example, Jason Peacey, 'The Exploitation of Captured Correspondence and Anglo-Scottish Relations in the British Civil Wars', *Scottish Historical Review*, 79 (2000), 213–32; Joad Raymond, *Pamphlets and Pamphleteering in Early Modern Britain* (Cambridge, 2003), p. 215. For the general phenomenon of unreliable news, and deliberate manipulation, see Jason Peacey, *Politicians and Pamphleteers: Propaganda during the English Civil Wars and Revolution* (Aldershot, 2004), esp. ch. 7.

32. *The Kings Cabinet opened*, p. 17.

33. Quoted in Gardiner, II, p. 258. For opposition of this kind to the Uxbridge treaty see [John Vicars], *The danger of treaties with popish-spirits* (London, 1645), Thomason date 4 January 1645, authorship attributed by Thomason.

34. *The Kings Cabinet opened*, pp. 43–4.

35. Ibid., p. 44.

36. Ibid., pp. 46–7.

37. Ibid., sig. A3v; Anon., *Some observations upon occasion of the publishing their majesties letters* (Oxford, 1645), pp. 1–2.

38. Anon., *A Key To the Kings cabinet* (Oxford, 1645), pp. 3–4.

39. Ibid., pp. 11–13.

40. Ibid., p. 3.

41. See, for example, Bruno Ryves, *Mercurius Rusticus* (London, 1685 edn), pp. 3, 10, 11, 14, 16, 66, 74, 78, 79–80, 105–6, 136–7, 181. In some of these cases the purpose was to destroy legal evidences – not just a breach of privacy but a threat to property rights.

42. Raymond, 'Popular Representations', pp. 58–9.

43. Gardiner, II, pp. 257–8.

44. Carlton, *Going to the Wars*, p. 146.

45. Wanklyn and Jones, *Military History*, pp. 255–6; Young and Holmes, *English Civil War*, pp. 251–2; Gardiner, II, pp. 254–5, 259–67.

46. Gentles, *New Model Army*, pp. 61–3; Gardiner, II, pp. 185–6, 264–5. For the clubmen see above, pp. 286–7.

47. Gentles, *New Model Army*, pp. 67–9.

48. Ibid., pp. 69–70; Young and Holmes, *English Civil War*, pp. 254–8; Wanklyn and Jones, *Military History*, p. 259.

49. Young and Holmes, *English Civil War*, p. 257.

50. Gentles, *New Model Army*, pp. 61–4, 70–72.

51. Young and Holmes, *English Civil War*, pp. 259–60; Gardiner, II, pp. 274–5.

52. Young and Holmes, *English Civil War*, pp. 251, 259–60; Stevenson, *Revolution and Counter-Revolution*, pp. 29–35.

53. Gentles, *New Model Army*, pp. 72–6; Young and Holmes, *English Civil War*, pp. 260–61; Gardiner, II, pp. 311–17. For the politics of the royalist command in these crucial months see Ian Roy, 'George Digby, Royalist Intrigue and the Collapse of the Cause', in Gentles, Morrill and Worden (eds.), *Soldiers, Writers and Statesmen*, pp. 68–90.

54. Young and Holmes, *English Civil War*, pp. 261–2; Stevenson, *Revolution and Counter-Revolution*, pp. 35–42; Gardiner, II, pp. 346–7, 356.

55. Young and Holmes, *English Civil War*, pp. 263–4; Gentles, *New Model Army*, pp. 76–8.

56. Quoted in Young and Holmes, *English Civil War*, pp. 263–4.

57. Young and Holmes, *English Civil War*, pp. 264–7.

14. Winners and Losers

1. Richard Gough, *The History of Myddle*, ed. David Hey (Harmondsworth, 1981), pp. 71–5; Charles Carlton, *Going to the Wars: The Experience of the English Civil Wars, 1638–1651* (London, 1992), p. 202. The population in 1563 was around 340 rising to 612 in 1676. There is no sign of rapid population growth before the 1630s, so that the population may well have been much less than 600: David Hey, *An English Rural Community: Myddle under the Tudors and Stuarts* (Leicester, 1974), pp. 41, 42, 48. It has been authoritatively estimated that during the 1640s around 18 per cent of the population was between 15 and 24 and 42 per cent between 25 and 59: E. A. Wrigley and R. S. Schofield, *The Population History of England 1541–1871: A Reconstruction* (Cambridge, 1989), p. 528. I have assumed a 1:1 sex ratio. Since the population of the village was growing during this period it may have been younger than average, but the total population is likely to be lower than the quoted figure.

2. Derived from the figures in Carlton, *Going to the Wars*, p. 204. These estimates are to be treated with caution of course, since contemporary estimates were inconsistent and often inaccurate, sometimes intentionally so: ibid., p. 203; Barbara Donagan, 'The Casualties of War: Treatment of the Dead and Wounded in the English Civil War', in Ian Gentles, John Morrill and Blair Worden (eds.), *Soldiers, Writers and Statesmen of the English Revolution* (Cambridge, 1998), pp. 114–32, at pp. 128–9. Carlton's estimates for population loss in England (3.7 per cent), Scotland (6 per cent) and Ireland (41 per cent) from battle and war-related disease suggest that the overall loss of life as a proportion of total population was greater than in the First World War (2.6 per cent, including deaths from Spanish influenza): *Going to the Wars*, p. 214. For the costs of Montrose's campaigns see also David Stevenson, *Revolution and Counter-Revolution in Scotland, 1644–1651* (London, 1977), pp. 41–2. In 1670 the combined population of Norwich, Bristol, York and Newcastle was about 64,000: E. A. Wrigley, *People, Cities and Wealth: The Transformation of Traditional Society* (Oxford, 1987), table 7.1.

3. Gough, *Myddle*, pp. 73–4. See also p. 134. Stories of such minor skirmishes abound in the papers in the Indemnity Committee (TNA, SP24).

4. Carlton, *Going to the Wars*, p. 207.

5. Peter Young and Richard Holmes, *The English Civil War: A Military History of the Three Civil Wars 1642–1651* (Ware, 2000), pp. 130–31; for a similar story, with a similar moral, see BL Sloane MS 1457, fo. 45r–45v.

6. Carlton, *Going to the Wars*, pp. 207–9.

7. Richard Wiseman, *Severall Chirurgicall Treatises* (London, 1676 edn), p. 441.

8. Ibid. For treatment more generally see Eric Gruber von Arni, *Justice to the Maimed Soldier: Nursing, Medical Care and Welfare for Sick and Wounded Soldiers and Their Families during the English Civil Wars and Interregnum, 1642–1660* (Aldershot, 2001) (for Wiseman see esp. pp. 185–8, 251–3); Donagan, 'Casualties', pp. 115–27; see also Carlton, *Going to the Wars*, pp. 221–4.

9. Donagan, 'Casualties', pp. 127–32, quotation at p. 129. For a gloomier view of the

maintenance of decent treatment of the physical remains of the fallen see Carlton, *Going to the Wars*, pp. 218–21.

10. Carlton, *Going to the Wars*, pp. 150, 206–7.

11. Ronald Hutton and Wylie Reeves, 'Sieges and Fortifications', in John Kenyon and Jane Ohlmeyer (eds.), *The Civil Wars: A Military History of England, Scotland and Ireland* (Oxford, 1998), pp. 195–233, at pp. 195–201.

12. Stephen Porter, *Destruction in the English Civil Wars* (Gloucester, 1994), ch. 2.

13. Victor Smith and Peter Kelsey, 'The Lines of Communication: The Civil War Defences of London', in Stephen Porter (ed.), *London and the Civil War* (Basingstoke, 1996), pp. 117–48. See also Keith Lindley, *Popular Politics and Religion in Civil War London* (Aldershot, 1997), pp. 238, 409; Valerie Pearl, *London and the Outbreak of the Puritan Revolution: City Government and National Politics 1625–1643* (Oxford, 1961), pp. 263–5; *A&O*, I, pp. 103–4. For Oxford's fortifications, which seem to have been a less popular enterprise, see Ian Roy, 'The City of Oxford 1640–1660', in R. C. Richardson (ed.), *Town and Countryside in the English Revolution* (Manchester, 1992), pp. 130–68, at pp. 145–6.

14. Martyn Bennett, *The Civil Wars Experienced: Britain and Ireland, 1638–1661* (London, 2000), p. 103; Hutton and Reeves, 'Sieges and Fortifications', pp. 212–19. For Exeter see Mark Stoyle, 'Whole Streets Converted to Ashes: Property Destruction in Exeter during the English Civil War', reprinted in R. C. Richardson (ed.), *The English Civil Wars: Local Aspects* (Stroud, 1997), pp. 129–44; Mark Stoyle, *From Deliverance to Destruction: Rebellion and Civil War in an English City* (Exeter, 1996).

15. Hutton and Reeves, 'Sieges and Fortifications', pp. 228–31.

16. For these (cautious) estimates, see Porter, *Destruction*, pp. 65–6; the combined population of Norwich, Bristol and York in 1670 was around 52,000: Wrigley, *People*, table 7.1.

17. Porter, *Destruction*, p. 77; M. D. Gordon, 'The Collection of Ship Money in the Reign of Charles I', *TRHS*, 3rd ser., IV (1910), 141–62, at p. 158.

18. Porter, *Destruction*, pp. 77–8.

19. Ibid., p. 79.

20. Ibid., chs. 5–6.

21. Stoyle, *Deliverance to Destruction*, pp. 90, 111–12. For Oxford see Roy, 'Oxford'; for Plymouth see Carlton, *Going to the Wars*, p. 211. For epidemics in general, including the plague, during the civil war see Paul Slack, *The Impact of Plague in Tudor and Stuart England* (Oxford, 1985), esp. ch. 3; for crisis mortality see Wrigley and Schofield, *Population History*, appendix 10, tables A10.1 and A10.2, figure A10.11. For plague at Newark see Bennett, *Civil Wars Experienced*, p. 117. See also Ann Hughes, *Politics, Society and Civil War in Warwickshire, 1620–1660* (Cambridge, 1987), p. 258.

22. Carlton, *Going to the Wars*, p. 211.

23. Joan Dils, 'Epidemics, Mortality and the Civil War in Berkshire, 1642–6', in Richardson (ed.), *Local Aspects*, pp. 145–55. For the figure of 100,000 see Carlton, *Going to the Wars*, pp. 210–11. Ian Gentles thinks it may be too low: 'The Civil Wars in England', in Kenyon and Ohlmeyer (eds.), *Civil Wars*, pp. 103–55, at pp. 106–7. For the national picture see Wrigley and Schofield, *Population History*, esp. table A10.2.

24. See above, pp. 317–18, 332, 378. For Hopton Castle see Carlton, *Going to the Wars*, pp. 168–9, 225, 258; Barbara Donagan, 'Atrocity, War Crime, and Treason in the English Civil War', *AHR*, 99 (1994), 1137–66, at p. 1152. See also Gardiner's florid pen portrait of Sir Anthony Ashley Cooper, a man of honour in command at Abbotsbury, Dorset, where quarter was refused to a garrison that had refused to surrender: Gardiner, II, pp. 94–8; Carlton, *Going to the Wars*, pp. 172–3. For the fear of 'turning Germany' see Ian Roy, 'England Turned Germany? The Aftermath of the Civil War in its European Context', reprinted in Peter Gaunt (ed.), *The English Civil War* (Oxford, 2000), pp. 249–67.

25. For the incidence of rape see Charles Carlton, 'Civilians', in Kenyon and Ohlmeyer

(eds.), *Civil Wars*, pp. 272–305, at pp. 292–5; Bruno Ryves reported no rapes, and only one attempted rape, despite his consistent concern to emphasize women's vulnerability to outrages: *Mercurius Rusticus* (London, 1685 edn), pp. 78–9 (see also pp. 97–8). For other examples see Ronan Bennett, 'War and Disorder: Policing the Soldiery in Civil War Yorkshire', in Mark Charles Fissel (ed.), *War and Government in Britain, 1598–1650* (Manchester, 1991), pp. 248–73, at p. 255; and, for the Bishops' Wars, David Cressy, *England on Edge: Crisis and Revolution 1640–1642* (Oxford, 2006), p. 85 (where it is associated with fornication and crime committed by men in arms rather than a means of fighting the war). For the resilience of codes of conduct see Donagan, 'Atrocity'; Barbara Donagan, 'Codes and Conduct in the English Civil War', *PP*, 118 (1988), 65–95; Barbara Donagan, 'The Web of Honour: Soldiers, Christians, and Gentlemen in the English Civil War', *HJ*, 44 (2001), 363–89.

26. For the scale of change see Michael J. Braddick, *Parliamentary Taxation in Seventeenth-Century England: Local Administration and Response* (Woodbridge, 1994), esp. intr., pp. 271–6; Michael J. Braddick, *The Nerves of State: Taxation and the Financing of the English State, 1558–1714* (Manchester, 1996), chs. 1, 9. The structure of public finance makes all these comparisons very difficult, particularly since the 1640s saw the collapse of one system and the birth of another: for a brief discussion see Michael J. Braddick, 'The Rise of the Fiscal State', in Barry Coward, (ed.), *A Companion to Stuart Britain* (Oxford, 2003), pp. 69–87.

27. Anthony Fletcher, *A County Community in Peace and War: Sussex 1600–1660* (London, 1975), pp. 336–8; Hughes, *Warwickshire*, pp. 260, 263–9. For other local studies of the financial impact see Ben Coates, *The Impact of the English Civil War on the Economy of London, 1642–50* (Aldershot, 2004), chs. 2, 5; Simon Osborne, 'The War, the People and the Absence of the Clubmen in the Midlands, 1642–1646', reprinted in Gaunt (ed.), *English Civil War*, pp. 226–48. For an overview see Bennett, *Civil Wars Experienced*; John Morrill, *Revolt in the Provinces: The People of England and the Tragedies of War 1630–1648*, 2nd edn (Harlow, 1999), pp. 84–5.

28. Donald Pennington, 'The War and the People', in John Morrill (ed.), *Reactions to the English Civil War 1642–1649* (Basingstoke, 1982), pp. 115–35, esp. pp. 127–30; Morrill, *Revolt in the Provinces*, 2nd edn, pp. 120–21.

29. John Morrill, *Cheshire 1630–1660: County Government and Society during the English Revolution* (Oxford, 1974), pp. 107–11; Morrill, *Revolt in the Provinces*, 2nd edn, pp. 120–21; see also Carlton, *Going to the Wars*, pp. 281–2; Peter Edwards, *Dealing in Death: The Arms Trade and the British Civil Wars, 1638–52* (Stroud, 2000), pp. 63–4; A. R. Warmington, *Civil War, Interregnum and Restoration in Gloucestershire 1640–1672* (Woodbridge, 1997), pp. 71–4; Bennett, *Civil Wars Experienced*. Quarter was not unregulated, even if it was unpaid – it was distinct from plunder. For evidence of local agreements see TNA, SP24/47 petition of farmers of Surrey; SP24/57 petition of Joane Johnson. The costs of quarter outlasted the war: Mary Coate, *Cornwall in the Great Civil War and Interregnum 1642–1660: A Social and Political Study* (Oxford, 1933), pp. 223–4.

30. Hughes, *Warwickshire*, p. 256. See also Martyn Bennett, 'Contribution and Assessment: Financial Exactions and the English Civil War, 1642–1646', *War and Society*, 4 (1986), 1–11.

31. Philip Tennant, 'Parish and People: South Warwickshire in the Civil War', reprinted in Richardson (ed.), *Local Aspects*, pp. 157–86.

32. TNA, SP24/47 petition of John Fettiplace. For these disputes and their implications see Ann Hughes, 'Parliamentary Tyranny? Indemnity Procceedings and the Impact of the Civil War: A Case Study from Warwickshire', *Midland History*, 11 (1986), 49–78.

33. Ian Roy, 'The Royalist Army in the First Civil War', unpublished D.Phil. thesis, Oxford (1963), pp. 138–9, 247–62; Carlton, *Going to the Wars*, pp. 188–9. For resentment of Goring see David Underdown, *Somerset in the Civil War and Interregnum* (Newton Abbot, 1973), chs. 4–5.

34. Edwards, *Dealing in Death*, ch. 4; for the supply of the New Model see also Ian Gentles, *The New Model Army in England, Ireland and Scotland, 1645–53* (Oxford, 1992), pp. 40–47. For the royalists see Roy, 'Royalist Army'; Ian Roy (ed.), *The Royalist Ordnance Papers, 1642–1646*, 2 vols., Oxfordshire Record Society, 43, 49 (Oxford, 1964, 1975).

35. Edwards, *Dealing in Death*, pp. 69, 71, 75.

36. Donald Woodward, 'Wage Rates and Living Standards in pre-Industrial England', *PP*, 91 (1981), 28–46; Woodward, *Men at Work: Labourers and Building Craftsmen in the Towns of Northern England, 1450–1750* (Cambridge, 1995).

37. Edwards, *Dealing in Death*, ch. 5.

38. Ibid., p. 136. For the following paragraph see also Pennington, 'War and the People', pp. 125–7.

39. Edwards, *Dealing in Death*, ch. 7.

40. Ibid., ch. 9; for Bateman and carriers' pay see ibid., pp. 228–9. In 1642 half of the Yorkshire gentry (relatively poor by national standards) had an income below £250 p.a.; in East Anglia in the 1630s the owner of 1,000 sheep (a pretty substantial operation) might make an annual profit of £140: Christopher Clay (ed.), *Chapters from the Agrarian History of England and Wales* (general editor Joan Thirsk), vol. 2: *Rural Society: Landowners, Peasants and Labourers 1500–1750* (Cambridge, 1990), pp. 56, 60. Cromwell was worth around £100 p.a. at the beginning of the 1630s, £300 by the end. The latter represented a respectable income for a Justice of the Peace: John Morrill, 'The Making of Oliver Cromwell', in John Morrill (ed.), *Oliver Cromwell and the English Revolution* (Harlow, 1990), pp. 19–48, at pp. 21–2.

41. John Morrill, 'Introduction', in Morrill (ed.), *The Impact of the English Civil War* (London, 1991), pp. 8–19, at p. 9.

42. Gentles, *New Model Army*, p. 40 and table 2.1; for the size of the royalist army at this point see above, p. 391.

43. Gentles, *New Model Army*, pp. 47–8.

44. For the reluctance of the royalists to use conscription, and the disappointing results when they did, see Roy, 'Royalist Army', pp. 185–9. There was little need for either side to resort to conscription in the Midland counties other than Worcester: Osborne, 'Clubmen in the Midlands', in Gaunt (ed.), *English Civil War*, p. 245. Gentles emphasizes conscription in maintaining infantry numbers, but it is clear from his account that many served voluntarily: *New Model Army*, pp. 34–8. In any case, volunteer and conscript were both paid, with the potential effects being outlined here.

45. Gentles, *New Model Army*, p. 29; Paul Slack, *Poverty and Policy in Tudor and Stuart England* (London, 1988), p. 171. We would need, though, a very detailed study to test the hypothesis: the geographical distribution of soldiers and of shortage and so on. There is, clearly, room for a systematic study of the effects of the war on the labour market, as on other aspects of the domestic economy. Coates, *London*, provides a model. For some suggestive comments see Hughes, *Warwickshire*, pp. 270–71; for the dearth see Steve Hindle, 'Dearth and the English Revolution: The Harvest Crisis of 1647–50', *EcHR*, 61 (2008), 64–98.

46. Gentles, *New Model Army*, table 2.1; population estimate derived from Wrigley and Schofield, *Population History*: 17 per cent of population between 15 and 24, 42 per cent between 25 and 59 (table A3.1, p. 528); total population 1646: 5,176,571 (table 7.8, p. 208). Assuming even sex ratios, the male population was 2,588,285, of whom 440,008 were 15–24 and 1,087,079 were 25–59.

47. Gentles, *New Model Army*, table 2.1. For the royalist figure see above, p. 391.

48. Gentles, *New Model Army*, table 2.1; Wrigley and Schofield, *Population History*, table A3.1, p. 528.

49. Gough, *History of Myddle*, p. 116.

50. John Walter and Roger Schofield, 'Famine, Disease and Crisis Mortality in Early Modern Society', in John Walter and Roger Schofield (eds.), *Famine, Disease and the Social Order*

in Early Modern Society (Cambridge, 1989), pp. 1–73; John Walter, 'The Social Economy of Dearth in Early Modern England', reprinted in John Walter, *Crowds and Popular Politics in Early Modern England* (Manchester, 2006), pp. 124–180.

51. Bennett, *Civil Wars Experienced*, pp. 113, 117.

52. TNA, SP24/38 petition of Thomas Catrowe (and associated papers); SP24/57 petition of Joane Johnson.

53. Donagan, 'Casualties', pp. 124–5; Arni, *Justice to the Maimed Soldier*, esp. pp. 11–12, 56–7, 148–51, 153–4.

54. Braddick, *Nerves of State*, esp. pp. 34–9; James Scott Wheeler, *The Making of a World Power: War and the Military Revolution in Seventeenth-Century England* (Stroud, 1999).

55. Philip Styles, 'The City of Worcester during the Civil Wars, 1640–60', reprinted in Richardson (ed.), *Local Aspects*, pp. 187–238, at pp. 197–202; see also Roy, 'Oxford', pp. 147–9.

56. In Cheshire, in fact, the net flow of money was into the county: Morrill, *Cheshire*, pp. 94–100; Gentles, *New Model Army*, pp. 40–47; Edwards, *Dealing in Death*, p. 137. The related question of corruption and peculation in the armies has received little attention: for some examples see TNA SP24/57 petition of George Key (forged debentures), SP24/76 petition of John Smith (extortion).

57. TNA SP24/47 petition of farmers of Surrey; Hughes, *Warwickshire*, pp. 270–71, 281–2; Braddick, *Parliamentary Taxation*, pp. 151–4; Pennington, 'War and the People', pp. 130–31; Colin Phillips, 'Landlord–Tenant Relationships 1642–1660', reprinted in R. C. Richardson (ed.), *Town and Countryside in the English Revolution* (Manchester, 1992), pp. 224–50, at pp. 238–9.

58. *Culpeper Letters*, pp. 118–19.

59. Barry Coward, *Oliver Cromwell* (Harlow, 1991), pp. 11, 12, 48.

60. Phillips, 'Landlord–Tenant Relationships', pp. 239–47; P. G. Holiday, 'Land Sales and Repurchases in Yorkshire after the Civil Wars, 1650–1670', reprinted in Richardson, *Local Aspects*, pp. 287–308; H. J. Habakkuk, 'Landowners and the Civil War', *EcHR*, 2nd ser., 18 (1965), 130–51; Joan Thirsk, 'The Sales of Royalist Land during the Interregnum', *EcHR*, 2nd ser., 5 (1952), 188–207; Coate, *Cornwall*, pp. 225–37. For other local examples see Underdown, *Somerset*, pp. 126–7; Morrill, *Cheshire*, pp. 111–17; Fletcher, *Sussex*, pp. 328–33. Set in a wider context by Christopher O'Riordan, 'Popular Exploitation of Enemy Estates in the English Revolution', *History*, 78 (1993), 183–200.

61. Ian Gentles, 'The Sales of Crown Lands during the English Revolution', *EcHR*, 2nd ser., 26 (1973), 614–35.

62. Anthony Fletcher, *Reform in the Provinces: The Government of Stuart England* (New Haven, Conn., 1986), pp. 12–14, 32.

63. Morrill, *Cheshire*, pp. 223–41; Hughes, *Warwickshire*, pp. 277–90. See Morrill, *Revolt in the Provinces*, 2nd edn, pp. 160–62.

64. Underdown, *Somerset*, ch. 7: these men were attacked as low-born, but it was truer to say that they were of lesser eminence than of no eminence. For other examples see Fletcher, *Sussex*, pp. 325–8; Coate, *Cornwall*, p. 221; Hughes, *Warwickshire*, ch. 9.

65. Underdown, *Somerset*, pp. 123–56; see, for example, Fletcher, *Sussex*, ch. 16, and, for the disruption of assizes, pp. 340–41; Bennett, 'War and Disorder', pp. 256–7 (Yorkshire); Hughes, *Warwickshire*, p. 170. This may have been less true of the towns: see, for example, John T. Evans, *Seventeenth-Century Norwich: Politics, Religion and Government, 1620–1690* (Oxford, 1979), pp. 131–8 (and, after 1649, 182–97). In Cheshire much effective action depended on the personal authority of William Brereton: Morrill, *Cheshire*, ch. 3, as with John Pyne in Somerset: Underdown, *Somerset*, ch. 7. Both men were of gentry backgrounds, however.

66. For Dowsing see pp. 313–14; for excisemen see Braddick, *Parliamentary Taxation*, ch. 4.

67. Gough, *History*, pp. 71–2, 133–4.

68. Bod. L, Ashmolean MS 184, fos 76v, 128r, 142r.

69. TNA SP24/38 petition of Matthew Ingelesbye; SP24/76 petition of Thomas Sheppard; SP24/57 petition of William Jennifer. For other examples see SP24/76 petition of Abraham Slack; SP24/47 petition of James Flood (who left service to go to the siege of Colchester). Apprenticeship disputes do not figure in the Gloucestershire indemnity cases, but they do appear in Warwickshire: Warmington, *Gloucestershire*, p. 89; Hughes, 'Parliamentary Tyranny?', p. 58. This may be another context for the decline in numbers entering service in the 1640s: Roy, 'England Turned Germany?', pp. 265–6.

70. For Marsworth see above pp. 100–101. For dependency see Paul Griffiths, *Youth and Authority: Formative Experiences in England 1560–1640* (Oxford, 1996), ch. 3, esp. pp. 147–69. See also Ilana Krausman Ben-Amos, *Adolescence and Youth in Early Modern England* (London, 1994); S. R. Smith, 'The London Apprentices as 17th Century Adolescents', reprinted in Paul Slack (ed.), *Rebellion, Popular Protest and the Social Order in Early Modern England* (Cambridge, 1984), pp. 219–31.

71. Gough, *History*, p. 71; see above, pp. 389, 406.

72. Gough, *History*, pp. 133–5.

73. For a good overview see Sara Mendelson and Patricia Crawford, *Women in Early Modern England* (Oxford, 1998), pp. 394–418. For petitioners see above, pp. 184–5, and Patricia Higgins, 'The Reactions of Women, with Special Reference to Women Petitioners', in Brian Manning (ed.), *Politics, Religion and the English Civil War* (London, 1973), pp. 179–222. For Alkin see Marcus Nevitt, *Women and the Pamphlet Culture of Revolutionary England, 1640–1660* (Aldershot, 2006), ch. 3. For the *Kings Cabinet opened* see above, pp. 379–83. For Hutchinson see Derek Hirst, 'Remembering a Hero: Lucy Hutchinson's *Memoirs* of Her Husband', *EHR*, 119 (2004), 682–92.

74. Gardiner, I, p. 296.

75. Sharon Achinstein, 'Introduction: Gender, Literature and the English Revolution', *Women's Studies*, 24:1–2 (1994), 1–13; Sharon Achinstein, 'Women on Top in the Pamphlet Literature of the English Revolution', *Women's Studies*, 24:1–2 (1994), 131–63; Rachel Trubowitz, 'Female Preachers and Male Wives: Gender and Authority in Civil War England', reprinted in James Holstun (ed.), *Pamphlet Wars: Prose in the English Revolution* (London, 1992), pp. 112–33; Susan Wiseman, ' "Adam, the Father of all Flesh": Porno-Political Rhetoric and Political Theory in and after the English Civil War', reprinted in ibid., pp. 134–57; Dagmar Freist, 'The King's Crown is the Whore of Babylon: Politics, Gender and Communication in Mid-Seventeenth-Century England', *Gender and History*, 7 (1995), 457–81; Dagmar Freist, *Governed by Opinion: Politics, Religion and the Dynamics of Communication in Stuart London, 1637–1645* (London, 1997). For newsbook representations see Joad Raymond (ed.), *Making the News: An Anthology of the Newsbooks of Revolutionary England, 1641–1660* (Moreton-in-Marsh, 1993), ch. 3.

76. Anon., *A discoverie of Six women preachers* (London, 1641), title page.

77. See, among many others, Anon., *A description of the Sect called the Familie of Love* (London, 1641); Anon., *The Adamites Sermon* (London, 1641); Clive Holmes, *Seventeenth-Century Lincolnshire* (Lincoln, 1980), p. 199. For other examples of this connection see Cressy, *England on Edge*, pp. 241–5.

78. Anon., *Calvers royall vision* (London, 1648), Thomason date 28 October 1648; Anon., *Thirteen strange prophecies* (London, 1648), Thomason date 10 August 1648; *Fourteene strange prophecies* (London, 1649), Thomason date 15 January 1649. For the maid of Worsop see Anon., *The Wonderfull works of God* (London, 1641), Fortescue date 21 November 1641.

79. Barbara Ritter Dailey, 'The Visitation of Sarah Wight: Holy Carnival and the Revolution of the Saints in Civil War London', *Church History*, 55 (1986), 438–55.

80. Keith Thomas, *Religion and the Decline of Magic: Studies in Popular Beliefs in Sixteenth- and Seventeenth-Century England* (Harmondsworth, 1991 edn), esp. pp. 151–66.

81. Keith Thomas, 'Women and the Civil War Sects', *PP*, 13 (1958), 42–62; Phyllis Mack, *Visionary Women: Ecstatic Prophecy in Seventeenth-Century England* (Berkeley, Calif.,

1992); Elizabeth Clarke, 'The Legacy of Mothers and Others: Women's Theological Writing, 1640–60', in Christopher Durston and Judith Maltby (eds.), *Religion in Revolutionary England* (Manchester, 2006), pp. 69–90.

82. See the special edition of *Women's Studies* edited and introduced by Sharon Achinstein, *Women's Studies*, 24:1–2 (1994); Trubowitz, 'Female Preachers'; Wiseman, ' "Adam, the Father of all Flesh" '. For petitioning see Higgins, 'Reactions of Women', in Manning (ed.), *Politics*, pp. 179–222, esp. pp. 209–12; Ann Hughes, 'Gender and Politics in Leveller Literature', in Susan D. Amussen and Mark A. Kishlansky (eds.), *Political Culture and Cultural Politics in Early Modern Europe: Essays Presented to David Underdown* (Manchester, 1995), pp. 162–88; Ann Marie McEntee, ' "The [un]civill-sisterhood of Oranges and Lemons": Female Petitioners and Demonstrators, 1642–53', reprinted in Holstun (ed.), *Pamphlet Wars*, pp. 92–111; Nevitt, *Women*, quotation at p. 5. The achievements of many of the women mentioned here are celebrated in Stevie Davies, *Unbridled Spirits: Women of the English Revolution: 1640–1660* (London, 1998).

83. Ian Gentles, 'The New Model Officer Corps in 1647: A Collective Portrait', *Social History*, 22 (1997), 127–44.

15. Remaking the Local Community

1. Cromwell had argued that 'if the army be not put into another method, and the war more vigorously prosecuted, the people can bear the war no longer, and will enforce you to a dishonourable peace': quoted in Ian Gentles, *The New Model Army in England, Ireland and Scotland 1645–1653* (Oxford, 1992), p. 6. See above, pp. 350–51.

2. Ronald Hutton, *The Royalist War Effort 1642–1646*, 2nd edn (London, 1999), p. 160.

3. Ibid., pp. 163–5; Gentles, *New Model Army*, pp. 61–6.

4. John Morrill, *Revolt in the Provinces: The People of England and the Tragedies of War*, 2nd edition (Harlow, 1999), p. 133; for the distinction between earlier and later movements see David Underdown, 'The Chalk and the Cheese: Contrasts among the English Clubmen', *PP*, 85 (1979), 25–48, at p. 28.

5. Hutton, *Royalist War Effort*, esp. pp. 160, 163–4; David Underdown, *Somerset in the Civil War and Interregnum* (Newton Abbot, 1973), esp. pp. 87–92, 98–100.

6. Hutton, *Royalist War Effort*, p. 161; Simon Osborne, 'The War, the People and the Absence of the Clubmen in the Midlands, 1642–1646', reprinted in Peter Gaunt (ed.), *The English Civil War* (Oxford, 2000), pp. 226–48, esp. pp. 227–39. Nowhere was unaffected by the war of course, and the clubman areas of Worcester certainly felt the burdens of war. On this point see also C. D. Gilbert, 'The Worcestershire Clubmen of 1645', *Transactions of the Worcestershire Archaeological Society*, 3rd ser., 15 (1996), 211–18, at p. 212.

7. Hutton, *Royalist War Effort*, pp. 160–61.

8. Underdown, *Somerset*, pp. 98–9.

9. Anthony Fletcher, *A County Community in Peace and War: Sussex 1600–1660* (London, 1975), p. 272.

10. Morrill, *Revolt in the Provinces*, 2nd edn, pp. 133–4.

11. Underdown, *Somerset*, esp. pp. 105–10, 115–16; Underdown, 'Chalk and the Cheese', esp. pp. 32–40; Hutton, *Royalist War Effort*, pp. 162–3. For other examples see Mark Stoyle, *Loyalty and Locality: Popular Allegiance in Devon during the English Civil War* (Exeter, 1994), ch. 6; Andrew Coleby, *Central Government and the Localities: Hampshire 1649–1689* (Cambridge, 1987), pp. 7–9.

12. Underdown, *Somerset*, pp. 106–8; C. D. Gilbert, 'Clubmen in South West Shropshire, 1644–5', *Transactions of the Shropshire Archaeological and Historical Society*, 68 (1993), 93–8, at pp. 95–6; Hutton, *Royalist War Effort*, pp. 163–4.

13. Underdown, *Somerset*, pp. 98–9; Underdown, 'Chalk and the Cheese', p. 29.

14. For this suggestion see Hutton, *Royalist War Effort*, p. 165.

15. Underdown, *Somerset*, p. 107; Hutton, *Royalist War Effort*, pp. 164–5, 171.

16. These manifestos reprinted in John Morrill, *Revolt of the Provinces: Conservatives and Radicals in the English Civil War, 1630–1650*, 1st edn (Harlow, 1980), pp. 196–7. Extracts are incorporated into the text of the second edition, but I have here referred readers to the fuller texts in the first edition.

17. Osborne, 'Clubmen in the Midlands'.

18. They are substantially reprinted in Morrill, *Revolt of the Provinces*, 1st edn, pp. 197–200.

19. Gilbert, 'Worcestershire Clubmen', p. 211.

20. Hutton, *Royalist War Effort*, pp. 162–3. For the royalist desire to use Grand Juries and quarter sessions, where possible, see Morrill, *Revolt in the Provinces*, 2nd edn, p. 78.

21. See Morrill, *Revolt of the Provinces*, 1st edn, pp. 199, 200.

22. Ibid., p. 197.

23. Gilbert, 'Clubmen in South West Shropshire', p. 94; see also Morrill, *Revolt in the Provinces*, 2nd edn, pp. 141, 148.

24. David Underdown, *Revel, Riot and Rebellion: Popular Politics and Culture in England, 1603–1660* (Oxford, 1985), pp. 158–9; Morrill, *Revolt in the Provinces*, 2nd edn, p. 143; Morrill, *Revolt of the Provinces*, 1st edn, pp. 197, 200; Gilbert, 'Worcestershire Clubmen', p. 212; Hutton, *Royalist War Effort*, pp. 162–3. Gilbert places less emphasis on anti-Catholicism, suggesting that this was more anti-unruly soldier than anti-Catholic in nature: 'Worcestershire Clubmen', p. 213.

25. Reprinted in Morrill, *Revolt of the Provinces*, 1st edn, p. 198; see also *Revolt in the Provinces*, 2nd edn, p. 141.

26. The demands of the Dorset and Wiltshire clubmen were published by order: *The Desires and Resolutions of the club-men of the counties of Dorset and Wilts* (London, 1645), Thomason date 12 July 1645. The Shropshire and Worcestershire manifestos were published in parliamentary newsbooks: Hutton, *Royalist War Effort*, p. 160; and the Wiltshire clubmen's petition of July 1645 survives in *LJ*: reprinted in Morrill, *Revolt of the Provinces*, 1st edn, pp. 196–7. Humphrey Willis, the Somerset leader, took his campaign against the county committee the following year into print: Underdown, *Somerset*, pp. 133–5. The published version of a sermon preached at the siege of Basing House by William Beech included 'a word of advice, full of love and affection' to the clubmen of Hampshire: William Beech, *More sulphure for Basing* (London, 1645). For a remarkably forthright denunciation see *A True relation of The Rising of the club-men in Sussex* (London, 23 September 1645).

27. Buchanan Sharp, *In Contempt of All Authority: Rural Artisans and Riot in the West of England, 1586–1660* (Berkeley, Calif., 1980), pp. 224–5, 240; Underdown, *Revel, Riot and Rebellion*, pp. 160–62.

28. Quoted in Sharp, *In Contempt*, p. 248.

29. Hutton, *Royalist War Effort*, p. 170.

30. Sharp, *In Contempt*, pp. 226–37.

31. Ibid., p. 250; see also Underdown, *Revel, Riot and Rebellion*, pp. 159–60. For Waltham and Windsor, see above, pp. 234–5.

32. Keith Lindley, *Fenland Riots and the English Revolution* (London, 1982), pp. 148–60, quotation at p. 149; see also Clive Holmes, 'Drainers and Fenmen: The Problem of Popular Political Consciousness in the Seventeenth Century', in Anthony Fletcher and John Stevenson (eds.), *Order and Disorder in Early Modern England* (Cambridge, 1985), pp. 166–95.

33. Quoted in Sharp, *In Contempt*, p. 249.

34. The title page noted that the manifesto had been read by a lawyer to a crowd of 4,000 'armed with clubs, swords, bills, pitchforks and other several weapons': *The Desires and Resolutions*, title page.

35. Sharp, *In Contempt*, p. 226.

36. Sharp's brief catalogue of violence makes surprisingly frequent reference to the presence of firearms: ibid., p. 226. This may have been true in any number of local communities. In April 1644 a nameless 'stout fellow' arrived in the Suffolk village of Walberswick to

keep commoners' cattle off the marshland claimed by his employer, Sir Robert Brooke. He started a fight in which he received mortal wounds and indirectly gave a name to 'Bloody Marsh'. It reopened a particularly violent round of dispute in a long-running contest over access to the lands, reflecting the dislocation of the legal system which had previously regulated and decided the issue: Peter Warner, *Bloody Marsh: A Seventeenth-Century Village in Crisis* (Bollington, 2000), esp. ch. 9.

37. Quoted in Morrill, *Revolt of the Provinces*, 1st edn, p. 196.
38. Underdown, *Revel, Riot and Rebellion*, p. 157.
39. Quoted in Morrill, *Revolt of the Provinces*, 1st edn, p. 196.
40. For the New Model see Gentles, *New Model Army*, pp. 61–6; for the fate of the Herefordshire movement see Hutton, *Royalist War Effort*, pp. 170–71; Morrill, *Revolt in the Provinces*, 2nd edn, pp. 148–51.
41. Michael J. Braddick, *Parliamentary Taxation in Seventeenth-Century England: Local Administration and Response* (Woodbridge, 1994), pp. 177–92, 285–6; Michael J. Braddick, *The Nerves of State: Taxation and the Financing of the English State, 1558–1714* (Manchester, 1996), pp. 168–9, 170–74.
42. Peter Edwards, *Dealing in Death: The Arms Trade and the British Civil Wars, 1638–52* (Stroud, 2000), p. 63.
43. There was a second disturbance on 4 July, another market day, which prompted the collector to make the complaint on which this account is based: reprinted in Braddick, *Nerves of State*, pp. 222–4. The second disturbance arose from a renewed attempt to collect the excise, prompted by a visit from the London commissioners: there is little doubt that the riots were connected with consideration of the problems through the formal channels.
44. Keith Lindley, *Popular Politics and Religion in Civil War London* (Aldershot, 1997), pp. 5–6; see above, p. 418.
45. For Haverford West see Morrill, *Revolt of the Provinces*, 1st edn, pp. 182–3; for women and grain riots see John Walter, 'Grain Riots and Popular Attitudes to the Law: Malden and the Crisis of 1629', reprinted in John Walter, *Crowds and Popular Politics in Early Modern England* (Manchester, 2006), pp. 27–66, at pp. 40–41.
46. Braddick, *Nerves of State*, pp. 223–4.
47. Ibid.
48. Braddick, *Parliamentary Taxation*, esp. p. 182. It was also true in the 1660s: ibid., pp. 211–20, 252–66; see also Braddick, *Nerves of State*, pp. 169–74, 221–6.
49. For the uneasy relationship between Leveller and army politics with regard to the excise see Michael J. Braddick, 'Popular Politics and Public Policy: The Excise Riot at Smithfield in February 1647 and Its Aftermath', *HJ*, 34 (1991), 597–626, at pp. 618–21. For a sensitive consideration of the possibilities for developing local connections between soldiers and civilians see Daniel C. Beaver, *Parish Communities and Religious Conflict in the Vale of Gloucester 1590–1690* (Cambridge, Mass., 1998), pp. 204–11.
50. Morrill, *Revolt in the Provinces*, 2nd edn, pp. 160–61, 164–6.
51. Ibid., pp. 166–9.
52. For Willis, see Underdown, *Somerset*, pp. 118, 133–7; Ann Hughes, *Politics, Society and Civil War in Warwickshire, 1620–1660* (Cambridge, 1987), pp. 251–2 for the use of print. For the interaction of local and national politics in disputes like this see Clive Holmes, 'Colonel King and Lincolnshire Politics, 1642–6', *HJ*, 16 (1973), 451–84.
53. Hughes, *Warwickshire*, ch. 6, esp. pp. 238–54, John Bryan quoted at p. 219.
54. William Cliftlands, 'The "Well-Affected" and the "Country": Politics and Religion in English Provincial Society, c. 1640–1654', unpublished Ph.D. thesis, Essex (1987), p. 261. For other examples see Braddick, *Parliamentary Taxation*, pp. 152–4.
55. A. R. Warmington, *Civil War, Interregnum and Restoration in Gloucestershire 1640–1672* (Woodbridge, 1997), esp. pp. 71–4; Fletcher, *Sussex*, pp. 333–6. For an overview of the histories of these committees, which emphasizes 'private battles' and bureaucratic and jurisdictional rivalries, see D. H. Pennington, 'The Accounts of the Kingdom,

1642–49', in F. J. Fisher (ed.), *Essays in the Economic and Social History of Tudor and Stuart England* (Cambridge, 1961), pp. 182–203; for the politics of accounts at Westminster see Jason Peacey, 'Politics, Accounts and Propaganda in the Long Parliament', in Chris R. Kyle and Jason Peacey (eds.), *Parliament at Work: Parliamentary Committees, Political Power, and Public Access in Early Modern England* (Woodbridge, 2002), pp. 59–78.

56. There is a huge literature on these issues. I have made this argument at greater length in Michael J. Braddick, *State Formation in Early Modern England c.1550–1700* (Cambridge, 2000), esp. pts 2–3. For a complementary account see Steve Hindle, *The State and Social Change in Early Modern England, c.1550–1640* (Basingstoke, 2000). Keith Wrightson, *English Society 1580–1680* (London, 1982) is of seminal importance. See also Keith Wrightson and David Levine, *Poverty and Piety in an English Village: Terling 1525–1700*, rev. edn (Oxford, 1995); Keith Wrightson, 'The Politics of the Parish in Early Modern England', in Paul Griffiths, Adam Fox and Steve Hindle (eds.), *The Experience of Authority in Early Modern England* (Basingstoke, 1996), pp. 10–46, and many of the other essays in that collection. An unusually clear statement of the values of village governors is reprinted in Steve Hindle, 'Hierarchy and Community in the Elizabethan Parish: The Swallowfield Articles of 1596', *HJ*, 42 (1999), 835–51. The treatment of the poor reveals these calculations with particular clarity. On that see, in particular, Steve Hindle, *On the Parish?: The Micro-Politics of Poor Relief in Rural England, c.1550–1750* (Oxford, 2004). For an important collection dealing with questions of community see Alexandra Shepard and Phil Withington (eds.), *Communities in Early Modern England: Networks, Place, Rhetoric* (Manchester, 2000); for urban communities see Phil Withington, *The Politics of Commonwealth: Citizens and Freemen in Early Modern England* (Cambridge, 2005), esp. pt 3. For Puritan fellowship see John Spurr, *English Puritanism 1603–1689* (Basingstoke, 1998), ch. 12. Beaver, *Parish Communities*, is particularly important in its emphasis on the role of ritual in the formation of parish communities, and offers a methodological complement to the works cited here.

57. TNA SP24/57 petition of Thomas Jenkins. Many of these disputes revolved around rights to tithe income: Ann Hughes, 'Parliamentary Tyranny? Indemnity Proceedings and the Impact of the Civil War: A Case Study from Warwickshire', *Midland History*, 11 (1986), 49–78, at pp. 61–2.

58. Morrill, *Revolt in the Provinces*, 2nd edn, pp. 156–9. See also Judith Maltby, 'Suffering and Surviving: The Civil Wars, the Commonwealth and the Formation of "Anglicanism", 1642–60', in Christopher Durston and Judith Maltby (eds.), *Religion in Revolutionary England* (Manchester, 2006), pp. 158–80, and the works cited there.

59. Martin Ingram, 'Puritans and the Church Courts', in Christopher Durston and Jacqueline Eales (eds.), *The Culture of English Puritanism, 1560–1700* (Basingstoke, 1996), pp. 58–91.

60. Alan Everitt's position in, *Suffolk and the Great Rebellion, 1640–60*, Suffolk Records Society, 3 (1960), is more subtle than is usually suggested. For Suffolk see also Clive Holmes (ed.), *The Suffolk Committee for Scandalous Ministers 1644–1646*, Suffolk Records Society, 13 (1970); Trevor Cooper (ed.), *The Journal of William Dowsing: Iconoclasm in East Anglia during the English Civil War* (Woodbridge, 2001). For Dowsing, see above, pp. 313–14.

61. James Sharpe, *Instruments of Darkness: Witchcraft in England 1550–1750* (London, 1996), pp. 128–9; the Essex trials are discussed in Alan Macfarlane, *Witchcraft in Tudor and Stuart England: A Regional and Comparative Study* (London, 1970), ch. 9; the fullest treatment is Malcolm Gaskill, *Witchfinders: A Seventeenth-Century English Tragedy* (London, 2005).

62. Charles Carlton, *Going to the Wars: The Experience of the English Civil Wars, 1638–1651* (London, 1992), p. 385.

63. The classic statements are Macfarlane, *Witchcraft*, chs. 10–16; Keith Thomas, *Religion and the Decline of Magic: Studies in Popular Beliefs in Sixteenth- and Seventeenth-Century*

England (Harmondsworth, 1991 edn), ch. 17. For subsequent revision see Sharpe, *Instruments*, chs. 6–7; Malcolm Gaskill, *Crime and Mentalities in Early Modern England* (Cambridge, 2000), esp. ch. 2; Diane Purkiss, *The Witch in History: Early Modern and Twentieth-Century Representations* (London, 1996), esp. ch. 4; Clive Holmes, 'Women: Witnesses and Witches', *PP*, 140 (1993), 45–78; Peter Rushton, 'Women, Witchcraft and Slander in Early Modern England: Cases from the Church Courts in Durham, 1560–1675', *Northern History*, 18 (1982), 116–32. For the general view outlined here, and further references, see Braddick, *State Formation*, esp. pp. 146–50.

64. Sharpe, *Instruments*, pp. 131–4.
65. Ibid., pp. 140–44.
66. Ibid., pp. 142–4; Macfarlane, *Witchcraft*, pp. 135–7.
67. Sharpe, *Instruments*, pp. 144–6; Macfarlane, *Witchcraft*, pp. 135–7.
68. Malcolm Gaskill, 'Witches and Witchcraft Prosecutions, 1560–1660', in M. Zell (ed.), *Early Modern Kent 1540–1640* (Woodbridge, 2000), pp. 245–77, at pp. 263–5.
69. Sharpe, *Instruments*, pp. 146–7.
70. Ibid., pp. 144–5.
71. Diane Purkiss, 'Desire and Its Deformities: Fantasies of Witchcraft in the English Civil War', *Journal of Medieval and Early Modern Studies* (1997), 103–32, at pp. 103–4.
72. *Signes and wonders from Heaven* (London, 1645), Thomason date 4 August 1645, pp. 54–5. For *Pharsalia* see above, pp. 54–5.
73. Sharpe, *Instruments*, pp. 134–7. He differs on this point from Macfarlane, *Witchcraft*, p. 139.
74. James Sharpe, 'Scandalous and Malignant Priests in Essex: The Impact of Grassroots Puritanism', in Colin Jones, Malyn Newitt and Stephen K. Roberts (eds.), *Politics and People in Revolutionary England: Essays in Honour of Ivan Roots* (Oxford, 1986), pp. 253–73; John Walter, 'Confessional Politics in pre-Civil War Essex: Prayer Books, Profanations, and Petitions', *HJ*, 44 (2001), 677–701; John Walter, ' "Abolishing superstition with sedition"?: The Politics of Popular Iconoclasm in England 1640–1642', *PP*, 183 (2004), 79–123; John Walter, 'Popular Iconoclasm and the Politics of the Parish in Eastern England, 1640–1642', *HJ*, 47 (2004), 261–90; John Walter, ' "Affronts & insolencies": The Voices of Radwinter and Popular Opposition to Laudianism', *EHR*, 122 (2007), 35–60; Cooper (ed.), *Journal of William Dowsing*.
75. *Signes and wonders*, p. 4. Two witches, in different locations, were said to have used witchcraft against parish officials who had tried to conscript their sons: Sharpe, *Instruments*, p. 133.
76. Gaskill, *Witchfinders*, p. 149; Carlton, *Going to the Wars*, p. 189; Purkiss, 'Desire and Its Deformities', p. 108; for Rupert as an incubus or devil see Anon., *The interpreter* (Oxford, 1643). There is a manuscript copy in HEH, EL 7801. For Rupert and responsibility for the war see above, p. 347.
77. Strafford's words as reported in William Lilly, *A collection of ancient and moderne prophesies* (1645), Thomason date 20 November 1645, p. 50; Perkins quoted in Genevieve Guenther, 'Why Devils Came When Faustus Called Them' (unpublished paper); Nathan Johnstone, *The Devil and Demonism in Early Modern England* (Cambridge, 2006), ch. 7. Wallington collected numerous stories of Cavaliers drinking to the health of the Devil, or reports of their being in league with the Devil: BL Sloane MS 1457, fos. 21r–29r.
78. Purkiss, 'Desire and Its Deformities', pp. 106–9, quotation at p. 109.
79. Quoted in Purkiss, 'Desire and Its Deformities', pp. 111–12, quotation at p. 112; for martial language see p. 115.
80. For the atrocity at Naseby see above, p. 378.
81. This explains, perhaps, the dramatic peak in witchcraft prosecutions in Devon during the 1650s: thirty-five of the known formal accusations (51 per cent of the total) came in that decade: Janet A. Thompson, *Wives, Widows, Witches and Bitches: Women in Seventeenth-Century Devon* (New York, 1993), ch. 4, esp. pp. 101–4. Other western counties also saw a peak in accusations after the war. Thompson suggests that this reflects

the 'homogenising' effect of the war, drawing the peripheries closer to the political and cultural concerns of the centre: p. 107.

82. Johnstone, *Devil*, esp. pp. 253–65.

83. For the relationship between witchcraft and anxieties about patriarchal order see Purkiss, *Witch in History*; Sharpe, *Instruments*, ch. 7.

84. For a study paying close attention to the role of ritual in the formation of community and resolution of conflict see Beaver, *Parish Communities*. See also the other works cited in n. 56 above.

85. For the survival of local administration see Anthony Fletcher, *Reform in the Provinces: The Government of Stuart England* (New Haven, Conn., 1986), esp. pp. 11–14, 96–7, 186–7, 243–5, 250–51, 257–60, 357; implementation of the Poor Law may have required more prompting from below than in previous years, in the absence of Privy Council oversight: Hindle, *On the Parish?*, pp. 253–6; Steve Hindle, 'Dearth and the English Revolution: The Harvest Crisis of 1647–50', *EcHR*, 61 (2008), 64–98.

16. Post-War Politics

1. Harrison quoted from Ian Gentles, *The New Model Army in England, Ireland and Scotland, 1645–1653* (Oxford, 1992), p. 68; Cromwell quoted from Barry Coward, *Oliver Cromwell* (Harlow, 1991), pp. 34, 40.

2. Barbara Taft, 'Walwyn, William (*bap.* 1600, *d.* 1681)', *ODNB*, 57, pp. 225–31; Andrew Sharp, 'Lilburne, John (1615?–1657)', *ODNB*, 33, pp. 773–83; Joseph Frank, *The Levellers: A History of the Writings of Three Seventeenth-Century Social Democrats: John Lilburne, Richard Overton, William Walwyn* (Cambridge, Mass., 1955), pp. 29–39; H. N. Brailsford, *The Levellers and the English Revolution* (London, 1961), ch. 5. For a selection of his writings see J. R. McMichael and Barbara Taft (eds.), *The Writings of William Walwyn* (Athens, Ga, 1989).

3. Sharp, 'Lilburne'; Brailsford, *Levellers*, ch. 6; Frank, *Levellers*, ch. 2.

4. Taft, 'Walwyn'; Sharp, 'Lilburne', p. 776; B. J. Gibbons, 'Overton, Richard (*fl.* 1640–1663)', *ODNB*, 42, pp. 166–71; Brailsford, *Levellers*, ch. 4; Frank, *Levellers*, pp. 39–44. For Overton and illegal printing in the early 1640s see also David Como, 'Secret printing, the Crisis of 1640, and the Origins of Civil War Radicalism', *PP*, 196, 61 (2008), 64–98.

5. Frank, *Levellers*, pp. 45–55; Pauline Gregg, *Free-Born John: The Biography of John Lilburne* (London, 1961), ch. 9. *A Helpe* and *The Araignement* are reprinted in William Haller (ed.), *Tracts on Liberty in the Puritan Revolution 1638–1647*, 3 vols. (New York, 1934), III, pp. 189–256; *A Helpe* is also reprinted in McMichael and Taft, *Writings of Walwyn*, pp. 131–42. For 'functional radicalization' see G. E. Aylmer (ed.), *The Levellers and the English Revolution* (London, 1975), pp. 13–14; the introduction contains a good brief outline of the history of the Leveller movement. See also Brailsford, *Levellers*; Frank, *Levellers*. For their political throught see Andrew Sharp, *The English Levellers* (Cambridge, 1998); David Wootton, 'Leveller Democracy and the Puritan Revolution', in J. H. Burns, with Mark Goldie (eds.), *The Cambridge History of Political Thought 1450–1700* (Cambridge, 1991), pp. 412–42.

6. Frank, *Levellers*, pp. 54–5.

7. Frank, *Levellers*, pp. 55–65; Gregg, *Free-Born John*, chs. 10–11. These pamphlets are reprinted in Aylmer, *Levellers*, pp. 56–67, and Haller, *Tracts*, III, pp. 257–307; *England's Lamentable Slaverie* is reprinted in McMichael and Taft, *Writings of Walwyn*, pp. 143–53.

8. J. C. Davis, 'The Levellers and Christianity', reprinted in Peter Gaunt (ed.), *The English Civil War* (Oxford, 2000), pp. 279–302; Rachel Foxley, 'Citizenship and the English Nation in Leveller Thought, 1642–1653', unpublished Ph.D. Thesis, Cambridge (2001), ch. 2; Rachel Foxley, 'John Lilburne and the Citizenship of "free-born Englishmen" ', *HJ*, 47 (2004), 849–74.

9. Brailsford, *Levellers*, p. xi; Frank, *Levellers*, pp. 51–2.

10. Brailsford, *Levellers*, p. xi. It is presumed in Gregg, *Free-Born John*, chs. 13–21.

11. Frank, *Levellers*, pp. 53–4; Brailsford, *Levellers*, pp. 53–4.

12. For a more cautious account of their relationship with democratic ideas see Wootton, 'Leveller Democracy'. For their relationship with the New Model Army see above, pp. 486–90, 508–9.

13. Frank, *Levellers*, p. 55.

14. Frank, *Levellers*, pp. 57–60; see also Andrew Sharp, 'John Lilburne and the Long Parliament's Book of Declarations: A Radical's Exploitation of the Words of Authorities', *History of Political Thought*, 9 (1988), 19–44; Andrew Sharp, 'John Lilburne's Discourse of Law', *Political Science*, 40:1 (1988), 18–33. For the *Exact collection* see above, pp. 272–3.

15. Frank, a believer in the usefulness of the term 'movement', thinks that the birth of the Leveller party was still two years away at this point: *Levellers*, p. 52.

16. Ann Hughes, *Gangraena and the Struggle for the English Revolution* (Oxford, 2004), esp. pp. 22–49; P. R. S. Baker, 'Edwards, Thomas (*c.*1599–1648)', *ODNB*, 17, pp. 965–8. See above, pp. 337–40.

17. Hughes, *Gangraena*, pp. 42–9, 131–7; Baker, 'Edwards'.

18. Hughes, *Gangraena*, esp. pp. 223–41, 333–67; Baker, 'Edwards'. For London politics and the remonstrance see Ian Gentles, 'The Struggle for London in the Second Civil War', *HJ*, 26 (1983), 277–305, esp. p. 280.

19. Hughes, *Gangraena*, pp. 151–69, 241–76, 305–8, 432–5.

20. Ibid., pp. 2–4; Baker, 'Edwards'. For the exchanges between Edwards and Walwyn, and Edwards's portrayal of Walwyn, Overton and Lilburne, see Frank, *Levellers*, pp. 69–76; Brailsford, *Levellers*, pp. 36–42.

21. The classic study is Christopher Hill, *The World Turned Upside Down: Radical Ideas during the English Revolution* (Harmondsworth, 1972): 'Now that the Protestant ethic itself, the greatest achievement of European bourgeois society in the sixteenth and seventeenth centuries, is at last being questioned after a rule of three or four centuries, we can study with a new sympathy the Diggers, the Ranters, and the many other daring thinkers who in the seventeenth century refused to bow down and worship it', p. 15.

22. For these arguments see also Michael J. Braddick, 'The English Revolution and Its Legacies', in Nicholas Tyacke (ed.), *The English Revolution c. 1590–1720* (Manchester, 2007) pp. 27–42. In addition to the works cited there, they are particularly informed by the approach of Hughes, *Gangraena*; Ann Hughes, 'The Meanings of Religious Polemic', in Francis J. Bremer (ed.), *Puritanism: Transatlantic Perspectives on a Seventeenth-Century Anglo-American Faith* (Boston, Mass., 1993), pp. 201–29; Steven Shapin, *A Social History of Truth: Civility and Science in Seventeenth-Century England* (Chicago, 1994).

23. A point made by Glenn Burgess, 'The Impact on Political Thought: Rhetorics for Troubled Times', in John Morrill (ed.), *The Impact of the English Civil War* (London, 1991), pp. 67–83, esp. pp. 67–8. For rhetorical creativity in radical religious writing see Nigel Smith, *Perfection Proclaimed: Language and Literature in English Radical Religion, 1640–1660* (Oxford, 1989); more generally, Nigel Smith, *Literature and Revolution in England, 1640–1660* (New Haven, Conn., 1994); Elizabeth Skerpan, *The Rhetoric of Politics in the English Revolution, 1642–1660* (Columbia, Mo., 1992).

24. See above, pp. 197–9, 207.

25. The manuscript copy, dated June 1646, is in HEH, HM 30303; for the published version see Josiah Ricraft, *A survey of England's Champions and Truth's Faithful patriots* (1647). The judgement on Newbury appears at p. 20 in both versions. The account of Marston Moor credits Manchester and Fairfax: Ricraft, *A survey*, p. 98.

26. For Ryves and *Mercurius Rusticus*, see above, pp. 282–4; [George Wharton], *Englands Iliads in a nut-shell* (London, 1645), Thomason date 24 July 1645; [Bruno Ryves], *Micro-chronicon* (London, 1647). Ryves's text is much fuller, but shares the basic outline and principal landmarks with Wharton's.

27. For an example of the genre see Anon., *The Apprentices VVarning-piece* (London, 1641); for examples of its political re-invention see, among many others, Thomas Morton,

Englands warning-piece (London, 5 August 1642); [James Cranford], *The teares of Ireland ... As a warning piece to her Sister Nations* (London, 1642); Anon., *A warning-piece To all His maiesties subjects of England* (reprinted in London, 1643), Thomason date 20 February 1643; Anon., *An Alarme to England: or A Warning-Piece* (London, 1647), Thomason date 8 April 1647; Alexander Mingzeis, *Englands Caveat: or Warning-piece* (London, 1647).

28. Sharon Achinstein, *Milton and the Revolutionary Reader* (Princeton, 1994); Hughes, 'Meanings of Religious Polemic', pp. 228–9.

29. Quoted in Paul Christianson, 'From Expectation to Militance: Reformers and Babylon in the First Two Years of the Long Parliament', *Journal of Ecclesiastical History*, 34 (1973), 225–44, at p. 243. It was not published until 1644. For the European Reformation context see Richard Popkin, *The History of Scepticism from Savonarola to Bayle*, rev. edn (Oxford, 2003), ch. 1.

30. William Prynne, *A vindication of psalme 105.15* (London, 1642).

31. John Milton, *Paradise Lost*, book ii, lines 559–61, quoted from Stephen Orgel and Jonathan Goldberg (eds.), *John Milton* (Oxford, 1991), pp. 355–618, at p. 389.

32. See, among many examples, John Taylor, *A Cluster of coxcombes* (London, 13 July 1642); Anon., *The Divisions Of the Church of England* (London, 1642); Anon., *A Discovery of 29. Sects* (London, 1641); [Alexander Ross], *Religions Lotterie or the Churches Amazement* (London, 1642). The second is attributed to Taylor by Wing and EEBO, but Bernard Capp discounts Taylor's authorship in his authoritative list of Taylor's publications: *The World of John Taylor the Water-Poet 1578–1653* (Oxford, 1994), p. 203.

33. Ephraim Pagitt, *Heresiography* (London, 1645). See, for comparison, the subtitle of Thomas Edwards, *The First and Second Part of Gangraena: A Catologue and Discovery of many of the Errors, Heresies and Blasphemies and pernicious Practices of the Sectaries of this time* (London, 1646).

34. For Benbrigge see above, pp. xxii–xxiii.

35. Clifford Geertz, 'Common Sense as a Cultural System', in Clifford Geertz, *Local Knowledge: Further Essays in Interpretive Anthropology* (New York, 2000 edn), pp. 73–93, at p. 75.

36. Angela McShane Jones, ' "Rime and Reason": The Political World of the English Broadside Ballad, 1640–1689', unpublished Ph. D. thesis, Warwick (2004), esp. intr., ch. 4.

37. Josiah Ricraft, *The peculier characters Of the orientall languages* (London, [1645]). On programmes of language reform both as a means of reducing public discussion to order and, more positively, to increase knowledge see Sharon Achinstein, 'The Politics of Babel in the English Revolution', reprinted in James Holstun (ed.), *Pamphlet Wars: Prose in the English Revolution* (London, 1992), pp. 14–44.

38. For *Macaria*, see above, pp. 156–8, and *Of Education*, pp. 341–3 above.

39. The best introduction to his career is Charles Webster, 'Introduction', in Charles Webster (ed.), *Samuel Hartlib and the Advancement of Learning* (Cambridge, 1970), which also reprints a number of crucial texts. For the wider intellectual context the standard work is Charles Webster, *The Great Instauration: Science, Medicine and Reform*, 2nd edn (Oxford, 2002); see also Charles Webster, *Utopian Planning and the Puritan Revolution: Gabriel Plattes, Samuel Hartlib and 'Macaria'* (Oxford, 1979); G. H. Turnbull, *Samuel Hartlib: A Sketch of His Life and His Relations to J. A. Comenius* (London, 1920); G. H. Turnbull, *Hartlib, Dury and Comenius: Gleanings from Hartlib's Papers* (London, 1947); Mark Greengrass, 'Samuel Hartlib and International Calvinism', *Proceedings of the Huguenot Society*, 25 (1993), 464–75; Mark Greengrass, Michael Leslie and Timothy Raylor (eds.), *Samuel Hartlib and Universal Reformation: Studies in Intellectual Communication* (Cambridge, 1994).

40. For the Society of Astrologers see Patrick Curry, *Prophecy and Power: Astrology in Early Modern England* (Princeton, 1989), pp. 40–44; Keith Thomas, *Religion and the Decline of Magic: Studies in Popular Beliefs in Sixteenth- and Seventeenth-Century England* (Harmondsworth, 1991 edn), quotation at p. 340.

41. In addition to Webster, *Advancement*, and Webster, *Great Instauration*, see, for the woollen tank, Timothy Raylor, 'Providence and Technology in the English Civil War: Edmund Felton and his Engine', *Renaissance Studies*, 7:4 (1993), 398–413, and for the saltpetre project Thomas Leng, *Benjamin Worsley (1618–1677): Trade, Interest and the Spirit in Revolutionary England* (Woodbridge, 2008). The torpedo was tested in 1655: John T. Young, *Faith, Medical Alchemy, and Natural Philosophy: Johann Moriaen, Reformed Intelligencer and the Hartlib Circle* (Aldershot, 1998), pp. 55–7. I am grateful to Tom Leng for this reference. For the failure of policies of agricultural improvement in this period see Joan Thirsk, 'Agrarian Problems and the English Revolution', in R. C. Richardson (ed.), *Town and Countryside in the English Revolution* (Manchester, 1992), pp. 169–97.

42. [Samuel Hartlib], *The Parliaments Reformation* (London, 1646), Thomason date 6 August 1646, quotations at pp. 1, 6. The pamphlet is reprinted in Webster, *Advancement*, pp. 111–18.

43. Ibid., p. 5. For the grant see Webster, *Advancement*, p. 49. The pamphlet is sub-titled *Or a Worke for Presbyters, Elders, and Deacons, to Engage themselves, for the Education of all poore Children, and imployment of all sorts of poore, that no poore body young nor old may be enforced to beg within their Classes in City nor Country.* See also Samuel Hartlib, *Londons Charitie Stilling The Poore Orphans Cry* (London, 1649); Hartlib, *Londons Charity inlarged* (London, 1650). This later scheme is discussed in Paul Slack, *From Reformation to Improvement: Public Welfare in Early Modern England* (Oxford, 1998), pp. 85–7.

44. Webster, *Advancement*, p. 49; Turnbull, *Hartlib*, pp. 48–51; for the Navigation Act and Down survey see Leng, *Worsley*.

45. Webster, *Advancement*, pp. 25–6. For Culpeper's politics see *Culpeper Letters*, pp. 105–402.

46. For Puritanism and science see Webster, *Great Instauration*, pp. xxi–xl, and the many works cited there. For Richard Wiseman see *Severall Chirurgicall Treatises* (London, 1676 edn); for dissection see Lisa Jardine, *On a Grander Scale: The Outstanding Career of Sir Christopher Wren* (London, 2002), pp. 55–7; for problems in the supply of corpses during the seventeenth century see Jonathan Sawday, *The Body Emblazoned: Dissection and the Human Body in Renaissance Culture* (London, 1996 edn), pp. 54–9; for Hobbes see Timothy Raylor, 'Thomas Hobbes and "The Mathematical Demonstration of the Sword" ', *Seventeenth Century*, 15 (2000), 175–98; for developments in nursing see Eric Gruber von Arni, *Justice to the Maimed Soldier: Nursing, Medical Care and Welfare for the Sick and Wounded Soldiers and Their Families during the English Civil Wars and Interregnum, 1642–1660* (Aldershot, 2001).

47. Robert Brenner, *Merchants and Revolution: Commercial Change, Political Conflict, and London's Overseas Traders, 1550–1653* (Cambridge, 1993), esp. chs. 8–13; for the Council of Trade and the Navigation Act see Leng, *Worsley*. This is discussed above, pp. 587–8.

48. For a brief introduction see Noel Malcolm, 'Hobbes, Thomas (1588–1679)', *ODNB*, 27, pp. 385–95; Noel Malcolm, *Aspects of Hobbes* (Oxford, 2002), ch. 1.

49. For the censorship ordinance see above, pp. 294–5; Debora Shuger, *Censorship and Cultural Sensibility: The Regulation of Language in Tudor–Stuart England* (Philadelphia, 2006), addresses the whole question of censorship in terms of civility rather than the nature of the views expressed; see also David Cressy, 'Book Burning in Tudor and Stuart England', *Sixteenth Century Journal*, 36 (2005), 359–74. For secrecy at the lower levels of government see Paul Griffiths, 'Secrecy and Authority in Late Sixteenth- and Seventeenth-Century London', *HJ*, 40 (1997), 925–51; see also the Swallowfield articles, reprinted in Steve Hindle, 'Hierarchy and Community in the Elizabethan Parish: The Swallowfield Articles of 1596', *HJ*, 42 (1999), 835–51, at p. 851 (article 26). For the ritual of burning see above, pp. 278–9.

50. For Dering see above, pp. 195–6, 278; for the *Book of Sports* see above, pp. 277–81;

for Williams see above, p. 341; for the catechism see above, p. 373; for the Scots' declarations see above, p. 471. For fuller discussion see Ariel Hessayon, 'Incendiary Texts: Radicalism and Book Burning in England, c. 1640–c. 1660', unpublished paper. I am grateful to Ariel Hessayon for allowing me to see this paper, and to Brian Cummings and Jason Peacey for discussing this issue with me.

51. Compare the texts of the R. Ram, *The souldiers catechisme*, 7th edn (1645) and R. Ram, *The soldiers catechisme*, 8th edition (1645); the title pages are otherwise indistinguishable. For the order for the burning of the soldiers' catechism published in Oxford 'counterfeiting that at London', see *The Kingdomes VVeekly Intelligencer*, no. 111, 29 July–6 August 1645, p. 887. It is also reported in *The Weekly Account*, 31 July–6 August 1645, pp. [5–6].

52. John Milton, *Areopagitica* (London, 1644), see above, pp. 341–3.

53. Ann Hughes, 'Parliamentary Tyranny? Indemnity Proceedings and the Impact of the Civil War: A Case Study from Warwickshire', *Midland History*, 11 (1986), 49–78.

54. TNA SP24/76 petition of Anne Smith. We might perhaps detect in the latter argument the hand of a lawyer or advocate.

55. TNA SP24/38 petition of William Caswall; SP24/57 petition of Thomas Johnson; SP24/57 petition of Thomas Jones. See also Ann Hughes, *Politics, Society and Civil War in Warwickshire, 1620–1660* (Cambridge, 1987), pp. 203–8, 289–90; David Underdown, ' "Honest" Radicals in the Counties, 1642–1649', in Donald Pennington and Keith Thomas (eds.), *Puritans and Revolutionaries: Essays in Seventeenth-Century History Presented to Christopher Hill* (Oxford, 1978), pp. 186–205; David Underdown, *Revel, Riot and Rebellion: Popular Politics and Culture in England, 1603–1660* (Oxford, 1985), pp. 217–20; Michael J. Braddick, *Parliamentary Taxation in Seventeenth-Century England: Local Administration and Response* (Woodbridge, 1994), pp. 152–6; David Scott, 'Politics and Government in York 1640–1662', in Richardson (ed.), *Town and Countryside*, pp. 46–68, esp. pp. 56–7; for the self-conscious adoption of this identity among those active for Parliament see William Cliftlands, 'The "Well-Affected" and the "Country": Politics and Religion in English Provincial Society, c. 1640–1654', unpublished Ph.D. thesis, Essex (1987).

56. TNA SP24/47 petition of William Flacke.

57. TNA SP24/76 petition of Francis Smith. Smith was being sued by a bookseller in Bury who had ordered the prayer book.

58. TNA SP24/57 petition of William Jackson; SP24/38 petition of Richard Carr (seven to eight years and for costs); SP24/76 Thomas Smallwood and Elizabeth Kent (three years); Hughes, 'Parliamentary Tyranny?', pp. 58–9, 64, 68. For the persistence of these partisan conflicts see also Ian Roy, 'The City of Oxford 1640–1660', in Richardson (ed.), *Town and Countryside*, pp. 130–68, at pp. 156–60.

59. TNA SP24/57 petition of the 'well-affected inhabitants' of St Ives. See also, for example, SP24/76 petition of John Smith; SP24/47 petition of the inhabitants of Farringdon Without (including Praisegod Barebon). Such cases are discussed by Robert Ashton, *Counter-Revolution: The Second Civil War and Its Origins, 1646–1648* (New Haven, Conn., 1994), pp. 215–23; Hughes, 'Parliamentary Tyranny?', p. 62; A. R. Warmington, *Civil War, Interregnum and Restoration in Gloucestershire 1640–1672* (Woodbridge, 1997), p. 89.

60. For some of the conventions of these exchanges see Joad Raymond, *Pamphlets and Pamphleteering in Early Modern Britain* (Cambridge, 2003), esp. pp. 206–14.

61. For the term bum-fodder: Margaret Spufford, *Small Books and Pleasant Histories: Popular Fiction and Its Readership in Seventeenth-Century England* (Athens, Ga, 1981), pp. 48–9; Alexandra Walsham, *Providence in Early Modern England* (Oxford, 1999), pp. 33–4. It was more usually, but not exclusively, associated with single-sheet ballads.

17. Military Defeat and Political Survival

1. Gardiner, III, pp. 103–4, 127. For the full text of the propositions see Gardiner, *CD*, pp. 290–306. There is a useful summary in David L. Smith, *Constitutional Royalism and the Search for Settlement, c. 1640–1649* (Cambridge, 1994), pp. 128–9; and a useful narrative in Robert Ashton, *Counter-Revolution: The Second Civil War and Its Origins, 1646–1648* (New Haven, Conn., 1994), pp. 7–17.

2. Smith, *Constitutional Royalism*, pp. 128–9.

3. Quoted in Austin Woolrych, *Britain in Revolution 1625–1660* (Oxford, 2002), p. 343; Gardiner, III, p. 127.

4. For a good summary of the position see David Underdown, *Pride's Purge: Politics in the Puritan Revolution* (Oxford, 1971), ch. 3, esp. pp. 73–5; Austin Woolrych, *Soldiers and Statesmen: The General Council of the Army and Its Debates, 1647–8* (Oxford, 1987), pp. 5–10. For the ordinances see Gardiner, III, pp. 137–8, 145. For anti-Scottish pamphlets see Ashton, *Counter-Revolution*, pp. 302–3.

5. Gardiner, III, pp. 79–80.

6. For Charles's views in this period see Richard Cust, *Charles I: A Political Life* (Harlow, 2005), pp. 423–9; Gardiner, III, pp. 131–2.

7. Quoted in Smith, *Constitutional Royalism*, pp. 129–30.

8. Gardiner, III, pp. 165–6; Cust, *Charles I*, pp. 426–7. For Culpeper and Presbyterian popery see *Culpeper Letters*, esp. pp. 144–5; for an earlier example see John Morrill, *Cheshire 1630–1660: County Government and Society during the English Revolution* (Oxford, 1974), p. 50. This alliance of royalism and anti-Presbyterianism was evident in other circles during 1647: the royalist judge David Jenkins struck up an unlikely friendship with John Lilburne while they were both in the Tower: Pauline Gregg, *Free-Born John: The Biography of John Lilburne* (London, 1961), ch. 17. See above, p. 490.

9. John Morrill, 'The Church in England, 1642–1649', reprinted in John Morrill, *The Nature of the English Revolution* (Harlow, 1993), pp. 89–114, esp. pp. 103–8.

10. Smith, *Constitutional Royalism*, pp. 129–32, quotation at p. 130; Cust, *Charles I*, pp. 424–6.

11. Ibid., esp. pp. 420–22, 438–9, 469–70.

12. For Ormond's position in Confederate politics see Micheàl Ó Siochrú, *Confederate Ireland, 1642–1649: A Constitutional and Political Analysis* (Dublin, 1999), esp. pp. 68–83.

13. Ibid., pp. 86–96; Gardiner, III, ch. 39; Patrick J. Corish, 'Ormond, Rinuccini, and the Confederates, 1645–9', in T. W. Moody, F. X. Martin and F. J. Byrne (eds.), *A New History of Ireland*, vol. 3: *Early Modern Ireland 1534–1691* (Oxford, 1976), pp. 317–35.

14. Ó Siochrú, *Confederate Ireland*, pp. 96–117; Gardiner, III, pp. 52–7, 151–3; Corish, 'Ormond', pp. 319–20.

15. Gardiner, III, ch. 44; Corish, 'Ormond', pp. 320–21.

16. David Stevenson, *Revolution and Counter-Revolution in Scotland, 1644–1651* (London, 1977), pp. 54–64.

17. Ibid., pp. 64–72. For the ambiguous relationship between royalism and Presbyterianism see Ashton, *Counter-Revolution*, ch. 8.

18. Stevenson, *Revolution and Counter-Revolution*, pp. 57–60, 64–6, 68; Gardiner, III, pp. 126–32; Cust, *Charles I*, pp. 412, 423.

19. Gardiner, III, pp. 151–3, 175–7, 178.

20. Gardiner, *CD*, pp. 306–8, quotations at pp. 306, 307.

21. Quoted in Cust, *Charles I*, p. 420.

22. Gardiner, *CD*, pp. 308–9, 311–16. For the circumstances of his answer in May see above, p. 492.

23. Gardiner, III, pp. 138, 144–5, 178–80, 182–5, 188–9; Stevenson, *Revolution and Counter-Revolution*, pp. 69, 72–81; Woolrych, *Britain in Revolution*, pp. 349–50.

24. Gardiner, III, pp. 130, 173, 182; Cust, *Charles I*, pp. 420–21.

25. Gardiner, III, p. 212.

26. Richard Wiseman, *Several Chirurgicall Treatises* (London, 1676 edn), p. 245.

27. Stuart Clark, *Thinking with Demons: The Idea of Witchcraft in Early Modern Europe* (Oxford, 1997), ch. 44.

28. Wiseman, *Chirurgicall Treatises*, p. 247. For the effectiveness of the royal touch, see Keith Thomas, *Religion and the Decline of Magic: Studies in Popular Beliefs in Sixteenth- and Seventeenth-Century England* (Harmondsworth, 1991 edn), pp. 242–4.

29. N. Woolf, 'The Sovereign Remedy: Touch-Pieces and the King's Evil', *British Numismatic Journal*, 49 (1980 for 1979), 99–121; N. Woolf, 'The Sovereign Remedy: Touch-Pieces and the King's Evil, part 2', *British Numismatic Journal*, 50 (1981 for 1980), 91–116.

30. Richards and Bloch read the many proclamations regulating the ceremony during the 1630s as evidence of Charles's withdrawal: Judith Richards, ' "His nowe Majestie" and the English Monarchy: The Kingship of Charles I before 1640', *PP*, 113 (1986), 70–96, esp. pp. 88–93; Marc Bloch, *The Royal Touch: Monarchy and Miracles in France and England*, trans. J. E. Anderson (New York, 1989), pp. 207–8. Sharpe argues convincingly that this was evidence of his commitment to the practice: Kevin Sharpe, *The Personal Rule of Charles I* (New Haven, Conn., 1992), pp. 217–18, 630–31.

31. It did not, though, incorporate the ceremony into the Book of Common Prayer, as is sometimes suggested: George MacDonald Ross, 'The Royal Touch and the Book of Common Prayer', *Notes and Queries*, 30:5 (1983), 433–5.

32. Sharpe, *Personal Rule*, pp. 642–3, 782. Charles had also wanted, on his visit to Scotland in 1641, to touch Scottish legislation with his sceptre to symbolize his consent. This was resisted: David Stevenson, *The Scottish Revolution, 1637–44: The Triumph of the Covenanters* (Edinburgh, 2003), pp. 233–4.

33. For other references see *A Perfect Diurnall* (19–26 April 1647), p. 1564 (Holmby); *Perfect Occurrences* (8–15 October 1647), p. 281; and, possibly, *A continuation of certain speciall and Remarkable Passages* (28 August–3 September 1647), Saturday, 29 August; *A Perfect Diurnall* (16–23 August 1647), p. 1702. He also touched at Windsor on the eve of his trial but the practice was halted by his captors: *Perfect Occurrences* (22–30 December 1648), p. 778. I am grateful to Keith Lindley for these references.

34. Bloch, *Royal Touch*, pp. 207–10, for a brief narrative. For the origins of the English rite see Frank Barlow, 'The King's Evil', *EHR*, 95 (1980), 3–27, which corrects most writing subsequent to Bloch. See, in general, Thomas, *Religion and the Decline of Magic*, pp. 227–35. Much later work is indebted to the labours of Raymond Crawfurd, *The King's Evil* (Oxford, 1911). Wiseman traced the power back to Edward the Confessor, as did the petition cited in n. 36 below.

35. J. C. D. Clark, *English Society 1688–1832: Ideology, Social Structure and Political Practice during the Ancien Regime* (Cambridge, 1985), pp. 160–67, 171; Thomas, *Religion and the Decline of Magic*, p. 228.

36. *To the Kings most Excellent Majesty. The Humble petition Of divers hundreds of the kings poore Subjects Afflicted with that grievous infirmitie called The Kings Evil* (London, 20 February 1643). In fact this petition was making a case for a peace party position: p. 8. Lilly had a number of enquiries about the King's Evil during the war: e.g. Bod. L, Ashmolean MS 184, fo. 7v, 16r. For post-regicide versions of a similar point, with obvious political implications, see *A Miracle of Miracles Wrought by the Blood of King Charles I* (London, 1649).

37. Gardiner, III, pp. 212–13. For popular royalism see Ashton, *Counter-Revolution*, pp. 205–15.

38. Gardiner, III, p. 242; *CJ*, v, 151.

39. Gardiner, III, pp. 139, 145, 147; Ian Gentles, *The New Model Army in England, Ireland and Scotland, 1645–1653* (Oxford, 1992), pp. 143–4. For the February ordinance see *A&O*, I, pp. 913–14. For the case against physical coercion of conscience see, for example, the Leveller argument: 'that no man for preaching or publishing his opinion in Religion,

in a peaceable way, may be punished or persecuted as heretical, by Judges that are not infallible, but may be mistaken as well as other men in their judgments, lest upon pretence of suppressing errors, Sects, or Schisms, the most necessary truths, and sincere professions thereof may be suppressed, as upon like pretence it hath been in all ages': the *Large Petition*, reprinted in G. E. Aylmer (ed.), *The Levellers in the English Revolution* (London, 1975), pp. 75–81, quotation at p. 79.

40. Ian Gentles, 'Political Funerals during the English Revolution', in Stephen Porter (ed.), *London and the Civil War* (Basingstoke, 1996), pp. 205–24, at pp. 210–17. See also V. F. Snow, *Essex the Rebel: The Life of Robert Devereux, the Third Earl of Essex 1591–1646* (Lincoln, Nebraska, 1970), pp. 489–94; Gardiner, III, pp. 147–9; J. S. A. Adamson, 'Chivalry and Political Culture in Caroline England', in Kevin Sharpe and Peter Lake (eds.), *Culture and Politics in Early Stuart England* (Basingstoke, 1994), pp. 161–97, esp. pp. 191–3.

41. Snow, *Essex*, p. 494; Gardiner, III, pp. 149–50; for the political complexion of the mourners see Gentles, *New Model Army*, p. 143.

42. John Morrill, 'The Army Revolt of 1647', reprinted in John Morrill, *The Nature of the English Revolution* (Harlow, 1993), pp. 307–31; John Morrill, 'Mutiny and Discontent in English Provincial Armies, 1645–1647', reprinted in ibid., pp. 332–58; Ashton, *Counter-Revolution*, ch. 2; for the post-war desire to establish control over the soldiery see Ronan Bennett, 'War and Disorder: Policing the Soldiery in Civil War Yorkshire', in Mark Charles Fissel (ed.), *War and Government in Britain, 1598–1650* (Manchester, 1991), pp. 248–73.

43. For this campaign see Valerie Pearl, 'London's Counter-Revolution', in G. E. Aylmer (ed.), *The Interregnum: The Quest for Settlement, 1646–1660* (London, 1972), pp. 29–56; Mark A. Kishlansky, *The Rise of the New Model Army* (Cambridge, 1979), esp. ch. 6; Underdown, *Pride's Purge*, esp. pp. 76–90; Gentles, *New Model Army*, ch. 6; Michael Mahony, 'Presbyterianism in the City of London, 1645–7', *HJ*, 22 (1979), 93–114; Ann Hughes, *Gangraena and the Struggle for the English Revolution* (Oxford, 2004), ch. 5; Elliot Curt Vernon, 'The Sion College Conclave and London Presbyterianism during the English Revolution', unpublished Ph.D. thesis, Cambridge (1999), chs. 2–3. Posterity has generally credited Holles with leadership, perhaps because of the survival of his published memoirs. Juxon referred to this parliamentary interest as the Stapletonian party: Keith Lindley and David Scott (eds.), *The Journal of Thomas Juxon, 1644–1647*, Camden, 5th ser., 13 (London, 1999), esp. p. 34; Kishlansky notes this too, *Rise*, pp. 15–16, although his account emphasizes the role of Holles. The New Model was not the only problem – the regional armies were also agitating for arrears: Morrill, 'Mutiny and Discontent'; Morrill, 'Army Revolt of 1647'.

44. Gentles, *New Model Army*, pp. 145–7. For the wider context see Ashton, *Counter-Revolution*, esp. chs. 2, 3, 7.

45. Ibid. For the offer of these terms to the King, and his insincere consideration of them, see Gardiner, III, pp. 213–15.

46. Ronald Hutton, *The Rise and Fall of Merry England: The Ritual Year 1400–1700* (Oxford, 1994), esp. pp. 203–12. See also Morrill, 'The Church in England'; Christopher Durston, 'Puritan Rule and the Failure of Cultural Revolution', in Christopher Durston and Jacqueline Eales (eds.), *The Culture of English Puritanism, 1560–1700* (Basingstoke, 1996), pp. 210–33; Christopher Durston, ' "Preaching and sitting still on Sundays": The Lord's Day during the English Revolution', in Christopher Durston and Judith Maltby (eds.), *Religion in Revolutionary England* (Manchester, 2006), pp. 205–25.

47. For the post-Reformation Protestant calendar, and its politics, see David Cressy, *Bonfires and Bells: National Memory and the Protestant Calendar in Elizabethan and Stuart England* (London, 1989).

48. Michael J. Braddick, 'Popular Politics and Public Policy: The Excise Riot at Smithfield in February 1647 and Its Aftermath', *HJ*, 34 (1991), 597–626, at p. 615. See also Hutton, *Merry England*, pp. 211–12, and, for the ritual year, ch. 1. For Shrove Tuesday and

disorder see Keith Lindley, 'Riot Prevention and Control in Early Stuart London', *TRHS*, 5th ser., 33 (1983), 109–26, esp. pp. 109–10.

49. W. G. Hoskins, 'Harvest Fluctuations and English Economic History 1620–1759', *Agricultural History Review*, 16 (1968), 15–31; Steve Hindle, 'Dearth and the English Revolution: The Harvest Crisis of 1647–50', *EcHR*, 61 (2008), pp. 64–98.

50. Braddick, 'Excise Riot', p. 611. For grain riots, popular politics and the response of the magistracy see John Walter, *Crowds and Popular Politics in Early Modern England* (Manchester, 2006), intr., chs. 1–5; John Walter and Keith Wrightson, 'Dearth and the Social Order in Early Modern England', reprinted in Paul Slack (ed.), *Rebellion, Popular Protest and the Social Order in Early Modern England* (Cambridge, 1984), pp. 108–28.

51. Braddick, 'Excise Riot', p. 611.

52. Michael J. Braddick, *Parliamentary Taxation in Seventeenth-Century England: Local Administration and Response* (Woodbridge, 1994), pp. 183–4. For the riot at Derby see above, pp. 422–3.

53. For the desire to return to normality see Gardiner, III, ch. 46; Underdown, *Pride's Purge*, pp. 76–8; Braddick, 'Excise Riot', pp. 610–11. Attacks on committee government were also a dimension of ideological battles: Ann Hughes, *Politics, Society and Civil War in Warwickshire, 1620–1660* (Cambridge, 1987), ch. 6.

54. Braddick, 'Excise Riot', p. 612.

55. Ibid., p. 597.

56. Ibid., pp. 612–14, quotation at p. 614.

57. Gardiner, III, p. 218.

58. Bod. L, Ashmolean MS 185, fo. 211r.

59. Gardiner, III, pp. 216–18; Corish, 'Ormond', pp. 322–3.

60. Bennett, 'War and Disorder', esp. pp. 260–66; Ann Hughes, 'Parliamentary Tyranny? Indemnity Proceedings and the Impact of the Civil War: A Case Study from Warwickshire', *Midland History*, 11 (1986), 49–78, at p. 58; Gregg, *Free-Born John*, p. 161. For local studies of tensions between soldier and civilian see A. R. Warmington, *Civil War, Interregnum and Restoration in Gloucestershire 1640–1672* (Woodbridge, 1997), pp. 81–91; Morrill, 'Army Revolt of 1647'; Morrill, 'Mutiny and Discontent'. A committee was established with powers to grant indemnity. Two thirds of its business in Gloucestershire was heard prior to 1650: Warmington, *Gloucestershire*, p. 89. For the committee see also John A. Shedd, 'Thwarted Victors: Civil and Criminal Prosecution against Parliament's Officials during the English Civil War and Commonwealth', *JBS*, 41 (2002), 139–69.

61. Gentles, *New Model Army*, pp. 140–48.

62. For a more detailed narrative see Joseph Frank, *The Levellers: A History of the Writings of Three Seventeenth-Century Social Democrats: John Lilburne, Richard Overton, William Walwyn* (Cambridge, Mass., 1955), pp. 77–124, although many of Frank's judgements now seem anachronistic; Aylmer, *The Levellers*, pp. 16–22; Andrew Sharp (ed.), *The English Levellers* (Cambridge, 1998), intr. The *Remonstrance* is reprinted in ibid., pp. 33–53; the *Large Petition* is reprinted in Aylmer, *The Levellers*, pp. 75–81, quotations at pp. 76, 79. For Lilburne's political thought see Rachel Foxley, 'Citizenship and the English Nation in Leveller Thought, 1642–1653', unpublished Ph.D. thesis, Cambridge (2001); Rachel Foxley, 'John Lilburne and the Citizenship of "free-born Englishmen"', *HJ*, 47 (2004), 849–74. For the resonance of the denial to the Lords of a negative voice see also *Culpeper Letters*, p. 145.

63. For the Levellers and petitioning see also Nigel Smith, *Literature and Revolution in England, 1640–1660* (New Haven, Conn., 1994), pp. 138–40. This line of argument is developed interestingly in David Zaret, *Origins of Democratic Culture: Printing, Petitions, and the Public Sphere in Early-Modern England* (Princeton, NJ, 2000), esp. ch. 8.

64. Gardiner, III, pp. 254–7.

65. Aylmer, *Levellers*, p. 75.

66. Gentles, *New Model Army*, pp. 148–9; Morrill, 'Army Revolt of 1647'; Morrill, 'Mutiny and Discontent'; Mark Kishlansky, 'Ideology and Politics in the Parliamentary Armies,

1645–9', in John Morrill (ed.), *Reactions to the English Civil War 1642–1649* (Basingstoke, 1982), pp. 163–83. Army activism was potentially in alliance with the Levellers and other London radicals, however, even if it was not a product of these outside agencies.

67. Woolrych, *Soldiers and Statesmen*, pp. 31–5; Gentles, *New Model Army*, pp. 150–51. These events are placed in the context of the increasing polarization of politics at Westminster and in the City by Kishlansky, *Rise*, chs. 5–6. See, here, pp. 157–60.

68. Woolrych, *Soldiers and Statesmen*, pp. 35–40; Kishlansky, *Rise*, pp. 159–60; Gentles, *New Model Army*, pp. 151–2; Gardiner, III, p. 231.

69. Woolrych, *Soldiers and Statesmen*, pp. 43–4.

70. The evidence and debate are summarized judiciously in Woolrych, *Soldiers and Statesmen*, pp. 55–65, with full references. See also Gentles: 'At the time the word "agitator" had none of its modern pejorative ring, and meant simply one who had been empowered to act on behalf of others', *New Model Army*, p. 159. A re-reading of key texts has suggested that Edward Sexby was not the central figure that he has subsequently claimed to be, and that the texts may reflect the role of some officers in channelling the army's grievances into a partisan political campaign, of sponsoring the emergence of the agitators: Michael Norris, 'Edward Sexby, John Reynolds and Edmund Chillenden: Agitators, "sectarian grandees" and the Relations of the New Model Army with London in the Spring of 1647', *Historical Research*, 76 (2003), 30–53.

71. Gentles, *New Model Army*, p. 152; for a detailed account of these events as a response to the triumph of the Holles–Stapleton group at Westminster, see Kishlansky, *Rise*, ch. 7, esp., here, pp. 206–9.

72. Gregg, *Free-Born John*, ch. 17. Lilburne was also close to Sir Lewis Dyve, another incarcerated royalist, and may have had a role in fostering approaches to the King in October. See also Gardiner, III, pp. 309–12.

73. Gardiner, III, pp. 239–40; Gentles, *New Model Army*, pp. 153–4.

74. Gentles, *New Model Army*, pp. 151, 154–7 and, for the comparison with the treatment of the Scots, p. 149.

75. Pearl, 'London's Counter-Revolution', pp. 45–6; Gentles, *New Model Army*, pp. 157–9. For the Presbyterian mobilization in London see Hughes, *Gangraena*, ch. 5; Vernon, 'Sion College', chs. 2–3.

76. For the *Book of Declarations* see above, pp. 510–11; for Husbands see above, pp. 272–3.

77. Stevenson, *Revolution and Counter-Revolution*, pp. 82–90.

78. Gardiner, *CD*, pp. 311–16.

79. Gardiner, III, pp. 251–3.

80. Woolrych, *Soldiers and Statesmen*, pp. 71–96; Gentles, *New Model Army*, pp. 161–4; Gardiner, III, pp. 247–9.

81. Gentles, *New Model Army*, pp. 165–7; Gardiner, III, pp. 254, 256–61, 262.

82. Pearl, 'London's Counter-Revolution', pp. 45–6.

83. Woolrych, *Soldiers and Statesmen*, pp. 106–12; Gentles, *New Model Army*, pp. 169–70.

84. Gentles, *New Model Army*, p. 170.

85. Woolrych, *Soldiers and Statesmen*, p. 112.

86. For a brilliant reading of this exchange see James Holstun, *Ehud's Dagger: Class Struggle in the English Revolution* (London, 2000), ch. 1. For the view that Joyce was appealing to the shared purpose and interests of the soldiery, not naked force, see Woolrych, *Soldiers and Statesmen*, pp. 107–10, 112.

87. Gardiner, III, p. 277. For his strategy more generally see Ashton, *Counter-Revolution*, p. 20.

88. Woolrych, *Soldiers and Statesmen*, pp. 100–105, 116–20.

89. Gardiner, III, pp. 279–85; Woolrych, *Soldiers and Statesmen*, pp. 113–15, 116–20.

90. Gardiner, III, pp. 278, 285–6; Woolrych, *Soldiers and Statesmen*, pp. 122–3, 125–6.

91. Braddick, 'Excise Riot', p. 615. Gardiner appears to misdate the ordinance to 8 July, although his interpretation of its motivation is the same: III, pp. 324–5. See *A&O*, I, p. 954; Hutton, *Merry England*, pp. 211–12.

92. Braddick, 'Excise Riot', pp. 615–16; *A&O*, III, p. lii.

93. Woolrych, *Soldiers and Statesmen*, p. 125.

94. Gardiner, III, p. 325.

95. Reprinted in part in J. P. Kenyon, *The Stuart Constitution, 1603–1688: Documents and Commentary* (Cambridge, 1966), pp. 295–301, quotations at pp. 296, 297; Woolrych, *Soldiers and Statesmen*, pp. 126–8.

96. Kishlansky estimated that one third of the senior officers left: *Rise*, p. 219. Woolrych thought this an over-estimate (*Soldiers and Statesmen*, pp. 133–6), a view confirmed by Gentles, *New Model Army*, pp. 167–8, 487 n. 218. In general, however, Kishlansky is right to point to a large exodus of officers in June 1647, many of them of relatively high status. For the continuing influence of officers of high status, however, see also Ian Gentles, 'The New Model Officer Corps in 1647: A Collective Portrait', *Social History*, 22 (1997), 127–44.

97. Woolrych, *Soldiers and Statesmen*, pp. 137–44; Gardiner, III, pp. 305–6. The other eight names were: Sir William Lewis, Sir John Clotworthy, Sir William Waller, Sir John Maynard, John Glyn, Colonel Edward Harley, Walter Long and Anthony Nicholl. For the charges see Kishlansky, *Rise*, pp. 250–55; Underdown, *Pride's Purge*, pp. 81–2.

98. Woolrych, *Soldiers and Statesmen*, pp. 148–50.

99. Kishlansky, *Rise*, pp. 250–55.

100. Gardiner, III, pp. 324–7; Woolrych, *Soldiers and Statesmen*, pp. 165–6.

101. Woolrych, *Soldiers and Statesmen*, pp. 153–67; Woolrych, *Britain in Revolution*, pp. 373–4. For the controversy over the authorship of the *Heads of Proposals* see J. S. A. Adamson, 'The English Nobility and the Projected Settlement of 1647', *HJ*, 30 (1987), 567–602; Mark A. Kishlansky, 'Saye what?', *HJ*, 33 (1990), 917–37; J. S. A. Adamson, 'Politics and the Nobility in Civil War England', *HJ*, 34 (1991), 231–55; Mark A. Kishlansky, 'Saye no more', *JBS*, 30 (1991), 399–448. See also John Morrill, *Revolt in the Provinces: The People of England and the Tragedies of War 1630–1648*, 2nd edn (Harlow, 1999), pp. 199–200; Smith, *Constitutional Royalism*, pp. 132–3.

102. Summarized in Smith, *Constitutional Royalism*, pp. 135–6. For the text see Gardiner, *CD*, pp. 316–26.

103. Woolrych, *Britain in Revolution*, p. 374.

104. Woolrych, *Soldiers and Statesmen*, pp. 169–74; Gardiner, III, pp. 327–8, 335–6.

105. Gardiner, III, pp. 336–40; Woolrych, *Soldiers and Statesmen*, pp. 172–4.

106. Gardiner, III, pp. 343–5; Gentles, *New Model Army*, pp. 190–91; Woolrych, *Soldiers and Statesmen*, pp. 181–2.

107. Gardiner, III, pp. 345–6, quotation at p. 345; Gentles, *New Model Army*, pp. 192–4; Woolrych, *Soldiers and Statesmen*, pp. 182–3.

108. Gardiner, III, pp. 347–52; Gentles, *New Model Army*, pp. 194–6.

109. Hughes, *Gangraena*, pp. 416–17; for the view that Edwards's campaign, the Presbyterian mobilization for a national church and against Independency, and the resulting cleavage among the godly were not inevitable products of irreconcilable aspiration see ibid., esp. pp. 326–33; for the fortunes of Presbyterians after its failure as a model for the national church in 1647 see Vernon, 'Sion College', chs. 4–7. The central arguments are set out in Elliot Vernon, 'A Ministry of the Gospel: The Presbyterians during the English Revolution', in Durston and Maltby (eds.), *Religion*, pp. 115–36.

110. Gardiner, II, p. 59.

111. An example each: *The Kings Maiesties letter intercepted* (London, 1647) revealed the King's negotiations with the French; *An answer to a letter concerning the kings going from Holdenby to the army* (London, 1647); *The declaration of the commissioners for the kingdom of Scotland* (London, 1647); *Vox militaris* (11 August 1647); *His Majesties declaration to all his subjects* (London, 20 December 1647).

112. For Norwich see John T. Evans, *Seventeenth-Century Norwich: Politics, Religion and Government, 1620–1690* (Oxford, 1979), pp. 155–72; Ashton, *Counter-Revolution*, pp. 368–75. For some important studies of local politics in these months see David Underdown, *Somerset in the Civil War and Interregnum* (Newton Abbot, 1973),

pp. 140–46; Clive Holmes, *Seventeenth-Century Lincolnshire* (Lincoln, 1980), pp. 187–99; Mary Coate, *Cornwall in the Great Civil War and Interregnum 1642–1660: A Social and Political Study* (Oxford, 1933), pp. 237–42, 338–40; Anthony Fletcher, *A County Community in Peace and War: Sussex 1600–1660* (London, 1975), pp. 269–89. For an overview see Ashton, *Counter-Revolution*, pp. 139–57. For the failure of the Presbyterian church organization see Morrill, 'The Church in England', pp. 155–8.

113. Anon., *Strange Newes from Scotland* ([London], 1647), Thomason date 24 September 1647, p. 3.

114. Ibid., pp. 4–5.

115. John Taylor, *The World turn'd upside down* (London, 1647), Thomason date 28 January, was a reissue of his *Mad Fashions*: Bernard Capp, *The World of John Taylor the Water-Poet 1578–1653* (Oxford, 1994), p. 202.

116. Anon., *A great fight in the church at Thaxted* (London, 1647), Thomason date 25 September 1647.

18. The Army, the People and the Scots

1. For the appointment of the new agents see Austin Woolrych, *Soldiers and Statesmen: The General Council of the Army and Its Debates 1647–1648* (Oxford, 1987), ch. 8; Austin Woolrych, 'The Debates from the Perspective of the Army', in Michael Mendle (ed.), *The Putney Debates of 1647: The Army, the Levellers and the English State* (Cambridge, 2001), pp. 53–78, at pp. 65–6; for the term 'Leveller', see Blair Worden, 'The Levellers in History and Memory', in ibid., pp. 256–82, appendix. Morrill and Baker question the closeness of the political alliance between Walwyn and the others prior to this date: John Morrill and Philip Baker, 'The Case of the Armie Truly Restated', in ibid., pp. 103–24, at pp. 119–20. This challenges the conventional view in most previous studies of the Levellers.

2. For the latter view see Morrill and Baker, 'Case of the Armie'. For a measured overview see Rachel Foxley, 'Citizenship and the English Nation in Leveller Thought, 1642–1653', unpublished Ph.D. thesis, Cambridge (2001), ch. 5. Foxley argues that the army and the Levellers employed similar metaphors and tropes: that they were literally speaking the same language.

3. Woolrych, *Soldiers and Statesmen*, pp. 160–65, 174–8.

4. Ibid., pp. 174–8, quotation at p. 177; Richard Cust, *Charles I: A Political Life* (Harlow, 2005), pp. 431–3; David L. Smith, *Constitutional Royalism and the Search for Settlement, c. 1640–1649* (Cambridge, 1994), pp. 132–6. For Scottish politics in these months see David Stevenson, *Revolution and Counter-Revolution in Scotland, 1644–1651* (London, 1977), pp. 88–93.

5. Woolrych, *Soldiers and Statesmen*, pp. 195–6; Gardiner, *CD*, pp. 326–7, quotation at p. 327.

6. Gardiner, III, pp. 366–9; Cust, *Charles I*, pp. 433–5.

7. For the reprinting of the *Heads of Proposals* see Woolrych, *Soldiers and Statesmen*, pp. 197–8. One edition of the *Book of Declarations*, acquired by Thomason on 2 October, reprints a Lords order of 27 September (*LJ*, ix, 450) giving sole benefit to the publishers. Another, presumably earlier, edition exists without this order on the title page. For an example of editing see Ian Gentles, *The New Model Army in England, Ireland and Scotland, 1645–1653* (Oxford, 1992), p. 480. n. 67.

8. Gardiner, III, p. 365; *LJ*, ix, 452; *A&O*, I, pp. 1021–2 (30 Sept. 1647), quotation at p. 1021. The *Large Petition* had also called for an end to name-calling as a necessary prelude to settlement: G. E. Aylmer (ed.), *The Levellers in the English Revolution* (London, 1975), p. 78.

9. For the porousness of early modern parliaments see Chris R. Kyle and Jason Peacey (eds.), *Parliament at Work: Parliamentary Committees, Political Power, and Public Access in Early Modern England* (Woodbridge, 2002).

10. Woolrych, *Soldiers and Statesmen*, p. 195 and n. 17; White was present at the Putney

debates on 29 October: C. H. Firth, *The Clarke Papers*, with a preface by Austin Woolrych (London, 1992 edn), p. 280.

11. For the attribution of authorship or co-ordination to Sexby see Morrill and Baker, 'Case of the Armie'. Woolrych expressed support for the view in 'The Debates', at p. 66; he was more convinced of Wildman's claims by the time he wrote *Britain in Revolution 1625–1660* (Oxford, 2002), p. 383.

12. Woolrych, *Soldiers and Statesmen*, pp. 191–3, 203–6; Morrill and Baker, 'Case of the Armie', pp. 108–10.

13. Reprinted in Don M. Wolfe (ed.), *Leveller Manifestoes of the Puritan Revolution* (New York, 1944), pp. 196–222, quotations at pp. 199, 212, 218, 220.

14. Morrill and Baker, 'Case of the Armie'.

15. Reprinted in Gardiner, *CD*, pp. 335–5, quotation at p. 334.

16. Woolrych, *Soldiers and Statesmen*, pp. 215–16 and n. 7.

17. Gardiner, III, pp. 367, 381.

18. Michael Mendle, 'Introduction', in Mendle (ed.), *Putney Debates*, p. 1: the blackout may have been, partially at least, officially imposed: Woolrych, *Soldiers and Statesmen*, p. 226 and n. 44. For Clarke see Woolrych, 'The Debates', p. 68.

19. For a detailed narrative of the debates see Woolrych, *Soldiers and Statesmen*, ch. 9. I have followed his summaries in *Britain in Revolution*, pp. 385–92 and 'The Debates', pp. 71–8. For the fullest published text see Firth (ed.), *Clarke Papers*, pp. 226–406; A. S. P. Woodhouse (ed.), *Puritanism and Liberty: Being the Army Debates (1647–9) from the Clarke Manuscripts with Supplementary Documents*, 2nd edn (London, 1974), pp. 1–123, contains very full extracts.

20. Woodhouse (ed.), *Puritanism and Liberty*, p. 11.

21. Ibid., p. 46.

22. Ibid., pp. 53–4.

23. For influential views of the controversy over the franchise see C. B. Macpherson, *The Political Theory of Possessive Individualism: Hobbes to Locke* (Oxford, 1962), pt III; Keith Thomas, 'The Levellers and the Franchise', in G. E. Aylmer (ed.), *The Interregnum: The Quest for Settlement 1646–60* (London, 1972), pp. 57–78; David Wootton, 'Leveller Democracy and the Puritan Revolution', in J. H. Burns, with Mark Goldie (eds.), *The Cambridge History of Political Thought 1450–1700* (Cambridge, 1991), pp. 412–42, esp. pp. 429–30; Patricia Crawford, ' "The poorest she": Women and Citizenship in Early Modern England', in Mendle (ed.), *Putney Debates*, pp. 197–218, esp. pp. 199–203; Morrill and Baker, 'Case of the Armie', pp. 117–19; Quentin Skinner, 'Rethinking Political Liberty', *History Workshop Journal*, 61:1 (2006), 156–70, esp. pp. 160–65.

24. Woolrych, *Britain in Revolution*, pp. 390–91.

25. Quoted in Gardiner, IV, pp. 5, 7; see also Woolrych, *Britain in Revolution*, p. 391. For blood guilt see Patricia Crawford, 'Charles Stuart, That Man of Blood', reprinted in Peter Gaunt (ed.), *The English Civil War* (Oxford, 2000), pp. 303–23, Ludlow quoted at p. 312; for blood guilt and the dangers of a weak peace in 1643 see above, p. 259.

26. Gardiner, IV, p. 9 for this vote.

27. Woolrych, *Britain in Revolution*, pp. 393–4, 395–8; this revises the case made by Mark A. Kishlansky, 'What Happened at Ware?' *HJ*, 25 (1982), 827–39.

28. Reprinted in W. C. Abbott, *Writings and Speeches of Oliver Cromwell*, 4 vols. (Cambridge, Mass., 1937), I, pp. 557–60, quotations at pp. 558, 559.

29. Cust, *Charles I*, pp. 434–5; Stevenson, *Revolution and Counter-Revolution*, pp. 88–94; Gardiner, IV, pp. 1, 9–10, 12–13, 15–16.

30. For incisive accounts of the politics see Stevenson, *Revolution and Counter-Revolution*, pp. 92–5; Cust, *Charles I*, pp. 434–5. See also Robert Ashton, *Counter-Revolution: The Second Civil War and Its Origins, 1646–1648* (New Haven, Conn., 1994), pp. 20–42.

31. Woolrych, *Soldiers and Statesmen*, p. 308; a similar suggestion was made at the General Council by Harrison: Gardiner, IV, p. 16.

32. Gardiner, IV, pp. 14–19.

33. For Taylor see above, p. 490. Some of the responses to the *Kings Cabinet opened* made a similar case: for example, Anon., *Some observations upon occasion of the publishing of their majesties letters* (Oxford, 1645), p. 4; Anon., *A Key To the Kings cabinet* (Oxford, 1645), pp. 10–11.

34. Gardiner, *CD*, pp. 328–32; for the politics of these crucial days see Woolrych, *Soldiers and Statesmen*, pp. 304–10.

35. Stevenson, *Revolution and Counter-Revolution*, p. 95; for this (relatively) sympathetic view of Charles's honesty see Cust, *Charles I*, esp. pp. 408–10, 438–9.

36. Cust, *Charles I*, p. 436; for the text see Gardiner, *CD*, pp. 335–47.

37. Woolrych, *Soldiers and Statesmen*, pp. 307–9; Gardiner, *IV*, pp. 33–4.

38. Stevenson, *Revolution and Counter-Revolution*, pp. 95–7. Developing hostility to the Covenanters' 'extra-national' interpretation of the Solemn League and Covenant can be traced in *Culpeper Letters*.

39. For the origins of the Engagement see Ashton, *Counter-Revolution*, pp. 316–26.

40. Gardiner, *CD*, pp. 347–52, quotation at pp. 349–50.

41. Gardiner, *IV*, p. 41.

42. Ibid.; for the text of Charles's rejection see Gardiner, *CD*, pp. 353–6, quotation at p. 355.

43. Gardiner, *CD*, p. 356; for the previous proposal see above, p. 510.

44. Woolrych, *Soldiers and Statesmen*, pp. 319–23, quotations at pp. 320, 321 (italics in the original). The regicide was to make clear, however, that a willingness to kill the King, or see him killed, could co-exist with a commitment to the preservation of the House of Lords: Blair Worden, *The Rump Parliament* (Cambridge, 1974), esp. pp. 49–50.

45. Gardiner, *IV*, pp. 52–6; Woolrych, *Soldiers and Statesmen*, pp. 320–23; Gentles, *New Model Army*, pp. 237–8: see the Commons order, *CJ*, v, 416, interpreted here as reviving the powers of the Committee of Both Kingdoms, with a reformed (all-English) membership and a new title. The Committee of Both Kingdoms was defunct after the Scots handed over the King at Newcastle and returned north: Mark A. Kishlansky, *The Rise of the New Model Army* (Cambridge, 1979), pp. 160–62, 164–7; Woolrych, *Britain in Revolution*, p. 352. It may not have been formally dissolved, however, and it is not clear from the order if it is being revived, or reconfigured. I am grateful to Ann Hughes and Mark Kishlansky for discussing this with me

46. Gardiner, *CD*, pp. 348–9.

47. Gardiner, *IV*, pp. 60–61; *A declaration of the Commons of England In Parliament assembled* [11 February 1648] (London, 1648), TT, E.427[9]; Alastair Bellany, 'The Murder of James I: Mutations and Meanings of a Political Myth, c. 1625–1660' (unpublished paper).

48. Charles Carlton, *Charles I: The Personal Monarch* (London, 1983), p. 328.

49. Gardiner, *III*, p. 309–10. For other indications of his apparent willingness to die rather than compromise his principles see Gardiner, *III*, pp. 134–7; and Cust, *Charles I*, esp. pp. 410, 421.

50. The authoritative study is M. D. Whinney, 'John Webb's Drawings for the Whitehall Palace', *Walpole Society*, 31 (1946 for 1942–3), 45–107, esp. pp. 45, 81–8. There is documentary evidence that Webb visited the King in Hampton Court and Carisbrooke. A surviving scheme, marked 'taken' by Charles I, belongs stylistically with the work of Webb rather than Jones, and obviously predates 1649. It is therefore supposed to be the one that arose from these visits of Webb. For fuller context see Simon Thurley, *The Lost Palace of Whitehall* (London, 1998), pp. 17–28; for the comparison with the Escorial see P. W. Thomas, 'Charles I of England: The Tragedy of Absolutism', in A. G. Dickens (ed.), *The Courts of Europe: Politics, Patronage and Royalty 1400–1800* (London, 1977), pp. 191–211, at p. 193. For earlier attributions of these designs see also J. Alfred Gotch, 'The Original Drawings of the Palace of Whitehall Attributed to Inigo Jones', *Architectural Review*, 31 (1912), 333–64; E. S. De Beer, 'Whitehall Palace: Inigo Jones and Wren', *Notes and Queries*, 177 (1939), 471–3. For Jones and Webb see John Newman, 'Jones,

Inigo (1573–1652)', *ODNB*, 30, pp. 527–38; John Bold, 'Webb, John (1611–1672)', *ODNB*, 57, pp. 837–40.

19. To Preserve That Which God Hath Manifestly Declared Against

1. David Stevenson, *Revolution and Counter-Revolution in Scotland, 1644–1651* (London, 1977), pp. 98–105; Robert Ashton, *Counter-Revolution: The Second Civil War and Its Origins, 1646–8* (New Haven, Conn., 1994), pp. 326–35.
2. Micheál Ó Siochrú, *Confederate Ireland, 1642–1649: A Constitutional and Political Analysis* (Dublin, 1999), ch. 5; Patrick J. Corish, 'Ormond, Rinuccini, and the Confederates, 1645–9', in T. W. Moody, F. X. Martin and F. J. Byrne (eds.), *A New History of Ireland*, vol. 3: *Early Modern Ireland 1534–1691* (Oxford, 1976), pp. 317–35, at pp. 323–30; summary in Austin Woolrych, *Britain in Revolution 1625–1660* (Oxford, 2002), p. 405; Gardiner, IV, pp. 102–10.
3. David Underdown, *Pride's Purge: Politics in the Puritan Revolution* (Oxford, 1971), p. 90.
4. Alan Everitt, *The Community of Kent and the Great Rebellion 1640–1660* (Leicester, 1966), pp. 231–3.
5. Ibid., p. 233.
6. Ian Gentles, *The New Model Army in England, Ireland and Scotland, 1645–1653* (Oxford, 1992), pp. 241–2.
7. Underdown, *Pride's Purge*, pp. 91–2. For Norwich see John T. Evans, *Seventeenth-Century Norwich: Politics, Religion and Government, 1620–1690* (Oxford, 1979), pp. 172–82.
8. Gardiner, IV, pp. 68–9, 94, 97–8; Ian Gentles, 'The Struggle for London in the Second Civil War', *HJ*, 26 (1983), 277–305, esp. pp. 287–9. There were many different versions of tip-cat.
9. Underdown, *Pride's Purge*, pp. 93–4. For anti-war sentiment and post-war religious disruption in Cornwall see Mary Coate, *Cornwall in the Great Civil War and Interregnum 1642–1660: A Social and Political Study* (Oxford, 1933), pp. 330–38.
10. Underdown, *Pride's Purge*, pp. 94–5, 99–100; Gentles, *New Model Army*, p. 241; for Essex see William Cliftlands, 'The "Well-Affected" and the "Country": Politics and Religion in English Provincial Society, c. 1640–1654', unpublished Ph.D. thesis, Essex (1987), pp. 77–9, ch. 4.
11. [William Davenant?], *London, King Charles his Augusta or City Royal* (London, 1648), Thomason date 7 March; Anon., *Coleman-Street Conclave Visited* (London, 1648), Thomason date 21 March; Anon., *Calendar-Reformation* (London, 1648), Fortescue date 27 March; Anon., *A true and perfect picture of our present reformation* (London, 1648), Fortescue date March; Anon., *Mistris Parliament Brought to Bed of a Monstrous Childe of Reformation* (London, 1648), Thomason date 29 April. The birth was assisted by the midwife Mrs London, the nurse Mrs Synod, and the gossips Mrs Schism, Mrs Privilege, Mrs Ordinance, Mrs Universall Toleration and Mrs Leveller; Anon., *Last will and testament* (London, 1648).
12. *Vindiciae, contra Tyrannos: a defence of Liberty against Tyrants* (London, 1648), Thomason date 1 March; *Queen Elizabeth's speech to her last parliament* (London, 1648), Thomason date 16 March. For the *Vindiciae* see Anne McLaren, 'Rethinking Republicanism: *Vindiciae, Contra Tyrannos* in Context', *HJ*, 49 (2006), 23–52; and the convincing riposte by George Garnett, 'Law in the *Vindiciae, Contra Tyrannos*: A Vindication', *HJ*, 49 (2006), 877–91. It was probably the product of a collaboration between Hubert Languet and Philippe Mornay, written in France between 1574 and 1577, and widely circulated in the rest of Europe thereafter. For the text and its history see George Garnett (ed.), *Brutus: Vindiciae, contra tyrannos or, Concerning the Legitimate Power of a Prince over the People, and of the People over a Prince* (Cambridge, 1994), esp., for the translations, pp. lxxiv–lxxxviii. For Walker see David Wootton, 'From

Rebellion to Revolution: The Crisis of the Winter of 1642/3 and the Origins of Civil War Radicalism', in Richard Cust and Ann Hughes (eds.), *The English Civil War* (London, 1997), pp. 340–56, at p. 352.

13. Ashton, *Counter-Revolution*, pp. 455–68.

14. Andrew Coleby, *Central Government and the Localities: Hampshire 1649–1689* (Cambridge, 1987), p. 13. See, in general, Ashton's account of the insurgents' aims: *Counter-Revolution*, pp. 12–13.

15. Gardiner, IV, p. 123.

16. For these militias see Sarah Barber, ' "A bastard kind of militia", Localism, and Tactics in the Second Civil War', in Ian Gentles, John Morrill and Blair Worden (eds.), *Soldiers, Writers and Statesmen of the English Revolution* (Cambridge, 1998), pp. 133–50.

17. For the paralysis these considerations might cause see Gentles, 'Struggle for London'. For other examples see Clive Holmes, *Seventeenth-Century Lincolnshire* (Lincoln, 1980), pp. 200–203; Anthony Fletcher, *A County Community in Peace and War: Sussex 1600–1660* (London, 1975), pp. 291–2; Evans, *Norwich*, pp. 172–82. Numerous local studies demonstrate the presence of these grievances without support for Charles as a necessary corollary, and not always as a source of anti-army feeling. See, for example, John Morrill, *Cheshire 1630–1660: County Government and Society during the English Revolution* (Oxford, 1974), ch. 5; Stephen K. Roberts, *Recovery and Restoration in an English County: Devon Local Administration 1646–70* (Exeter, 1985), pp. 5–13; A. R. Warmington, *Civil War, Interregnum and Restoration in Gloucestershire 1640–1672* (Woodbridge, 1997), pp. 146–55.

18. Gardiner, IV, pp. 83–6, 99–101; Stevenson, *Revolution and Counter-Revolution*, pp. 103–5.

19. Ashton, *Counter-Revolution*, pp. 422–38.

20. John Morrill, *Revolt in the Provinces: The English People and the Tragedies of War 1630–1648*, 2nd edn (Harlow, 1999), pp. 174–6, 205–8.

21. Woolrych, *Britain in Revolution*, p. 407; Morrill, *Revolt in the Provinces*, 2nd edn, p. 176; Gentles, *New Model Army*, pp. 242–3.

22. Gardiner, IV, pp. 125–6; Woolrych, *Britain in Revolution*, pp. 407–8, quotation at p. 407; Austin Woolrych, *Soldiers and Statesmen: The General Council of the Army and Its Debates, 1647–1648* (Oxford, 1987), pp. 330–35; Gentles, *New Model Army*, pp. 257–8.

23. Gardiner, IV, pp. 132, 145, 154–5, 167.

24. Ibid., pp. 125, 127–8; Underdown, *Pride's Purge*, pp. 97–8.

25. Woolrych, *Soldiers and Statesmen*, pp. 330–35; Underdown, *Pride's Purge*, pp. 96–7.

26. Everitt, *Kent*, pp. 235–40.

27. Ibid., pp. 240–59. For the naval revolt see Bernard Capp, *Cromwell's Navy: The Fleet and the English Revolution, 1648–1660* (Oxford, 1989), ch. 2; Ashton, *Counter-Revolution*, pp. 438–48.

28. Everitt, *Kent*, pp. 259–60; Capp, *Cromwell's Navy*, pp. 20–22.

29. Everitt, *Kent*, esp. pp. 251–4.

30. Ibid., pp. 258–65; Gardiner, IV, pp. 133–42; Gentles, *New Model Army*, pp. 247–9.

31. Gardiner, IV, pp. 146–9; Gentles, *New Model Army*, pp. 249, 251–3.

32. Gardiner, IV, pp. 149–54; Gentles, *New Model Army*, pp. 253–5.

33. Gardiner, IV, p. 145; Gentles, *New Model Army*, p. 242; Morrill, *Revolt in the Provinces*, 2nd edn, pp. 171–3. See, in general, Ashton, *Counter-Revolution*, chs. 10, 12.

34. Gardiner, IV, pp. 156–62.

35. Ibid., pp. 145–6, 173–4.

36. Ibid., pp. 145–6.

37. Ibid., pp. 164–6, 170–73, 194–5, 210–11.

38. Gentles, *New Model Army*, pp. 258–60; Woolrych, *Britain in Revolution*, p. 415. For the difficulties of recruitment in Scotland see Stevenson, *Revolution and Counter-Revolution*, pp. 105–11.

39. Woolrych, *Britain in Revolution*, pp. 415–16; Gentles, *New Model Army*, p. 260. For the following see also Malcolm Wanklyn, *Decisive Battles of the English Civil War: Myth and Reality* (Barnsley, 2006), chs. 16–17.

40. For varying estimates of the size of the armies see Gentles, *New Model Army*, p. 261; Woolrych, *Britain in Revolution*, pp. 416–17; Wanklyn, *Decisive Battles*, p. 191.

41. Woolrych, *Britain in Revolution*, pp. 416–18; Gentles, *New Model Army*, pp. 261–4; Wanklyn, *Decisive Battles*, pp. 194–9.

42. *CJ*, vi, 5.

43. Woolrych, *Britain in Revolution*, pp. 417–18; Gentles, *New Model Army*, pp. 261–4; Gardiner, IV, pp. 210–11.

44. Barbara Donagan, 'Myth, Memory and Martyrdom: Colchester 1648', *Essex Archaeology and History*, 34 (2004), 172–80, quotations at p. 173. For accounts of the siege see also Gardiner, IV, pp. 197–208; Gentles, *New Model Army*, pp. 256–7; Ashton, *Counter-Revolution*, pp. 473–5.

45. When Magdeburg was stormed on 20 May 1631 there was slaughter among the civilian population and the city was torched. As with the Irish risings of 1641, estimates of the extent of the devastation vary, partly because the events were immediately interpreted in the light of the larger confessional battle. For the memorialization and propaganda impact of this catastrophe see Hans Medick, 'Historical Event and Contemporary Experience: The Capture and Destruction of Magdeburg in 1631', trans. Pamela Selwyn, *History Workshop Journal*, 52 (2001), 23–48. Commonly cited estimates of population loss vary from two thirds of its population of 30,000 (Thomas Munck, *Seventeenth-Century Europe*, 2nd edn (Basingstoke, 2005), p. 18) to 96 per cent (Richard Bonney, *The European Dynastic States 1494–1660* (Oxford, 1991), p. 203).

46. Donagan, 'Myth', pp. 173–4. For the laws of war see also Barbara Donagan, 'Codes and Conduct in the English Civil War', *PP*, 118 (1988), 65–95; Barbara Donagan, 'Atrocity, War Crime, and Treason in the English Civil War', *AHR*, 99 (1994), 1137–66.

47. Donagan, 'Myth', p. 174.

48. Ibid., pp. 174–5.

49. Ibid., pp. 175–6; Fairfax quoted from Gardiner, IV, p. 205.

50. Donagan, 'Myth', pp. 176–9.

51. Gentles, *New Model Army*, pp. 270–72. This account is to be preferred to that of Gardiner, IV, p. 232, and those that followed it. For the initial reporting of the incident as an atrocity, and as direct revenge for the deaths of Lucas and Lisle, see *A full and exact relation of the Horrid murder committed on the body of Col Rainsborough* (London, 1648), Thomason date 3 November 1648, esp. pp. 2–3, 4. Details varied: *The Moderate* (31 October–7 November 1648), pp. [7–8]; *Packets of letters from Scotland, and the North parts of England* (London, 1648), Thomason date 8 November 1648, p. 1. See also Ian Gentles, 'Political Funerals during the English Revolution', in Stephen Porter (ed.), *London and the Civil War* (Basingstoke, 1996), pp. 205–24, at pp. 217–18.

52. Gardiner, IV, pp. 125–6; Woolrych, *Britain in Revolution*, pp. 407–9; Woolrych, *Soldiers and Statesmen*, pp. 330–35, quotation at p. 334.

53. Woolrych, *Soldiers and Statesmen*, pp. 325–8.

20. The Occasioner, Author, and Continuer . . .

1. David Underdown, *Pride's Purge: Politics in the Puritan Revolution* (Oxford, 1971), p. 97; Gardiner, IV, pp. 116, 122–4; *CJ*, v, pp. 551–2, quotation at p. 552; *LJ*, x, 247.

2. Gardiner, IV, pp. 168–9, 172.

3. Underdown, *Pride's Purge*, pp. 100–105.

4. Robert Ashton, *Counter-Revolution: The Second Civil War and Its Origins, 1646–1648* (New Haven, Conn., 1994), pp. 139–57; David Underdown, *Revel, Riot and Rebellion: Popular Politics and Culture in England, 1603–1660* (Oxford, 1985), pp. 229–32; David Underdown, ' "Honest" Radicals in the Counties, 1642–1649', in Donald Pennington and

Keith Thomas (eds.), *Puritans and Revolutionaries: Essays in Seventeenth-Century History Presented to Christopher Hill* (Oxford, 1978), pp. 186–205, esp. pp. 199–203.

5. For a sympathetic view see Richard Cust, *Charles I: A Political Life* (Harlow, 2005), pp. 437–42.

6. Gardiner, IV, pp. 209–10; Underdown, *Pride's Purge*, pp. 100–105.

7. David Stevenson, *Revolution and Counter-Revolution in Scotland, 1644–1651* (London, 1977), pp. 115–22.

8. Underdown, *Pride's Purge*, p. 109; Gardiner, IV, p. 213.

9. Underdown, *Pride's Purge*, p. 108. The source for this story is Ludlow's memoirs, which may not be reliable – they were later recollections and subject also to some massaging for publication in rather different times: Blair Worden, *Roundhead Reputations: The English Civil Wars and the Passions of Posterity* (Harmondsworth, 2001), esp. ch. 2. I am grateful to Ann Hughes for pointing this out to me.

10. Gardiner, IV, pp. 212–13; Underdown, *Pride's Purge*, p. 110. For the local political context of the Somerset petition see Underdown, *Somerset in the Civil War and Interregnum* (Newton Abbot, 1973), ch. 8, esp. p. 151.

11. Underdown, *Pride's Purge*, p. 112.

12. Gardiner, IV, pp. 214–22; Underdown, *Pride's Purge*, pp. 111–15; David L. Smith, *Constitutional Royalism and the Search for Settlement, c. 1640–1649* (Cambridge, 1994), pp. 138–40; Cust, *Charles I*, pp. 442–8.

13. Gardiner, IV, pp. 222–6; Cust, *Charles I*, pp. 444–5.

14. David Scott, *Politics and War in the Three Stuart Kingdoms, 1637–49* (Basingstoke, 2004), p. 185.

15. For the importance of fears about a renewal of war in England on the basis of a peace in Ireland, and their impact on English politics, see J. S. A. Adamson, 'The Frighted Junto: Perceptions of Ireland, and the Last Attempts at Settlement with Charles I', in Jason Peacey (ed.), *The Regicides and the Execution of Charles I* (Basingstoke, 2001), pp. 36–70.

16. For discussions of the text see Ian Gentles, *The New Model Army in England, Ireland and Scotland, 1645–1653* (Oxford, 1992), pp. 274–6; Gardiner, IV, pp. 233–6; Underdown, *Pride's Purge*, pp. 115–17, 123–7; Austin Woolrych, *Britain in Revolution 1625–1660* (Oxford, 2002), pp. 423–4, quotation at p. 424. Extracts are reprinted in A. S. P. Woodhouse, *Puritanism and Liberty: Being the Army Debates (1647–9) from the Clarke Manuscripts with Supplementary Documents*, 2nd edn (London, 1974), pp. 456–65. In general, calls for justice did not necessarily imply the killing of the King: Sean Kelsey, 'The Death of Charles I', *HJ*, 45 (2002), 727–54, esp. pp. 729–33. Kelsey also suggests that the passage quoted from the *Remonstrance* might be ambiguous: 'The Ordinance for the Trial of Charles I', *Historical Research*, 76 (2003), 310–31, at p. 313.

17. *A remonstrance of his excellency Thomas Lord Fairfax, Lord Generall of the Parliaments forces and of the Generall Councell of officers* (London, 1648), p. 24.

18. For the importance of this argument see Patricia Crawford, 'Charles Stuart, That Man of Blood', reprinted in Peter Gaunt (ed.), *The English Civil War* (Oxford, 2000), pp. 303–23.

19. Quoted from Gentles, *New Model Army*, p. 275.

20. *A remonstrance of his excellency*, p. 16. This clause follows directly from that quoted by Gentles, who sees a clearer intent behind the calls for justice to be exacted from the King.

21. Ibid., pp. 47–51, quotation at p. 47.

22. This may relate to the classical republican view that popular sovereignty was equivalent to reason, which should restrain interest (the equivalent of passion or will): Blair Worden, 'Classical Republicanism and the Puritan Revolution', in Hugh Lloyd-Jones, Valerie Pearl and Blair Worden (eds.), *History and Imagination: Essays in Honour of H. R. Trevor-Roper* (London, 1981), pp. 182–200, esp. pp. 193–4.

23. *A remonstrance of his excellency*, p. 36.

24. *A remonstrance or declaration of the army* (London, 1648).

25. *A remonstrance of his excellency*, p. 64.

26. For example, John Vernon, *The Swords Abuse Asserted* (1648); [Clement Walker], *Animadversions upon the armies remonstrance* (Huntington Library copy dated 4 January 1648, authorship attribution EEBO), refutes the historical account, makes a good case against the lawfulness of regicide (p. 15) and makes Gentles's point about who 'the people' defended by the army are (p. 22) (see Gentles, *New Model Army*, p. 276); *The recoyle of ill-cast and ill-charged ordinances* (1648); [Nedham], *A plea for the king, and kingdome* (1648), engages with the detail but highlights the principle – his defence of the King was not intended to save Charles's life, but was a defence against the threat to government posed by this version of *salus populi*. On the other side of the argument, *The humble ansvver of the general councel of the Officers of the army* (1648) justified the purge of Parliament, not in terms of justice on the King, but of a purging of interests in order to secure a settlement which defended the public good.

27. Gardiner, IV, pp. 236–45; Underdown, *Pride's Purge*, pp. 118–23, 129.

28. Underdown, *Pride's Purge*, pp. 126–7; Gentles, *New Model Army*, p. 274.

29. Underdown, *Pride's Purge*, pp. 130–32.

30. Gentles, *New Model Army*, pp. 276–8, 280; Charles Carlton, *Charles I: The Personal Monarch* (London, 1983), pp. 339–42.

31. Underdown, *Pride's Purge*, pp. 131, 133–40.

32. Ibid., pp. 140–42; Gentles, *New Model Army*, p. 281.

33. Underdown, *Pride's Purge*, pp. 143–8, 152, 208–20; Blair Worden, *The Rump Parliament* (Cambridge, 1974), pp. 23, 387–92.

34. Gentles, *New Model Army*, pp. 283–5.

35. Underdown, *Pride's Purge*, pp. 150–63; Gardiner, IV, p. 275. For the mixed political profile of the purged parliament see Worden, *Rump*, ch. 2. For the triumph of radicals in London see Robert Brenner, *Merchants and Revolution: Commercial Change, Political Conflict and London's Overseas Traders, 1550–1653* (Cambridge, 1993), pp. 533–47.

36. Underdown, *Pride's Purge*, pp. 178–82; Underdown, *Somerset*, pp. 146–50; Anthony Fletcher, *A County Community in Peace and War: Sussex 1600–1660* (London, 1975), pp. 292–3.

37. Adamson, 'Frighted Junto', pp. 43–5. In fact the Confederate alliance was by this time unravelling under the weight of its own contradictions: Micheál Ó Siochrú, *Confederate Ireland, 1642–1649: A Constitutional and Political Analysis* (Dublin, 1999), ch. 6.

38. Adamson, 'Frighted Junto', esp. pp. 40–52; Sean Kelsey, 'The Trial of Charles I', *EHR*, 118, 477 (2003), 583–616, esp. pp. 587–8. For the navy see Bernard Capp, *Cromwell's Navy: The Fleet and the English Revolution, 1648–1660* (Oxford, 1989), esp. pp. 43–6.

39. Underdown, *Pride's Purge*, p. 168; Adamson, 'Frighted Junto', pp. 46–7, 58, 60, 61.

40. Kelsey, 'Trial', p. 593; Kelsey, 'Death', pp. 740–42.

41. Gardiner, IV, pp. 281–5; Gentles, *New Model Army*, pp. 285–94. Extracts are reprinted in Woodhouse, *Puritanism and Liberty*.

42. Underdown, *Pride's Purge*, pp. 166–72; Gentles, *New Model Army*, pp. 294–300.

43. Gentles, *New Model Army*, pp. 292–3, 300; Underdown, *Pride's Purge*, pp. 164–5.

44. Phyllis Mack, *Visionary Women: Ecstatic Prophecy in Seventeenth-Century England* (Berkeley, Calif., 1992), esp. pp. 78–9; Manfred Brod, 'Politics and Prophecy in Seventeenth Century England: The Case of Elizabeth Poole', *Albion*, 31 (1999), 395–413; Manfred Brod, 'Poole, Elizabeth (*bap.* 1622?, *d.* in or after 1668)', *ODNB*, 44, p. 837. For women and prophecy see above, pp. 409–11.

45. Brod, 'Politics and Prophecy', esp. pp. 411–12.

46. *Clarke Papers*, II, pp. 150–54, quotations at pp. 150, 151, 152, 154. The vision was later published: Elizabeth Poole, *A vision* (London, 1648).

47. *Clarke Papers*, II, pp. 163–70, quotations at pp. 164, 165; Poole, *A vision*, p. 6.

48. Crawford, 'Charles Stuart'.

49. For the diversity of opinion on these issues see Underdown, *Pride's Purge*, ch. 7; Worden, *Rump*, esp. chs. 1–3; David Scott, 'Motives for King-Killing', in Peacey (ed.), *Regicides*,

pp. 138–60; John Morrill and Philip Baker, 'Oliver Cromwell, the Regicide and the Sons of Zeruiah', in ibid., pp. 14–35.

50. Gentles, *New Model Army*, pp. 300–302, quotation at p. 302.

51. Gardiner, IV, pp. 288–91, quotation at p. 290; *CJ*, vi, 110–11.

52. Gardiner, *CD*, pp. 357–8; Kelsey, 'Trial', pp. 588–94; Kelsey, 'Death', pp. 743–4. For a full discussion of the tensions over the purpose and meaning of the enabling legislation see Kelsey, 'Ordinance'.

53. Kelsey, 'Trial', pp. 595–8; Kelsey, 'Death', pp. 733–4; C. V. Wedgwood, *The Trial of Charles I* (London, 1964), esp. pp. 123–7. For the full range of motives in allowing reporting of the trial see Jason Peacey, 'Reporting a Revolution: A Failed Propaganda Campaign', in Peacey (ed.), *Regicides*, pp. 161–80. For a sample of reports see Joad Raymond (ed.), *Making the News: An Anthology of the Newsbooks of Revolutionary England, 1641–1660* (Moreton-in-Marsh, 1993), ch. 5.

54. The charges are reprinted in Kelsey, 'Trial', pp. 598–601; Kelsey, 'Death', pp. 734–5; Gardiner, *CD*, pp. 371–4, quotation at pp. 373–4.

55. 'he has been the author and continuer of a most unjust war, and is consequently guilty of all the treason it contains and of all the innocent blood, rapine, spoil, and mischief to the kingdom acted or occasioned thereby': *A remonstrance of his excellency*, p. 24; for the phrase quoted in the text see p. 23.

56. Kelsey, 'Trial', pp. 598–602; Kelsey, 'Death', pp. 734–5. For detailed accounts of the proceedings see also Wedgwood, *Trial*, chs. 6–8 and Gardiner, IV, chs. 70–71.

57. Kelsey, 'Trial', p. 616.

58. Ibid., pp. 602–10; Kelsey, 'Death', pp. 743–5.

59. Kelsey, 'Trial', pp. 607–10; for the text of the King's reasons see Gardiner, *CD*, pp. 374–6.

60. Kelsey, 'Trial', pp. 610–12; Kelsey, 'Death', pp. 745–9.

61. Kelsey, 'Trial', p. 614; Gardiner, IV, pp. 311–13.

62. Kelsey, 'Death', pp. 749–51.

63. Kelsey, 'Death', pp. 750–51; Gardiner, IV, pp. 316–18; for the element of negotiation in court, including the possibility of pardon, see Cynthia Herrup, *The Common Peace: Participation and the Criminal Law in Seventeenth-Century England* (Cambridge, 1987), ch. 6; for the exercise of discretion as an aspect of power in legal contexts see Krista J. Kesselring, *Mercy and Authority in the Tudor State* (Cambridge, 2003): in this case to pardon Charles would have been further to subject him to a higher authority.

64. Gardiner, IV, pp. 278–80; Ian Gentles, 'Harrison, Thomas (*bap.* 1616, *d.* 1690)', *ODNB*, 25, pp. 529–33.

65. *Perfect Occurrences* (22–30 December 1648), p. 778 (I am grateful to Keith Lindley for this reference); Kelsey, 'Death', pp. 731–2; Clarendon, IV, pp. 479, 483, 485.

66. Gardiner, IV, pp. 299–300, quoting the *State Trials*. Clarendon has it as 'No, nor the hundredth part of them', IV, p. 486.

67. Gardiner, IV, p. 301.

68. Clarendon, IV, p. 487; Gardiner, IV, p. 300.

69. Clarendon, IV, p. 488.

70. Wedgwood, *Trial*, ch. 8; Kelsey, 'Trial', pp. 614–15; Gardiner, IV, pp. 319–23.

71. Gardiner, IV, p. 323; Wedgwood, *Trial*, p. 193.

72. Wedgwood, *Trial*, p. 196.

73. TNA, SP24/71 petition of Darcy Roades; SP24/75 petition of Thomas Sharpe. For Warwickshire politics following the regicide see Ann Hughes, *Politics, Society and Civil War in Warwickshire, 1620–1660* (Cambridge, 1987), ch. 8. In Lincolnshire, for example, it was accepted with 'sullen resentment', and there was no evidence of opposition in formerly royalist Cornwall: Clive Holmes, *Seventeenth-Century Lincolnshire* (Lincoln, 1980), pp. 203–5; Mary Coate, *Cornwall in the Great Civil War and Interregnum 1642–1660: A Social and Political Study* (Oxford, 1933), p. 250.

74. Diary entries 16 August 1648, 4 February 1649: Alan Macfarlane, *The Diary of Ralph*

Josselin 1616–1683, British Academy Records of Social and Economic History, new series, III (Oxford, 1976), pp. 130, 155. A transcript is online at http://linux02.lib.cam.ac.uk/earlscolne/documents/diary.htm

75. Underdown, *Pride's Purge*, p. 190.

76. But he noted this in embarrassment, having met an old schoolfellow who he feared might have remembered this: Robert Latham and William Matthews (eds.), *The Diary of Samuel Pepys: A New and Complete Transcription*, vol. I: 1660 (London, 1970), p. 280.

77. Wedgwood, *Trial*, pp. 184–5; *CSPD, 1660–61*, p. 67, and see also pp. 65, 109, 124, 184; for William Walker see also David Wootton, 'From Rebellion to Revolution: The Crisis of the Winter of 1642/3 and the Origins of Civil War Radicalism', reprinted in Richard Cust and Ann Hughes (eds.), *The English Civil War* (London, 1997), pp. 340–56, at p. 352.

78. Wedgwood, *Trial*, pp. 204–5.

79. Elizabeth Skerpan Wheeler, '*Eikon Basilike* and the Rhetoric of Self-Representation', in Thomas N. Corns (ed.), *The Royal Image: Representations of Charles I* (Cambridge, 1999), pp. 122–40; Cust, *Charles I*, pp. 446–7; Kevin Sharpe, 'The King's Writ: Royal Authors and Royal Authority in Early Modern England', in Kevin Sharpe and Peter Lake (eds.), *Culture and Politics in Early Stuart England* (Basingstoke, 1994), pp. 117–38, at pp. 136–8; Kevin Sharpe, ' "So hard a text"?: Images of Charles I, 1612–1700', *HJ*, 43 (2000), 383–406; Andrew Lacey, 'Elegies and Commemorative Verses in Honour of Charles the Martyr, 1649–60', in Peacey (ed.), *Regicides*, pp. 225–46, and the references in his n. 2. For a convenient modern edition see P. A. Knachel (ed.), *Eikon Basilike: The Portraiture of His Sacred Majesty in His Solitudes and Sufferings* (Ithaca, NY, 1966). For the cult of King Charles more generally see Andrew Lacey, *The Cult of King Charles the Martyr* (Woodbridge, 2003). For the healing power of his blood see *A Miracle of Miracles Wrought by the Blood of King Charles I* (London, 1649).

Epilogue

1. Thomas May, *The history of the parliament Of England, which began November the third, MDCXL* (London 1647), title page, sig. A3r.

2. Ibid., sig. A3v–A4r.

3. Ibid., sig. B1r.

4. Ibid., sig. A3r–v.

5. Lois Spencer, 'The Politics of George Thomason', *The Library*, 5th ser., 14 (1959), 11–27; Joad Raymond, *Pamphlets and Pamphleteering in Early Modern Britain* (Cambridge, 2003), pp. 161–2, 192–6.

6. For modern views of May's history see J. G. A. Pocock, 'Thomas May and the Narrative of Civil War', in Derek Hirst and Richard Strier (eds.), *Writing and Political Engagement in Seventeenth-Century England* (Cambridge, 1999), pp. 112–44; Nigel Smith, *The Poems of Andrew Marvell* (Harlow, 2003) esp. pp. 116–18.

7. May, *History*, sig. B2v.

8. See above, p. 580.

9. Based on a search of ESTC, 14 April 2007.

10. 'Exit tyrannus Regum ultimus, anno primo restitutae libertatis Angliae 1648': Nicola Smith, *The Royal Image and the English People* (Aldershot, 2001), ch. 3, esp. p. 68 (my translation). For the legislation and other examples see Julie Spraggon, *Puritan Iconoclasm during the English Civil War* (Woodbridge, 2003), pp. 81, 209–10, 238–9, 262–3; C. V. Wedgwood, *The Trial of Charles I* (London, 1964), pp. 209–10. For the sale of the crown jewels see Anna Keay, 'Toyes and trifles', *History Today* (July 2002).

11. Margaret Aston, 'Puritans and Iconoclasm, 1560–1660', in Christopher Durston and Jacqueline Eales (eds.), *The Culture of English Puritanism, 1560–1700* (Basingstoke, 1996), pp. 92–121; Keith Thomas, 'Art and Iconoclasm in Early Modern England', in Kenneth Fincham and Peter Lake (eds.), *Religious Politics in post-Reformation England:*

Essays in Honour of Nicholas Tyacke (Woodbridge, 2006), pp. 16–40; Jerry Brotton, *The Sale of the Late King's Goods: Charles I and His Art Collection* (Basingstoke, 2006), pp. 234–8.

12. Smith, *Royal Image*, pp. 69–70, 73–5, 79, and for Cromwell, ch. 8. This memorialization of Cromwell goes to the heart of subsequent attempts to make sense of the wars: Blair Worden, *Roundhead Reputations: The English Civil Wars and the Passions of Posterity* (Harmondsworth, 2001), ch. 11. For the Act of Oblivion and the erasure of memories of the wars see David Norbrook, *Writing the English Republic: Poetry, Rhetoric and Politics, 1627–1660* (Cambridge, 1999), esp. pp. 1–22; Jonathan Scott, *England's Troubles: Seventeenth-Century English Political Stability in European Context* (Cambridge, 2000), esp. intr., ch. 1.

13. This is a large subject, of course. For important recent studies emphasizing the intellectual and cultural creativity of the 1650s see Sean Kelsey, *Inventing a Republic: The Political Culture of the English Commonwealth, 1649–1653* (Manchester, 1997); Scott, *England's Troubles*, esp. chs. 10–16; Jonathan Scott, *Commonwealth Principles: Republican Writing of the English Revolution* (Cambridge, 2004); Norbrook, *Writing the English Republic*.

14. John Pocock, quoted in J. C. Davis, 'Political Thought during the English Revolution', in Barry Coward (ed.), *A Companion to Stuart Britain* (Oxford, 2003), pp. 374–96, at p. 374.

15. *A true and strange relation of fire* (London, 1639), p. 8. Butter was a news pioneer, a key figure in the heroic accounts of the rise of the news industry. His output of news pamphlets included a number of stories of natural wonders, some of which made direct connections with current affairs. Prior to 1640, they were mainly foreign events (e.g. *Good Newes to Christendome* [London, 1620]), but it was not impossible to make a connection between earthquake and fire in the Terceiras (Azores) in 1638 and Charles's troubles. In 1659 Butter published a pamphlet relating a strange atmospheric phenomenon above London, which coincided with Charles's departure after the attempt on the Five Members: *A Letter with a Narrative, written to the right Hon:ble Thomas Allen* (London, 1659).

Bibliography of Secondary Works

I have not included modern editions of sixteenth- and seventeenth-century materials except where there is extensive editorial comment upon which I have drawn.

Achinstein, Sharon, 'The Politics of Babel in the English Revolution', reprinted in James Holstun (ed.), *Pamphlet Wars: Prose in the English Revolution* (London, 1992), pp. 14–44.

Achinstein, Sharon, 'Introduction: Gender, Literature and the English Revolution', *Women's Studies*, 24:1–2 (1994), 1–13.

Achinstein, Sharon, *Milton and the Revolutionary Reader* (Princeton, 1994).

Achinstein, Sharon, 'Women on Top in the Pamphlet Literature of the English Revolution', *Women's Studies*, 24: 1–2 (1994), 131–63.

Adamson, J. S. A., 'The English Nobility and the Projected Settlement of 1647', *HJ*, 30 (1987), 567–602.

Adamson, J. S. A., 'The Baronial Context of the English Civil War', *TRHS*, 5th series, 40 (1990), 93–120.

Adamson, J. S. A., 'Politics and the Nobility in Civil War England', *HJ*, 34 (1991), 231–55.

Adamson, J. S. A., 'Chivalry and Political Culture in Caroline England', in Kevin Sharpe and Peter Lake (eds.), *Culture and Politics in Early Stuart England* (Basingstoke, 1994), pp. 161–97.

Adamson, J. S. A., 'Of Armies and Architecture: The Employments of Robert Scawen', in Ian Gentles, John Morrill and Blair Worden (eds.), *Soldiers, Writers and Statesmen of the English Revolution* (Cambridge, 1998), pp. 36–67.

Adamson, J. S. A., 'The Frighted Junto: Perceptions of Ireland, and the Last Attempts at Settlement with Charles I', in Jason Peacey (ed.), *The Regicides and the Execution of Charles I* (Basingstoke, 2001), pp. 36–70.

Adamson, John, 'The Triumph of Oligarchy: The Management of War and the Committee of Both Kingdoms, 1644–1645', in Chris R. Kyle and Jason Peacey (eds.), *Parliament at Work: Parliamentary Committees, Political Power and Public Access in Early Modern England* (Woodbridge, 2002), pp. 101–27.

Adamson, John, *The Noble Revolt: The Overthrow of Charles I* (London, 2007).

Appleby, Andrew B., *Famine in Tudor and Stuart England* (Liverpool, 1978).

Archer, Ian W., *The Pursuit of Stability: Social Relations in Elizabethan London* (Cambridge, 1991).

Archer, Ian, 'Popular Politics in the Sixteenth and Early Seventeenth Centuries', in Paul Griffiths and Mark S. R. Jenner (eds.), *Londinopolis: Essays in the Cultural and Social History of Early Modern London* (Manchester, 2000), pp. 26–46.

Arni, Eric Gruber von, *Justice to the Maimed Soldier: Nursing, Medical Care and Welfare for Sick and Wounded Soldiers and Their Families during the English Civil Wars and Interregnum, 1642–1660* (Aldershot, 2001).

Asch, Ronald G., 'Wentworth, Thomas, First Earl of Strafford (1593–1641)', *ODNB*, 58, pp. 142–57.

Ashton, Robert, 'From Cavalier to Roundhead Tyranny, 1642–9', in John Morrill (ed.), *Reactions to the English Civil War 1642–1649* (Basingstoke, 1982), pp. 185–207.

Ashton, Robert, *Counter-Revolution: The Second Civil War and Its Origins, 1646–1648* (New Haven, 1994).

Aston, Margaret, *England's Iconoclasts*, Vol. 1: *Laws Against Images* (Oxford, 1988).

Aston, Margaret, 'Puritans and Iconoclasm, 1560–1660', in Christopher Durston and Jacqueline Eales (eds.), *The Culture of English Puritanism, 1560–1700* (Basingstoke, 1996), pp. 92–121.

Aston, Margaret, 'Iconoclasm in England: Official and Clandestine', reprinted in Peter Marshall (ed.), *The Impact of the English Reformation 1500–1640* (London, 1997), pp. 167–92.

Atherton, Ian, '"The itch grown a disease": Manuscript Transmission of News in the Seventeenth Century', in Joad Raymond (ed.), *News, Newspapers and Society in Early Modern Britain* (London, 1999), pp. 39–65.

Atherton, Ian, 'The Press and Popular Political Opinion', in Barry Coward (ed.), *A Companion to Stuart Britain* (Oxford, 2003), pp. 88–110.

Atherton, Ian, and Julie Sanders (eds.), *The 1630s: Interdisciplinary Essays on Culture and Politics in the Caroline Era* (Manchester, 2006).

Aylmer, G. E. (ed.), *The Interregnum: The Quest for Settlement, 1646–1660* (London, 1972).

Aylmer, Gerald, *The State's Servants: The Civil Service of the English Republic 1649–1660* (London, 1973).

Aylmer, G. E. (ed.), *The Levellers in the English Revolution* (London, 1975).

Baker, P. R. S., 'Edwards, Thomas (c.1599–1648)', *ODNB*, 17, pp. 965–8.

Barber, Sarah, '"A bastard kind of militia": Localism, and Tactics in the Second Civil War', in Ian Gentles, John Morrill and Blair Worden (eds.), *Soldiers, Writers and Statesmen of the English Revolution* (Cambridge, 1998), pp. 133–50.

Barber, Sarah, *Regicide and Republicanism: Politics and Ethics in the English Revolution, 1646–1659* (Edinburgh, 1998).

Barber, Sarah, 'Marten, Henry (1601/2–1680)', *ODNB*, 36, pp. 908–12.

Barlow, Frank, 'The King's Evil', *EHR*, 95 (1980), 3–27.

Barnard, Toby, 'Butler, James, First Duke of Ormond (1610–1688)', *ODNB*, 9, pp. 153–63.

Barnes, Thomas G., 'County Politics and a Puritan *Cause Célèbre*: Somerset Church Ales, 1633', *TRHS*, 5th ser., 9 (1959), 103–22.

Barnes, Thomas G., *Somerset 1625–1640: A County's Government during the 'Personal Rule'* (Chicago, 1961).

Barnes, Thomas G., 'Deputies not Principals, Lieutenants not Captains: The Institutional Failure of Lieutenancy in the 1620s', in Mark Charles Fissel (ed.), *War and Government in Britain, 1598–1650* (Manchester, 1991), pp. 58–86.

Barratt, John, *Cavaliers: The Royalist Army at War, 1642–1646* (Stroud, 2000).

Beaver, Daniel C., *Parish Communities and Religious Conflict in the Vale of Gloucester 1590–1690* (Cambridge, Mass., 1998).

Beaver, Daniel C., 'The Great Deer Massacre: Animals, Honor, and Communication in Early Modern England', *JBS*, 38 (1999), 187–216.

Beaver, Daniel C., '"Bragging and daring words": Honour, Property and the Symbolism of the Hunt in Stowe, 1590–1642', in Michael J. Braddick and John Walter (eds.), *Negotiating Power in Early Modern Society: Order, Hierarchy and Subordination in Britain and Ireland* (Cambridge, 2001), pp. 149–65.

Beaver, Daniel C., 'Sacrifice, Venison and the Social Order in Waltham Forest, 1608–1642' (unpublished paper).

Beier, A. L., David Cannadine and James M. Rosenheim (eds.), *The First Modern Society: Essays in English History in Honour of Lawrence Stone* (Cambridge, 1989).

Beier, A. L. and Roger Finlay (eds.), *London 1500–1700: The Making of the Metropolis* (London, 1986).

Bell, Mark, 'Freedom to Form: The Development of Baptist Movements during the English Revolution', in Christopher Durston and Judith Maltby (eds.), *Religion in Revolutionary England* (Manchester, 2006), pp. 181–201.

Bellany, Alastair, '"Rayling Rymes and Vaunting Verse": Libellous Politics in Early Stuart England, 1603–1628', in Kevin Sharpe and Peter Lake (eds.), *Culture and Politics in Early Stuart England* (Basingstoke, 1994), pp. 285–310.

Bellany, Alastair, 'Libels in Action: Ritual, Subversion and the English Literary Underground, 1603–42', in Tim Harris (ed.), *The Politics of the Excluded, c. 1500–1850* (Basingstoke, 2001), 99–124.

Bellany, Alastair, 'Basting the Lambe: Witchcraft, Court Scandal and the Lynching of the Duke's Devil, June 1628', *PP* (forthcoming).

Bellany, Alastair, 'The Murder of James I: Mutations and Meanings of a Political Myth, c.1625–1660' (unpublished paper).

Ben-Amos, Ilana Krausman, *Adolescence and Youth in Early Modern England* (London, 1994).

Bennett, Martyn, 'Contribution and Assessment: Financial Exactions and the English Civil War, 1642–1646', *War and Society*, 4 (1986), 1–11.

Bennett, Martyn, 'Between Scylla and Charybdis: The Creation of Rival Administrations at the Beginning of the English Civil War', reprinted in Peter Gaunt (ed.), *The English Civil War* (Oxford, 2000), pp. 167–83.

Bennett, Martyn, *The Civil Wars Experienced: Britain and Ireland, 1638–1661* (London, 2000).

Bennett, Ronan, 'War and Disorder: Policing the Soldiery in Civil War Yorkshire', in Mark Charles Fissel (ed.), *War and Government in Britain, 1598–1650* (Manchester, 1991), pp. 248–73.

Bertrand Taithe and Tim Thornton (eds.), *Prophecy: The Power of Inspired Language in History 1300–2000* (Stroud, 1997).

Binns, Jack, 'Cholmley, Sir Hugh, First Baronet (1600–1657)', *ODNB*, 11, pp. 504–5.

Black, Joseph, ' "Pikes and Protestations": Scottish Texts in England, 1639–40', *Publishing History*, 42 (1997), 5–19.

Blackwood, B. G., 'Parties and Issues: The Civil War in Lancashire and East Anglia', reprinted in R. C. Richardson (ed.), *The English Civil Wars: Local Aspects* (Stroud, 1997), pp. 261–85.

Bliss, Robert M., *Revolution and Empire: English Politics and the American Colonies in the Seventeenth Century* (Manchester, 1990).

Bloch, Marc, *The Royal Touch: Monarchy and Miracles in France and England*, trans. J. E. Anderson (New York, 1989).

Bold, John, 'Webb, John (1611–1672), *ODNB*, 57, pp. 837–40.

Bonney, Richard, *The European Dynastic States 1494–1660* (Oxford, 1991).

Boulton, Jeremy, *Neighbourhood and Society: A London Suburb in the Seventeenth Century* (Cambridge, 1987).

Boulton, Jeremy, 'London 1540–1700', in Peter Clark (ed.), *The Cambridge Urban History of Britain*, vol. 2: *1540–1840* (Cambridge, 2000), 315–46.

Bowen, Lloyd, 'Representations of Wales and the Welsh during the Civil Wars and Interregnum', *Historical Research*, 77 (2004), 358–76.

Boynton, Lindsey O., *The Elizabethan Militia, 1558–1638* (London, 1967).

Braddick, Michael J., 'Popular Politics and Public Policy: The Excise Riot at Smithfield in February 1647 and Its Aftermath', *HJ*, 34 (1991), 597–626.

Braddick, Michael J., 'State Formation and Social Change: A Problem Stated and Approaches Suggested', *Social History*, 16:1 (1991), 1–17.

Braddick, Michael J., *Parliamentary Taxation in Seventeenth-Century England: Local Administration and Response* (Woodbridge, 1994).

Braddick, Michael J., *The Nerves of State: Taxation and the Financing of the English State, 1558–1714* (Manchester, 1996).

Braddick, Michael J., *State Formation in Early Modern England, c. 1550–1700* (Cambridge, 2000).

Braddick, Michael J., '"Upon this instant extraordinarie occasion": Military Mobilisation in Yorkshire in the Armada Year and Thereafter', *HLQ*, 61 (2000 for 1998), 429–55.

Braddick, Michael J., 'Administrative Performance: The Representation of Political Authority in Early Modern England', in Braddick and John Walter (eds), *Negotiating Power in Early Modern Society: Order, Hierarchy and Subordination in Britain and Ireland* (Cambridge, 2001), pp. 166–87.

Braddick, Michael J., 'The Rise of the Fiscal State', in Barry Coward (ed.), *A Companion to Stuart Britain* (Oxford, 2003), pp. 69–87.

Braddick, Michael J., 'The English Revolution and Its Legacies', in Nicholas Tyacke (ed.), *The English Revolution c. 1590–1720* (Manchester, 2007), pp. 27–42.

Braddick, Michael J., and John Walter (eds.), *Negotiating Power in Early Modern Society: Order, Hierarchy and Subordination in Britain and Ireland* (Cambridge, 2001).

Brailsford, H. N., *The Levellers and the English Revolution* (London, 1961).

Brayshay, Mark, Philip Harrison and Brian Chalkley, 'Knowledge, Nationhood and Governance: The Speed of the Royal Post in Early-Modern England', *Journal of Historical Geography*, 24 (1998), 265–88.

Bremer, Francis J., 'Williams, Roger (*c.*1606–1683)', *ODNB*, 59, pp. 293–7.

Brenner, Robert, *Merchants and Revolution: Commercial Change, Political Conflict, and London's Overseas Traders, 1550–1653* (Cambridge, 1993).

Brewer, John, *The Sinews of Power: War, Money and the English State, 1688–1783* (London, 1989).

Brod, Manfred, 'Politics and Prophecy in Seventeenth Century England: The Case of Elizabeth Poole', *Albion*, 31 (1999), 395–413.

Brod, Manfred, 'Poole, Elizabeth (*bap.* 1622?, *d.* in or after 1668)', *ODNB*, 44, p. 837.

Brooks, Christopher W., *Pettyfoggers and Vipers of the Commonwealth: The 'Lower Branch' of the Legal Profession in Early Modern England* (Cambridge, 1986).

Brooks, Christopher, 'Interpersonal Conflict and Social Tension: Civil Litigation in England, 1640–1870', in A. L. Beier, David Cannadine and James M. Rosenheim (eds.), *The First Modern Society: Essays in English History in Honour of Lawrence Stone* (Cambridge, 1989), pp. 357–99.

Brotton, Jerry, *The Sale of the Late King's Goods: Charles I and His Art Collection* (Basingstoke, 2006).

Brown, Christopher, and Hans Vlieghe (eds.), *Van Dyke, 1599–1641* (London, 1999).

Brown, Keith M., 'Aristocratic Finances and the Origins of the Scottish Revolution', *EHR*, 104 (1989), 46–87.

Brown, Keith M., *Kingdom or Province? Scotland and the Regal Union, 1603–1715* (Basingstoke, 1992).

Broxap, Ernest, *The Great Civil War in Lancashire (1642–51)*, 2nd edn (Manchester, 1973).

[Bulmer, T.], *History, Topography, and Directory of East Yorkshire (with Hull)* (Preston: T. Bulmer and sons, 1892).

Burgess, Glenn, 'The Impact on Political Thought: Rhetorics for Troubled Times', in John Morrill (ed.), *The Impact of the English Civil War* (London, 1991), pp. 67–83.

Burgess, Glenn, *The Politics of the Ancient Constitution: An Introduction to English Political Thought, 1603–1642* (Basingstoke, 1992).

Burns, J. H., with Mark Goldie (eds.), *The Cambridge History of Political Thought 1450–1700* (Cambridge, 1991).

Cameron, Euan, *The European Reformation* (Oxford, 1991).

Campbell, Gordon, 'Milton, John (1608–1674)', *ODNB*, 38, pp. 333–49.

Canny, Nicholas, 'What Really Happened in Ireland in 1641?', in Jane H. Ohlmeyer (ed.), *Ireland from Independence to Occupation 1641–1660* (Cambridge, 1995), pp. 24–42.

Canny, Nicholas, *Making Ireland British 1580–1650* (Oxford, 2001).

Capp, Bernard, *Astrology and the Popular Press: English Almanacs 1500–1800* (London, 1979).

Capp, Bernard, *Cromwell's Navy: The Fleet and the English Revolution, 1648–1660* (Oxford, 1989).

Capp, Bernard, *The World of John Taylor the Water-Poet 1578–1653* (Oxford, 1994).

Capp, Bernard, 'Naval Operations', in John Kenyon and Jane Ohlmeyer (eds.), *The Civil Wars: A Military History of England, Scotland and Ireland* (Oxford, 1998), pp. 156–91.

Carlton, Charles, *Charles I: The Personal Monarch* (London, 1983).

Carlton, Charles, *Going to the Wars: The Experience of the English Civil Wars, 1638–1651* (London, 1992).

Carlton, Charles, 'Civilians', in John Kenyon and Jane Ohlmeyer (eds.), *The Civil Wars: A Military History of England, Scotland and Ireland* (Oxford, 1998), pp. 272–305.

Christianson, Paul, 'From Expectation to Militance: Reformers and Babylon in the First Two Years of the Long Parliament', *Journal of Ecclesiastical History*, 34 (1973), 225–44.

Christianson, Paul, *Reformers and Babylon: English Apocalyptic Visions from the Reformation to the Eve of the Civil War* (Toronto, 1978).

Clark, J. C. D., *English Society 1688–1832* (Cambridge, 1985).

Clark, Peter, *English Provincial Society from the Reformation to the Revolution: Religion, Politics and Society in Kent, 1500–1640* (Hassocks, 1977).

Clark, Stuart, *Thinking with Demons: The Idea of Witchcraft in Early Modern Europe* (Oxford, 1997).

Clarke, Aidan, 'Selling Royal Favours, 1624–32', in T. W. Moody, F. X. Martin and F. J. Byrne (eds.), *A New History of Ireland*, vol. 3: *Early Modern Ireland 1534–1691* (Oxford, 1976), pp. 233–42.

Clarke, Aidan, 'The Government of Wentworth, 1632–40', in T. W. Moody, F. X. Martin and F. J. Byrne (eds.), *A New History of Ireland*, vol. 3: *Early Modern Ireland 1534–1691* (Oxford, 1976), 243–69.

Clarke, Aidan, 'The Breakdown of Authority, 1640–41', in T. W. Moody, F. X. Martin and F. J. Byrne (eds.), *A New History of Ireland*, vol. 3: *Early Modern Ireland 1534–1691* (Oxford, 1976), pp. 270–88.

Clarke, Aidan, with R. Dudley Edwards, 'Pacification, Plantation and the Catholic Question', in T. W. Moody, F. X. Martin and F. J. Byrne (eds.), *A New History of Ireland*, vol. 3: *Early Modern Ireland 1534–1691* (Oxford, 1976), pp. 187–232.

Clarke, Elizabeth, 'The Legacy of Mothers and Others: Women's Theological Writing, 1640–60', in Christopher Durston and Judith Maltby (eds.), *Religion in Revolutionary England* (Manchester, 2006), pp. 69–90.

Clay, C. G. A., *Economic Expansion and Social Change. England 1500–1700*, 2 vols. (Cambridge, 1984).

Clay, Christopher (ed.), *Rural Society: Landowners, Peasants and Labourers 1500–1750*, vol. 2 of *Chapters from the Agrarian History of England and Wales* (general editor Joan Thirsk) (Cambridge, 1990).

Clegg, Cyndia, 'Burning Books as Propaganda in Jacobean England', in Andrew Hadfield (ed.), *Literature and Censorship in Renaissance England* (Basingstoke, 2001), pp. 165–86.

Clifford, C. A., 'Ship Money in Hampshire: Collection and Collapse', *Southern History*, 4 (1982), 91–106.

Cliftlands, William, 'The "Well-Affected" and the "Country": Politics and Religion in English Provincial Society, c. 1640–1654', unpublished Ph.D. thesis, Essex (1987).

Clifton, Robin, 'The Popular Fear of Catholics during the English Revolution', *PP*, 52 (1971), 23–55.

Clifton, Robin, 'Fear of Popery', in Conrad Russell (ed.), *The Origins of the English Civil War* (London, 1973), pp. 144–67.

Coate, Mary, *Cornwall in the Great Civil War and Interregnum 1642–1660: A Social and Political Study* (Oxford, 1933).

Coates, Ben, *The Impact of the English Civil War on the Economy of London, 1642–50* (Aldershot, 2004).

Coffey, John, 'Henderson, Alexander (*c.*1583–1646)', *ODNB*, 26, pp. 288–93.

Coffey, John, 'Johnston, Sir Archibald, Lord Wariston (*bap.* 1611, *d.* 1663)', *ODNB*, 30, pp. 338–46.

Coffey, John, 'The Toleration Controversy during the English Revolution', in Christopher Durston and Judith Maltby (eds.), *Religion in Revolutionary England* (Manchester, 2006), pp. 42–68.

Cogswell, Thomas, *The Blessed Revolution: English Politics and the Coming of War, 1621–1624* (Cambridge, 1989).

Cogswell, Thomas, 'England and the Spanish Match', in Richard Cust and Ann Hughes (eds.), *Conflict in Early Stuart England: Studies in Religion and Politics 1603–1642* (Harlow, 1989), pp. 107–33.

Cogswell, Thomas, 'A Low Road to Extinction?: Supply and Redress of Grievances in the Parliaments of the 1620s', *HJ*, 33 (1990), 283–303.

Cogswell, Thomas, 'The Politics of Propaganda: Charles I and the People in the 1620s', *JBS*, 29:3 (1990), 187–215.

Cogswell, Thomas, 'War and the Liberties of the Subject', in J. H. Hexter (ed.), *Parliament and Liberty from the Reign of Elizabeth to the English Civil War* (Stanford, 1992), pp. 225–51.

Cogswell, Thomas, 'Underground Verse and the Transformation of Early Stuart Political Culture', in Susan D. Amussen and Mark A. Kishlansky (eds.), *Political Culture and Cultural Politics in Early Modern England: Essays Presented to David Underdown* (Manchester, 1995), pp. 277–300.

Cogswell, Thomas, 'Phaeton's Chariot: The Parliament Men and the Continental Crisis in 1621', in J. F. Merritt (ed.), *The Political World of Thomas Wentworth, Earl of Strafford, 1621–1641* (Cambridge, 1996), pp. 24–46.

Cogswell, Thomas, *Home Divisions: Aristocracy, the State and Provincial Conflict* (Manchester, 1998).

Cogswell, Thomas, '"Published by Authoritie": Newsbooks and the Duke of Buckingham's Expedition to the Île de Ré', *Huntington Library Quarterly*, 67:1 (2004), 1–25.

Cogswell, Thomas, 'John Felton, Popular Political Culture, and the Assassination of the Duke of Buckingham', *HJ*, 49 (2006), 357–83.

Cogswell, Thomas, Richard Cust and Peter Lake (eds.), *Politics, Religion and Popularity in Early Stuart Britain: Essays in Honour of Conrad Russell* (Cambridge, 2002).

Coleby, Andrew, *Central Government and the Localities: Hampshire 1649–1689* (Cambridge, 1987).

Collinson, Patrick, *The Elizabethan Puritan Movement* (London, 1967).

Collinson, Patrick, *The Religion of Protestants: The Church in English Society 1559–1625* (Oxford, 1982).

Collinson, Patrick, *The Birthpangs of Protestant England: Religious and Cultural Change in the Sixteenth and Seventeenth Centuries* (Basingstoke, 1988).

Collinson, Patrick, 'William Shakespeare's Religious Inheritance and Environment', reprinted in Patrick Collinson, *Elizabethan Essays* (London, 1994), pp. 219–52.

Collinson, Patrick, 'The Theatre Constructs Puritanism', in David L. Smith, Richard Strier and David Bevington (eds.), *The Theatrical City: Culture, Theatre and Politics in London, 1576–1649* (Cambridge, 1995), pp. 157–69.

Collinson, Patrick, 'From Iconoclasm to Iconophobia: The Cultural Impact of the Second English Reformation', reprinted in Peter Marshall (ed.), *The Impact of the English Reformation 1500–1640* (London, 1997), pp. 278–308.

Como, David R., 'Predestination and Political Conflict in Laud's London', *HJ*, 46 (2003), 263–94.

Como, David R., *Blown by the Spirit: Puritanism and the Emergence of an Antinomian Underground in Pre-Civil-War England* (Stanford, Calif., 2004).

Como, David, 'Secret Printing, the Crisis of 1640 and the Origins of Civil War Radicalism', *PP* 196 (2007), 37–82.

Como, David R., and Peter Lake, 'Puritans, Antinomians and Laudians in Caroline London: The Strange Case of Peter Shaw and Its Contexts', *Journal of Ecclesiastical History*, 50 (1999), 684–715.

Cooper, Trevor, (ed.), *The Journal of William Dowsing: Iconoclasm in East Anglia during the English Civil War* (Woodbridge, 2001).

Cope, Esther, 'Politics without Parliament: The Dispute about Muster Masters' Fees in Shropshire in the 1630s', *HLQ*, 45 (1982), 271–84.

Corish, Patrick J., 'The Rising of 1641 and the Catholic Confederacy, 1641–5', in T. W. Moody, F. X. Martin and F. J. Byrne (eds.), *A New History of Ireland*, vol. 3: *Early Modern Ireland 1534–1691* (Oxford, 1976), pp. 289–316.

Corish, Patrick, J., 'Ormond, Rinuccini, and the Confederates, 1645–9', in T. W. Moody, F. X. Martin and F. J. Byrne (eds.), *A New History of Ireland*, vol. 3: *Early Modern Ireland 1534–1691* (Oxford, 1976), pp. 317–35.

Cowan, Edward J., *Montrose: For Covenant and King* (London, 1977).

Cowan, Edward J., 'The Making of the National Covenant', in John Morrill (ed.), *The Scottish National Covenant in Its British Context 1638–51* (Edinburgh, 1990), pp. 68–89.

Coward, Barry, *Oliver Cromwell* (Harlow, 1991).

Crawford, Patricia, *Denzil Holles, 1598–1680: A Study of His Political Career* (London, 1979).

Crawford, Patricia, 'Charles Stuart, That Man of Blood', reprinted in Peter Gaunt (ed.), *The English Civil War* (Oxford, 2000), 303–23.

Crawford, Patricia, '"The poorest she": Women and Citizenship in Early Modern England', in Michael Mendle (ed.), *The Putney Debates of 1647: The Army, the Levellers and the English State* (Cambridge, 2001), pp. 197–218.

Crawford, Raymond, *The King's Evil* (Oxford, 1911).

Cressy, David, *Literacy and the Social Order: Reading and Writing in Tudor and Stuart England* (Cambridge, 1980).

Cressy, David, *Bonfires and Bells: National Memory and the Protestant Calendar in Elizabethan and Stuart England* (London, 1989).

Cressy, David, *Birth, Marriage and Death: Ritual, Religion, and the Life-Cycle in Tudor and Stuart England* (Oxford, 1997).

Cressy, David, *Agnes Bowker's Cat: Travesties and Transgressions in Tudor and Stuart England* (Oxford, 2000).

Cressy, David, 'The Protestation Protested, 1641 and 1642', *HJ*, 45 (2002), 251–79.

Cressy, David, 'Lamentable, Strange, and Wonderful: Headless Monsters in the English Revolution', in Laura Lunger Knoppers and Joan B. Landes (eds.), *Monstrous Bodies/Political Monstrosities in Early Modern Europe* (Ithaca, NY, 2004), pp. 40–63.

Cressy, David, 'Book Burning in Tudor and Stuart England', *Sixteenth Century Journal*, 36 (2005), 359–74.

Cressy, David, *England on Edge: Crisis and Revolution 1640–1642* (Oxford, 2006).

Croft, Pauline, 'Trading with the Enemy, 1585–1604' *HJ*, 32 (1989), 281–302.

Cromartie, A. D. T., 'The Printing of Parliamentary Speeches November 1640–July 1642', *HJ*, 33 (1990), 23–44.

Cromartie, Alan, *The Constitutionalist Revolution: An Essay on the History of England, 1450–1642* (Cambridge, 2006).

Curry, Patrick, 'Lilly, William (1602–1681)', *ODNB*, 33, pp. 794–8.

Curry, Patrick, *Prophecy and Power: Astrology in Early Modern England* (Princeton, 1989).

Cust, Richard, *The Forced Loan and English Politics 1626–1628* (Oxford, 1987).

Cust, Richard, 'Politics and the Electorate in the 1620s', in Richard Cust and Ann Hughes (eds.), *Conflict in Early Stuart England, 1603–1642* (Harlow, 1989), pp. 134–67.

Cust, Richard, 'News and Politics in Early Seventeenth-Century England', reprinted in Richard Cust and Ann Hughes (eds.), *The English Civil War* (London, 1997), pp. 233–60.

Cust, Richard, 'Charles I and Popularity', in Thomas Cogswell, Richard Cust and Peter Lake (eds.), *Politics, Religion and Popularity in Early Stuart Britain: Essays in Honour of Conrad Russell* (Cambridge, 2002), pp. 235–58.

Cust, Richard, *Charles I: A Political Life* (Harlow, 2005).

Cust, Richard, 'Charles I and Providence', in Kenneth Fincham and Peter Lake (eds.), *Religious Politics in Post-Reformation England: Essays in Honour of Nicholas Tyacke* (Woodbridge, 2006), 193–208.

Cust, Richard, '"Patriots" and "Popular Spirits": Narratives of Conflict in Early Stuart Politics', in Nicholas Tyacke (ed.), *The English Revolution c. 1590–1720* (Manchester, 2007), pp. 43–61.

Cust, Richard, 'The "Public Man" in Late Tudor and Early Stuart England', in Peter Lake and Steven Pincus (eds.), *The Politics of the Public Sphere in Early Modern England* (Manchester, forthcoming).

Cust, Richard, and Ann Hughes (eds.), *Conflict in Early Stuart England: Studies in Religion and Politics, 1603–1642* (Harlow, 1989).

Cust, Richard, and Ann Hughes (eds.), *The English Civil War* (London, 1997).

Cust, Richard, and Peter G. Lake, 'Sir Richard Grosvenor and the Rhetoric of Magistracy', *Bulletin of the Institute of Historical Research*, 54 (1981), 40–53.

Dailey, Barbara Ritter, 'The Visitation of Sarah Wight: Holy Carnival and the Revolution of the Saints in Civil War London', *Church History*, 55 (1986), 438–55.

Daly, James, 'The Implications of Royalist Politics 1642–1646', *HJ*, 27 (1984), 745–55.

Davies, Julian, *The Caroline Captivity of the English Church* (Oxford, 1992).

Davies, Stevie, *Unbridled Spirits: Women of the English Revolution: 1640–1660* (London, 1998).

Davis, J. C., *Utopia and the Ideal State: A Study of English Utopian Writing, 1516–1700* (Cambridge, 1981).

Davis, J. C., 'The Levellers and Christianity', reprinted in Peter Gaunt (ed.), *The English Civil War* (Oxford, 2000), pp. 279–302.

Davis, J. C., 'Political Thought during the English Revolution', in Barry Coward (ed.), *A Companion to Stuart Britain* (Oxford, 2003), pp. 374–96.

De Beer, E. S., 'Whitehall Palace: Inigo Jones and Wren', *Notes and Queries*, 177 (1939), 471–3.

Dils, Joan, 'Epidemics, Mortality and the Civil War in Berkshire, 1642–6', reprinted in R. C. Richardson (ed.), *The English Civil Wars: Local Aspects* (Stroud, 1997), pp. 145–55.

Dixon, C. Scott, 'Popular Astrology and Lutheran Propaganda in Reformation Germany', *History* (1999), 403–18.

Donagan, Barbara, 'Providence, Chance and Explanation', *Journal of Religious History*, 11 (1981), 385–403.

Donagan, Barbara, 'Godly Choice: Puritan Decision-Making in Seventeenth-Century England', *Harvard Theological Review*, 76 (1983), 307–34.

Donagan, Barbara, 'Codes and Conduct in the English Civil War', *PP*, 118 (1988), 65–95.

Donagan, Barbara, 'Understanding Providence: The Difficulties of Sir William and Lady Waller', *Journal of Ecclesiastical History*, 39:3 (1988), 433–44.

Donagan, Barbara, 'Atrocity, War Crime, and Treason in the English Civil War', *AHR*, 99 (1994), 1137–66.

Donagan, Barbara, 'Halcyon Days and the Literature of War: England's Military Education before 1642', *PP*, 147 (1995), 65–100.

Donagan, Barbara, 'The Casualties of War: Treatment of the Dead and Wounded in the English Civil War', in Ian Gentles, John Morrill and Blair Worden (eds.), *Soldiers, Writers and Statesmen of the English Revolution* (Cambridge, 1998), pp. 114–32.

Donagan, Barbara, 'Casuistry and Allegiance in the English Civil War', in Derek Hirst and Richard Strier (eds.), *Writing and Political Engagement in Seventeenth-Century England* (Cambridge, 2000), pp. 89–111.

Donagan, Barbara, 'The Web of Honour: Soldiers, Christians, and Gentlemen in the English Civil War', *HJ*, 44 (2001), 363–89.

Donagan, Barbara, 'Myth, Memory and Martyrdom: Colchester 1648', *Essex Archaeology and History*, 34 (2004), 172–80.

Donagan, Barbara, 'Troubled Consciences: Choice and Allegiance in the English Civil War' (unpublished paper).

Donald, Peter, 'New light on the Anglo-Scottish Contacts of 1640', *Historical Research*, 62:148 (1989), 121–9.

Donald, Peter, *An Uncounselled King: Charles I and the Scottish Troubles, 1637–41* (Cambridge, 1990).

Donaldson, Gordon, *The Making of the Scottish Prayer Book* (Edinburgh, 1954).

Donaldson, Gordon, *The Scottish Reformation* (Cambridge, 1960).

Donaldson, Gordon, 'The Scottish Church, 1567–1625', in A. G. R. Smith (ed.) *The Reign of James VI and I* (London, 1972), pp. 40–56.

Durston, Christopher, 'Puritan Rule and the Failure of Cultural Revolution', in Christopher Durston and Jacqueline Eales (eds.), *The Culture of English Puritanism, 1560–1700* (Basingstoke, 1996), pp. 210–33.

Durston, Christopher, '"Preaching and sitting still on Sundays": The Lord's Day during the English Revolution', in Christopher Durston and Judith Maltby (eds.), *Religion in Revolutionary England* (Manchester, 2006), pp. 205–25.

Durston, Christopher, and Jacqueline Eales (eds.), *The Culture of English Puritanism, 1560–1700* (Basingstoke, 1996).

Durston, Christopher, and Judith Maltby (eds.), *Religion in Revolutionary England* (Manchester, 2006).

Eales, Jacqueline, *Puritans and Roundheads: The Harleys of Brampton Bryan and the Outbreak of the English Civil War* (Cambridge, 1990).

Eales, Jacqueline, '"So many sects and schisms": Religious Diversity in Revolutionary Kent, 1640–60', in Christopher Durston and Judith Maltby (eds.), *Religion in Revolutionary England* (Manchester, 2006), pp. 226–48.

Edwards, Peter, *Dealing in Death: The Arms Trade and the British Civil Wars, 1638–52* (Stroud, 2000).

Elliott, J. H., 'The Year of the Three Ambassadors', in Hugh Lloyd-Jones, Valerie Pearl and Blair Worden (eds.), *History and Imagination: Essays in Honour of H. R. Trevor-Roper* (London, 1981), pp. 165–81.

Engberg, Jens, 'Royalist Finances during the English Civil War, 1642–6', *Scandinavian Economic History Review*, 14:2 (1966), 73–96.

Evans, John T., *Seventeenth-Century Norwich: Politics, Religion and Government, 1620–1690* (Oxford, 1979).

Everitt, Alan, *Suffolk and the Great Rebellion, 1640–60*, Suffolk Records Society, 3 (1960).

Everitt, Alan, *The Community of Kent and the Great Rebellion 1640–60* (Leicester, 1966).

Everitt, Alan, 'The Local Community and the Great Rebellion', reprinted in R. C. Richardson (ed.), *The English Civil Wars: Local Aspects* (Stroud, 1997), pp. 15–36.

Falvey, Heather, 'Crown Policy and Local Economic Context in the Berkhamsted Common Enclosure Dispute, 1618–42', *Rural History*, 12 (2001), 123–58.

Faraday, M. A., 'Shipmoney in Herefordshire', *Woolhope Naturalists' Field Club*, 41 (1974), 219–29.

Fielding, John, 'Arminianism in the Localities: Peterborough Diocese 1603–1642', in Kenneth Fincham (ed.), *The Early Stuart Church, 1603–1642* (Basingstoke, 1993), pp. 93–113.

Fielding, John, 'Opposition to the Personal Rule of Charles I: The Diary of Robert Woodford, 1637–1641', reprinted in Peter Gaunt (ed.), *The English Civil War* (Oxford, 2000), pp. 104–27.

Fielding, John, 'Sibthorpe, Robert (d. 1662)', *ODNB*, 50, pp. 500–501.

Fincham, Kenneth, 'The Judges' Decision on Ship Money in February 1637: The Reaction of Kent', *Bulletin of the Institute of Historical Research*, 57:136 (1984), 230–7.

Fincham, Kenneth (ed.), *The Early Stuart Church, 1603–1642* (Basingstoke, 1993).

Fincham, Kenneth, and Peter Lake, 'The Ecclesiastical Policies of James I and Charles I', in Kenneth Fincham (ed.), *The Early Stuart Church, 1603–1642* (Basingstoke, 1993), pp. 23–49.

Fincham, Kenneth, and Peter Lake (eds.), *Religious Politics in Post-Reformation England: Essays in Honour of Nicholas Tyacke* (Woodbridge, 2006).

Finlay, Roger, and Beatrice Shearer, 'Population Growth and Suburban Expansion' in A. L. Beier and Roger Finlay (eds.), *London 1500–1700: The Making of the Metropolis* (London, 1986), pp. 37–59.

Firth, C. H., *Cromwell's Army: A History of the English Soldier during the Civil Wars, the Commonwealth and the Protectorate* (London, 1967 edn).

Fissel, M. C., *The Bishops' Wars: Charles I's Campaigns against Scotland 1638–1640* (Cambridge, 1994).

Fissel, M. C., *English Warfare, 1511–1642* (London, 2001).

Fletcher, Anthony, 'Petitioning and the Outbreak of the Civil War in Derbyshire', *Derbyshire Archaeological Journal*, 113 (1973), 34–8.

Fletcher, Anthony, *A County Community in Peace and War: Sussex 1600–1660* (London, 1975).

Fletcher, A. J., 'Concern for Renewal in the Root and Branch Debates of 1641', Derek Baker (ed.), *Renaissance and Renewal in Christian History: Papers Read at the Fifteenth Summer Meeting and Sixteenth Winter Meeting of the Ecclesiastical History Society* (Studies in Church History, 14) (Oxford, 1977), pp. 279–86.

Fletcher, Anthony, *The Outbreak of the English Civil War* (London, 1981).

Fletcher, Anthony, 'National and Local Awareness in the County Communities', in Howard Tomlinson (ed.), *Before the English Civil War: Essays on Early Stuart Politics and Government* (London, 1983), pp. 151–74.

Fletcher, Anthony, *Reform in the Provinces: The Government of Stuart England* (New Haven, Conn., 1986).

Fletcher, Anthony, and Diarmaid MacCulloch, *Tudor Rebellions*, 5th edition (Harlow, 2004).

Forster, G. C. F., 'Faction and County Government in Early Stuart Yorkshire', *Northern History*, 11 (1976 for 1975), 70–86.

Fortescue, G. K. (ed.), *Catalogue of the Pamphlets, Books, Newspapers, and Manuscripts Relating to the Civil War, the Commonwealth and the Restoration, Collected by George Thomason, 1640–1661*, 2 vols (London, 1908).

Foster, Andrew, 'The Clerical Estate Revitalised', in Kenneth Fincham (ed.), *The Early Stuart Church, 1603–1642* (Basingstoke, 1993), pp. 93–113.

Foster, E. R., 'Printing the Petition of Right', *HLQ*, 38 (1974–5), 81–3.

Foster, Roy, *Modern Ireland 1600–1972* (London, 1988).

Fox, Adam, *Oral and Literate Culture in England, 1500–1700* (Oxford, 2000).

Foxley, Rachel, 'Citizenship and the English Nation in Leveller Thought, 1642–1653', unpublished Ph.D. thesis, Cambridge (2001).

Foxley, Rachel, 'John Lilburne and the Citizenship of "Free-Born Englishmen" ', *HJ*, 47 (2004), 849–74.

Frank, Joseph, *The Levellers: A History of the Writings of Three Seventeenth-Century Social Democrats: John Lilburne, Richard Overton, William Walwyn* (Cambridge, Mass., 1955).

Frearson, Michael, 'Communications and the Continuity of Dissent in the Chiltern Hundreds during the Sixteenth and Seventeenth Centuries', in Margaret Spufford (ed.), *The World of Rural Ddissenters, 1520–1725* (Cambridge, 1995), pp. 273–87.

Freist, Dagmar, 'The King's Crown is the Whore of Babylon: Politics, Gender and Communication in Mid-Seventeenth-Century England', *Gender and History*, 7 (1995), 457–81.

Freist, Dagmar, *Governed by Opinion: Politics, Religion and the Dynamics of Communication in Stuart London, 1637–1645* (London, 1997).

Furgol, Edward M., 'Scotland Turned Sweden: The Scottish Covenanters and the Military Revolution', in John Morrill (ed.), *The Scottish National Covenant in Its British Context 1638–1651* (Edinburgh, 1990), pp. 134–54.

Games, Alison, 'Migration', in David Armitage and Michael J. Braddick (eds.), *The British Atlantic World, 1500–1800* (Basingstoke, 2002), pp. 31–50.

Gardiner, Samuel R., *History of England from the Accession of James I to the Outbreak of the Civil War 1603–1642*, 10 vols. (London, 1884).

Garnett, George (ed.), *Brutus: Vindiciae, contra tyrannos or, Concerning the Legitimate Power of a Prince over the People, and of the People over a Prince* (Cambridge, 1994).

Garnett, George, 'Law in the *Vindiciae, Contra Tyrannos*: A Vindication', *HJ*, 49 (2006), 877–91.

Gaskill, Malcolm, *Crime and Mentalities in Early Modern England* (Cambridge, 2000).

Gaskill, Malcolm, 'Witches and Witchcraft Prosecutions, 1560–1660', in M. Zell (ed.), *Early Modern Kent 1540–1640* (Woodbridge, 2000), pp. 245–77.

Gaskill, Malcolm, *Witchfinders: A Seventeenth-Century English Tragedy* (London, 2005).

Gaunt, Peter (ed.), *The English Civil War* (Oxford, 2000).

Geertz, Clifford, 'Common Sense as a Cultural System', in Clifford Geertz, *Local Knowledge: Further Essays in Interpretive Anthropology* (New York, 2000 edn), pp. 73–93.

Geneva, Ann, *Astrology and the Seventeenth-Century Mind: William Lilly and the Language of the Stars* (Manchester, 1995).

Gentles, Ian, 'The Sales of Crown Lands during the English Revolution', *EcHR*, 2nd series, 26 (1973), 614–35.

Gentles, Ian, 'The Struggle for London in the Second Civil War', *HJ*, 26 (1983), pp. 277–305.

Gentles, Ian, *The New Model Army in England, Ireland and Scotland, 1645–1653* (Oxford, 1992).

Gentles, Ian, 'Political Funerals during the English Revolution', in Stephen Porter (ed.), *London and the Civil War* (Basingstoke, 1996), pp. 205–24.

Gentles, Ian, 'The New Model Officer Corps in 1647: A Collective Portrait', *Social History*, 22 (1997), pp. 127–44.

Gentles, Ian, 'The Civil Wars in England', in John Kenyon and Jane Ohlmeyer (eds.), *The Civil Wars: A Military History of England, Scotland, and Ireland 1638–1660* (Oxford, 1998), pp. 103–55.

Gentles, Ian, 'The Iconography of Revolution: England 1642–1649', in Ian Gentles, John Morrill and Blair Worden (eds.), *Soldiers, Writers and Statesmen of the English Revolution* (Cambridge, 1998), pp. 91–132.

Gentles, Ian, 'Harrison, Thomas (*bap.* 1616, *d.* 1690)', *ODNB*, 25, pp. 529–33.

Gentles, Ian, John Morrill and Blair Worden (eds.), *Soldiers, Writers and Statesmen of the English Revolution* (Cambridge, 1998).

Gibbons, B. J., 'Overton, Richard (*fl.* 1640–1663)', *ODNB*, 42, pp. 166–71.

Gibson, J. S. W. and A. Dell (eds.), *The Protestation Returns 1641–2 and Other Contemporary Listings* (Birmingham, 1995).

Gilbert, C. D., 'Clubmen in South West Shropshire, 1644–5', *Transactions of the Shropshire Archaeological and Historical Society*, 68 (1993), 93–8.

Gilbert, C. D., 'The Worcestershire Clubmen of 1645', *Transactions of the Worcestershire Archaeological Society*, 3rd series, 15 (1996), 211–8.

Glow, Lotte, 'The Committee of Safety', *EHR*, 80 (1965), 289–313.

Glow, Lotte, 'Peace Negotiations, Politics and the Committee of Both Kingdoms, 1644–1646', *HJ*, 12 (1969), 3–22.

Goldie, Mark, 'The Unacknowledged Republic: Officeholding in Early Modern England', in Tim Harris (ed.), *The Politics of the Excluded, c. 1500–1850* (Basingstoke, 2001), pp. 153–94.

Goodare, Julian, *State and Society in Early Modern Scotland* (Oxford, 1999).

Goodare, Julian, 'Charles I: Comment', *PP* (forthcoming).

Gordon, M. D., 'The Collection of Ship Money in the Reign of Charles I', *TRHS*, 3rd series, IV (1910), 141–62.

Gotch, J. Alfred, 'The Original Drawings of the Palace of Whitehall Attributed to Inigo Jones', *Architectural Review*, 31 (1912), 333–64.

Graham, Michael F., *The Uses of Reform: 'Godly Discipline' and Popular Behaviour in Scotland and Beyond* (Leiden, 1996).

Graves, Michael A. R., *Tudor Parliaments: Crown, Lords and Commons, 1485–1603* (Harlow, 1985).

Green, Ian, 'The Persecution of "Scandalous" and "Malignant" Parish Clergy during the English Civil War', *EHR*, 94 (1979), 507–31.

Green, Ian M., ' "For children in yeeres and children in understanding": The Emergence of the English Catechism under Elizabeth and the Early Stuarts', *Journal of Ecclesiastical History*, 37 (1986), 397–425.

Green, Ian, *The Christian's ABC: Catechisms and Catechizing in England c. 1530–1740* (Oxford, 1996).

Green, Ian, *Print and Protestantism in Early Modern England* (Oxford, 2000).

Greengrass, Mark, 'Samuel Hartlib and International Calvinism', *Proceedings of the Huguenot Society*, 25 (1993), 464–75.

Greengrass, Mark, Michael Leslie and Timothy Raylor (eds.), *Samuel Hartlib and the Universal Reformation: Studies in Intellectual Communication* (Cambridge, 1994).

Gregg, Pauline, *Free-Born John: The Biography of John Lilburne* (London, 1961).

Griffiths, Paul, *Youth and Authority: Formative Experiences in England 1560–1640* (Oxford, 1996).

Griffiths, Paul, 'Secrecy and Authority in Late Sixteenth- and Seventeenth-Century London', *HJ*, 40 (1997), 925–51.

Griffiths, Paul, 'Politics Made Visible: Order, Residence and Uniformity in Cheapside, 1600–45', in Paul Griffiths and Mark S. R. Jenner (eds.), *Londinopolis: Essays in the Cultural and Social History of Early Modern London* (Manchester, 2000), pp. 176–96.

Griffiths, Paul, Adam Fox and Steve Hindle (eds.), *The Experience of Authority in Early Modern England* (Basingstoke, 1996).

Griffiths, Paul, and Mark S. R. Jenner (eds.), *Londinopolis: Essays in the Cultural and Social History of Early Modern London* (Manchester, 2000).

Guenther, Genevieve, 'Why Devils Came When Faustus Called Them' (unpublished paper).

Guy, John, 'The Origins of the Petition of Right Reconsidered', *HJ*, 25 (1982), 289–312.

Habakkuk, H. J., 'Landowners and the Civil War', *EcHR*, 2nd ser., 18 (1965), 130–51.

Haigh, Christopher, *English Reformations: Religion, Politics and Society under the Tudors* (Oxford, 1993).

Haigh, Christopher, 'The Troubles of Thomas Pestell: Parish Squabbles and Ecclesiastical Politics in Caroline England', *JBS*, 41 (2002), 403–28.

Harris, Tim (ed.), *The Politics of the Excluded, c. 1500–1850* (Basingstoke, 2001).

Hart, James S., *Justice upon Petition: The House of Lords and the Reformation of Justice 1621–1675* (London, 1991).

Herrup, Cynthia, *The Common Peace: Participation and the Criminal Law in Seventeenth-Century England* (Cambridge, 1987).

Hessayon, Ariel, 'Incendiary Texts: Radicalism and Book Burning in England, c.1640–c.1660' (unpublished paper).

Hexter, Jack H., *The Reign of King Pym* (Cambridge, Mass., 1941).

Hey, David, *An English Rural Community: Myddle under the Tudors and Stuarts* (Leicester, 1974).

Hibbard, Caroline, *Charles I and the Popish Plot* (Chapel Hill, NC, 1983).

Hibbard, Caroline, 'Henrietta Maria (1609–1669)', *ODNB*, 26, pp. 392–406.

Hibbard, Caroline, 'Henrietta Maria in the 1630s: Perspectives on the Role of Consort Queens in *Ancien Régime* Courts', in Ian Atherton and Julie Sanders (eds.), *The 1630s:*

Interdisciplinary Essays on Culture and Politics in the Caroline Era (Manchester, 2006), pp. 92–110.

Higgins, Patricia, 'The Reactions of Women, with Special Reference to Women Petitioners', in Brian Manning (ed.), *Politics, Religion and the English Civil War* (London, 1973), 179–222.

Hill, Christopher, *The World Turned Upside Down: Radical Ideas During the English Revolution* (Harmondsworth, 1975).

Hill, Christopher, *Milton and the English Revolution* (New York, 1977).

Hill, Christopher, *A Turbulent, Seditious and Factious People: John Bunyan and His Church, 1628–1688* (Oxford, 1988).

Hindle, Steve, 'Hierarchy and Community in the Elizabethan Parish: the Swallowfield Articles of 1596', *HJ*, 42 (1999), 835–51.

Hindle, Steve, *The State and Social Change in Early Modern England, c.1550–1640* (Basingstoke, 2000).

Hindle, Steve, 'Exhortation and Entitlement: Negotiating Inequality in English Rural Communities, 1550–1650', in Michael J. Braddick and John Walter (eds.), *Negotiating Power in Early Modern Society: Order, Hierarchy and Subordination in Britain and Ireland* (Cambridge, 2001), pp. 102–22.

Hindle, Steve, *On the parish?: The Micro-Politics of Poor Relief in Rural England, c.1550–1750* (Oxford, 2004).

Hindle, Steve, 'Dearth and the English Revolution: The Harvest Crisis of 1647–50', *EcHR*, 61 (2008), 64–98.

Hirst, Derek, *The Representative of the People: Voters and Voting in England under the Early Stuarts* (Cambridge, 1975).

Hirst, Derek, *England in Conflict, 1603–1660: Kingdom, Community, Commonwealth* (London, 1999).

Hirst, Derek, 'The Defection of Sir Edward Dering, 1640–1641', reprinted in Peter Gaunt (ed.), *The English Civil War* (Oxford, 2000), pp. 207–25.

Hirst, Derek, 'Reading the Royal Romance: Or, Intimacy in a King's Cabinet', *Seventeenth Century*, 18 (2003), 211–29.

Hirst, Derek, 'Remembering a Hero: Lucy Hutchinson's *Memoirs* of Her Husband', *EHR*, 119 (2004), 682–92.

Hirst, Derek, and Richard Strier (eds.), *Writing and Political Engagement in Seventeenth-Century England* (Cambridge, 2000).

Holiday, P. G., 'Land Sales and Repurchases in Yorkshire after the Civil Wars, 1650–1670', reprinted in R. C. Richardson (ed.), *The English Civil Wars: Local Aspects* (Stroud, 1997), pp. 287–308.

Holmes, Clive (ed.), *The Suffolk Committees for Scandalous Ministers 1644–1646*, Suffolk Records Society, vol. 13 (Ipswich, 1970).

Holmes, Clive, 'Colonel King and Lincolnshire Politics, 1642–6', *HJ*, 16 (1973), 451–84.

Holmes, Clive, *The Eastern Association in the English Civil War* (Cambridge, 1974).

Holmes, Clive, 'The County Community in Stuart Historiography', *JBS*, 19:2 (1980), 54–73.

Holmes, Clive, *Seventeenth-Century Lincolnshire* (Lincoln, 1980).

Holmes, Clive, 'Drainers and Fenmen: The Problem of Popular Political Consciousness in the Seventeenth Century', in Anthony Fletcher and John Stevenson (eds.), *Order and Disorder in Early Modern England* (Cambridge, 1985), pp. 166–95.

Holmes, Clive, 'Parliament, Liberty, Taxation, and Property', in J. H. Hexter (ed.), *Parliament and Liberty: From the Reign of Elizabeth to the English Civil War* (Stanford, Calif., 1992), pp. 122–54.

Holmes, Clive, 'Women: Witnesses and Witches', *PP*, 140 (1993), 45–78.

Holstun, James (ed.), *Pamphlet Wars: Prose in the English Revolution* (London, 1992).

Holstun, James, *Ehud's Dagger: Class Struggle in the English Revolution* (London, 2000).

Hopper, Andrew, '"The popish army of the north": Anti-Catholicism and Parliamentarian Allegiance in Civil War Yorkshire, 1642–46', *Recusant History*, 25:1 (2000), 12–28.

Hopper, Andrew, '"Fitted for Desperation": Honour and Treachery in Parliament's Yorkshire Command, 1642–1643', *History*, 86 (2001), 138–54.

Hopper, Andrew, *'Black Tom': Sir Thomas Fairfax and the English Revolution* (Manchester, 2007).

Hopper, Andrew, 'The Wortley Park Poachers and the Outbreak of the English Civil War', *Northern History*, 44 (2007), 93–114.

Hoskins, W. G., 'Harvest Fluctuations and English Economic History 1620–1759', *Agricultural History Review*, 16 (1968), 15–31.

Howell, Roger, *Newcastle Upon Tyne and the Puritan Revolution: A Study of the Civil War in North England* (Oxford, 1967).

Howell, Roger, 'Neutralism, Conservatism and Political Alignment in the English Revolution: The Case of the Towns, 1642–9', in John Morrill (ed.), *Reactions to the English Civil War 1642–1649* (Basingstoke, 1982), pp. 67–87.

Howell, Roger, 'Newcastle and the Nation: The Seventeenth-Century Experience', reprinted in R. C. Richardson (ed.), *The English Civil Wars: Local Aspects* (Stroud, 1997), pp. 309–29.

Hughes, Ann, 'The King, the Parliament and the Localities during the English Civil War', *JBS*, 24 (1985), 236–63.

Hughes, Ann, 'Parliamentary Tyranny? Indemnity Proceedings and the Impact of the Civil War: A Case Study from Warwickshire', *Midland History*, 11 (1986), 49–78.

Hughes, Ann, *Politics, Society and Civil War in Warwickshire, 1620–1660* (Cambridge, 1987).

Hughes, Ann, 'Local History and the Origins of the Civil War', in Richard Cust and Ann Hughes (eds.), *Conflict in Early Stuart England, 1603–1642* (Harlow, 1989), pp. 224–53.

Hughes, Ann, 'Coventry and the English Revolution', reprinted in R. C. Richardson (ed.), *Town and Countryside in the English Revolution* (Manchester, 1992), pp. 69–99.

Hughes, Ann, 'The Meanings of Religious Polemic', in Francis J. Bremer (ed.), *Puritanism: Transatlantic Perspectives on a Seventeenth-Century Anglo-American Faith* (Boston, Mass., 1993), pp. 201–29.

Hughes, Ann, 'Gender and Politics in Leveller Literature', in Susan D. Amussen and Mark A. Kishlansky (eds.), *Political Culture and Cultural Politics in Early Modern Europe: Essays Presented to David Underdown* (Manchester, 1995), pp. 162–88.

Hughes, Ann, *The Causes of the English Civil War*, 2nd edition (Basingstoke, 1998).

Hughes, Ann, *Gangraena and the Struggle for the English Revolution* (Oxford, 2004).

Hughes, Ann, 'Greville, Robert, Second Baron Brooke of Beauchamps Court (1607–1643)', *ODNB*, 23, pp. 792–5.

Hutton, Ronald, 'The Structure of the Royalist Party, 1642–1646', *HJ*, 24 (1981), 553–69.

Hutton, Ronald, *The Rise and Fall of Merry England: The Ritual Year 1400–1700* (Oxford, 1994).

Hutton, Ronald, *The Royalist War Effort 1642–1646*, 2nd edition (London, 1999).

Hutton, Ronald, and Wylie Reeves, 'Sieges and Fortifications', in John Kenyon and Jane Ohlmeyer (eds.), *The Civil Wars: A Military History of England, Scotland and Ireland* (Oxford, 1998), pp. 195–233.

Ingram, Martin, 'Puritans and the Church Courts', in Christopher Durston and Jacqueline Eales (eds.), *The Culture of English Puritanism, 1560–1700* (Basingstoke, 1996), pp. 58–91.

Ingram, Martin, 'Reformation of Manners in Early Modern England', in Paul Griffiths, Adam Fox and Steve Hindle (eds.), *The Experience of Authority in Early Modern England* (Basingstoke, 1996), pp. 47–88.

Israel, Jonathan I., *Radical Enlightenment: Philosophy and the Making of Modernity, 1650–1750* (Oxford, 2001).

James, Mervyn, *Society, Politics and Culture: Studies in Early Modern England* (Cambridge, 1986).

Jankovic, Vladimir, 'The Politics of Sky Battles in Early Hanoverian Britain', *JBS*, 41 (2002), 429–459.

Jansen, Sharon, *Political Protest and Prophecy under Henry VIII* (Woodbridge, 1991).

Jardine, Lisa, *On a Grander Scale: The Outstanding Career of Sir Christopher Wren* (London, 2002).

Johnstone, Nathan, *The Devil and Demonism in Early Modern England* (Cambridge, 2006).

Jones, Colin, Malyn Newitt and Stephen K. Roberts (eds.), *Politics and People in Revolutionary England: Essays in Honour of Ivan Roots* (Oxford, 1986).

Jones, David Martin, *Conscience and Allegiance in Seventeenth Century England: The Political Significance of Oaths and Engagements* (Woodbridge, 1999).

Keeble, N. H., 'Baxter, Richard (1615–1691)', *ODNB*, 4, pp. 418–33.

Kelsey, Sean, *Inventing a Republic: The Political Culture of the English Commonwealth, 1649–1653* (Manchester, 1997).

Kelsey, Sean, 'The Death of Charles I', *HJ*, 45 (2002), 727–54.

Kelsey, Sean, 'The Ordinance for the Trial of Charles I', *Historical Research*, 76 (2003), 310–31.

Kelsey, Sean, 'The Trial of Charles I', *EHR*, 118, 477 (2003), 583–616.

Kennedy, D. E., *The English Revolution 1642–1649* (Basingstoke, 2000).

Kent, Joan R., *The English Village Constable, 1580–1642* (Oxford, 1986).

Kenyon, John, *The Civil Wars of England* (London, 1989 edn).

Kenyon, John, and Jane Ohlmeyer (eds.), *The Civil Wars: A Military History of England, Scotland, and Ireland 1638–1660* (Oxford, 1998).

Kesselring, Krista J., *Mercy and Authority in the Tudor State* (Cambridge, 2003).

Kesselring, Krista J., 'Deference and Dissent in Tudor England: Reflections on Sixteenth-Century Protest', *History Compass*, 3:1 (2005).

Ketton-Cremer, R. W., *Norfolk in the Civil War: A Portrait of a Society in Conflict* (London, 1969).

Kilburn, Terence, and Anthony Milton, 'The Public Context of the Trial and Execution of Strafford', in J. F. Merritt (ed.), *The Political World of Thomas Wentworth, Earl of Strafford, 1621–1641* (Cambridge, 1996), pp. 230–51.

Kingdom, Robert M., 'Calvinist Resistance Theory, 1550–1580', in J. H. Burns, with Mark Goldie (eds.), *The Cambridge History of Political Thought 1450–1700* (Cambridge, 1991), 193–218.

Kishlansky, Mark A., *The Rise of the New Model Army* (Cambridge, 1979).

Kishlansky, Mark, 'Ideology and Politics in the Parliamentary Armies, 1645–9', in John Morrill (ed.), *Reactions to the English Civil War 1642–1649* (London, 1982), pp. 163–83.

Kishlansky, Mark A., 'What Happened at Ware?', *HJ*, 25 (1982), 827–39.

Kishlansky, Mark A., *Parliamentary Selection: Social and Political Choice in Early Modern England* (Cambridge, 1986).

Kishlansky, Mark A., 'Saye What?', *HJ*, 33 (1990), 917–37.

Kishlansky, Mark A., 'Saye No More', *JBS*, 30 (1991), 399–448.

Kishlansky, Mark, 'Tyranny Denied: Charles I, Attorney General Heath, and the Five Knights' Case', *HJ*, 42 (1999), 53–83.

Kishlansky, Mark, 'Charles I: A Case of Mistaken Identity?', *PP*, 189 (2005), 41–80.

Kitson, Frank, *Old Ironsides: The Military Biography of Oliver Cromwell* (London, 2004).

Kupperman, Karen Ordahl, *Providence Island 1630–1641: The Other Puritan Colony* (Cambridge, 1993).

Kyle, Chris R., and Jason Peacey (eds.), *Parliament at Work: Parliamentary Committees, Political Power, and Public Access in Early Modern England* (Woodbridge, 2002).

Kyle, Chris R., and Jason Peacey, '"Under cover of so much coming and going": Public Access to Parliament and the Political Process in Early Modern England', in Chris R. Kyle and Jason Peacey (eds.), *Parliament at Work: Parliamentary Committees, Political Power, and Public Access in Early Modern England* (Woodbridge, 2002), 1–23.

Lacey, Andrew, 'Elegies and Commemorative Verses in Honour of Charles the Martyr,

1649–60', in Jason Peacey (ed.), *The Regicides and the Execution of Charles I* (Basingstoke, 2001), pp. 225–46.

Lacey, Andrew, *The Cult of King Charles the Martyr* (Woodbridge, 2003).

Lake, P. G., 'Calvinism and the English Church, 1570–1635', *PP*, 114 (1987), 32–76.

Lake, Peter, 'Anti-Popery: The Structure of a Prejudice', in Richard Cust and Ann Hughes (eds.), *Conflict in Early Stuart England, 1603–1642* (Harlow, 1989), pp. 72–106.

Lake, Peter, 'Defining Puritanism – Again?', in Francis J. Bremer (ed.), *Puritanism: Transatlantic Perspectives on a Seventeenth-Century Anglo-American Faith* (Boston, Mass., 1993), pp. 3–29.

Lake, Peter, 'The Laudian Style: Order, Uniformity and the Pursuit of Holiness in the 1630s', in Kenneth Fincham (ed.), *The Early Stuart Church, 1603–1642* (Basingstoke, 1993), pp. 161–85.

Lake, Peter, 'Popular Form, Puritan Content?: Two Puritan Appropriations of the Murder Pamphlet from Mid-Seventeenth-Century London', in Anthony Fletcher and Peter Roberts (eds.), *Religion, Culture and Society in Early Modern Britain: Essays in Honour of Patrick Collinson* (Cambridge, 1994), pp. 313–34.

Lake, Peter, ' "A Charitable Christian Hatred": The Godly and Their Enemies in the 1630s', in Christopher Durston and Jacqueline Eales (eds.), *The Culture of English Puritanism, 1560–1700* (Basingstoke, 1996), pp. 145–83.

Lake, Peter, *The Boxmaker's Revenge: 'Orthodoxy' and 'Heterodoxy' and the Politics of the Parish in Early Stuart London* (Manchester, 2001).

Lake, Peter, 'Puritans, Popularity and Petitions: Local Politics in National Context, Cheshire, 1641', in Thomas Cogswell, Richard Cust and Peter Lake (eds.), *Politics, Religion and Popularity in Early Stuart Britain: Essays in Honour of Conrad Russell* (Cambridge, 2002), pp. 259–89.

Lake, Peter, ' "The monarchical republic of Elizabeth I" Revisited (by Its Victims) as a Conspiracy', in Barry Coward and Julian Swann (eds.), *Conspiracies and Conspiracy Theory in Early Modern Europe from the Waldensians to the French Revolution* (Aldershot, 2004), pp. 87–111.

Lake, Peter, 'Anti-Puritanism: The Structure of a Prejudice', in Kenneth Fincham and Peter Lake (eds.), *Religious Politics in Post-Reformation England: Essays in Honour of Nicholas Tyacke* (Woodbridge, 2006), pp. 80–97.

Lake, Peter, and David R. Como, ' "Orthodoxy" and Its Discontents: Dispute Settlement and the Production of "Consensus" in the London (Puritan) "Underground" ', *JBS*, 39 (2000), 34–70.

Lake, Peter, and Steve Pincus, 'Rethinking the Public Sphere in Early Modern England', *JBS*, 45 (2006), 270–92.

Lake, Peter, and Michael C. Questier, 'Agency, Appropriation and Rhetoric under the Gallows: Puritans, Romanists and the State in Early Modern England', *PP*, 153 (1996), 64–107.

Lake, Peter, with Michael Questier, *The Antichrist's Lewd Hat: Protestants, Papists and Players in Post-Reformation England* (New Haven, Conn., 2002).

Lamont, William, 'Prynne, William (1600–1669)', *ODNB*, 45, pp. 489–94.

Langelüddecke, Henrik, 'Law and Order in Seventeenth-Century England: The Organization of Local Administration during the Personal Rule of Charles I', *Law and History Review*, 15 (1997), 49–76.

Langelüddecke, Henrik, ' "Patchy and spasmodic"?: The Response of Justices of the Peace to Charles I's Book of Orders', *EHR*, 113 (1998), 1231–48.

Langelüddecke, Henrik, ' "The chiefest strength and glory of this kingdom": Arming and Training the "Perfect Militia" in the 1630s', *EHR*, 118 (2003), 1264–1303.

Laqueur, Thomas, 'Crowds, Carnival and the State in English Executions, 1604–1868', in A. L. Beier, David Cannadine and James M. Rosenheim (eds.), *The First Modern Society: Essays in English History in Honour of Lawrence Stone* (Cambridge, 1989), pp. 305–55.

Larminie, Vivienne, 'Maynwaring, Roger (1589/90?–1653)', *ODNB*, 37, pp. 612–14.

Laurence, Anne, *Parliamentary Army Chaplains, 1642–1651* (Woodbridge, 1990).

Lee, Maurice, Jr, *The Road to Revolution: Scotland under Charles I, 1625–37* (Urbana, Ill., 1985).

Leng, Thomas, *Benjamin Worsley (1618–1677): Trade, Interest and the Spirit in Revolutionary England* (Woodbridge, 2008).

Lindley, Keith J., 'The Impact of the 1641 Rebellion upon England and Wales, 1641–5', *Irish Historical Studies*, 18:70 (1972), 143–76.

Lindley, Keith, 'The Part Played by Catholics', in Brian Manning (ed.), *Politics, Religion and the English Civil War* (London, 1973), pp. 127–76.

Lindley, Keith, *Fenland Riots and the English Revolution* (London, 1982).

Lindley, Keith, 'Riot Prevention and Control in Early Stuart London', *TRHS*, 5th ser., 33 (1983), 109–26.

Lindley, Keith, *Popular Politics and Religion in Civil War London* (Aldershot, 1997).

Liu, Tai, 'Burges, Cornelius (*d.* 1665)', *ODNB*, 8, pp. 751–5.

Lockyer, Roger, *The Early Stuarts: A Political History 1603–1642* (London, 1989).

MacCulloch, Diarmaid, *The Later Reformation in England, 1547–1603* (Basingstoke, 1990).

MacCulloch, Diarmaid, *Reformation: Europe's House Divided 1490–1700* (London, 2003).

Macfarlane, Alan, *Witchcraft in Tudor and Stuart England: A Regional and Comparative Study* (London, 1970).

Macinnes, Allan I., 'The Scottish Constitution, 1638–1651: The Rise and Fall of Oligarchic Centralism', in John Morrill (ed.), *The Scottish National Covenant in Its British Context 1638–1651* (Edinburgh, 1990), pp. 106–33.

Macinnes, Allan I., *Charles I and the Making of the Covenanting Movement, 1625–1641* (Edinburgh, 1991).

Macinnes, Allan I., *The British Revolution, 1629–1660* (Basingstoke, 2005).

Mack, Phyllis, *Visionary Women: Ecstatic Prophecy in Seventeenth-Century England* (Berkeley, Calif., 1992).

Macpherson, C. B., *The Political Theory of Possessive Individualism: Hobbes to Locke* (Oxford, 1962).

Maddison, R. E., '"The King's Cabinet Opened": A Case Study in Pamphlet History', *Notes and Queries*, 211 (1966), 2–9.

Mahony, Michael, 'Presbyterianism in the City of London, 1645–7', *HJ*, 22 (1979), 93–114.

Makey, Walter, *The Church of the Covenant, 1637–1651: Revolution and Social Change in Scotland* (Edinburgh, 1979).

Malcolm, Joyce Lee, 'All the King's Men: The Impact of the Crown's Irish Soldiers on the English Civil War', *Irish Historical Studies*, 21 (1979), 239–64.

Malcolm, Noel, *Aspects of Hobbes* (Oxford, 2002).

Malcolm, Noel, 'Hobbes, Thomas (1588–1679)', *ODNB*, 27, pp. 385–95.

Maltby, Judith, *Prayer Book and People in Elizabethan and Early Stuart England* (Cambridge, 1998).

Maltby, Judith, 'Suffering and Surviving: The Civil Wars, the Commonwealth and the Formation of "Anglicanism", 1642–60', in Christopher Durston and Judith Maltby (eds.), *Religion in Revolutionary England* (Manchester, 2006), pp. 158–80.

Manning, Brian (ed.), *Politics, Religion and the English Civil War* (London, 1973).

Manning, Brian, 'The Aristocracy and the Downfall of Charles I', in Brian Manning (ed.), *Politics, Religion and the English Civil War* (London, 1973), pp. 37–80.

Manning, Brian, *The English People and the English Revolution* (Harmondsworth, 1976).

Manning, Brian, *Aristocrats, Plebeians and Revolution in England, 1640–1660* (London, 1996).

Marsh, Christopher W., '"Common Prayer" in England 1560–1640: The View from the Pew', *PP*, 171 (2001), 66–94.

Marshall, Peter (ed.), *The Impact of the English Reformation 1500–1640* (London, 1997).

Marshall, Peter, *Beliefs and the Dead in Reformation England* (Oxford, 2002).

Marshall, Peter, *Reformation England 1480–1642* (London, 2003).

McEntee, Ann Marie, '"The [un]civill-sisterhood of Oranges and Lemons": Female Petitioners and Demonstrators, 1642–53', reprinted in James Holstun (ed.), *Pamphlet Wars: Prose in the English Revolution* (London, 1992), pp. 92–111.

McGrath, Patrick, 'Bristol and the Civil War', reprinted in R. C. Richardson (ed.), *The English Civil Wars: Local Aspects* (Stroud, 1997), pp. 91–128.

McKenzie, Andrea, 'Martyrs in Low Life? Dying "Game" in Augustan England', *JBS*, 42 (2003), 167–205.

McLaren, Anne, 'Rethinking Republicanism: *Vindiciae, Contra Tyrannos* in Context', *HJ*, 49 (2006), 23–52.

McMichael, J. R., and Barbara Taft (eds.), *The Writings of William Walwyn* (Athens, Ga., 1989).

McRae, Andrew, *God Speed the Plough: The Representation of Agrarian England, 1500–1660* (Cambridge, 1996).

McShane Jones, Angela, '"Rime and Reason": The Political World of the English Broadside Ballad, 1640–1689', unpublished Ph.D. thesis, Warwick (2004).

Medick, Hans, 'Historical Event and Contemporary Experience: The Capture and Destruction of Magdeburg in 1631', trans. Pamela Selwyn, *History Workshop Journal*, 52 (2001), 23–48.

Mendelson, Sara, and Patricia Crawford, *Women in Early Modern England* (Oxford, 1998).

Mendle, M. J., 'Politics and Political Thought 1640–1642', in Conrad Russell (ed.), *The Origins of the English Civil War* (London, 1973), pp. 219–45.

Mendle, Michael, *Dangerous Positions: Mixed Government, the Estates of the Realm, and the Making of the Answer to the XIX Propositions* (Tuscaloosa, 1985).

Mendle, Michael, 'The Ship Money Case, *The case of shipmony*, and the Development of Henry Parker's Parliamentary Absolutism', *HJ*, 32 (1989), 513–36.

Mendle, Michael, 'Henry Parker: The Public's Privado', in Gordon J. Schochet, P. E. Tatspaugh and Carol Brobeck (eds.), *Religion, Resistance and Civil War: Papers Presented at the Folger Institute Seminar 'Political Thought in Early Modern England, 1600–1660'* (Washington, DC, 1990), pp. 151–77.

Mendle, Michael, 'The Great Council of Parliament and the First Ordinances: The Constitutional Theory of the Civil War', *JBS*, 31 (1992), 133–62.

Mendle, Michael, 'Parliamentary Sovereignty: A Very English Absolutism', in Nicholas T. Phillipson and Quentin Skinner (eds.), *Political Discourse in Early Modern Britain* (Cambridge, 1993), pp. 97–119.

Mendle, Michael, 'De Facto Freedom, De Facto Authority: Press and Parliament, 1460–1643', *HJ*, 38 (1995), 307–332.

Mendle, Michael, *Henry Parker and the English Civil War: The Political Thought of the Public's 'Privado'* (Cambridge, 1995).

Mendle, Michael, 'Introduction', in Michael Mendle (ed.), *The Putney Debates of 1647: The Army, the Levellers and the English State* (Cambridge, 2001), pp. 1–15.

Mendle, Michael (ed.), *The Putney Debates of 1647: The Army, the Levellers and the English State* (Cambridge, 2001).

Merritt, J. F. (ed.), *The Political World of Thomas Wentworth, Earl of Strafford 1621–1641* (Cambridge, 1996).

Merritt, J. F., *The Social World of Early Modern Westminster: Abbey, Court and Community, 1525–1640* (Manchester, 2005).

Milton, Anthony, 'The Church of England, Rome and the True Church: The Demise of a Jacobean Consensus', in Kenneth Fincham (ed.), *The Early Stuart Church, 1603–1642* (Basingstoke, 1993), pp. 187–210.

Milton, Anthony, *Catholic and Reformed: Roman and Protestant Churches in English Protestant Thought, 1600–1640* (Cambridge, 1995).

Milton, Anthony, '"The unchanged peacemaker"?: John Dury and the Politics of Irenicism in England, 1628–1643', in Mark Greengrass, Michael Leslie and Timothy Raylor (eds.),

Samuel Hartlib and the Universal Reformation: Studies in Intellectual Communication (Cambridge, 1994), pp. 95–117.

Milton, Anthony, 'Thomas Wentworth and the Political Thought of the Personal Rule', in J. F. Merritt (ed.), *The Political World of Thomas Wentworth, Earl of Strafford 1621–1641* (Cambridge, 1996), pp. 133–56.

Milton, Anthony, 'Laud, William (1573–1645)', *ODNB*, 32, pp. 655–70.

Moody, T. W., F. X. Martin and F. J. Byrne (eds.), *A New History of Ireland*, vol. 3: *Early Modern Ireland 1534–1691* (Oxford, 1976).

Morley, Claude, 'Solemn League and Covenant in Suffolk', *East Anglian Miscellany* (1945), 30–35.

Morrill, John, *Cheshire 1630–1660: County Government and Society during the English Revolution* (Oxford, 1974).

Morrill, John, *Revolt of the Provinces: Conservatives and Radicals in the English Civil War, 1630–1650*, 1st edition (Harlow, 1980).

Morrill, John (ed.), *Reactions to the English Civil War 1642–1649* (Basingstoke, 1982).

Morrill, John (ed.), *Oliver Cromwell and the English Revolution*, (Harlow, 1990).

Morrill, John, 'The Making of Oliver Cromwell', in John Morrill (ed.), *Oliver Cromwell and the English Revolution* (Harlow, 1990), pp. 19–48.

Morrill, John, 'The National Covenant in Its British Context', in John Morrill (ed.), *The Scottish National Covenant in Its British Context 1638–51* (Edinburgh, 1990), pp. 1–30.

Morrill, John, 'Introduction', in John Morrill (ed.), *The Impact of the English Civil War* (London, 1991), pp. 8–19.

Morrill, John (ed.), *The Impact of the English Civil War* (London, 1991).

Morrill, John, *The Nature of the English Revolution* (Harlow, 1993).

Morrill, John, 'The Church in England, 1642–1649', reprinted in John Morrill, *The Nature of the English Revolution* (Harlow, 1993), pp. 89–114.

Morrill, John, 'The Ecology of Allegiance', reprinted in John Morrill, *The Nature of the English Revolution* (Harlow, 1993), pp. 224–41.

Morrill, John, 'The Army Revolt of 1647', reprinted in John Morrill, *The Nature of the English Revolution* (Harlow, 1993), pp. 307–31.

Morrill, John, 'Mutiny and Discontent in English Provincial Armies, 1645–1647', reprinted in John Morrill, *The Nature of the English Revolution* (Harlow, 1993), pp. 332–58.

Morrill, John, 'The Unweariableness of Mr Pym: Influence and Eloquence in the Long Parliament', in Susan Dwyer Amussen and Mark A. Kishlansky (eds.), *Political Culture and Cultural Politics in Early Modern England: Essays Presented to David Underdown* (Manchester, 1995), pp. 19–54.

Morrill, John, *Revolt in the Provinces: The People of England and the Tragedies of War 1630–1648*, 2nd edition (Harlow, 1999).

Morrill, John, 'William Dowsing and the Administration of Iconoclasm in the Puritan Revolution', in Trevor Cooper (ed.), *The Journal of William Dowsing: Iconoclasm in East Anglia during the English Civil War* (Woodbridge, 2001), pp. 1–28.

Morrill, John, 'Devereux, Robert, Third Earl of Essex (1591–1646)', *ODNB*, 15, pp. 960–9.

Morrill, John, 'Dowsing, William (*bap.* 1596, *d.* 1668)', *ODNB*, 16, pp. 817–19.

Morrill, John, 'Holles, Denzil, First Baron Holles (1598–1680)', *ODNB*, 27, pp. 708–14.

Morrill, John, and Philip Baker, 'The Case of the Armie Truly Re-stated', in Michael Mendle (ed.), *The Putney Debates of 1647: The Army, the Levellers and the English State* (Cambridge, 2001), pp. 103–24.

Morrill, John, and Philip Baker, 'Oliver Cromwell, the Regicide and the Sons of Zeruiah', in Jason Peacey (ed.), *The Regicides and the Execution of Charles I* (Basingstoke, 2001), pp. 14–35.

Morrill, John, and John Walter, 'Order and Disorder in the English Revolution', in Anthony Fletcher and John Stevenson (eds.), *Order and Disorder in Early Modern England* (Cambridge, 1985), pp. 137–65.

Naphy, William G., 'Plague-Spreading and Magisterially Controlled Fear', in William G.

Naphy and Penny Roberts (eds.), *Fear in Early Modern Society* (Manchester, 1997), pp. 28–43.

Nevitt, Marcus, *Women and the Pamphlet Culture of Revolutionary England, 1640–1660* (Aldershot, 2006).

Newman, John, 'Jones, Inigo (1573–1652)', *ODNB*, 30, pp. 527–38.

Niccoli, Ottavia, *Prophecy and People in Renaissance Italy* (Princeton, NJ, 1990).

Norbrook, David, 'Lucan, Thomas May, and the Creation of a Republican Literary Culture', in Kevin Sharpe and Peter Lake (eds.), *Culture and Politics in Early Stuart England* (Basingstoke, 1994), pp. 45–66.

Norbrook, David, *Writing the English Republic: Poetry, Rhetoric and Politics, 1627–1660* (Cambridge, 1999).

Norbrook, David, *Poetry and Politics in the English Renaissance*, revised edition (Oxford, 2002).

Norris, Michael, 'Edward Sexby, John Reynolds and Edmund Chillenden: Agitators, "Sectarian Grandees" and the Relations of the New Model Army with London in the Spring of 1647', *Historical Research*, 76 (2003), 30–53.

Notestein, Wallace, 'The Establishment of the Committee of Both Kingdoms', *AHR*, 17 (1912), 477–95.

Oakley, Francis, 'Christian Obedience and Authority, 1520–1550', in J. H. Burns, with the assistance of Mark Goldie (eds.), *The Cambridge History of Political Thought 1450–1700* (Cambridge, 1991), pp. 159–92.

Ó hAnnracháin, Tadhg, 'Plunkett, Sir Nicholas (1602–1680)', *ODNB*, 44, pp. 645–6.

Ohlmeyer, Jane H., 'Introduction: A Failed Revolution?', in Jane H. Ohlmeyer (ed.), *Ireland from Independence to Occupation 1641–1660* (Cambridge, 1995), pp. 1–23.

Ohlmeyer, Jane H. (ed.), *Ireland from Independence to Occupation 1641–1660* (Cambridge, 1995).

Ohlmeyer, Jane, 'The Civil Wars in Ireland', in John Kenyon and Jane Ohlmeyer (eds.), *The Civil Wars: A Military History of England, Scotland, and Ireland 1638–1660* (Oxford, 1998), pp. 73–102.

O'Riordan, Christopher, 'Popular Exploitation of Enemy Estates in the English Revolution', *History*, 78 (1993), 183–200.

Osborne, Simon, 'The War, the People and the Absence of the Clubmen in the Midlands, 1642–1646', reprinted in Peter Gaunt (ed.), *The English Civil War* (Oxford, 2000), pp. 226–48.

Ó Siochrú, Mícheál, *Confederate Ireland, 1642–1649: A Constitutional and Political Analysis* (Dublin, 1999).

Peacey, Jason, 'The Exploitation of Captured Correspondence and Anglo-Scottish Relations in the British Civil Wars', *Scottish Historical Review*, 79 (2000), 213–32.

Peacey, Jason (ed.), *The Regicides and the Execution of Charles I* (Basingstoke, 2001).

Peacey, Jason, 'Reporting a Revolution: A Failed Propaganda Campaign', in Jason Peacey (ed.), *The Regicides and the Execution of Charles I* (Basingstoke, 2001), pp. 161–80.

Peacey, Jason, 'Politics, Accounts and Propaganda in the Long Parliament', in Chris R. Kyle and Jason Peacey (eds.), *Parliament at Work: Parliamentary Committees, Political Power, and Public Access in Early Modern England* (Woodbridge, 2002), pp. 59–78.

Peacey, Jason, '"Fiery Spirits" and Political Propaganda: Uncovering a Radical Press Campaign of 1642', *Publishing History*, 55 (2004), 5–36.

Peacey, Jason, 'The Paranoid Prelate: Archbishop Laud and the Puritan Plot', in Barry Coward and Julian Swann (eds.), *Conspiracies and Conspiracy Theory in Early Modern Europe: From the Waldensians to the French Revolution* (Aldershot, 2004), pp. 113–34.

Peacey, Jason, *Politicians and Pamphleteers: Propaganda During the English Civil Wars and Revolution* (Aldershot, 2004).

Peacey, Jason, 'Popularity and the Politician: An MP and His Public, 1640–1644' (unpublished paper).

Peacock, John, 'The Image of Charles I as a Roman Emperor', in Ian Atherton and Julie Sanders (eds.), *The 1630s: Interdisciplinary Essays on Culture and Politics in the Caroline Era* (Manchester, 2006), pp. 50–73.

Pearl, Valerie, *London and the Outbreak of the Puritan Revolution: City Government and National Politics 1625–1643* (Oxford, 1961).

Pearl, Valerie, 'London's Counter-Revolution', in G. E. Aylmer (ed.), *The Interregnum: The Quest for Settlement, 1646–1660* (London, 1972), pp. 29–56.

Peck, Linda Levy, *Consuming Splendor: Society and Culture in Seventeenth-Century England* (Cambridge, 2005).

Peltonen, Markku, *Classical Humanism and Republicanism in English Political Thought, 1570–1640* (Cambridge, 1995).

Peltonen, Markku, 'Citizenship and Republicanism in Elizabethan England', in Martin van Gelderen and Quentin Skinner (eds.), *Republicanism: A Shared European Heritage*, vol. 1: *Republicanism and Constitutionalism in Early Modern Europe* (Cambridge, 2002), pp. 85–106.

Pennington, D. H., 'The Accounts of the Kingdom, 1642–49', in F. J. Fisher (ed.), *Essays in the Economic and Social History of Tudor and Stuart England* (Cambridge, 1961), pp. 182–203.

Pennington, Donald, 'The War and the People', in John Morrill (ed.), *Reactions to the English Civil War 1642–1649* (London, 1982), pp. 115–35.

Pennington, D. H., and I. A. Roots (eds.), *The Committee at Stafford, 1643–1645: The Order Book of the Staffordshire County Committee*, Collections for a History of Staffordshire, 4th ser., 1 (Manchester, 1957).

Perceval-Maxwell, Michael, *The Outbreak of the Irish Rebellion of 1641* (Dublin, 1994).

Pestana, Carla G., *The English Atlantic in an Age of Revolution, 1640–1661* (Cambridge, Mass., 2004).

Phillips, Colin, 'Landlord–Tenant Relationships 1642–1660', reprinted in R. C. Richardson (ed.), *Town and Countryside in the English Revolution* (Manchester, 1992), pp. 224–50.

Phillips, Colin, 'The Royalist North: The Cumberland and Westmorland Gentry, 1642–60', in R. C. Richardson (ed.), *The English Civil Wars: Local Aspects* (Stroud, 1997), pp. 239–59.

Pitman, Jan, 'Tradition and Exclusion: Parochial Officeholding in Early Modern England, a Case Study from North Norfolk, 1580–1640', *Rural History*, 15 (2004), 27–45.

Pocock, J. G. A., 'Thomas May and the Narrative of Civil War', in Derek Hirst and Richard Strier (eds.), *Writing and Political Engagement in Seventeenth-Century England* (Cambridge, 1999), pp. 112–44.

Pooley, Roger, 'Saltmarsh, John (*d.* 1647)', *ODNB*, 48, pp. 770–1.

Popkin, Richard, *The History of Scepticism from Savonarola to Bayle*, revised edn (Oxford, 2003).

Porter, Stephen, *Destruction in the English Civil Wars* (Gloucester, 1994).

Porter, Stephen (ed.), *London and the Civil War* (Basingstoke, 1996).

Purkiss, Diane, *The Witch in History: Early Modern and Twentieth-Century Representations* (London, 1996).

Purkiss, Diane, 'Desire and Its Deformities: Fantasies of Witchcraft in the English Civil War', *Journal of Medieval and Early Modern Studies* (1997), 103–32.

Purkiss, Diane, *The English Civil War: Papists, Gentlemen, Soldiers, and Witchfinders in the Birth of Modern Britain* (New York, 2006).

Questier, Michael, 'Arminianism, Catholicism and Puritanism in England during the 1630s', *HJ*, 49 (2006), 53–28.

Quintrell, B. W., 'The Making of Charles I's Book of Orders', *EHR*, 95 (1980), 553–72.

Raylor, Timothy, 'Providence and Technology in the English Civil War: Edmund Felton and His Engine', *Renaissance Studies*, 7:4 (1993), 398–413.

Raylor, Timothy, 'Thomas Hobbes and "The Mathematical Demonstration of the Sword"', *Seventeenth Century*, 15 (2000), 175–98.

Raymond, Joad (ed.), *Making the News: An Anthology of the Newsbooks of Revolutionary England, 1641–1660* (Moreton-in-Marsh, 1993).

Raymond, Joad, *The Invention of the Newspaper: English Newsbooks 1641–1649* (Oxford, 1996).

Raymond, Joad (ed.), *News, Newspapers and Society in Early Modern Britain* (London, 1999).

Raymond, Joad, 'Popular Representations of Charles I', in Thomas N. Corns (ed.), *The Royal Image: Representations of Charles I* (Cambridge, 1999), pp. 47–73.

Raymond, Joad, *Pamphlets and Pamphleteering in Early Modern Britain* (Cambridge, 2003).

Reeve, L. J., 'The Legal Status of the Petition of Right', *HJ*, 29 (1986), 257–77.

Reeve, L. J., *Charles I and the Road to Personal Rule* (Cambridge, 1989).

Reeve, John, 'Secret Alliances and Protestant Agitation in Two Kingdoms: The Early Caroline Background to the Irish Rebellion', in Ian Gentles, John Morrill and Blair Worden (eds.), *Soldiers, Writers and Statemen of the English Revolution* (Cambridge, 1998), pp. 19–35.

Richards, Judith, '"His nowe Majestie" and the English Monarchy: The Kingship of Charles I before 1640', *PP*, 113 (1986), 70–96.

Richardson, R. C. (ed.), *Town and Countryside in the English Revolution* (Manchester, 1992).

Richardson, R. C. (ed.), *The English Civil Wars: Local Aspects* (Stroud, 1997).

Roberts, Stephen K., *Recovery and Restoration in an English County: Devon Local Administration 1646–70* (Exeter, 1985).

Ross, George MacDonald, 'The Royal Touch and the Book of Common Prayer', *Notes and Queries*, 30:5 (1983), 433–35.

Roy, Ian, 'The Royalist Army in the First Civil War', unpublished D.Phil. thesis, Oxford (1963).

Roy, Ian, 'The City of Oxford 1640–1660', in R. C. Richardson (ed.), *Town and Countryside in the English Revolution* (Manchester, 1992), pp. 130–68.

Roy, Ian, 'George Digby, Royalist Intrigue and the Collapse of the Cause', in Ian Gentles, John Morrill and Blair Worden (eds.), *Soldiers, Writers and Statesmen of the English Revolution* (Cambridge, 1998), pp. 68–90.

Roy, Ian, 'England Turned Germany?: The Aftermath of the Civil War in Its European Context', reprinted in Peter Gaunt (ed.), *The English Civil War* (Oxford, 2000), pp. 249–67.

Roy, Ian, 'Rupert, Prince and Count Palatine of the Rhine and Duke of Cumberland (1619–1682)', *ODNB*, 48, pp. 141–54.

Rusche, Harry, 'Merlini Anglici: Astrology and Propaganda from 1644 to 1651', *EHR*, 80 (1965), 322–33.

Rusche, Harry, 'Prophecies and Propaganda, 1641 to 1651', *EHR*, 84 (1969), 752–70.

Rushton, Peter, 'Women, Witchcraft and Slander in Early Modern England: Cases from the Church Courts in Durham, 1560–1675', *Northern History*, 18 (1982), 116–32.

Rushton, Peter, 'The Matter in Variance: Adolescents and Domestic Conflict in the Pre-Industrial Economy of Northeast England, 1600–1800', *Journal of Social History*, 25 (1991), 89–107.

Russell, Conrad, *Parliament and English Politics 1621–1629* (Oxford, 1979).

Russell, Conrad, *The Causes of the English Civil War* (Oxford, 1990).

Russell, Conrad, 'Parliamentary History in Perspective, 1604–1629', reprinted in Conrad Russell, *Unrevolutionary England, 1603–1642* (London, 1990), pp. 31–57.

Russell, Conrad, 'The Theory of Treason in the Trial of Strafford', reprinted in Conrad Russell, *Unrevolutionary England, 1603–1642* (London, 1990), pp. 89–109.

Russell, Conrad, 'The Ship-Money Judgments of Bramston and Davenport', reprinted in Conrad Russell, *Unrevolutionary England, 1603–1642* (London, 1990), pp. 137–44.

Russell, Conrad, 'Arguments for Religious Unity in England, 1530–1650', reprinted in Conrad Russell, *Unrevolutionary England, 1603–1642* (London, 1990), pp. 179–204.

Russell, Conrad, 'The First Army Plot of 1641', reprinted in Conrad Russell, *Unrevolutionary England, 1603–1642* (London, 1990), pp. 281–302.

Russell, Conrad, *The Fall of the British Monarchies 1637–1642* (Oxford, 1991).

Russell, Conrad, 'Sir Thomas Wentworth and Anti-Spanish Sentiment, 1621–1624', in J. F. Merritt (ed.), *The Political World of Thomas Wentworth, Earl of Strafford, 1621–1641* (Cambridge, 1996), pp. 47–62.

Russell, Conrad, 'Pym, John (1584–1643)', *ODNB*, 45, pp. 624–40.

Russell, Conrad, 'Russell, Francis, Fourth Earl of Bedford (*bap.* 1587, *d.* 1641)', *ODNB*, 48, pp. 241–50.

Ryrie, Alec, 'Congregations, Conventicles and the Nature of Early Scottish Protestantism', *PP*, 191 (2006), 45–76.

Ryrie, Alec, *The Origins of the Scottish Reformation* (Manchester, 2006).

Sacks, David Harris, 'Bristol's "Wars of Religion"', in R. C. Richardson (ed.), *Town and Countryside in the English Revolution* (Manchester, 1992), pp. 100–129.

Salt, S. P., 'Dering, Sir Edward, First Baronet (1598–1644)', *ODNB*, 15, pp. 874–80.

Sawday, Jonathan, *The Body Emblazoned: Dissection and the Human Body in Renaissance Culture* (London, 1996 edn).

Scally, John J., 'Hamilton, James, First Duke of Hamilton (1606–1649)', *ODNB*, 24, pp. 839–46.

Schen, Claire S., 'Constructing the Poor in Early Seventeenth-Century London', *Albion*, 32 (2000), 450–63.

Schen, Claire, *Charity and Lay Piety in Reformation London, 1500–1620* (Aldershot, 2002).

Scott, David, 'Politics and Government in York 1640–1662', in R. C. Richardson (ed.), *Town and Countryside in the English Revolution* (Manchester, 1992), pp. 46–68.

Scott, David, '"Hannibal at our gates": Loyalists and Fifth-Columnists during the Bishops' Wars – the Case of Yorkshire', *Historical Research*, 70 (1997), 269–93.

Scott, David, 'Motives for King-Killing', in Jason Peacey (ed.), *The Regicides and the Execution of Charles I* (Basingstoke, 2001), pp. 138–60.

Scott, David, *Politics and War in the Three Stuart Kingdoms, 1637–49* (Basingstoke, 2004).

Scott, David, 'Hotham, John (1610–1645)', *ODNB*, 28, pp. 259–61.

Scott, David, 'Hotham, Sir John, First Baronet (1589–1645)', *ODNB*, 28, pp. 257–9.

Scott, Jonathan, *England's Troubles: Seventeenth Century English Political Stability in European Context* (Cambridge, 2000).

Scott, Jonathan, *Commonwealth Principles: Republican Writing of the English Revolution* (Cambridge, 2004).

Seaver, Paul, *Wallington's World: A Puritan Artisan in 17th Century London* (London, 1985).

Seaward, Paul, 'Hyde, Edward, First Earl of Clarendon (1609–1674)', *ODNB*, 29, pp. 120–38.

Shaaber, Matthias Adam, *Some Forerunners of the Newspaper in England, 1476–1622* (Philadelphia, Pa., 1929).

Shagan, Ethan Howard, 'Constructing Discord: Ideology, Propaganda, and English Responses to the Irish Rebellion of 1641', *JBS*, 36:1 (1997), 4–34.

Shagan, Ethan Howard, 'Rumours and Popular Politics in the Reign of Henry VIII', in Tim Harris (ed.), *The Politics of the Excluded, c. 1500–1850* (Basingstoke, 2001), pp. 30–66.

Shapin, Steven, *A Social History of Truth: Civility and Science in Seventeenth-Century England* (Chicago, 1994).

Sharp, Andrew, 'John Lilburne and the Long Parliament's Book of Declarations: A Radical's Exploitation of the Words of Authorities', *History of Political Thought*, 9 (1988), 19–44.

Sharp, Andrew, 'John Lilburne's Discourse of Law', *Political Science*, 40:1 (1988), 18–33.

Sharp, Andrew (ed.), *The English Levellers* (Cambridge, 1998).

Sharp, Andrew, 'Lilburne, John (1615?–1657)', *ODNB*, 33, pp. 773–83.

Sharp, Buchanan, *In Contempt of All Authority: Rural Artisans and Riot in the West of England, 1586–1660* (Berkeley, Calif., 1980).

Sharp, Buchanan, 'Rural Discontents and the English Revolution', in R. C. Richardson (ed.), *Town and Countryside in the English Revolution* (Manchester, 1992), pp. 251–72.

Sharpe, James A., '"Last dying speeches": Religion, Ideology and Public Execution in Seventeenth-Century England', *PP*, 107 (1985), 144–67.

Sharpe, James, 'Scandalous and Malignant Priests in Essex: The Impact of Grassroots Puritanism', in Colin Jones, Malyn Newitt and Stephen K. Roberts (eds.), *Politics and People in Revolutionary England: Essays in Honour of Ivan Roots* (Oxford, 1986), pp. 253–73.

Sharpe, James, *Instruments of Darkness: Witchcraft in England 1550–1750* (London, 1996).

Sharpe, Kevin, 'The Image of Virtue: The Court and Household of Charles I 1625–1642', in David Starkey and D. A. L. Morgan, John Murphy, Pam Wright, Neil Cuddy, and Kevin Sharpe (eds.), *The English Court: From the Wars of the Roses to the Civil War* (London, 1987), pp. 226–60.

Sharpe, Kevin, *The Personal Rule of Charles I* (New Haven, Conn., 1992).

Sharpe, Kevin, 'The King's Writ: Royal Authors and Royal Authority in Early Modern England', in Kevin Sharpe and Peter Lake (eds.), *Culture and Politics in Early Stuart England* (Basingstoke, 1994), pp. 117–38.

Sharpe, Kevin, '"An image doting rabble": The Failure of Republican Culture in Seventeenth-Century England', in Kevin Sharpe and Steven M. Zwicker (eds.), *Refiguring Revolutions: Aesthetics and Politics from the English Revolution to the Romantic Revolution* (Berkeley, Calif., 1998), pp. 25–56.

Sharpe, Kevin, '"So hard a text"?: Images of Charles I, 1612–1700', *HJ*, 43 (2000), 383–406.

Sharpe, Kevin, and Peter Lake (eds.), *Culture and Politics in Early Stuart England* (Basingstoke, 1994).

Shaw, Dougal, 'St Giles' Church and Charles I's Coronation Visit to Scotland', *Historical Research*, 77 (2004), 481–502.

Shaw, W. A., *A History of the English Church during the Civil Wars and under the Commonwealth*, 2 vols. (London, 1900).

Shedd, John A., 'Thwarted Victors: Civil and Criminal Prosecution against Parliament's Officials during the English Civil War and Commonwealth', *JBS*, 41 (2002), 139–69.

Sheils, William, 'English Catholics at War and Peace', in Christopher Durston and Judith Maltby (eds.), *Religion in Revolutionary England* (Manchester, 2006), pp. 137–57.

Shepard, Alexandra, and Phil Withington (eds.), *Communities in Early Modern England: Networks, Place, Rhetoric* (Manchester, 2000).

Shuger, Debora, *Censorship and Cultural Sensibility: The Regulation of Language in Tudor–Stuart England* (Philadelphia, Pa., 2006).

Sizer, J. R. M., 'Stewart, John, First Earl of Traquair (c.1599–1659)', *ODNB*, 52, pp. 718–20.

Skerpan, Elizabeth, *The Rhetoric of Politics in the English Revolution, 1642–1660* (London, 1992).

Skerpan Wheeler, Elizabeth, '*Eikon Basilike* and the Rhetoric of Self-Representation', in Thomas N. Corns (ed.), *The Royal Image: Representations of Charles I* (Cambridge, 1999), pp. 122–40.

Skinner, Quentin, *The Foundations of Modern Political Thought*, vol. 2: *The Age of Reformation* (Cambridge, 1978).

Skinner, Quentin, 'Motives, Intentions and the Interpretation of Texts', reprinted in James Tully (ed.), *Meaning and Context: Quentin Skinner and His Critics* (Princeton, NJ, 1988), pp. 68–78.

Skinner, Quentin, 'Language and Social Action', reprinted in James Tully (ed.), *Meaning and Context: Quentin Skinner and His Critics* (Princeton, NJ, 1988), pp. 119–32.

Skinner, Quentin, 'Classical Liberty and the Coming of the English Civil War', in Martin Van Gelderen and Quentin Skinner (eds.), *Republicanism: A Shared European Heritage*, vol. 2: *The Values of Republicanism in Early Modern Europe* (Cambridge, 2002), pp. 9–28.

Skinner, Quentin, 'Rethinking Political Liberty', *History Workshop Journal*, 61:1 (2006), 156–70.

Slack, Paul, 'Books of Orders: The Making of English Social Policy, 1577–1631', *TRHS*, 5th series, 30 (1980), 1–22.

Slack, Paul, *The Impact of Plague in Tudor and Stuart England* (Oxford, 1985).

Slack, Paul, *Poverty and Policy in Tudor and Stuart England* (London, 1988).

Slack, Paul, *From Reformation to Improvement: Public Welfare in Early Modern England* (Oxford, 1998).

Smith, A. H., *County and Court: Government and Politics in Norfolk, 1558–1603* (Oxford, 1974).

Smith, David L., *Constitutional Royalism and the Search for Settlement, c. 1640–1649* (Cambridge, 1994).

Smith, David L., *The Stuart Parliaments, 1603–1689* (London, 1999).

Smith, Nicola, *The Royal Image and the English People* (Aldershot, 2001).

Smith, Nigel, *Perfection Proclaimed: Language and Literature in English Radical Religion, 1640–1660* (Oxford, 1989).

Smith, Nigel, *Literature and Revolution in England 1640–1660* (New Haven, Conn., 1994).

Smith, S. R., 'The London Apprentices as 17th Century Adolescents', reprinted in Paul Slack (ed.), *Rebellion, Popular Protest and the Social Order in Early Modern England* (Cambridge, 1984), pp. 219–31.

Smith, Victor, and Peter Kelsey, 'The Lines of Communication: The Civil War Defences of London', in Stephen Porter (ed.), *London and the Civil War* (Basingstoke, 1996), pp. 117–48.

Smuts, R. M., 'Public Ceremony and Royal Charisma: The English Royal Entry in London, 1485–1642', in A. L. Beier, David Cannadine and James M. Rosenheim (eds.), *The First Modern Society: Essays in English History in Honour of Lawrence Stone* (Cambridge, 1989), pp. 65–93.

Snow, Vernon F., *Essex the Rebel: The Life of Robert Devereux, the Third Earl of Essex 1591–1646* (Lincoln, Nebraska, 1970).

Sommerville, Johann, 'Ideology, Property and the Constitution', in Richard Cust and Ann Hughes (eds.), *Conflict in Early Stuart England: Studies in Religion and Politics, 1603–1642* (Harlow, 1989), pp. 47–71.

Sommerville, Johann, *Royalists and Patriots: Politics and Ideology in England 1603–1640*, rev. edn (London, 1999).

Spencer, Lois, 'The Politics of George Thomason', *The Library*, 5th ser., 14 (1959), 11–27.

Spraggon, Julie, *Puritan Iconoclasm during the English Civil War* (Woodbridge, 2003).

Spufford, Margaret, *Small Books and Pleasant Histories: Popular Fiction and its Readership in Seventeenth-Century England* (Athens, Ga., 1981).

Spufford, Margaret, 'Puritanism and Social Control', in Anthony Fletcher and John Stevenson (eds.), *Order and Disorder in Early Modern England* (Cambridge, 1985), pp. 41–57.

Spufford, Margaret (ed.), *The World of Rural Dissenters, 1520–1725* (Cambridge, 1995).

Spurr, John, *English Puritanism 1603–1689* (Basingstoke, 1998).

Stater, Victor L., 'The Lord Lieutenancy on the Eve of the Civil Wars: The Impressment of George Plowright', *HJ*, 29 (1986), 279–96.

Stevenson, David, *Revolution and Counter-Revolution in Scotland, 1644–1651* (London, 1977).

Stevenson, David, 'The English Devil of Keeping State: Élite Manners and the Downfall of Charles I in Scotland', in Roger Mason and Nicholas Macdougall (eds.), *People and Power in Scotland: Essays in Honour of T. C. Smout* (Edinburgh, 1992).

Stevenson, David, *The Scottish Revolution, 1637–44: The Triumph of the Covenanters* (Edinburgh, 2003).

Stevenson, David, 'Graham, James, First Marquess of Montrose (1612–1650)', *ODNB*, 23, pp. 189–95.

Stevenson, David, 'Monro, Sir George, of Culrain and Newmore (d. 1694)', ODNB, 38, pp. 649–50.

Stewart, Richard W., 'Arms and Expeditions: The Ordnance Office and the Assaults on Cadiz (1625) and the Isle of Rhé (1627)', in Mark Charles Fissel (ed.), War and Government in Britain, 1598–1650 (Manchester, 1991), pp. 112–32.

Stewart, Richard Winship, The English Ordnance Office 1585–1625: A Case Study in Bureaucracy (Woodbridge, 1996).

Stoyle, Mark, Loyalty and Locality: Popular Allegiance in Devon during the English Civil War (Exeter, 1994).

Stoyle, Mark, From Deliverance to Destruction: Rebellion and Civil War in an English City (Exeter, 1996).

Stoyle, Mark, 'Whole Streets Converted to Ashes: Property Destruction in Exeter during the English Civil War', reprinted in R. C. Richardson (ed.), The English Civil Wars: Local Aspects (Stroud, 1997), pp. 129–44.

Stoyle, Mark, Soldiers and Strangers: An Ethnic History of the English Civil War (New Haven, Conn., 2005).

Styles, Philip, 'The City of Worcester during the Civil Wars, 1640–60', reprinted in R. C. Richardson (ed.), The English Civil Wars: Local Aspects (Stroud, 1997), pp. 187–238.

Taft, Barbara, 'Walwyn, William (bap. 1600, d. 1681)', ODNB, 57, pp. 225–31.

Tennant, Philip, 'Parish and People: South Warwickshire in the Civil War', reprinted in R. C. Richardson (ed.), The English Civil Wars: Local Aspects (Stroud, 1997), pp. 157–86.

Thirsk, Joan, 'The Sales of Royalist Land during the Interregnum', EcHR, 2nd ser., 5 (1952), 188–207.

Thirsk, Joan, 'Agrarian Problems and the English Revolution', in R. C. Richardson (ed.), Town and Countryside in the English Revolution (Manchester, 1992), pp. 169–97.

Thomas, Keith, 'Women and the Civil War Sects', PP, 13 (1958), 42–62.

Thomas, Keith, 'The Levellers and the Franchise', in G. E. Aylmer (ed.), The Interregnum: The Quest for Settlement, 1646–60 (London, 1972), pp. 57–78.

Thomas, Keith, Religion and the Decline of Magic: Studies in Popular Beliefs in Sixteenth- and Seventeenth-Century England (Harmondsworth, 1991 edn).

Thomas, Keith, 'Art and Iconoclasm in Early Modern England', in Kenneth Fincham and Peter Lake (eds.), Religious Politics in Post-Reformation England: Essays in Honour of Nicholas Tyacke (Woodbridge, 2006), pp. 16–40.

Thomas, P. W., 'Charles I of England: The Tragedy of Absolutism', in A. G. Dickens (ed.), The Courts of Europe: Politics, Patronage and Royalty 1400–1800 (London, 1977), pp. 191–211.

Thompson, Janet A., Wives, Widows, Witches and Bitches: Women in Seventeenth-Century Devon (New York, 1993).

Thurley, Simon, The Lost Palace of Whitehall (London, 1998).

Todd, Margo, The Culture of Protestantism in Early Modern Scotland (New Haven, Conn., 2002).

Tolmie, Murray, The Triumph of the Saints: The Separate Churches of London, 1616–1649 (Cambridge, 1977).

Trevor-Roper, Hugh, 'Three Foreigners: The Philosophers of the Puritan Revolution', reprinted in Hugh Trevor-Roper, Religion, the Reformation, and Social Change, and Other Essays (London, 1984), pp. 237–93.

Trevor-Roper, Hugh, 'The Fast Sermons of the Long Parliament', reprinted in Hugh Trevor-Roper, Religion, the Reformation, and Social Change, and Other Essays (London, 1984), pp. 297–344.

Trevor-Roper, Hugh, Europe's Physician: The Various Life of Sir Theodore de Mayerne (New Haven, Conn., 2006).

Trim, David, 'Calvinist Internationalism and the English Officer Corps, 1562–1642', History Compass, 4/6 (2006), 1024–48.

Trubowitz, Rachel, 'Female Preachers and Male Wives: Gender and Authority in Civil War

England', reprinted in James Holstun (ed.), *Pamphlet Wars: Prose in the English Revolution* (London, 1992), pp. 112–33.

Tuck, Richard, *Philosophy and Government 1572–1651* (Cambridge, 1993).

Turnbull, G. H., *Samuel Hartlib: A Sketch of His Life and His Relations to J. A. Comenius* (London, 1920).

Turnbull, G. H., *Hartlib, Dury and Comenius: Gleanings from Hartlib's Papers* (London, 1947).

Twigg, J. D. 'The Parliamentary Visitation of the University of Cambridge 1644–1645', *EHR*, 98 (1983), 513–28.

Tyacke, Nicholas, *Anti-Calvinists: The Rise of English Arminianism c. 1590–1640* (Oxford, 1987).

Tyacke, Nicholas, *Aspects of English Protestantism, c. 1530–1700* (Manchester, 2001).

Tyacke, Nicholas, 'The Fortunes of English Puritanism, 1603–40', reprinted in Nicholas Tyacke, *Aspects of English Protestantism, c. 1530–1700* (Manchester, 2001), pp. 111–31.

Tyacke, Nicholas, 'Puritanism, Arminianism and Counter-Revolution', reprinted in Nicholas Tyacke, *Aspects of English Protestantism, c. 1530–1700* (Manchester, 2001), pp. 132–59.

Tyacke, Nicholas, 'The Rise of Arminianism Reconsidered', reprinted in Nicholas Tyacke, *Aspects of English Protestantism, c. 1530–1700* (Manchester, 2001), pp. 160–75.

Tyacke, Nicholas (ed.), *The English Revolution c. 1590–1720* (Manchester, forthcoming).

Underdown, David, *Pride's Purge: Politics in the Puritan Revolution* (Oxford, 1971).

Underdown, David, *Somerset in the Civil War and Interregnum* (Newton Abbot, 1973).

Underdown, David, '"Honest" Radicals in the Counties, 1642–1649', in Donald Pennington and Keith Thomas (eds.), *Puritans and Revolutionaries: Essays in Seventeenth-Century History Presented to Christopher Hill* (Oxford, 1978), pp. 186–205.

Underdown, David, 'The Chalk and the Cheese: Contrasts among the English Clubmen', *PP*, 85 (1979), 25–48.

Underdown, David, 'The Problem of Popular Allegiance in the English Civil War', *TRHS*, 5th ser., 31 (1981), 69–94.

Underdown, David, *Revel, Riot and Rebellion: Popular Politics and Culture in England, 1603–1660* (Oxford, 1985).

Underdown, David, 'A Reply to John Morrill', *JBS*, 26 (1987), 468–79.

Underdown, David, *Fire from Heaven: Life in an English Town in the Seventeenth Century* (London, 1992).

Vallance, Edward, 'Protestation, Vow, Covenant and Engagement: Swearing Allegiance in the English Civil War', *Historical Research*, 75 (2002), 408–24.

Vallance, Edward, *Revolutionary England and the National Covenant: State Oaths, Protestantism and the Political Nation, 1553–1682* (Woodbridge, 2005).

Vernon, Elliot Curt, 'The Sion College Conclave and London Presbyterianism during the English Revolution', unpublished Ph.D. thesis, Cambridge (1999).

Vernon, Elliot, 'A Ministry of the Gospel: The Presbyterians during the English Revolution', in Christopher Durston and Judith Maltby (eds.), *Religion in Revolutionary England* (Manchester, 2006), pp. 115–36.

Walsham, Alexandra, 'The Parochial Roots of Laudianism Revisited: Catholics, Anti-Calvinists and "Parish Anglicans" in Early Stuart England', *Journal of Ecclesiastical History*, 49 (1988), 620–51.

Walsham, Alexandra, *Providence in Early Modern England* (Oxford, 1999).

Walsham, Alexandra, *Charitable Hatred: Tolerance and Intolerance in England, 1500–1700* (Manchester, 2006).

Walter, John, 'Anti-Popery and the Stour Valley Riots of 1642', in David Chadd (ed.), *History of Religious Dissent in East Anglia, III* (Norwich, 1996), pp. 121–40.

Walter, John, *Understanding Popular Violence in the English Revolution: The Colchester Plunderers* (Cambridge, 1999).

Walter, John, 'Confessional Politics in Pre-Civil War Essex: Prayer Books, Profanations, and Petitions', *HJ*, 44 (2001), 677–701.

Walter, John, '"Abolishing Superstition with Sedition"?: The Politics of Popular Iconoclasm in England 1640–1642', *PP*, 183 (2004), 79–123.

Walter, John, 'Popular Iconoclasm and the Politics of the Parish in Eastern England, 1640–1642', *HJ*, 47 (2004), 261–90.

Walter, John, *Crowds and Popular Politics in Early Modern England* (Manchester, 2006).

Walter, John, 'Grain Riots and Popular Attitudes to the Law: Maldon and the Crisis of 1629', reprinted in John Walter, *Crowds and Popular Politics in Early Modern England* (Manchester, 2006), pp. 27–66.

Walter, John, 'A "rising of the people"?: The Oxfordshire Rising of 1596', reprinted in John Walter, *Crowds and Popular Politics in Early Modern England* (Manchester, 2006), pp. 73–123.

Walter, John, 'The Social Economy of Dearth in Early Modern England', reprinted in John Walter, *Crowds and Popular Politics in Early Modern England* (Manchester, 2006), pp. 124–180.

Walter, John, 'Public Transcripts, Popular Agency and the Politics of Subsistence in Early Modern England', reprinted in John Walter, *Crowds and Popular Politics in Early Modern England* (Manchester, 2006), pp. 196–222.

Walter, John, 'The English People and the English Revolution Revisited', *History Workshop Journal*, 61 (2006), 171–182.

Walter, John, '"Affronts & insolencies": The Voices of Radwinter and Popular Opposition to Laudianism', *EHR*, 122 (2007), 35–60.

Walter, John, and Roger Schofield, 'Famine, Disease and Crisis Mortality in Early Modern Society', in John Walter and Roger Schofield (eds.), *Famine, Disease and the Social Order in Early Modern Society* (Cambridge, 1989), pp. 1–73.

Walter, John, and Keith Wrightson, 'Dearth and the Social Order in Early Modern England', reprinted in Paul Slack (ed.), *Rebellion, Popular Protest and the Social Order in Early Modern England* (Cambridge, 1984), pp. 108–28.

Wanklyn, Malcolm, *Decisive Battles of the English Civil War: Myth and Reality* (Barnsley, 2006).

Wanklyn, Malcolm, and Frank Jones, *A Military History of the English Civil War, 1642–1646: Strategy and Tactics* (Harlow, 2005).

Warmington, A. R., *Civil War, Interregnum and Restoration in Gloucestershire 1640–1672* (Woodbridge, 1997).

Warmington, Andrew, 'Massey, Sir Edward (d. 1674)', *ODNB*, 37, pp. 208–11.

Warner, Peter, *Bloody Marsh: A Seventeenth-Century Village in Crisis* (Bollington, 2000).

Watt, Tessa, *Cheap Print and Popular Piety, 1550–1640* (Cambridge, 1991).

Watt, Tessa, 'Piety in the Pedlar's Pack: Continuity and Change, 1578–1630', in Margaret Spufford (ed.), *The World of Rural Dissenters, 1520–1725* (Cambridge, 1995), pp. 235–72.

Watts, M. R., *The Dissenters*, vol. 1: *From the Reformation to the French Revolution* (Oxford, 1978).

Webb, John, 'The Siege of Portsmouth in the Civil War', reprinted in R. C. Richardson (ed.), *The English Civil Wars: Local Aspects* (Stroud, 1997), pp. 63–90.

Webster, Charles, 'Introduction', in Charles Webster (ed.), *Samuel Hartlib and the Advancement of Learning* (Cambridge, 1970).

Webster, Charles, 'The Authorship and Significance of Macaria', *PP*, 56 (1972), 34–48.

Webster, Charles, *Utopian Planning and the Puritan Revolution: Gabriel Plattes, Samuel Hartlib and 'Macaria'* (Oxford, 1979).

Webster, Charles, *The Great Instauration: Science, Medicine and Reform*, 2nd edition (Oxford, 2002).

Wedgwood, C. V., *The King's War 1641–1647* (London, 1958).

Wedgwood, C. V., *The Trial of Charles I* (London, 1964).

Wheeler, James Scott, 'Four Armies in Ireland', in Jane H. Ohlmeyer (ed.), *Ireland from Independence to Occupation 1641–1660* (Cambridge, 1995), pp. 43–65.

Wheeler, James Scott, *The Making of a World Power: War and the Military Revolution in Seventeenth-Century England* (Stroud, 1999).

Whinney, M. D., 'John Webb's Drawings for the Whitehall Palace', *Walpole Society*, 31 (1946 for 1942–3), 45–107.

White, Michelle Anne, *Henrietta Maria and the English Civil Wars* (Aldershot, 2006).

White, Peter, *Predestination, Policy and Polemic: Conflict and Consensus in the English Church from the Reformation to the Civil War* (Cambridge, 1992).

Whiteman, Anne, 'The Protestation Returns of 1641–1642. Pt. 1: The General Organisation', *Local Population Studies*, 55 (1995), 14–26.

Whiteman, Anne, and Vivian Russell, 'The Protestation Returns, 1641–1642. Pt. 2: Partial Census or Snapshot? – Some Evidence from Penwith Hundred, Cornwall', *Local Population Studies*, 56 (1996), 17–29.

Wilson, John Frederick, *Pulpit in Parliament: Puritanism during the English Civil Wars, 1640–8* (Princeton, NJ, 1969).

Wiseman, Susan, '"Adam, the Father of all Flesh": Porno-Political Rhetoric and Political Theory in and after the English Civil War', reprinted in James Holstun (ed.), *Pamphlet Wars: Prose in the English Revolution* (London, 1992), pp. 134–57.

Withington, Philip, *The Politics of Commonwealth: Citizens and Freemen in Early Modern England* (Cambridge, 2005).

Wolffe, Mary, 'Chudleigh, James (1617–1643)', *ODNB*, 11, pp. 571–2.

Wolffe, Mary, 'Chudleigh, Sir George, Baronet (1582–1658)', *ODNB*, 11, pp. 570–1.

Wood, Andy, 'Beyond Post-Revisionism?: The Civil War Allegiances of the Miners of the Derbyshire "Peak Country"', *HJ*, 40 (1997), 23–40.

Wood, Andy, *Riot, Rebellion and Popular Politics in Early Modern England* (Basingstoke, 2002).

Woodward, Donald, 'Wage Rates and Living Standards in Pre-Industrial England', *PP*, 91 (1981), 28–46.

Woodward, Donald, '"Here Comes a Chopper to Chop Off His Head": The Execution of Three Priests at Newcastle and Gateshead, 1592–1594', *Recusant History*, 22 (1994), 1–6.

Woodward, Donald, *Men at Work: Labourers and Building Craftsmen in the Towns of Northern England, 1450–1750* (Cambridge, 1995).

Woolf, N., 'The Sovereign Remedy: Touch-Pieces and the King's Evil', *British Numismatic Journal*, 49 (1980 for 1979), 99–121.

Woolf, N., 'The Sovereign Remedy: Touch-Pieces and the King's Evil, Part 2', *British Numismatic Journal*, 50 (1981 for 1980), 91–116.

Woolrych, Austin, *Commonwealth to Protectorate* (Oxford, 1982).

Woolrych, Austin, *Soldiers and Statesmen: The General Council of the Army and Its Debates, 1647–1648* (Oxford, 1987).

Woolrych, Austin, 'The Debates from the Perspective of the Army', in Michael Mendle (ed.), *The Putney Debates of 1647: The Army, the Levellers and the English State* (Cambridge, 2001), pp. 53–78.

Woolrych, Austin, *Britain in Revolution 1625–1660* (Oxford, 2002).

Wootton, David (ed.), *Divine Right and Democracy: An Anthology of Political Writing in Stuart England* (Harmondsworth, 1986).

Wootton, David, 'Leveller Democracy and the Puritan Revolution', in J. H. Burns, with Mark Goldie (eds.), *The Cambridge History of Political Thought 1450–1700* (Cambridge, 1991), pp. 412–42.

Wootton, David, 'From Rebellion to Revolution: The Crisis of the Winter of 1642/3 and the Origins of Civil War Radicalism', reprinted in Richard Cust and Ann Hughes (eds.), *The English Civil War* (London, 1997), pp. 340–56.

Worden, Blair, *The Rump Parliament* (Cambridge, 1974).

Worden, Blair, 'Classical Republicanism and the Puritan Revolution', in H. Lloyd-Jones, V. Pearl and Blair Worden (eds.), *History and Imagination: Essays in Honour of H. R. Trevor-Roper* (London, 1981), pp. 182–200.

Worden, Blair, 'Oliver Cromwell and the Sin of Achan', in Derek Beales and Geoffrey Best (eds.), *History, Society and the Churches: Essays in Honour of Owen Chadwick* (Cambridge, 1985), pp. 125–45.

Worden, Blair, 'The "Diary" of Bulstrode Whitelocke', *EHR*, 108 (1993), 122–34.

Worden, Blair, 'The Levellers in History and Memory', in Michael Mendle (ed.), *The Putney Debates of 1647: The Army, the Levellers and the English State* (Cambridge, 2001), pp. 256–82.

Worden, Blair, *Roundhead Reputations: The English Civil Wars and the Passions of Posterity* (Harmondsworth, 2001).

Wormald, Jenny, *Court, Kirk and Community: Scotland, 1470–1625* (Edinburgh, 1997).

Wright, Stephen, 'Carew, Sir Alexander, Second Baronet (1609–1644)', *ODNB*, 10, pp. 40–41.

Wrightson, Keith, 'Aspects of Social Differentiation in Rural England, c.1580–1660', *Journal of Peasant Studies*, 5:1 (1977), 33–47.

Wrightson, Keith, 'Two Concepts of Order: Justices, Constables and Jurymen in Seventeenth-Century England', in John Brewer and John Styles (eds.), *An Ungovernable People?: The English and Their Law in the Seventeenth and Eighteenth Centuries* (London, 1980), pp. 21–46.

Wrightson, Keith, *English Society 1580–1680* (London, 1982).

Wrightson, Keith, 'The Politics of the Parish in Early Modern England', in Paul Griffiths, Adam Fox and Steve Hindle (eds.), *The Experience of Authority in Early Modern England* (Basingstoke, 1996), pp. 10–46.

Wrightson, Keith, *Earthly Necessities: Economic Lives in Early Modern Britain* (New Haven, Conn., 2000).

Wrightson, Keith, and David Levine, *Poverty and Piety in an English Village: Terling 1525–1700*, revised edition (Oxford, 1995).

Wrigley, E. A., 'A Simple Model of London's Importance in Changing English Society and Economy, 1650–1750', reprinted in E. A. Wrigley, *People, Cities and Wealth: The Transformation of Traditional Society* (Oxford, 1987), pp. 133–56.

Wrigley, E. A., and R. S. Schofield, *The Population History of England 1541–1871: A Reconstruction* (Cambridge, 1989).

Young, John T., *Faith, Medical Alchemy, and Natural Philosophy: Johann Moriaen, Reformed Intelligencer and the Hartlib Circle* (Aldershot, 1998).

Young, Peter, and Richard Holmes, *The English Civil War: A Military History of the Three Civil Wars 1642–1651* (Ware, 2000).

Zaret, David, 'Petitions and the "Invention" of Public Opinion in the English Revolution', *American Journal of Sociology*, 101 (1996), 1497–1555.

Zaret, David, *Origins of Democratic Culture: Printing, Petitions, and the Public Sphere in Early-Modern England* (Princeton, NJ, 2000).

Index

Page numbers in *italics* refer to illustrations. Other than in the entry under his name, Charles I is referred to as C.